COOKING AND DINING IN TUDOR AND EARLY STUART ENGLAND

Frontispiece. Henry VIII's hall-place kitchen, Hampton Court Palace, 1531.

Cooking and Dining in Tudor and Early Stuart England

Peter Brears

PROSPECT BOOKS
2015

First published in Great Britain in 2015 by Prospect Books,
26 Parke Road, London SW13 9NG.
(https://prospectbooks.co.uk)

British Library Cataloguing in Publication Data:
A catalogue entry of this book is available from the British Library.

Typeset and designed by Tom Jaine.

ISBN 978-1-909248-32-8

Printed and bound in Malta by the Gutenberg Press Ltd, Malta.

Table of Contents

Acknowledgements

Although I had previously published works on Tudor and Stuart cookery, my major study commenced 25 years ago, when the Historic Royal Palaces Agency asked me to put Henry VIII's magnificent kitchens at Hampton Court Palace back into practical use, just as in the 1530s. Over the following years, living in the Palace and working as a Tudor master cook for weeks at a time, provided me with a unique body of practical experience, giving real insights into the masses of surviving evidence from the period. For this I offer my most grateful thanks to all the staff of Historic Royal Palaces who assisted in the project, and especially to Marc Meltonville and 'the lads in the Kitchen', whose enthusiasm, tireless energy, skill and friendship made the whole challenging slog so successful, popular and, for me in particular, highly informative.

Anyone who undertakes a detailed study of this period has to rely heavily on the published works of generations of historians, past and present. Although there has been no personal communication between us, I would like to record my enormous debt of gratitude to Dr David Starkey, Dr Simon Thurley, Dr Marc Girouard and the late Dr Joan Thirsk for the vast wealth of great scholarship that they have made available through their many books and articles. I also wish to thank Dr Alan Borg, the late Dr Ian Goodall, Mr John Malden and Mr John Allen for their helpful information, and particularly Dr Chris Woolgar for the use of his transcription of the second Northumberland Household Book. As always, the librarians and archivists of the Yorkshire Archaeological Society have been constantly helpful.

Some of the descriptions and drawings of buildings, fixtures and fittings given in the following pages are a by-product of my professional work for the National Trust, English Heritage and the owners of great country houses. However, I also wish to thank the many museum curators, home-owners and others, too numerous to mention individually, for the ready access they have given me to their collections and properties.

As is now usual, I must thank Mrs Susan Houghton for her great assistance in bringing this book to its eventual completion, and to Mr Tom Jaine, for all his care in its design and publication, as well as to Catheryn Kilgarriff, the publisher.

To all of these, I offer my most grateful thanks.

Peter Brears
Leeds,
December, 2014.

A Note on the Recipes

Anyone who has taken an intelligent interest in food history as presented in period dramas and cooked by celebrity chefs on television and other London-based media already knows that Tudor food was particularly obnoxious. Not only were its ingredients made up of unmentionable animal parts, but they were rotten and cooked in squalor. To add to the mess, table manners were non-existent, even Henry VIII ravaging his food like a wild beast before throwing the remains about his chamber. Seeing actors and presenters recreating such scenes is thoroughly nauseating, especially to those who know that they lack all historical knowledge and integrity. They are nothing more than figments of the imagination of those who seek celebrity and lucre. The real tragedy is that their antics have successfully buried one certain truth: the food culture of upper-class Tudor and Stuart England was of top international status, exemplary in its preparation, presentation and consumption.

At the start of this period, cooking and dining still followed long-established medieval practices, but over the next century and a half the cooks and their employers enjoyed a unique burst of energetic experimental research and developments. Freed from medieval conventions, provided with new foodstuffs, and not yet confined by the classical European cuisine of later centuries, they explored every aspect of technique, flavour, texture, shape, colour and scent. Their results have to be experienced to be fully appreciated. This can produce interesting reactions, however, since it makes us question that comfortable relationship between our mouths and our minds which we have inherited along with many other aspects of our culture. We know that apples are sweet, and onions are savoury, and we like both in their respective roles, but what if we cook them together to obtain a perfect mid-flavour? Is it pleasant – certainly! – but how can we define it? Is it a sweet or a savoury? Where would we place it on the menu? The only reason why bacon should not be cooked with cream, rosewater, orange zest and sugar is the indoctrination of our palates, but such conditioning did not apply in the sixteenth and early seventeenth centuries. It is very important to appreciate this basic fact in order to approach the recipes in this book with the open mind they deserve and require. Their products can be both interesting and challenging, but rarely dull.

All food is essentially sensory, being experienced through a combination of its taste, texture, temperature, aroma and appearance. Each of these is subject to considerable variation according to the characteristics of the raw ingredients, the techniques used to prepare and cook them, and the skill of the cook. It can therefore be reasonably argued that we can never recapture the truly authentic food experiences of the past unless we literally work from the ground up. Given this caveat, and using ingredients as close to period varieties as possible, it is still feasible to recreate dishes which are almost identical to those described in early recipe books and menus. To do so is not only a fascinating gustatory experience, but it helps to reveal that, just as in art, architecture and music, there are tastes which clearly define their period and culture.

In the following pages all the recipes are given in modernized rather than original forms. The reason for this is that they were usually written as aides-mémoire by cooks who assumed that their reader had a great deal of prior knowledge and experience. Oven temperatures and cooking times were rarely given, for example, while quantities, even if provided, were frequently suited to serving a large household, not a modern family meal or dinner party. The original recipes also assumed ready access to large roasting-hearths, wood-fired 'beehive' ovens and built-in boilers, for which we now have to substitute modern domestic ovens and hobs. To accommodate these changes the modernized recipes give their reduced quantities in both imperial and metric measures. Spoon measures all represent their level, rather than heaped volumes, while medium-sized eggs have been used throughout. The temperatures given in centigrade, fahrenheit and gas marks are those for standard ovens, and should therefore be reduced accordingly when using one which is fan-assisted.

The recipes have been selected to demonstrate the characteristic dishes of the period using foodstuffs which are currently available and acceptable. This explains the absence of swan, suckling pig, brains, chitterlings and the like. However, no allowance has been made for modern alternatives to saturated fats, readers being left to substitute low-fat or vegetarian versions of ingredients as they choose. It is important to use raw materials of good quality, organic fruit, vegetables, meats, eggs and dairy produce usually giving better and probably more authentic results.

The period covered by this book is one of the most interesting in English food history. Its recipes are well worth reviving today, not just because they represent a virtually unknown aspect of the country's cultural history, but because they are really excellent, interesting and satisfying in their own right.

Introduction

The period 1500–1660 was one of unprecedented change. Henry Jenkins of Bolton-on-Swale in Yorkshire experienced them all. Born around 1501 (although there are no parish registers to prove it), he had carried arrows for the battle of Flodden as a youth in 1513, and then lived on through to his eventual death, aged 169, in 1670. He grew up in a stable England, one that enjoyed a rich, unified culture, its religion, social structure and government all firmly, apparently immovably, fixed by centuries of custom and practice. He then saw everything change beyond belief. Monasteries closed, churches were stripped, the Pope was declared Antichrist, war swept the land laying waste to castles, mansions and many smaller houses, and a king was killed as a republic replaced a monarchy. There were years of poverty and plague on an unremembered scale, and even the very landscape changed as sheep farming destroyed villages, and new mansions arose, built by new men with new ideas. His lifetime spanned all these immense changes, as England was transformed from a completely medieval society to one embracing every aspect of early modern life.

As far as his own food was concerned, much remained relatively stable. Locally grown wheat, barley, rye and oats continued to provide bread, cakes, porridge and ale, and local herds the fresh and salt beef, bacon, milk and cheese, as in past and future centuries. But although not a wealthy man, he would also have probably enjoyed a number of dishes virtually unknown in his youth. These might have included fruit cakes, boiled cereal puddings, pastries, pickles and sugary gingerbreads and preserves. He would have seen changes in his tableware too, as turned ash-wood cups and wooden trenchers were replaced by new pottery versions, lead-glazed to give their attractive, glossy and non-porous finishes. As for his table manners, they would have continued in the old medieval style, rumours of effeminate fork-flourishing posers probably causing much raising of eyebrows and shaking of heads.

Had he ever entered any of the noble and gentry houses of the region, such as nearby Kiplin Hall, built around 1625 by Lord Baltimore, founder of Maryland, he would have discovered that a completely new style of cooking had been introduced from the mid-sixteenth century. Quite amazingly, it had rapidly destroyed the centuries-old recipes, culinary practices and vocabulary of high-quality medieval cookery. Even though the connection at first appears remote, this change may be positively attributed to the dissolution of all monasteries and chantries in the late 1530s. Within a few years their lands had been sold to great magnates, and successively on to others down the social scale. These new owners rapidly concentrated their entrepreneurial skills on exploiting the potential of their estates, either by expanding previous monastic enterprises, or opening up new mines, metal and glass works and other ventures, or by agricultural activities. Instead of being asked to support the Church and its vast entourage of clergy, the large revenues generated by these lands now went directly into the pockets of their owners. Some were re-invested in further money-making schemes, but this still left a very substantial surplus available for pleasure and show.

Across the country, new or re-built houses sprang up throughout the late sixteenth and early seventeenth centuries, their kitchens, halls and parlours all filled with the best new equipment, furniture, textiles and tableware. Regional centres, such as York, Chester, Bristol and Norwich, now began to supply a whole range of luxury goods and services, everything which the aspiring new families needed to confirm their place in society. Each city developed its own 'season', usually associated with sittings of the courts, which drew in every affluent family from the surrounding countryside. Some set up temporary home in rented rooms, while others established their own town-houses for use mainly at these annual gatherings. While husbands conducted their legal and financial business, wives busied themselves with socializing and shopping, organizing dinners, visiting fashionable houses and events, and buying clothes, foods and tableware. The boys might also be given fencing lessons and, along with the girls, tuition in other social skills such as music and dancing. All these activities were highly enjoyable, making the old country routines seem dull in comparison. As a result, the wealthy began to spend an increasing amount of time either at their provincial centre or, if at all possible, in London itself.

Here the expenses were high, but the potential for political, social and commercial advancement was unparalleled. The country's finest range of craftsmen and shops were concentrated here, offering every conceivable variety of luxury goods and services. It was also the seat of the Court, the focus of the nation's prestige and fashion. All this activity drew in people from all over England, mainly internal migration boosting the population of the capital from around 5,000 to 20,000 in the latter half of the sixteenth century. The authorities repeatedly ordered families to return to their country estates, where their roles as administrators, justices of the peace and leaders of local society were being neglected, but with little effect. The social life of the capital was far too attractive, especially for the new generation of wealthy wives who, apparently unlike their medieval noble predecessors, enjoyed cooking luxurious meals both for their families and for their dinner guests.

In this fashionable world, novelty was everything. If searching for printed sources for recipes up to the 1570s, there were only two to choose from. Richard

Pynson's *Boke of Cokery* of 1500 was virtually identical to *A Noble Boke Off Cookry ffor a Prynce Houssolde*, a manuscript of around 1470 probably transcribed from an earlier source. The other was the anonymous *A Proper Newe Booke of Cokerye* published by Richard Lant in 1546. Both were essentially medieval in character, the only decidedly modern recipes in the latter being for short pastry tarts, and for 'a Cover Tarte After the Frenche Fashyon'. If new recipes were required, neither of these books would be of much use, and so had to be discovered elsewhere, particularly from overseas. Up to the mid-sixteenth century England still held lands in France, Henry VIII's military and political expeditions there bringing knowledge of that country's developing cookery to many of his court. His own Yeoman Cook for the King's Mouth in the 1540s was Pero le Doulce, otherwise Pero the Frenchman, while as early as 1526 'Giggots' of mutton had appeared in his diet, evidence of a growing French influence.[1]

Other countries also exerted an influence on English cooks. The Portuguese, for example, contributed various recipes from the 1550s, these including sweet dumplings, called Fystes and balls of light pastry called Farts.[2] A number of other sweetmeat recipes probably originated from Portugal, since it was a major source of the highly prized, thick, sweet quince paste called *marmelado*. Spain certainly provided recipes for more conserved quinces, and for its *olla podridas* (i.e.'rotten pots'). These had first been experienced by ambassadors to the Spanish court, Lord Herbert of Cherbury seeing their mixed stewed meats built up in tall cones, each topped by a sparrow. By the early seventeenth century instructions for English versions were appearing here in print.[3] There were also a few recipes adopted from Italy, Germany, Holland, and even Turkey.[4] All of these introductions, when combined with numerous home-produced developments, ensured that England's long tradition of medieval dishes went into a rapid decline from the mid-sixteenth century, becoming virtually extinct in polite households by around 1600.

It now appears surprising to discover that some quintessentially English everyday foods, those which sustained the nation up to the mid-twentieth century, were purely French in origin. These included all stews or casseroles made with chopped meats and vegetables. Robert May first published these in 1660 as 'stews of Beef, in the French Fashion', along with 'hashes' reincarnating the remains of the Sunday roast, but actually true French *hachis*.[5] This period also saw the introduction of all our modern forms of pastry, our fruit loaves, fruit cakes, sweet boiled puddings, milk puddings, and even our scrambled eggs on toast.[6] It was this country's major period of culinary revolution, one which largely established what we were to eat, and how we were to cook, over the next three to four hundred years.

The same elements which had instigated this change in our diet, also brought profound changes to the ways in which all polite households organized themselves. Throughout the medieval period the status of every family was confirmed by the size of its almost entirely male domestic staff, and by its close relationships, both with superior families from whom it received patronage, and inferior families to whom it provided patronage. The centuries-old feudal system had used this principle to control the whole of society, from monarch down to peasant. By accepting young boys and girls of the immediately lower rank into their households, and bringing them up as a blend of adoptees and domestic servants, each tier of family had established life-long, multi-generational relationships of great strength. Often extended into the arrangement of marriages and part- or full-time domestic employment, this system had produced an extremely well-established and cohesive medieval society. Everybody knew their place, and accepted its responsibilities, including those of hospitality and providing support for poorer neighbours and tenants.

There had always been some flexibility, allowing families to rise and fall according to their means, but this was hardly able to cope with the influx of the numerous newly wealthy entrepreneurial class. Unlike the established families, they inherited neither responsibilities for, nor relationships with, those who lived on their newly acquired estates. Most did not wish to provide employment for extensive numbers of serving men and retainers as these were now seen more as a drain on financial resources than as a source of status and influence. Why support hangers-on, when the costs of their wages and keep could be enjoyed in the form of fine clothes, fashionable luxuries, and high living in London? As food prices rose, the old established families began to see what their new rivals were doing, and decided to follow their lead. The practice of keeping 'secret house' in a lodge by the country house while annual accounts and refurbishments were completed was now replaced by longer periods of absence in London or one of the lesser provincial capitals. By the late sixteenth and early seventeenth centuries the effects of these changes was being felt throughout the country, many writers lamenting the passing of the old hospitable ways of life. To Thomas Haywood:[7]

> in good hospitality, there can be nothing found that's ill, he that's a good house-keeper keeps a good table, a good table is never without good stooles, good stooles never without good guests, good guests never without good cheere, good cheere cannot be without good digestion, good digestion keeps men in good health, and therefore all good people, that bear good minds as you love goodnesses, be sure to keepe good meat and drinke in your houses and so you shall be called good men, and nothing can come on't but good, I warrant you.

Robert Herrick's *Panegyric to Sir Lewis Pemberton* also rejoiced in his subject's hospitality:[8]

> ... To the worn Threshold, Porch, Hall, Parlour, Kitchin,
> The fat-fed smoking Temple, which in
> The wholesome savour of thy mighty Chines
> Invites to supper him who dines,
> Where laden spits, warp't with large Ribbs of Beefe,
> Not represent, but give reliefe
> To the lanke Stranger, and sowre Swain;
> Where both may feed, and come again.
> For no black-bearded Vigil from thy doore
> Beats with a button'd-staffe the poore;
> But from thy warm-loving-hatching gates each may
> Take friendly morsels, and there stay
> To Sun his thin-clad members, if he likes,
> For there no Porter keep'st who strikes.
> No commer to thy Roofe his *Guest-vite* wants;
> Or staying there is scourg'd with taunts
> Of some rough Groom, who, (quirkt with Corns) says, Sir,
> Y'ave dipt too long i'th' Vinegar;
> And with our Broth and bread, and bits, Sir, fried,
> Y'ave fared well, pray make an end;
> Two days y'ave larded here; a third, yee know,
> Makes guests and fish smell strong; pray go
> You to some other chimney, and there take
> Essay of other goblets, make
> Merry at another's hearth ...

Similarly an early seventeenth-century poem *The Old and the New Courtier* epitomizes the different approaches to housekeeping and hospitality practised by country gentlemen of Elizabeth's and James' reigns respectively. Now the old weapon-hung hall, the setting for bountiful entertainment, was rebuilt for the display of paintings and a shove-ha'penny board which never bore food. The fifty-two blue-capped and livery-badged household serving men were now dispersed, their places taken by a new gentleman-usher, two waiters to carry up the food, and a waiting gentle*woman* who kept her fellow servants on short rations. Where six cooks had been kept busy, there was now just a French cook 'to devise kickshaws and toys', the buttery hatch now dispensing its ales and beers not every day, but only once every five or six days:[9]

With an old fashion, when Christmas was come,
To call in all his neighbours with a bagpipe or a drum,
And good cheer enough to furnish out every old room,
And beer and ale would make a cat speak, and a wise man dumb.
Like an old Courtier of the Queen's
And the Queen's old Courtier
With a new fashion when Christmas was drawing on,
Upon a new journey they must all to London be gone,
And leave none to keep house in the country, but their new man John,
Who relieves all his neighbours with a great thump on the back with a cold stone.
Like a new Courtier of the King's
And the King's new Courtier.

This decay in hospitality was described in far greater detail in a book by 'I.M.' entitled *A Health to the Gentlemanly Profession of Servingmen: or, The Servingman's Comfort* of 1598. He starts by celebrating their qualities as chosen men of some status, often second sons of good breeding, displaying the wit, discretion and policy necessary for taking charge of their master's business affairs and worldly goods. They were strong, nimble and active, making ideal companions in fights, the hunting field and sports, as well as in undertaking all his domestic administration and table-service. They also dispensed his hospitality to visitors and to the poor, whenever he was absent from home. In return they received their keep, livery-clothing, a wage, an old-age pension and, most importantly, their master's protection and respect. Now, however, they were seen as expensive burdens, not worth their former remuneration, rewards or companionable status. Even the food and drink they received was reduced in both quality and quantity:[10]

> Where are the great Chines of staulled Beefe: the great blacke Jackes of doble Beere: the long Haull tables fully furnished with good victuals: and multitude of good fellowes assembling to ... men of worth: In a worde, they are all banyshed with the spirit of the Butterie, they are as rare in this age, as common in former tymes ... Now for [the three-year old fat] Beefe, Mutton, Veale, Pigge, Goose and Capon, which was the substaunce of their provision in those dayes ... so that there was good cheere with plentie for them that sate, good reversions [i.e. left-overs] for them that wayted, and great reliefe for the poore amongst those full platters. Now these bountifull and substantiall dyshes are changed into cates of lesse cost ... Goose-giblets [Pigs-trotters, etc.] to satisfie and content them that are served, yet not what shall answere the hungrie appetites of the attendaunts ... small are the broken meates that remayne to relieve the poore.

These changes took place gradually, as individual households decided either to reduce the number of their serving men to a minimum or, especially in noble houses, to continue the maintenance of large numbers to reflect their status. The general trend still remained constant, with gentlemanly serving men being replaced by fewer low-status servants who provided only basic domestic services, but none of the former companionship and loyalty to their employers.

The departure of numerous higher-status, trustworthy manservants left a considerable vacuum in many lesser noble and gentry houses. Their masters still required someone to maintain overall control of their domestic affairs, and the obvious people to do this were their constantly available, financially dependant, yet totally unwaged companions – their wives. Royal and noble wives had usually been provided with their own, separate households, leaving the main household in the sole charge of ranks of serving men who reported directly to their masters. Henry Percy 9th Earl of Northumberland, certainly believed that this was still the best policy:[11]

> The great discomodite of all I will beginne with, that is [that your wife] will have the commande of all your servants ... [Keep] that power in your selfe.
>
> The things that great mens wyfes ought to endevor, and are most proper for them in house affairs, is, to bring upp their children well ... to tender their helthes and education, and to obey their husbands. [Also] to see that their women ... kepe the linnen sweete; to have care that when great personages shall visitt, to sit at an ende of a table, and carve handsomly.
>
> The kitching, buttry, or pantry, are not places proper for them: a dary is tolerable; for soe may yow have perhaps a dische of butter, a soft cheese, or some clouted crème, once in a sommer. Poultry and fed fowle I have sene their huswifry stretche to, in overlooking their darymaydes; for the commendation of a fatt pulletts legge of my Ladyes owen carving, to a good pallate is a great vertue in a belly-god's estimation.

If a wife were to be given control of the household accounts, he thought that she would cut the essentials in order to spend on her own vanities: 'the beefe-potts would be translated into wardropps, and multitudes of servants into a few privat baudes, ether to their passions or their persons, [e.g.] Jewells.' However, such misogynist opinions were anathema to many of the Earl's contemporaries. Thomas Fuller celebrated the benefits of wifely care in *The Good Wife* of 1652;[12]

> She keeps home ... if she have not her husband's company ... For the house is the woman's centre. In her husband's absence, she is wife and deputy-husband ... At his return he finds all things so well ... The heaviest work of her servants

she maketh lightly by orderly and seasonably enjoining it. Wherefor her service is counted a preferment, and her teaching better than wages.

Ladies' diaries of the period confirm their expanding role as capable domestic managers, both instructing their servants in all household matters, and leading them by practical example. Around 1600 Lady Margaret Hoby recorded her days spent in supervising the sowing of wheat, measuring corn in the granary, catching trout or crayfish, gathering apples, pulling hemp, potting honey, preserving, and candlemaking.[13] These and a whole series of other tasks were of paramount importance in this age of domestic self-sufficiency.

Despite the Earl of Northumberland's reservations, many well-to-do ladies were excellent practical cooks, more than capable of running their kitchens and producing excellent food. Instead of competing with their established household cooks, who prepared all the ordinary, everyday meals, they concentrated on a limited number of high-quality dishes for their own dinner tables, along with the more delicate baking of cakes, pastries and biscuits and expensive sugar confectionery for banquets of sweetmeats. In order to replicate such cookery, especially when enjoyed at dinners taken away from home, they collected recipes, and carefully transcribed them into their own manuscript recipe books. Some of these are of exceptional size and quality, far exceeding any of the man-authored printed recipe books of Elizabethan or Jacobean date. Their instructions for marketing, noting how to determine the desirable qualities of most foodstuffs, show that they had a deep understanding of raw materials and knew how to obtain the best value for their money. Their many recipes, often neatly indexed, might be attributed to a particular source, such as a lady donor, or its locality; for this is the period in which Banbury Cakes, Shrewsbury Cakes, Oxfordshire Cakes and the like make their first appearance.

Other recipes were transcribed from printed cookery books, that of the late-Elizabethan Mrs Beale including a number from *The Good Huswifes Handmaide for the Kitchin*, first published in 1588, for example.[14] Recognizing the growing culinary interests of wealthy, fashionable ladies, the London publishers now began to issue titles deliberately designed to serve this new, expanding market. They included:

M.R.	*The Widdowes Treasure*, 1584
?	*The Good Huswife's Jewell* [in 2 parts], 1585
?	*The Good Hous-Wives Treasurie*, 1588
A.W.	*A Book of Cookrye*, 1591
Sir Hugh Plat	*Delights for Ladies*, 1600

Similar volumes were to appear throughout the seventeenth century, still addressing the same lady-cooks, and providing them with a range of recipes clearly intended for the dining parlour and banquet-house rather than the hall. Some were also 'Plentifully furnished with precious and approved secrets in Phisicke and Chirurgery, for the health and pleasure of Mankinde.'[15]

Although beyond the scope of this book, the role of ladies in preserving the health of the nation throughout this period cannot be over-stated. The Dissolution had effectively destroyed the country's medieval health service, particularly by the closure of major monastic hospitals. Since they had nowhere else to go, and still expected the protection of their landlords, the bulk of the community now turned to literate, educated ladies to provide the same level of care. Many major houses had prepared their own medicines before the Dissolution, the Earls of Northumberland having 28 different 'waters' in their stillroom in 1512, for example, while Sir William Webster, the chaplain, was distilling strawberry and other waters for the Willoughbys of Wollaton Hall, Nottingham, in 1524. In the 1540s some former monks became peripatetic distillers of medicinal waters, travelling from one country house to another from violet-time in spring through to late autumn.[16] Using such potions, either made up from instructions in printed recipe books, or recorded in their own hand-written volumes, the ladies regularly dosed their family, friends and local communities. They also practised quite serious surgical procedures. The entries in Lady Margaret Hoby's diaries give a clear indication of the levels of medical care she had to provide.[17]

> 30/1/1600: 'I dressed a poore boies legge that came to me ... after I dressed the hand of one of our servants that was verie sore Cutt';
> 12/7/1600: 'I made readie a pugatione for my Cosine Isons woman';
> 18/9/1600: 'gave a poore woman of Caton a salve for hir arm';
> 26/8/1601: [a couple from Silpho brought their new-born baby to her, as it had no anus] 'earnestly intreated to Cutt the place to see if any passhage could be made, but although I Cutt deepe and seerched there was none to be found.'

While such ladies were expanding their own roles in the management of their households, moving into previously male-dominated activities, a similar change was taking place in the lower ranks. As well-bred serving men departed from gentry houses, along with all-male kitchen staffs, their places were now gradually being taken by women. New words now entered the English language to identify their new roles. The first recorded 'Woman-coke' appeared in 1530, the 'Kitchenmaid' in 1550, the 'Kitchen-wench' in 1590, the female 'Housekeeper' in 1607 and 'Scullion-wench' in 1602.[18]

As we have seen, the sixteenth and early seventeenth centuries saw enormous changes in the recipes we used to cook our food, in the staffing of our households, and the growing roles of women in domestic management. Another change was just as important, that of newly available foodstuffs. England's medieval gardeners had produced a useful range of culinary vegetables and herbs but had not kept up with their Continental contemporaries. Market gardening had made great advances in Holland and Flanders, Catherine of Aragon bringing in Flemish gardeners to raise her salads, while Catherine Parr regularly sent to Flanders for her salad-stuffs. The growing demand for fresh vegetables led to the establishment of market gardens in England, particularly to serve the London markets. Writing in 1651, Robert Child told how old men in Surrey remembered 'the first gardeners that came into these parts & plant cabages, collerflours and to sowe turneps, carrots and parsnips, and to sow Raithe peaze, all of which time were great varieties, we having few or non in England but what came from Holland and Flanders.'[19] The results of these developments, coupled with those promoted by the ladies and professional gardeners of private households, made a wide range of vegetables, herbs and fruits available for kitchen use. The following lists include all those which Robert May required to complete the recipes in his *Accomplisht Cook* of 1660:

VEGETABLES	HERBS	FRUITS
Artichokes, Globe,	Alexanders	Apples
Artichokes, Jerusalem (fr. c.1620)	Balm	Apples, Codlings
Asparagus	Bloodwort	Apples, Pippins
Beans, French & Garden	Borage	Apricots
Beetroot	Burnet	Barberries
Cabbages, White Cabbages	Camomile	Cherries
Cauliflowers	Chervil	Damsons
Carrots	Corn-Salad	Gooseberries
Chives	Garlic, Wild Garlic	Grapes
Coleworts, Red Coleworts	Marigold Flowers	Lemons
Cucumbers	Marjoram	Medlars
Endive, White Endive	Mint	Melons
Gourds	Parsley	Oranges
Lettuce, Cabbage Lettuce	Pennyroyal	Pears
Melons, Musk Melons	Purslane	Plums
Mushrooms, Champignons	Rosemary	Quinces
Onions	Sage, Red Sage	Raspberries
Parsnips	Samphire	Strawberries

Peas, Crucifix Peas	Savory	Wardens
Pumpions [Pumpkins]	Scurvy-grass	
Potatoes, Sweet Potatoes	Sorrel	
Skirrets	Succory	
Spinach	Tansy	
Turnips	Thyme	
Watercress		

Of these, the most important relatively recent introductions were citrus fruits and potatoes. Oranges and lemons had been great rarities in fifteenth-century England but, now imported in much larger quantities from the Iberian peninsular, they provided a welcome and versatile alternative to vinegar in contributing a sharp flavour to a variety of dishes. When combined with sugar, they also produced a number of excellent banquet sweetmeats, while their raw juice made a piquant sauce for capon and other meats. As for potatoes, two separate plants had been introduced here during the later sixteenth century. The Sweet – Spanish – or, to Gerard the herbalist, common-potato *Ipomoea batatos* had been imported from Central America into Spain in the 1550s, whence it was carried into England, where it soon acquired a popular reputation as an aphrodisiac as well as a nutritive vegetable. By 1595 it was reported that these sweet 'Potato Roots are now so common among us, that even husbandmen buy them to please his wife. They nourish mightily, ... engendering much flesh, blood, and seed, but without increasing wind and lust.'[20] They must have been imported in quantity since they could not flourish in this climate except as specially tended garden plants. John Goodyer made a special note of those he saw growing at his brother-in-law's house at Sheet, Hampshire, in 1637. The Virginian potato *Solanum tuberosum* was certainly being grown in England by the 1590s, but its role as one of Britain's staple foods was not to be realized for a further two hundred years. It is interesting to find baked potatoes appearing on dinner and supper menus from October to December, 1605. Since sweet potatoes were not seen in season during these months, they must have been Virginian, but potatoes remained a comparative rarity on English tables throughout this period.[21]

The range of farmed and game animal foods changed very little between 1500 and 1660, the only significant introduction being the turkey, which probably arrived here from Mexico and Central America in the 1520s. Archbishop Cranmer listed it as a great bird for the table in 1541, while in 1550 William Strickland of Boynton was granted a turkey as his heraldic crest, its colouring being described as white feathers, red crest and wattles, and black legs.[22] Over the following years the turkey effectively replaced the peacock as a main item of poultry. Herons, bitterns, swans, cygnets and most wild birds were still eaten, as were seagulls. The latter were caught in the winter months and fattened in the poultry-yards to rid them of their distinctive fishiness. In 1590 these cost the enormous sum of 5s. each when bought for the Lords of the Star Chamber.[23]

A wide variety of fish and shellfish were also eaten:

SEA FISH	SHELLFISH	FRESHWATER FISH
Bass	Cockles	Bream
Conger eel	Crabs	Carp
Flounder	Crayfish	Eel
Gurnard	Lobsters	Perch
Halibut	Mussels	Pike
Herring	Oysters	Salmon
Lamprey	Prawns	Tench
Ling	Scallops	Trout
Mackerel	Shrimps	
Pilchard		
Plaice		
Rocket [Red Gurnard]	AMPHIBIANS	
Salmon	Frogs	
Smelt	INVERTEBRATES	
Sole	Snails	
Sprat	REPTILES	
Sturgeon	Tortoise	
Turbot		
Weever		

Most of these had a long history of culinary use here, but frogs' legs, snails and tortoises were never popular, their appearance in Robert May's repertoire being a direct result of his five years in France.[24]

Having set the scene, the following chapters each consider a different aspect of Tudor and Jacobean domestic economy, cookery and table service. It continues the story of English food, as commenced in my *Cooking and Dining in Medieval England* of 2008, and follows its general arrangement and approach. Having explored the planning and control of the whole household, which took place in the Counting House, it goes on to follow each successive step through to the service of meals. At every stage it draws on the widest range of archival, archaeological and architectural sources to present as complete an account as is currently feasible. Food history is primarily a multi-disciplinary subject, none of its contributory studies being sufficient within themselves to present an accurate and balanced account of the culinary past. It is also an essentially practical subject, no amount of scholarship compensating for a lack of kitchen experience. Fortunately I have been able to spend years in operational historic kitchens, being the first person to run Henry VIII's kitchens at Hampton Court Palace since 1737, for example. Only by using such buildings for their original purposes, living in them for weeks at a time, commissioning their practical equipment and using it to produce meals, has it been possible to fully appreciate the true integrity of all the extremely diverse sources of relevant information.

Similarly, it is imperative that anyone working in food history should avoid treating recipes merely as texts for archival studies. To appreciate what they actually mean, they must be experienced with all the senses, since the flavours, textures, shapes, colours and scents and techniques they reveal tell us much about the characteristic tastes of previous ages. The interpretation of the accounts, inventories and household regulations surviving in record offices is also improved by a working knowledge of cookery, catering and personnel management. The maintenance of adequate supplies, cleanliness and discipline has always been essential to the operation of every culinary organization. Henry VIII and his officers were well aware both of this fact, and of their responsibility for establishing the court's management procedures as a precedent which all others should follow.[25] The survival of their household regulations or ordinances provides an excellent starting point from which to explore the complex practices required to sustain one of the largest courts in Europe.

Figure 1. The back gate & counting house, Hampton Court Palace. The administrative staff of the royal household had their offices on the first floor, so that they might literally oversee everyone and everything entering and leaving the service wing. (1) Counting House (The Greencloth); (2–5) Comptroller's Lodgings; (6) Scullery Office; (7–8) Pastry Office; (9) Clerk of the Kitchen's Office; (10–11) Clerks Comptroller; (12–13) Cofferer's Office.

CHAPTER ONE

The Counting House

Throughout history food has always been a hard-won and relatively expensive commodity. Essential for supporting human life, its constant supply was only maintained by efficient means of production, acquisition and storage. In rural society as a whole, from labourer to lord, it was still possible to live on carefully rationed home-grown produce, with a surplus to spare to pay for rents, other essentials and, if fortunate, some luxuries too. For many others, however, especially if living in towns and cities, the bulk of their food had to be purchased from shops, markets or merchants. This meant that in either case an efficient means of financial control was absolutely essential, both for the continuity of supplies, and for regulating the size and content of meals year after year. Failure to do this could lead only to poverty, illness, starvation and eventual death.

By the early sixteenth century, the principles of managing domestic finances were already well developed. They were succinctly set down by Dr Andrew Boorde in his *Compendyous Regyment or Dyetary of Helth* of 1542:[1]

> Who soever he be that wyll kepe an howse, he must ordre the expenses of his howse according to the rest of his [income, or] shal fal to poverte ... as it is dayly sene by experyence of many men; wherefore they [who] eschewe such prodygalyte and inconvenyence, must devyde his [income] into 3 equal porcyons or partes. The first part must serve to provyde for meate and drynke, & all other necessary thynges for the sustencyon of the howseholde. The second porcyon [must be] for apparell, servants' wages and alms. The 3rd porcyon must be reserved for urgent causes in tyme of nede, as in sycknesse, reparacyon of howses [etc.]

Francis Bacon also believed in this method of financial planning:[2]

> Riches are for spending, and spending for honour and good actions – therefore extraordinary expence must be limited by the worth of the occasion. Ordinary expence ought to be limited by a man's estate ... and not subject to deceit and abuse of servants ... his ordinary expences ought to be but half of his receipts, and if he thinks to wax rich, but to the third part. He ... need both choose

well those whom he employeth, and change them often; for new are more timorous and less subtle.

These were not abstract concepts, but formed the practical basis for the management of most households. Around 1600, for example, the Hippisley family of Ston Easton, Somerset, recorded that the first part of their income should be spent on food, clothes, heating and household goods, and the second on pleasure, building and improvement of their farms and parks.[3]

In most large households, the income received from rents, court fees, business ventures and other sources was collected by the receiver, his cash and records, along with those of every other income-producing department, being subject to periodic inspection by the auditor. The auditor then informed the head of the household and his senior officers of his findings and the totals received, before recording all the relevant details in a permanent account book.[4] In order to keep the auditor away from the other staff and their influence as he completed this task, he was frequently provided with his own audit chamber, which might have just his bed, a few chairs or stools, and a long table on which to set out his papers.[5]

Now that they knew what financial resources were available, the head officers of the household could meet together to determine the budgets for their forthcoming expenditure. The room in which they gathered each day for this and similar purposes was usually called the counting house in the largest households, but it might also be known as the 'checker', or simply as 'the officers' chamber'.[6]

Here a large table was set up, its top being covered with a green baize cloth marked out in squares, on which accounts could be calculated using small round counters in a similar manner to the beads on an abacus. Usually the counting house table was rectangular, but that at Petworth House in Sussex, probably of early sixteenth century date, was 'round ... of wainscott with a round table in yt. the counting house having deskes and seats round it.'[7] In the royal household the table was flanked by settles with shoulder-height screens, openings being left at each end for access. A drawing of 1472 shows one in use, the Lord Steward and Treasurer being seated alongside the Comptroller and Clerks of the Greencloth who are completing their records using round counters and a rectangular standish or inkwell.[8] The early-1530s accounts for fitting out the counting house over the back gate at Hampton Court describe:[9]

A pair of timbers for a table in the newe counting house
for an iron trestle for the same table
for 2 locks for the cupboard in the same table
for 6 heart rings [handles] for tills in the same table

and also the purchase of its covering of green cloth.

In 1588 the Earl of Leicester's counting house at Leicester House in London similarly had a deal-boarded frame-built table covered with green table-carpets.[10] The table at the Earl of Rutland's controller's chamber at Belvoir Castle also had its top covered with four yards of green cloth costing a shilling a yard in 1542, showing how widely this practice was followed.[11] The 1576 inventory of Thomas Prestwood, a wealthy merchant in Exeter, lists the counting tables or boards to be found in his three counting houses:[12]

In the Counting house
One Iron Cheste 40*s.*
Two Iron fawcelettes [taps] 5*s.*
One other Chest 3*s.* 4*d.*
A quysshen 12*d.*
One countinge borde with shelves 4s
other tryffles as glasses 5*s.*

In the Countinge house adjoyning to the [Higher] Chamber
A borde and shelves 12*d.*

In the Countinge house by the hall with the bookes
[2 Geneva bibles, 2 service books, Calvin, Hall's *Chronicle*, books in English, French & Latin]
A table and sealings 20*s.*
A pare of ballaunce and weights 20*d.*
A pyle of weights 6*s.* 8*d.*
A great weight of brasse 2*s.*
A pare of gold ballaunce 12*d.*
Item certeyne tables [etc.] 26*s.* 8*d.*

In the royal household, the green tablecloth had already transferred its name to the group of important head officers and clerk which met around it every morning as the Board, or Court, of the Greencloth. As the household ordinances clearly stated, 'at the green-cloth ys alwey represented the Kinges power touching matters of thys household.'[13] It even had its own coat of arms, a key and a white stick arranged as a diagonal cross, to demonstrate its right to open, close and administer justice throughout the household, all on a green background which represented the green cloth.

The internal management of the royal household had been subject to some 460 years of continuous development by 1526, when its practices were thoroughly revised for Henry VIII by his Chancellor, Cardinal Wolsey.[14] In the Eltham Ordinances the Lord Steward, who had previously supervised the household, was replaced by a Lord Great Master, in the person of George Talbot, Earl of Shrewsbury. He was directly responsible to the King for introducing job descriptions, defining disciplinary procedures and promoting the maximum level of efficiency. He was supported by the Treasurer, Sir William Fitzwilliam, who supervised the sourcing and control of all the households' resources and maintaining its discipline. Next came the Comptroller, Sir Henry Guilford, who managed the Treasurer's finances, agreed the specifications and prices of all goods inward, authorized payments and audited the accounts of each department of the household. To signify that these three head officers held their authority directly from the King, each carried a white staff of office, giving them the combined title of the White Sticks. They each sat on the Privy Council, and attended the King each day.

The White Sticks may be considered as the directors of the royal household, with the Cofferer as the chief executive who effectively ran the administration. He received the money required to fund the household, issued it to the purchasing officers, paid their invoices and ensured that quarterly and annual records of expenditure were prepared for audit. Following reforms introduced by Thomas Cromwell in 1539–40, he also had to check the expenditure on a daily, weekly and quarterly basis, settle the accounts every month and, most importantly, pay all the wages of the household staff.[15] A new tier of management was introduced at the same time, with two Great Masters and a clerk to supervise the management of the King's and the Queen's households, presenting their accounts to the head officers every six weeks.

The bulk of the clerical work was undertaken by a series of clerks. Every morning the Clerk of the Greencloth noted down each department's expenditure for the previous day in his book of expenses and then entered their totals in the main docket. This parchment volume provided the information he needed to prepare periodic reviews of expenditure, and complete the Cofferer's book of accounts for each year. Although primarily responsible for recording financial transactions, he also maintained the rules of the counting house and, once or twice a week in the company of a Clerk Comptroller, inspected every room in the household's use to see that everything was in order and that only authorized personnel were present.

The Clerk Comptrollers were chiefly concerned with the acquisition and control of foodstuffs and other domestic supplies. At the start of each year the head officers took their advice when setting down in a book kept for this purpose in the counting house the approved prices, quantities and qualities of everything they required. Using this as a guide, the purveyors or purchasing officers of the various departments then arranged the contracts for wheat for the Bakehouse, wine for the Cellar, ale for the Buttery, poultry for the Poultry and meat and fish for the Acatry. Additional fresh supplies were also brought in by the Clerk of the Markets. When these goods and their accounts had been inspected by the Greencloth, the Clerk Comptrollers checked them for quality and entered their quantities in the Book of Records. Every day these entries were compared with what had been used during the previous day to ensure that no excess consumption had taken place. A further check was carried out at the end of every month, so that the contents of every department could be confirmed. These records then enabled the clerks to complete the Book of Comptrollment, the final record of purchased supplies, ready for inclusion in the Cofferer's year-end accounts.

The Clerk Comptrollers' other duties were largely concerned with personnel matters. Every three months they drew up lists of the names and wages of every member of staff, and used this to check for any unauthorized absences, and for everyone being where they should be. They also ensured that only the correct wages were given, and that only the permitted perquisites of office were taken.

Supervised by a Clerk Comptroller, the Clerk of the Spicery controlled six separate departments – the Spicery itself, the Confectionery for sugarwork and fruit, the Wafery for wafers, the Chaundry for candles and the like, the Ewery for linens, and the Laundry for washing. Every day he had to report the previous day's expenditure and consumption of supplies to the Greencloth, with further monthly and yearly accounts, ready for the Cofferer.

Finally, there came the Clerk of the Kitchen, who supervised all those departments responsible for cooking and serving the food. These included the Woodyard for fuel, the Poultry, the Pastry, the Kitchen, the Saucery, the Scullery for utensils, the Pantry for bread, the Buttery for beer and the Cellar for wine. He too had to present his daily, weekly, monthly and yearly accounts to the Greencloth. His day probably started around 5 a.m. when, in the presence of a Clerk of the Greencloth and a Clerk Comptroller, he entered the larders to see the meat or fish cut into the correct number of pieces to serve everyone at dinner and their transfer to the cooks. He then accompanied the Clerk Comptroller into the kitchen, to issue instructions for their cooking. Before 8 a.m., he had to present his previous day's accounts to the clerks in the counting house, so they could be checked by the White Sticks at the Greencloth before 9 a.m. Just before 10 a.m., he joined the Clerk of the Greencloth, the Clerk Comptroller and the Surveyor at the kitchen dressers, to see that every dish for every course was properly cooked, served and accounted for. He did the same at 4 p.m. when supper was served, and then toured the larders and kitchens, to check the quantities of food remaining in store.

The whole series of procedures just described may seem over-complicated for the management of a kitchen – until the sheer scale of the operation is fully appreciated. In 1539–40 the total costs for a single year comprised:

The King's Side food	£7035	0*s.*	10¾*d.*
The Queen's Side food	£4158	12*s.*	8½*d.*

Food for the Household	£6367	17*s*.	0¾*d*.
Fuel, equipment, etc.	£4445	2*s*.	6*d*.
Total	£22,006	3*s*.	2*d*.

In the early twenty-first century, this is the equivalent of some £7,000,000, which shows why such careful accounting was essential.

During the reigns of Edward VI, Philip and Mary, and Elizabeth, the same basic management structure still remained in place, but became more expensive and less efficient as the officers increasingly sought to line their own pockets rather than protect the interests of the household. Silver dishes were stolen, wines were served to unauthorized people, food was carried out of the court, cooks took large pieces of meat under the pretence of testing it for poisons, and courtiers' servants were provided with free bed and board. In 1604 James I banned all these abuses, reduced the number of dishes served at meals, and reiterated many of the 1539–40 ordinances in order to control and diminish the excessive levels of expenditure.[16] The same principles were followed by Charles I and by his Board of the Greencloth. In 1630 he had granted a tierce of 42 gallons of sack to his poet, Ben Jonson, but the Greencloth decided not to pay up. In retaliation, he attacked them in verse:[17]

> ... would the King but grant
> His poet leave to sing his Household true,
> He'd frame such ditties of their store, and want,
> Would make the very green-cloth to look blue;
> And rather wish, in their expence of sack,
> So the allowance from the King to use
> As the old bard should no canary lack.
> 'Twere better spare a butt, than spill his muse,
> For in genius of a poet's verse
> The King's fame lives. Go now, deny this tierce.

Within a few years such requests were in vain, for the Civil Wars had completely swept away the monarchy and its long-established household.

Since Tudor and Stuart nobles frequented the royal court, some of them serving as senior household officers, they regularly observed the excellence of its accounting principles. Clearly their own establishments were much smaller in every way, but their need to explore strict economies was just as great. This led them to adopt as many controls on finance and materials as served their particular needs. There was never any single standard approach, each household developing its own distinct methodology.

The house books of Francis Clifford, 4th Earl of Cumberland, of Skipton Castle and Londesborough House in Yorkshire, provide a good example of noble accountancy.[18] Using a separate page for each day of the week, commencing on Sunday, the clerk started a column down the left margin with a priced list of everything which had been received into the kitchen. These started with the *Caterparcels*, all the goods and services bought in from external sources, including foodstuffs, utensils, repairs, and their associated transport costs. The *Stores* detailed what had been brought in from the existing stocks in the garners, larders and pantries, or from the estate. *Venison* listed the deer from the parks, or received as gifts, while *Bakemeats* listed the pies and pastries from the bakehouse. Down the right-hand side of the same page he then made a list of the *Old Remains*, the foods left in the kitchen from the previous day, together with the *New Remains*, the quantities remaining at the end of that day's cooking. If the *Old Remains* listed eleven rabbits, and the *New Remains* ten rabbits, for example, it proved that only one rabbit had been used on that day. By contrast, if five chickens were in the *Old Remains*, and sixty-four in the *New Remains*, it showed that at least fifty-nine chickens had been brought in. Finally the clerk added the names of all *Persons Extraordinary* to record all the visitors served in addition to those comprising the established household, in order to explain the additional expenditure incurred.

Every Saturday night this information was used to produce the weekly account. To do this each page was divided into eleven vertical columns:

1: *Particulars*, listing each separate item purchased or issued into the kitchen during the previous week.
2: *Old Remains*, the quantities of each food remaining in the kitchen at the end of the previous week, e.g. 38 qtrs of beef.
3: *Value* of the old remains e.g. £2 18*s*. 0*d*.
4: *Caterparcels*, being the quantities of new supplies purchased for the kitchen.
5: *Value* of the caterparcels.
6: *Store*, showing the new supplies issued into the kitchen from the household's own sources, e.g. 35 quarters of beef.
7: *Value* of the stores, e.g. £2 17*s*. 8*d*.
8: *Expenditure*, being the quantity of any item used or 'spent' during the previous week, e.g. 36 quarters of beef.
9: *Value* of the spent items, e.g. £2 15*s*. 8*d*.
10: *New Remains*, the quantity of all foods currently in the kitchen, calculated by adding columns 2 and 6, and subtracting column 8,

e.g.	2. *Old Remains*	38 qtrs. beef
	6. *Store*	35 ditto
	Total	73 ditto
	less 8. *Spent*	36 ditto
	10. *New Remains*	37 ditto

11: *Value* of the new remains , calculated by adding columns 3 and 7, and subtracting column 9, e.g.

3. *Value of Old Remains*	£2	18*s*.	0*d*.
7. *Value of Stores*	£2	17*s*.	8*d*.
Total	£5	15*s*.	8*d*.
Less 9. *Value Spent*	£2	15*s*.	8*d*.
11. *Value of New Remains*	£3	0*s*.	0*d*.

Having completed this exercise for some forty items of food and other supplies, columns 3, 5, 7, 9, and 11 were each added up separately. Then, by adding the totals of columns 3, 5, and 7 together, and subtracting that of column 11, the net cost of the week's supplies was obtained. If all was correct, this figure should be exactly the same as that in column 9.

The clerk then went on to list each separate joint of venison received into the larder, each individual pie and pasty from the bakehouse, and every 'extra-ordinary' dish cooked in the kitchen. Finally he listed how many people were in the household, and how many additional meals had been served to visitors. In the week ending 17 August 1628, for example, there were 66 in the household, consuming 462 dinners and 462 suppers, and extra people who consumed 233 dinners and 207 suppers, a total of 1564 meals. With food being cooked and served in such large quantities, accurate book-keeping was absolutely essential.

Other households preferred a much simpler system. In her 'Kitchen Booke Conteyning the expences of my howse in London beginning upon Satterdaie XI of April 1601,' Mrs Magdalene Herbert kept a daily list of what she had *Bought*, with its prices and a total.[19] Next came what she had *Spent* (used) that day, including the quantities served at *Dinner* and *Supper*, with its *Expenditure*, and what *Remained* in the kitchen. Every Saturday she used these entries to produce an itemized list of what she had spent up to the previous evening, to discover:

The Somme disbursed the weeck past is	£6	7*s*.	11½*d*.
The Somme Received with the last Remaynder is	£8	16*s*.	7*d*.
The Somme Now Remayning is just	£2	8*s*.	7½*d*.

Another even more basic method was just to list expenditure every day, week or fortnight, quarter, and year.[20]

In addition to such formal accounts, there might be others kept by the lady of the house to record all those necessary but irregular payments needed to keep everything running smoothly. According to her memorial in Tavistock parish church, Devon, Rachel, Countess of Bath, had 'in domestic ... affairs a genius exceeding that of a man', vast praise in such a masculine era. Like many of her status, she carefully recorded both the amounts of cash she received and the various ways in which it was expended, everything being periodically totalled in order to exert a tight control of her budget. In 1639, for example, she paid for the services of carpenters, masons, chandlers, poulterers, butchers, herb-, milk- and washer-women, the hire of a cook, and the purchases of a table, tablecloth and tableware. She had nothing to do with the bulk purchase of food and materials, or the wages of the permanent staff, however, since these remained in the control of the steward.

At this level of catering no counting house was required, all domestic paperwork being readily housed in a piece of furniture appropriately called a counter. These frequently appear in inventories, but are difficult to identify among surviving tables and other practical furnishings. One early sixteenth-century form resembles a small, long-legged chest, its flat top being mounted on bearers so as to slide backwards or forwards in order to give access to its otherwise enclosed interior.[21] For most ordinary families, even this was unnecessary, for financial controls were more verbal than clerical. As John Fitzherbert instructed farmers' wives in 1534, they needed to:[22]

> buy all manner of necessary things belonging to households, and to make true reckoning and account to her husband what she hath received and what she hath paid. And if the husband go to the market to buy or sell (as they often do), he then to show his wife in like manner, For if one of them should use to deceive the other, he deceiveth himself, and he is not like to thrive, and therefore must be true either to other.

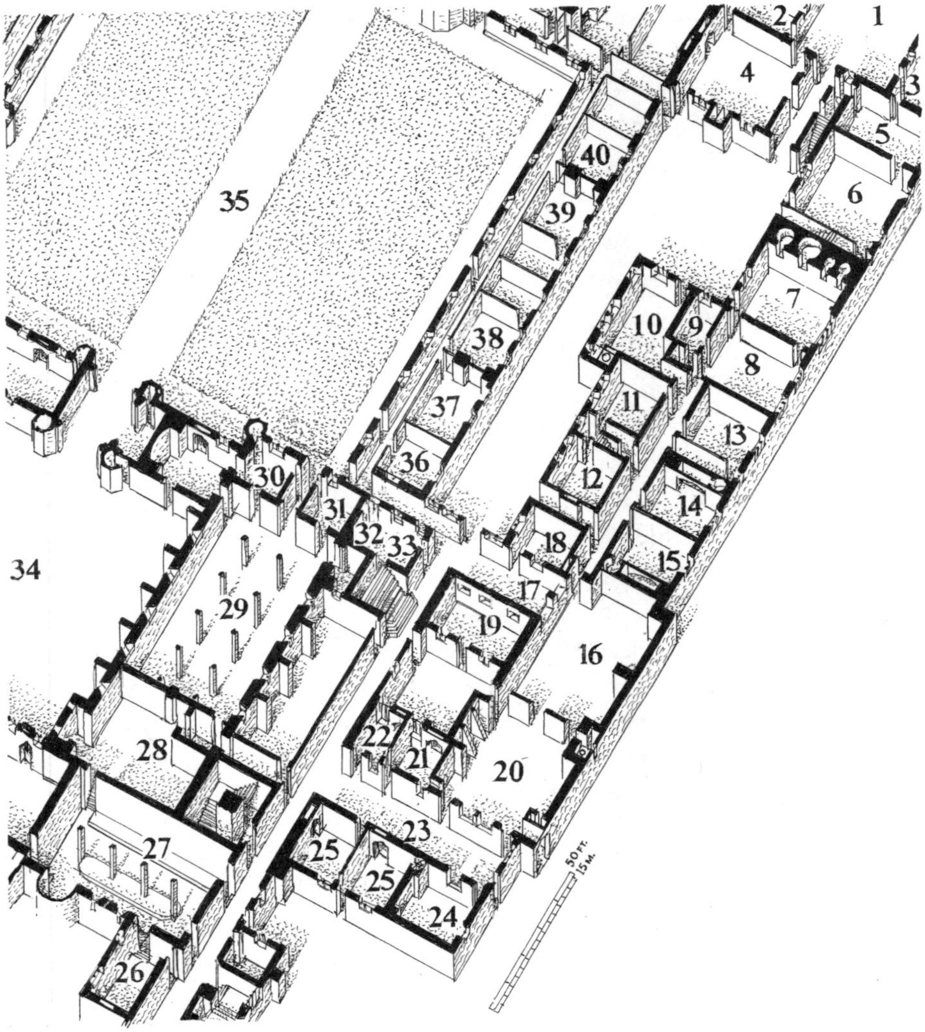

Figure 2. Henry VIII's kitchens at Hampton Court Palace, 1531. The kitchens were designed as a highly efficient and controllable production-line, commencing at the back gate (top right), and progressing via: (1) Greencloth Yard; (2) Chandlery; (3) King's Coal House; (4) Clerk Comptroller's Room; (5) Bottle House; (6) Dry Fish House; (7) Pastry Bakehouse; (8) Pastry Workhouse; (9) Pastry Boulting House (?); (10) Boiling House; (11–12) Wet Larders; (13) Dry Larder; (14–15) Hall-place Kitchen Workhouses; (16) Hall-place Kitchen; (17) Hall-place Kitchen Surveying Place; (18) Hall-place Dresser Office; (19) Pewter Scullery; (20) Lords'-side Kitchen; (21) Lords'-side Kitchen Dresser Office; (22) Silver Scullery; (23) The Great Space; (24) Lords'-side Workhouse (?); (25) Clerk of Kitchen's Lodgings; (26) Drinking House; (27) Great Wine Cellar; (28) Privy Cellar; (29) Beer Cellar; (30) Great Buttery; (31) Privy Buttery; (32) Pantry; (33) Almonry; (34) Fountain Court; (35) Base Court; (36–40) Lodgings.

CHAPTER TWO

Planning for Cooking

The best early sixteenth century advice for those planning a new house was provided by Dr Andrew Boorde in 1542. Having selected a firm, well-drained site, well away from any nuisances and plentifully supplied with fresh air, fresh water and plenty of firewood, the builder was to orientate the house to take the best advantages of the winds. The south winds brought corrupt and evil vapours, which the north wind purged, while easterly winds were temperate, brisk and fragrant. Any house should therefore have its best residential rooms facing east, rather than south. This brought further benefits which Boorde does not mention, enabling the kitchens to be set along the cool northern façade where the prevailing south-western winds would carry off their smoke and smells. The hall and chambers could also be positioned to receive the best of the daylight at mealtimes.

As for the internal arrangements, Boorde advised:[1]

> Make the hall under such a fashion that the parler be anexed to the head of the hall. And the buttery and pantry to be at the lower end of the hall, the cellar under the pantry, sette somewhat abase; the kychen set somewhat abase from the buttery and pantry, commyng with an entry by the wall of the buttery, the pastry-house and the larder-house anexed to the kychen. Then devyde the lodgynges by a cyrcuyt of the quadryngall courte, and let the gate-howse be opposyt or agaynst the hall-dore (not dyrectely) but the hall-dore standing abase, and the gate-howse in the mydle of the front entryng in to that place: let the pryve chambre be anaxed to the chambre of astate, with other chambres necessarye ... If there be an utter courte made, make it quadryngyal, with howses of easementes [latrines] and but one stable for horses of pleasure, & se no fylth nor dong be within the courte, nor cast at the backe-syde. Also ... the slaughter-howse [and] a dayery (if any be kept) shulde be elongated the space of a quarter of a myle from the place. And also the bake-howse and brew-howse shulde be a dystaunce from the place and from other buyldyng ... And in no wyse let not the fylth of the kychen descende into the moote.

In 1624 Sir Henry Wotton offered further directions regarding the location of certain service rooms in relation to the cardinal points. He agreed that the north side should be used for 'all that need a coole and a fresh temper, as *Cellars, Pantries, Butteries, Granaries*.' However, those 'Offices which require heat, *Kitchens, stillatories, stoves*, rooms for Baking, Brewing, Washing or the like', should face the south.[2]

Further good advice was given at the opening of the seventeenth century by Francis Bacon, Lord Verulam. His ideal house was to be built to live in, not to look at, function being preferred to symmetry, unless both could be achieved in unison. Approaching across three grassed courts, a visitor would see a high central prospect tower flanked by two symmetrical wings, each with 40-foot-high rooms set over 16-foot-high basements. One wing was to be a banqueting suite, leading through to a series of fashionable long galleries, while the other should house a household sequence of chapel, hall, and winter and summer parlours, leading to presence and bed chambers. Behind the façade there were to be two rectangular grass courts, the first flanked by galleries and chambers, and the second by privy chambers and galleries set upon cloister-like arcades. As for the services, the kitchens, bakehouse, brewery and other rooms were linked to it only by some low galleries. The wine and beer cellars, buttery, pantry and the privy kitchen for producing meals solely for the prince or lord were to be much more conveniently situated, however, in the basement below the hall and parlours.[3]

The advice given by writers such as Boorde and Bacon was not purely new theory, but was obviously based on an observation of the most successful institutional and domestic buildings of earlier periods. Monasteries had determined the best way of arranging their residential and service rooms around rectangular courtyards back in the eleventh and twelfth centuries, for example. Similarly, architects such as John Lewyn had developed such plan-forms for sophisticated, high-status residences in the fourteenth century.

Having previously considered the great care and attention to detail with which household officers managed their kitchen accounts, we should expect that they would demand that any new building should fulfil their exacting requirements. They were ideally placed to make such demands, being responsible for paying the architects' and masons' wages and bills. It is not surprising, therefore, to observe that many suites of service rooms incorporate features which show that they were constructed to satisfy every nuance of financial, commodity and personnel control.

When planning any major house, one primary decision had to be made: were the service rooms to be incorporated into the main residential block, or were they to be moved out into a separate wing? The advantage of the former was an unencumbered exterior enclosing a compact, convenient interior, while the latter kept all the unwelcome problems of deliveries, noise, smoke and smells well away from the resident owners and their guests. In extremely large houses and palaces the great numbers to be catered for demanded such huge suites of kitchen offices that they had to be physically separate. This explains the appearance of separate kitchen wings in the now-demolished Henrician palaces at Beaulieu, Nonsuch and Oatlands.[4] The finest of them all still remains intact at Hampton Court, where it was commenced by Cardinal Wolsey shortly after 1514 and brought to its magnificent completion by Henry VIII in 1529–32.

Designed to feed some 800 courtiers and 230 servants, it forms a 400- by 90-foot block running parallel to the north side of the base court.[5] Entered by its own gatehouse on the west front, it commenced with a porters' lodge and jewel house for currency, with the counting house above. Next came various stores, the pastry and boiling house, the larders and kitchens, and finally the dressers from which the food was distributed. The respective positions of each department, office, window and door were specifically designed to meet the needs of the administrative officers, giving them visual control of every important doorway and passage. Neither person nor object could enter or leave unseen or unchecked. In every aspect it promoted the greatest degree of efficiency and security, achieving modern production-line factory standards centuries before the first great textile and engineering works. This is clearly demonstrated by the following flow-chart:

Hampton Court Palace

ADMINISTRATIVE OFFICES	PRACTICAL OFFICES
Back Gate	
2 Jewel Houses	Porter
Counting House	
Spicery	Comptroller's Cellar
Chandlery	King's Coal House
Clerk Comptroller	Bottle House
Clerk of the Kitchen	Dry Fish House
Scullery Office	Confectionery
	Pastry Bakehouse
Pastry & Scullery Offices	Pastry Workhouse – Boulting House?
Boiling House Officers	Boiling House
	Wet Larder
	Dry Larder
Cooks' Lodgings?	2 Hall-place Workhouses

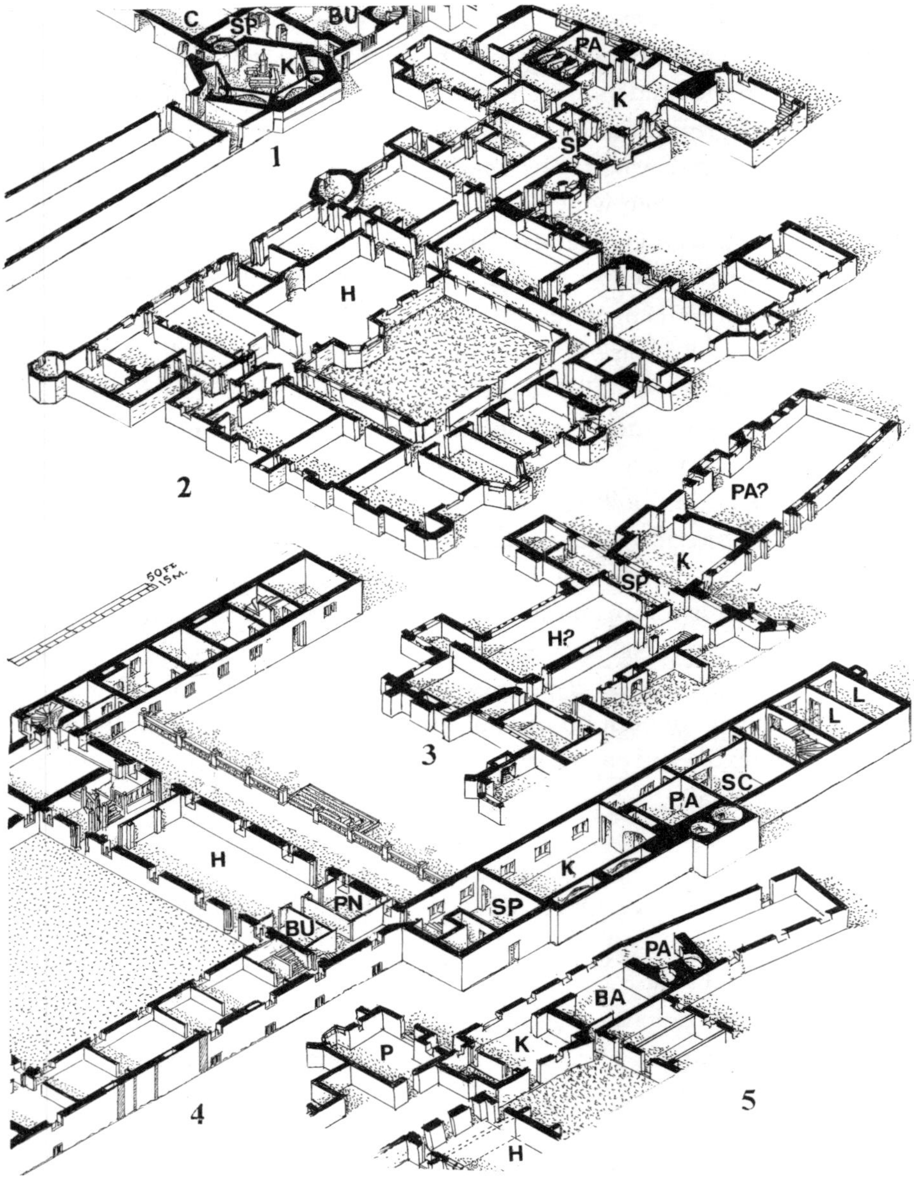

Figure 3. Tudor kitchen wings. To keep the noise, bustle, smell and smoke away from the residential areas, many Tudor houses placed their kitchens in extended service wings, as at, (1) Cowdray House, Sussex, 1520s; (2) Hengrave Hall, Suff., 1528–38; (3) Hinchingbrooke, Hunts., 1538–45; (4) Syon House, Middlesex, post 1547; and (5) Fawsley, Northants., pre 1542. (BA: Bakehouse; BU: Buttery; C: Cellar; H: Hall; K: Kitchen; L: Larder; PA: Pastry; PN: Pantry; SC: Scullery; SP: Surveying Place.)

Hall-place Surveying Place	Hall-place Kitchen
Lords'-side Dresser Office	Lords'-side Kitchen – Boiling House
Silver Scullery	
Lords'-side Surveying Place	
Clerk of Kitchen's Lodging	Lords'-side Workhouse
Surgeon's, etc., Lodgings	Wafery
	Wine Cellar
Great Hall	Pantry – Bread Store
(Minor Courtiers and Servants)	
Great Watching Chamber	Buttery – Beer Cellars
(Senior Courtiers & Officers)	

A number of noble and upper-gentry houses also used separate kitchen service wings. One early example is at Cowdray House in Sussex. Started by Sir Robert Owen in 1520–30, it has a hexagonal kitchen separated from the rest of the property by a small courtyard. From this Sir William Fitzwilliam, treasurer to Henry VIII, extended a further wing of sculleries, larders and other service rooms. Unfortunately they were converted into estate cottages in the early twentieth century, leaving no evidence of their original internal arrangements.[6] Sir Thomas Kytson, Sheriff of London, built a similar 80-foot-long kitchen wing at Hengrave Hall, Suffolk, between 1528 and 1538, but this has been demolished, and is only known from historic plans.[7] Good sixteenth-century examples still survive elsewhere, however, including those at Sir Thomas Knightley's Fawsley Hall built before 1542 and Lewis Watson's Rockingham Castle of around 1550, both in the delightful ironstone masonry of Northamptonshire.[8]

Further north, there is another fine kitchen service wing at Walter Strickland's Sizergh Castle in Cumbria.[9] He was a rising gentleman, his estate income, probably boosted by plunder from expeditions against the Scots, enabling him to field 200 mounted soldiers whenever required. Around 1560 he extended his medieval defended house on a virtually noble scale, with a 148-foot kitchen wing. The end room housed a brewhouse/bakehouse, followed in succession by a pastry, milkhouse, dry larder, huge three-fireplace kitchen with a hatch leading into a surveying place, and then the stairs up to the hall and chambers.

Some of the houses converted from monastic buildings after the Dissolution also added kitchen wings. In Huntingdonshire, Thomas Cromwell's nephew Sir Richard Williams built one at the former Hinchingbrooke nunnery between 1538 and 1545.[10] Extending northwards, it had preparation rooms at its outer end, then a two-fireplace kitchen and a door and serving hatch into a surveying place at the lower end of the hall. At Syon, Middlesex, the great abbey church was converted after 1547 into a house for Edward, Duke of Somerset, Protector

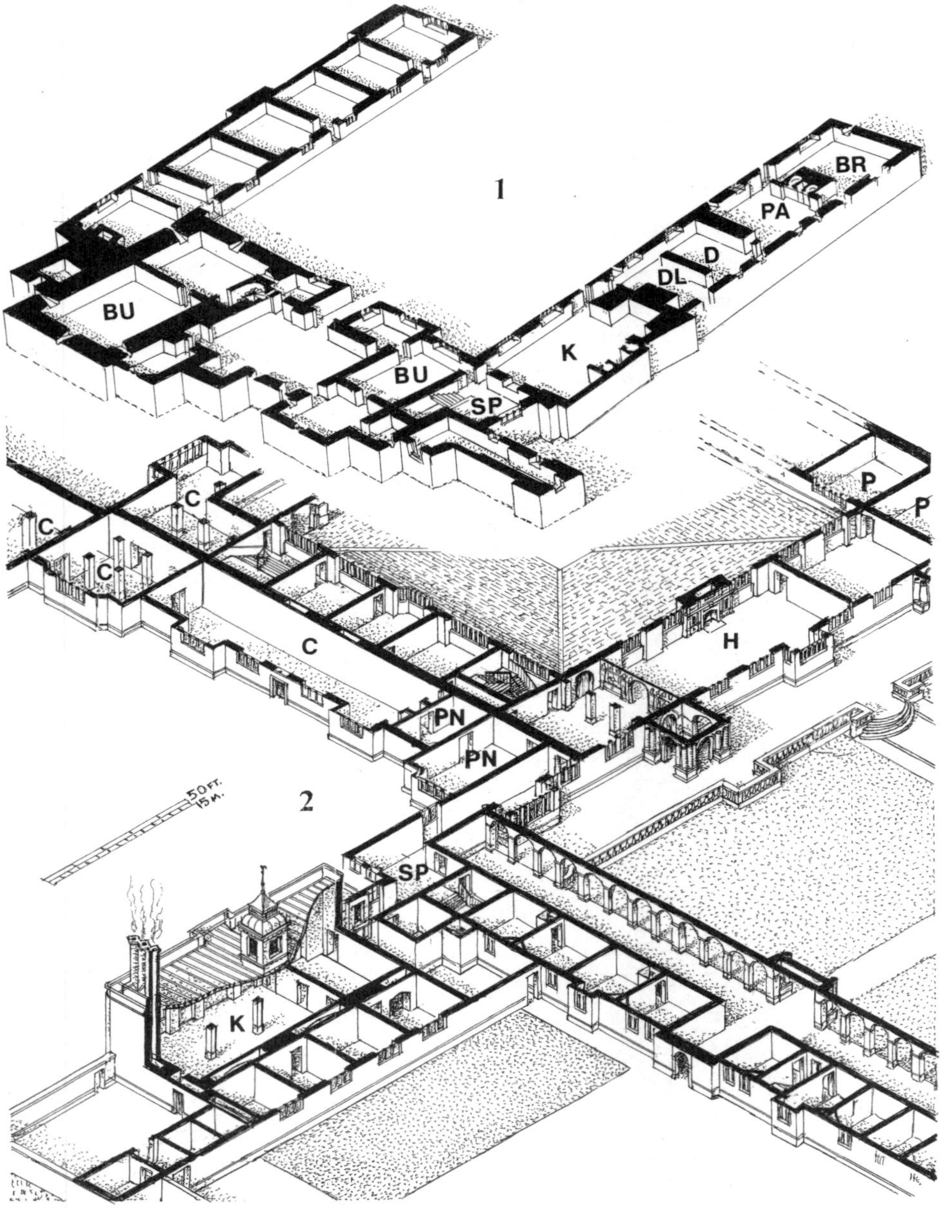

Figure 4. Large kitchen wings. Intended to serve large numbers of soldiers for service on the Scottish borders, Walter Strickland's kitchens at Sizergh Castle, Cumbria, (top) were built on a large scale c. 1560, as were those at the Earl of Suffolk's Audley End of c. 1603–16 (bottom), but for entertaining royalty. (BR: Brewhouse; BU: Buttery; C: Cellar; D: Dairy; DL: Dry Larder; H: Hall; K: Kitchen; PN: Pantry; S: Surveying Place.)

of the young Edward VI and the most powerful man in the land.[11] His kitchen wing on the north-west corner of the great stone-faced courtyard house began with sculleries and larders, then a pastry with two ovens, a three-fireplace kitchen, a surveying place with its own clerk's office, and stairs up to the hall.

Similar kitchen wings were still being built in the seventeenth century, Sir Simon Clarke adding one to the south of Salford Hall, Warwickshire, shortly after 1606.[12] This was very modest when compared to the 150-foot wing built on to the north façade of Audley End, Essex, *c.* 1603–1616.[13] Designed by Bernard Johnson for Thomas Howard, Earl of Suffolk, it was of exceptionally high architectural quality. The kitchen alone measured some 50 by 30 feet, its high, flat lead roof being surmounted by an elegant square-domed cupola to extract the hot air and cooking fumes. Now replaced by a much more modest kitchen wing, only its surveying place survives today.

Many owners of great houses had preferred to keep their kitchens within their main residential blocks, off the lower end of the hall, as Boorde suggested. Two of the finest, the Duke of Buckingham's Thornbury Castle, in Gloucestershire, and Lord Darcy's Temple Newsam near Leeds were both completed in the second decade of the sixteenth century.[14] Both had an impressive gatehouse at the centre of their symmetrical façade, this leading into a rectangular court. The wing to the left housed the domestic offices at ground level, with the kitchen at the junction with the buttery, pantry and great hall wing. The right wing, meanwhile, was occupied by the parlours, great chambers and principal bedchambers. Their major difference in culinary planning is the location of the privy kitchen for preparing the lord's food. At Thornbury it extends from one side of the household kitchen, while at Temple Newsam it occupies a more usual position directly below the lord's chamber.

Most courtyard houses of this type, such as Compton Wynyates, Warwickshire, of *c.* 1522, Ingatestone Hall, Essex, of *c.* 1538, Cadhay, Devon, *c.* 1545–50, and Burton Agnes Hall, Yorkshire, *c.* 1601–10, have a simple sequence of service rooms.[15] It starts with larders, a kitchen at the angle of the courtyard, then butteries, pantries, the screens passage, and on into the hall and dining chambers.

The remaining major plan-form, again following well-established medieval precedents, was to add cross-wings to a long hall block so as to produce either an H or an E-shaped outline. In the mid-sixteenth century most followed the usual arrangement of kitchen and service rooms in one cross-wing at the bottom end of the hall, next to the entrance porch. Then came the hall, followed by the dining and other residential chambers, to complete a very practical sequence of rooms. Unfortunately this did not satisfy the growing taste for perfect symmetry in a façade. To do this, it would be necessary to move the porch into a central

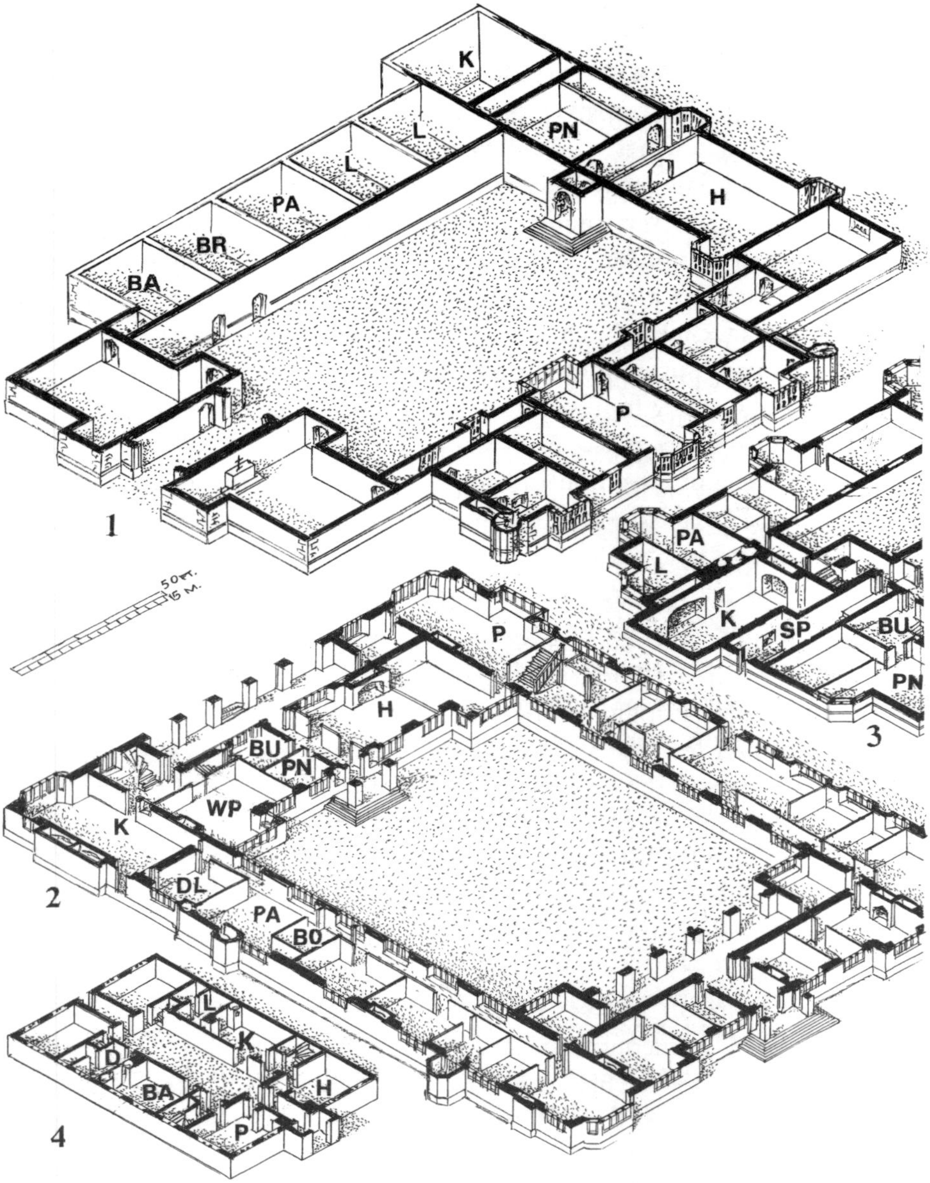

Figure 5. Kitchens in courtyard houses. In houses built around central courtyards, the kitchen offices retained their usual relationship with the hall and chambers as at (1) Temple Newsam, Leeds, 1513; (2) Slaugham Place, Sussex, 1578; (3) the original place for Burton Agnes, Yorks., 1601; (4) John Smythson's design for a house for Mr Diball, 1622. (BA: Bakehouse; BU: Buttery; D: Dairy; DL: Dry Larder; H: Hall; K: Kitchen; L: Larder; P: Parlour; PA: Pastry; PN: Pantry; SP: Surveying Place; WP: Winter Parlour.)

position by inserting further rooms towards the kitchen offices to exactly match the length of the hall. These might include butteries, lodging rooms, or a 'winter parlour'.

Today the word 'parlour' means a polite sitting room, inventory evidence suggesting that many parlours were of this type, especially if off the upper end of the hall. However, of the forty 'winter parlours' named on the plans of the architect John Thorpe, over half were beyond the lower end of the hall, close to the kitchen, and frequently next to the buttery. At Slaugham Place in Sussex it was called the winter parlour or hinds' hall, while at Burghley-on-the-Hill it was the 'Lesser Hall for hynds'.[16] From around 1400 a hind was a domestic servant, only later becoming a farm labourer. This suggests that these winter parlours may have functioned as servants' halls for those lower servants not entitled to dine with the house servants in the hall.

In the service wing itself there might be only a kitchen and larders, perhaps with a boulting house and a pastry, all that was needed for immediate use, but not sufficient to store year-long supplies. Good examples of this plan include Doddington, Lincolnshire, of 1593–1600, Montacute, Somerset, late 1590s, Somerhill, Kent, *c.* 1610, and Aston Hall, Birmingham, of 1618.[17]

From the early sixteenth century, it was realized that there could be advantages in exploiting naturally sloping sites for great houses. By setting the kitchen offices along their lower sides, they could enjoy the benefits of windows and ground-level doors in their external walls, while their inner walls could be dug into the earth as full or semi-basements. As well as reducing the visual impact of the offices as seen from the façade or inner courtyard, this arrangement could permit them to have higher ceiling heights, or allow the main ground floor level to run almost continuously above them. This arrangement was adopted at Temple Newsam, Leeds, before 1520, Parham House, Sussex, of 1577, and Fountains Hall, Yorkshire, in 1611, to give just a few examples.[18]

As the social distinction between masters and servants began to increase in the Elizabethan period, architects began to move more of the service rooms and their staffs into purposely built full or semi-basements. Servants might still dine in the hall as before, but now 'Upstairs' was being separated from 'Downstairs', establishing a precedent which was to be followed for the next 400 years. The houses looked much more impressive, set on their basement storeys, entered by way of fine external stairs, and now without any need for straggling, asymmetrical separate kitchens and service wings. Those above stairs also benefited from warmer and drier ground floors, better views, and far less chance of encountering a servant.

One of the earliest houses to have major service rooms in its basement was Shaw House, Newbury, Berkshire.[19] Built in the 1570s, its features suggest

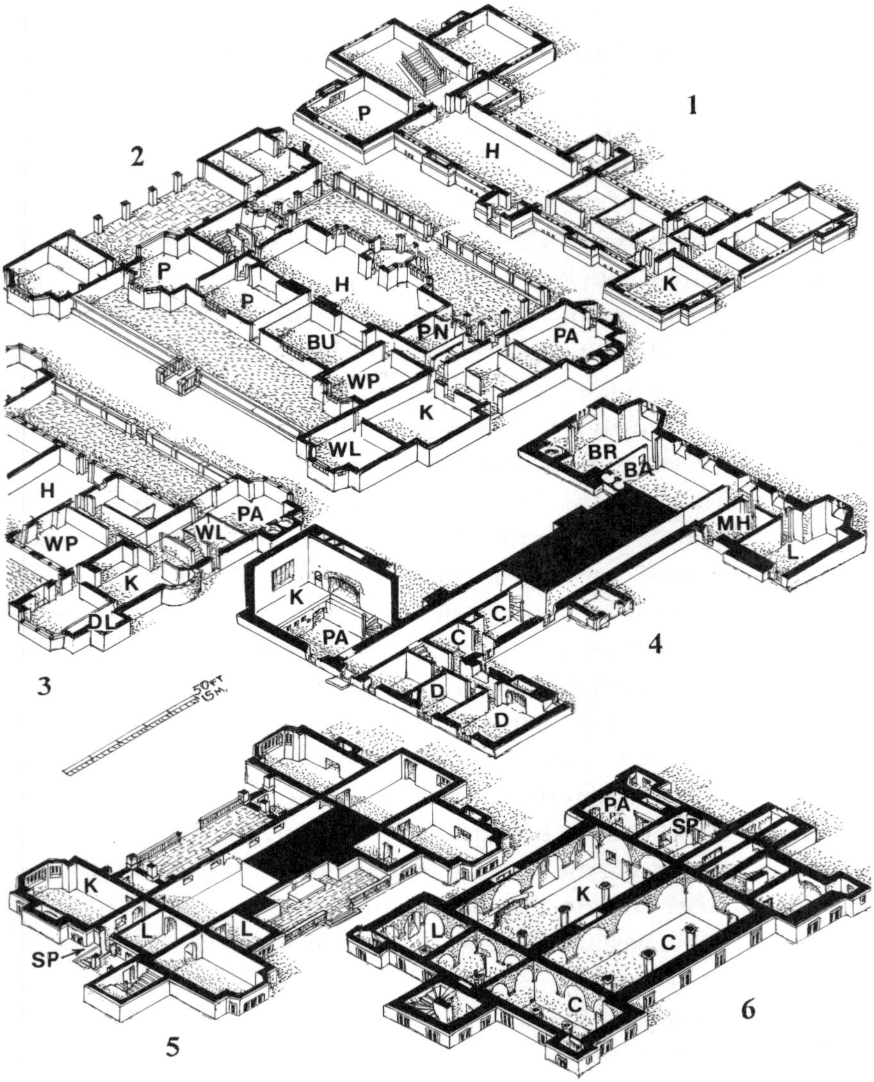

Figure 6. Kitchens in H-plan houses, & basement kitchens. In H-plan houses the kitchen wing was set at right-angles to the hall, a convenient arrangement which suited the growing demand for symmetrical façades, as at (1) Doddington Hall, Lincs., of 1593–1600; (2) John Thorpe's Holland House, Kensington c. 1605–14; and (3) his Somerhill, Kent, c. 1610–13. Placing the service rooms in basements added height to a house, and added a form of underfloor heating for the residential rooms. (4) Shaw House, Newbury, Berks., 1570s; (5) Ham House, Middlesex, 1610; and (6) Slingsby Castle, Yorks., c. 1630. (BA: Bakehouse; BR: Brewhouse; BU: Buttery; C: Cellar; D: Dairy; H: Hall; K: Kitchen; L: Larder; MH: Malt House; P: Parlour; PA: Pastry; PN: Pantry; SP: Surveying Place; WP: Winter Parlour.)

some connection with the circle of the architect Robert Smythson, perhaps being designed by Humphrey Lovell, Queen Elizabeth's master mason. The kitchen remained in the low end cross-wing, but the two-oven pastry, beer and candle cellars, milkhouse, larder, bakehouse, brewhouse and malthouse were all consigned to the basement. From this period basement service rooms became much more popular, as may be seen by those at Barlborough Hall, Derbyshire, of 1583, Heath Old Hall, Yorkshire, of *c.* 1584, Chastleton, Oxfordshire, of 1602, and Ham House, Surrey, of 1610.[20]

Between the 1580s and the 1630s the major developments in domestic planning in England were led by a single dynasty of great architects, the Smythsons. Robert Smythson had worked for Sir John Thynne on the rebuilding of Longleat, Wiltshire, from 1568, but his major houses were undertaken for the Earl or Countess of Shrewsbury, commencing with Worksop Manor, Nottinghamshire, completed in 1586.[21] Here there was a logical linear sequence of back door, pastry, boiling place, kitchen, surveying place, buttery and pantry, screens passage and hall, all on the ground floor, then a flight of steps up the the dining chamber. This was all very conventional, but only two years later at Hardwick Old Hall, Derbyshire, he produced a revolutionary plan with the hall at right-angles to the main façade, rather than parallel to it, as in every earlier house.[22] It was flanked by larders, pastry, kitchen, surveying place, buttery and other offices, to one side, and what were possibly upper-servants' bedchambers to the other, leaving the upper storey solely for residential purposes. The same general arrangement was followed in Hardwick New Hall when it was commenced in 1590.[23] It too had a rectangular plan, extended with tower-like bay windows to each end of its perfectly symmetrical façade. Here too the hall retained its central position, with a wet larder, dry larder, pastry, scullery, little kitchen, surveying place and buttery to its north, and the pantry, nursery and upper servants' bedchambers to the south. As in other houses in this group, it was not so much that the (servants') hall and service rooms had been sunk into the ground, as that the residential chambers had risen above them.

The taste for classical architecture became far more refined in the opening decades of the seventeenth century, leading to further developments in domestic design. One was the introduction of the double-pile plan, where the rooms were set to each side of a central spine-wall, rather than having two external walls. This enabled houses to become rather more compact, as opposed to linear in plan. In the 1620s John Smythson built two major double-pile houses for members of the Cavendish family. At Slingsby Castle, Yorkshire, the basements to the north of the spine wall housed a larder, cooks' room, a huge two-fireplace kitchen, a pastry and a surveying place, while those to the south

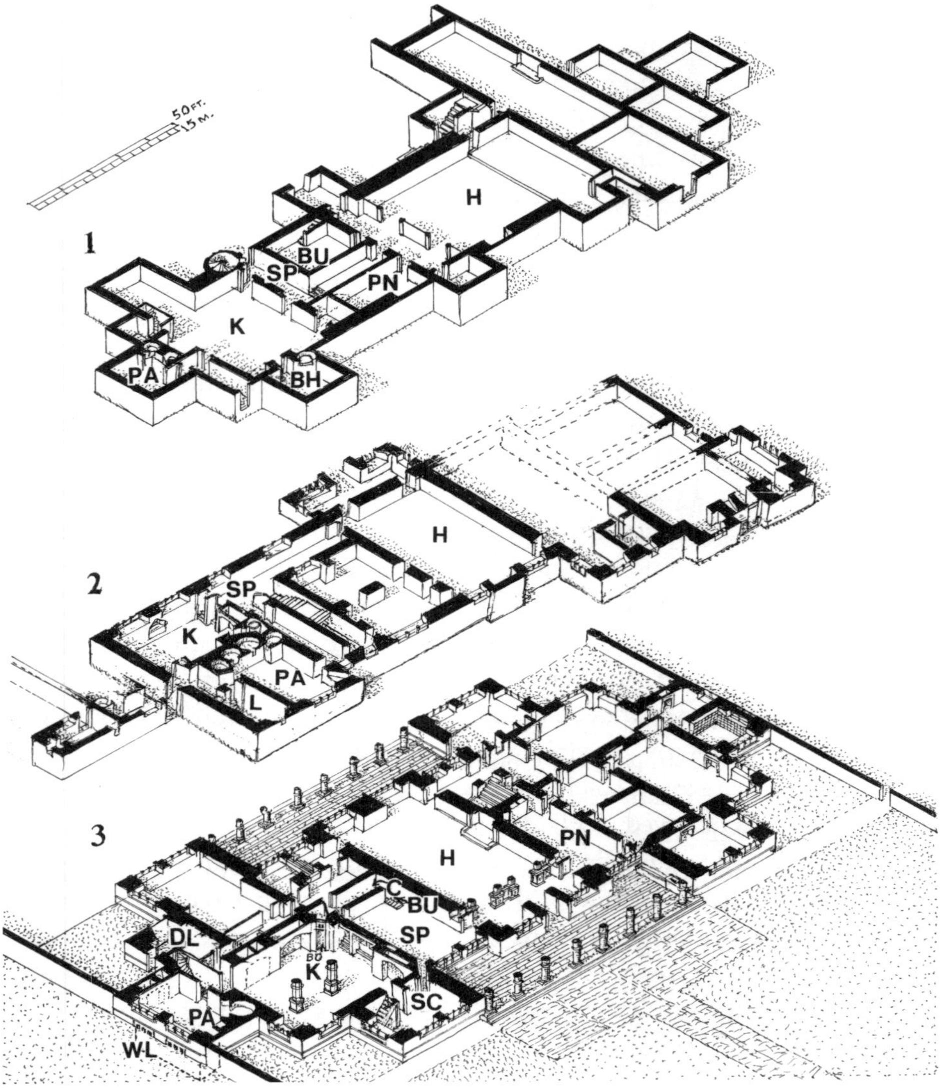

Figure 7. Three high houses of the Midlands. Built in the 1580s, Worksop Manor (1) retained the usual arrangement of late-medieval services, while at Hardwick Old Hall (2) of c. 1587–90 Robert Smythson experimented with a new design with a screens-passage and hall turned at 90 degrees. This placed the kitchen, buttery and pantry doors along one side of the hall, quite an inconvenient arrangement. These problems were fully solved in his Hardwick New Hall (3) of 1590–97, which incorporated all the services into a very efficient yet flexible plan. (BH: Bake House; BO: Boiling House; BU: Buttery; C: Cellar; D: Dairy; H: Hall; K: Kitchen; L: Larder; PA: Pastry; PN: Pantry; SC: Scullery; SP: Surveying Place; WL: Wet Larder.)

contained the cellars and stores.[24] Similarly at Bolsover Castle, Derbyshire, also in the 1620s, he designed a double-pile residential range running along the steep scarp overlooking the surrounding lowlands.[25] Here stairs descending from the courtyard led to an enfilade of doorways running against the west side of the spine wall, forming a long corridor linking each room, doors through the spine wall giving access to individual rooms to the east. This facilitated a very efficient sequence of service rooms. First on the east, was an office probably used by the clerk of the kitchen, having a small fireplace, wall cupboards, and a hatch cut through to the silver scullery. Next came the privy kitchen, the main kitchen, linked to the pastry with one hatch, and to the surveying place by another. These were followed by a boiling house, the stairs up to the dining areas, and a suite of three rooms, probably used as larders. In this way the kitchen department was able to operate in a completely practical and secure manner. The cellars for wine and ale had their own separate internal and external entrances at the north end of the block.

Contemporary architects working in the Palladian court style led by Inigo Jones found the double-pile plan with a half-buried basement storey both aesthetically pleasing and very practical. This is clearly seen in houses such as Chevening, reputedly designed by Jones in the 1620s, but perhaps by Edward Carter.[26] The style was continued into the middle of the century by Jones' nephew and pupil John Webb. In 1654 the Countess of Rutland had him prepare designs for the new Belvoir Castle to replace that which had been demolished at the end of the Civil War. The 250-foot, nineteen-bay east façade was to have a grand central portico and terminal pavilions in a very advanced and competent composition, but the final building had none of these embellishments. From a functional point of view Webb's basement offices were efficient, with external doors for supplies leading to the dairy and larders, then a very large kitchen with sculleries, pastry and other offices, and service stairs leading up to the hall and to the dining chamber. The ale and wine cellars, meanwhile, occupied a physically separate area at the south end of the basement, with their own access stair. The whole wing was remodelled by James Wyatt in the early nineteenth century, and is now only known from manuscript drawings and plans.[27]

Around 1650 Sir Roger Pratt, an amateur architect freshly back from seeing the new Palladian houses of Italy and France, designed a new house for his cousin Sir George Pratt at Coleshill, Berkshire.[28] Externally it was an aesthetic masterpiece of enormous influence, but its greatest innovations were all concealed within. The double-pile basement plan was similar to those at Bolsover and Belvoir but now a central corridor ran the length of the house, with an external door at each end. Ale and wine cellars occupied the centre of the western

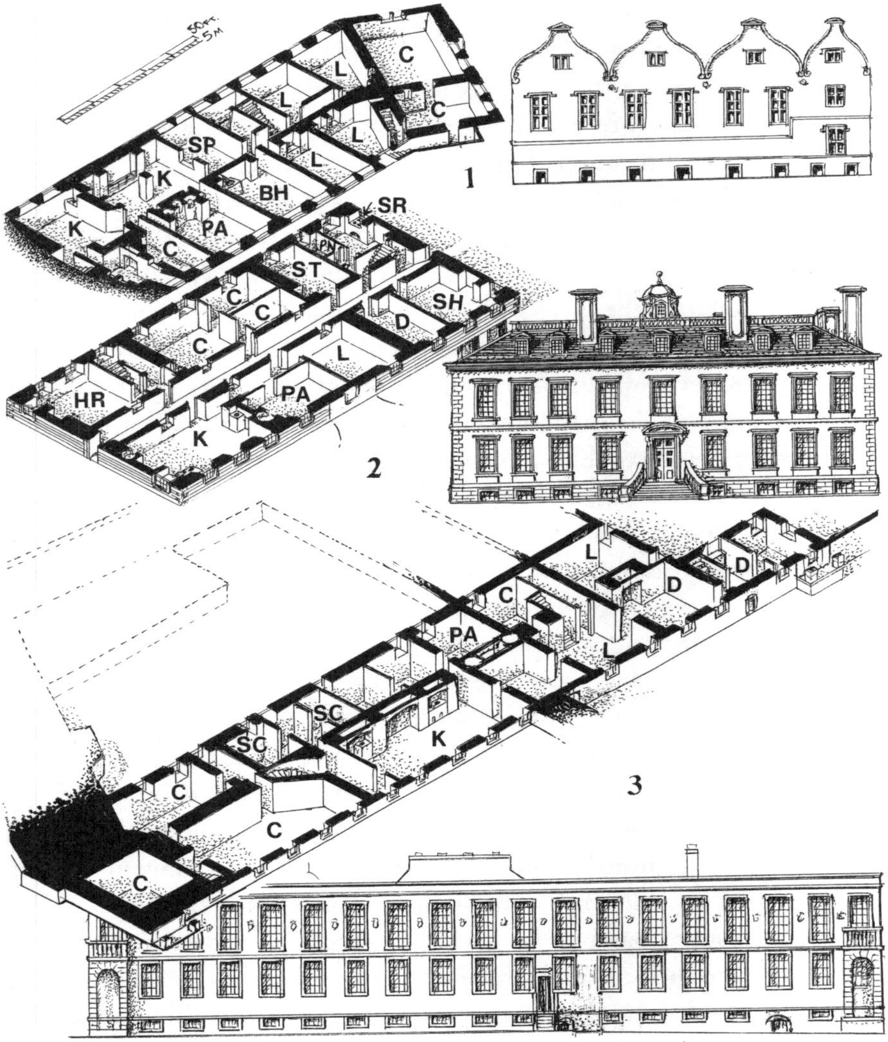

Figure 8. Later basement kitchens. The introduction of double-pile houses in the early 17th century, and the setting of formal Palladian façades over rusticated service basements, enabled efficient kitchen plans to be developed. At John Smythson's Terrace Range at Bolsover Castle, c. 1613 (1) a series of doorways created a spinal corridor, while Sir Roger Pratt's Coleshill of c. 1650 (2) incorporated a through-passage, with rooms set off to each side. John Webb's massive 250ft east range at Belvoir Castle of 1655–68 (3) used doorways along its outer wall as its corridor with appropriate linking doors to the lesser service rooms against its inner wall. (BH: Boiling House; C: Cellar; D: Dairy; HR: Housekeeper's Room; K: Kitchen; L: Larder; PA: Pastry; PK: Privy Kitchen; PN: Pantry; SC: Scullery; SH: Servants' Hall; SP: Surveying Place; SR: Still Room; SS: Silver Scullery.)

side, with the essentially female housekeeper's room, dairy and stillroom to each end. On the east side, an interconnecting larder, pastry and kitchen served a stair ascending to the upper floors. The real surprise lay in the north-east corner however, for here was probably the first basement-level servants' hall in England. Societal shifts had exchanged the gentlemen and yeomen servants of former generations for cheaply waged, lower status male and female servants, who had little in common with their master. On his part, he certainly did not wish them to occupy the same rooms as he did, and so they now spent their working days below stairs, and their nights in the garrets in the roof-space. Upstairs, visitors still entered a hall, but its dining facilities for servants were no longer there. Instead there was a grand imperial staircase, sweeping up to a landing and the great dining-room on the first floor. From this time on, Pratt's Coleshill ensured that the English country house, and the life led within it, would never be the same.

From the medieval period many major families chose to spend their time well away from the formality and constant responsibilities experienced in their great houses. Life could be quite enjoyable with a few friends and a reduced number of servants when travelling, when hunting and fishing, when the main house was being cleaned and the accounts made up, or when there was a simple need for a little privacy. Visiting households might also appreciate separate accommodation. The solution was to build a lodge, a small but largely complete residence either adjacent to the house, or a short ride away. Some, like the Hunting Tower at Chatsworth, were close to the main house, and small in scale, so that they had no need for any meaningful domestic offices. Others were intended to accommodate a small household for perhaps a week or more. As their function was essentially one of pleasure, most lodges were built to excellent architectural standards, adopting the form of a tower topped with flat lead roofs and turrets for recreation and enjoying the distant views. In the early seventeenth century Lord Exeter built a lodge at Wothorpe, Northamptonshire, as his place 'to retire to out of the dust while his great house was a sweeping'.[29] This was only a short ride away from Burghley House, but others could be more distant. Sir Thomas Wortley built Wharncliffe Lodge in 1510 in his great chase near Sheffield. Here 'he lie for most of the grease time [i.e. when the deer were fattest], and the worshipful of the county did resort unto him, having with him pastime and good cheer'.[30]

The facilities to provide such good living were set either in a basement or a back room, well out of sight. Their configuration had to fit into the plan, which might be a simple rectangle, or else adopt a more unusual or symbolic shape, such as a cross. Within this constraint, the services had to resemble those of a

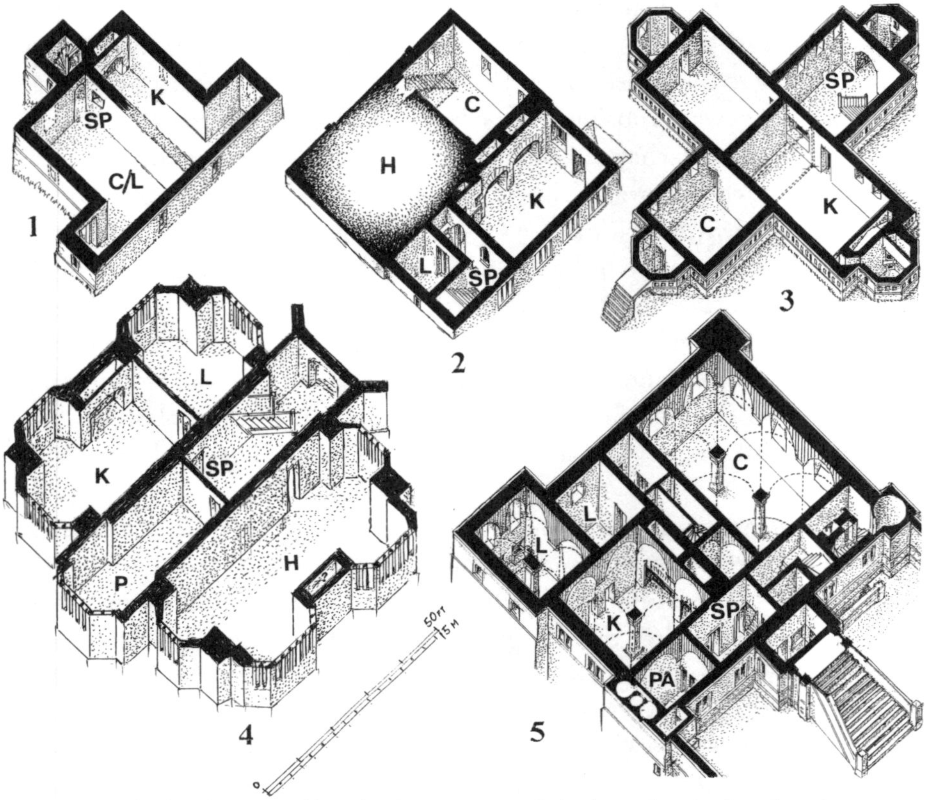

Figure 9. Lodge kitchens. Building kitchens to provide high-quality food within the compact groundplans of lodges required much ingenuity. (1) Dob Park, Otley, Yorks., late 16th cent.; (2) Lodge Park, Gloucs., c. 1630; (3) Lyveden New Bield, Northants, 1594; (4) Westwood Park, Worcs., c. 1600; and (5) the Little Castle at Bolsover, Derbys., c. 1613. (C: Cellar; K: Kitchen; L: Larder; P: Parlour; PA: Pastry; SP: Surveying Place.)

great house, but in miniature, with larders, kitchens, pastries, cellars and other offices, secure serving hatches and surveying places. Usually, on the ground floor there would be a buttery and pantry and hall to accommodate the servants and grooms, the higher status dining chambers being in the upper storeys.

Lodges could vary considerably in the scale and quality of their design and construction. The Little Castle of 1612–14 at Bolsover Castle in Derbyshire is certainly our finest surviving example, its pseudo-fortified façade containing some of John Smythson's richest interiors.[31] Others, now demolished or ruined, may certainly have matched its opulence, as may be judged by the unfinished Lyveden New Bield, Northamptonshire, probably designed by Robert Stickelles, clerk of the works at Richmond, or John Dutton's recently restored Lodge Park, Gloucestershire.[32] The majority must have been much simpler, as at Newark

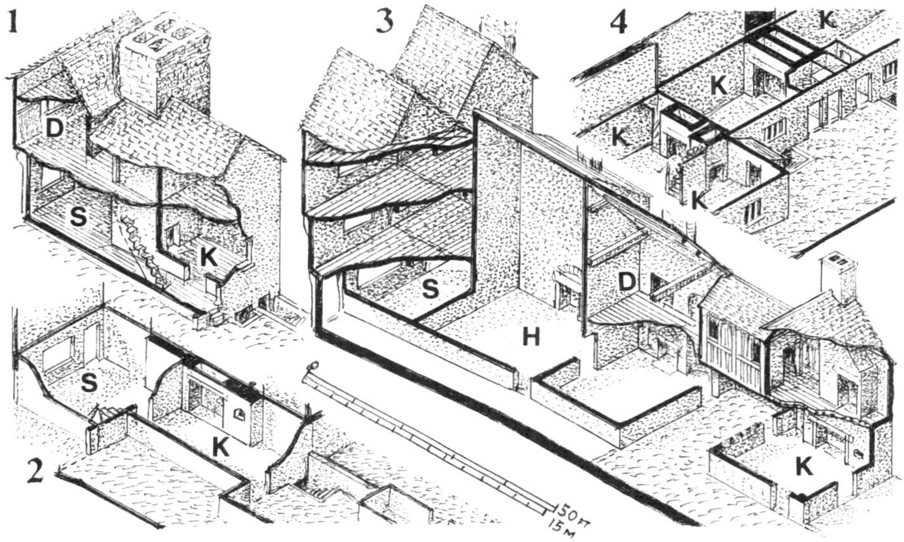

Figure 10. Town-house kitchens. In towns it was important to keep front rooms available for shops, and so the kitchens were relegated to the back rooms, as at (1) the former Bratley's shop, Pontefract, Yorks. of the late 16th–early 17th cent.; (2) Christopher Askwith's shop in London's Smithfield in 1612, and (3) 38 North Street, Exeter, of the late 16th cent., which has a typical courtyard to separate the detached kitchen at the rear. In crowded back yards the kitchen was also the sole living room, as at (4) Phesant Court, Cowe Lane, London, in 1612. (D: Parlour; H: Hall; K: Kitchen; P: Parlour; S: Shop.)

Park, Gloucestershire, or the Vavasour family's Dob Park overlooking the Forest of Knaresborough in Yorkshire.[33]

Changes in domestic planning were not restricted to major houses, for the sixteenth and early seventeenth centuries saw developments in the properties occupied by the minor gentry, yeomen and farmers. Some still used detached kitchens. A manorial survey of Ingatestone, Essex, showed that two-thirds of the houses there had one in 1556. Most were twenty to thirty feet long, twelve to sixteen feet wide, and seven feet to the eaves, with brick chimneys and tiled roofs.[34] In Rotherfield, Sussex, a third of the houses had detached kitchens in 1567, demonstrating their continued use.[35]

One of the problems of defining the purpose of these buildings is our understanding of the word 'kitchen'. We now use it solely to mean a room in which food is cooked, but it formerly included rooms in which food preparation and such associated activities as brewing, baking might take place, and food might be stored. In some areas up to half the 'kitchens' listed in contemporary inventories could be of this kind, having no hearth, the actual cooking being

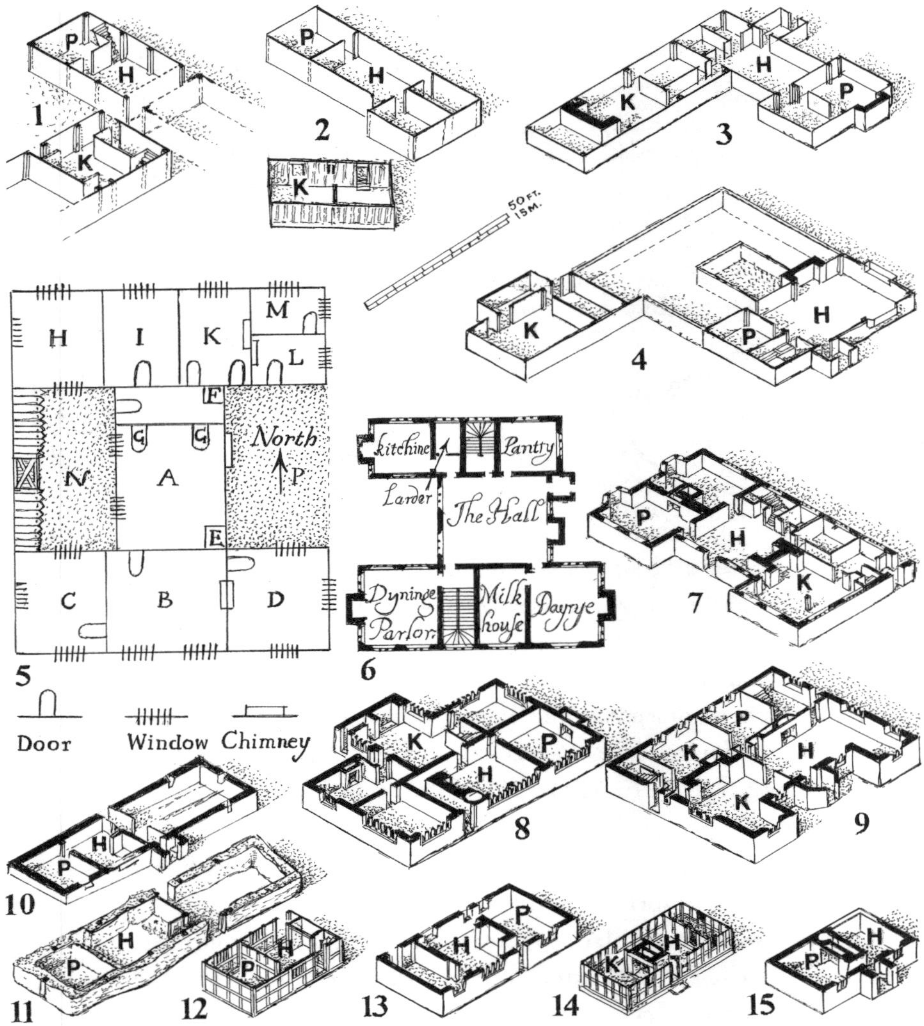

Figure 11. Kitchens in smaller houses & cottages. The houses of the minor gentry and yeomen had a number of house-plans which mirrored those of great houses, but on a smaller scale. Some had detached kitchens, as at (1) Hassocks, Moreton, Essex, 16th cent., or (2) Dorwell Beech, Mountfield, Sussex, mid-late 16th cent. Others had projecting kitchen wings, as at (3) Bugsall, Salehurst, Sussex, c. 1650 and (4) Wardsbrook, Ticehurst, Sussex, c. 1565. The late medieval H-plan continued, as in the plan published in Gervase Markham's English Husbandman *of 1613 at (5), where A: Hall, B: Dining Parlour for Strangers, C: Inward Closet for the Mistress, D: Stranger's Lodging, E: Stair to rooms over Parlour, F: Stair to Goodman's Room, G: Screen in Hall, H: Inward Cellar or Larder, I: Buttery, K: Kitchen & brewing lead, L: Dairy House, M: Milkhouse, N: Forecourt, O: [Back Court], over Kitchen & Buttery, P: Pump; or (6) John Smythson's 'Newe Platt at Twyforde,' Leics., of the early*

carried out over the household's main fire in the family living-room, variously called the hall, houseplace, housebody or fire-house.[36] Probably the best clues for determining the usage of a detached kitchen, in the absence of sound inventory evidence, are its distance from the main house, and the presence of a cooking hearth. Those at Hancocks, Essex, and Darwell Beech, Mountsfield, Sussex, were most probably used for food preparation and/or cookery, being only a few feet away from their hall. Others could be up to 40 feet away. One at Great Worge, Brightling, Sussex, was described in 1567 as having separate rooms for dressing meat, for baking, firing an oven and a malt kiln, and for dairy work, but none for food preparation. The use of detached kitchens obviously varied according to their region, household and date. Most appear to have been going out of use as the sixteenth century progressed, records of the manor of Ticehurst, Sussex, recording their demolition between 1560 and 1609, only eight still surviving in 1618.

The decline of detached kitchens took place at a period when the traditional halls, open to the rafters, were being replaced by comfortable single-storey, ceiled rooms, with chambers on the floor above. Draughty screens passages were being replaced by porches, and unheated service rooms into convenient in-door kitchens. These features were incorporated into most new-built houses, some placing the kitchen adjacent to the hall, some to a rear wing, in accordance with numerous local plan-forms.

In smaller houses retaining an H or E-shaped plan, the kitchen, along with the pantries and butteries, was usually in a cross-wing at the low end of the hall, while the parlours were set symmetrically opposite. As in great houses, double-pile plans were becoming more popular by the early seventeenth century, so that kitchens and ancillary rooms could be set alongside and behind the hall. This enabled true back doors to be introduced for service use, leaving front doors solely for the family and their guests. It also permitted a very practical two-kitchen system to be introduced. The back-kitchen, perhaps fitted with a cooking

17th century. Further houses moved towards a double-piled plan: (7) Horton Hall, Staffs., 1643, which had its bakehouse in the basement; (8) Stockton House, Wilts., 1622; or (9) The Nunnery, Arthington, Yorks., of 1585.

Peasant houses or cottages might still have cross-passages, now with a hearth and chimney to one side and livestock at the other as at (10) Lettaford, Devon, early mid-16th cent., or (11) Wharram Percy, Yorks., early 16th cent. Others had a hall with a fireplace against the end wall, e.g. (12) Poplar Cottage, Waslington, Sussex, mid-17th cent.; or a double-sided chimney stock forming a lobby just inside their central doors: (13) Topham's Farm, Coniston, Yorks., 1630, (14) Pendean, Midhurst, Sussex, late 16th cent., and (15) Chapel Farm, Wapley, Gloucs., of 1636. (H: Hall; P: Parlour; K: Kitchen.)

hearth, oven and boiler, usually served as a combined scullery, washhouse, bakehouse, brewhouse and food preparation room. Having relegated most of these hot, steaming and often dirty operations to the rear, the front kitchen was free to provide the family with a very warm,clean and comfortable multi-purpose informal living-room. Here prepared food could be cooked or sometimes baked in a large fireplace, supervised by the womenfolk. Here too they could look after babies and children, serve everyday meals, and carry out all the multifarious tasks of sewing, spinning, and other womanly responsibilities.

In the smallest houses the functions of both back and front kitchens had to be combined into a single room, as in the hall-kitchens of medieval longhouses. By the sixteenth century most still had an unheated parlour at one end, but the fire at the other was now contained within a back wall and side screen, above which rose a pyramidal timber-framed smokehood. Behind the back wall an entry or cross-passage ran through the house, separating the living quarters from a shippon or cow-byre. Most cottages had a similar combination of a hall-kitchen and parlour, but without the cross-passages and byres, and more frequently with upper floors. As expectations of domestic comfort increased, the parlours gained a fireplace which backed onto that of the hall-kitchen in a central stack. By setting the entrance doors in line with the stack to form a lobby or baffle-entry, there was ready access both from the outside, and from one room to the other. It can be difficult to determine how such cottages were actually used, despite the frequent description of their rooms as 'halls', 'kitchens' or 'parlours'. In theory, these represented three distinct functions, but in practice each family would have cooked, dined and entertained in either or both of the rooms according to their personal preference, just as in the urban terrace houses of later centuries.

CHAPTER THREE

Wood, Coals, Turves and Fires

At the opening of the sixteenth century, most country families relied entirely on fuels which they could harvest for themselves either from their own lands or, by manorial custom, from the nearby woods and commons. Only the largest cities had to import their fuel from greater distances, much of London's supplies being shipped in and sold by its Company of Woodmongers, active from the fourteenth century.[1] Local environmental conditions determined which fuel predominated, but every available resource was exploited.

The best all-round fuel was wood, since it gave excellent heat and flame, burnt on any flat surface and, if well-dried, gave off little smoke, and that more aromatic than foul. In addition, its ashes produced strong alkali lyes for laundry use and soap making. As a marketable commodity, wood was sold in a number of standard forms, each being defined by statute in the assizes of wood and charcoal passed by Henry VIII's parliament in 1543 and Elizabeth I's in 1601.[2] Major households sometimes transcribed these into their own accounts, to ensure that their purchasing officers were fully aware of the standard quantities they should acquire.[3]

Billets were narrow round logs 3 feet 4 inches long, the 'single' being 9 inches in circumference and the 'double' or 'cast' 12 inches in Henry's reign, these being reduced to 7 inches and 10 inches with a 'cast of two' of 14 inches in the 1580s. Tall wood or talshides were larger logs 4 feet long, either round, halved or quarter-split. They were sold in numbered sizes according to their circumference, a Henrician talshide no. 1 being 20 inches round, no. 2, 26 inches, no. 3, 32 inches, and so forth. By the Elizabethan statute, these had been reduced to:

Number	*Round log*	*Half-split*	*Quarter-split*
1.	16″ girth	19″ girth	18″ girth
2.	23″ girth	27″ girth	26″ girth
3.	28″ girth	33″ girth	32″ girth
4.	33″ girth	39″ girth	38″ girth

Faggots were bundles of much smaller branches and twigs 3 feet long, their ends being bound with bands 27 inches long (24 inches under Elizabeth) excluding the knot, to give around 8 inches in diameter. They were usually composed of hedge-trimmings, the extremities of felled trees and so forth, but some made them for their own use from the 'clensinge of the groundes wherein such rubbidge doth growe as briers, brambell, blackthorne and shrubbs of all sortes, which are to be fagotted, and good fewell for bakinge and bruinge.'[4] Both broom and whin, an alternative name for furze or gorse, were similarly harvested:[5]

24–2–1619: 'For 300 broom fagots in Brampton parke 18d'
20–1–1631: 'To Richard Hayton for cutting sixe loades of broome & whinns for fewell at Corbye 2s'
'certayne of brome Facketts 5s.'[6]

'Bavins' were usually longer versions of the faggot, while 'kids' were smaller, both being held together by only one binding rather than two.

Other vegetation used as fuel included ling or heather 'pulled' from the moors between July and October, and sedge, the grassy rush- or flag-like plants of fens and marshes.[7] Many manuscript sources also mention turf, a word now exclusively used for pared strips of grass including both roots and soil. In the past, 'turf' as a fuel might be the coarse vegetation pared from unenclosed land, the distinct layer between the vegetation and the subsoil, rich in roots and the like, or a block of the underlying peat. Where there are references to both turf and peat, it shows that the clerks were differentiating the upper, fibrous, unrotted layers from the lower, compacted and uniform layers which provided the better fuel. Judging from later examples, the peat-spades had L-shaped iron blades mounted on wooden shafts, so that they could cut the peat vertically or horizontally into long, rectangular-sectional strips. They appear in inventories as both turf spades and peat spades, along with the turf wains and peat sledges used to transport them back to the house.[8]

Peat cutting or 'graving' started in April and May.[9] The freshly-cut blocks were then laid out on the surface to dry, being turned and stacked until they had shrunk and become rock-hard by July. It was important to keep them in this condition once stored away in a stack or a peat-house, for if too damp they crumbled and became difficult to burn.

Another form of readily available vegetable fuel was called cassons. They appear in inventories such as those of Charytye Norman and John Pescodd of South Cave, Yorkshire, along with turf and firewood.[10] They were nothing more than dried cow dung, which gave a good clear, swift and odourless heat.[11]

If a particularly clear, bright, smokeless fire was required, especially in stoves or the chafing dishes used at table, the only practical fuel was charcoal. This was made by baking wood in a low-oxygen atmosphere to drive off all its moisture and volatile substances to convert it to an almost pure carbon. The timber was first cut into logs which were dried for months before being built up into a close-packed circular stack around a central vertical stake. After the whole had been covered first in grass, bracken, rushes and the like, and then with damp earth and ashes, the stake was pulled out and red-hot charcoal and other kindling inserted in its place. After one or more days, depending on the variety and humidity of the wood, the white smoke emanating from the stack was replaced by a blue haze, showing that the process had been completed. After sealing the clamp and allowing it to cool, the covering layers were removed so that the charcoal might be extracted.

Most large households made charcoal for their own use and for sale, the only expenditure being that of employing someone skilled in the craft. In the summer of 1607, for example, the Earl of Cumberland at Skipton Castle, Yorkshire, was paying 'yong Tyngle the Colier' 14–15*s*. 'for seting of two killes of Charcole in Crokerise'.[12] The best charcoal, known as 'white charcoal' despite its blackness, was best made in January and February:[13]

> for white charcole the lightest gorwood [i.e. cordwood] is best and metest for it, vidz. Willowe, sallowe, maple, beech, birtch, ashe, aulder, and such like, which is to bee taken and clifted [i.e. split] ... about two or three fingers thicke, and a foote and a half longe, and soe to be well and thoroughlie dried upon a kilne, which donne maketh a verie hott fier and sweete without stuffinge smoak or suffocating as other charcole doth.

In the mid-sixteenth century the royal household was buying its charcoal by the 'quarter' of eight bushels, the other measure being the sack of four bushels.[14] Charcoal was also being sold by the load. In Essex Sir William Petre employed Robert Marshall, collier, to hew and coal seven loads, each to contain two dozen and three-quarters [of a dozen] at 22*d*. the dozen, and costing 5*s*. the load. This shows that the load was 33 sacks, or 132 bushels, enough to fill a 5-feet-6-inch cubic box. By the mid-seventeenth century the load was stated to be 30 sacks of 3 bushels, or 90 bushels, approaching the volume of a 5-foot cube.[15] Since it was a relatively expensive fuel, the chambers of Henry VIII, Queen Anne, and the Princess Mary were the only ones to be heated with charcoal in 1540.[16] At Hampton Court the coalhouse was located at one side of the Greencloth Yard, from whence it was delivered to the royal apartments in specially made, measured and marked baskets containing 2.6 bushels.[17] Their shape is not recorded, but this volume suggests that they may have been about 1 foot 6 inches in diameter by about 1 foot 10 inches deep, a convenient size to carry upstairs.

The provisioning of such fuels was a year-round task. January and February were occupied in felling, hedging and clearing scrub, so that in March, April, and May:[18]

> is all kinde of provision of fewell to be sortede and brought home, vidz. charcole to bee kepte drie in house, bavin and faggott to bee well stackede for bakinge and bruinge, billet and logwoode to bee pilede in large stakes for the house use in generall [in the steward's charge]

> Get home with thy fuel, made ready to set,
> The sooner the easier, carriage to get …
> Or otherwise linger the carriage thereon
> Till (where as ye left it) the quarter be gone

June and July, the driest months before the onset of the busy harvest-time, were ideal for gathering:[19]

> For turf and for sedge, for to bake and to brew;
> For charcoal and sea-coal, and also for thack
> For tall-wood and billet, as yearly ye lack.

In town, where demand for fuel was now at its lowest, this was the cheapest time to buy in fuel which would be excessively expensive over the coming winter:[20]

> His firing, in summer, let citizen buy,
> Lest buying, in winter, make purse for to cry,
> For carman [carter] and collier harp both on a string
> In winter they cost, to be with thee to bring.

After harvest, it was time to gather in the haulm, the stalks of wheat and rye from which the ears had been reaped that could be used to heat an oven or brewing furnace, and then to:[21]

> House charcoal and sedge, chip and coal of the land,
> Pile tall-wood and billet, stack all that hath band.
> Blocks, roots, pole and bough, set upright to the thatch,
> The nearer more handsome, in winter to fetch.

> In stacking of bavin, and piling of logs,
> Make under thy bavin a hovel for hogs,
> And warmly enclose it all saving the mouth,
> And that to stand open, and full to the south.

From this time to the end of the year, it was 'good to fell all such woode as is fittinge for use … that then such woode so cut downe may be faggotted for provision of the house.'[22]

This seasonal gathering of fuel had been practised for millenniums, carefully managed nature keeping the entire population warm and well fed. It was expected to continue in this self-sufficient, perpetually renewable way for ever. However, some Elizabethan commentators were having to contemplate an entirely new problem:[23]

> if woods go so fast to decay in the next hundred years of grace as they have done and are like to do … it is to be feared that the fenny bote, [such as] broom, turf, gale, heath, firze, brakes, whins, ling, dies, hassocks, flags, straw, sedge, reed, rush, and also sea coal will be good merchandise even in the city of London.

A number of different factors had now combined to produce a great shortage of firewood. The most obvious were the rapid rise in population and a considerable drop in temperature from the late sixteenth to the late seventeenth centuries, when even great rivers such as the Thames froze solid in winter. The passage of the land and its resources from the church and monasteries into lay hands had aggravated the situation through the increased use of timber for industrial purposes. New landlords and entrepreneurs now used up their woodland in sinking new mines, setting up iron furnaces and forges, and developing products for both local and international trade. In addition, the State had to build up a new and robust navy to protect itself from invasions from Catholic Europe. This required the felling of thousands of acres of established woodland.

In 1554 Parliament tried to blame the great shortage of firewood on its export to Europe 'by reason whereof the said [wood is] grown into a wonderful dearth and extreme price, to the great detriment of the common wealth of this your highness realm, and your faithful subjects of the same', but its export ban had little effect.[24] England's demands for firewood had completely outstripped available resources. The sole solution was to exploit its only other potential source of fuel, mineral coal. If rich seams had not been available, it would have been impossible for the country to have kept its people well fed and warm, or to have developed as a great industrial and economic power in succeeding centuries.

In the north-east, coal had been mined and shipped down the east coast to London and beyond from the mid-fourteenth century.[25] It had been mainly used for industrial processes such as lime burning and salt boiling, but as other fuels became scarcer, it slowly made its way into halls and kitchens. By the fifteenth century coal was being burned in York and the Yorkshire Wolds, their supplies coming from the west Yorkshire mines, which along with all those in other regional coalfields, expanded to meet the demands of the growing domestic market. The use of coal in the kitchens of major households in the early sixteenth century is well documented, but anyone consulting accounts should be aware that until the end of the seventeenth century the word 'coal' was used for both the mineral and charcoal. Confirmation of which was actually being described only comes from its particular context, or from the use of a qualifying term such as digged, earth, pit, sea, or stone-coal.

Coal from Newcastle was sold in bulk by the chaldron or chalder, a measure containing 36 bushels weighing 53 hundredweight, and by the quarter or quarter-chaldron of around thirteen hundredweight, smaller quantities were calculated in mets, two-bushel measures of some three hundredweight. When the Earl of Northumberland's household was in residence in one of its castles around 1512, it burned six bushels, almost nine hundredweight, in its kitchens every day.[26] Further down the coast at Hunstanton, Norfolk, the Le Strange family obtained 'a grette grate for ye kechyn' in 1520, then bought coal to burn in it:[27]

> 28–6–1522 to Mr Baxters seint of Newcastell for 20 chalder of coles [53 tons] ... £5 6*s*. 8*d*.
> to Robt. Banyard, Willm. Osborne & John Cawston for 2 days caryeng of the same coles wt your bottes from ye shippe to ye shore 3*s*. 8*d*.
> to Edward Spencer for 2 dayes caryeng pte of the same coles from the botes upon the Clyffe 2*s*.

In smaller households the new expense of buying coals instead of collecting their fuel for free, brought additional pressure to bear on their meagre resources. As one aged husbandman of Burnley, Lancashire, complained in 1526, no one had 'any nede in tyme past to get Coles for there fuell by reason they hedde plenty of woode from the forests and turves at theyre liberty which now be decayed and restrayned from theym.'[28] However, for him and hundreds of thousands of others, there was no alternative. This explains the massive increase in coal production throughout this period as illustrated by the following estimates:[29]

Coalfield	*1550s*	*1680s*
Durham & Northumberland	65,000 tons	1,255,000 tons
Midlands	65,000	850,000
Cumberland	6,000	100,000
Kingswood Chase & Somerset	10,000	100,000

Forest of Dean	3,000	25,000
Devon & Ireland	1,000	17,000
Total	*130,000* tons	*2,347,000* tons

In Newcastle alone, coal exports rose from 33,000 tons in 1563–4 to 529,000 tons in 1658–9. As a contemporary verse truly claimed:[30] 'England's a perfect World, has Indies too! / Correct your Maps: Newcastle is Peru.'

Both coal dealers and householders found that their coal-houses rapidly accumulated quantities of slack, this being made up of the dust and small chips of coal eroded from the larger, clean-burning lumps. It readily absorbed moisture and was difficult to ignite, unless placed on top of a burning fire, where it often gave off masses of foul smoke and then effectively stifled the fire below. This property was useful if ever a fire had to be 'banked up' last thing at night, so that it might be readily revived next morning, but otherwise slack represented the loss of much valuable fuel.

To remedy this situation Sir Hugh Plat published *A new cheape and delicate Fire of Cole-balles* in 1603. His method involved strewing alternate layers of coal dust and loam onto a paved floor and turning them over with a shovel or spade until they could be made into balls, as if 'making snowballs'. After drying for a few days, these could then be placed on the fire to produce a good enduring heat. This practice was revived by Richard Gesling in 1644 as *Artificial Fire, or Coale for Rich and Poore. This being the offer of an Excellent new Invention.*[31] His basic recipe comprised three loads of red brick marl, half a chaldron of best seacoal, three sackfuls of small seacoal, four trusses of chopped straw, and sufficient water to combine these together to the consistency of brick-clay. This mixture was then either moulded like house-bricks, but only half the thickness, or into balls, both using four sacks of coal or charcoal dust to stop them sticking to the moulds, the hands, or to each other. Those who could not afford to use so much coal could replace much of it with sawdust, cow or horse dung, peat, or well-dried turves cut from Greenwich or Hounslow heaths.

From the later sixteenth century coal was the main fuel for general cookery in most parts of the country. Only those areas where alternatives remained available, the peaty uplands and levels, the wooded hill country, parks and forests, or where bulk transport was prohibitively expensive, did the older traditional fuels remain in use.

The use of coal produced vast quantities of foul sulphurous smoke in every town and city. It drove Elizabeth I from London in 1574, the same year that a brewer and dyer were thrown into gaol for burning coals in Westminster, but such actions did not improve the situation.[32] Housewives found that coal introduced far more work into their kitchens. Fine wood-ash dissolved in water

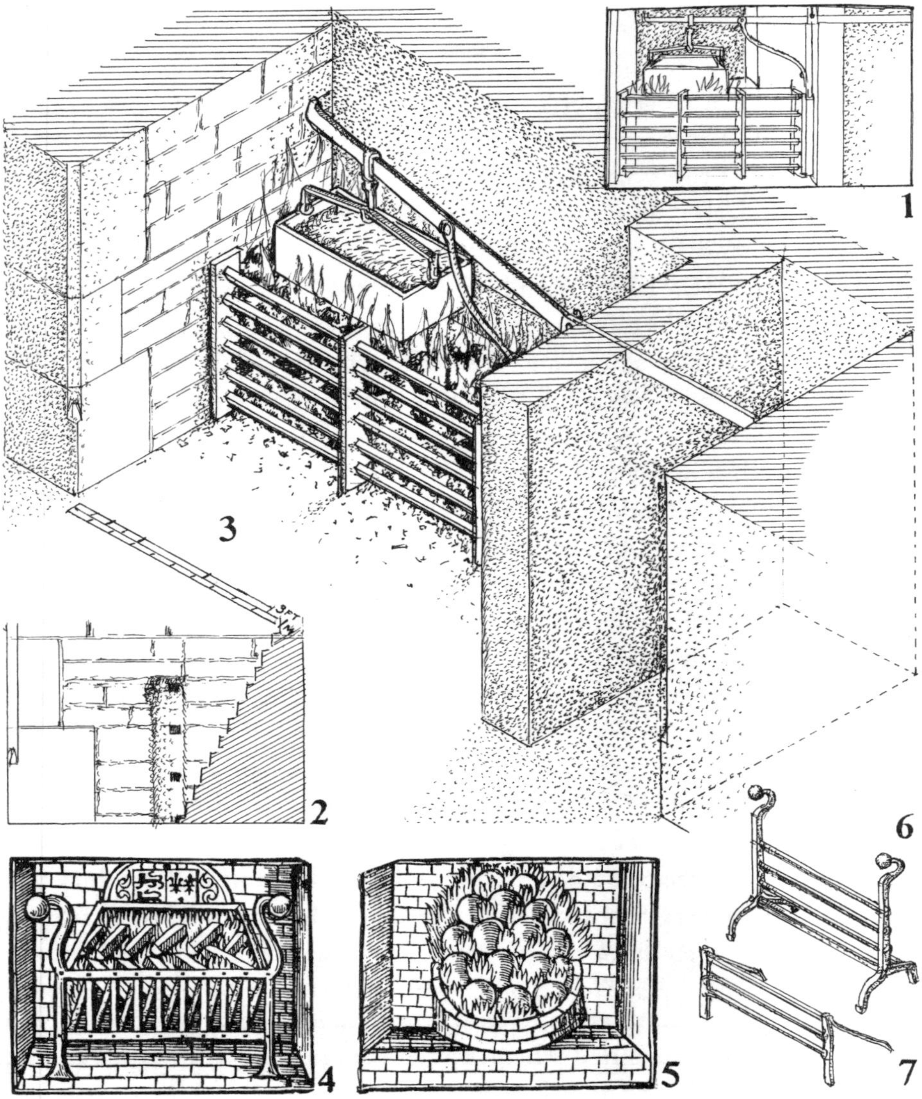

Figure 12. Roasting ranges. John Smythson's design of the 1620s for a roasting range for Bolsover Castle (1 & 3) conforms exactly to its sockets cut into the side wall of the kitchen fireplace there (2). When installed, it would have been ideal for roasting or boiling over a coal fire, or one made of Richard Gosling's 'Artificial Coal' of 1644 (4 & 5). Smaller ranges (6 & 7), made from the early 17th century, were probably intended to support a coal fire between a pair of masonry hobs.

and could be wiped off the bottom of cooking pots with a wet cloth, but coal coated them in a mixture of foul soot and tar, insoluble and as messy as printers' ink. Remembering the 1570s, Arthur Standish confirmed that even 'the poorest sort scorned to eat a piece of meat roasted with sea coal, which now [in 1613] the best magistrates are constrained to do.'[33] No one except those in the coal trade liked the change from wood to coal. In the City of London, the wives complained 'O Husband, we shall never bee well, we nor our Children, whilst wee live in the smell of this *Cities Seacole smoke*, Pray, a Country house for our health, that we may get out of this *stinking Seacole smell*.' They only ceased to protest when the Civil War blockade cut off the supplies from Newcastle. Then these 'Nosed *Dames*' cried 'Would to *God* we had Seacole, O the want of Fire undoes us, O the sweet Seacole fire we used to have, how we want thee now, no fire to your Seacoale.'[34]

Within kitchens, the introduction of coal brought with it the need for new resources. Unlike wood, coal required a good under-draught to burn effectively, and so had to be raised up in an iron frame. The word grate originally indicated the iron grid place across a window or drain opening, but it was now applied to firebaskets. To qualify this new specific usage, the clerks used terms such as grates 'for fire', 'wherein coals of fire must lie', 'to burn coals in the kitchen', and other terms.[35] It is probable that the first generation of grates were a series of horizontal bars mounted between two vertical end-posts resembling the andirons used when burning logs. This type continued in use into the twentieth century, often fitted between a pair of masonry hobs.[36]

In the late 1620s John Smythson drew a detailed design for a very large grate of this kind for the terrace-range kitchen at Bolsover Castle. A close examination of the surviving fireplace there reveals the slots cut in the masonry to house its end-posts. Each one was pierced with six holes to hold the diagonally-set horizontal firebars. Three of these bars had bosses or nuts at the left end, and three at the right, so that the grate could be assembled before being set in place, and subsequently dismantled whenever the bars needed to be replaced. The brick fireback sloped at 30 degrees to the vertical, so that the glowing coals were always pressed against the firebars as they settled and shrank into cinders. It provides extremely rare, probably unique evidence of the first generation coal-burning kitchen grates designed for both boiling and roasting.[37]

The transition from wood to coal initially required no change in the design of chimney flues in stone or brick-built kitchens. However, there were many small houses and cottages which had never before needed chimneys to carry away the smoke from their cooking fires. Their occupants were quite used to living with the fumes rising from the wood, peat or other fuel burning in the

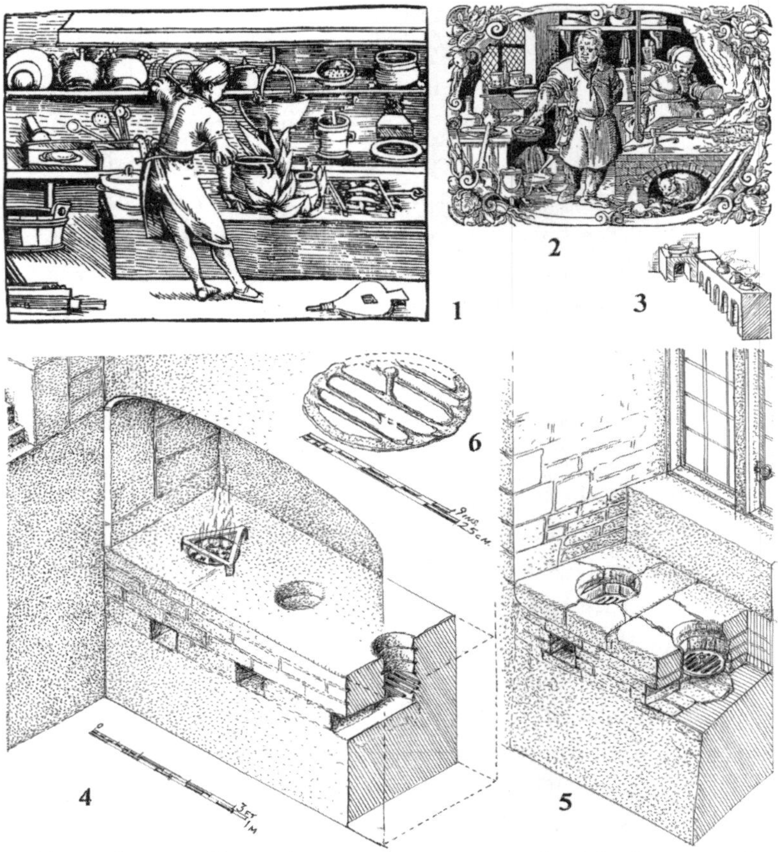

Figure 13. Charcoal stoves. Charcoal stoves are seen in a number of 16th-century Continental publications, such as: (1) Hans Burghmair's woodcut of 1542; (2) Joss Amman's woodcut in Marx Rumpolt's Ein new Kochbuch *of 1581; (3) Bartolomeo Scappi's* Opera *of 1570. Surviving English examples are extremely rare, but probably include: (4) in the 1620s Terrace Range at Bolsover Castle;, and (5) in St Nicholas Priory, Exeter. The latter, probably of the mid-17th century, still has its iron grid (6), with a knob by which it might be lifted out with its embers when being cleaned out.*

middle of their living-rooms. Early sixteenth-century Cheshire farmhouses still 'had their fires in the midst of the house, against a hob of clay', while in Cornwall the cottages had 'scarcely any chimnies, other than a hole in the wall to let out the smoke.' Elsewhere Joseph Hall described a house:[38]

> Of one bays width, God wot! A silly cote,
> Whose thatched spars are furr'd with skittish soote
> A whole inch thick shining like a black-moor's brow,
> Though smoke that down the head-les barrel blows.

In Essex, such problems had already been solved by the introduction of chimneys, as Harrison recorded in his *Description of England* of 1577:[39]

> [Older people remembered that] in their young days there were not above two or three [chimnies], if so many in most uplandish towns in the realm ... but each made his fire against a reredos in the hall, where he dined and dressed his meat ... [but now a] multitude of chimneys [are] lately erected.

Archaeological evidence for this change was discovered when excavating the deserted village of Wharram Percy on the Yorkshire Wolds. The first house to have a chimney instead of an unenclosed hearth was built here in the late fifteenth / early sixteenth centuries, when coal had already come into use. It extended almost two-thirds across the partition wall backing on the the cross-passage entrance bay, a screen at right-angles enclosing its open end.[40] By comparison with similar examples which survived locally up to the twentieth century, it would have had a long mantle-beam across its open side facing into the hall. This supported a half-pyramid timber-framed chimney hood which effectively funnelled the smoke up and away over the thatch.

The soot which collected in such chimneys, and even more intensely in masonry chimney flues, had to be swept away at regular intervals. If allowed to accumulate, it not only retarded the rising smoke, but created a dangerous fire-risk. Household accounts therefore include payments such as the following from Hunstanton in 1519: 'pd. to John le Scott of Ryngstede [Rinstead, two miles away], for sweepyng of ye Kethyn Chymne 2*d*.'[41] November was the best month for chimney sweeping, since:[42]

> The chimney all sooty, would now be made clean,
> For fear of mischances, so oftentime seen;
> Old chimney and sooty, if fier once take,
> By burning and breaking, some mischief may make.

In contrast, the burning of charcoal produced no soot, its fumes being perfectly transparent, unless it was damp. Like coal, it needed a good draught to keep it alight, and so was burned in containers having either firebars or ventilation holes. In major households these took the form of stoves or furnaces, table-height masonry benches with a series of fireplaces sunk into their top surfaces. They are illustrated in Continental woodcuts of the 1540s and in manuals on distillation, but are difficult to trace with any certainty in contemporary accounts. A Tudor 'stove' might also be a room-heating device or a vapour bath, for example. In 1616 Gervase Markham described a form of cooking stove with its fireplace bottom 'made in the fashion of a Gridyron' so that the ashes would 'not stay behind to

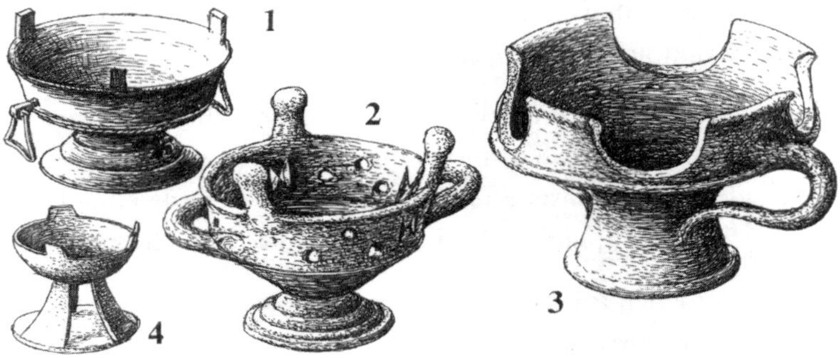

Figure 14. Chafing dishes. Used for minor cooking in the kitchen or heating food at the table, chafing dishes were small firebaskets designed to hold dishes on their three knobs over a bed of glowing charcoal. These examples are (1) of bronze, early 16th century, (2–4) of earthenware from Potterton, Yorkshire, early 16th century, from London and from Donyatt, Somerset, early-mid-17th century.

choake up the fire'. Beneath this there was an ashpit at floor level with an opening which allowed the updraught to enter, and the ashes to be removed.[43] These details were confirmed by Richard Tomlinson in 1657, the fire being set in the upper part over a grate with an ashpit below 'to receive the ashes, give ventilation to the coals and extract the ashes.'[44] Since this arrangement continued unchanged for centuries it is not possible to date surviving examples on stylistic grounds, but it is probable that those in the kitchens at St Nicholas' Priory in Exeter and Bolsover Castle are of the second quarter of the seventeenth century. Both have round fireplaces, provision for iron grids, and a draught / ash-hole opening to their front faces. In use, all stewpans, frying-pans and other utensils would have to be supported on a low iron trivet, otherwise their bases would stifle the draught, and put out the fires.

Cooking over charcoal is very similar to cooking over gas, both giving a relatively clean and controllable heat. After use, the bottoms of the pots may usually have their thin layer of ash simply wiped or washed away, unless the charcoal has given off minor tarry deposits. The only real disadvantage is the fume. Although invisible, it is scorching, hot and toxic, as any cook who has received a face-full from a strong draught knows only too well. Unless carried away, any large concentration would certainly induce drowsiness, unconsciousness and death. For this reason the stoves were usually set either into a wide fireplace and chimney or beneath a window, always with good light to enable the cook to see what he was doing.

Whenever additional stewing facilities were needed, or in kitchens where there was no stove, small portable stoves called chafing dishes provided a very practical solution. Three brass examples were used in Archbishop Parker's kitchens in the 1570s, for example, while Izaak Walton instructed that his fish should 'be boiled gently over a Chafing-dish with wood coals.' Professional cooks such as John Saulter of Bury St Edmunds, also found them invaluable, his pair being valued at a shilling each in 1576.[45] Some cast and turned brass or bronze examples may have been imported from the Continent, but others, such as those from Ouseden in Suffolk or Wigmore Grange, Shropshire, appear to have been made in England in the sixteenth century. They have a bowl-shaped body to hold the burning charcoal. With three projections rising above the rim to support a dish or frying-pan, and holes pierced through the base into an integral pedestal, these allowing for the necessary up-draught, and a means of collecting the fine ashes.[46]

As in the medieval period, most chafing dishes were made of glazed earthenware. They were similar in shape and size to the metal examples, with bowls around seven to nine inches in diameter, their designs changing slightly from one pottery to another. Those made on the Hampshire/Surrey border in the early-mid-seventeenth century had rounded knobs above their rims, and sometimes piercings around their bowls, for example, while some of those from Donyatt in Somerset had deeply-scalloped rims to perform the same function. Rather smaller versions, with bowls only around four or five inches in diameter were unsuitable for cooking, and so were most probably used as dish-warmers to keep food hot as it stood on the dining table. In Yorkshire, elegant yellow-glazed examples were made in early sixteenth-century 'Cistercian ware', others made on the Hampshire / Surrey borders in the mid to late seventeenth century with very shallow bowls and rims cut into a zig-zag crenellation.[47]

Whichever fuel was to be burned, it first had to be ignited, usually starting with a small quantity of dry, flammable kindling to establish the required body of heat.[48] To create the initial flame, a piece of flint was held in one hand a few inches above a small heap of tinder composed of dry tow, rotten wood, charred linen or fungus. A 'steel' forged to hook over the knuckles of the other hand was then brought sharply down onto the edge of the flint, sending sparks into tinder which, with gentle blowing, started to smoulder and glow. At this point a splinter of wood called a match, its ends dipped in sulphur, was put against the glow, causing it to burst into flame. The use of 'fyre yrons, flynte stones, Tinder, and Brimstone' in this way was well established by the early sixteenth century, but one of the best descriptions was provided by Nicholas Breton in 1626:[49]

> The maid ... groaps for the tinder box, where after a conflict between the steel and the stone, she begets a spark, at last the candle lights on his match; then upon and old rotten foundation of broken boards she erects an artificial

fabrick of the Black Bowels of New-Castle soyle, to which she sets fire with as much confidence as the Romans to their Funeral Pyles.

KITCHEN LIGHTING

As food was usually prepared and cooked in daylight hours, most kitchens relied on windows for illumination. In ordinary houses they were indistinguishable from those of any other room, but in great houses they were set high in the walls, up against the wallplate or ceiling. Here they could more effectively throw their light across the centre of the floor, prevent pilfered food from being carried away, and leave the lower parts of the walls free for fireplaces, dressers and other furniture. As the use of glass became more widespread, windows were now usually fully or half-glazed. In 1591, for example, the kitchen of Richard Sweete, an Exeter merchant, had its window of seven lights all half-glazed, and priced at threepence the square foot.[50] Slots to receive leaded lights for full glazing are to be found in the mullions of most Tudor and Stuart kitchen windows, demonstrating that this was a widespread practice.

For early mornings and late nights, particularly over the dark winter months, it was necessary to use artificial light. Since the hearths were almost at floor level, their flames only lit the undersides and edges of the tables and dressers, leaving their worktops in complete shadow. References to lighting equipment and materials in kitchens are relatively uncommon, probably because the former were of little value, and the latter would be drawn from general domestic supplies. Candles were certainly used, the kitchen serving the Star Chamber in the Palace of Westminster using 10lb costing 3*s*. 4*d*. in the autumn of 1590.[51] These would have been purchased from a professional wax-chandler, but many households, both great and small, preferred to make them from their own tallow or wax either by dipping the wicks, or encasing them in metal or pottery moulds.[52] In 1541 the Earl of Rutland's clerks 'paide for 2 dozen lynkes of rosen floresshid with waxe for the kechyn at 4*d*. the lb conteynyng 32lb. 7*s*.'[53] Each of these 1lb 5oz 3½*d*. links would be made by dipping lengths of tow or linen rag into hot wax and rolling them to produce a rod about three-quarters of an inch (2 cm) in diameter. In use, they were mounted on the spike of a portable iron cresset, where they produced a much stronger light than any candle. Even so, all kitchens remained rather too gloomy to operate easily after dark.

CHAPTER FOUR

Water Supplies

> But he ... whiche will dwell at pleasure, and for proffyte and halth of his body, he must [have] water ... anexed to his place or howse ... for to wasshe and to wrynge, to bake and to brewe, and dyvers other causes, specyally for peryll, the whiche myghte fall by fyre.

As Andrew Boorde advised in 1542, anyone selecting the site for a new mansion or house had to ensure that it could draw on a sufficient supply of fresh water. Without this necessity it would be impossible to prepare food and drink, to wash and clean, or to fight fires if they spread from the hearth into timbers and thatch. In order of preference, he thought that rainwater was best, then that from clean streams running over gravel, clean rivers and fresh springs. Well water was not recommended, but worst of all was still pond water, especially if muddy or polluted with froth or a carpet of green duckweed.[1]

Collecting rainwater as it dripped from the eves would provide householders with their easiest source of clean water, even if this supply could be quite restricted in quantity. In York, for example, William Carter was using the water tub in the garth of his Stonegate inn in 1581, this being preferable to water drawn from backyard wells and the heavily polluted Ouse.[2] Rainwater collecting in such small houses might be as simple as the 'square and rounde pipes of cesternes from the gutters', which took a London plumber and his two labourers eight days to erect at Ashley House, Walton-on-Thames, in 1602. Here the lead storage cistern for the house, which also had a conduit supply, weighed almost half a ton, its waters serving seven brass taps around the property.[3]

In contrast, larger and more prosperous establishments, those with large areas of roof drained by efficient gutters and fall-pipes, could collect quite substantial amounts. Each square foot of roof collected half a gallon of water per inch of annual rainfall, so that a large mansion might easily obtain 1000 or 1500 gallons a year, some 20 to 30 pints a day, purely from this source. Unfortunately the archaeology of Tudor and Stuart rainwater collection is still in its infancy, but evidence of its importance is demonstrated by Henry VIII's system at Windsor Castle. Here, in 1532–3, the water from the lead-covered roofs was

Figure 15. Conduits. The Combe Hill conduit at Kingston, Surrey (1) provided water from springs into two settling tanks before piping it to Hampton Court Palace via four tampkins (right) which allowed for further sediment to settle, and relieved pressure on the lead pipes. Smaller tampkins still survive near Bolsover Castle (2). The cistern tower and overflow of c. 1588 on the brink of the hill at Hardwick Old Hall (3) controlled the supply of water into the nearby kitchen, while at Cowdray House (4) the conduit took the form of a column in the middle of the kitchen floor. The Elizabethan woodcut of a public conduit in London (5) shows maids and wives collecting their water in buckets, while a professional watercarrier uses a tall tankard over his shoulder to fill a large soe resting on the ground. In some regions earthenware buckets were used, (6) coming from Goldsmith Street, Exeter, c. 1660, and (7) from the Horton kiln, Dorset.

piped into a series of massive brick-vaulted cisterns beneath the new terrace built along the north façade, providing an excellent self-replenishing supply.

From the early sixteenth century Henry VIII ordered new waterworks for many of his palaces: Greenwich in 1515, Beaulieu in 1522, St James's in 1531–2, Woodstock in 1532–3, and Hampton Court in 1538–45.[4] These all relied on spring water however, which demanded the presence of copious springs at a higher level, and the construction of long, gravity-fed pipelines down to the service areas of the individual properties. One of the best examples still survives largely intact close to Hampton Court Palace. As the old supply was inadequate to serve the greatly extended kitchens and services, it was decided to take water from the three springs some three miles away formerly used by the recently suppressed Merton Abbey. Each of the springs was now enclosed within a substantial brick conduit house to protect it from pollution and frost. After passing through primary and secondary settling tanks, the water descended into a deep tertiary tank, and then along a duct into a fourth tank set beneath a 'tampkin' some 80 feet away. Further tampkins, small roofed buildings each housing a settling tank, were built at intervals along the rest of the leaden pipeline. Their purposes included the absorption of water-hammer effects along the pipe, the extraction of the finest sediments, and the ability to isolate sections of the pipe in case of damage or leaks. Finally, having passed beneath the Thames, the pipes arrived at the Palace, to supply water to various taps and cisterns in the service areas.[5] The contours of the ground around Nonsuch Palace enabled an even more efficient system to be installed, a conduit from the Little Park gravity-feeding 'a very large cistern of lead' housed in the second storey of the elegant western turret of the inner courtyard. From here many individual supply-pipes ran off to supply the needs of the whole house.[6]

Similar systems were constructed to serve major private houses. Around 1500 a tunnel was driven into the hillside at Petworth Park to springs deep in the sandstone. After passing through a two-foot layer of gravel in a ten- by six- by six-foot-high stone-lined chamber, the water entered a three-inch lead pipe, and ran down to a large stone reservoir, which still stands in its original building in the Wood Yard at Petworth House. From here, pipes led off to serve both the 'cestern of lead with a curbe of wood about yt to receive the cundit water commyng into the said kitchen,' and a conduit in the town. The main problem with such supplies was that they could become sources of great contention, and subject to vandalism. At Petworth, the inhabitants had to be fined in order to stop them using the conduits to water their horses or wash their roots, fish and bullocks' entrails in the cisterns. When a dispute broke out between the Earl of Northumberland and his tenants in 1592, they came 'in violent manner, broke and entred those Conduit House and hedds apperteyning and ... stopped and restrayned the water for my necessary euse, supposing the same thieve lewde behaviours not to come to light ....'[7] In spite of such difficulties, most large houses, having nearby springs, found it best to install conduit systems and gain an effective self-acting water supply.

Since everyone today is used to turning taps on and off, it is easy to forget that self-acting systems, whether from springs or water-powered pumps, run constantly. This made it necessary to divert the surplus waters away as quickly as possible through copious drains. Since Hardwick Old Hall stood at the top of a very steep hill, William Sanderton, plumber, placed the conduit-fed cistern in an elegant arched structure, probably designed by Robert Smythson, on the very brink of the scarp. From here, supply pipes could top up cisterns in the kitchen, and offices while the surplus could overflow into a short shaft below, and run off down the slope. Completed on 10 December 1591, the system cost £23 6*s.* 8*d.*[8]

Where the land was flat, more elaborate drains were required, these also being utilized for flushing away kitchen and other waste. At Hampton Court Palace, where separate conduit-fed cisterns were fitted in the boiling-house, wet-larder and kitchen in 1530, great underground 'sinks' or drains were constructed. Measuring fourteen feet high by ten feet wide, with brick walls and vaulted roofs, they carried off the cisterns' overflow, collected dirty water and waste from grates in the floors, then conveyed them beneath the moat (to avoid polluting it) and on into the Thames.[9] Private householders were equally concerned to provide themselves with good drains. At Ingatestone Hall in Essex Sir William Petre 'devised with himself [around 1540] for the sure avoiding and ready conveyance of all such waters [from his springs and conduits] to make divers vaults and gutters of brick, very large, under the ground, round about the whole situation of the house, conveying the waters from every office ... the rain water or otherwise ... unto the lowest part of the river southwards.'[10]

Other houses had even more sophisticated systems. At Cowdray in West Sussex, the spring water collected in an elevated cistern in the conduit house, together with that from the roofs,apparently ran to the various offices in two-foot-wide centrally divided ducts, one side bringing in the water, and the other carrying it away.[11]

In towns and cities, most of the medieval river- or spring-sourced conduit supplies continued in use, many of those installed by monastic houses passing into civic control after the Dissolution, as at Bath, Gloucester, Grantham and Southampton. As populations increased and old systems began to decay, new and more plentiful sources had to be developed using either communal, commercial or charitable funding. Some of these were extremely large-scale and complex undertakings. In 1584–5, for example, with the aid of Sir Francis Drake, its M.P., Plymouth obtained an act 'to digge and myne a diche or trenche conteyninge in bredth between six or seven foot over in all places ... necessaire conveyenge of the same ryver [Mewe als. Mevye] to the said towne'. Drake was paid £200 to complete the seventeen-mile leat between 1590 and 1591, after which both wooden and leaden pipes provided the town and its passing shipping with an excellent supply.[12]

A similar scheme was proposed for London in 1609 by one of its wealthy goldsmiths, Sir Hugh Middleton. With the backing of the Corporation, and half the expenses in return for half the income from James I, the New River, ten feet wide and four feet deep, was cut the 38 miles from Chadwell in Hertfordshire to a reservoir at Islington. When opened in 1613, it fed wooden mains to supply a number of existing conduits, as well as pumps in the streets, becoming the largest and probably purest of all the City's sources of water.[13]

Since such watercourses offered few opportunities to celebrate the munificence demanded by their construction, their point of delivery, the spouts and cisterns in the streets, were frequently of the highest architectural standard. John Scriven's conduit erected in Gloucester in 1636 was a gothic octagon with an open crown on top, rising 25 feet into the air; Hobson's conduit erected in Cambridge in 1614 is a classical hexagonal tower surmounted by a conical roof and parapet embellished with the royal arms, putti and strapwork panels; while the Oxford city conduit of 1617 is a substantial hexagon, its flying buttresses supporting a huge polygonal drum, each face having a carved figure in its arched niche. Along with others of the same quality elsewhere, such structures reflect the pride taken in the provision of clean water for all. Without such conduits, citizens of cities as large as York had to largely rely on river-water for cooking and cleaning, despite its heavy pollution of sewage, offal and filth.[14]

Water was one of the most difficult of all essential supplies to be brought into a kitchen, being heavy, slopping around in any container, and leaking away through the smallest of holes. Small quantities were probably still being carried from nearby supplies in earthenware pitchers or stoneware cruses, but for general purpose a coopered bucket bound with either wooden or iron bands was much more satisfactory. Its use was still quite laborious, however, Richard Madox recording how, in the cold of early January, 1582, he came with his brother and manservant, 'by the wel with 60 buckets to [the house at Handsworth, Staffs.], where we found Mrs Stanford at Dinner.'[15]

If larger quantities were to be carried, especially from the urban conduits, buckets were replaced by tankards. Thomas Platter described these in 1599 as 'special wooden iron-bound vessels with broad bottoms and narrow tops, which poor labourers carry to and fro the houses on their shoulders and sell.'[16] These professional water-carriers included the Company of Water Tankard Bearers of London, which had 4,000 members by the opening of the sixteenth century, and the Water Drawers and Leaders of the Dee in Chester, who petitioned the Crown for a charter of incorporation in 1582.[17] Having filled their tankards at the conduit, they slung them over their right shoulders, grasping the handles with their right hands. A staff in their left hands then passed over their left shoulders and under the base of the tankards, so that they could maintain good balance as they walked, and readily dispense to customers as required without the need of stooping. Many great and middle-ranking households found it more convenient and economical to buy their own tankards, so that they could collect water from the conduits without having to pay the tankard-bearers' fees. In 1615, Thomas Heywood's play *The Poor Apprentices of London* has Charles, a haberdasher's apprentice, acting as water-bearer along with his other chores; 'Faith', he cries, 'as soon as I heard but the messenger say my father must up and twitch me, I left my tankard to guard the conduit, and away came I.'[18] Like his contemporaries, he probably used a large stoneware jug to bail the water from the conduit cistern into his tankard; 'Paide for an other grete stone cruse for ye kechyn, because the first was broken at the conduit in filling of John Turner's tankerde, 6d.'[19]

If sufficient labour was available, the tankard could be superseded by the soe. This was a very large iron-bound coopered tub, two of its staves being extended above the rim and bored through to form strong handles. When filled, a stout staff was thrust through these staves, so that it could be hoisted up on to the shoulders of two men, before being carried off to its destination. If left unattended, it was very easy for a child to overbalance and fall in while trying to get a drink: the parish registers of St Michael le Belfrey in York recording the death of one who 'by misfortune drowned in a soo of water' in 1581.[20]

When water had to be carried for greater distances, it was much better to use horses and water-bougets, pairs of leather bags secured to a cross-bar so as to hang down each side of the animal. Their characteristic profile had been adopted as an heraldic device in the medieval period, but they also remained in practical use throughout the sixteenth and early seventeenth centuries. In 1541, for example, the Earl of Rutland's accounts show payments 'For 2 halters for the water budgies 2*d*. For shoyng of the water budges horse'; while one house in Knaresborough still listed 'a pair of water bags' among its contents in 1660.[21]

When all these vessels were being filled, the conduits became bustling centres of communal life. A late-Elizabethan woodcut entitled *Tittle Tattle* shows a crowd of women around a London conduit, some queuing, some filling their buckets, and others fighting like cats:[22]

At the conduit striving for their turn,
The quarrel it grows great,
That up in arms they are at last,
And one another beat

The language used here was similarly colourful, as Ben Jonson's character, Oliver Cob, the water-bearer in *Every Man in his Humour*, clearly showed.

Such time-wasting, vexatious trouble could be avoided by digging a private well, provided that there was water close to the surface, and someone who could find it. The payment 'To Baldwyne for his charge in sekinge for Water 1*s*. 10*d*.,' recorded in the Le Strange accounts in the 1540s probably refers to the employment of a dowser who would use his traditional rod to find the best place to start digging. He was obviously successful, for the same account records a further 1*s*. 8*d*. 'for a bucket and the ropes for the welle in the kechinge'.[23]

When a well was out of doors and fairly shallow, the medieval device of a large beam, pivoted at its centre, with a heavy weight at one end and a chain and bucket at the other, still remained in use. St Mary's Well in the outer ward of Scarborough Castle was of this type, as shown on an early sixteenth-century survey. As the well as only sixteen feet deep and perhaps nine feet down to water level, it was quite a simple matter to pull the chain down, plunging the bucket into the water, and then pull it up, aided by the heavy counterweight.[24]

Most small wells relied on the traditional hand-cranked 'beame or rounde wood whereabout the cord of a well is winded, some do call it a winch', as described by Claudius Hollyband in 1580.[25] In most cases, the well-rope terminated in a few feet of iron chain fastened to the half-round iron handle which hinged across the mouth of the well-bucket. The weight of the chain and handle was a matter of great importance, since without it the bucket would float on the surface of the water, rather than capsizing and filling ready for being drawn back to the surface. Since the weight of the wet well-rope, chain and bucket could be considerable, the earlier practice of hanging two buckets on the same winch, so that one counterbalanced the other, was still continued. The well-house at Nonsuch had been provided with 'a faire well of great depth, a large cisterne of lead, and a wheel for winding up the water, with two large and strong buckets well bound with iron', for example.[26] Shakespeare was familiar with such systems, describing in *Richard II*:[27]

a deepe Well,
That owes two Buckets, filling one another,
The emptier ever dancing in the ayre,
The other downe unseene, and full of water

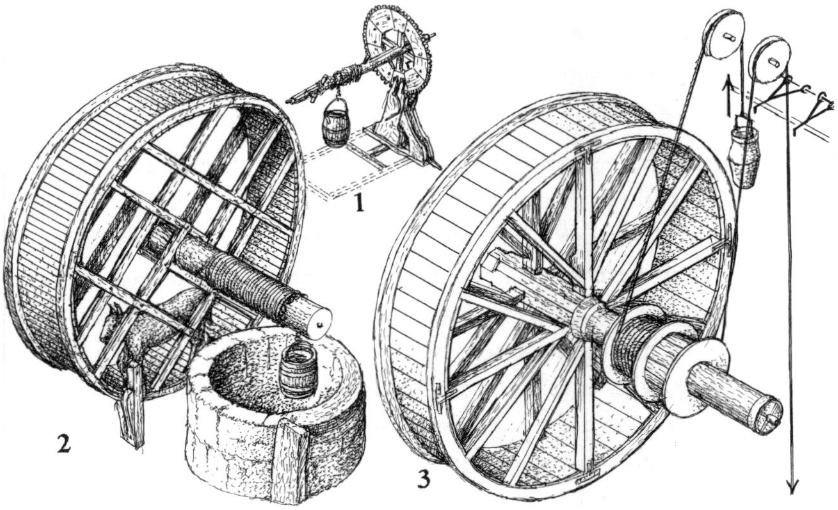

Figure 16. Winches and donkey wheels. Where wells were particularly deep, as on chalk downlands, mechanical devices were essential for raising water up to the surface. The two-man winch from Lower Wield Farm, Alton, Hants. (1) was fitted over a 300ft well. The Carisbrooke Castle donkey wheel of 1587 (2) serves a 160ft well, while the 16th-century example at Greys Court, Oxfordshire (3) serves one of 200ft.

In most parts of the country, where there was a relatively high water-table, these simple winches were quite adequate, but they were far too slow and laborious where there were only deep wells. If the geology was mainly of chalk, particularly in the south and south-east, the home counties and in east Yorkshire, most rainwater was instantly absorbed, and could only be retrieved by digging wells perhaps 200–300 feet deep. Should a hand-wound winch be used, it had to incorporate an effective gearing system and a brake to make the best use of time and effort. One constructed at Lower Wield Farm near Alton, Hampshire, had a large wooden gear-wheel mounted at one end of its winch, this being turned by a much smaller gear-wheel operated by two men, each winding his own strong iron crank. Raising sufficient water for domestic and agricultural use from the 300-foot well must have been one of the most laborious and boring of all daily chores.[28]

From the early mid-sixteenth century much larger well-winches began to be installed over the deepest excavations, their power being provided by a large cylindrical tread-wheel mounted at one end of their massive horizontal shafts. D'Acres' *Art of Water Drawing* of 1660 described them as 'Certain great hollow wheels hanging perpendicularly, in which men tread (called by some tread-wheels) not unlike unto a dog in a spit wheel.'[29] Now a man, or more usually a donkey, could climb inside the wheel, and rotate it by walking forward, using their own body-weight to raise the well-bucket. One of the best-documented and best-known of these is at Carisbrooke Castle on the Isle of Wight. Rebuilt in 1587 at a cost of £16, it has a wheel fifteen and a half feet in diameter, a long rope wound around its winch-shaft enabling its heavy bucket to raise water from the 160-foot well with relatively little effort. John Taylor, the Water Poet, saw a similar wheel in use at Dover Castle in 1623:[30]

> And in a wheele I saw a comely asse
> Dance like a dogge that's turning of a spit,
> And draw as it were from the infernall pit,
> (Whose deepe abisse is perpendicular)
> One hundred fathome (oer well neere as farre)
> So christaline, so cleere, and coole a water,
> That will in summer make a man's teeth chatter,
> And when to see it up, I there had stood,
> I drank thereof, and found it sweet and good ...

This well is actually 380 feet deep, rather than the reputed 600 feet, quoted here, and just over a yard in diameter, so there was only room for a single bucket, in the normal manner. At Greys Court, Oxfordshire, the twelfth-century, 200-foot well was much wider, and so permitted two buckets to be used, so that one counterbalanced the other, greatly reducing the effort required. Built in the sixteenth century, it had a pair of large pulleys mounted on its shaft to keep each well-rope separate from the other. Instead of descending directly into the well, each rope passed over its pulley, so that as one bucket descended, the other was raised up to engage a hook, which tipped its load into a collecting tank, providing a head of water for household use. Once the bucket had tipped, a lever brake was applied so that the donkey could stop, be led out, turned around, and brought back into the treadwheel, ready to raise the fully laden lower bucket, this routine being repeated until the tank was full.[31]

Rather surprisingly, the use of lift and force pumps, known here in the Roman period, was hardly ever employed for water-raising in medieval England. They were used on board fifteenth-century ships to expel bilge-water, so it is interesting to speculate if the 'plumpmaker' recorded in Bristol in 1490 was serving the nautical, rather than the domestic trade. Well-pumps first enter written records in the late fifteenth and early sixteenth centuries. In Coventry, there was a 'plum-house by the well-yard yate' in 1480; in 1505–6, Oriel College, Oxford, paid a shilling 'for the reparacion of the plump'; while in 1517 the

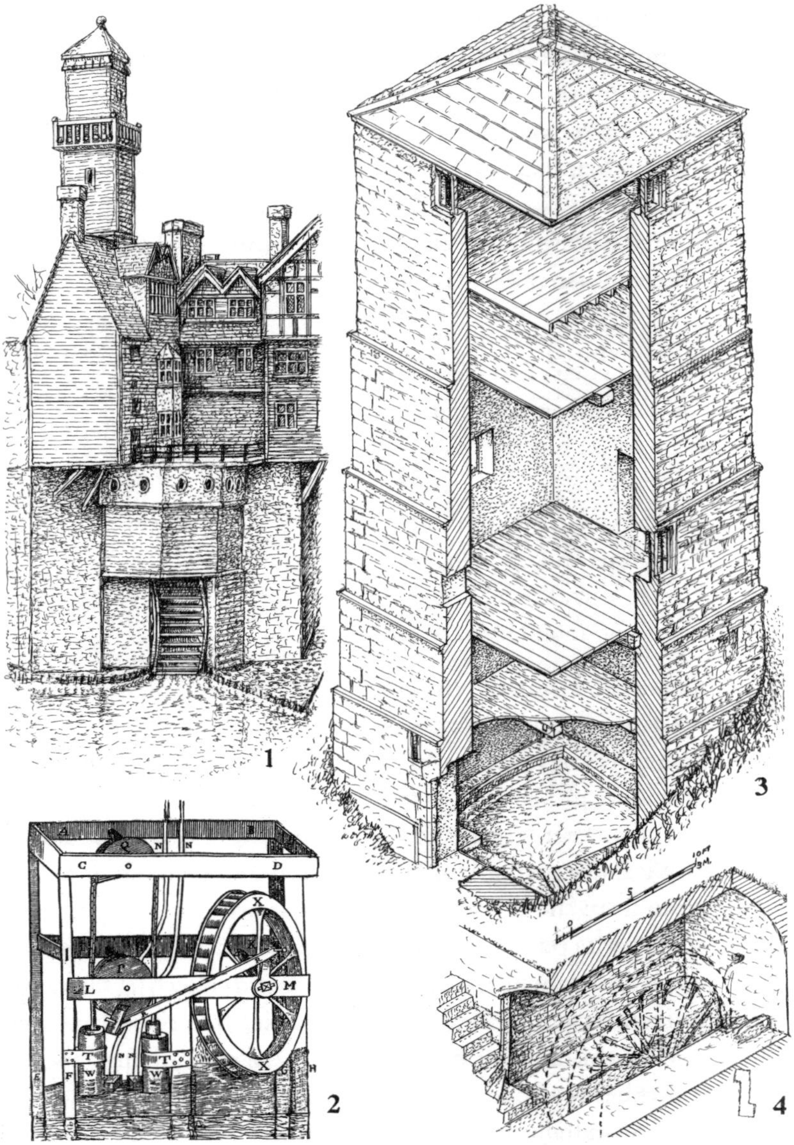

Figure 17. Water-powered lift and force pumps. From the late 16th century self-acting pumps operated by waterwheels were being used to provide domestic water supplies. Peter Morris the Dutchman's waterwheel and watertower (1) and pumps (2) were installed at the north end of London Bridge in 1582. Dame Mary Bolle's early 17th-century water tower at Heath Old Hall, Wakefield (3) collected water from a spring and used this source to turn a wheel in an underground chamber (4) to pump the water to a header tank at the top of the tower. From here a lead pipe carried it along an inverted syphon up to the Hall.

churchwardens of Yatton, Somerset, paid a pound for 'drawing up ye plumpe to ye well'.[32] Hand pumps were also used to raise water from conduit supplies up to domestic offices. John Carpenter supplied one for 'the back court by the new office' at Hampton Court in 1530, while another was erected in the centre of the kitchen at Cowdray House about the same time.[33] When Henry VIII established Ashridge, Hertfordshire, as a nursery for the infants Edward and Elizabeth in 1539, a dog-powered pump, probably worked by a treadwheel, was used to raise its water from the well, such records confirming the increasing use of pumps.[34]

One of the most impressive remains of a domestic pumping system of this period still stands on the edge of Heath Common, just to the south of Wakefield. It takes the form of a square tower some 50 feet high built for Dame Mary Bolles in the mid-seventeenth century. Her will of 1662 describes it as 'The Water Tower or Conduit, lately built, with the lead works & iron works belonging it'. A door in its base gives access to a cistern which is constantly filled by an extremely copious spring. Its overflow was directed into a subterranean chamber close by, where it operated an eighteen-foot diameter waterwheel, which in turn powered force-pumps which raised the water back up to a second cistern at the top of the tower. From here, a lead pipe descended down to ground level, before ascending to fill a third cistern at the side of the porters' lodge and brewhouse at Heath Old Hall, some 200 yards away on top of a high bluff overlooking the lower Calder valley. It continued to provide the Hall with an excellent water supply until the sinking and draining of coal mines nearby in the mid-nineteenth century caused the spring to fail, after which the pump, second cistern and pipeworks were all removed, leaving the tower and pump chamber still intact.[35]

The first major use of force pumps to provide a public supply was commenced by Peter Morice or Morris, a Dutchman, in London in 1582. After an initial demonstration, during which he threw a jet of water over the steeple of St Magnus the Martyr, he was permitted to build waterwheels in, eventually, the five northern arches of London Bridge. When these rotated, first one way, and then the other as the tide ebbed and flowed, they worked pumps which raised the river-water up into a high cistern in a wooden water-tower at the bridgehead. From here pipes carried it both to private houses in the eastern end of the city, and to public conduits near the churches of St Mary Magdalene (1583) and St Nicholas Cole Abbey[36] (1593). Further force-pumps, at least two worked by horses, were then set up by Bevis Bulmer on the banks of the Thames at Broken Wharf, their pipes serving private houses around West Cheap, St Paul's and Fleet Street. Much of the water brought into London by the New River Company was also raised by pumps, thirteen deep wells being exploited in this way to complement the gravity-fed supplies from 1613.[37]

By the middle of the seventeenth century the combination of new leats, winches and pumps had enabled many of the major towns and country houses to provide themselves with copious supplies of water for domestic use. In small towns and rural areas, however, the medieval sources continued as before, but, whatever its source, it was still unwise to drink any unboiled unless it came directly from a pure spring or hillside stream.

CHAPTER FIVE

The Dairy

In practical terms, the role of the dairy was to convert fresh, rapidly souring milk into a number of nourishing foodstuffs, some to be eaten almost immediately, and others preserved for long-term use. It differed from most other domestic offices, however, since it was a distinctly female department. The dairymaids' pristine cleanliness, early rising, ample fresh air and a clear skin, naturally inoculated by cowpox from the devastation of smallpox, gave them a seemingly idyllic appearance and lifestyle. Sir Thomas Overbury's 'fair and happy milkmaid' was:[1]

> a country wench, that is so far from making herself beautiful by art, that one look of her's is able to put all face physic out of countenance. She knows a fair look is but a dumb orator to command virtue, therefore minds it not. All her excellences stand in her so silently, as if they had been stolen upon her without her knowledge. The lining of her apparel (which is herself) is far better than the outsides of [silk] tissue; for though she be not arrayed in the spoil of the silkworm, she is decked out in innocency, a far better wearing

Richard Braithwaite was proud to boast of the same qualities in his wife:[2]

> Oft have I seen her from the Dayry come
> Attended by her maids, and hasting home
> To entertain some Guests of Quality,
> She would assume a state so modestly
> Sance affect[at]ion, as she struck the eye
> With admiration of the stander by.

In 1595 Henry Percy, 9th Earl of Northumberland, while condemning the interference of great men's wives in kitchens, butteries and pantries, considered that their presence in 'a dary is tolerable; for soe may yow have perhaps a dische of butter, a soft cheese, or some clouted crème in a summer.'[3] Noble ladies had already discovered that a dairy offered a welcome refuge from the stuffy formalities of a great house. It also gave them some of the attractive attributes of the dairymaid, an English advantage later pursued by Marie Antoinette at the Petit

Figure 18. Dairy utensils. Milk from the cow was first strained through a piece of cloth stretched across the hole in the bottom of a bowl-shaped strainer supported on a 'brig' over a cream-pan, such as this 16th-century Netherlands redware example from Newcastle-upon-Tyne (1). The cream was then skimmed off with a fleeting dish (2), and perhaps used to make wassails served in wooden wassail bowls (3), as presented by Richard Rogers to his friends at the Toge Inn, just outside Hampton Court Palace, in the early 17th century, or smaller bowls (4). Cream was also a principal ingredient of syllabubs, served in spouted syllabub glasses (5). Most cream was worked in wooden plunge churns to make butter, as seen in the Grete Herball *of 1526 (6). Smaller churns were made of glazed earthenware, as excavated from Sandal Castle, 1640s (7), and the Fulmodeston pottery in Norfolk, 16th century (8).*

Trianon. Even as early as 1570 it was being reported that Elizabeth I, 'hearying ... a certaine milke mayde singing pleasauntly, wished herself to be a milke mayde as she was.'[4]

While out on his fishing expeditions Izaak Walton had also been charmed by the songs he had heard them singing in the meadows. These were the popular ballads of the city, each rapidly carried into the country, 'till at last it grows common there too, as every poor milkmaid can chant and chirp it under her cow, which she useth, as a harmless charm, to make her let down her milk.' One song by Martin Parker, a London ballad-writer of the 1620s–50s, was entitled *The Milkemaid's Life*. It praised the merry lasses that carried the milking pail, on mountain or in dale, for no sickness doth them assail, before describing their traditional May Day customs:[5]

Upon the first of May
With garlands fresh and gay;
With mirth and music sweet,
For such a season is meet,
They pass the time away:
They dance away sorrow
And all the day thorow,
Their legs do never fail;
They nimbly Their feet do ply
And bravely try The victory
In honour o' th' milking pail

In reality, the life of a dairymaid was usually healthy and involved work both indoors and out, but its pleasures were tempered by the demands of working long hours in the cold and wet. It was usual to start work at 3 a.m., milk in the fields perhaps as early as 4 a.m., but no later than 5–6 a.m., start making butter and cheese at 7 a.m., and clean the equipment by 8 a.m., only finishing off after evening milking at 6–7 p.m., and setting the milk for the following day.[6] It was with good reason that Henry Best, an East Riding farmer, advised his son to 'make choise of such as are good milkers, and to have care [beware] of such as are of a sluggish and sleepie disposition for dainger of fire, and neaver to hyre such as one too neare their freinds, for occasion is sayd to make a theefe.'[7]

MILK

The actual process of milking usually took place in the open air, where there was always a risk of the cow moving away, as well as kicking. For these reasons it was hobbled with a cow-tie, a short length of rope with a loop at one end and a wooden toggle at the other which could be rapidly looped around the back legs. With it thus secured, the milkmaid could squat on her low stool, wipe the teats, and begin to express the milk into a deep, round coopered vessel with one long projecting stave or handle. Known as a milking kit, eshin, piggin or skeel, it was held firmly in place between the knees, the stave pressing against the stool until full of milk, when it was lifted onto a pad on the dairymaid's head and carried back to the dairy for processing.

Opinions on the risks or benefits of drinking raw milk differed considerably. Erasmus' translation of Plutarch advised that it 'engendereth dyseases', while Andrew Boorde considered both cow and sheep milk to be good, especially if boiled and sweetened with a little sugar.[8] Similarly Sir Thomas Elyot noted that those who had taken milk and butter since childhood had a better complexion, physique and resistance to sickness than others who had drunk wine or ale. However, for those with delicate stomachs, he suggested that they should have it milked directly into cups primed with a few leaves of mint and a little sugar or honey. Like most of his contemporaries, he recognized that milk was not so much a single substance as a combination of different elements; the rich cream, acidic whey and cheesy curds, which he must have regularly seen being separated in the dairy.[9]

CREAM

Since cream contained more fat and less water than the remainder of the fresh milk, it naturally floated to the surface where it formed an increasingly firm layer. To utilize this property, the dairymaids poured the milk into shallow vessels offering a broad surface area. Described as milk basins, milk skeels, cream pans or dishes, they might be made of wood, which was best in very cold dairies, of earthenware, best for long-keeping, or of lead, which produced most cream.[10] Turned wooden milk basins were still in common use, Lady Mary Lister having twenty-one in her dairy in 1626.[11] However, earthenware dishes with glazed interiors were probably the most economical and practical, being made at many local potteries, and also imported into the eastern counties from the Netherlands. In March 1624 the Howard family purchased three cream dishes for just a penny each, ready for the busy summer season.[12] Shallow rectangular lead milk-trays measuring about 3 feet by 2 feet 4 inches (1 m x 73 cm) were more convenient for large dairies, since the risen cream remained on their surfaces once the skim-milk had been drained off through a central plug-hole. They were much more expensive, however, six standing on wooden frames at Speke Hall, Liverpool, being valued at some 11*s*. 8*d*. in 1624.[13] Having been scalded to ensure absolute cleanliness, all of these vessels were first bridged by a light wooden frame shaped like a letter H but with two cross-bars and known as a silebrig or brig.[14] This was to support a sile or strainer, a turned wooden bowl having a large hole and footrim at its base across which a piece of linen cloth was tied to filter out any grass, grit, cowhairs or bovine dandruff. Once the milk had passed through, it was left for about twelve hours before a shallow saucer-like fleeting dish was used to skim off the cream and transfer it into a cream-pot ready for immediate use or short-term storage.[15] The result was what we would now call single cream, the thicker double cream being obtained by deferring the fleeting for a further day or so.

Cream formed the chief dish at a whole series of annual festivities. As Andrew Boorde explained in 1542: 'Clowtyd crayme and rawe crayme put together, is eaten more for a sensuall appetyde then for any good nowrishment. Rawe crayme undecocted, eaten with strawberyes or hurts, is a rural mannes banket.'[16] The delicious combination of strawberries and cream offered even greater sensual pleasures to the readers of Robert Herrick's poems, in which 'A Strawberry … half drown'd in Creame' was nothing less than one of his Julia's nipples:[17]

Wo'd yee have fresh Cheese and Cream?
Julia's Breast can give you them:
And if more; Each *Nipple* cries
To your Cream, here's *Strawberries.*

The first of the cream-eating festivals was Twelfth Night, 6 January, when it appeared in turned wooden wassail-bowls passed around the assembled company, perhaps being brought in by the maids who were rewarded with gifts of money.[18] In more rustic establishments it was served in a milking pail, as described in John Bale's play *Kynge John* of around 1550:[19]

Wassayle, wassayle out of the milking payle
Wassayle, wassayle, as white as my nayle
Wassayle, wassayle, in snowe, frost and hayle …
Wassayle, wassayle, that never will fayle.

TO MAKE A WASSEL[20]

4 slices white bread 1 inch/2.5 cm thick
1pt/600ml muscatel
1pt/600ml double cream
2 cloves
2 egg yolks
2tbs sugar
½oz/12g blanched almonds, sliced
½tsp mixed ground cinnamon and ginger

Trim the crusts from the bread, cut into cubes and use to line a deep dish. Pour the muscatel into a pan, cover, and heat gently. Beat the yolks into 6tbs of the cream, bring the remaining cream to the boil with the cloves, and leave to simmer for 5 minutes.

Pour the hot wine over the bread, and sprinkle with half the sugar. Remove the cream from the heat, beat in the yolks, pour over the bread, stick the almonds into its surface, and finally sprinkle on the remaining sugar mixed with the spices. Serve hot.

May Day morn cream awaited those who had set off before daybreak to gather the May-blossom as in Herrick's verse:[21]

A deal of youth, ere this is come
Back, and with white-thorn laden home,
Some have dispatched their cakes and cream,
Before that we have left to dream

After the completion of sheep-shearing in June in the Cotswolds, the King of the Shepherds, he whose flock had lambed earliest, presided over the shepherds' feast. Here the more plentiful cream now appeared in various forms, as described by Michael Drayton:[22]

In his gay bauldric sits at his grassy board
With flawns, curds, clouted cream and country dainties stor'd
And whilst the bag-pipe plays, each lusty jocund swain
Quaffs sillibubs in cans, to all upon the plain ...
And at our shepherd's board that's cut out of the ground
My fellow swains and I together at it round,
With green-cheese, clouted cream, with flawns, and custards stored,
Whig, cider, and white whey, I domineer, a lord ...

Once the pea and grain harvest was safely gathered in, all the workforce was invited to a churn- or kirn-supper, this alternative title for a harvest-home being derived from the distribution of cupfuls of cream served out of a large churn.[23] On Henry Best's East Yorkshire farm it was served in platters:[24]

> and every one [had] a spoone. Then after all they have hotte cakes and ale, for they bake cakes and send for ale against that time. Some will cut their cake and putte [it] into the creame, and this feast is called the Creame-potte or Creame-kitte, for on the morninge that they gott all done, the workfolke will aske theire dames if they have a good store of Creame, and say that they must have the Creame kitte anon.

Cream also appeared at the wakes described by Herrick:[25]

Tarts and Custards, Creames and Cakes,
Are the Junketts still at Wakes:

The late sixteenth and early seventeenth centuries saw a remarkable development in the range of cream-based recipes. *A Proper Newe Book of Cokerye* of 1557/8 could only offer 'a Dyshefull of Snowe', which beat up the whites of eggs, then whisked them with cream, sugar and rosewater to make a light foam which was piled on a branch of rosemary stuck upright into an apple.[26] This was still around in 1660, by which time it had been joined by dozens of completely new recipes producing a whole range of new flavours and textures.[27] Some were extremely laborious and time-consuming, as when raw milk or thin cream was whisked for over an hour to produce the most delicate of froths. The following selection has been chosen to demonstrate the major techniques of the period, starting with simple whipping. Such creams might be served on white delftware cream dishes.

WHIPPED CREAM[28]

1pt/600ml whipping cream	*1tbs sugar*

Whisk three-quarters of the cream until firm but not turning to butter and place on three or four pieces of freshly rinsed linen cloths each resting on a saucer. Leave in a cool place for 2 to 3 hours, then turn out onto a dish, remove the cloths, pour the remaining cream around them and sprinkle with sugar.

LORD ST ALBANS' CREAME FOUETTE[29]

Whip as in the recipe above. Just before serving sprinkle sugar across a dish, spread on half the cream, sprinkle on more sugar, add the remaining cream, and more sugar over the top.

A VERY GOOD CREAM[30]

½pt/300ml single cream	*2tbs rosewater*
½pt/300ml whipping cream	*2tbs sugar*

Bring the single cream to the boil, stir in the rosewater and sugar until dissolved and leave to go cold. Whip the whipping cream until firm, mix into the boiled cream, and serve.

Syllabubs were whipped creams delicately curdled with wine and given additional flavouring. They were best served in small glass cups provided with two handles and a narrow spout from which to suck up any delicious whey which might collect beneath. Sir Kenelm Digby owned seven of such syllabub glasses to set on a great glass plate, as well as a white delftware syllabub pot with a cover.[31]

TO MAKE A WHIP SYLLABUB[32]

1pt/600ml single cream	*3tbs dry sherry*
1 egg white	*2oz/50g sugar*

Whisk all together until thick, spoon into glasses, and leave in a cool place for a few hours or overnight to become firm.

MY LADY MIDDLESEX'S SYLLABUB[33]

1pt/600ml double cream
7fl.oz/200ml Rhenish white wine
2tbs dry sherry
4oz/100g caster sugar
sprigs of rosemary or broad parings of lemon zest

Whisk the cream, wines and sugar together until thick, spoon into glasses, and insert a piece of either rosemary or lemon zest into each one. Leave overnight in a cool place to become firm.

Other syllabubs were made in the fields when the maids directed jets of milk directly from the teats into piggins, primed with sweetened cider. The dairy at Speke Hall had '3 sellibub piggins 6*d*' specifically for this purpose in 1624, but those who have tried this method have discovered that it produces a creamy whey below a floating mass of clotted, stringy curd of a kind usually found on a baby's bib.[34] It was preferable to use more refined recipes of this period which half-filled the syllabub pots with sweetened cider and a little nutmeg before throwing in two or three tablespoonfuls of cream at a time, stirring once, and then leaving it to stand for two hours in a cool place.[35] Similar but lighter dishes could be made with sack.

SACK CREAMS[36]

1pt/600ml single cream
3tbs dry sherry
1tbs caster sugar
pinch ground nutmeg

Boil the cream, remove from the heat, and stir continuously while adding the sherry little by little. Stir in the sugar and nutmeg, pour into a dish, and leave to cool before serving.

Other creams were thickened with eggs.

A GOOD DISH OF CREAM (WITH EGG WHITES)[37]

1pt/600ml single cream
1 stick cinnamon
½ nutmeg, sliced
2oz/50g sugar
3 egg whites, lightly beaten
2tbs orange flower water
3 slices white bread, with the crusts removed

Simmer the spices with ¾ of the cream for 5 minutes until well flavoured. Beat the eggs with the remaining cream, stir them into the hot cream, boil up twice, and strain into a sieve lined with a piece of freshly rinsed muslin. When cold, beat the curd with the orange flower water and heap on the bread arranged on a dish.

A MESS OF FINE CREAM (WITH YOLKS)[38]

1pt/600ml single cream
3 yolks and 1 white of egg
2tbs rosewater
1½oz/37g sugar

Beat the eggs into the cream and stir continuously while gently heating until thickened, but not boiling. Pour into a sieve lined with freshly rinsed muslin, and leave to drain and cool. Gather up the edges of the muslin to enclose the thickened cream, hold it over a clean bowl, and squeeze the cream through the muslin. Beat in the rosewater and sugar, turn into a dish, and sprinkle with sugar just before serving.

In the east of England similar creams were served on sliced white bread to become fools, the direct ancestors of both the trifle and the fruit fools of later centuries.

TO MAKE A NORFOLK FOOL[39]

12 thin slices white bread
6 egg yolks
2pt/1.2l double cream
2 sticks cinnamon
3 blades of mace
6 dates, sliced
3tbs sugar

Trim the crusts from the bread, and use a few slices to line a dish. Beat the yolks with ¼pt/150ml of the cream. Bring the remaining cream to the boil, simmer for 5 minutes with the mace and cinnamon, remove the spices and take the cream off the heat. Beat in the egg yolk and cream liaison.

Pour one third of the cream into the dish, add a layer of bread, then a further third of the cream, the remaining bread, and the last of the cream. Stick with the dates, and sprinkle with sugar.

ELIZABETH CROMWELL'S FOOL[40]

Make the cream to the recipe above, but line the dish with small slices of bread soaked in dry sherry 10 minutes before gently pouring in the cream.

A number of very fine creams were made by setting with rennet. They included junkets and Danske creams, but unfortunately the modern practice of heat-treating virtually all milk and cream sold in England, though making them safer, renders them unsuitable for producing good results.[41]

Further creams were enriched with stewed, sweetened and other puréed fruits, including plums, quinces, gooseberries, strawberries, raspberries or red currants, this apple cream providing typical instructions:

APPLE CREAM[42]

1pt/600ml single or double cream
1 stick cinnamon
1¼lb/550g apples, peeled & sliced
4tbs claret
grated zest of a lemon
3oz sugar
pinch ground ginger

Bring the cream and cinnamon to the boil, allow to cool, then remove the cinnamon.

Simmer the remaining ingredients until the apples may be beaten to a pulp (pass through a sieve for a smoother cream), and leave to cool. Beat the cream and apple mixture together, pour into a dish and serve.

Clotted cream was made in all parts of the country, but was already a regional speciality in Devon and Cornwall. Here it was made 'by setting the milk over an easie fire untill it is come to a thicker heade.'[43] The equipment required is described in recipes as either a brass pan or kettle, or 'a great earthen milk pan set … upon a charcoal fire well kindled.'[44] A fuller list is provided in the inventory of William Chappell's milkhouse at his barton (farm) at Broad Clyst near Exeter. Here were five earthen pitchers to hold the milk and cream, two cloam 'chaffers' (earthenware chaffing dishes) for the burning charcoal and three pancrocks (bowls) in which to heat the milk and cream.[45] The latter were probably of north-Devon heat-proof gravel-tempered earthenware ideal for the simplest method of making clotted cream. This involved merely standing the pan and whole milk in embers and skimming some twelve hours later.[46] Other methods are more convenient for use today:

CLOTTED CREAM[47]

2pt/1.2l full cream milk, preferably Jersey milk,
which has not been homogenized
1pt/600ml double cream (not 'extra-thick')
3tbs rosewater

Pour the ingredients into a broad ceramic baking dish, place this over a large pan half-filled with water and heat on the stove until the water is just simmering. Turn down the heat to the very gentlest simmer and leave for two hours.

Remove the dish to a cool place and leave for 36 hours, then use a knife to cut the cream into squares and around the edge, lift it out with a slice, arrange on a plate, and sprinkle with sugar just before serving.

It might also have either sugar or honey stirred into it.

BUTTER

The main product of cream was butter. In the West Country well-flavoured butter was made by working clotted cream with the flat of the hand in a shallow wooden skeel, but elsewhere single cream was processed in a churn.[48] Barnaby Googe described a churn as 'A vessel rather deepe than big, round and Cilinder fashion: although in some places they have other kindes of Charnes low and flat wherein ... they so shake the milke.'[49] Most were cooper-made from oak, as seen in contemporary woodcuts, but others were made in earthenware, being thrown to the identical shape with raised bands in imitation of the hazel or iron bindings of their wooden alternatives. All churns were provided with a lid. This was pierced in the centre to take the churn – or cruddle-staff, the wooden rod fitted with a piston-like circular dasher at its base with which the cream was agitated. Having set the churn in a cool place in summer or a warm place in winter, it was filled with cream and churned with swift strokes until the butter began to form.[50] This could take some time, even an hour or two, maids in the reign of Philip and Mary being instructed by priests to speed the process by chanting three times:[51]

> Come, butter, come,
> Come, butter, come.
> Peter standing at the gate
> Waiting for a butter cake
> Come, butter, come.

As the butter began to form, the churn was opened and the hand used to remove the globules which had accumulated around the lid and sides. Now the churn-staff was worked slowly until the butter had gathered into a single mass, which could be lifted out into a turned wooden bowl partly filled with clean cold water. Cradling the bowl in one arm, the dairymaid beat and turned the butter with her free hand until all the buttermilk had been extracted, leaving nothing but the butter. Slashing this with a knife removed any remaining hairs, after which the butter was ready for use.

If intended for the table, a few drops of the extracted oils of sage, cinnamon, nutmeg or mace might be beaten in to impart their characteristic flavours.[52] The use of carved wooden butter-prints to impress an ornamental design on individual pats of butter probably originated in the late Elizabethan period, for by 1616 the word 'butter-print' had already attained the secondary meaning of a child or offspring. Lady Mary Lister had two in her dairy in 1626, but unfortunately no provenanced English examples appear to have survived from this period.[53]

In the early sixteenth century the use of butter instead of lard as a spread on bread was still considered to be a Continental habit. 'To my butter I take good bread,' boasted Andrew Boorde's 'Buttermouth Fleming', describing this 'unhealthy' Dutch habit.[54] In 1567 one such Fleming told his wife in Ypres that his fellow countrymen living in Norfolk were having to make their own butter, for in England they used pig's fat.[55] The practice here was changing, however, with little children eating 'bread smeared with butter in the Flemish fashion, given them by their mothers. And although this is general throughout the island, it is more observed in the kingdom of England than elsewhere.'[56] By the 1620s the term 'bread-and-butter' was used to indicate childhood, Beaumont and Fletcher's *The Humble Lieutenant* calling 'Ye Bread-and-butter rogues, do ye run from me?'[57]

If the butter was to be preserved, no water was used in the beating, only salt after the buttermilk had been removed. It had then to be made up in various regulated vessels and quantities. The usual measures used in the butter trade were the kilderkin and firkin casks, and the pot. An Act of Parliament of 1662 stated that:

> by Custome time out of mind used every Kinderkin of Butter ought to [weigh] One hundred and thirty two pounds gross ... that is ... One hundred and twelve pounds of Neat butter and the Cash Twenty pounds. The Firkin of Butter ought to weigh Sixty and four pounds viz Fifty and six pounds of good and Merchantable Butter Neat and the Cash Eight pounds And the Pott of Butter ought to weigh Twenty pounds viz Fourteen pounds of good and Merchantable Butter Neat and the Pott Six pounds.'

Some recipes also mention 'a dish of butter' as a recognized quantity, its price in accounts showing that this represented one pound in weight.[58]

If packed into kilderkins or firkins a narrow stick might be used to spear a hole through the butter from top to bottom before it was covered with a strong cold brine and closed up. Sometimes the brine was first boiled with a couple of branches of rosemary to impart a pleasant and distinctive flavour.[59] For potting it was necessary to :[60]

> take cleane earthen pots, exceedingly well leaded [i.e. glazed] ... and cast salt into the bottome of it: then lay in your butter, and presse it downe hard within the same, and when your pot is filled, then cover the top thereof with salt so no butter be seene: then closing up the pot let it stand where it may be cold and safe.

In some areas the pots held a gallon (4.8l) of butter, as in Exeter where 'gallonde Crocks of earth' filled with butter cost around two shillings in the 1570s.[61]

The finished butter was now ready for use in frying, baking, potting, and other uses, as well as for the table. For the latter, Sir Hugh Plat advised making 'sundry sorts of most daintie butter having a lively taste of Sage, Cinamon, Nutmegs, Mace &c.' by incorporating a few drops of their respective oils.[62]

The buttermilk left in the churn made a pleasant drink, but could also produce curds. Once a third of its volume of hot fresh milk had been poured into it and it had cooled for around a day, they could be skimmed off and eaten. Cream, ale, wine or beer made good accompaniments, or they might be baked in cheesecakes. The clear, sharp liquid 'whig' left by the curds made 'an excellent coole drinke and a wholesome; any may very well be drunke a summer through ... and will slake the thirst of any labouring man as well.'[63]

CHEESE

At this period four main varieties of cheese were made in England, all based on curded milk. The most basic was hard cheese made from skimmed or 'floted' milk which gave it a hot, dry flavour, and made it hard to penetrate, let alone eat and digest.[64] Those made in Essex and Suffolk had a particularly evil reputation since:[65]

Those that made me were uncivil;
They made me harder than the devil.
Knives won't cut me, fire won't sweat me,
Dogs bark at me, but can't eat me.

Although most cheeses were sold by the 224lb 'wey' of 32 x 7lb 'cloves', in Suffolk the wey was 256lb, and in Essex 336lb of 42 cloves.

Next came whole milk 'soft' cheese, eaten neither fresh nor aged, and with the same degree of solidity as a modern traditional cheese. In 1577 Barnaby Googe considered that the best of these were 'the Cheshyre, and the Shropsyre, then the Banbury'.[66] Cheshire was already being sold in London in the sixteenth century, those bought for the Privy Council dining at the Star Chamber costing five shillings each in 1590.[67] Shakespeare knew the Banbury well, calling Slender 'You Banbury Cheese!'[68] To Thomas Cogan this was the best cheese 'for therin you shall neither taste the rennet nor salt, which be the two special properties of good cheese.'[69] It was so rich that it need only be chopped up and sugared before being baked as a cheesecake.[70] Cheddar cheese only gained its high reputation in the seventeenth century, when farmers around Cheddar Gorge in Somerset formed a club for combining their milk to make large, slow-maturing, well-flavoured cheeses. However, they remained relatively scarce and expensive well into the 1660s.

Figure 19. A carved wooden cheese sinker of 1603.

To start the cheesemaking process Gervase Markham described how milk was brought up to blood heat either in a cheese kettle over the fire, or by adding boiling water to it in a tub.[71] Rennet was then stirred in, this being made from the full stomach of a suckling calf, the cheeseclip- or earning-bag, and its curdled contents. Having been separately cleaned, washed and salted, they were re-assembled and sealed down in a pot for a full year. In June, 1641, Lord Huntingdon's steward recorded the payment 'For a steen for Sues[an] to put her rindell bag in 3*d*.'[72] The alternative 'sluttish, naught and unwholesome [practice of] hanging them up in chimney corners (as coarse Huswives do)' was certainly not best practice. When required for use the curds were removed, ground with egg yolks, cream, saffron, cloves and mace, replaced in the bag, and submerged in a brine flavoured with saxifrage and walnut leaves, other recipes adding sage and clary too.[73] After two weeks the rennet was so strong that only four spoonfuls would curdle at least twelve gallons (28.8l) of milk in about half an hour.

Once the curd had formed it was broken up and mashed with a dish and pressed to the bottom of the kettle or tub, so that most of the watery whey could be baled out. The remaining curds were then packed into a cylindrical coopered cheese-vat pierced with numerous drain-holes, a piston-like wooden cheese-board, follower or sinker placed on top, and left under a light weight to express the surplus whey. Once firm, the cheese was removed, wrapped in a freshly rinsed cheesecloth, replaced in the vat, and put under greater pressure in a cheesepress, for half an hour. Over the next day it was removed, wrapped in a fresh dry cheesecloth, and replaced five or six times, being so firm at the end of another day's pressing that it could be handled without a cheesecloth. After being rubbed with salt for two mornings and regularly turned in the resulting brine for two or three more days, the cheese was set on a table or shelf and turned and rubbed with a dry cloth every day until ready for a final pressing and transfer to the cheese-room, -chamber or -loft for storage, sale, or use. Most large dairies had cheese 'ladders', 'crutches' or 'heckes, the long and round racke wheron cheese is dried', while some used a 'grated Save [slatted wooden shelf] hung by a pulley to the top of the Dairie House or Store-house; and serveing to keepe cheese, white-meates [dairy produce] ... in'.[74] In smaller households the cheese-store might occupy a servants' bedroom, one Atkinson at Calverley Old Hall near Leeds having to share his nights with 43 cheeses and a mass of butter.[75]

There were many different recipes for making similar soft cheeses, some adding cream, some scalding the curd with hot whey, and some using the milk from the second crop of hay for 'eddish' cheese.[76] For hard 'floater' or skim-milk hard cheeses the almost sour milk might have to be warmed by adding hot water, since direct heat would throw up a curd unsuitable for keeping.[77]

The third major class of cheese was called green cheese, not from its colour, but from its freshness. Like the moon, such cheeses were white. Nettle cheeses were of this type, ordinary full-milk curds set to drain half an inch/1.2cm deep in a cheese-vat before being placed between layers of nettle leaves which were turned and changed every two days for about a week.[78] Creamier slipcoat cheeses were often drained on layers of the parallel stems of *Juncus* field rushes, or of long, broad grass.[79] This method was also used to imitate 'Frenche Angelot [which] is yet green. It is more deintie, as men doo saye it is so fat: it is but creame'.[80] The other class of cheese made in England was called spermys, for which the curds were mixed with the juices of various herbs, each milk-wife flavouring her own according to her personal taste.[81] The only equivalent today is sage Derby. Together with imported Dutch, Auvergne and Parmesan cheeses, prosperous Tudor and Stuart diners enjoyed an excellent choice of cheeses to serve at the end of their meals.

The whey which remained after cheesemaking could be drunk in-house, given to the poor, fed to the pigs, or converted into curds. When a quantity was heated almost to boiling point successive batches of buttermilk were poured in, each forming curds which were skimmed off into a colander to drain. Usually they were then either eaten with cream and sugar, or were baked as cheesecakes.[82]

SUBSTITUTE DAIRY PRODUCTS

In medieval England it was customary to abstain from dairy produce when fasting at Lent and other holy days. As a result substitute milk, cream and butter were made from other ingredients. The best of these were delicious in their own right. They continued to be made after the religious restrictions were relaxed from the mid-sixteenth century, after which some actually incorporated real cream. The easiest substitute for cow's milk was almond milk.

SIMPLE ALMOND MILK[83]

8oz/225g blanched (or ground) almonds

Finely chop the almonds, if whole. Mix the almonds with 2pt/1.2l warm water, leave to cool for 1 hour, then grind (or blend) until smooth. Spread a large piece of very fine muslin or cloth across a sieve over a bowl, pour in the almond mixture, gather the cloth over the almonds and squeeze out as much liquid as possible. Grind the almonds again with a further 1pt/600ml warm water and strain as before. (It may be flavoured with a little rosewater, salt and/or sugar, or made with light stock if for a savoury dish.)

ALMOND BUTTER[84]

1 batch of almond milk made to the recipe above
6tbs rosewater — *2tsp salt*
2tsp caster or icing sugar — *pinch of saffron*

Pour the milk into a pan, heat until just about to boil, stir in the salt and rosewater, allow to boil up once, then leave to cool. Pour into a fresh piece of fine cloth (or filter-paper) and hang up to drain. When it has stopped dripping mix in the sugar, saffron and a little more rosewater before transferring to a small dish. This produces some 6oz/175g of the butter. It may also have 2–3tbs white wine vinegar added when just boiling, have a little sweet white wine beaten in when finished, and garnished with raisins, borage leaves, violets or red comfits after dishing.

According to Andrew Boorde this butter 'rejoyceth the herte, doth comforte the brayne, & doth qualyfye [cool] the heate of the lyver.' Its pleasant alternative, bean butter, was also 'used moche in Lent.'[85] The following recipe produces much more luxurious results.

A RARE ALMOND CREAM[86]

13fl.oz/400ml single cream	*2tbs dry sherry*
5oz/125g almond paste	*2tbs rosewater*
2 eggs, lightly beaten	*pinch ground nutmeg*

Put all the ingredients into a pan and beat over a gentle heat until the almond paste has completely dissolved and the mixture is hot, but not boiling, or it will curdle. Pour into a dish and leave to go cold.

Just before serving sprinkle with sugar and the freshly squeezed juice of an orange.

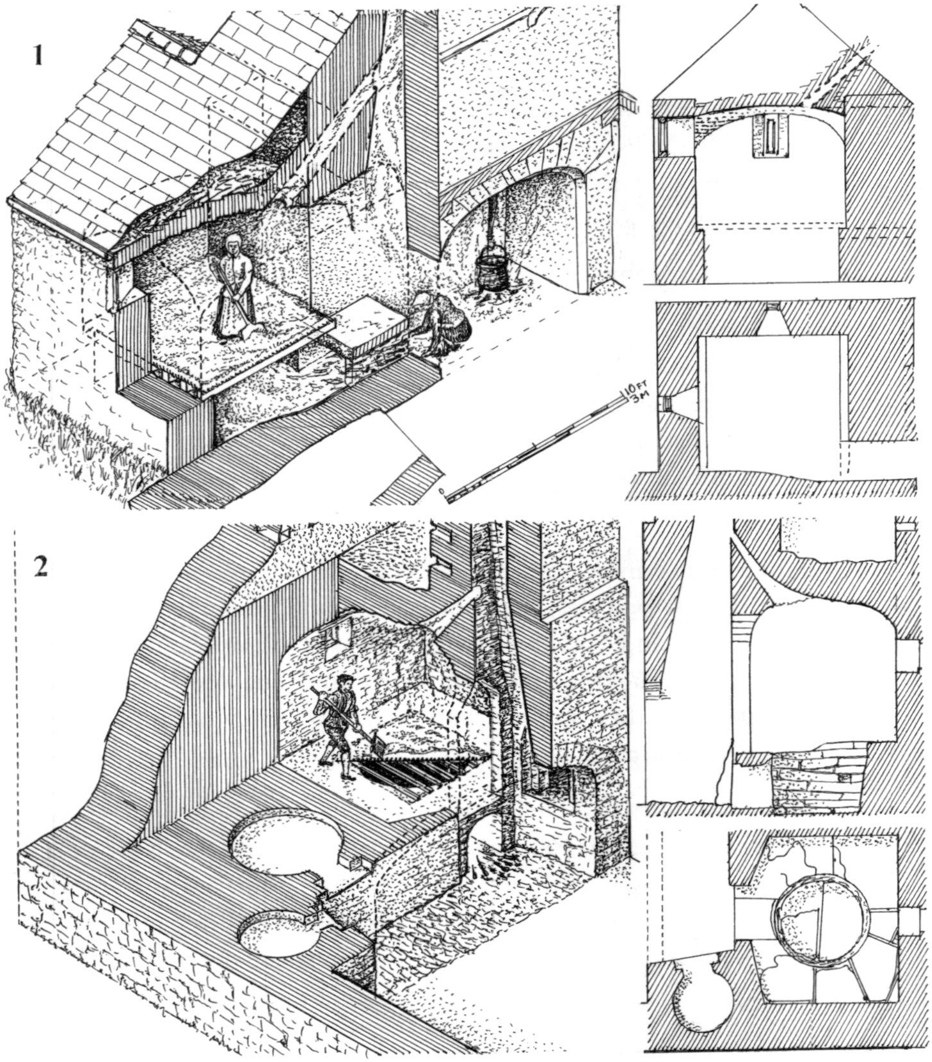

Figure 20. Domestic malt kilns. In the West Country malt kilns were frequently built as part of the kitchen chimney stack: (1) Ware Farm, Ugborough, Devon, mid–late 16th century; (2) Yarde Farm, Malborough, Devon. Note the ducts drawing the hot vapour up into the main kitchen fireplace flue, and the dovecot above the malt kiln at Malborough.

CHAPTER SIX

The Brewhouse

Ale and beer were the staple drinks of the majority of the population, a source of nourishment, and a major source of pleasure and sociability. As praised by John Taylor, the Water Poet:

> the vigorous spirit of the Buttry, Nappy, Nut-browne, Berry-browne, Ale Alelendo [has] Aleaborate operation to elevate & exhillarate the vitals, put alemental Raptures and Enthusiasms in the most capitall Perricranion, in such Plentitude, that the meanest and most illiterate Plowjogger could speedily play the Rhetorician, and speak Alequently, as if he were mounted up into the Aletitude.[1]

Throughout the country a number of commercial brewers enjoyed high reputations for their strong ales, these including Hull 'cheese', Eastbourne 'rug', Holborn 'dagger' ales, and Yorkshire 'stingo'.[2] These and other professionally brewed ales might be bought in as and when required, but were often found to be more expensive and more suspect than their home-brewed equivalents. In 1592 Robert Greene described how brewers,

> grow to be worth forty thousand pounds by selling of sodden water, what subtiltie have you in making your beare to spare the malt and put in more of the hoppe to make your drink (be barley never so cheap) not a whit the stronger and yet never sell a whit the more measure for monie, you can, when you have taken all the harte of the malt awaye, then clap on store of water, tis cheape ynough, and mashe out a tunning of small beare, so thin that it scoures a man's maw.[3]

To avoid these problems, and to provide the ales and beers best suited to their particular tastes, budgets and needs, most households of whatever size and status preferred to brew at home.

MALT

The first necessity was to convert the starch content of cereal grains into soluble sugars by the process of malting. Sometimes this was undertaken by a professional maltster, as when William Middleton of Stokeld employed Gregory of Wetherby to convert his grain into malt at a shilling a quarter in 1581.[4] It was just as usual, however, to carry out the malting at home, this being a valued skill in a housewife or female servant. In 1610 the justices of Rutland set the wages of a woman who could make malt at a shilling a year more than those who lacked this skill.[5] Any grain might be selected, barley being the most popular, with wheat, bigg (4-rowed barley) or oats being often chosen, according to local preference. In April 1569 the garner of Sir William Strickland's Sizergh Castle stored 35 bushels of bigg malt valued at £6 2*s.* 6*d.*, 28 bushels of haver (oat) malt at £3, and 60 bushels of malt in course of preparation at £10, demonstrating the great quantities required by the household of a major gentleman.[6]

As William Harrison described in 1577:

> Our malt is made all yeare long in some great townes, but in gentlemen's and yeomen's houses, who commonlie make sufficient for their owne expenses onelie, the winter half is thought most meet for that commoditie ... each one indevereth to make it of the best barlie, which is steeped in a cesterne in greater or less quantitie, by the space of three daies and three nights, until it be thoroughly soaked. This being donne, the water is drained off from it by little and little, till it be quite gone. Afterward they take it out and laieng it upon the clene floore on a round heape, it resteth so until it be readie to shoot at the roote end, which maltsters call 'coming'. When it beginneth, therefor, to shoote in this manner, they saie it is 'come', and then foorthwith they spread it abroad, first thick and afterwards thinner and thinner upon the said floore ... and there it lieth (with turning every day foure or five times) by the space of one and twenty daies at the least. ... [Then] they carie it to a kill covered with haire cloth, where they give it gentle heats (after they have spread it there verie thin abroad) till it be dry, in the meane while they turne it often that it may be uniformelie dried. For the more it be dried (yet must it be done with a soft fire), the sweeter and better the malt is, and the longer it will [keep].[7]

The required equipment appears in numbers of household inventories, the 'cistern' frequently being described as a 'steepvat' if made as a coopered tub, or as a 'steeplead' if made of lead.[8] None of these is known to survive from this period, but their surrounding masonry walls are to be found on many monastic sites. That at Fountains Abbey is some eighteen feet in diameter, brick-built and skimmed with cement, probably intended to support a lead liner. Any flagged or cobbled surface might serve as a malting floor, whether specially constructed adjacent to a malt kiln, or within any ordinary domestic kitchen.

Most malt kilns or 'kills' were rectangular buildings having a walk-way around a square or circular pit set into its centre, this being a few feet deep and heated by a fireplace. Usually the kilns were associated with outbuildings such as barns, brewhouses or bakehouses, as was the sixteenth-century example in the south-east corner of the bailey at Middleham Castle in Yorkshire. In contrast, many of those found in the West Country were built into the back or side of the main kitchen fireplace, conveniently located for the housewife or her maid. These have been mistakenly christened 'bacon-smoking chambers' by vernacular architecture 'experts', who should know better. When required for use, a few bars or branches of wood were laid across the pit to support a piece of specially woven horsehair cloth known as a kiln-hair or dry-hair. In 1549 the steward at Haddon Hall, Derbyshire, went to Chesterfield in order to buy his 'Kylne hayre of 26 yards for to drye Maulte wt. After 8*d*. ye yerde 16*s*. 4*d*.'[9] A low fire was then lit in its fireplace, its fuel being,

> wood alone, or strawe alone [or] with wood and straw together, but all of straw is most excellent ... Such also as use both indifferentlie doo barke, cleave, and drye their wood in an oven ... and this is the second place [with] that which is made with dried furze, broome etc.[10]

The purpose of the fire was to produce a stream of warm dry air to drive the moisture off the malt spread over the kiln-hair, until each grain was hard, yellowish, and would write like a piece of chalk once bitten in half. If the fire got too hot it would set fire to the kiln-hair and ruin the whole laborious operation. This explains why the malts of this period were always light and unroasted. If a darker malt was needed, it could only be made by stirring the pale malt in a hot cauldron until it reached the desired darker shade. Once the malting had been completed, the kilns were frequently used as storage areas, items including tools, hides, wool, harness, coal and cheese frequently being listed in kilns when inventories were being prepared.[11]

Having been removed from the kiln and spread out to cool, the malt had to be ground in a mill to produce 'grist'. Most families would be obliged to have this essential process carried out at a manorial mill to produce income for its lord. In 1579, for example, the Wakefield Burgess Court levied a fine of one shilling on all those who should use the mill, but chose not to. Here, as in most other areas, householders measured their grain, had it ground at the mill and saw the miller extract an agreed quantity as his fee. If four independent burgesses found that he had extracted too much 'mulcture', or milled the grain badly, he had to reimburse the same quantity of grain and himself pay a shilling fine.[12]

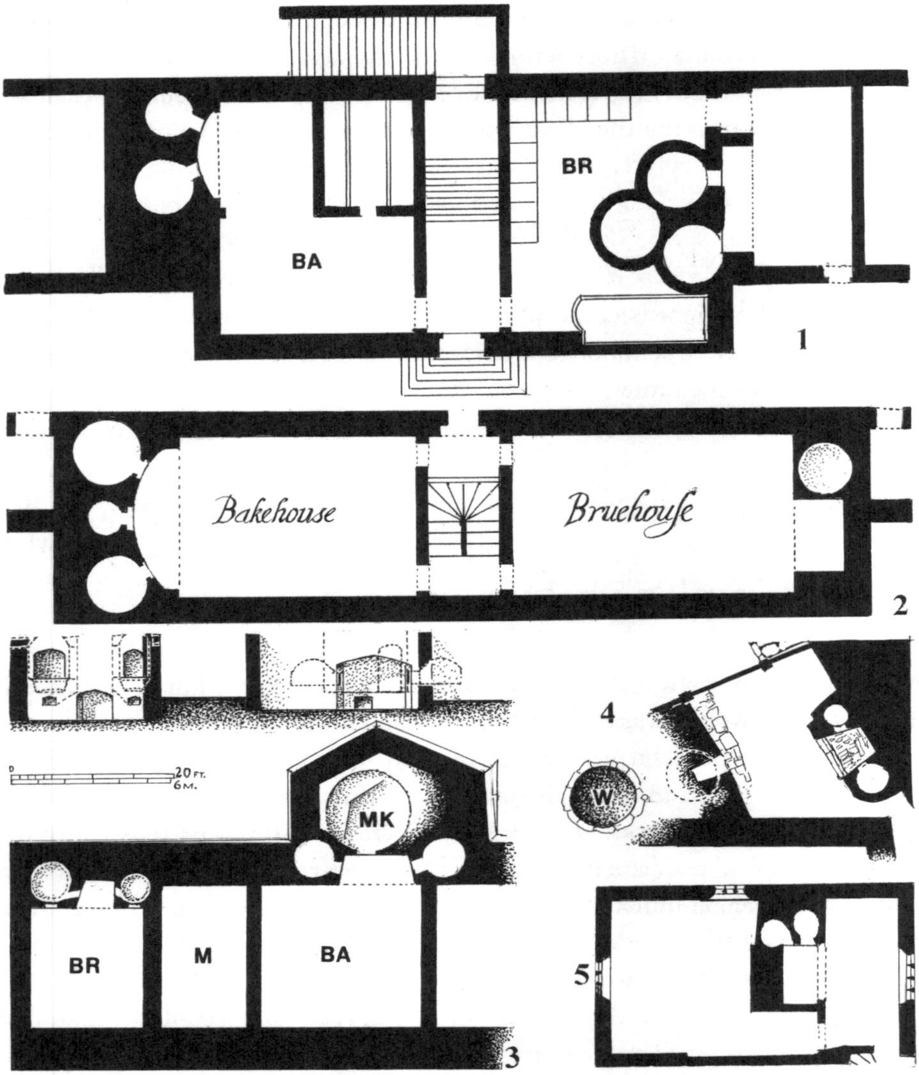

Figure 21. Brewhouses and bakehouses. Since they required the same facilities and working conditions, brewhouses and bakehouses were frequently built into the same block. (1) a design by Robert Smythson, late 16th century; (2) Smythson's Wollaton Hall, c. 1580; (3) Raglan Castle, 1549–89; (4) Sandal Castle mid-16th–17th century; (5) Horton Hall, Staffordshire, 1643. (BA: Bakehouse; BR: Brewhouse; M: Malthouse/Malting Floor; MK: Malt Kiln; W: Well.)

In other communities this restriction had already begun to break down by the early sixteenth century. In 1547 the Kingsthorpe manorial court was permitting 'All those p'sons that have quernes [hand-mills] shal suffer noebody to grynde theirat above a tollflat.' Those who ground any more were fined threepence a tollflat.[13] From about this period more querns begin to appear in probate inventories, those in the East Riding village of South Cave including:

1570	a pair of whernes	
1575	a pair of whernstones	12*d*
1577	1 pair of malt quernes[14]	

Elsewhere there might be a quern for communal use. Alice Pechye of Soham bequeathed her quern 'common to everie poore man who hath neede, and helpinge the reperacon of the same' in 1547.[15]

Most of the gentry and nobility sent their malt and corn to their own wind- and water-mills, but some still found a domestic horse-mill to be more convenient. These were of particular use in castles, where total self-sufficiency was still essential for the purpose of defence. Belvoir Castle's 'timber for the horse mylne' cost 38*s*. in 1540, while Stockton-on-Tees Castle's malthouse, kiln, brewhouse and horse-mill was a stone building measuring 48 x 39 feet, with walls 12 feet high.[16] In preparation for the siege of Scarborough Castle in 1654 a new horse-mill was built in the old Norman chapel, its circular paved horse-walk being discovered in later excavations.[17] In all of these, the horses worked 'with no rest ... endlesse, a perpetualle racke, or horse-mill ... still going round as in a ring.'[18]

After being ground, the malt grist was carefully stored ready for use, some larger properties having a separate, dry and secure upstairs room for this purpose. Francis Clarke had malt and peas valued at £100 in his malt chamber at Sharlston Hall near Wakefield in 1656, this probably being stored in his large meal-chest or ark worth £1.[19]

BREWING

The actual brewing took place in a separate brewhouse in all major households, although most cottagers carried out identical but smaller-scale activities around the fireplaces of their kitchen/living-rooms. If possible, the brewhouse stood next to the bakehouse at the service end or its enclosing yard. This offered mutual advantages, since both used grain, fuel, water and yeast, both worked unsocial hours, produced smoke and smells, and had to be kept warm in order to keep their yeasts alive and active. The earlier brewhouses, which were designed to produce ales made solely of malt and water, only needed one boiling furnace,

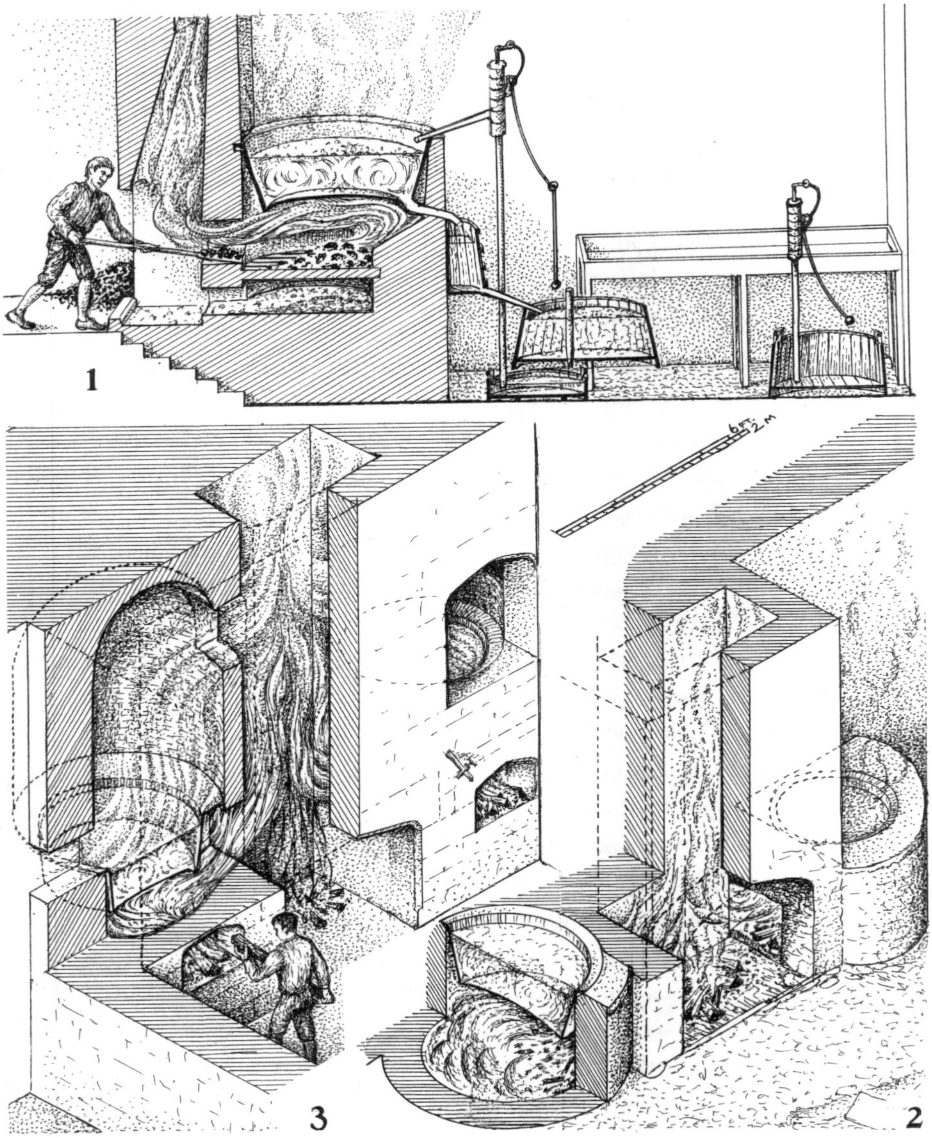

Figure 22. Brewing furnaces. In Robert Smythson's design of c. 1600 (1) the traditional concave-bottomed boiler feeds hot water into the mash tun, from where the sweet wort drained into the underback, ready to be pumped back into the boiler for boiling with hops. A cooler and fermenting vat stand in the background. At Raglan Castle of 1549–89 (2), there were separate boilers for the water and the wort, each with an external duct which drew in fresh air and carried the steam away up the central flue. At Sir Francis Drake's brewhouse at Buckland Abbey, Devon (3) the two boilers were set each side of a central fireplace.

sometimes known as a copper or a lead. Some still had lead upper parts and flashings to prevent the liquids soaking into the surrounding masonry, but most were of copper or brass.[20] Compared to the deeply domed profiles of boiling-house and laundry coppers, those used in brewing were remarkably shallow, their depth being about a third of their diameters, while their bases were concave rather than convex. This shape concentrated the heat of their fires into the centre of the coppers, ensuring the obligatory rolling boil and efficient convection of their contents. A good brewing copper represented a large investment of capital, usually being the most expensive fitting to be found in the service rooms. That bought in London by Richard Croft for the Howard family of Naworth in Cumbria in 1633 was of 'copper weighinge 2cwt 2lb (with nayles [rivets?] to it) at 15*d*. a pounde £17– 5– 6*d*.'[21] Being of sheet metal it must have been of great size, and a real problem to deliver up to the edge of the Lake District.

Once mounted over a fireplace within an encircling masonry furnace, burning logs or bundles of brushwood were thrust beneath, their flames licking the base of the copper before leaving the upper part of the fireplace and ascending an open chimney above. As with the boilers in boiling houses, this was the most efficient way of heating the brewing liquor. By the late sixteenth century, the decreasing availability of firewood and the increasing use of coal by his leading Midlands patrons led the architect Robert Smythson to design coal-burning brewing coppers. These had a fireplace set into a chimney in an adjacent room, a grate in the fireback supporting the burning coals just beneath the base of the copper, the flames and smoke then being drawn away up the chimney. In this way all the dirt and fumes were totally excluded from the brewhouse, leaving it clean and relatively cool.

Since the increasingly popular beer required the ale to be given a second boiling with hops, the use of the old single-boiling coppers became more and more problematic. The solution was to add a second copper with about half the volume of the main installation specifically for boiling the ale with the hops. As demonstrated by the excavated remains of Sir Francis Drake's brewhouse at Buckland Abbey, Devon, it became convenient to set the fireplaces of each copper into a low furnace at each side of a common chimney, so that both could be fired from the same point.[22] At Raglan Castle a more sophisticated system was introduced. Here both coppers were set at a much higher level, each probably being filled by the use of a pump. This arrangement provided space for a separate fireplace beneath each copper, the flames then passing through flues into a central chimney. Instead of being left open, the top of each copper was surmounted by a tall domed chamber, each having a duct just above the rim of the copper to draw in cold fresh air. Having absorbed the surplus steam, this was then drawn away through high-level ducts into the central chimney-stack. As a result, the brewhouse was a drier and pleasanter place in which to work.

In 1635 Charles I granted two patents for improved designs of boiling coppers. One, awarded to his groom of the Privy Chamber and two Westminster brewers, could boil some 1,900 gallons 'with halfe the fuell they now spende, as alsoe for the removall and taking away of the great annoyance of smoake, which ariseth from brewhouse … also with sea coales.' The other, granted to Captain Thornese Francke, claimed to save more than a third of the usual quantity of fuel, and was re-granted to him in 1660 for further 'perfection' of brewing furnace design.[23]

The other equipment required in a well-equipped brewhouse, such as that of the Earl of Northumberland at Petworth in Sussex in 1632, included:

1. a large open tub called a mashvat, fitted with a plug to drain its contents into
2. a large open tub called an underback, placed beneath;
3. a jet, or large ladle and
4. a shoot, or gutter, to transfer liquids to
5. a cooler, a large shallow vessel with a broad surface area, in which liquids were rapidly cooled before being transferred to
6. a sweet wort vat, where yeast was added from
7. a starting tub, to ferment, and then into
8. a tun and two hogsheads mounted on
9. 3 stillings, or long barrel-stands;
10. a branding iron used here for marking each barrel with the half-moon badge of the Percy family.

There were also faggots to heat the copper, a coal rake and an iron fork to manage the fire, a wire screen to clean the malt, a basket for hops, and a set of scales and weights to measure out the ingredients.[24]

ALE

The usual method of brewing ale commenced with:

1. filling the copper with water and bringing it up to the boil in order to sterilize it;
2. running the water, called liquor, into a mashvat, leaving it to cool to around 62–68°C/144–155°F, pouring in the ground malt, stirring it with a mash paddle or 'masheroe',[25] covering it to keep warm, and leaving for about two hours to release the malt sugars;
3. removing the plug from the mashvat, a wicker strainer called a bettony

Figure 23. Strong ale cask. In the greatest households, strong, long-keeping ales were kept in large casks with carved heads. This example bears the portrait of Charles I.

or betwell holding back the malt as the liquid, now called sweet wort, drained into

4. the underback, from whence it was transferred to the cooler, and then into the sweet wort or guilevat, and the yeast stirred in, so that the sugars could be fermented into alcohol.
5. When fermentation had largely ceased, a jet ladle and shoot gutter transferred the wort into barrels, with the aid of a funnel called a tundish.
6. Two successive batches of water were meanwhile being boiled in the copper and mashed with the remaining malt to produce weaker batches. These were usually cooled and fermented separately to produce three different strengths of ale, although they might also be mixed together to make a single large batch of medium-quality ale.

The following recipe produces identical results on a smaller scale.

TO BREW 5 GALLONS OF ALE OF 3 STRENGTHS

1 boiling vessel of 20pt/12l capacity

1 brewing thermometer

4 tubs each of 30pt/15l capacity with a corked hole at the base.

1 sieve

1 large, thick blanket

6lb/2.7kg (12pt/7.2l) ground pale malt

6tsp/30g dried real-ale yeast

Allow some 8 hours to complete the mashing and preparation, and 6 days to completion.

Boil 16pt/9.5l water, allow to cool to 62–68°C/145–155°F, and pour into one of the tubs at the same time as pouring in most of the malt. Stir for 10 minutes, cover and wrap with the blanket, then leave to stand for two hours.

Gently withdraw the cork and allow a narrow stream of the wort to drain out through the sieve into another of the tubs.

When the wort stops running, re-cork the first tub, and repeat the two stages above, running a second batch into another tub, and finally a third batch into the last tub.

When each of the three batches has cooled to 16°C/60°F stir in 2tsp of the yeast into each one, cover, and leave at this temperature to ferment for the next 5 days, skimming the yeast off the tops on the third day for potential use for further brews or breadmaking.

Remove to a cool place, allow to clear, then run off the ales without disturbing the sediment.

This will produce some

10pt/6l wort of *c.* 0.085 specific gravity giving an excellent strong light ale of around 10% alcohol by volume, which would keep several months when barrelled;

14pt/8.4l wort of *c.* 0.025 specific gravity of lighter ale of around 3% alcohol by volume, which might keep a week or two;

15pt/9l wort of *c.* 0.005 specific gravity of small ale having well under 1% alcohol by volume with a slightly malt and almost mild lemon flavour, good to quench the thirst, but only keeping a few days before turning sour.

Lacking the sharp flavour of hops, ales were often flavoured with herbs. While on his *Pennyles Pilgrimage* of 1618 John Taylor had visited the house of John Pinner in Manchester, where he enjoyed;

Good ale of Hisope, 'twas not Esope fable;
Then we had Ale of Sage, and Ale of Malt,
With Ale of Rosemary, and Bettony,
And two more, or else I needs must lye,
But to conclude this drinking and ye tale,
We had a sort of Ale called scurvy Ale,'[26]

The latter, made with scurvy-grass, *Cochlearia officinalis*, was 'frequently drunk in the mornings as physic-drink', while the sage ale was being sold at a penny a pint in the mid-seventeenth century.[27] The practice of adding herbs continued long after the introduction of hops, the accounts of the Howard family including the payment of a shilling 'To the brewer, which was owinge for bagges for putting in hearbes for my Lord's beare' in October, 1640.[28] The most famous medicated ale was invented by Dr Butler, physician to James I. This was a mixture of:

4oz/100g senna	*small handfull agrimony*
4oz/100g Polypodium vulgare	*small handfull maiden*
2oz/50g sasparilla	*4pt/2.4l scurvygrass*

all beaten in a mortar, packed into a thin canvas bag and hung in 10 gallons/45litres of ale as it fermented. This was reputed to help digestion, clear the lungs, promote sleep, and improve the memory.[29] Other special and herbed ales could have quite different effects, as Ben Jonson discovered during a heavy hangover:

What wild ingredients did the woman choose
To mad her drink with all; it made me loose
My wits before I quenched my thirst: there came
Such whimsies in my head, and such a flame
Of Fiery drunkenness had singed my nose,
My beard shrank in for fear ... [30]

BRAGGOT

The practice of converting some of the strong ale wort into an even stronger heavily herbed and spiced honey ale continued from the medieval period. Known as braggot, it was popular at weddings, John Kaye of Woodsome Hall near Huddersfield buying in a quantity for the double wedding of two of his daughters in February, 1584.[31] The following recipe is based on that which Mr Webb, the royal brewer, made and demonstrated to Sir Kenelm Digby in 1663.

TO MAKE BRAGGOT[32]

the first batch of c. 10pt/6l wort prepared as in the previous recipe

8oz/225g clear honey	*3tsp bruised stick cinnamon*
1tsp each chopped rosemary, thyme, savory, marjoram and parsley	*2tsp dried real ale yeast*
	1 nutmeg, crushed
6tsp grated root ginger	*10 cloves*

Bring the wort to the boil, stir in the honey until dissolved, cover, simmer for 45 minutes, skim, then add the herbs and half the spices, cover and simmer for a further hour, then leave to cool for about 15 minutes.

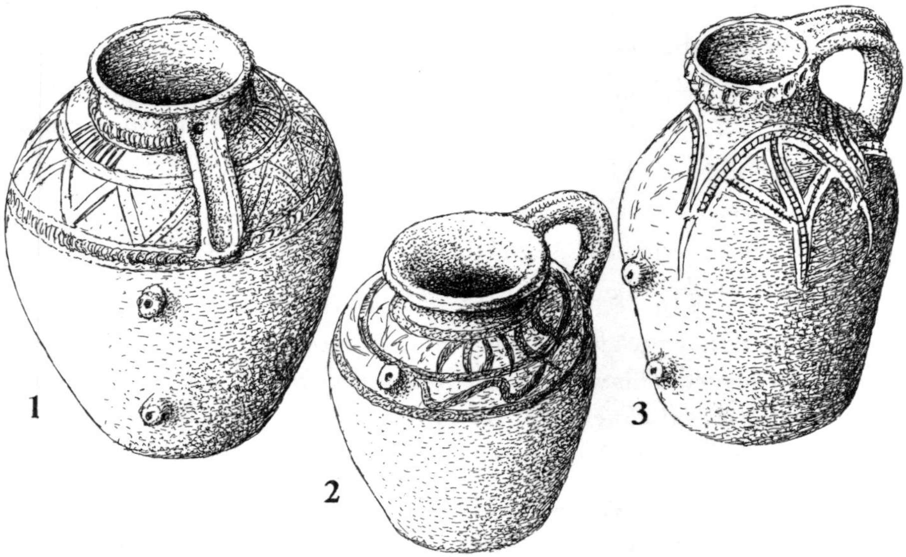

Figure 24. White ale pots. Since the white ales of the West Country produced a thick white sediment, the pots for keeping them during their short lives had a number of high-level spigot-holes to enable the clearer ale to be drawn off. (1) from St Germans, Cornwall, has a hole at the top of its fluted handle, to carry off any excess fermentation; (2) from Totnes, Devon; (3) from Donyatt, Somerset.

Strain off the herbs and spices, leaving behind any dregs, and pour the clear liquid into a clean vessel. When cooled to about 16°C/60°F stir in the yeast, cover, and keep at the same temperature to ferment for the next three days, while it continues a strong fermentation.

Skim off the yeast and pour the clear liquid into a large jar or demijohns containing the remaining spices enclosed in small muslin bags, cork very tightly, or fit an air-trap, and leave for a month in a cooler place to finish fermenting.

The braggot may now be drunk, but will keep in good condition if bottled, lightly corked, and kept cool.

WHITE ALE

Unlike such richly flavoured strong ales, the white ales of Cornwall and Devon had quite different qualities, described by Andrew Boorde in 1542:

Iche cham a Cornyshe man, ale che can brew;
It wyll make one to kaeke, also to spew;
It is diche [watery] and smoky, and also it is dyn [cloudy],

It is lyke wash, as pygges had wrestled dryn …
There ale is starke nought, loking whyte & thycke … [33]

This was made in small quantities for immediate consumption, but unfortunately no early recipes are known to have survived. However, it may be brewed according to the instructions recorded by Charles Vancouver in 1808.

WHITE ALE

1 boiling vessel of 15pt/8l capacity; 1 brewing thermometer; 2 tubs of 30pt/15l capacity; 1 sieve; 1 large, thick blanket

13pt/7l pale malt
½ an egg, beaten
5oz/125g flour
2tsp real ale brewer's yeast
pinch of salt

Mash the malt with 13pt/7l water in one tub as described in the ale recipe on p. 108. Run off into the other tub, leave to cool to 16°C/60°F, and stir in the remaining ingredients. Cover, leave in a cool place for 24 hours before drinking.

The resulting ale has the colour of milky tea, with a thick creamy sediment. It is highly alcoholic and has a scent similar to that of barley wine. Since it still retains active yeasts, it can have the extreme laxative effects described by Andrew Boorde, but remains one of the easiest and speediest-made of all intoxicating liquors.

BEER

By the late fifteenth century Flemish immigrants had already introduced a new ingredient into English brewing, the hop. The flowers of this field and garden crop provided oils which gave ale a pleasant bitter taste and greatly increased its keeping properties. At first hops had to be imported from the Low Countries, but their cultivation in England began around 1524 when Flemings developed the first Kentish hop-gardens.[34] Within a few decades many wealthy families had started to grow their own hops in other parts of the country, some being encouraged by the publication of Reynolde Scot's *Perfite Platforme of a Hoppe Garden* of 1574. By the later 1570s Lord North had established a hopground at Kirtling in Cambridgeshire, for example, while the Howard family had one at Kirkoswald in Cumbria by 1612.[35] Even so, most households continued to purchase imported hops throughout this period.

When hops were boiled with ale wort, before it was fermented, the resulting drink changed its name from 'ale' to 'beer'. It was more troublesome to make, since each brew had to be boiled and mashed just like ale, but then the three batches of decreasing strength had to each be given a second boiling with the hops in order to absorb their flavour and other properties.

The strengths of the first mashings drawn off the malt was much greater than those of most modern beers, as may be seen from the following calculations of the weight of malt and corn allowed to each gallon of water:

Modern bitters[36]	*c.* 1 to 1.7lb with 0.5 to 1oz hops
Modern barley wine	*c.* 2lb with 1oz hops
1547 single beer[37]	1.67lb with 0.3oz hops
1547 double beer	3.35lb with an unknown quantity of hops
16th century beer[38]	3.32lb with 0.3oz hops
1587 beer[39]	7.20lb with 0.4oz hops
1615 March beer[40]	9.32lb with an unknown quantity of hops
1615 strong ale (beer)[41]	18.29lb with an unknown quantity of hops
1615 bottled ale (beer)[42]	12.8lb with an unknown quantity of hops

As the last two references show, the meaning of 'ale' was changing from an unhopped drink to a very strong and hopped beer from around the late sixteenth century, then retaining this later definition through to modern times.

Each brewer or ale-wife used their own particular recipes while still retaining the old-established practice of drawing three separate batches of wort from the same batch of ground malt. The following recipe demonstrates the usual method used in a two-boiler brewhouse, but with its quantities reduced to a convenient modern domestic scale.[43]

TO BREW 5 GALLONS OF BEER OF 3 STRENGTHS, SIXTEENTH CENTURY

You will need: *2 boiling vessels, one of 20pt/11l and one of 18pt/10l capacity (as boiling coppers); 1 brewing thermometer; 5 tubs each of 30pt/15l capacity with a corked hole in the base (to serve as underbacks/mash tubs/fermenting vats); 1 sieve; 1 large, thick blanket*

For the beer:

4lb 12oz/2.1kg ground pale malt
15oz/425g kibbled wheat
15oz/425g medium oatmeal
2oz/50g hops
6tsp dried real ale yeast

I have numbered the stages, so that the recipe may be followed more easily.

1. Put 16pt/9.5l water into the larger vessel (as a copper), bring to the boil and leave to cool to *c.* 65–68°C/150–155°F.

2. Run the water into one of the tubs (as a mash vat) with the malt, stir in thoroughly, cover with the blanket and leave for about 2 hours.
3. Meanwhile put a further 16pt/9.5l water into the larger vessel, bring to the boil and leave to cool to *c.* 65–68°C/150–155°F.
4. Run the first wort from stage 2 into another of the tubs (as the underback).
5. Run the water from stage 3 onto the malt, cover with the blanket and leave for about 2 hours.
6. Transfer the first wort from stage 4 into the smaller vessel (as the smaller copper), stir in 1oz/25g of the hops, cover, and simmer for 2 hours (being careful it does not boil over), then run it through a sieve into another tub (as a cooler).
7. Run the second wort from stage 5 off into one of the tubs (as the underback).
8. Put a further 16pt/9.5l water into the larger vessel, bring to the boil and leave to cool to *c.* 65–68°C/150–155°F.
9. Transfer the first wort from stage 6 into another of the tubs (as a fermenting vessel), when at 16°C/60°F stir in 2tsp of the yeast and leave to ferment.
10. Transfer the second wort from stage 7 into the smaller vessel, stir in 1oz/25g of the hops, cover, and simmer for 2 hours (being careful that it does not boil over), then run through a sieve into another tub (as cooler).
11. Run the third batch from stage 8 onto the malt, cover, and leave for a further two hours, before being run off into another of the tubs (as the underback).
12. Run the second wort from stage 10 into another of the tubs (as a fermenting vessel), stir in 2tsp of the yeast and leave to ferment.
13. Transfer the third wort from stage 11 into the smaller vessel, stir in 1oz/25g of the hops, cover, and simmer for 2 hours (being careful that it does not boil over), then run through a sieve into another tub (as cooler).
14. Transfer the third wort from stage 13 into a tub (such as the cleaned-out-mash-vat or another fermenting tub), stir in 2tsp of the yeast, and leave to ferment.
15. At this stage there are three tubs (fermenting vessels), each with a different strength of beer, which are covered and left to ferment in a warm place for some 5 days. They are then transferred to separate casks in the cool of the cellar and left to settle ready for use. This recipe produces some 10pt/6l strong 'ale', 14pt/8.4l beer and 15pt/9l of small beer.

Instead of keeping the three batches separate to produce three strengths of beer, some household brewers mixed the three worts together to make a uniform beer of their chosen strength and flavour. At first the hopped beers had been treated with considerable suspicion. In the 1540s Andrew Boorde found them not only cold, perhaps even fatal, to many Englishmen, but also making them 'fat, and doth inflate the belly, as it doth appere by the Dutche men's faces & belyes'.[44] By the reign of Elizabeth I, however, beers had become so popular as to largely replace the earlier un-hopped ales, Reynolde Scot claiming in 1574 that:

> If your ale may endure a fortnight, your beer through the benefit of the hop, shall endure a month and what grace it yeildeth to the taste, all men may judge that hath sense in their mouths ... ale giveth place unto [beer] and ... most of our countrymen do abhore and abandon ale as a loathsome drink.[45]

MEAD, METHEGLIN & HYDROMEL

Mead was made by fermenting a solution of honey and water, metheglin being a herbed or spice mead, as was hydromel. Despite their different names, there was no real distinction between them, for each might be made with the same wide range of ingredients and variations in strengths. *The Closet of Sir Kenelm Digby Open'd*, compiled before 1665, includes a hundred recipes, the weakest having some 16fl.oz or 1pt (480 or 600ml) honey per gallon (4.8l), while the strongest had 2pt 12fl.oz (1.5l) or even 3pt 4fl.oz (1.9l) of honey per gallon.[46] Some contained no additional yeasts, some stirred in yeasts or spread them on floating slices of toast, while others obtained their fermentation by tunning in old sack-casks. The following recipes are typical of both lightly and heavily flavoured meads.

GOOD MEAD[47]

2pt/1.1l honey
1 egg white
2 nutmegs, sliced
1½tsp dried yeast

Beat the egg white into 1 gallon/4.4l cold water, stir in the honey, slowly bring to the boil, removing all scum as it rises. Add the nutmeg, cover, and simmer for 10 minutes, then leave to cool to around 65°C/150°F, then stir in the yeast, cover, and leave in a warm place for about 4–5 days until fermentation has subsided. Pour into sterilized demijohns fitted with an air-lock (instead of the traditional cask) and leave in a cool place for 2 months before use or bottling.

MY LORD HERBERT OF CHERBURY'S MEAD[48]

6 sprigs rosemary
half a nutmeg
1tbs crushed blade mace
1tsp cloves
6in/15cm stick cinnamon
½oz/12g root ginger, sliced
1 egg white & its crushed shell
4fl.oz/120ml honey
1½tsp dried yeast

Boil the rosemary and spices in 1 gallon/4.4l water for 1 hour, then leave to cool to around 65°C/150°F.

Thoroughly beat the egg white, shell and honey into the water, return to the heat, removing all the scum as it rises to the boil.

Strain the clear liquid into a clean vessel, leave to cool to 65°C/150°F, then stir in the yeast and leave in a warm place for 4–5 days until the fermentation has subsided. Pour into a sterilized demijohn fitted with an airlock and leave in a cool place for 3 weeks before drinking or bottling.

Much more basic meads were made by taking all the combs from a hive and, having extracted as much of their honey as possible, boiling them in three gallons of water. On removing the valuable beeswax, the remaining liquid was either fermented on its own, or used to mash a quantity of malt and a few hops and fermenting the resulting liquid as if it was a beer.

CIDER & PERRY

Cider, made from apples or sometimes apples mixed with pears, and perry, made from pears alone, were essentially drinks of the poor throughout the sixteenth century. As Richard Drake of Little Malvern, Worcestershire, recorded in 1585, the cottagers there were so poor that they were obliged to gather 'crabbes, payres and such other fruites as the wodde of the Common doth yealde to pownde to make drink.'[49] Such drinks were considered to be decidedly unhealthy, being cold and flatulent, upsetting the stomach, but still being relatively harmless if drunk during the hot work of the harvest field.[50] Their use was largely restricted to counties with rich soils and mild climates, including Kent and Sussex, and from Shropshire down through Herefordshire, Worcestershire, Gloucestershire, Somerset and Devon.

Having been gathered, the ripe fruit was heaped up to soften, pounded into a pulp called pomace, carefully enclosed in a strong horse-hair cloth to form a rectangular 'cheese', then pressed in large wooden presses to extract the juice. The first pressing might produce a cider of reasonable quality, but dilution was widespread, either by adding water, or by soaking poor apples in water before they were pressed.[51] Alternatively water was mixed with pomace after it had been removed from the press, and then given a second pressing. Called ciderkin, this made 'a good drinke to coole the thirst of the poore labourer.'[52] However, John Evelyn still found 'new cider and all diluted watered ciders are great enemies of the teeth, and cause violent pains in them, and rheums in the head.'[53]

It was only from the late 1640s, perhaps as a result of the disruption of the wine trade during the Civil War, that gentlemen began to plant specialized cider orchards and make good quality cider and perry. This was not just for home-consumption, but for sale as a means of drawing increased profit from the land.

Some cider recipes were closely related to those usually restricted to wine-making, boiling the fruit to a pulp before straining off and fermenting its liquor.[54] One of the best contemporary descriptions of cidermaking was published in Gervase Markham's *The English Hus-wife* of 1615. Having picked out all the stalks, rotten parts and other refuse, the fruit was crushed 'in the presse mill which is made with a mil-stone running round in a circle' usually pulled round by a horse.[55] The pomace was then pressed, the first running being transferred to casks for use, and the residue soaked in water for a further day or two before being re-pressed to produce small perry or cider.

By 1664, when Sir Paul Neale FRS published his 'Discourse on Cider' in John Evelyn's *Sylva*, these basic methods had been greatly improved. His recipe started with pearmains, pippins, golden pippins, codlings, red-streaks and ginet-moils, which were picked, heaped for three weeks, stamped, and strained into a large covered wooden vat. After twelve hours the juice was run off into a barrel for a further day, this process being repeated up to three times until there was no further sediment, and it was clear enough to be bottled and carried down into the cellar. Here they were protected from frost by hay or straw, while in hot weather, which might cause secondary fermentation and exploding bottles, they were embedded in sand. By these improved methods it was now possible to enjoy fine sparkling ciders throughout the entire year.[56]

VERJUICE

In October 1540, the Manners' steward, 'Payed to 6 women for gatheryng of crabbs at 2*d*. per piece 12*d*. To 6 women agayne for 3 days for stampyng of crabbs at 3*d*. the day the pece 4*s*. 6*d*.'[57] It was autumn, and they had been gathering and crushing crab apples in order to make a very sour culinary ingredient and table-condiment called verjuice.

Having picked the crab apples when their cores were turning black, they were heaped for a short while to sweat, had the stalks, rotten parts and rubbish picked clean, were tipped into a long trough and beaten with large mallets until reduced to a mush. This was then packed into a horsehair bag and pressed in a verjuice 'brake', usually a lever-press weighted with a heavy stone. Grooves in a flat stone beneath the bag conveyed the verjuice into a tub, whence it was poured into a cask and stored in a cool place ready for use in a similar manner to vinegar.[58] As Thomas Tusser advised, October was the time to, 'Be suer of vergis (a gallon at least), / So good in the kitchen, so needful for beast.'[59]

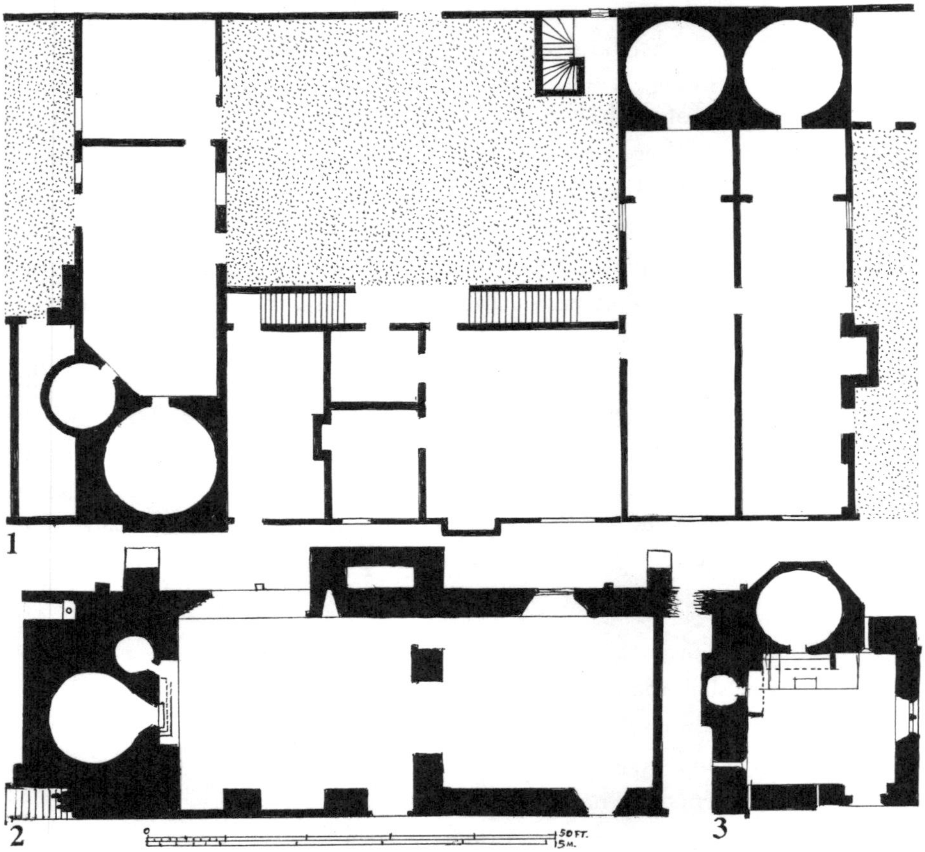

Figure 25. Bakehouses. Royal bakehouses had to be especially large to meet the demands of perhaps 1,000 people a day. That at Hampton Court (1) of 1529 was half-timbered with masonry ovens for the Great Bakehouses (right) and Privy Bakehouse, (left), separated by the Bread House and stairs up to the Granary. The Middleham Castle bakehouse (2) and the Wressle Castle bakehouse (3) date from the early 16th century.

CHAPTER SEVEN

The Bakehouse

The purpose of the bakehouse was to make all the bread required in the household, where it formed one of the most important every-day foods. Following Old Testament prophets, early seventeenth-century writers confirmed its status, Penkethman stating that 'Bread is worth all, being the Staffe of life.'[1] 'Gentyll bakers', pleaded Andrew Boorde, 'make good breade, for good breade doth comforte, confyrme, and doth stablysshe a mannes herte ... sophystycate [adulterate] not your breade made of pure whete ....'[2] Meanwhile Gervase Markham instructed every English housewife to 'looke into her Backe-house, and to the baking of all sorts of bread, either for Masters, Servants, or Hinds, and to ordering and compounding of the meale for each severall use.'[3] Although bread was a staple food, it was by no means a standard product, its character being governed partly by the availability of different bread-corns, which varied from one region to another, and partly by the status of those it was to feed.

> And though white and browne be both at one price,
> With browne shalt thou fede least white might make thee nice.
> The lordes will always that people note and see
> Between them and servauntes some diversitie.
> Though it to them turne no profit at all,
> If they have pleasour, the servant shall have small.[4]

In large establishments, where many people had to be provided with bread of the appropriate qualities, a well-staffed, well-equipped and well-administered bakehouse was an absolute necessity. The royal household had been successfully operating the country's largest bakery for centuries, its regulations therefore being largely confirmed rather than revised during the sixteenth and early seventeenth centuries. The administrative head of the Bakehouse was its clerk. He prepared all the accounts for submission to the Counting House, checked its officers' fees, and made sure that all its loaves were of the correct weight. It was the sergeant, however, who took charge of all the more practical matters. His four yeoman purveyors were responsible for buying the best wheat on the market at the best of prices, and arranging for its delivery into the royal garners. As it was carried in, the sergeant and/or the clerk checked that it was all of good quality and of the correct weight, refusing all that was sub-standard. Being already threshed, and thus subject to outbreaks of mould, the yeoman garnetor and his labourers turned it regularly to keep it well aired, and reed it in a riddle to remove all the dirt, stalks and other rubbish. This ensured that it was quite pure before he sent it off to the mill. On its return to the Bakehouse as meal, the sergeant checked it again, in case the miller had illegally extracted any by way of a fee. If accepted, he then sent it on to the two bakehouses. The Privy Bakehouse, which served the monarch and senior members of the court, was staffed by two yeomen and two grooms, while the Great Bakehouse had a yeoman, a groom and five conducts to bake for everyone else. Both performed every operation, starting with boulting the meal to remove the coarsest bran, which the sergeant claimed as his fee. After further boulting to provide white flour for manchets and 'wholemeal' flour for cheat loaves, it was seasoned well, 'not drowning it with too much water, weighing the same into the Oven, that every Loaf may weigh and keepe its full weight, after it is baked … [and] not be rashly handled in drawing it out of the Oven, nor in putting it into the Storehouse for fear of breaking of the Bread, whereby there shall come wast.'[5]

Nobles operated their bakehouses in a very similar manner to make almost identical breads, but on a smaller scale. At Petworth, for example, the Earl of Northumberland employed a baker and an under-baker to provide all the household's bread in the 1620s.[6] When appointing such staff, it was always best to get the candidates to come to the house, see them in action, and taste their products, before either accepting or rejecting them. In 1541 Sir William Bassett's baker went through this process when applying for a similar post at Belvoir Castle, being paid 20*d.* for 'his servys doone at the bakehouse for the triall of his conyng.'[7] Similarly in 1653, Sir Ralph Verney instructed his steward that 'my cook comes down tomorrow … If there is not wooden dishes to make white bread, buy a dozen, he will show you the size. Buy a bushel of white wheat for bread and crusts. Let him try 2 or 3 times to make French bread and after the first or second time send me a loaf of each sort to judge of.'[8] Lesser households might employ a baker, but in most gentry, yeoman and peasant homes, bread-making remained a decidedly female occupation. The housewives who enjoyed the services of a serving maid as described by Thomas Churchyard could reckon themselves fortunate:[9]

> And raising paste, she passed still
> As soon as flour came from the mill,
> She made the goodiest cakes thereof

And baked as fair a household loaf
As e're was seen or set on board.

The quantities of grain and flour used each year in large domestic bakehouses could be vast. In 1594–5 the Earl of Cumberland's bakers converted over 16 tons of wheat into loaves, around 3.25 tons into 4,568 'cast' of white manchets, and almost 13 tons into 8,829 'cast' of sieved wholemeal loaves. The number of loaves to the 'cast' is still uncertain, and was probably variable. In the Earl's bakehouse it was 26oz of wheat for manchets and 52oz for wholemeal, while William Harrison described it as 22.6oz for manchets, and Lady Gray 22.4oz for manchets.[10] Given that a number of recipes have 16oz (1lb or 454g) manchets, these figures suggest that a cast may have been two loaves.

In the largest houses the bakehouse was usually consigned to an outer court, adjacent to the brewhouse, so that its activities did not intrude on the owner, his family or guests. Early sixteenth-century examples are recorded in this position at Eltham Palace, Kent, Raglan Castle, Monmouth, Nottingham Castle, and the immediately post-Dissolution additions to Lacock Abbey, Wiltshire, to list just a few of many.[11] The greatest of all was built in the outer court of Hampton Court Palace in 1529. Measuring some 110 x 65 feet (36 x 21 metres), it had an outer yard probably for storing its fuel, stables for purveyors' horses, and an inner yard for the reception of corn, whence two staircases led up to dry, first-floor granaries. The yard walls, chimney stacks and huge ovens, two each in the Privy and Great Bakehouses, were all of fireproof brick, the remainder being timber-framed beneath tiled roofs.[12] Most great houses of the late sixteenth and early seventeenth centuries continued to have external bakehouses, as at the Smythsons' Hardwick and Wollaton. Internal basement bakehouses, such as that at Shaw House, Newbury, of the 1570s, were extremely rare.

When examining household inventories of this period, it becomes clear that many owners found it best to store much of their bread-corn within their houses. After harvest the sheaves were carefully built up in weatherproof thatched stacks in the farm yard. Here they would keep in good condition until the following March, if intended for a cash sale to the millers. If threshed out of the ears, the grain had a tendency to go mouldy, even if regularly aired by being turned with a shovel. It was therefore much better to thresh it for household use just before it was needed.[13] It was then heaped into bushel measures, the surplus scraped off level with a straight-edge called a strike, and poured into a sack for transport to the mill. At Elmswell, Henry Best insisted that the miller first clean it by kneeling on the ground, and shaking batches in a reeing sieve or coarse riddle, so that the chaff or head-stalks rose to the surface and dust and dirt fell away, leaving only the pure grain. Having poured this into the hopper feeding the millstones, the miller then scooped out four pints per bushel, this being his mulcture, or payment-in-kind for providing his services.[14]

Before being used, the freshly milled meal usually had to undergo further grading. In cottages, this might take place on a cloth on the living-room floor, while in larger houses there might be a boulting room specially equipped for this purpose. In 1624 Speke Hall near Liverpool had in its boulting house five sacks, two pipes (casks) to boult in, a hogshead for storing wheat, a tub for storing 'seeds' (oat husks), two barrels for bran, a meal sieve, a 'tem' sieve, a searce, a peck and a 1.5 bushel measure and two balance scales and weights.[15] Others had more or less, depending on the quantities of meal which they had to process.

Like grain, the ground meal rapidly went sour or developed mould if exposed to damp air for a period, and so it had to be firmly packed down into containers for storage. Barrels and tubs might suffice in smaller houses, but huge oak chests were necessary where larger quantities were required. One of the finest is the 'great garnar, an irelome [partly filled with] 30 busshels [38.5cu.ft.] meale £4 10*s*' which William Strickland left in the bakehouse at Sizergh in Westmorland in 1569. Still in the house, it is an immensely long panel-fronted chest, its sloping top having four hatches each giving access to a separate meal-box.[16] A rather more typical example remains at East Riddlesden Hall, West Yorkshire. Probably made in 1648 for John Murgatroyd, and listed among his 'one wheate Arke £1, four meil Arkes £4' in 1662, it has pegged tenon joints.[17] These allow it to be dismantled for removal from one room to another, and a lid which, when removed and inverted, forms a hand-barrow for carrying in the sacks of meal. If used as in later years, a servant would stand in it as it was filled, using his stockinged feet to pack the meal down into a compact, almost airtight mass.

On being scooped out of such arks, the meal had to be graded. This involved an initial shaking through a meal-sieve, a piece of open-weave, probably horse-hair, cloth supported within a hoop of wood. Having extracted the coarser husk of the grain, variously known as bran, chizel, gurgeon, pollard, sharps or treat, it left a flour of some 85 per cent wholemeal. This in turn could be shaken through a temse, searce or sieve, also a hoop of wood, but now bottomed with finer-meshed linen boulting cloth, to extract the finer fragments of bran. The temsed flour this produced was satisfactory for most good general baking, but not that of the highest quality. To drive the finest flour through the finest boulting cloth needed more pressure, and a far more vigorous action than could be achieved in an open-topped temse. Instead, the coarsely temsed flour had to be placed on a square of fine boulting cloth, which was then rolled up, grasped at each end, and rapidly flicked up and down to expel a cloud of fine flour-dust. In many boulting houses this was carefully swept up from the floor using a hand-broom and the feathery wing of a goose, but in others it was caught in a variety of receptacles:

> 'in your Bake-house you shall have a faire boultinge house with large Pipes [105 gallon barrels], to boulte meale in ... boulters, searces, raunges and meale sive of all sorts both fine and coarse' (Markham, 1615);
>
> 'a bultynge pype coverid with a yarde of canvasse' (1534);
>
> '2 barrels, a temse & a meale sive' (1606);
>
> 'one chist, one meyll syve, on ryenge syve, one temse ... ' (1558);
>
> 'an olld arke [chest] to bowt melle in & 2 temses & a bowlt clothe' (1581).[18]

Clearly it would be much more efficient if the boulting process could be mechanized and enclosed, so that all the flour could be retained, rather than scattered around the bakehouse. The solution was the boulting machine, as illustrated in John Penkethman's *Artachthos* of 1638.[19] Wholemeal poured into a hopper at one end entered a sloping cylindrical frame lined with successively coarser meshes. A series of brushes turned by an external hand-crank then worked the meal through them, delivering separate batches of flour, each of a different degree of fineness. Since the whole was enclosed within a rectangular wooden casing, there was now hardly any loss.

Having prepared the flour, the next stage was to convert it into dough using a variety of implements, as listed in a number of bakehouse inventories. The following examples are all of Bess of Hardwick's properties in 1601:

> 'too kneading troughes, a Chest to put bran in, fyve long tables, a breade bynge, a Coffer, a payre of bellowses, a brandyiron, a brass pan, a kytt.' (Chatsworth)
>
> 'fowre long bordes, a brass kettle, a trevet, two kites, a kymnell, a kneading trough, three tubbes for flower.' (Hardwick Old Hall)[20]

The brandiron and trivet were used to hold the pan or kettle over the fire, heating water to luke-warm before mixing into the flour. The kneading troughs were plank-built, with sides sloping outwards from the base, while kimnels were shallow coopered tubs, Henry Best's having a one-bushel capacity.[21] Kits, meanwhile, were smaller tubs, one stave projecting upwards as a handle, intended for carrying in the required water. Other bakehouse inventories include, '1 brake', or 'a brak.'[22] This was a kneading machine, consisting of a knee-high rectangular bench for the dough, above one side of which was hinged a long, stout pole. By sitting on one end of the pole, meanwhile grasping it with both hands and working it with a progressive rotary motion, the baker was able to 'brake' or knead the dough, extending its gluten and making it much more elastic. The dough was then transferred to the tables or benches, where knives, prickers and scales were ready for moulding it into loaves.

The ovens were usually built into one wall of the bakehouse, with their flat floors about hip-height above the ground. Their interiors were dome- or beehive-shaped, without any internal flues, and usually constructed of fireproof stone or brick:

> 'To Christopher Wayn … getting and breaking stones for to make the new oven in the bakehouse 2*s.* 6*d.*' (Earl of Cumberland's accounts, 1607)
>
> 'The soales [floors] of your large ovens [should be] of one or two intire stones than of many brickes and the mouth made narrow, square and easie to be covered' (Markham 1615)
>
> 'The charge of the Oveyns: Bricks 48 thousand at severall prices £22 13*s.* Lime 474 bushells at severall prices £8 6*s.* 20 bricke lears at 11 days a peece at 18*d.* The daye a man £16 10*s.* 20 labourers at 11 days a peece at 12*d.* per diem £11' (Harefield, 1602)[23]

The latter account covers the costs of building a huge temporary oven at Harefield, ready for the visit of Queen Elizabeth to her Lord Keeper's house. Such structures were essential for even relatively short-term but extremely populous events, the best illustration of one in use appearing in the mid-sixteenth century painting of *The Field of the Cloth of Gold* in the Royal Collection. Like all other ovens, they had rectangular door openings, with a ledge protruding across the sill, on which a stopper in the form of a slab of stone or wood could stand, often held in place by a cross-bar fitted into sockets in each jamb.

In the West Country a new kind of oven was introduced around the opening years of the seventeenth century. Built of thick slabs of gravel-tempered clay, fired into hard, robust pottery in the Barnstaple and Bideford kilns, they probably represent a permanent, portable form of earlier, unfired clay-built ovens. They had the same flat floor, domed roof and flat front of masonry ovens, but had close-fitting doors cut out of their fronts, and were incised with a number, which indicated their capacity in bushels. Some were built into the walls of cottage fireplaces, being easier and cheaper to install than the complete masonry ovens, but others could be used freestanding, either indoors, or externally under a sheltering roof.[24]

Whichever kind of oven was used, it was always heated in the same way, the burning fuel being thrust to the back of its interior with an iron-tipped 'furgon' or fork. Faggots, tied bundles of small-diameter branches, were the usual fuel in large households, but thorn or blackthorn gave good results, producing a clear, bright heat. Tusser advised the more economical straw or haulm. As reaping with a sickle had only removed the heads and upper parts of the wheat and rye crops, the haulm, or remaining straw, could be scythed in August as bedding for livestock or as fuel for ovens or boiling-furnaces:

> With straw wisp and pease-bolt [pea stalks],
> Some brew and do bake ...
> Mow haulm to burn, To serve thy turn,
> To bake thy bread, to burn under lead.[25]

Once hot enough, as judged mainly by practical experience, the embers were removed with an oven-rake, and the fine ash with a bundle of wet rags fastened to the end of a long pole. This was the malkin, which gave such scope to Elizabethan and Jacobean writers:

> 'the clout wherewith they clense or sweepe the Oven, called a Maukin' (1580)
>
> 'He helde betweene both his hands a durty malkin, such as bakers sweepe their ovens withall' (1590)
>
> 'Blacke, foule and ugly like bakers malkins' (1620)
>
> 'a beard filthier than a bakers mawkin that he sweepes his oven' (1607)[26]

The loaves were then inserted on the rectangular wood or iron blade of a long-handled peel, and the door set in place, its edges sealed with mud applied with a trowel. When baked, the peel came into use once more, removing the loaves, probably into bread-baskets called maunds, ready for carrying into the pantry.

The loaves baked in Tudor and Jacobean homes varied greatly in their composition and size. Unlike the products of commercial bakers, which were closely regulated by government-, civic-, and guild-enforced assize laws, all households were free to make any kind of bread they liked, at any size found convenient. Their loaves did, however, fall into a number of widely recognized categories, the finest of all being the manchet loaf. Andrew Boorde did 'love manchet breade ... the whiche be well mowlded and throwe baken, the brande abstractyed and abjected, and that is good for old ages.'[27] It was made from the finest boulted flour, mixed with warm water, raised with yeast, and moulded 'first with strong kneading, then with rouling too and fro, and last of all wheeling or turning it round about, that it may sit the closer.'[28] Alternatively one should 'knead it very well together both with your hands, and through the brake, or for want thereof, fold it in a cloth, and with your feet tread it a good space together, then letting it lie an hour or thereabouts to rise.'[29] By this time it had

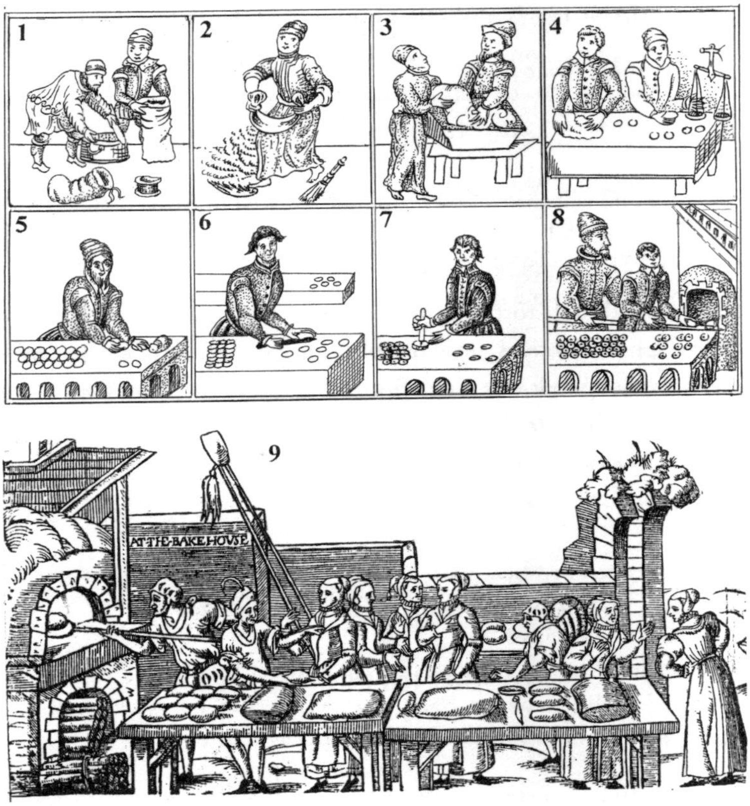

Figure 26. Baking. The 1598 Ordinances of the York Bakers' Company show the making of manchets: (1) measuring the wheat with a bushel and strike; (2) boulting the flour; (3) kneading the dough; (4) weighing the dough; (5) moulding the manchets; (6) slashing the sides; (7) pricking the tops; (8) baking. At a public bakehouse in London (9), the maids pass their mistresses' loaves to the baker, who feeds them into his oven.

been divided into individual loaves, each being weighed on the scales, or judged by experience, to a uniform size. In some households they might weigh 6oz (150g) or 1lb (450g) each, while in the royal household they were most probably of around 24oz (675g) flour, made up to weigh 30oz (850g) into the oven, and 27oz (775g) after being baked. These are approximate figures, based on the probable weight of a quarter of flour, that is eight bushels.[30] After being moulded, each loaf was scotched or given a shallow cut around its midriff, and pricked or stabbed down through the centre. This caused the loaf to rise vertically rather than expand horizontally, giving a lighter crumb, and allowing more to be packed into the oven at one baking.

A MANCHET, AS FOR THE ROYAL HOUSEHOLD

1½lb/675g (strong) white flour
1tsp/5g salt
¾pt/450ml water at 24°C/75°F
1tsp/5g sugar
1tsp/5g dried yeast

Sift the flour and salt into a bowl, and make a well in the centre.

Beat the sugar and yeast into the water, pour into the flour, then stir in, and knead for 10 minutes to produce a soft dough.

Return the dough to the bowl, cover with a light cloth, and leave at 21°C/70°F for 1–1½ hours, until doubled in size.

Knead the dough for 2–3 minutes on a floured board, mould into a ball or fat oval, place on a greased baking sheet with the smooth side uppermost, make a cut around its midriff, and form a dimple down through the middle.

Cover with a light cloth and return to the warm for a further 30–60 minutes until risen.

Bake in an oven pre-heated to 230°C/450°F/gas mark 8 for some 20–25 minutes, then remove and leave on a grid to cool down.

LADY ARUNDEL'S MANCHET[31]

2lb 12oz/1.3kg (strong) white flour
2tsp/10ml salt
12fl.oz/400ml water at 24°C/75°F
12fl.oz/400ml milk at 24°C/75°F
2½oz/65g butter
2tbs/30ml sugar
1tbs/15g dried yeast
1 egg, beaten

Make as in the recipe above, rubbing the butter into the flour at the start, and adding the egg by beating it into the milk before mixing with the flour.

After the first rising, it may be moulded into twelve 6oz manchets, or five weighing approximately 1lb, before cutting, proving and baking.

FRENCH BREAD[32]

Follow the recipe above, but add another beaten egg, and leave out the butter. Make up as either short rolls, or bake in metal or fireproof ceramic substitutes for Robert May's 'little wooden dishes'.

The second quality of bread was called cheat. Made after the abstraction of the coarser bran, to leave some 50 per cent wholemeal, or thereabouts, it was not so prestigious as manchet, but was still held in good repute, even appearing on monarchs' tables.[33] This was the 'Franklins' Bread of England, most nourishing, middle size, between Gentlemans' Rolls and little manchets, or great rolls used

Figure 27. Baking. This woodcut from 'The Assyse of Breade' (1) shows bakers weighing and moulding, tying faggots and baking. John Penkethman's Mysterie and Trade of Baking *(2) of 1638 illustrates all the processes of manchet-making. The Assyse also depicts each of the bakers' products: (3) the farthing wastell; (4) the farthing symnel; (5 & 6) the farthing and halfpenny white loaves; (7 & 8) the halfpenny and penny wheaten loaves; (9) the halfpenny household loaf.*

in Yeomans' houses'.[34] Instead of being raised with ale-yeast, it used a sourdough culture. This was made by keeping back a little dough from each baking, allowing it to go sour, then dissolving it in warm water, mixing this to a batter with some of the meal in the dough trough, and leaving it overnight to form a 'sponge' ready to knead into the remaining meal next day. Since this can be an unreliable method for those who do not practise it regularly, the following recipe substitutes modern dried yeast, along with a mixture of the white and wholemeal flours available today to obtain a close replica of the original cheat loaves. There are few clues as to their size in individual households, the quantities here coming from the Earl of Cumberland's accounts of 1594–5 which suggest they were about 3lb, or twice that of his manchets.[35]

A CHEAT LOAF

1lb/450g (strong) white flour
1lb/450g (strong) wholemeal flour
16fl.oz/550ml water at 24°C/75°F
1tbs/15g dried yeast
1tbs/15ml salt

Mix the flours in a bowl, and make a well in the centre.

Mix the yeast with ½pt/300ml of the water, leave for 15 minutes, mix again, pour into the flour, and work in sufficient from the sides to form a smooth batter.

Cover with some of the flour, cover, and leave in a warm place overnight. Next morning add the remaining warm water, and the salt to the batter, and immediately knead all together to form a smooth dough.

Turn the dough out onto a floured board, knead for 20 minutes, place in a bowl, cover with a light cloth, and leave to rise for about an hour until doubled in size.

Return to the board, knead for 5 minutes, form into a ball, place on a greased baking sheet, cover again, and leave to rise for about a further 30 minutes.

Bake in a pre-heated oven at 230°C/450°F/gas mark 6 for a further 30–40 minutes until baked, then remove and leave to cool on a grid.

Next in quality came the ravelled cheat, which:

> retaineth most of the grosse, and lesse of the pure substance of the wheat and this being more sleightly wrought-up is used in the halles of the nobilitie and gentrie only [it is] generally made that out of one bushel of meale, after 22lbs [about half its total weight] of brande sifted and taken from it, whereunto they ad gurgeons, that rise from the manchet, they make 30 cast, every loaf

> weighing 18 ounces into the oven, and 16 ounces out, and beside, they so handel the water that everie bushel of meale they add only 22 or 23 pound of water.[36]

RAVELLED CHEAT LOAVES

Follow the recipe above, using 1lb 10oz/725g 100% wholemeal (strong) flour and 6oz/175g (strong) white flour, with a minimum of water, and form the finished dough into two round loaves.

This was followed by 'Brown bread of the colour … baked up as it cometh from the mill, so that neither the bran nor the flour are in any way diminished.'

BEST BROWN LOAVES[37]

Follow the cheat loaf recipe above, using only 100% wholemeal (strong) flour, with a little less water, and form into either one large, or two smaller loaves.

And finally, among the pure wheat breads, the second-best brown bread which:

> hath little or no flour left therein at all … it is not only the worst and weakest of all the other sorts, but also appointed in old time for servants, slaves and inferior kind of people to feed upon. Hereafter likewise because it is hard and dry and brickle (for it will hardly be made up into loaves) some add a portion of rye meal in our time.[38]

Bolted rye bread was highly recommended in William Vaughan's *Haven of Health* of 1617, especially in summertime 'in the beginning meate, for it keepeth the belly loose and for this cause it is so used at the tables of Princes: It must not be eaten but in small quantitie, rather for the diet and health sake, then to satisfie hunger.'[39]

A further range of breads was made of mixed grains and pulses. In contrast to the wheat breads of the gentry, their 'household and poor neighbours in some shires are forced to content themselves with rye, or barley, yea, in times of dearth, many with bread made either of beans, peas or oats, or of all together, and some acorns among.'[40] At Henry Best's Elmswell farm these were made from two different combinations. The first, probably for his own family's consumption, was of maslin, a blend of wheat and rye, tempsed or sieved to extract the coarse bran. The second, brown bread probably for his servants, was of equal volumes of rye, barley and pea-meal mixed together before being ground at the mill. His poor neighbours made their breads of either one part peas to four parts rye, or equal volumes of peas and maslin to 'make hearty bread'.[41]

In the 1530s a new kind of bread began to appear in England.[42] This was spice bread, richer, spicier, and sweeter than any previous loaf, and now containing quantities of dried fruits. It rapidly became very popular, especially at funeral entertainments. In York it probably led to the decline of that city's famous 'mayne bread' in the 1550s, the council deciding in 1595 that this really was 'by reason that spyced cakes are of late growne into great use then heretofore hath bene.'[43] In London in 1595 the authorities banned all commercial bakers from making or selling 'any spice cakes ... or other spice bread ... except it be at burials, or on Friday before Easter, or at Christmas, upon pain of forfeiture of all such spiced bread to the poor.'[44] This was due to their sizes not being governed by the assize of bread, and therefore beyond the City's control. In the Commonwealth some cities even banned spice cake at funerals, in order to conserve their ingredients in times of scarcity.

Some spice breads were just that, being ordinary manchet loaf doughs, into which further ingredients were kneaded.

SPICED BREAD 1654[45]

1 batch of manchet dough, prepared as on p. 127

8oz/225g butter, in pieces	*8oz/225g currants*
4oz/100g sugar	*pinch of mace*

Knead all together after the dough has completed its first rising, then continue baking as instructed.

Others were made of new, richer doughs, and were much, much larger, one of Sir Kenelm Digby's recipes weighing 45lb (20.25kg) into the oven. Still being raised with yeast, others were made using two distinct techniques. In one, the butter was rubbed into the flour, before adding any liquids. The following recipes exemplify these variations in composition and method.

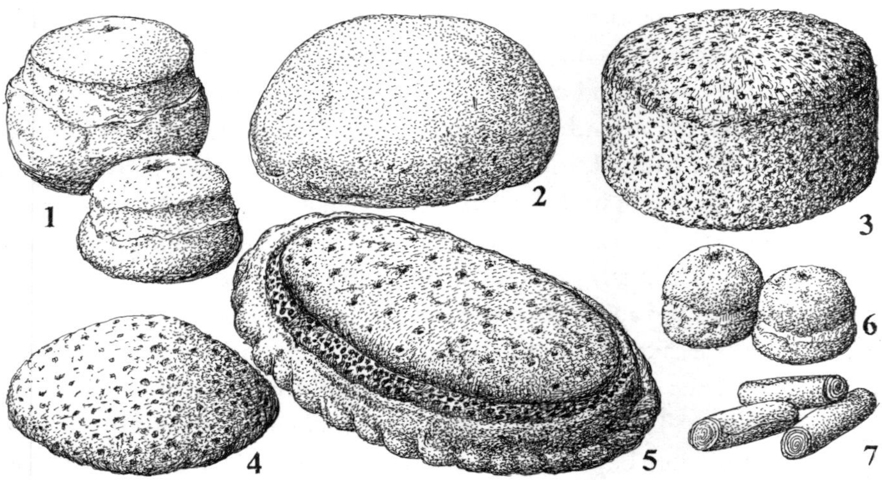

Figure 28. Tudor & early Stuart bakery: (1) manchets; (2) cheat loaf; (3) Oxfordshire cake; (4) Wood Street cake; (5) Banbury cake; (6) buttered curd loaves; (7) leavened bread.

OXFORDSHIRE CAKE, 1655 [46]
(one-tenth full size)

1lb 6oz/625g (strong) white flour
2½oz/60g sugar
½tsp/2.5ml cinnamon
½tsp/2.5ml mixed nutmeg & mace
pinch of salt
5oz/150g butter
1¼tsp/7g dried yeast
8fl.oz/240ml cream
2tbs/30ml dry sherry
2tbs/30ml rosewater
2 eggs, separated
10oz/275g currants
3oz/75g raisins

Mix the flour, sugar, salt and spices, and rub in the butter. Beat the yeast, cream, sherry, rosewater, two yolks and one white together (and warm, while stirring, to 24°C/75°F).

Make a well in the flour mixture, pour in the liquid, work all together, turn out on to a floured board, knead for 10 minutes, return to the bowl, and leave in a warm place to rise for some 30 minutes.

Knead in the currants and raisins, form into a ball, place in a greased 9in/23cm cake tin, cover, and return to the warm to rise for up to an hour, then bake at 200°C/400°F/gas mark 6 for 50 minutes (cover with greaseproof paper after the first 10 minutes).

On removing from the oven, beat the remaining egg white with a little rosewater, brush this over the top of the cake, sprinkle with a little sugar, put it back into the oven for a minute or two to glaze, then remove and cool.

In the second technique, the dry and wet ingredients were mixed separately, then worked together to form the dough. The following recipe instructs how 'To make a Cake the way of the Royal Princess, the Lady Elizabeth, daughter to King Charles the first.' She was only thirteen when she last met her father on the day before his execution, but may have been given this recipe by her mother some years before.

THE LADY ELIZABETH'S CAKE[47]
(one-sixth full size)

1lb/450g (strong) white flour	*3.5fl.oz/100ml cream*
¼tsp/1.25ml nutmeg	*4oz/100g butter*
pinch of salt	*1 egg yolk, beaten*
1¼tsp hydrolyzed 'instant' yeast	*3tbs/45ml rosewater*
1½oz/40g sugar	*10oz/275g currants*

Mix together the flour, nutmeg, salt and dried yeast. Melt the butter and sugar in the cream, and, when the temperature is below 24°C/75°F, beat in the yolk and rosewater.

Make a well in the flour mixture in a bowl, pour in the liquid, work in with a little more water if necessary to form a smooth dough. Turn this out onto a floured board, knead for 10 minutes, replace in the bowl, cover, and leave to rise in a warm place for some 40–50 minutes, then knead in the currants, place in a greased 8in/20cm cake tin, and return to the warm for some 40 minutes to rise again.

Bake at 220°/425°F/gas mark 7, for some 30 minutes (covering with greaseproof paper after the first 10 minutes).

A particular spice cake played a part in one of the many dramatic episodes of the Civil War. In 1648 King Charles instructed Colonel Joseph Bamfield to organize the escape of his second son, James, Duke of York, from his incarceration in St James's Palace. Having secured the keys to the garden gate there, James let himself out, boarded a coach with the Colonel, drove down to the Thames, and was rowed down to the steps by London Bridge. On entering a house nearby, he met Ann Murray, who rapidly dressed him in the specially made maid's clothes which formed his disguise. Just before setting off, Ann gave him 'a Woodstreet cake (which I knew he loved) to take to the barge, with as much haste as could be.' This then sustained him as he boarded his ship at Gravesend, and escaped to the Continent.[48] Presumably these cakes took their name from a baker operating in Wood Street, in the Cripplegate ward of the City.

WOOD STREET CAKE[49]
(half full size)

1lb 12oz/775g plain white flour
pinch of salt
1½tsp mixed clove, mace & nutmeg
12oz/325g currants
8oz/225g raisins, chopped
2tsp hydrolyzed 'instant' yeast
5 egg yolks
1tbs/15ml rosewater
6oz/175g butter
½pt/300ml cream
5tbs/75ml warm water

Mix the dry ingredients. Melt the butter in the cream, and beat in the yolks, rosewater and water, before pouring into the dry ingredients, and continuing as in the recipe above.

Mould the dough into a round cake on its baking sheet, thick in the middle, thinner round the sides, stab it vertically with a knife or skewer, and leave it to rise.

Bake at 220°C/425°F/gas mark 7 for some 40 minutes (cover with greaseproof paper after the first 10 minutes).

Finally, glaze the top with sugar dissolved in rosewater.

Some spiced cakes were specifically made for wedding feasts, 'Bryde cakes' entering English vocabulary around 1550.[50] Eighty years later, John Aubrey remembered that, 'When I was a little boy (before the Civill Warres) I have seen (according to the custome then) the Bryde and Bride-groome kisse over the Bride-cakes at the Table: it was about the latter end of dinner; and the cakes were layd one upon another, like the picture of the Sew bread in the old Bibles.'[51] To have been piled in this way, the cakes would have been circular, and relatively flat. The earliest recipe for a bride cake was published in *The Queen's Closet Open'd* of 1655. Entitled 'The Countess of Rutland's Receipt of making the rare Banbury Cake which was so much praised at her Daughter's (The Right Honourable Lady Chaworth's) Wedding', it is a rather plain spiced cake, its distinguishing feature being an outer crust of plain dough to protect the currant-rich filling within. Weighing some 30lb, such cakes took the form of deep oval slabs, their perimeter seams being rolled like those of a modern Cornish pasty. Four of them appear in Joris Hoefnagel's painting of *A Wedding Feast in Bermondsey* of *c.* 1570. Each is cradled in a long napkin suspended from its attendant's neck, as they precede the musicians, the pot of rosemary and the remainder of the wedding procession.

THE COUNTESS OF RUTLAND'S BANBURY CAKE[52]
(one-sixth full size)

2lb 13oz/1.28kg (strong) white flour
3tsp each ground mace, nutmeg & cinnamon
3tsp hydrolyzed 'instant' yeast
2 yolks & 1 white of egg
1tbs rosewater
6oz/170g butter
2lb/900g currants

Mix the flour, spices and yeast in a bowl and make a well in the centre.

Beat the eggs and rosewater in a measuring jug and make up to 1pt/600ml with warm water. Pour this into the flour, and work in with the butter cut in small pieces to produce a smooth dough. Knead for 10 minutes, then cover and leave in a warm place for 15 minutes to rise.

Cut off a third of the dough, and set to one side.

Break the remaining dough into pieces, layer with the currants in a bowl, knead until all are completely incorporated, and form into an oval cake about 2in/5cm thick.

Divide the remaining plain dough in two, and roll each half out 3 inches bigger than the currant dough, all round.

Place the first piece of plain dough on a large greased baking sheet, set the currant dough on top, brush all the upper surfaces with water, set the second piece of plain dough on top, pat it to shape over the currant dough, then roll the edges together and pinch them, as when making a Cornish pasty.

Prick the cake completely through, all over, with a skewer, make a deep cut into the sides all the way round, cover, and leave to rise for a further 50–60 minutes.

Bake at 200°C/400°F/gas mark 6 for some 50 minutes until baked, then remove from the oven, and leave to cool.

Rastons were one of medieval England's richest breads, each loaf having its top cut off, the crumb inside scooped out, soaked in butter, and replaced inside. Once their tops had been put back, they were served to the table piping hot. Their name disappeared in the late sixteenth century, while they themselves were transformed into a group of small loaves variously entitled 'buttered loaves of cheese curds', 'cheese loaves', 'curd loaf', 'buttered loaves' and the like. Their recipes were subject to much variation, most including fresh curds, flour, eggs, salt and yeast, and some being further enriched with sugar, spices and butter. Once baked, they were usually sliced across, soaked in melted butter, and then re-assembled with sugar, spices, rosewater, cream or other things between each layer, and re-heated just before being served.

BUTTERED CURD LOAVES[53]

8oz/225g (strong) white flour
½tsp mixed ground mace & clove
1tsp hydrolyzed 'instant' yeast
pinch of salt & pepper
8oz/225g cottage cheese
2 eggs, beaten
1oz/25g butter, melted

Mix the spices, yeast, salt & pepper into the flour and make a well in the centre.

Rub the cottage cheese through a sieve, beat in the eggs and melted butter, pour into the flour, work together to form a dough, knead for 5 minutes, then cover and leave in a warm place for about 15 minutes to rise.

Knead the dough, break into 12 pieces, and form each into a ball. Make a cut all round them some ½in/1cm from the base, and stab them down the centre with a skewer. Place them on a greased baking sheet, allowing space for each to expand, and return to the warm for a further 30 minutes to rise.

Bake at 200°c/400°F/gas mark 6 for 15 minutes, then remove from the oven.

To Serve

4oz/100g butter, melted
4oz/100g sugar

Cut each loaf in turn into 4 horizontal slices, soak each one in the butter, and re-assemble as a loaf, sprinkling sugar between each layer. Place on a fireproof dish, re-heat in the oven for 5 minutes, then serve immediately.

Variations

Add 6tbs/90ml sherry, white wine, cream or rosewater to the melted butter.

'Leavened Bread' was similar, but took the form of cylindrical rolls of paper-thin pastry.

LEAVENED BREAD[54]

8oz/225g plain white flour
6 egg yolks, beaten
½oz/12.5g butter, melted
4oz/100g butter
2oz/50g sugar
pinch cinnamon & ginger

Sift the flour into a bowl, and work in the yolks and ½oz/12.5g butter, with a little water if necessary, to form a firm dough.

Knead the dough until smooth, and roll out on a floured board to form a large paper-thin rectangle. Melt the remaining butter in a clean frying-pan, and use a little to brush all over the pastry.

Roll the pastry up from one edge like a scroll, cut into 3in/7.5cm lengths, flatten these slightly, and bake at 200°C/400°F/gas mark 6 for 30 minutes

Re-melt (but do not brown) the butter in the pan, add the hot rolls from the oven, toss in the butter for a few minutes, then transfer to a hot dish, sprinkle with the sugar and spices, and serve piping hot.

In the colder and wetter parts of England, where it was difficult to grow wheat, oats, barley and rye were the chief bread corns. As they lacked wheat's rich gluten content, they were much more difficult to knead and raise, being far more suitable for unleavened or lightly leavened flatbreads. These were described in Gerard's *Herbal* of 1597:[55]

> Avena Vesca, common Otes, is called Vesca, a Vescendo, [Latin *vescor* to feed on] because it is used in many countries to make sundry sorts of bread, as in Lancashire, where it is the chiefest bread corne for Jannocks, Haver cakes, Tharffe cakes, and for those which are called Oten cakes; and for the most part they call the grain Haver, whereof they likewise make drinke for want of Barley.

Thomas Muffet agreed:[56]

> Had Galen seen the Oaten Cakes of the North, the jannocks of Lancashire and the Grues of Cheshire, he would have confesed that Oats and Oatmeal are not only meal for Beasts, but also for tall, fair and strong Men and Women.

Jannock, the thick, unleaved oatcake, was made in all the counties of northern England, from the Border down to Cheshire, Derbyshire and Yorkshire. In Manchester in 1586 they weighed 1lb avoirdupois each, and just a century later the Manchester Court Leet was still concerning itself with their size and quality, one Gilbert Lowe being fined 2*s*. 6*d*. for selling 'Gannack bread not marketable.'[57] Throughout the same region, and also in Staffordshire, East Anglia and in Hampshire, Wiltshire, Somerset and Devon, the almost identical item went by the alternative title of bannock.[58]

Traditionally, the oatmeal was mixed with water in a kneading, haver-meal or oatmeal trough, or oatmeal stock, these items being frequently listed in probate inventories of the period. From here they were formed into thick cakes, perhaps eight inches in diameter, using a flat bakboard as a working surface, and a large, thin square paddle called a spittle to transfer them to the bakestone over the fire.

The required utensils included;

'ottmeal trought'	(South Cave, Yorks., 1587)
'a haver meal trough'	(South Cave, Yorks., 1588)
'An otte meal stocke'	(South Cave, Yorks., 1611)
'a kneding basyn ... a backboard'	(Richmondshire, Yorks., 1563)
'one backstone and one spetil'	(Lancashire, 1531)[59]

The earliest bakestones were smooth, thin, fireproof slabs quarried wherever suitable seams outcropped onto the surface. In 1647 Captain Adam Eyre recorded in his diary that on 1 November he 'went to James Mitchell, to Hartcliffe, to get one of them to come and hew me a backstone tomorrow, or the next day.'[60] The main source, however, was at Delph near Saddleworth on the Yorkshire–Lancashire border. From at least the fourteenth century they had been carried on packhorses to many distant markets, examples being found in the mid-sixteenth century levels of the Constable's Lodgings at Sandal castle near Wakefield. Peacham's 1606 'blue stones, such as they make Haver or oten cakes upon' were probably from Delph.[61] Others were made of iron, for example the 'two Iron bakestones' recorded at North Bierley, Yorkshire in 1656, and 'an Iron bake stone' noted at Eshton, Yorkshire in 1656.[62] These were probably about a foot (30cm) in diameter, like most later examples, but some must have been much larger. When the Earl of Thanet was modernizing Skipton Castle in December 1648, Thomas Chamberlaine provided:[63] 'To one Baxton 34lb at 3d per lb. 8*s*. 6*d*. To making it 1*s*. 6*d*.' The weight suggesting it may have measured some 2 feet by 5 feet (60 x 150cm), suitable for mounting on its own table-height stove, rather than for hanging over the fire.

TO MAKE JANNOCK

1lb/450g medium oatmeal
1tsp salt
½pt/300ml water

Put the meal in a basin, mix in the salt, make a hole in the centre, and mix in the water, adding a little more if necessary, to form a stiff dough.

Turn out onto a meal-sprinkled board, and pat or roll out to about 8in/20cm diameter.

Gently heat a bakestone or girdle until a few drops of water dropped onto it bubble away in 3–4 seconds, and slide on the jannock. Bake for about 10 minutes, turn over (using pieces of strong cardboard or thin board), and bake for a further 10 minutes on the other side, moving it regularly to ensure no scorched hot-spots develop.

Thick cakes of this kind were often finished by standing in front of the fire to ensure they cooked through. This may be replicated by placing them in an oven at 150°C/300°F/gas mark 2 for 10 minutes.

Thin haver or oat cakes were made as in previous centuries, their recipes being published in the author's *Cooking & Dining in Medieval England*.

In south-western counties a different form of hearth baking was carried out using utensils called bake-pans. In his *Garden of Health* of 1579 William Langham had instructed that food should be baked 'under a bake-pan of earth'.[64] Such pans have been excavated from Barnstaple, external handles near their bases enabling them to be used when inverted.[65] Their traditional Cornish name was simply 'baker', while in Devon it was 'wovering pan'.[66] First a 'flat ire' (Cornwall), or a 'baking iron' (Devon), a thick iron sheet some 15 inches (38cm) diameter with a handle at each side, was placed on a brandis, a fire-welded three-legged frame, standing on the hearth. A fire of sticks, brambles, furze, peats, bracken, hay or even chaff was then lit beneath it and continued for about 20 minutes before being allowed to die down. The iron was then dropped down onto the hearth. Alternatively the iron could be laid on the hearth from the start, the fire lit on top of it, and brushed cleanly to one side once it was hot. Whichever method was used, the bread, bannock or pastry was then placed on the iron, covered first by the baker or wovering pan, then by the remaining burning fuel, and left, perhaps for an hour, until completely baked.

By using such regional techniques, each developed over centuries to make the best possible use of locally available bread corns and fuels, every level of society was able to provide itself with a sufficient supply of bread. Even so, a single bad harvest or an exceptionally good one could make corn either unaffordably expensive or plentifully cheap. In 1557, for example, the scarcity of wheat had driven its price up to £2 13*s*. 8*d*. a quarter on the London markets, this falling to a mere 5*s*. after the harvest. As a result, the weight of each penny loaf rose from 11oz/300g to 56oz/1.6kg, indicating the volatility of the markets and their influence on the bread consumption of major sections of the community. Clearly there were many advantages in growing one's own corn, whether as a great lord or as a subsistence farmer.

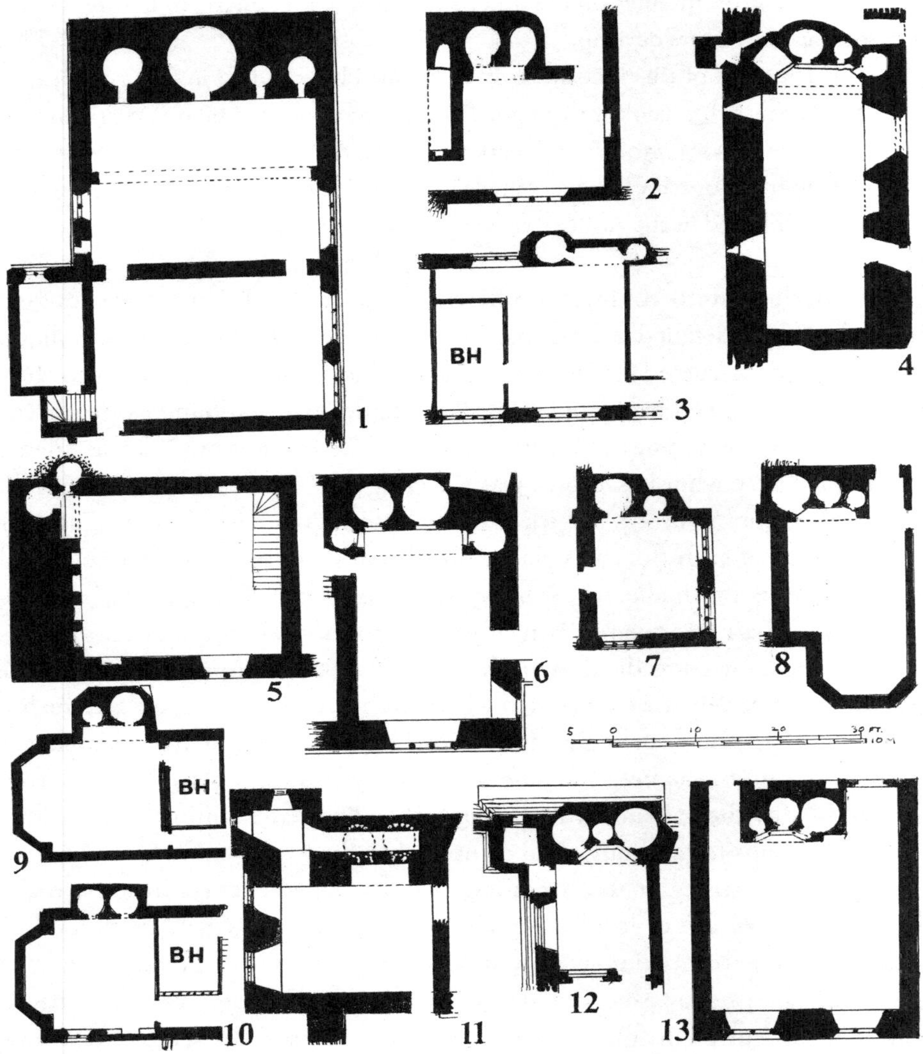

Figure 29. Pastries. As pies, pastries and tarts grew in popularity, a separate kitchen called the pastry became an essential facility in every fashionable house, its size and number of ovens varying according to its anticipated output. (1) Hampton Court, 1530, with ovens built by Gabryell Dalton; (2) Berry Pomeroy, Devon, c. 1600; (3) Slaugham Place, Sussex, pre 1579; (4) Middleham Castle, Yorkshire, 16th cent.; (5) Shaw House, Newbury, Berkshire, 1570s (beneath the kitchen); (6) Hardwick Old Hall, Derbyshire, 1588; (7) Beaufort House, Chelsea, 1595–9; (8) Burton Agnes, Yorkshire, 1601–10; (9) Holland House, Kensington, London, 1605–14; (10) Somerhill, Kent, c. 1610; (11) Slingsby Castle, Yorkshire, c. 1630; (12) the Little Castle, Bolsover, Derbyshire, c. 1613; (13) the Terrace Range, Bolsover Castle, c. 1629. (BH: the boulting-house, where flours were sifted and stored.)

CHAPTER EIGHT

The Pastry

Few domestic offices saw such a transformation in their use and produce as the pastry. Almost every large medieval kitchen had had a pastry oven or two set into its walls, sometimes with a well-lit bench or table close by on which to mix, knead and raise pies and pastries.[1] It didn't matter if these activities took place amid the heat and bustle of boiling, roasting, frying and grilling, for virtually all the early pastries used a crude hot-water crust made with nothing but flour and boiling water. Once dried off to firmness in the oven, the piecrusts were taken out, filled with their chosen contents, and replaced to bake until cooked through. At table, only their fillings were consumed, the crusts, the disposable cookware of the day, being given either to the poor or to the dogs.

From the early mid-sixteenth century new, more sophisticated and more palatable forms of pastry began to be introduced, with a much greater variety of fillings. Baked meats, pies, pastries, custards and tarts both sweet and savoury now appeared in far more intricate and interesting forms which demanded higher standards of care and craftsmanship. It was soon realized that preparation of pastry-work required its own specialized space, one which was sufficiently cool to enable good buttery shortcrusts and puff pastes to be made, an impossibility in a hot kitchen.

The pastry ovens of all the medieval monarchs had been under the direct control of their master cooks, but by the time of Henry VIII's Eltham Ordinances of 1526 there was a separate office of the Pastry staffed by a sergeant, clerk, six yeomen, their grooms, and six 'conducts' or labourers.[2] At major palaces such as Hampton Court new pastries were built on a lavish scale. There, in 1529–30, the staff were provided with offices and lodging rooms on the first and second floors, warm and dry over their three workhouses. The smallest of these was probably a storehouse and boulting house for the various flours and other ingredients to be used here, the second would be the main pastry-working room, and the third the oven-house. Gabryell Dalton built a row of four 'beehive' ovens into its western wall, the largest being over 12 feet (4m) in diameter.[3] Each had a shallow domed roof made of tiles set on edge, ideal for retaining the heat required to bake their contents. Above their mouths a huge half-pyramid-shaped

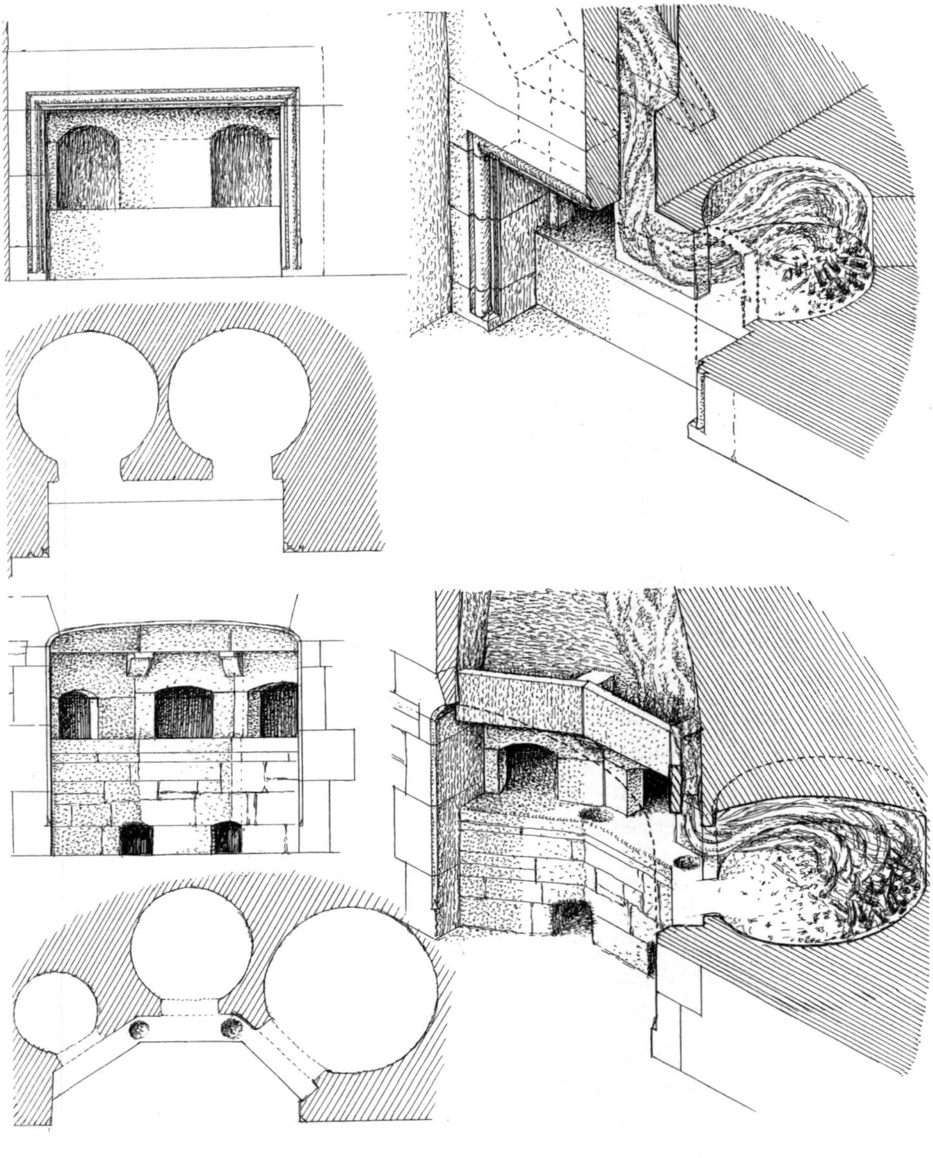

Figure 30. Pastry ovens. Late Tudor and Stuart architects took great care to produce pastry ovens which were both well-designed and efficient. That at Berry Pomeroy Castle, Devon, of c. 1600 (top) is quite basic in its construction. In contrast John Smythson's pastry oven in the Terrace Range of Bolsover Castle of c. 1629 (bottom) shows many improvements, including internal smoke-hoods, and chutes to convey embers from the doors of the ovens directly into ashpits below.

hood was constructed to carry away all the smoke and fumes as they were fired up to temperature. The whole pastry office was obviously designed by someone who really knew their profession, particularly appreciating the advantages of having separate ovens which could be used to meet the variable demands of household catering.

Some major private houses, such as Temple Newsam near Leeds, were built with pastry offices around 1513, from which time they became increasingly popular.[4] By 1542 Andrew Boorde recognized that a 'pastry-howse anexed to the kychen' was now a standard facility.[5] It is therefore unsurprising that Shakespeare should have provided Romeo's parents with a pastry in which to bake their quinces and dates in 1592.[6] Some pastries formed part of an extending kitchen wing, some a part of the cross-wing at the lower end of the hall, and others part of the new suites of cellar/basement offices being constructed after *c.* 1580. In some of the earlier pastries, such as that at Slaugham Place in Sussex, dating from before 1574, the oven-mouths were set in the sidewalls of ordinary fireplaces, so that their smoke might be drawn directly up the chimney flue.[7] In their fully developed form, however, three or four ovens were set in the angled jambs and back of a fireplace-like recess. A shelf at the mouth of each oven provided both support for the oven door, and a shaft by which the embers could be raked directly into an ash-pit below. Above, vertical stone slabs were set out on corbels to channel the smoke up the chimney rather than out into the pastry workhouse. Some of the best of these were designed by John Smythson for Bolsover and Slingsby Castles. At the latter he also introduced a narrow chamber directly over the ovens to provide an ideally warm and dry environment for the storage of perishable ingredients.

Even in quite modest houses, in rural areas and in town centres, the spread of home bakery fed an increasing demand for ovens. A single oven in the side or back wall of the kitchen fireplace was usually sufficient, but in some older houses it was more convenient to build a new fireplace and an oven back-to-back with the original fireplace. This is illustrated in some of the early Jacobean plans of central London properties, such as Ralph Treswell's survey of West Smithfield.[8]

In both large and small houses, single pies and pastries could be baked without going to the trouble and expense of heating up the oven. Instead, the embers would be raked away to expose a section of the hearthstone, the pie or pastry set down on it, probably on a plate or dish, and a cylindrical vessel called a bake-pan place on top. Once covered with glowing embers, this acted as a miniature oven. In 1579 William Langham referred to baking 'under a bake-pan of earth', showing that they were made of pottery, but it has proved impossible to identify any excavated examples with any degree of certainty. Since such pans

Figure 31. Bakeware. Since crusts made of pastry were rarely intended to be eaten, it made good sense to replace them with permanent 'crusts' of glazed earthenware in identical shapes. In this way these ceramic vessels retain the pinched rims of their contemporary pastry originals. (1) yellow-glazed earthenware, Potovens, Yorkshire, mid–late 16th cent.; (2) yellow-glazed earthenware, Sandal Castle, Yorkshire, mid–late 16th cent.; (3) yellow-glazed earthenware, Waltham Abbey, Essex, c. 1600; (4) yellow-glazed earthenware, Waltham Abbey, Essex, 16th cent; (5–7) yellow-glazed earthenware, Totnes, Devon, c. 1600; (8) yellow-glazed earthenware, Coventry, late 16th–17th cent.; (9) pasty-pan, Exeter, Devon, late 16th–early 17th cent.; (10) custard-pan, yellow glazed earthenware, London, early–mid-17th cent.; (11) stew pot, red glazed earthenware, Winchester, Hampshire, late 16th cent.; (12–13) stew pots, yellow and green-glazed earthenwares, London, early–mid-17th cent.; (14) pie dish, sheet-iron, Basing House, Hampshire, 1640s; (15) pastry-jigger, wrought iron, found in the thatch of a house near Kirby Moorside, Yorkshire, mid-17th cent?; (16) pastry-jigger-cum-spoon, cast brass, mid-17th cent?

apparently gave fiercer top heat than an oven, some writers recommended placing pieces of butter on the tops of tarts and the like, to prevent them from burning.[9]

In the West Country, the early seventeenth-century demand for ovens was met in a completely different way. By mixing coarse river gravel into their local clay, the potters on the north Devon coast produced a robust and fireproof ceramic which they used to make baking ovens. Each resembled a traditional beehive in shape, but with a flattened face to the front, from which was cut a rectangular two-handled door. Whether freestanding in the hearth, or built into its masonry, they were used just like ordinary bread ovens, except that their temperature could be checked by rubbing a stick across the dome, emitting sparks from the hot surface. These ovens proved so popular that they were shipped into Devon and Cornwall, Wales and Ireland, and across to the American colonies.[10]

Most inventories suggest that pastries were usually furnished quite simply. In 1594, that at Bedford House, Exeter, had:

> Two plancks standing on fowre Tressels made fast in the grownd. One other little short planck wth. fowre legges. A shelf made fast on thre pinnes. Five little shelves standing behind the dore one above the other. One great planck behind the dore and no tressells belonging to it. One Oven Stopper.[11]

At Chatsworth House, Derbyshire, the pastry contained only 'a longe borde, a hogshed' in 1601, the hogshead probably being used for boulting the flour, as there was no separate boulting house here.[12] Sometimes inventories list vast amounts of unrelated equipment, not because it was being used in that location, but for the simple reason that a pastry provided an ideal secure storage area when the family was absent. In 1596 the pastry at Ashby-de-la-Zouche Castle housed 123 pewter dishes, for example, while the Parliamentary survey of Hampton Court pastry in 1659 listed unrelated pots and pans, only the '8 great dishes tinned ... 4 peales, 1 raker' being appropriate to the function of the office.[13] A better impression of the required equipment comes from the items listed in the recipes of Robert May. These include a large paste board, a rolling pin and a jagging iron to shape the doughs, and the patty pans, deep dishes, wooden baking dishes and pie plates in which to bake them.[14]

Pie plates could be quite large. In 1617 the Earl of Northumberland bought eighteen made of 774 ounces of solid silver. This suggests that each one was probably around eighteen inches (45cm) in diameter, quite suitable for baking pies in such a major household.[15] Other metallic pie and pastry dishes might be made either of pewter or of tinned brass. In 1653 Sir Ralph Verney ordered his cook to be shown 'what brass baking pans are in my house and also latten pans for puddings or tarts', but unfortunately no provenanced examples appear to have survived.[16] Tinned sheet-iron baking dishes were also used, one being recovered from the Civil War demolition debris at Basing House, Hampshire.[17]

Many baking dishes and pans were made of lead-glazed earthenware, being direct descendants of the 'traps' of the medieval period.[18] Produced in a variety of forms, they were closely observed copies of contemporary piecrusts, their thumb-crimped or jagged wheel-cut rims following those traditionally made by the pastry-cooks. When cylindrical, or with slightly flaring walls, they were ideal for baking all kinds of puddings and pies, but others were specifically made as rectangular patty-pans for pasties, or long collars of beef and similar joints.[19] Such vessels were very economical, requiring neither bases nor walls of pastry, only lids. They took no time to prepare, never leaked or collapsed in the oven, could be served directly onto the table and, after a quick wash, were ready for immediate re-use.

From the second half of the sixteenth century some earthenware baking dishes were being made with close-fitting lids, so that their contents might be baked without any form of crust whatsoever. Today we would recognize them as casseroles. However, French cooks such as La Varenne defined their '*castrolles*' as kettles made in the form of a great tourte pan or as a kind of dripping pan, suggesting something quite different such as a large shallow metal boiling pot, ideal for stewing fish and similar items. This is confirmed by recipes for cooking flatfish such as plaice, flounders and dabs 'in castrolle'.[20] In England, the alternative term 'stewpot' referred both to the stewing vessel and to its contents, whether hung over the fire or baked in the oven. The advantage of the latter, soaking in a uniform, all-round gentle heat, was that it enabled semi-liquid to quite solid foods to be cooked tenderly and with little risk either of burning or evaporating most of their delicious juices. Some even had lids which fitted over their rims, so that they could be sealed down with a strip of pastry to conserve all their steam.[21]

When cooking and serving Tudor and early Stuart meals it is important to appreciate that the primary function of the pastry cases which enclosed pies and pastries, flans and tarts was to provide ovenproof vessels in which to bake their contents. If served directly onto the table, any lids were first cut away so that their contents might be spooned or cut out onto individual plates, leaving their empty cases as waste. Only those pastries which were made with the recently introduced fine butter pastry, paste-royal or puff-paste, were suitable for being sliced and served to be eaten with their contents.

A number of pastries were blind-baked to act solely as serving vessels. Their individual fillings were first baked in pies of coarse pastry before being poured into the finer cases for serving at the table. Some might take the form of small individual tarts, each shaped so as to form symmetrical patterns when set out on a dish, while others might have multiple compartments set on a single large base.[22]

Since pastries were now being made both large and small, to hold liquids or solids, to be edible or virtually inedible, to be used quickly or stored for months, to hold food while in the oven or only on the table, the simple flour and hot-water crust of the medieval period was now obsolete, except for baked custards. In its place the cooks developed a whole range of new pastries, each designed to fulfil its particular function. The following selection includes all the main varieties, and demonstrates the amazing developments in English pastry-work which took place largely from the 1580s. It commences with the coarsest and works its way through to the most complex.

1. RYE HOT-WATER CRUST FOR VERY LARGE PIES[23]

1lb/450g rye flour | *½pt/300ml boiling water*

Make a well in the flour, pour in the water, mix together with a strong wooden spatula, then knead smooth, cover, and allow to go cold. Knead again just before using.

2. RYE HOT-WATER CRUST WITH BUTTER OR LARD FOR VERY LARGE PIES[24]

Make as above, but with 3oz/75g lard or butter boiled in ½pt/300ml water.

3. RYE COLD-BUTTER CRUST FOR VENISON PASTIES[25]

1lb/450g rye flour
4oz/100g butter
1tsp salt; ½tsp ground black pepper
about 5–6tbs cold water

Rub the butter into the flour, salt and pepper, work in sufficient cold water to form a stiff dough, and knead until smooth.

4. RYE COLD-BUTTER CRUST WITH EGG FOR VENISON PASTY[26]

1lb/450g rye flour
5½oz/140g butter
1 egg, beaten
about 2–3tbs cold water

Make as in 3 above, adding the egg with the water.

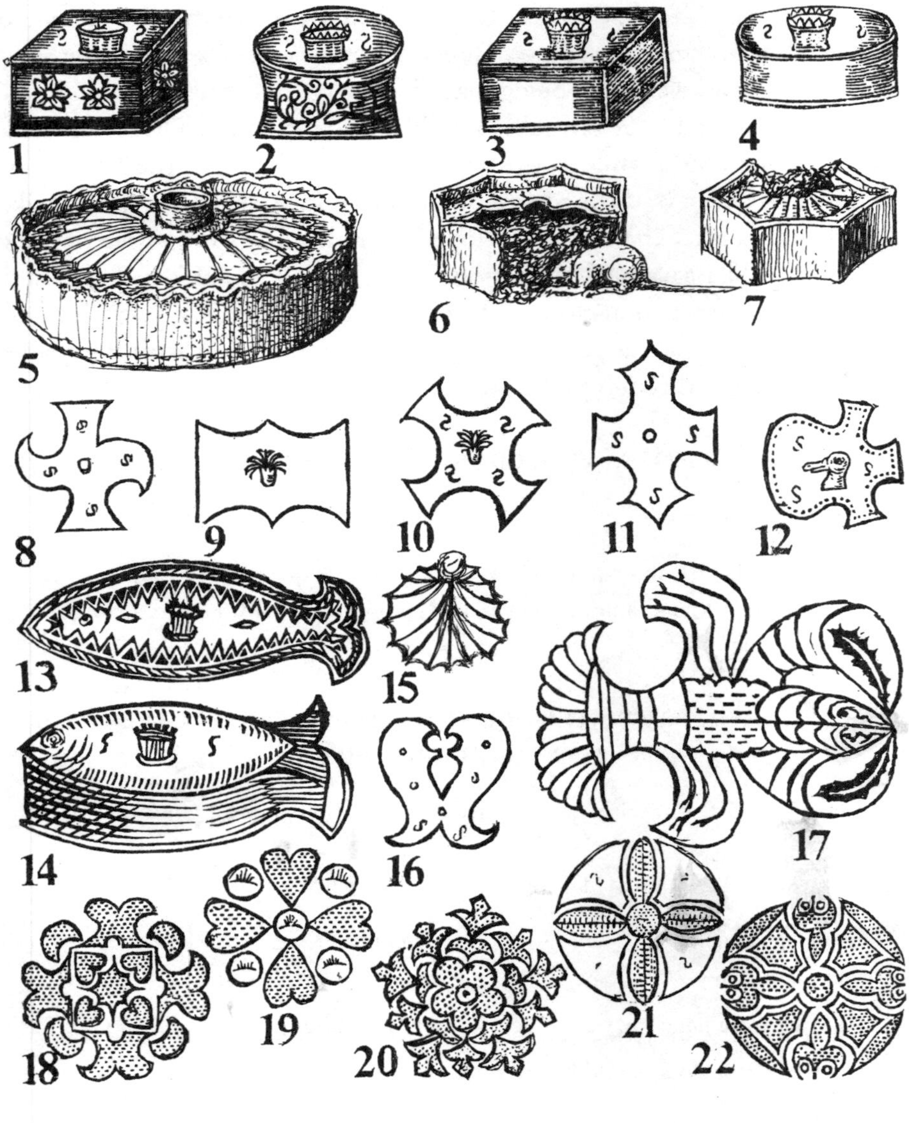

Figure 32. Pie designs. Wenceslaus Hollar depicted a number of pies in his 1665 engravings of Aesop's Fables *(5–7), the others shown here coming from Robert May's* Accomplisht Cook *of 1660. (1 & 2) red deer; (3 & 4) veal; (8) neat's tongue; (9) chaldron; (10) lumber; (11) chicken; (12) land or sea-fowl; (13) carp; (14) salmon; (15–16) oyster; (17) lobster; (18–22) minced pies.*

5. WHOLEWHEAT HOT-WATER CRUST FOR LARGE BIRDS, VEAL AND LAMB[27]

1lb/450g wholewheat flour
3oz/75g butter
½pt/300ml boiling water or stock

Make a well in the flour, pour in the butter melted in the water, mix together, knead until smooth.

6. WHOLEWHEAT COLD-WATER CRUST FOR VENISON PASTIES[28]

1lb/450g wholewheat flour
about 8fl.oz/240ml cold water

Make a well in the flour, pour in the cold water, mix in, then knead until smooth.

7. HOT-WATER CRUST FOR CUSTARDS[29]

1lb/450g plain flour
½pt/300ml boiling water

Make as 1 above.

8. HOT-WATER CRUST WITH BUTTER FOR PIES OF SMALLER BIRDS[30]

1lb/450g plain flour
3oz/75g butter
9fl.oz/250ml boiling water

Make as 1 above, boiling the butter in the water.

9. HOT-WATER CRUST WITH BUTTER AND EGGS FOR VENISON PASTY AND PIES[31]

1lb/450g plain flour
2 egg yolks
3oz/75g butter
9fl.oz/250ml boiling water

Drop the yolks into the flour, mix, then rub in until completely absorbed. Make a well in the centre, pour in the butter boiled with the water, mix and knead until smooth.

Figure 33. Pie, tart & custard designs. As illustrated by Robert May in 1660, these pastries were for: (1–5) florentines (shallow pies); (6) strawberry tart; (7) gooseberry tart; (8) stoned fruit tart; (9) plum tart; (10–12) tarts royal; (13–14) laid tarts; (15–19) cut-laid tarts; (20–25) custards.

10. HOT-WATER CRUST WITH EGGS FOR TOWERS AND THE LIKE[32]

12oz/350g flour
2 egg yolks and 1 white
7fl.oz/210ml boiling milk

Make as in 9 above.

11. HOT-WATER CRUST WITH ALE, SUGAR AND SAFFRON FOR PIES AND OTHER THINGS[33]

1lb/450g plain flour
1 egg, beaten
2tbs caster sugar
pinch of salt
pinch of saffron
3oz/75g butter
8fl.oz/240ml brown ale

Make as in 9 above.

12. HOT-WATER CRUST FOR LENT[34]

1lb/450g plain flour
9fl.oz/250ml boiling almond milk
3tbs olive oil
pinch of saffron

Make as in 9 above.

13. COLD-BUTTER CRUST FOR TARTS, PIES AND OTHER THINGS[35]

1lb/450g plain flour
5oz/150g butter
1 egg, beaten
about 5–6tbs cold water

Rub the butter into the flour, then work in the egg and water to form a stiff paste, then knead lightly.

14. PASTE ROYAL[36]

1lb/450g plain flour
2oz/50g sugar
large pinch of saffron
½tsp ground cinnamon
3oz/75g butter
¼pt/150ml almond milk
1tbs rosewater
1tbs beaten egg

Mix the dry ingredients, rub in the butter, mix the liquids and egg, then work sufficient into the flour, sugar and spice to form a pastry, *or*, for a shorter paste royal, take:

1lb/450g plain flour
2oz/50g sugar
8oz/225g butter
¼pt/150ml white wine
1tbs rosewater
1 large egg, beaten

Make as above.

15. COLD-WATER CRUST FOR CHEESECAKES[37]

9oz/250g flour
3oz/75g butter
1 egg yolk
4tbs cold water

Make as in 13 above.

16. EARLY PUFF PASTE FOR TARTS, FRENCH PUFFINS AND SIMILAR[38]

1lb/450g plain flour
4oz/100g butter
8 egg whites, or the yolks and 2tbs icing sugar

Sift the flour into a bowl (with the sugar, if chosen), make a well in the centre, and work in the eggs, with either a little cold water or flour, to produce a firm dough. Form into a long roll, cut into twelve pieces, roll each into a ball, squash flat, and roll out on a floured board until as thinly as possible. Cut each piece to the same size using a plate or pan lid as a template. Warm and beat the butter until soft and semi-liquid, but not oiled. Brush this over each sheet in turn, piling them six high in two stacks, one to form the bottom of a covered tart, the other to form the lid. Alternatively, stack twelve high and cut as small round cakes to bake as puffins, dusting their tops with sugar before serving.

17. PUFF PASTE FOR PASTIES, CUT AND CUT-LAID TARTS[39]

1lb/450g flour
1 egg
5fl.oz cold water
12oz/325g butter

Cool all the ingredients for 30 minutes, then mix the egg and water into the flour and lightly knead to form a medium-consistency dough. Roll out on a cool floured board to form a rectangle twice as long as broad. Lightly knead the butter until of the same consistency as the pastry and divide into five pieces. Use one piece to dot one end-half of the pastry with small pieces, dust with flour, fold the plain end of the pastry over, to form a square, turn 90°, and roll out again to the original size. Repeat this process until all the butter has been used up, and the pastry is of the required thickness, then leave in a cool place for at least 30 minutes to rest. Cut to shape and use according to the particular recipe. Always bake at 220°C/425°F/gas mark 7, for at lower temperatures the butter will melt out before the pastry has set.

Given this extensive range of pastries, the cooks could now incorporate all manner of ingredients into pastry goods to serve the needs of their households. A typical week's output at the Earl of Cumberland's pastry in August 1628 included eighteen (venison?) pasties, four red deer pies, eleven umble pies, a trout pie, four codling apple pies, one gooseberry and two cherry tarts, in addition to an elaborate laid tart.[40] Each of the different types of pastry appearing in this list will now be discussed, described, and provided with period recipes. In almost every example, however, it has been necessary to greatly reduce the quantities of the ingredients to suit the size of modern domestic ovens, only professional bakers now having the facilities required to work on the massive scale originally specified.

PASTIES AND PIES

Today everyone is familiar with pasties, tens of thousands being sold every day from fast-food outlets throughout the country. Their combination of rich pastry and substantial hot fillings, all in a compact hand-held form, make them ideal for eating in the street. In considering the pasties of sixteenth- and seventeenth-century England, it is important to realize that they were of an entirely different scale and quality, and often served the additional functions of preserving and transporting large and expensive joints of meat.

Of all pastries, the most prestigious of all was the venison pasty. As Andrew Boorde boasted:

> I have gone rownde aboute Crystendome, and overthwarte Crystendom, & a thousande or two and more myles out of Crystendom, yet there is not so moche pleasure for harte & hynde, bucke and doe, and for roo bucke and doo, as in Englande ... I pray God to sende me parte of the fleshe to eate ... I am sure it is a lordes disshe, and I am sure it is good for an Englysshe man, for it doth anymate hym to be as he is, whiche is, stronge and hardy, but I do advertyse every man, for all my wordes, not to kyll, and so to eate of it, excepte it be lefully, for it is a meate for great men. And great men do not set so much by the meate, as they do by the pastyme of kylling of it.[41]

Venison pasties were made at most times of the year except Lent, but were especially associated with feasts at weddings and Christmas. The Petres at

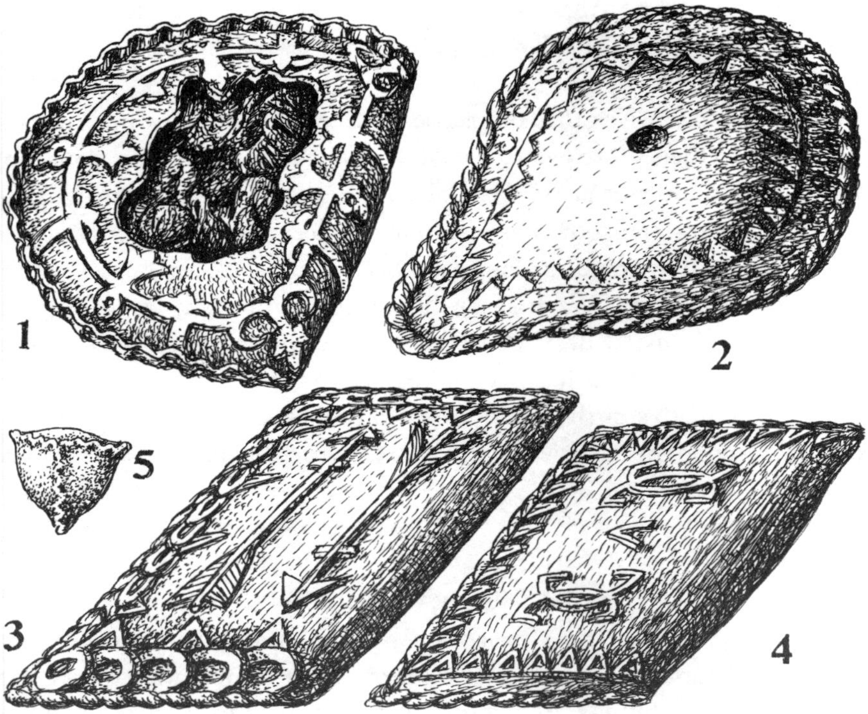

Figure 34. Pasties. Most large pasties were used to bake single joints of meat, the crust retaining all their juices and flavours. One in Hollar's Aesop's Fables *of 1665 (1) shows how the crust was broken open to reveal its contents. Robert May's pasties were intended to contain a leg of wild boar (2), red deer (3) and any kind of head or ox-cheek (4). Thomas Dawson's pasties of 1596 (5) contained individual portions of a rich spiced trout paste.*

Ingatestone in Essex ate six over the Christmas period of 1551–2, for example, and the Willoughbys at Wollaton sixteen on Christmas Day alone in 1547.[42] They were massive constructions, those for sides or half-haunches of red deer each requiring some 24lb of rye flour made up into pastry, and fallow deer 15lb.[43]

There are many recipes for venison pasty, some first parboiling the meat and soaking it in vinegar, some beating it with a rolling pin, some larding it, some slashing it and others leaving it intact before coating it in spices.[44] Within its inch-thick pastry it was lined above and below with either butter or suet, sealed down and decorated, placed on sheets of 'cap'-paper, and slid into the oven on an appropriately long pasty-peel.[45] Red deer pasties were then baked for about 8 or 9 hours, or overnight, and those of fallow deer about 4½ hours. A hole cut through their highest point served both to release their steam while cooking, and also to allow either vinegar, claret or melted butter to be poured in afterwards. If not to be served hot, this hole could be sealed with a little raw pastry, enabling the contents to remain in good condition for weeks if stored in a cool place. At Wollaton Hall the kitchen accounts for 1587 show that meat pasties might be at least a month old before being served.[46]

VENISON PASTY[47]

1½ batches of pastries 3, 4, 5, 6, 9 or 17 (pp. 148–9)

1½lb/675g venison joint	*½tsp salt*
2oz/50g fat bacon	*pinch ground cloves*
¼tsp each ground pepper & nutmeg	*2 bay leaves*
2oz/50g butter	*1 egg, beaten*

Cut the bacon into strips and insert (i.e. lard) into the upper side of the joint, then stab the meat a few times with a pointed knife, and rub in a mixture of all the spices and salt. Roll the pastry out to form a rectangle about 18 x 12in/45 x 30cm. Dot one half with half the butter and the bay leaves, place the joint on top and smear with the remaining butter. Dampen the edges of the pastry, fold the vacant end over the top, seal down the edges, trim off the surplus pastry, and crimp the cut edges like a Cornish pasty. Use the trimmings to add decorations and a border around a hole cut in the centre of the top. Brush with the beaten egg, and bake at 150°C/300°F/gas mark 2 for 2 hours until tender.

This recipe tops up the pasty with clarified butter for keeping, but advises that claret should be poured in with a little butter if it is to be eaten while still hot.

Since the original pasties were so large, they had to be served on specially made pasty plates. The favourite part was the corner, where the fattest of the venison was usually to be found. In 1625 Massinger's cook Furnace, had announced that 'there came last night, from the forest of Sherwood, The fattest stag I ever cooked ... A stag, sir; part of it prepared for dinner, And baked in puff-paste.' On hearing this Master Greedy, a hungry Justice of the Peace, responded with the demand, 'Do you heare, Master Cook. Send but a corner of that immortal pasty, And I, in thankfulness, will, by your boy, Send you a brace of threepences ... Think of Pie-corner, Furnace!'[48]

Since venison was such a high-status meat, those who could not obtain it developed various ways of simulating it from the inferior beef or mutton. This could be done either by parboiling in beer, vinegar and turnsole, a red vegetable dye, or by covering it with fresh blood, before putting it into its pasty.[49] Avoiding this deception, something of the flavour of venison could be achieved by baking the inner organs of the deer known as umbles or humbles. When either coarsely chopped with sweet herbs or cut as small as dice with bacon, nutmeg and butter, they made a satisfying, if not prestigious pasty or pie.[50]

Both beef, especially ox-cheek, and mutton were baked as pasties, but lamb and pork were also excellent when cooked in this way.[51]

LAMB PASTY[52]

1 batch of pastry no. 13 (p. 151)	*1oz/25g suet*
1lb/450g lean lamb	*¼tsp each ground nutmeg & clove*
1tsp salt	*1tbs white wine*
¼tsp pepper	*1tbs white wine vinegar*
1tsp thyme	*1tbs sugar*
½tsp ground mace	*1 egg yolk, beaten*

Trim the fat and sinew from the lamb and season with a mixture of the salt, pepper, thyme and mace. Roll the pastry into a rectangle about 16 x 12in/40 x 30cm spread the suet over one half, leaving a broad border all around and arrange the lamb in a level layer on top. Dampen the edges of the pastry, fold the vacant end of the pastry over the lamb, seal the edges, trim off the surplus, and crimp the edges as for a Cornish pasty. Transfer to a greased baking sheet, use the pastry trimmings to make a decorative border around the crimped edges and a central hole. Bake at 200°C/400°F/gas mark 6 for 20 minutes, then reduce to 180°C/350°F/gas mark 4 for a further 20 minutes. Beat together the remaining ingredients, pour into the pasty, shake the liquid in, then serve hot.

PORK PASTY AS A BOAR'S HEAD[53]

2½ batches of pastry no. 13 (p. 151)	
2½lb/1.1kg lean pork	*1tsp ground black pepper*
2½lb/1.1kg fat bacon	*1tbs salt*
4tbs chopped sage	*2 eggs, beaten*
2tsp ground ginger	*1oz/25g butter*
2tbs white wine vinegar	*3–4 bay leaves*

Finely mince the pork and bacon, knead with the herbs, spices, vinegar and eggs to form a stiff dough, and model into the shape of a boar's head topped with the bay leaves and butter. Roll about a quarter of the pastry into a pear shape, place on a baking sheet, and place the 'head' on top of it. Roll the remaining pastry into a very large pear shape, place over the 'head', and dampen and seal the joints all round to form a completely enclosed pasty. Trim off the surplus pastry, and use to model the snout, tusks, eyes and ears. Bake at 150°C/300°F/gas mark 2 for about 2½ hours, then leave to go cold. When served with an apple in its mouth, it would be carved like a real boar's head, slicing vertically from the neck, working towards the snout.

TO BAKE [A LEG OF PORK AS] WILD BOAR[54]

2 batches of pastry nos. 5, 6 or 13 (pp. 149 or 151)

1 leg of pork, about 4½lb/2kg	*6 cloves, ground*
3oz/75g fat bacon	*1tsp salt*
½tsp each ground nutmeg, ginger and black pepper	*6 bay leaves*
	1oz/25g each lard & butter

Cut the bacon into strips, roll in the mixed ground spices and salt, and insert into cuts made in the flesh of the leg. Roll the pastry into two pear-shaped pieces and place the leg on top of one. Smear the top of the meat with the butter and lard and then scatter the bay leaves. Dampen the edges of the bottom pastry, put the other half over the top of the joint, trim away any surplus, then crimp the edges as for a Cornish pasty. Use the trimmings to form the applied decoration (as you did with the previous recipe), and cut a round hole at the top. Place on a baking sheet and bake at 180°C/350°F/gas mark 4 for about 3 hours, until tender when tested with a skewer inserted through the top hole.

Fish was rarely baked in pasties, the main exceptions being salmon – with its crust modelled to represent the whole fish – and trout in individual pasties.[55]

TROUT PASTIES[56]

half a batch of pastry no. 13 (p. 151)

4 trout fillets	*½tsp ground cinnamon*
5 dates, chopped	*1tbs sugar*
¼tsp ground ginger	*4oz/100g butter*

Cover the fillets with boiling water and poach for 10–15 minutes until tender. Drain, remove any bones that may remain, then beat with the remaining ingredients to form a smooth paste. Roll out the pastry, cut into eight large triangles, place a ball of the paste in the centre of each one, moisten the edges, bring the points together over the paste, then pinch the joints to form triangular pasties. Prick each one around the top, and bake at 180°C/350°F/gas mark 4 for about 20–25 minutes. They may be brushed with a little butter followed by a sprinkling of caster sugar and cinnamon just before serving.

Moving on from pasties to pies, these too were often of great size and quality, the largest having foot-high, inch-thick walls of rye pastry. By the first half of the seventeenth century they were being made not only in standard round or square forms, but also to much more complicated shapes, each designed to inform the cook, the servants and the diners of their respective contents.[57] The trouble and expense of making such pies could be very great. In February 1605 a lamprey pie was baked at Berkeley Castle for despatch to Lord Berkeley at his house in Coventry. Its four lampreys cost 6*s.*, its spices 1*s.* 6*d.*, onions 6*d.*, butter 1*s.* and some 18lb of wheatmeal flour 1*s.* 6*d.*, the total, inclusive of other expenses, coming to 11*s.* 10*d.* [59p], about £100 in modern currency.[58]

All manner of meat, fish, fruit, vegetables and dairy produce were baked in pies, having either raised or slab-built walls. Contemporary illustrations show that the holes cut in the centres of their lids were surrounded with chimney-like pastry 'funnels'. These retained the internal juices and allowed the steam to escape during baking, as well as acting as convenient handles for raising the lids when serving their contents at table. Just as importantly, they allowed 'lears' or liaisons to be poured in as they emerged from the oven. This practice, virtually unknown today, allowed raw batters of wine, vinegar, spices, eggs and other ingredients to be shaken into the pie juices and gently cooked in their remaining heat to create smooth and flavoursome integral sauces. The following recipes are typical.

FRENCH LAMB STEAK PIE[59]

1 batch of pastry no. 5, 6, or 13 (pp. 149, 151)
1lb/450g lamb steaks, the fat, skin and gristle cut away
8oz/225g minced lamb
1oz/25g butter
2tbs cider vinegar
½tsp each thyme, sage and either pennyroyal or mint
1 egg yolk
sage or bay leaves
2oz/50g fresh white breadcrumbs
2oz/50g raisins
1oz/25g suet
juice of an orange or lemon

Raise two-thirds of the pastry, or use to line a loose-bottomed cake tin, to produce a pie some 7in/18cm in diameter and 3in/7cm high. Layer the steaks in the bottom, with a little pepper and salt, dot with the butter, and sprinkle with the cider vinegar.

Thoroughly mix and knead the mince, herbs, yolk, crumbs, raisins and suet to form a firm paste, divide into twelve, roll each piece in a little flour to make balls, and pack these on top of the steaks. Use the remaining pastry to make a lid, close the top of the pie, cut a hole in the centre, surround with a tall 'funnel', and bake at 150°C/300°F/gas mark 2 for 2 hours. Remove from the oven, cut out the lid, stick each ball with a fried sage leaf or a bay leaf, pour in the orange or lemon juice, and serve immediately.

Alternative filling[60]

Use 2lb/900g of lamb steaks, season them with salt, pepper, nutmeg and cinnamon, layer with raisins and sliced prunes, and top with orange slices, dates, whole mace and 2oz/50g butter. When baked, pour in a hot lear of 1oz/25g butter and 1tbs sugar melted in 3tbs white wine, and serve immediately.

TO BAKE A HEN WITH BACON[61]

1 batch of pastry no. 13 (p. 151)
1tsp salt
½tsp mace, ground
2tsp thyme leaves
a few barberries
1 egg, beaten
1¾lb/800g chicken off the bone
8 rashers bacon
2tsp sage, chopped
2tsp ground pepper
1oz/25g butter
4tbs claret
1 egg yolk

Raise two-thirds of the pastry, or use to line a loose-bottomed cake tin to produce a pie some 7in/18cm diameter and 3in/7cm high. Beat the salt, mace, thyme and barberries into the egg, and mix in the chicken pieces. Separate the rashers. Cut each in half, and dust with the sage and pepper. Arrange the chicken and bacon in layers in the pie, topping off with the bacon and butter. Use the remaining pastry to make a lid, sealing it in place, surrounding a hole in the centre with a 'funnel' of pastry, and bake at 150°C /300°F/gas mark 2 for 1½ hours, pouring in the claret after the first 45 minutes. When cooked, cut the lid off, ladle the pie juices onto the yolk, beat together, pour back into the pie with a little more butter, and shake together just before serving hot.

A CHICKEN PIE[62]

1 batch of pastry no. 13 (p. 151)
3oz/75g currants
3oz/75g raisins
6 prunes, sliced
2tbs sugar
2 blades mace, broken up
½tsp ground cinnamon
1½lb/675g chicken off the bone
1½oz/35g butter
1 egg, beaten
1tbs white wine
1 tbs rosewater
1tbs white wine vinegar
large pinch cinnamon

Raise two-thirds of the pastry, or use to line a loose-bottomed cake tin to produce a pie some 7in/18cm diameter and 3in/7cm high. Mix the dried fruit, mace, ½tsp cinnamon and half the sugar, put a little of this mixture into the pie, then layer it with the chicken, finishing off with the fruit mixture, and the butter in pieces. Bake at 150°C/300°F/gas mark 2 for 1½–1¾ hours until the meat is tender. Beat the remaining ingredients together, cut the lid out of the pie, pour them in, and shake or agitate until incorporated with the pie juices, then serve hot.

NEAT'S TONGUE PIE[63]

1 batch of pastry no. 13 (p. 151)
1 2½–3lb/1–1.4kg ox tongue
2tsp salt
1tsp ground black pepper
1tsp ground cinnamon
1tsp ground ginger
1tsp broken blade mace
2oz/50g dates, chopped
1 small onion, minced
4oz/100g currants
2oz/50g butter
2oz/50g sugar
2tbs cider vinegar or verjuice

Cover the tongue with water, bring to the boil, skim, simmer 2 hours, plunge into cold water, peel off the skin, slice thinly, and cut into diamond shapes. Mix these with the remaining ingredients.

Raise two-thirds of the pastry, or use to line a loose-bottomed cake tin to produce a pie some 7in/18cm diameter and 3in/7cm high. Fill with the tongue mixture, use the remaining pastry to form a lid, sealing this in place and using the trimmings to provide both decoration and a 'funnel' around the central hole. Bake at 180°C/350°F/gas mark 4 for about 2 hours.

PIE OF BALD MEATS [GREENS] FOR FISH DAYS[64]

1 batch of pastry no. 13 (p. 151)
8oz/225g spinach, lettuce, cabbage and beet tops
1 hard-boiled egg yolk
2oz/50g raisins, chopped
1oz/25g grated hard cheese
2oz/50g fresh white breadcrumbs
½tsp salt
½tsp ground cinnamon
¼tsp ground ginger
1tbs sugar
3 raw egg yolk
1oz/25g melted butter

Line a 2pt/1l baking dish with half the pastry, covering the brim. Remove the coarser parts of the greens and shred the remainder into long, thin strips. Thoroughly mix with the mashed hard yolk and the other ingredients, pack into the dish, cover with the remaining pastry, cut a hole in the centre, and decorate the top with the trimmings cut into ornamental designs. Bake at 150°C /300°F/gas mark 2 for 45–50 minutes, brushing the top with a little butter and sprinkling on a little fine sugar just before serving hot.

FRIDAY PIES[65]

Follow the recipe above, filling it with:

6oz/150g beet or other green leaves, finely chopped
12oz/325g apples, peeled, cored and finely chopped
4oz/100g raisins
½tsp ground ginger
½tsp salt
large pinch black pepper
1oz/25g melted butter
and finally sprinkling in:
1tbs sugar
juice of 1 orange

SALMON PIE[66]

1½ batches pastry no. 7 (p. 149)
1½lb/675g salmon
1tsp salt
½tsp mixed ground pepper & nutmeg
3oz/75g butter
8 cloves
1 egg, beaten

Raise three-quarters of the pastry on a baking sheet, making it in the shape of a fish about 10–12in/26–30cm long, with vertical walls. Trim the salmon to fit (having removed the bones and skin), season with the spices, and lay on half the butter and cloves in the pie. Top with the remaining butter. Use the remaining pastry to form a lid, and the trimmings to provide it with tail-fins, an eye, and a funnel around a central hole. Brush with the beaten egg and bake at 150°C/300°F/gas mark 2 for 1 hour 45 minutes, until the fish is tender, then remove from the oven and serve either hot or cold.

Both fresh and dried fruits were essential for pie-making, as the Young Shepherd in Shakespeare's *The Winter's Tale* discovered when his sister sent him off to the shops. 'Let me see: what am I to buy for our sheepshearing feast? Three pound of sugar, five pound of currants, rice ... I must have saffron to colour the warden pies: mace: dates ... nutmegs, seven: a race or two of ginger, but that I may beg: four pound of prunes, and as many raisins o'th' sun.'[67]

WARDEN PIES

Wardens were hard cooking pears, their great advantage being that they kept well, avoiding the uncertain and rapid transit from unripe to ripe and then rotten often experienced with softer varieties. They were a popular Christmas dish, the Petres enjoying eight warden pies on Christmas Day 1551, while Elizabeth I frequently received them as New Year presents from her Sergeant of the Pastry.[68]

A WARDEN OR PEAR PIE[69]

1 batch of pastry no. 13 (p. 151)
1½lb/675g hard pears, peeled and cored
1 clove for each pear
½tsp ground ginger
½tsp ground cinnamon
3tbs sugar

Parboil the pears in water for 10–15 minutes or until just tender when tested with a skewer. Raise the pastry or line a loose-bottomed cake tin to produce a pie some 7in/18cm diameter and 3in/7cm high. Add the pears, each with a clove stuck in the bud end, and sprinkle with the mixed spices and sugar. Cover with a pastry lid, sealing the edges and cutting a hole in the centre, then bake at 150°C/300°F/gas mark 2 for 40–50minutes. Alternatively, ripe pears may be cored, sliced, and baked in the same way, but without parboiling.

TAFFETA TART [A PIPPIN PIE][70]

1 batch of pastry no. 13 (p. 151)
2lb/900g pippins
3oz/75g sugar
1tsp fennel seed
grated zest of 1 lemon
1tbs rosewater
½oz/12g butter

Roll out half the pastry and use it to line a 2pt/1l baking dish, covering the rim. Peel, core and slice the apples, and pack into the dish with a sprinkling of the fennel seed, zest and 2oz/50g sugar between each layer. Use the remaining pastry to form a lid, using the trimmings to decorate the rim and provide a 'funnel' to the central hole. Bake at 200°C/400°F/gas mark 6 for 30–35 min. Remove from the oven, brush with the rosewater, butter and half the remaining sugar melted together, sprinkle on the remaining sugar, return to the oven for a few minutes to cook the glaze, then serve either hot or cold.

MINCE OR SHRED PIES

The association of pies of minced meats with Christmas appears to have developed in the mid-sixteenth century. In 1573, Thomas Tusser confirmed that 'Beef, mutton, and Pork, shred pies of the best' already formed an essential part of 'Christmas Husbandly Fare'.[71] By the time of Robert Herrick, writing in the early seventeenth century, they appear to have become the favourite target of food thieves who used long flesh-hooks to extract them through the bars of locked larders:

Come guard the Christmas pie
That the Thief, though ne'er so sly
With his flesh hooks don't come nigh
    To catch it
From him who all alone sits there
Having his eyes still in his ear,
And a deal of nightly fear
    To watch it.[72]

Around 1600 one of the best Christmas pies was stolen from the larder of 'Old Hobson, the merry Londoner'. Believing that the culprit was one of his servants, he called them all into his hall for a seasonal celebration, plying them with drink until all were drunk. Having them seated around a fully laden table, he asked why 'he that stole the pye is not yet sat?', to which one replied 'Yes, that I doe!', so confirming his guilt.[73]

By 1651 Puritan influence had identified shred pies as symbols of Popery, and so tried to suppress their use. However,

No matter for Plumb-porridge, or Shrid-pies
Methought they had this Motto 'Though they stir
And preach us down, sub pondex cressit virtus.'
    [under consideration, they grow in valour] [74]

This was certainly the case at Haddon Hall, Derbyshire, where they purchased 'one quarter of beyffle for to make pyes agenst Crysmas 6*d*.' on 22 December 1650.[75]

[MINCE OR SHRED] PIES OF MUTTON OR BEEF[76]

1 batch of pastry no. 13 (p. 151)
1½lb/675g lean mutton or beef, finely chopped or minced

2oz/50g raisins	*½tsp ground cloves*
2oz/50g currants	*1tsp ground mace*
2oz/50g prunes, chopped	*½tsp ground black pepper*
4oz/100g suet	*pinch of saffron*

Raise two-thirds of the pastry, or use to line a loose-bottomed cake tin to produce a pie some 7in/18cm diameter and 3in/7cm high. Thoroughly mix all the ingredients, pack into the pie, and use the remaining pastry to make a lid, the trimmings forming any decoration and a 'funnel' around the central hole. Bake at 180°C/350°F/gas mark 4 for some 2 hours. Serve either hot or cold.

APHRODISIAC PIES

Elizabethan dieticians such as Henry Buttes listed all those foodstuffs which provoked Venus, including chestnuts, artichokes, oysters and eggs. Others considered sparrows, sweet or Spanish potatoes and candied sea-holly roots, called eringoes, to be even more effective.[77] For a really good party all of these could be combined with hot and urine-provoking spices to fill large pies. Sir Theodore Mayerne, physician to both Henri IV of France and the first three Stuart monarchs, recommended this typical recipe:[78]

'A CITY OF LONDON PIE'

Take eight marrow bones, eighteen sparrows, one pound of potatoes, a quarter of a pound of eringoes, two ounces of lettuce stalks, forty chestnuts, half a pound of dates, a peck of oysters, a quarter of a pound of preserved citron, three artichokes, twelve eggs, two sliced lemons, a handful of picked barberries, a quarter of an ounce of whole pepper, half an ounce of nutmeg, half an ounce of whole cinnamon, a quarter of an ounce of whole cloves, half an ounce of mace, a quarter of a pound of currants; Liquor when it is baked with white wine, butter and sugar.'

Thomas Dawson's 'tarte that is a courage to a man or woman' of 1596/7 was based on potatoes, quinces, dates, egg-yolks and the brains of cock sparrows to achieve similar results.[79] Such pies were soon being made as bride pies for wedding feasts. That published by Robert May took the form of a huge, open-topped blind-baked tart, each of its six concentric compartments having a separate pie-baked filling poured into it just before serving. The outer circle was of egg-mincemeat tarts, then came compartments of artichokes, stuffed larks, prawns and cockles, oysters, and a rich mixture which included cocks' testicles and combs, lambs' testicles, more oysters and other prized offal. The central compartment was filled with live birds or snakes beneath an upper crust 'which will seem strange to the beholders, which cut up the pie at the Table. This is only for a Wedding to pass away the time.'[80] Today the scale of such pies and the problems associated with their ingredients make them almost impossible to recreate accurately. However, the simpler sweet potato pie is easy to prepare. In John Fletcher's Jacobean play *Love's Cure*, Her Ladyship is asked if she would like 'a potato pie? 'Tis a good stirring dish for an old lady after a long lent.'[81]

[SWEET] POTATO PIE[82]

1 batch of fine butter pastry no. 13 (p. 151)
1½lb/625g sweet potatoes
1½oz/37g butter (for bone marrow)
3oz/75g raisins
5 dates
1oz/25g candied orange peel
½tsp mixed ground nutmeg, cinnamon and ginger
1oz/25g candied citron
3tbs sugar
2tsp white wine vinegar
2tbs dry sherry
1 egg yolk

Boil the potatoes for 20 minutes until tender, cool in cold water, and rub off the thick skins before cutting into pieces less than 1in/2.5cm square. Mix with the dried fruit, peel, spices and 2 tablespoonfuls of the sugar.

Use two-thirds of the pastry to line a loose-bottomed 8in/40cm diameter sandwich tin. Pack with the potato mixture, top with 1½oz/37g butter, add the lid made from the remaining pastry, dampening and pinching the brim, cut a hole in the centre, and surround with a 1½in/4cm high tube or funnel made from the remaining pastry.

Bake at 200°C/400°F/gas mark 6 for 20 minutes, then reduce to 180°C/350°F/gas mark 4 for a further 40 minutes. Remove from the oven, pour in the lear made with the remaining sugar, the vinegar, sherry and egg beaten with the remaining butter, melted. Shake the pie from side to side, sprinkle the top with icing sugar, return to the oven for 5 minutes, then remove and serve either hot or cold.

Figure 35. Pastry for a grand salad. Using rye pastry, William Rabisha made twelve stepped supports, four pastry rings and a castle which were then assembled as shown here. Each ring was then dressed with a different salad of young lettuce, spinach, water-cress and flower-buds. Separate segments of contrasting colours of almonds, barberries, par-boiled currants and raisins, and pickled samphire, olives, capers, broom-buds and cucumbers (gherkins) were then arranged around the base. A tree of wax, of green pastry, or of pastry brushed with egg-yolk and sprinkled with fresh green herbs, and stuck with flowers, was then set in the castle. Finally the two cruets of oil and two of vinegar held by the figures on the balconies were opened at the table, so that the diners could see their contents run down into the salads below. The smaller tower (top right) was provided with a base and served as a pie-case so that, after being baked, it could be filled with cold preserved fruits or other foods.

PASTRY CASTLES

The sixteenth and seventeenth centuries saw a revival of chivalric pageantry in fashionable material culture. Imitation castles were theatrically attacked and defended at the courtly celebrations of all the Tudors and early Stuarts, while in the reign of James I even the most luxurious of houses and lodges began to be built in castle form, bristling with turrets and battlements.[83] In fourteenth-century England cooks had baked pastry castelettes, each tower containing a different filling, a form which could now be up-dated and improved to create the most exciting and impressive dishes for great feasts.[84] Some time before 1607 Anthony Brewer had seen:

Ramparts of pastry crust, and forts of pies
Entrench'd with dishes full of pastry stuffe
Hath Gustus made and planted ordinance,
Strange ordinance, cannons of hollow canes,
Whose powder's rape seed, charged with turnip shot.[85]

Furnace, the cook in Massinger's *A New Way to Pay Old Debts* of 1625, set near Nottingham, '[Could] raise fortifications in the pastry / Such as might serve for models in the Low Countries / Which, if they had been practiced at Breda, / Spinola might have thrown his cap at it, and ne'er took it / With six eggs and a strike of rye meal, / I had kept the town till doomsday, perhaps longer.'[86] Robert May had a similar excellent reputation as one, 'Who can in paste erect (of finest flour) / A compleat Fort, a Castle, or a Tower.'[87]

May's most spectacular castle appears to have been strongly influenced by an entertainment for the Prince of Wales in 1610, when mock warships and 'a great castle builded upon the water' exchanged cannon-fire, followed by a firework display. In May's table-top version, the castle had 'Battlements, Portcullises, Gates and Draw-Bridges, made of Paste-board, the Guns and Kickses, and covered in coarse paste ... guild over in spots ... with guilt bay-leaves on the turrets and tunnels.' To face this he made 'the likeness of a Ship in Paste-board, with flags and streamers, the Guns belonging to it of Kickses, bind them about with packthread, and cover them with close parts proportionable to the fashion of Cannon with Carriages ... with such holes and trains of [gun]powder that they may all take Fire'. This was set in a sea of salt, on which floated rosewater-filled eggs for the ladies to throw at each other to perfume the air after the battle. Next the accompanying pies were opened, discharging live frogs from one, and live birds from another, the latter flying towards the lighted candles, and putting them out. Having made 'the Ladies to skip and shreek [with] much delight and pleasure to the whole company', and given ample opportunity for bonding and groping, the candles were re-lit, and a sweetmeat banquet brought in with music.[88]

In contrast to May's cannon-firing pastry castles, those of his contemporary William Rabisha held all manner of foods, from which diners could help themselves. At their simplest, they were single round 'Battlely' pies, 'Castle fashion', their diverse contents changing from one season to another.[89] In the month of May, for example, they would include rabbits, bacon, chickens, pigeons, lamb-stones, sweetbreads, forcemeat balls, ox-pallates, oysters, marrow, egg yolks, blanched chestnuts, pine nuts, pistachios, onions and butter, inserted in that order. After baking, the lid was removed, a batter of white wine, anchovies, egg yolks, broth and butter was shaken in, and the contents garnished with sprigs of pastry. Next came groups of towers:

PASTRY TOWERS[90]

For each individual tower take:

12oz/350g flour	*7fl.oz/210ml milk*
2 egg yolks and 1 white	*candied orange peel*

Drop the yolks into the flour, mix, then rub in until completely absorbed. Bring the milk to the boil, pour in, mix, then turn out on to a floured board and knead for 3–5 minutes until smooth.

Roll into a rectangle 12in/30cm by 6in/15cm, with one long edge thick, and the other thinner. Trim exactly to size, cut battlements along the thinner edge, score or impress the pattern of coursed masonry across the surface, and cut out a few round or cross-shaped firing-loops. Gather up the trimmings, knead, and form into a disc about 5in/12cm diameter.

Cut two pieces of writing or greaseproof paper 18 x 7in/45 x 18cm, and form each into a loose roll. Turn the battlemented pastry over, prick lightly, brush the thick edge and both ends with egg white, and roll into a cylinder around one length of paper, securing the ends together. Stand it vertically on the pastry disc, trim the surplus from the base, encircle with the other piece of paper, pull it tight, and tie with a piece of string.

Transfer to a baking sheet and bake at 200°C/400°F/gas mark 6 for 20–25 minutes, removing the inner paper after 15 minutes. Remove from the oven, allow to cool, then remove the outer paper. Garnish the battlements and loops with strips of orange peel, and fill up with cold preserved fruits and the like just before serving. Up to six of these could encircle a taller central tower to fill a large dish.

Rabisha's grandest castle used rye pastry as a construction medium to build up a stepped conical mount, each tier decked with a different variety of green salad. At its foot, extending to the rim of its great dish, was a 'moat' of pickles, each colour arranged symmetrically. The real tour-de-force, however, was the castle at the top of the mount. Statues representing the four seasons stood on balconies extending from its walls, each holding a glass cruet from which oil and vinegar flowed onto the salad when delivered to the table. From the centre of the castle sprouted a green tree of wax or pastry, the whole being brushed with egg yolk as an adhesive for a final coating of green herbs and coloured flowers in summer. For autumn, the colours reflected those of fallen leaves, the castle having details carved from carrots and turnips, while for winter white predominated, the tree and other elements looking as if they had been covered in snow.[91]

CHEWETS

Originating in the medieval period, each of these individual-sized small pies originally had a hand-pinched rim which made it look like a small *chou* or cabbage, hence the name.[92] By the early seventeenth century they were being made in straight-sided crusts which expanded from a pronounced base up to a slightly wider rim, the flat lid being pierced by a central hole.[93] They were filled with either minced meat or fish.

CHEWETS OF VEAL, TONGUE, POULTRY, SALMON, AND OTHER MEATS[94]

1 batch of pastry no. 8 (p. 149)
8oz/225g veal or other meat or fish, finely minced
3oz/75g suet
6oz/150g currants
1oz/25g sugar
1oz/25g dates, sliced
½tsp each ground nutmeg, cinnamon & black pepper
¼tsp ground ginger
1tbs caraway seed
1tbs candied orange peel
2tbs rosewater
2tbs lemon juice (verjuice)
1tsp salt

Mix all the ingredients, pack into pie cases raised about 2½in/6cm diameter and 2in/5cm high. Dampen the edges, apply the lids, cut a hole in the centre and bake at 200°C/400°F/gas mark 6 for 1 hour.

FLORENTINES

The florentine, which apparently originated in Florence, was a distinctive form of pastry introduced into England before 1570.[95] It continued to be made into the late Georgian period, the best description being of one made at Potton in Bedfordshire around 1770. It 'consisted of an immensely large dish of pewter, or such-like metal, filled with good baking apples, sugar and lemon to the brim; with a roll of rich paste as a covering – pie-fashion. When baked, before serving up, the upper crust ... was taken off and divided into sizeable triangular portions, which were again arranged around the dish in order, by way of garnish, and ... a full quart of well-spiced ale was poured in, hissing hot.'[96] With the exception of the ale this was a true English florentine, a pie-cum-tart baked in a deep, wide-rimmed metal dish.

Instructions for making them all line the dish and rim with fine butter or puff pastry, insert the contents, then add a lid with some form of decoration. Some had their upper crusts cut with pierced patterns, some were 'carved about the brim' in elaborate designs, while others were given a grid of twisted strips of puff-paste, the direct ancestors of today's 'lattice pies'.[97] Those made by the Countess of Newport had their dishes lined with thin pastry, but thicker at the brim. Once filled, the lid was added so as to 'over-reach the brim with some carved pastry work to grace it, which must go up with a border like lace growing a little way upwards upon the Cover, which is a little arched up, and hath a little hole in the top ... to pour in' [broth].[98] Fortunately Robert May illustrated nine of their tops, confirming how the pastry was decorated around their brims.[99]

Their fillings were almost identical to those of ordinary pies and pasties, ranging from mincemeats, tongue, poultry and game, to spinach, apples and rice.

A FLORENTINE OF MUTTON OR VEAL[100]

1 batch of pastry no. 13 or 17 (p. 151–152)

1½lb/675g leg of mutton or veal	*large pinch black pepper*
1 medium onion finely chopped	*1 pinch nutmeg*
2oz/50g fresh white breadcrumbs	*1 clove garlic, chopped*
6 thin rashers of streaky bacon	*½tsp salt*
¼tsp each of marjoram, thyme, savory, parsley & rosemary	*2 egg yolks, beaten*
	bay leaves

Slice the meat across the grain and mix with all the remaining ingredients except the bay leaves. Roll out half of the pastry and use to line a round 2pt/1l baking dish with a broad rim. Fill with the mixture (add a lid made of the remaining pastry), trim the edges, and use the trimmings to form a raised border, with eight narrow twisted strips extending towards the centre like spokes. For pastry 13 bake at 180°C/350°F/gas mark 4 for 1½ hours. For pastry 17 bake at 220°C/425°F/gas mark 7 for the first 30 minutes, then reduce to 180°C/350°F/gas mark 4 for a further hour. Stick the bay leaves into the top just before serving.

A FLORENTINE OF RICE[101]

1 batch of pastry no. 13 or 17 (p. 151–152)

4oz/100g short-grained rice	*2tbs rosewater*
2 sticks cinnamon	*6 dates, minced*
½pt/300ml milk	*2oz/50g suet*
3oz/75g currants	*3tbs sugar*
½tsp mixed ground cinnamon, nutmeg, clove, mace & ginger	*3 yolks & 1 white of egg*
	3tbs cream

Simmer the rice and cinnamon sticks in 1pt/600ml water for 15 minutes, drain, return to the pan with the milk, and stir over a gentle heat for 30 minutes more, until thick and creamy. Leave until cold, then stir in the remaining ingredients. Meanwhile, use two-thirds of the pastry to line a round 2pt/1l baking dish and prick the base. Fill with the mixture, roll out the remaining pastry, cut in ½in/1.5cm strips with a jagging iron, twist each in turn, and use to form a chequer or grid pattern across the florentine, dampening and fixing the ends onto the edge of the pastry base, and sealing them down beneath a further strip applied all round the brim. For pastry 13 bake at 150°C/300°F/gas mark 2 for 40 minutes. For pastry 17 bake at 220°C/425°F/gas mark 7 for 30 minutes. A lozenge/kissing comfit was stuck into each square of the top and the whole sprinkled with sugar just before serving.

TARTS

Unlike pasties and pies, tarts were usually open-topped, making them more suitable for baking sweet or creamy mixtures, where the evaporation of the juices was beneficial, rather than detrimental. The following recipes illustrate just a few of their many fillings.

BACON TART[102]

8in/20cm blind-baked pastry flan case
6oz/150g dry-cured bacon
1oz/25g fresh white breadcrumbs
½pt/300ml single cream
2 eggs, beaten
1oz/25g candied orange & citron peel
1tbs rosewater
2tsp sugar
¼tsp each ground nutmeg, cinnamon & ginger
½tsp salt

Chop and process the bacon until it is a smooth paste, beat in the remaining ingredients, pour into the case, and bake at 150°C/300°F/gas mark 2 for 45 minutes, then serve either hot or cold.

CHEESE TART[103]

1 batch of pastry no. 13 (p. 151)
1lb/450g Cheshire or similar cheese
6 egg yolks
4oz/100g butter, melted

Use half the pastry to form an 8in/20cm diameter 1in/2.5cm high tart. Blend the cheese with the yolks, beat in the butter, and pour into the tart. Use the remaining pastry to form a cut lid, seal in place, and bake at 180°C/350°F/gas mark 4 for 50 minutes. Serve hot, since it is very solid when cold.

ALMOND TART[104]

8in/20cm blind-baked pastry flan case
5oz/125g ground almonds
3tbs rosewater
13fl.oz/400ml single cream
2 yolks & 1 white of egg
½tsp mixed ground cinnamon & mace
3tbs caster sugar
1oz/25g shredded candied orange & citron peel

Grind or blend the almonds, rosewater and a third of the cream until smooth, stir in the remaining ingredients, transfer to a pan and stir continuously over a gentle heat until it has thickened. Turn into the flan case, smooth the top, and bake at 150°C/300°F/gas mark 2 for some 25 minutes until the top has just risen but is still uncoloured. Serve cold.

PRUNE TART[105]

8in/20cm blind-baked pastry flan case
12oz/350g pitted prunes
4oz/100g fresh white breadcrumbs
½pt/300ml red wine
½tsp ground cinnamon
1tsp ground ginger
4oz/100g sugar
1tbs rosewater

Soak the prunes overnight, then simmer for 10–15 minutes until tender, drain, grind/blend with the remaining ingredients to form a smooth, thick paste. Turn into the flan case, and bake at 150°C/300°F/gas mark 2 for 20 minutes. It may be garnished with small biscuits or caraway comfits before serving.

STRAWBERRY TART[106]

1 8in/20cm blind-baked pastry flan case
1lb/450g fresh strawberries, the stalks and haulm removed
¼tsp mixed ground cinnamon and ginger
6tbs red wine
2tbs sugar

Arrange the strawberries neatly in the flan case, sprinkle with the spices mixed into the wine, then sprinkle with the sugar, and bake at 150°C/300°F/gas mark 2 for 30 minutes. Sprinkle with a little caster sugar and serve hot.

In addition to these simple tarts, the cooks made much more ornamental forms. For double tarts, the lid, usually of puff-paste, was baked separately after having flower-shaped symmetrical designs cut in its upper surface using a penknife. As Elizabeth Cromwell's recipe instructed, the lid of the basic pie or tart was removed as it came out of the oven, after which one should have 'a lid cut in flowers ready, lay it on and garnish it with preserves of damson, raspberries, apricots and cherries, and place a preserved quince in the middle and strew it with sugar biscuits.'[107] Robert May gave designs for related 'cut-laid' tarts made by applying strips of puff paste onto the secondary lid, so that the space in between could be filled with multi-coloured preserves.[108]

Laid tarts presented a similar appearance, but were individual tarts, round, square, diamond, heart, flower or fleur-de-lis-shaped in plan arranged either in a formal pattern within a large dish, or baked on a common base as a single multi-celled tart.[109]

LAID TARTS[110]

2 batches of pastry no. 10 (p. 151)

Roll a third of the pastry as a large round ¼in/7mm thick on a sheet of oven paper. Next prepare a full-sized paper pattern of the intended design to fit it, with a 4in/10cm-diameter round 'tower' in the centre. Roll out the rest of the pastry to the same thickness, and cut out a rectangle 12½ x 4in/32 x 10cm, using a knife for three sides, and a jagging iron for one long side. Form this into a tower, the jagged side to the top, and fix in the centre of the large sheet. Cut the remaining pastry into strips 1½in/4cm high, with their upper edges jagged, folding them into the required shapes on the paper pattern, before fixing them onto the pastry base. When all is complete, run the jagging iron around the perimeter to remove all the surplus pastry. Using a sharp skewer, prick the insides and bases of all the pastry walls to prevent them from blistering in the oven. Bake at 150°C/300°F/gas mark 2 for about 30 minutes, when it just starts to colour, then remove and leave to cool.

The laid tarts were then filled with 'tart stuffs' of various colours, all of which had been pre-cooked in readiness.

BLACK TART STUFF[111]

12oz/350g pitted prunes
2 pippins, peeled, cored & sliced
½pt/300ml claret
1 piece root ginger
1 clove
1 sprig rosemary
1 small piece cinnamon
2tbs rosewater
3tbs sugar

Simmer the prunes and spices in the claret for some 20 minutes until very tender, then rub through a sieve into a clean pan. Add the rosewater and sugar, simmer until thick, stirring constantly, then either pour into a blind-baked tart case, or seal in sterilized jars for future use.

RED TART STUFF[112]

1lb/450g pippins, weighed after peeling, coring, & slicing
12oz/350g sugar — *2 sticks cinnamon*

Place all the ingredients into a pan, just cover with water, and simmer very gently, stirring more often as the colour deepens until it is 'as red as Ruby'. This will take about an hour or more. Remove the cinnamon and either seal in sterilized jars for future use, or allow to cool before filling a blind-baked tart case, decorating the surface with slips of candied orange or citron. (If the stuff is too thick, beat in 2 or 3 tablespoons of rosewater before storing or using.)

DARK YELLOW TART STUFF (1)[113]

8oz/225g drained apricots, stewed or tinned
4oz/100g sugar — *2tbs white wine*

Rub the apricots through a sieve, add the sugar and wine, bring to the boil, and use either immediately or seal in sterilized jars.

LIGHT YELLOW TART STUFF (2)[114]

½pt/300ml single cream — *3tbs rosewater*
2 large eggs, beaten — *2oz/50g sugar*
a pinch of each of ground ginger, mace and nutmeg

Beat the cream, egg and spices together, stir over a gentle heat to form a thick custard, remove from the heat, rub through a sieve, beat in the remaining ingredients to form a smooth paste, and use while freshly made. If preferred, the spices and rosewater might be replaced by 3tbs dry sherry.

WHITE TART STUFF[115]

Use the previous recipe, but replace the whole eggs with 3 egg whites, and cook to a soft curd before draining and rubbing through the sieve. If making both yellow and white tart stuff, the separated yolks and whites of 3 eggs may be used.

GREEN TART STUFF[116]

Use greengages or gooseberries either stewed or made into jams, or make a green spinach tart stuff.

4oz/100g spinach
½pt/300ml single cream
1tbs dry sherry
pinch each of ground cinnamon, and nutmeg
3 egg yolks
2tbs rosewater
2oz/50g sugar

Plunge the spinach into boiling water, boil for 4 minutes, drain, and rub through a sieve. Beat the pulp into the remaining ingredients and cook gently while stirring to form a green custard (do not boil).

CUSTARDS

Most custards were made of rich cream, flavoured with spices, sugar and a little dried fruit, all thickened with eggs. Some were simply stirred in a pan or cooked in a dish over boiling water on a stove, but since they readily curdled if even slightly over-heated, the preference was to bake them in pastry cases.[117] Even this gentler method had its own restrictions,however, for large baked custards cook unevenly, their centres still being raw when their outer edges are over-cooked to a hard curd. To ensure that this does not happen, the cooks developed pastry cases in which the custard mixture was never more than about 3in/7.5cm wide. The smallest were individual round custard tarts known as doucets, while the largest used symmetrical designs of scrolls, leaves and trefoils, each a few inches broad to become 'double bordered custards' perhaps 18in/45cm across. Although appearing excessively fanciful today, their complex plans were entirely functional, ensuring that their expensive fillings were evenly cooked, and that they could be easily divided into individual portions at table.[118]

BAKED CUSTARD[119]

The following quantities are for making four doucets, but may be increased proportionately for double-bordered custards.

1½ batches of pastry no. 7 (p. 149)
1pt/600ml double cream
5 eggs, beaten
4oz/100g sugar
¼tsp ground cinnamon
large pinch ground ginger
½tsp salt

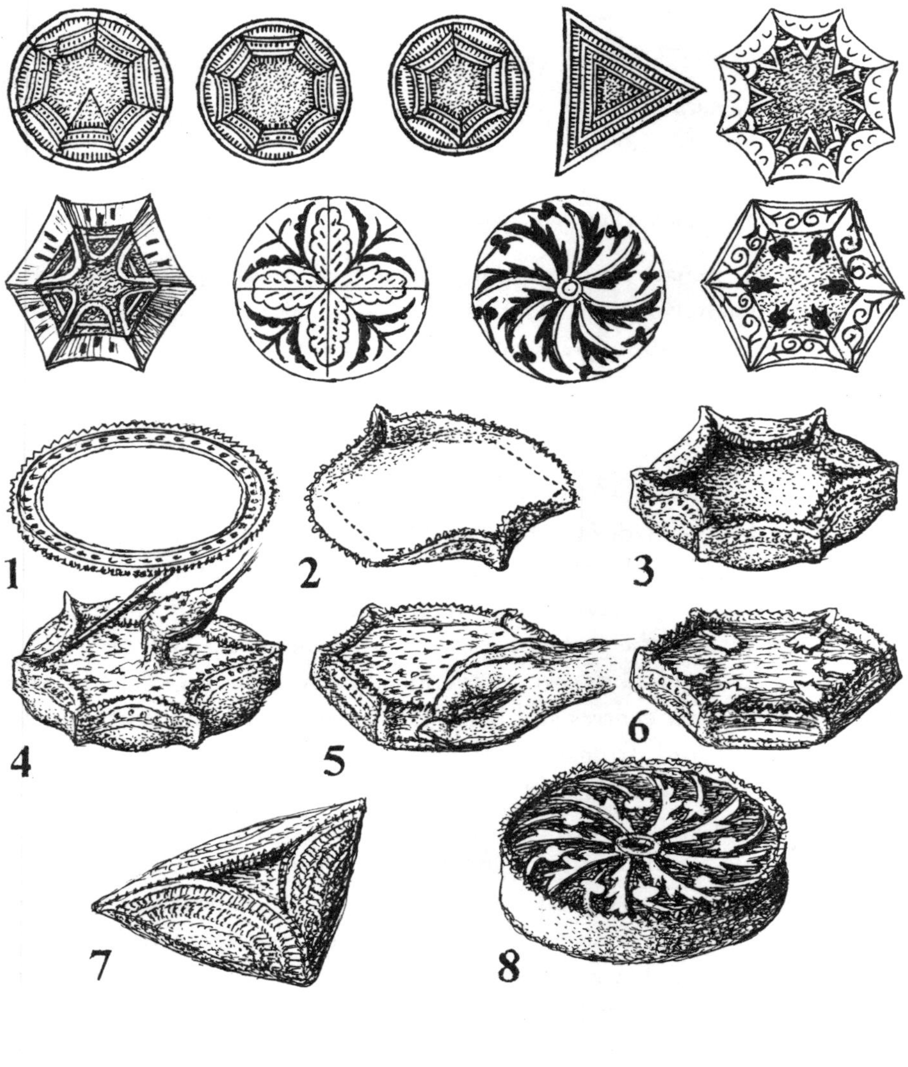

Figure 36. Cheesecakes. As illustrated by Robert May (top two rows), the rich curd mixtures of cheesecakes were baked either in polygonal pastry cases or round pastry flans. To make the polygonal cases, first roll out the pastry, cut it into a large disc and incise decoration around its perimeter (1). Turn over and nip up opposing corners (2) and a number of corners on each side (3). Spoon in the mixture, raising each 'flap' so that it rests on the mixture (4). If preferred, the sides of the cheesecakes can be worked to give them a straight profile (5) and pastry decorations added just before baking (6). Alternatively the cheesecakes can be made as simple triangles (7) or as flans with pastry decorations (8).

Use the pastry to make four pastry cases some 3in/7.5cm in diameter and height with a jagged rim. Prick the base and the interior all over with a sharp skewer, and blind bake, with an internal paper collar for support, at 150°C/300°F/gas mark 2 for 30 minutes. Beat the remaining ingredients together, ladle into cases (traditionally this was done when still in the oven, to avoid spillage) and continue to bake at the same temperature for a further 15 minutes (but longer for double-bordered custards) until set, then remove and leave until cold.

Alternatives

1. Use a blend of saffron, clove, mace, cinnamon and ginger as the spicing.[120]
2. Put 1–2oz/25–50g mixed currants, sliced dates and raisins in the mixture.
3. Add 1oz/25g melted butter to the mixture.[121]
4. Stick the top of the cold custard with muscadines (kissing comfits) or sliced dates, and sprinkle with sugar.
5. Use thick almond milk instead of cream for Lent.[122]
6. For double-bordered custards, make the walls 3in/7.5cm high, and use beaten egg yolk to join the borders to the base and to each other. Use a jagging-iron when cutting the top edge of the standing strips of pastry, and to trim the surplus pastry from the base just before baking.

CHEESECAKES

Sweetened cheese tarts had been made in the late medieval period, but more refined cheesecakes only appeared around the middle of the sixteenth century.[123] They soon developed a very distinctive type of pastry crust, and a range of fillings, some losing all traces of cheese or curds, using fresh breadcrumbs or ground almonds instead. The following are typical, with cheese, curds, or other fillings.

A ROBERT MAY CHEESECAKE[124]

5oz/125g Edam or Gouda
7½oz/210g cottage cheese, drained
1½oz/37g caster sugar
1 egg, beaten
¼tsp mixed ground cinnamon, and mace
2tbs cream
2tbs ground almonds
pinch of saffron
a few pistachios (optional)

Finely chop the Edam or Gouda, mix with everything else except the pistachios, and grind or blend until perfectly smooth. Bake as below.

ELIZABETH CROMWELL'S CHEESECAKES[125]

7½oz/210g cottage cheese, drained
¼pt/150ml double cream
1 egg, beaten
1oz/25g sugar
¼tsp mixed ground clove & nutmeg
2oz/50g currants
1oz/25g melted butter
1tbs rosewater

Beat together, then bake as below.

CHEESECAKES WITHOUT CHEESE[126]

3 eggs, beaten
3tbs sugar
4tbs flour
large pinch ground cinnamon
pinch of salt
¾pt/450ml single cream
1½oz/37g butter
3tbs currants

Beat the eggs, sugar, flour, cinnamon and salt in a basin, until completely smooth. Bring the cream, butter and currants to the boil, pour into the eggs while beating vigorously, return to the pan, and beat over a gentle heat until smooth and thick, then cover and leave to cool. Bake as below.

TO BAKE CHEESECAKES[127]

9oz/250g flour
3oz/75g butter
1 egg yolk
4 tbs cold water

Rub the butter into the flour, then add the yolk and water, work in with a round-ended knife, gather together, knead lightly, and divide into three equal-sized balls.

Roll out each ball into an 8in/20cm disc, cover with a plate of this size, and trim the edge with a pastry-jagger. Using a skewer, lightly scribe a design around the perimeter (see fig. 36), then turn face down on a baking sheet. Lightly rub the outer inch (2.5cm) with egg white, then pinch up two opposing corners, and one, two or three corners between each, to form a square, hexagonal or octagonal pastry.

Spoon in a third of the cheesecake batters above, little by little, raising each side of the rim in turn, so that the batter runs beneath it, rather than overflows. Using the side of the thumbs, push in the sides to form a narrow ledge just above the base, and make the walls stand more vertically. Float any cut-out pastry decoration on the surface.

Bake in an oven pre-heated to 180°C/350°F/gas mark 4 for 30 minutes (15–20 minutes for the last recipe above) and serve either hot or cold.

BAKING IN POTS

The foot-high rye pastry venison pies were so hard after their prolonged baking that some cooks managed to preserve them ready for use over the coming year by topping them up with clarified butter.[128] It was soon realized that glazed earthenware pots were even better for this purpose. A probable example excavated from the Civil War debris of Basing House, Hampshire, took the form of a 16-inch (41cm) cylinder with projecting rim ideal for tying down some form of cover. Instructions for potting venison commence with larding and seasoning the joint, setting it in the pot with lard and butter, covering the top with a pastry cover and 'funnel', and baking for 6 hours. On removal from the oven, the pot was inverted to drain all the juices, the interior wiped clean, the venison put back inside, covered by some 2 inches (5cm) of clarified butter, and finally had a piece of sheep leather tied over the top to complete an airtight seal.[129]

In the early mid-seventeenth century baking pots were being used to cook 'collars' or rolls of spiced venison, beef, veal, mutton, pork and goat for immediate use. For this purpose the pots had to be very large, a single collar of a flank of beef being about 12 inches (30cm) in diameter by 18 inches (45cm) high.[130]

TO BAKE BEEF[131]

3lb/1.35kg beef joint, such as silverside
1 onion, sliced
2oz/50g butter
1tbs mixed parsley, savory, marjoram, lemon thyme, sage and pennyroyal (or mint)
2tsp salt
large pinch black pepper
½ bottle claret

Bone and trim the meat, beat it with a rolling pin, rub in the pepper and salt, form into a roll, tie with string or twine, and put into a close-fitting casserole or cooking pot with the remaining ingredients. Seal the top with a piece of cooking foil in place of pastry, and bake at 170°C/325°F/gas mark 3 for 2½–3 hours, until tender when tested with a skewer. The original recipe then covers the drained joint with clarified butter for long-term storage, but for present-day use it may be rested and carved hot, or left to cool, then drained and pressed for serving cold.

Smaller earthenware pots enabled puddings to be baked rather than boiled, as they had been previously. Most were probably ordinary bowls or other vessels, but some must have been purpose-made, the 1631 inventory of Thomas Parker of South Cave, Yorkshire, including his' 3 puddinge pye poots'.[132] Their contents included most of the fruit, cereals or vegetables usually baked in pastry cases, as well as others made from oatmeal.[133]

DOROTHIE LACON'S SWEET OATMEAL PUDDING[134]

6oz/175g coarse oatmeal
¾pt/450ml milk
½oz/12g butter
2 large eggs, beaten
3oz/75g currants
3oz/75g raisins
3tbs orange flower water
4tbs sugar
¼tsp salt
pinch grated nutmeg

Bruise the oatmeal in a mortar, or 2–3 minutes in a food processor (or use rolled oats). Bring the milk and butter to the boil, and stir into the oatmeal to form a smooth mixture, cover, and leave overnight. Beat in the remaining ingredients, pour into a buttered 2pt/1l baking dish, and bake at 150°C/300°F/gas mark 2 for 50–60 minutes. (Serve with cream.)

SAVOURY OATMEAL PUDDING[135]

Follow the previous recipe, but replace the dried fruit, orange flower water and sugar with a finely chopped leek and ¼tsp each of ground ginger and cinnamon.

WHITEPOTS

These ancestors of the bread pudding were a west-country speciality, the local May Day games here being led by 'Whitepot Queens' in the 1520s.[136] After Charles Blount, Lord Mountjoy, was created Earl of Devonshire at James I's coronation, he appears to have introduced the whitepot into the Home Counties. Lady Elinor Fettiplace, a Berkshire gentlewoman who wrote up her recipes shortly after 1604, thus included a classic whitepot as 'The Lord of Devonshire his pudding'.[137] Mid-seventeenth-century printed versions state that they should be baked either in a dish or a broad shallow basin, while Robert May advised using vertical-sided multi-lobed dishes, illustrating the shape he preferred.[138] Almost identical dishes, presumably for whitepots, were made in the mid-seventeenth-century potteries of the Hampshire-Surrey border, their rims being notched to resemble jagged pastry.[139] One of these has been excavated from central Exeter, reinforcing the west-country origins of this pudding.[140]

The whitepot could be made to various recipes, some being a set custard on broad thin slices of bread, some using crumbed bread, and some being cooked between a pair of dishes set over a pan of boiling water, but the following is both early and typical:

MY LORD OF DEVONSHIRE HIS PUDDING[141]

1pt/600ml single cream
3 eggs, beaten
3tbs sugar
¼tsp ground cinnamon
¼ nutmeg, grated
2tbs rosewater
half a white loaf
2oz/50g butter (for bone marrow)
2oz/50g raisins
2tbs currants

Beat the cream, eggs, sugar, spices and rosewater together. Thinly slice the loaf, removing the crusts, place a layer in the bottom of a 2pt/1l ceramic dish, dot with some of the butter and dried fruit, and continue in layers until all is in the dish. Pour in the cream mixture, and bake at 150°C/300°F/gas mark 2 for about 45 minutes until set. The top was stuck with 'muscadoes' (kissing comfits) just before being served.

Although this chapter has described most types of pastry introduced in the later sixteenth and early seventeenth centuries, it has only given a small fraction of the extant recipes, many of which are now accessible in reprinted cookery books of the period. However, those which have been included here clearly demonstrate how important the pastry workhouses had become, producing vast amounts of high-quality dishes for their respective households.

CHAPTER NINE

The Boiling House

In cottages all boiling could be carried out in a single ceramic or metal pot placed over the fire. When catering for several hundred people dining in large houses and palaces, however, a whole boiling department had to be set up with its own rooms, staff and administration.

The usual foods cooked in the boiling house might include beef, mutton, pork and bacon, along with some of the larger fishes. Being required in bulk, frequently at times of the year when fresh supplies were scarce, many of these foods were either purchased in their salted form, or were salted down from the fresh carcasses brought into the larders.

There were three major sources of salt. The best large-crystal sea-salt was imported from around Bourgneuf near Nantes in the Bay of Biscay. This 'Bay salt' was best for dry-salting, as it dissolved more slowly than most other varieties. The salts produced in England were evaporated from either sea-water, or the brine which emerged from springs in the Cheshire wiches around Northwich. Some of the largest industrial-scale saltings were set up around the mouth of the Tyne, where Newcastle coals were both cheap and plentiful. At one of these visited by Sir William Brereton in 1635, the brine was boiled in large riveted sheet-iron pans, each 15 feet by 10 feet 6 inches, by 2 feet 3 inches deep (4.6 x 3.05 x 0.7m), and set over a furnace. Every 36 hours their brine was reduced to salt worth about £1 10*s*., using two and a quarter tons of coal. Taking all expenditure into account, he calculated that the 250 pans working here, in 'such a cloud of smoak, as amongst these workes you cannot see to walke', were producing £600 a year profit, showing the importance of the industry.[1] As at other saltings, there was an excellent distribution system both by sea, and by a host of long-distance pack-horse tracks which still retain the title of salt-ways or saltersgates today.

The quantities of salt bought in by large households could be immense. Every year Henry VIII's court required 60 quarters (three-quarters of a ton) of bay salt costing £20, and the same of white salt at £13 6*s*. 8*d*.[2] It was more usual to sell salt by the peck, or two-gallon measure, rather than by weight. The Howard household at Naworth bought in almost 150 pecks in 1612, for example.[3]

Figure 37. Henrician boiling equipment. The painting of The Field of the Cloth of Gold *(1), dating from around 1545, shows the great copper boiling pots in use with implements similar to the skimmer (2) and ladle (3) recovered from the* Mary Rose. *The boiler and its furnace from the* Mary Rose *(4) appear to be unique survivals from this period.*

The vast majority of this would be used for either dry-salting, rubbing in the crystals and the brine as it was drawn from the meat's own juices, or wet-salting, by soaking in a pre-prepared brine. The latter was apparently the technique favoured in the royal household, a furnace for boiling brine being installed in the flesh larder at Greenwich in 1534.[4] Since it avoided rubbing each joint individually, this method was particularly suitable for large-scale catering.

The actual boiling process took place in large metal boiling vessels variously known as beef-pots, cauldrons, kettles or pans. Portable examples for use in the kitchen fireplace or while on campaign ranged in volume from only a few gallons up to perhaps 250 or 300 gallons. The great hemispherical kettles seen in the field-kitchen in the painting of *The Field of the Cloth of Gold*, probably removed from royal palace use, and perhaps even the same '6 very large copper pots tinned' listed at Hampton Court in 1659, were of around this size. Mounted over the fire on strong iron brandreths or frames, they were practical, but not particularly efficient. This was because the heat of the flames was largely lost either to open air or up the chimney. It was far better to set the pot within a hollow masonry casing called a furnace, so that the flames and hot air were compelled to transfer most of their heat into the food before being allowed to escape.

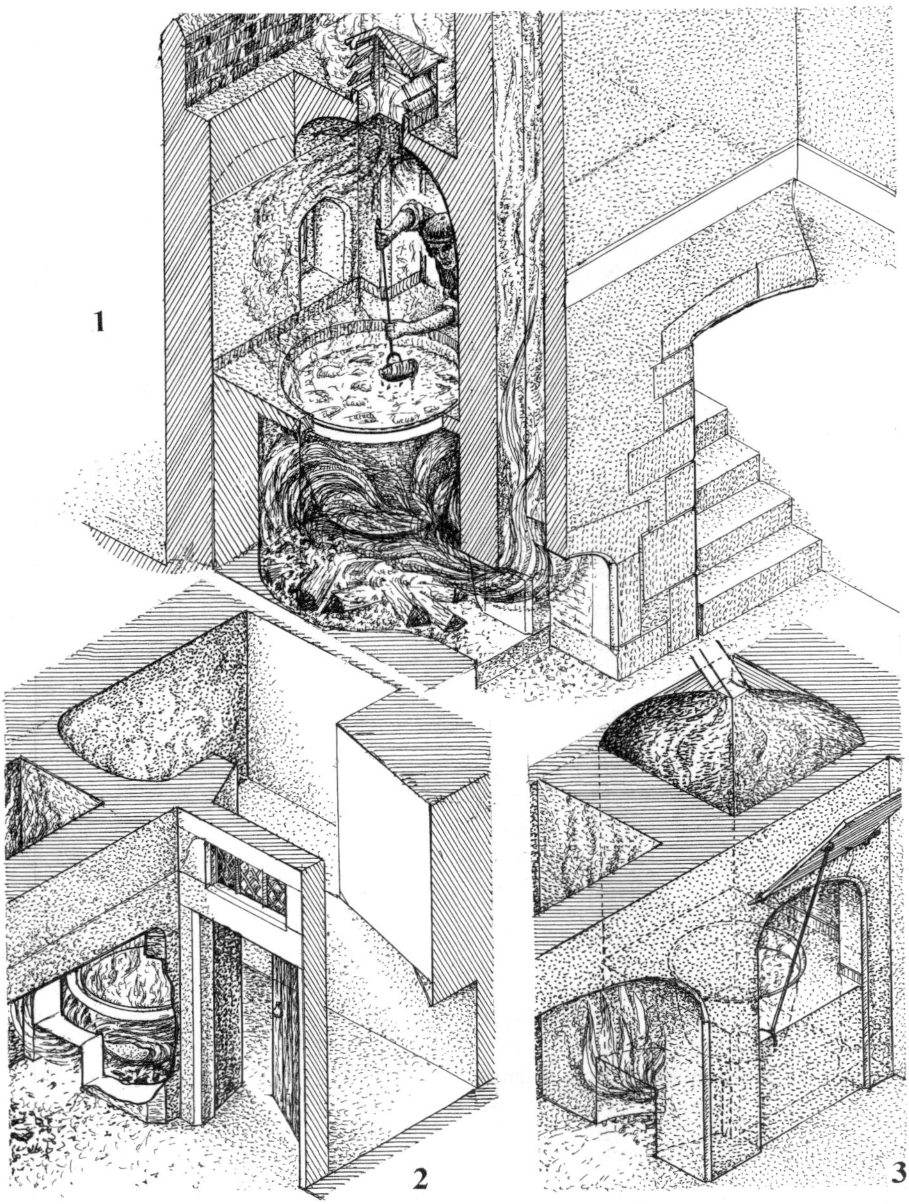

Figure 38. Boiling houses. The boiling houses of 1530–31 at Hampton Court Palace (1), of 1588 at Hardwick Old Hall, Derbyshire (2), and of Wollaton Hall, Nottingham (3) all had single openings which admitted fuel and draught, and also emitted the smoke and flames. This ensured a highly efficient transfer of heat into the contents of their boilers. The flue rising from the top of the Wollaton boiler passed into the main kitchen flue alongside, the up-draught providing an effective means of extracting the steam.

Few secular examples of small furnaces of this period have survived, but there is good archaeological evidence for one of post-medieval date in the kitchen of Bowhill, Exeter. Built into one corner of the fireplace, it had a masonry base measuring some 40 x 45 inches, and walls 36 inches high (102 x 115 x 91cm). Once the pot had been encased in this furnace, flames from the burning logs thrust beneath would completely envelop its base before emerging from the top of its firemouth, leaving their soot on the fireback, which can still be seen there today.[5] A rather improved method involved setting the furnace in a separate niche about the size of a sentry box cut into the wall just to one side of the kitchen fireplace, so that its smoke could be pulled away up the main chimney. Since there was no fireplace in the front wall of the furnace, this arrangement enabled the cooks to fill and empty the pot without any risk of being burned. In addition, the steam rising from the pot was carried off by a ventilation duct at the top, which fed into the chimney at a higher level. Because these pots were fixtures, they formed part of the freehold of a property, and so, although listed in probate inventories, they were not valued as part of the deceased's estate, in contrast to all portable goods.

> 'one panne for boilling beyf
> one pane for boilling of beif (heyrelomes)'
> [Lord Wharton of Healaugh, Yorkshire, 1568]
> 'one furnace pann for beefe 10s. The beef kettle ...'
> [Sir W. Fairfax of Gilling, Yorkshire, 1594]
> 'the boyling beef potte' [in the inner kitchen]
> [Francis Willoughby of Wollaton Hall, Nottinghamshire, 1601][6]

Other inventory references show that a different type of furnace was also in use, one which was built into a separate room called a boiling house:

> 'Yet of the great Kittchen ... A great beef pann made fast in the little howse
> by the Chimney like unto a ffurnes'
> [Earl of Bedford, Bedford House, Exeter, 1594]
> 'In the boyling house: three brass pans'
> [Countess of Shrewsbury, Hardwick Old Hall, 1601][7]

Both designed by the Smythson architects, the boiling houses at Hardwick Old Hall, *c.* 1588, and New Hall, *c.* 1590, still survive remarkably intact. They are small rooms set into the corners of their kitchens, to one side of the main fireplaces from which their beef pots were fuelled. Both have lockable doors, surmounted by glazed windows to allow the cook to keep the boiling beef perfectly secure at all times. This arrangement also enabled the boiling houses

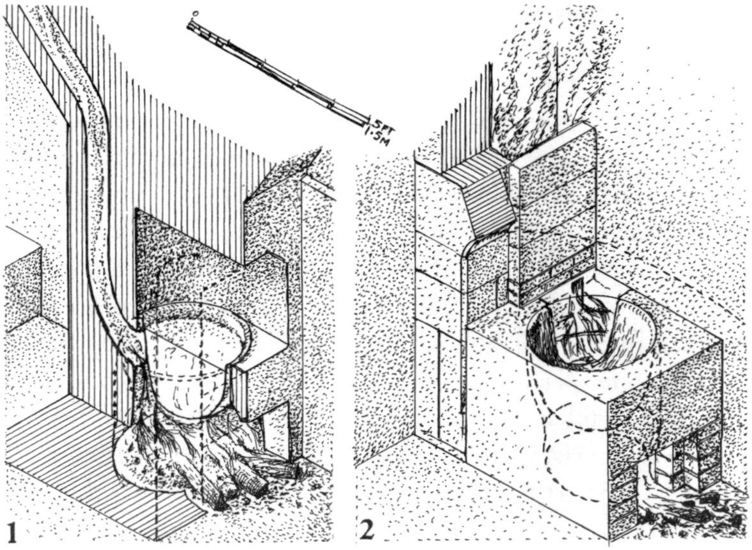

Figure 39. Boiling Furnaces. The boiling furnaces of c. 1600 at Berry Pomeroy, Devon, (1) and c. 1629 at Bolsover Castle, Derbyshire (2), had flues to create a through up-draught to carry away all their fumes. They kept the kitchen smoke-free, even though much of their heat was lost up the chimneys.

to serve as storerooms in which valuable kitchen equipment could be stored whenever the household was living elsewhere. In 1601, the New Hall boiling house contained pans, kettles, a mortar, frying-pan, colander, chopping and mincing knives, a cleaver, a grater, ten spits and other things, all safe from pilfering or misuse.[8]

There was very little development in the design of boiler furnaces between the fifteenth and mid-seventeenth centuries, virtually every example being fired like a bread-oven. Burning wood was still thrust in at the firemouth, clear air then rushing in at ground level to feed the fire, while the smoke and flame issued from the top of the same opening, having heated the pot. However, at the Duke of Somerset's new mansion at Berry Pomeroy in Devon, a completely new system was introduced, probably for the first time, in 1548. Here the furnace was set into the side wall of the kitchen fireplace, but now it had a separate flue which directed the flame around the pot, and then upwards to emerge high up in the adjacent chimney stack. Not only did this keep the top of the pot clear of soot and dirt, but it made it much safer for those adding and removing joints or other foods. Even so, at least a century was to pass before this development became more widely adopted.[9]

Figure 40. The larder. Larders were used to store both fresh and preserved meats and fish ready for use in the kitchen. The 1601 inventory of the Wollaton Hall larder, seen here, included a square table, a trestle table, a powdering or salting tub, a [hanging?] safe and a number of shelves. The stone wall-shelves were ideal for salting.

The largest and busiest boiling houses in England were those of the royal palaces. Fortunately, that built at Hampton Court in 1530 remains largely complete, even if divided by later partitions. Measuring some 25 feet by 15 feet (7.6 x 4.6m) it was provided with an outer door for bringing in the fuel, and an inner door leading in from the larders of meat and fish, and then along a corridor to the hall-place dresser hatches. The furnace fireplace in the end wall heated a large copper pot installed in September 1531.[10] Probably a baffle directed the flames backwards under the pot, up its back surface, and then forward round both sides of the top before rising into a chimney set in the thickness of the front wall. This ensured the maximum transfer of heat from the fire into the pot, and that no smoke ever entered the boiling house. A short flight of steps to one side gave access to the open top of the pot, where the staff could carry out their duties in relative comfort, a vent above removing all the steamy vapours.

In Elizabeth's reign, the boiling house became a separate department under the Master Cook.[11] It was headed by a clerk, two yeomen, three grooms and two pages. These 'Boylers' had to 'dresse Meate well and seasonably, that it be neither raw, over much boyled ... but soe as it may be for the King's honour and best contenting those to whom it shall be served'. In addition to their regular wages

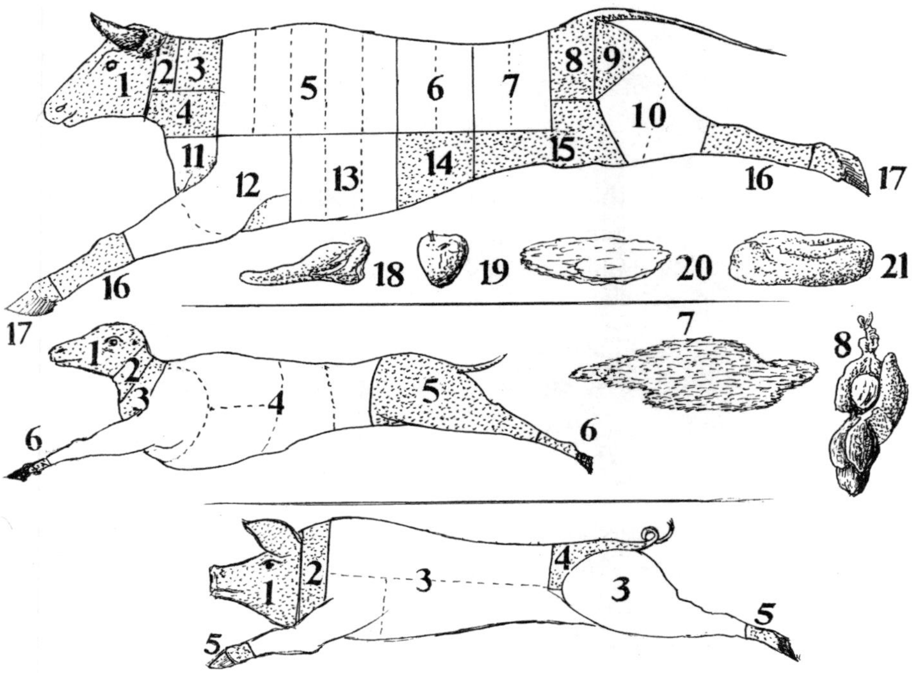

Figure 41. Butchery. Each morning the carcasses were chopped into a number of separate joints, each of a carefully calculated size to serve messes of four people. In Elizabeth I's larders they were divided in the following manner:
Oxen: *(1) head, (2) crag or neck, (3) clods, 2 joints, (4) chines, 4 joints, (5) shoulders, 4 joints, (6) livery pieces, 10 joints, (7) sirloins & fillets, 8 joints, (8) rump chine, (9) rump, (10) hind quarter to arse bone, (11, 13, 14, 15) belly pieces, 2, (12) legs to first joint, (16, 17) shin and feet, (18–21) offal of tongue and paunch. All the stippled parts were claimed as fees by the servants, the sergeant of the larder taking 1, 10, 11, 13, 14, and parts of 2 & 3, while the yeomen and grooms of the larder and kitchen had parts of 2, 9 & 13.*
Muttons & Sheep: *(1) head, (2) scrag end, (3) neck, (4) 10 messes of mutton, (5) rump, (6) hind knuckles, (7) feet, (8) offal of the caul and pluck ('gathers'). The heads of lambs went to the master cooks and of muttons to the yeomen and grooms. The latter also took the necks, rumps, hind knuckles, feet and offal, while the grooms of the kitchen and larder had two joints of the scrag end.*
Pigs: *(1) head, (2) neck, (3) 13 messes of pork, (4) chine, (5) feet. All the stippled parts were claimed by the sergeant of the larder.*

and keep, they also received perquisites in kind. All the fat coming from beef boiled in the palaces went to the Master Cook, while all that left in kettles and pans when emptying the boiling pot or lead went to the boiling house staff. In smaller households this fat, known either as kitchen fee or kitchen stuff, might remain a cook's perquisite, or else be sold off for the benefit of his employer. Five pots of kitchen stuff were sold for 6*s.* 10*d.* from the Tawstock kitchens of the Earl of Bath in October 1651, for example.[12]

Early each morning the chief officers and clerks supervised the cutting of the meat or fish, and its transfer from the larders to the boiling house. Here it was plunged into water (boiling for fresh supplies, and cold for salted) and briefly brought to the boil. At this point it threw off a thick, foamy scum, which had to be carefully removed in order to keep the stock clear. This was executed using a skimmer, a shallow-dished and pierced non-ferrous metal disc mounted on the end of a long handle, usually of wood. After being cooked to tenderness, the joints were removed using a flesh-hook, a long handle tipped with a row of sharp curved iron hooks. It was then usual to stir in a mixture of chopped pre-cooked herbs and oatmeal, instantly converting the stock into gallons of hot, nutritious and well-flavoured pottage ready to be served into the hall as the first course.

The main food cooked here was beef. Tudor society, informed by its own experience backed up by professional medical opinion, knew that this was the ideal food for labourers and servants. In 1542 Andrew Boorde stated that,[13]

> Beefe is a good meate for an Englysshe man, so be it the beest be yonge, & that it be not kowe-flesshe; For olde beefe and kowe-flesshe doth ingender melancolye and leprous humoures. Yf it be moderatly powderyd [salted], that the groose blode by salte may be exhaustyd, it doth make an Englysshe man stronge.

Similarly, in 1599 Henry Buttes confirmed that it was most suitable for youth, labourers and great exercisers, provided that it was young, fat and tender beef, used to pulling ploughs, and had been salted for 24 hours. Thomas Muffet, meanwhile, thought it so 'tough, hard, heavy, and of ill nourishment, requiring rather the stomach of another *Hercules* (who is said to have fed chiefly of Bull's flesh) than of any ordinary and common ploughman.'[14]

The production of beef followed a regular annual cycle. Calves born in the spring were weaned at about 50 days, then put out to pasture separately from the other cattle. Some, chiefly bull-calves, were then eaten as veal or young calf, the remainder needed for neither draught nor dairy production being fed on grass in the fields until autumn, and then on hay, pease-straw and other fodder ready to provide a regular supply of fresh winter beef. Winter-feeding of this kind was a relatively expensive process, but some beasts could be maintained in this way for three to five years to serve urban markets.[15] Cattle bones recovered from the mid-sixteenth-century Free Grammar School in Coventry suggest that of the beefs eaten there, one-fifth were veal, two-fifths were three- to five-year-olds, and the rest elderly draught or dairy animals.[16] The main period of mature beef consumption commenced on All-Souls Day, 1 November:

At Hallontide, slaughter-time entereth in,
And then doth the husbandman's feasting begin.
From thence till Shrovetide, kill now and then some ...
Their offall for household the better will come.
For Easter, at Martilmas [11 November] hang up a beef
For stall-fed and pease-fed play pickpurse the thief.
With that and the like, ere an grass beef come in
Thy folk shall look cheerly, when others look thin.[17]

Some beef-joints were cooked without any initial salting;

A POTTAGE CALLED SKINKE[18]

2lb/900g joint of beef
1 marrow bone, chopped in two
5tbs fine oatmeal
2tsp mixed & bruised cloves, mace & peppercorns
1 bouquet garni of marjoram, rosemary, thyme, savory, sage & parsley
1tsp salt
1 large peeled onion
pinch of ground saffron
large slice of white bread
1 large bread roll (manchet)

Bring 2pt/1.2l water to the boil in a large pan, put in the beef and marrow bone, return to the boil, skim off all the scum, and reduce to a gentle simmer.

Stir in the spices, bouquet, salt, onion, and the oatmeal mixed in ¼pt/150ml cold water, cover, and continue cooking for some 75 minutes until tender, adding the saffron towards the end of this time.

Place the slice of bread in the centre of a deep dish, arrange the sliced and toasted bread roll around the rim, then put the joint in the middle, the marrow bones to the sides, and strain the stock into the dish.

The production of pottages made of large joints of meat simmered in their own stocks was one of the most important of all cooking operations at this period. As Gervase Markham stressed, 'as our House wife is intended to be generall, one that can as well feed the poore as the rich, we first beginne with those wholesome boild-meats, which are of use in every good mans house.'

ORDINARY POTTAGE[19]

2lb/900g joint of meat — *1½tsp salt*

3tbs fine oatmeal finely chopped with 6tbs leaves of parsley, spinach, spring onion, endive, violet, succory, strawberry, bugloss, and marigold; **or** *spinach, thyme, parsley, onion and savory, with a large pinch of ground clove and of mace;* ***or, in winter,*** *capers and samphire*

Wash the meat, put in a large pan, cover with cold water, bring to the boil, skim, then stir in the herbs and oatmeal mixed in a little cold water, reduce to a gentle simmer, cover and stir from time to time until the herbs and oatmeal are completely incorporated into the stock. After an hour, add the salt, then continue cooking for a further 15 minutes until the meat is tender. Pour all into a deep dish, on sops or cubes of bread if desired, and serve.

Variations

1. Grind the herbs and oatmeal in a non-metallic pestle and mortar to form a perfectly smooth paste. Moisten this with a little hot water from the pot, grind again, so that no fragment of the herbs may be seen, before adding to the pot.
2. Instead of using chopped herbs, add a selection of whole inner leaves of lettuce, cauliflower, cabbage, spinach, endive and succory, with a sliced onion. Before serving, stir in a little vinegar (for verjuice) to taste.
3. Replace the herbs with 2 sliced onions, and add 2 tablespoonsful of more oatmeal

Other joints were green-salted, being rubbed with salt for a week in summer, or a fortnight in winter before use, as in the following:

ELIZABETH CROMWELL'S BOILED BEEF[20]

2lb/900g joint of beef
4oz/100g sea salt
3tbs mixed herbs, finely chopped
3tbs suet
½ nutmeg, grated
1 small cabbage or equivalent of root vegetables
1pt/600ml milk
4oz/100g butter

Figure 42. Salting & Smoking. Breughel's Die Klugheit *of 1559 (1) shows how joints of pork were dry-salted in shallow tubs before being packed into a large cask for long-term preservation. Similar processes would have been followed in many English homes. Specially made glazed earthenware ham-pans were used for salting in 16th century Hereford (2), but larger salting troughs were used in major households. The dug-out wooden example (3) is at Haddon Hall, Derbyshire, and the stone one (4) of 1613 at Bolsover Castle, Derbyshire. The first specially built smoking chambers were constructed in the late 16th century. One at Berry Pomeroy Castle, Devon, of the 1580s–90s (5) has a hatch with a sliding door to feed smoke from the kitchen fire and oven up into the chamber.*

Rub the salt into the meat, place in a deep dish in a cool place, and rub in its brine for 5 minutes a day for a week.

Knead the herbs, suet and nutmeg to a stiff paste, stuff this into deep stabs made in the meat, then plunge into a pan of boiling water, return to the boil, skim, and reduce to a gentle simmer for 75 minutes until tender.

Twenty minutes before it is ready, simmer the cabbage or vegetables in the milk with 1 tsp salt until tender, then drain.

Place the joint in a deep dish with the quartered cabbage or vegetables and strain in some of the stock, before topping with the softened butter.

There are 'rich Farmers houses', wrote Thomas Muffett in 1655, 'that keep beefe a whole twelve-month till they eat it'.[21] This might be wet-salted and kept in barrels by householders for their own use, or by contractors for general sale or use on military expeditions. For the latter, a 105-gallon (478l) cask called a 'pipe' would hold 400 two-pound (900g) joints sufficient to serve 1,600 individual meals. A recipe of the 1580s soaked the joints in brine for 36 hours, drained them on a hurdle while the brine was re-boiled and cooled, soaked them for 60 hours, and then put them back on the hurdle for two or three days.[22] A barrel was then prepared by placing a cross of sticks in its base to serve as a drainer, and then filled with the joints, each being wiped dry and dusted with dry salt before packing down and sealing, ready for transport or storage.

Large joints or flitches of dry- or wet-salted beef were also prepared, forming one of the most common of all everyday winter meals. Andrew Boorde considered these to be particularly harmful.[23]

> Martylmas beef, whiche is called 'hanged beef' in the rofe of a smoky howse, is not laudable; it may fyll the bely, and cause a man to drynke, but it is evyll for the stone and evyll of dygestyon, and maketh no good juce. If a man have a peace hangynge by his side, and another in his bely, that the whiche doth hange by the syde shall do hym more good.

In contrast, most of his contemporaries found the sight of such meats gave them a sense of comfortable security against future hunger. To keep the flitches in good condition, it was essential that they were stored in a dry, well ventilated but frost-free environment. This is confirmed by the locations in which they are listed in probate inventories:

'The Kytching; 5 bacon flickes & 2 Beoffe Flickes	10s.'
'The kitchyne; 17 beafe flakes & 4 baycon flakes	£3'
'The Kitchinge chamber; salt beefe and lard	£2 10s.'
'The Hall house; Six beefe flickes with other peeces	£2 10s.'

'Chamber over the hall; Thirteene Beefe flitches & seven Bacon flitches	£6 13*s*. 4*d*.'
'The buttry; in flesh at the balks	5*s*.'[24]

When hung in a smoky room, the flitches gradually absorbed a piquant smoky taste. For those who began to appreciate this flavour, it could be enhanced by hanging the meat high in a smoky chimney over a wood fire, where it also dried out more rapidly in the constant draught of warm air. From the mid-sixteenth century the salt-cured and smoked hams, gammons and flitches imported from Westphalia in western Germany, as well as the smoked pork sausages of Bologna in northern Italy, were considered to be among the finest delicacies imported into England.

One of the first published descriptions of Continental practice was provided by Sir Kenelm Digby, who had visited Frankfurt in 1620–23.[25] After being dry-salted in a tub for about a week, the meat was wiped dry and hung in a room 'where they keep a fire, either on a hearth, or that smoak cometh out of a stove into the room (as most of the rooms do smoak) but hang them not in the Chimney, that the hot smoak striketh upon them; but if you have a very large Chimney hang them pretty high and aside that the smoak may not come upon them. After a while (when they are dry) take them thence, and hang them from the smoak in a warm room.' As he stresses, the meat should only be heated sufficiently to dry out and absorb the smoky favour, but never enough to melt its fat.

By the late sixteenth century, some large houses were building smoke-chambers in their kitchen chimneys, where the meats could be enveloped in cool smoke rising from the cooking fires and ovens below. A fine example survives at Sir Edward Seymour's 1580–90 kitchen at Berry Pomeroy in Devon. Here a sliding shutter at head height, directly over a pastry oven, allows a controlled volume of smoke to fill a mural chamber above, and then exhaust through a small window into the open air. At the vernacular level, smoking chambers of this period are now relatively uncommon. The usual practice, as described in most recipes, was simply to hang the salted joints up in an open chimney, high above the fire. In houses such as Manor Farm, Templecombe, Devon, a door into the front of the chimney stack at first floor level provided a convenient means of access, but elsewhere a ladder would have to be put up the chimney to insert and remove the joints. At Scow Hall, Fewston, North Yorkshire, a timber partition rising above one end of the lintel-beam created a narrow open-topped smoking chamber, while at Durrett's Farmhose, Broomfield, Somerset, a chamber in a similar position, but constructed in the side wall of the chimney flue, performed the same function.[26]

Mutton, especially from wethers, castrated rams a year or two old, might also appear in the boiling house. When castration took place over the midsummer period, Henry Best of Elmwell's labourers would 'carry with them a baskett, and therein a poder-platter and table-napkin, to save the lambes stones in; which are accounted a very dainty dish, beinge fryed with parsley, then after they are fryed brown, your are to take of[f] the two uppermost filmes, and to eat nothinge but the innermost kernells, and these, being thus handled, are called Anchitricoes.' In contrast, Robert May parboiled and minced them, fried them in a spicy, creamy cheese batter, and served them with sugar and rosewater.[27]

'In this realme, if it be yonge, [mutton] is a right temperate meate, and maketh good juyce, and therefore it is used more than any other meate in all diseases,' confirmed Sir Thomas Elyot, 'And yet it is not lyke good in all places, nor the shepe whiche beareth fynest wolle, is not the sweetest in eatynge, nor the most tender.'[28] By the early sixteenth century some major landowners had cleared crop-raising villages to make way for sheep pastures, some individuals holding up to 24,000 sheep. In addition they had raised carcass prices from 2*s.* 4*d.* (12p) or 3*s.* (15p) to 4*s.* (20p) or 6*s.* (30p) each. As stated in the Act of 1533 which reduced individual flocks to no more than 2,000 sheep, 'by reason whereof a marvellous multitude and number of people of this realme be not able to provide meat, drink, and clothes necessary for themselves, their wives and children, but be so discouraged with misery and poverty, that they fall daily to theft, robbery, ... or pitifully die of hunger, and cold.'[29]

Whether home-grown or purchased from the markets, the mutton carcasses were butchered by having their heads cut off ready for making a variety of sheeps-head broths.[30] They were then split in two down the spine, and usually chopped into the scrag end and middle of neck for chops, the best end for cooking whole as a rack or divided into chops, the shoulder, the saddle or loin, the chine, and the leg. The thin lower part of the ribs, the breast of lamb, was also chopped off horizontally.[31] The racks, loins and chines made the best pottages, the shoulders and legs usually being roasted on the bone. Most of the other joints were suitable for boiling, either fresh or salted, using almost identical recipes to those given for beef.[32] Edward Topsell's *Historie of foure-footed beastes* of 1607 confirms that 'In many places they salt their Muttons when they are killed, and so eat them out of the pickle.' The 'pickle' indicates wet-salting in brine.[33]

Pork, both fresh and preserved, made a valuable contribution to the meals taken by all levels of society. Thomas Tusser's verses tell of its place in the rural economy where every October:

If vent of the market-place serve thee not well,
Set hogs up a fatting, to drover to sell.

And November:

Let hog, once fat, lose nothing of that,
When [its] meat is gone, Hog falleth anon
Still fat up some, Till Shrovetide come.
Now pork and souse Bears tack in house,
Put barley a malting, Lay flitches a salting.
Through folly, too beastly, Much bacon is reasty.[34]

Pigs were regularly slaughtered throughout the year, providing an excellent supply of fresh meat and offal, but November was the time for salting down fat hogs to supply the house through to the onset of Lent. Their meat was preserved in a variety of ways, the hind legs being salted to produce gammons we now call ham, the sides boned and salted to make bacon, the lard brined, the shoulder pickled as brawn, and the head cured and stuffed.

For bacon hogs, the sides were scalded and scraped to remove all hair and dirt, after which they were covered in salt for three weeks or a month. After being hung up in a cool, well-ventilated place and rubbed dry, they shortly began to grow moist. Having been dried in a warm part of a chimney, near the heat of the fire, or set in an oven after the bread had been drawn, they were hung up once more. By repeating this process as necessary it was possible to keep them in good condition for at least nine months.[35] In the boiling house the bacon was used to make the following recipe:

BACON & PEASE POTTAGE, ENGLISH FASHION[36]

2lb/900g bacon joint
8oz/225g dried peas
large bundle of mint, tied
4 slices white bread

Soak the peas in 2pt/1.2l cold water overnight, then drain. Place them in a pan with a further 2pt/1.2l fresh water, the bacon and the mint, cover, and simmer very gently for some 2–3 hours until the peas are tender.

Remove the mint, place the bacon on crustless squares of bread in a deep dish, pour on the pease and serve.

To preserve the lard, the layer of fat between the skin and the flesh down both flanks, it was usually dry-salted for some three days to remove the blood. Sufficient salt was then dissolved in water by beating with a paddle until it formed a brine strong enough to float a fresh egg. Once submerged in this, the lard could be kept ready for use for two or three years, provided the brine was replaced from time to time.[37] Alternatively it could be rendered down and stored in pigs' bladders.

The preparation of brawn, the cured flesh-meat originally of a wild boar, but usually from a domesticated example by the sixteenth century, commenced months before it was served at Christmas. Thomas Muffet advised farmers to 'Shut up a young boar, of a year and a half old, in a little room at harvest-time, feeding him with nothing but sweet whey, and giving him every morning clean straw to lie upon, but lay it not thick: so before Christmas he will be sufficiently brawned with continual lying, and prove exceeding fat, wholesome and sweet.'[38] William Harrison then continued:

> It is made commonly of the forepart of a tame boar ... the rest is nothing so fat, and therefore it beareth the name of souse only, and is commonly reserved for the servingman and hind .... When the boar is cut out each piece is tied up either with bulrushes, ozier, peels, tape inkle, or such like, and then sodden in lead or cauldron together, till they be so tender that a man may thrust a bruised rush or straw clean through the fat: which being done, they take it up and lay it abroad to cool. Afterward, putting it into clean vessels, they pour either good small ale or beer mingled with verjuice and salt thereto till it be covered, and so let it lie (now and then altering the sousing drink lest it should wax sour) till occasion serve to spend it out of the way.[39]

TO MAKE BRAWN[40]

4lb/1.8kg pork joint, ideally cut as a rectangle from the back to the belly, the belly end 1in/2.5cm wider than the back, boned out and retaining its skin
pared and chopped zest of 2 lemons
6tbs fine oatmeal
6tbs fine sea salt
6tbs bran

Soak the joint in cold water in a cool place for two days, scraping off any bristles, then rinse clean.

Spread the lemon zest and 1tbs salt on the flesh side and form into a roll, the thick back-meat in the centre, bind in place with broad linen tape, then sew within white cloth (or bandage tightly) to form a neat cylinder.

Plunge into boiling water, and simmer for some 3½hours until cooked through, then allow the brawn to cool to luke-warm in its stock.

Remove the cloth from the brawn, and press it into a close-fitting cylindrical vessel, such as a deep cake-tin or pan, to retain its shape, and leave in a cool place until perfectly cold.

Meanwhile boil 5pt/2.5l water with the oatmeal, bran and remaining salt, and leave until cold, before using to cover the brawn. It was originally left in a strong brine for some weeks before serving, but for modern use only two or three days' soaking is sufficient.

Variations

1. Replace the lemon zest, oatmeal and bran with sage, nutmeg, mace and breadcrumbs mixed with sharp orange juice, and boil with 1 bottle white wine, 1tsp mace, 2 tsp ginger, peel of 1 lemon and a bouquet garni, retaining this to soak the brawn in when cold.
2. Add 1 tsp each of clove, mace and nutmeg, 1tbs salt, 3 large stalks of rosemary and 1tbs mixed herbs to the boiling liquor, omitting the above ingredients. Mix this with a bottle of light ale for soaking the brawn. This was Elizabeth Cromwell's recipe.[41]

If a small pig had had its sides rolled as two collars, and the head boiled in a similar manner, the head was placed in the middle of a large dish, with a collar to each side, stuck with two sprigs of rosemary, large-crystal sea-salt being sprinkled around as garnish.[42] For major feasts the garnish was much more elaborate.

TO GARNISH A BRAWN[43]

1 brawn, prepared as in the previous recipe, and sliced across the grain of the meat
20 x ½in/1cm squares of gold and silver foils
30 bay leaves, preferably freshly picked
½pt/300ml each of red and yellow jelly, preferably made by dissolving 2tsp/10ml gelatin in clear stock or consommé, with red and yellow colouring
2 lemons, halved, and patterns cut in their peels
2 small oranges
a few grapes
1 large branch of rosemary
2 cooked beetroot
3tbs flour or 1 tin gold spray

Arrange the brawn as a shallow mound filling the centre of a large dish, dot the central 6in/15cm area with the foil squares, and surround these with three concentric rings of bay-leaves, stuck in vertically on their stalks.

Form a symmetrical border of jelly, lemon, orange, grape and beetroot around the edge of the dish.

Cut the bottom of the rosemary branch as a sharp point, then either rinse with the water and sprinkle with the flour, to resemble hoar frost, or spray with gold, to replace the original gold leaf, and stick this into the middle of the brawn.

Even more prestigious than the brawn was the boar's head. To make this, the meat and skin was peeled off the skull, cured, stuffed with cured strips of belly pork and fillet with a rich pork forcemeat, bound into shape, and simmered until cooked through.[44] Once cold, it was blackened to look like a wild boar and elaborately garnished. An account at Belvoir Castle records the purchase of 'goldfoylle for the bores hede 10*d*.' in January 1542, while at Hengrave Hall in Suffolk payments in December 1545 included '3 sheets of thick grose paper to decke the bores heade in Christmas 12*d*. More payd to Bushe of Bury, paynter, for paynting of the bores heade with sundry colors 12*d*.'[45] Sprigs of rosemary and bay formed the most essential element however. In his play *The Wonderful Year 1603* Dekker described Londoners trying to ward off the plague with 'rue and wormwood stip't into their ears and nostrils, looking like so many bores heads stuck with brandes of rosemary, to be served in for the brawne at Christmas.'[46] Robert Herrick also described:

At Christmas time
Then if you would send up the brawner's head,
Sweet rosemary and bays around it spread.
His foaming tusks let some large pippins grace,
Or 'midst these thun'dring spears an orange place,
Sauce, like himself, offensive to its foes.
The roguish mustard, dangerous to the nose:[47]

As it was carried up from the screens passage to the top table in the hall, it was celebrated by its own old-established carol, this version appearing in Wynkyn de Worde's *Christmasse Carolles* of 1521:

The bore's head in hande bring I
With garlandes gay and rosemary.
I pray you all sing merely
Qui estis in convivio

The bore's head, I understande,
Is the chefe servyce in this lande.
Loke wherever it be fande
Servite cum Cantico

Be gladde, lords, both more and lasse,
For this hatth ordeyned our stewarde,
To chere you all this Christmasse,
The bores head with mustards![48]

Boar's head and brawn were usually served and cut in slices, but thick slices were also put on a plate, heated in a hot oven, and served with a sauce of orange juice, pepper, gravy and beaten butter.[49]

The most exclusive meat which, due to its size, might appear in the boiling house was the haunch of venison, a cut which comprised half the deer, extending from the lower ribs down to the back knuckle. During the Commonwealth it was frequently prepared for the Protector's table. After being salted it was stuffed with seasonal herbs, spices, suet and egg yolks, boiled in the pot, and placed on sippets on a large dish with three or four cauliflowers. Surrounded by an inner border of stewed spinach, and an outer border of finely chopped curly parsley, it was finally garnished with barberries and sauced with a hot mixture of the stock, vinegar, nutmeg and melted butter.[50]

In medieval England, the religious practice of abstaining from meat on Fridays, Saturdays, Lent, and the eves of saints' days had meant that fish was eaten on almost half the days of the year. The mid-sixteenth century Protestant governments at first cancelled fish-days, as symbols of Popery, but then found it expedient to rapidly restore them for practical and political purposes. The price of meat was rising rapidly, taking it out of the reach of many of the poor, while the increasing threat of invasion from Spain meant that there was a pressing need for a ready supply of new ships and trained seamen. As a result, the Friday fish day was extended into Saturday in 1548 with Wednesdays being added in 1585 as Armadas became an imminent probability. In 1593, when the statutes were re-introduced, a £1 fine or a month's imprisonment was imposed on anyone discovered eating flesh on fish days, unless licensed for medical reasons. Those who failed to inform on their families or neighbours faced a fine of 13*s.* 4*d.* (66p). It was essential that the boiling house should therefore be able to prepare large quantities of fish for at least three days of the week for most of this period.

Sources of freshwater fish were clearly inadequate to meet this demand, and so the anticipated expansion of deep-sea fishing became a reality. Inshore fishing continued as before, as did the great east-coast herring fishery centred on Yarmouth. By following the shoals as they came down from Shetland in early June, sufficient supplies were accumulated to meet the almost nation-wide demands at the huge autumn fair. After gutting, the fish were brined for fifteen hours, 900 then being packed between layers of salt in each barrel before sealing down to exclude air. These were the 'white herring' of household accounts:[51]

> '3 barrels of Whight herring £3–3–6*d*' (Lord North, 1575)
> 'White Herrings, 1 barrel £1–1–0*d*' (Earl of Cumberland, 1629)[52]

Any surplus brined herrings at Yarmouth were hung up in smoky sheds to dry out and change colour. In 1599 Thomas Nash celebrated:

> The puissant red herring, the golden Hesperides red herring, the red herring of red herrings ... it is wholesome in a frosty morning, it is most precious fish merchandise, because it can be carried through all Europe. Nowhere are they so well cured as at Yarmouth. The poorer sort make it three parts their sustenance. It is every man's money, from the king to the peasant. The sound [roe/melt] is good for the stone. A red herring drawn on the ground leadeth hounds upon a false scent. A broiled herring is good for rheumatism. A fishery is a great nursery for seamen, and brings more ships to Yarmouth than assembled at Troy to fetch back Helen.[53]

They were usually sold in casks holding a 'cade' of six 'long hundreds' of 120 fish, 720 to the cade. For instance: '2 cades [1,440] Redd Herring £1' (1575), and 'Red Hearing dem [½] Cade [360] 7*s*.' (1629).[54] Such fish might possibly have been eaten raw, but it was much better to broil them, heating them through on a gridiron over the embers.

The boiling house was much better equipped to deal with quantities of large deep-sea fish. In February and March Bristol ships set off to Ireland, Shetland and the Faroes, returning in time for the autumn markets with supplies of cod, both salted before air-drying, and packed down in barrels with salt to cure as 'green-fish'. Some English ships also ventured as far as Iceland, where, Andrew Boorde tells us, 'The people be good fyshers; muche of theyr fyshe they do barter wyth English men, for mele, lases, and shoes, & other pelfery.'[55] These northern and Baltic fishing grounds were neither an English nor a Scottish preserve however, the Dutch effectively dominating them, probably providing much of the salt fish sold in the east-coast ports. Around 1500 fishermen from Devon and Dorset began to make seasonal voyages to the east coast of Newfoundland, setting up temporary settlements there, these becoming permanent from 1610. Here their catch could be gutted and air-dried, and the livers rendered down to extract the valuable oil.

Wherever it came from, it was important for every household to buy in an adequate supply at autumn fairs, before the deep-sea fisheries closed down, and winter weather turned the roads into rivers of mud. Sufficient had to be stored up to serve fish-days and Lent over the next six months. The basic air-dried cod was called stock-fish, an appropriately Dutch/Baltic word. The better-eating varieties were described as either ling, organ-ling, or haberdine. Thought to be of different species, most were more probably all basic cod, but of contrasting sizes and qualities. Thomas Muffet suspected this, believing that the organ-ling that stood 'every Fish-day as a cold supporter at my Lord Mayor's Table, ... is nothing but a long Cod, whereof the greater size is called Organ Ling, and the [lesser], because it is no larger than a Cod, yet hath the taste of Ling.'[56] Even so, the difference in quality was palpable, superior persons 'Differing as much from other people ... as Stockfish or Poor John [salted and dried hake] is from the large organe ling.'[57]

In the royal household organ ling, along with salted sturgeon, salmon, lampreys and eels, was restricted to the monarch's tables, all others at court having ordinary ling.[58] These were purchased by the Sergeant of the Acatery, assisted by two clerks and the Yeoman Keeper of the Salt Store, who had to carry stock sufficient to feed the court every fish-day, and throughout Lent.[59] Similar provisions were made in virtually every other household across the country:

> [August] Let haberden lie, In pease-straw dry.
> When harvest is ended, take shipping or ride,
> Ling, salt fish and herring, for Lent to provide
> To buy it at first, as it cometh to road,
> Shall pay for thy charges, thou spendeth abroad.
>
> Chuse skilfully salt-fish, not burnt at the stone,
> But such as be good, or else let it alone,
> Get home that is bought, and go stack it up dry,
> With pease-straw between it, the safer to lie.
>
> [December] Both salt-fish and ling-fish, (if any ye have),
> Through shifting and drying, from rotting to save;
> Lest winter with moistness do make it relent,
> And put it to hazard, before it be spent.
>
> Broom faggot is best to dry haberden on,
> Lay board upon ladder if faggots be gone,
> For breaking (in turning) have very good eye,
> And blame not the wind, so the weather be dry.[60]

Being more like slabs of oak than any food, pieces of stockfish required tough treatment to make them edible. This involved laying them on a block and beating them to pliability using either a heavy mallet or a short length of thick rope. This was often followed by an overnight soak in cold water, and simmering for several hours. After draining it could then be dished up in large pieces, have melted butter poured over, and be served with mustard as its accompanying sauce.[61] Even with this treatment, it remained a distinctly worthy but rather unattractive dish. Ben Jonson drew on this in *Every Man Out of Humour*, describing one who 'lookes like … a dried Poule of Ling upon Easter-eve, that has furnisht the table all lent.'[62]

Most modern salt cod is much more delicate, and may be prepared as follows:[63]

TO DRESS STOCKFISH

1lb/900g salt cod, soaked overnight and drained
½tsp salt
4oz/100g butter
4tbs parsley or spring onion, finely chopped

Place the pieces of fish in a broad, shallow pan, barely cover with water, cover and simmer very gently for 10–15 minutes until just cooked. Use a slice to transfer them into a colander, and gently shake them to separate the flakes.

Arrange the flakes row-by-row in a dish, scattering a little salt and parsley or spring onions, then melt the butter, pour it over the fish, and serve immediately with mustard as accompaniment.

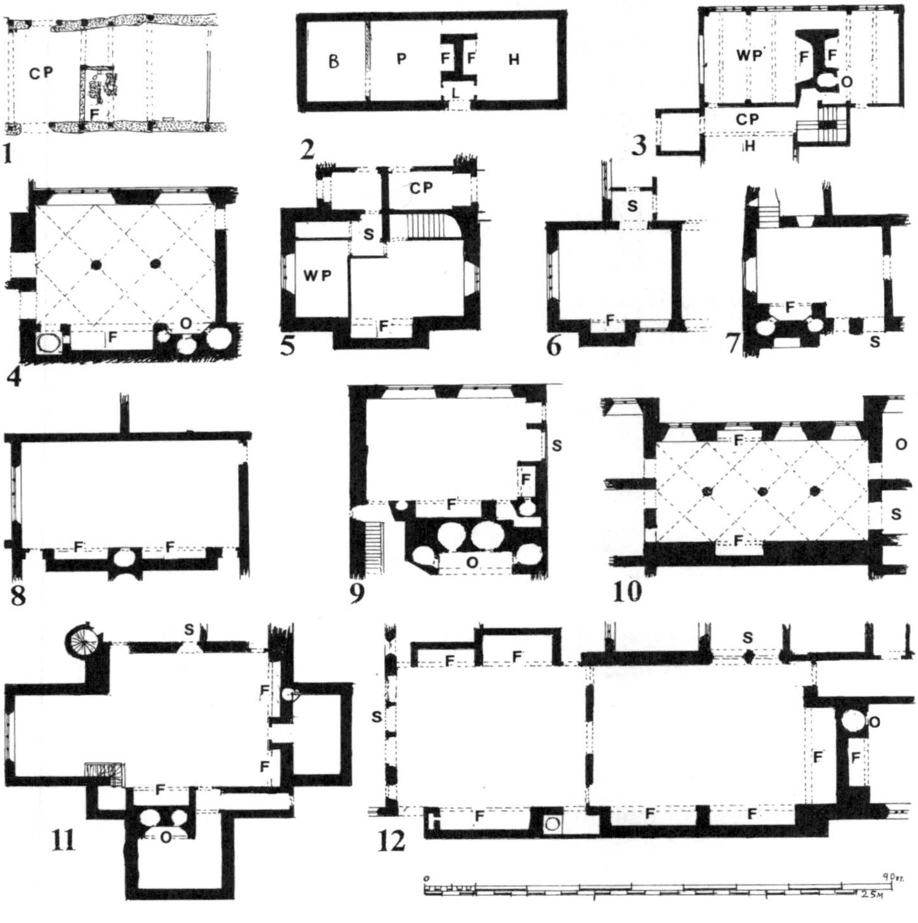

Figure 43. Kitchen plans. The size and facilities of a kitchen varied according to the wealth and status of its builder, as may be seen in the following examples. (1) Wharram Percy, Yorkshire, early 16th cent.; (2) 16th cent. plan of a Suffolk house; (3) Preston Court, Gloucs., c. 1585; (4) Wollaton Hall, Nottingham, 1580; (5) Wilderhope, Shropshire, c. 1580; (6) Doddington Hall, Lincs., c. 1593–1600; (7) Berry Pomeroy, Devon, 1580s–90s; (8) Copped Hall, Essex, after 1564; (9) Hardwick Old Hall, Derbys., 1587–90; (10) Slingsby Castle, Yorks., c. 1630; (11) Worksop Manor, Notts., 1580s; (12) Hampton Court Palace, c. 1530. (B: Buttery; CP: Cross Passage; F: Fireplace; H: Hall; L: Lobby; O: Oven; S: Surveying Place; WP: Winter Parlour.)

CHAPTER TEN

The Kitchen

As in all other periods of English history, the size and structure of each individual kitchen directly reflected the scale and status of the household it served. At peasant level very few rooms were devoted solely to the preparation of food – thus qualifying for the title of kitchen. Instead, cooking formed just one of the multifarious activities carried out in the main family living-room, the name of which varied from region to region. In Cumbria it was usually a 'firehouse', in Yorkshire and Lancashire a 'house' or a 'housebody', while in other areas it was a 'houseplace', or a 'hall', where members of the family might cook, eat, work and sleep together. Sometimes an additional unheated service room, often called a 'buttery' or a 'dairy', performed the combined functions of pantry, larder, buttery, dairy, scullery, wash-house and general store for various household goods. A further room, usually called a parlour, served as a best bedroom, where clothes and linens and the like were frequently stored. Whether built of mud, clay, stone, or cruck or square-framed timbering, simple houses arranging some of these different rooms under one long roof had become common throughout medieval England, and still remained in general use. Their most significant development during the late fifteenth and early sixteenth centuries was centred around their hearths. Instead of having the fire burning in the centre of the living-room floor, leaving its smoke to escape as best it could, it was usually moved to a cross-wall and provided with a wattle-and-daub superstructure to carry the smoke up through the roof. Such changes were clearly demonstrated in the excavation of a house at Wharram Percy in East Yorkshire. When completed around 1500, it was a single-storey block with internal measurements of about 76 feet by 18 feet. This contained a parlour of 13 feet, a cross-passage-cum-porch of 18 feet and a 25-foot byre for the cattle, all in line under a long cruck-framed thatched roof. Here, the central hearth was replaced by a fireplace built against the wall of the cross-passage.

A survey of the rural houses of Lancashire has found that the total exclusion of cooking from the main living-room was rare, being confined to the highest level of yeoman family, where the distinction between yeoman and gentry classes was least distinct. Some two-thirds of yeomen still cooked in their 'housebodies', and although they had rooms called 'kitchens' or 'butteries', these were sometimes unheated and were general-purpose rooms for domestic work and storage.[1] The same practices were to be found in many other parts of the country, where rooms specifically called kitchens and used as such remained rare at ordinary yeoman level. A sixteenth-century house-plan from Suffolk, and the almost identical Pendean cottage now at the Weald and Downland Museum in Sussex, both show a sequence of a 'hall' with a large fireplace as a living-room-kitchen, a parlour as a sitting-room with a smaller fireplace, and then a 'buttery' or 'milkhouse' or 'bakehouse' or 'brew-house' as the multifunctional unheated service room.

The removal of cooking activities from the hall, housebody or other general purpose living-room into a kitchen devoted solely to the preparation of food was still one of the main differences between homes of the yeoman and those of the gentry. At gentry level, the increasing use of masonry fireplaces and chimneys caused most of the formerly detached, freestanding medieval kitchens to be abandoned, their place being taken by new ones integrated into the service rooms off the bottom ends of the halls. Most of the older houses were updated in this way, by adding or replacing kitchen wings, or by inserting masonry chimneys into a pre-existing structure. As many new gentry houses were built in the late-sixteenth and seventeenth centuries, most included a single large kitchen just across the screens passage from the hall. However, by the early seventeenth century the use of the hall was beginning its long transformation from a common dining-room into its present role as an entrance hall usually incorporating a staircase. Increasingly seen as a reception room, its former community of servants was now being relegated to a separate ground-floor service room off the screens passage and variously known as a winter parlour or front kitchen. This served as a servants' hall-cum-cooking area, often supplemented by a back kitchen-cum-scullery, both with a large fireplace for cooking. Away from the formality of the hall, these appear to have been much more comfortable, convivial and convenient for the cooks and servants, and removed them further from their masters' dining-parlours.[2]

The new great houses built by the leading Tudor gentry and nobility needed much larger kitchens to serve households which might vary from a few score on ordinary days up to hundreds at great feasts. To construct them demanded a huge investment in materials and workmanship, and was not undertaken lightly. Whenever a new suite of kitchen offices was to be built, it was essential to commission a master mason or architect to draw up a plan, then obtain the client's approval before compiling a detailed estimate of the basic costs. In 1615, the 9th Earl of Northumberland asked Robert Floode, his disburser for apparel, and Robert Dee, to undertake these preliminaries for a magnificent new house at Petworth in Sussex. After passing through the great courts, the visitor to the proposed mansion would have faced a very impressive façade fronted by an open-arcaded ground-floor corridor. Its central doorway led directly into the cross-passage of the great hall that extended to the left, while service doors to the right led to the buttery, pantry, pastry, surveying place, and kitchen. The whole of this great service wing was apparently to be of two or three storeys, built of brick and stone, and then requiring:

75ft Beer stone for the 3 ovens, & sawing it	£5	12*s.*	6*d.*
bricks, tiled top, lime & hair for the 3 ovens & building them	£2	0*s.*	0*d.*
lime & sand & building the kitchen, chimneys & arches	£1	8*s.*	0*d.*
3013ft tiles & mortar, & paving all the floors	£37	18*s.*	9*d.*
1692 yds plastering	£42	5*s.*	6*d.*
10 beams 43' x 15" & 330 joists to frame the middle storey of the kitchen	?	?	?
100 loads of timber to roof all the kitchen offices	?	?	?
840 yds fretting all the officers' lodgings over the kitchen	?	?	?
Total	£89	4*s.*	3*d.*

These accounts demonstrate the great expense of building a major kitchen wing. At Petworth, the Earl never completed this ambitious scheme, continuing to use his 29-foot-square kitchen until its eventual replacement by the present structure in the early eighteenth century.[3]

In most large, rectangular courtyard houses, the kitchen was set in the corner at the lower end of the hall, being separated from it by a screens passage, buttery and pantry. Most were at the same level as the hall, but some had their floors in the basement so that they could achieve high ceilings by rising up through the adjacent storeys. The arrangement of their fireplaces varied from one house to another, some having just a single fireplace in one wall, while others had two fireplaces either set side-by-side, or on adjacent walls. One would certainly be used for boiling and roasting, while the other might have been used to house a stewing stove for making the more delicate dishes. In addition there might be a boiling furnace or a pastry oven set into either the sides of the fireplace, or the adjacent walls, and also a dresser-hatch for despatching food into a surveying place.

In addition to these kitchens designed for general everyday use, others were intended to serve more specific needs. In the royal palaces, for example, there were separate kitchens to cook the meals served to the servants sitting in the

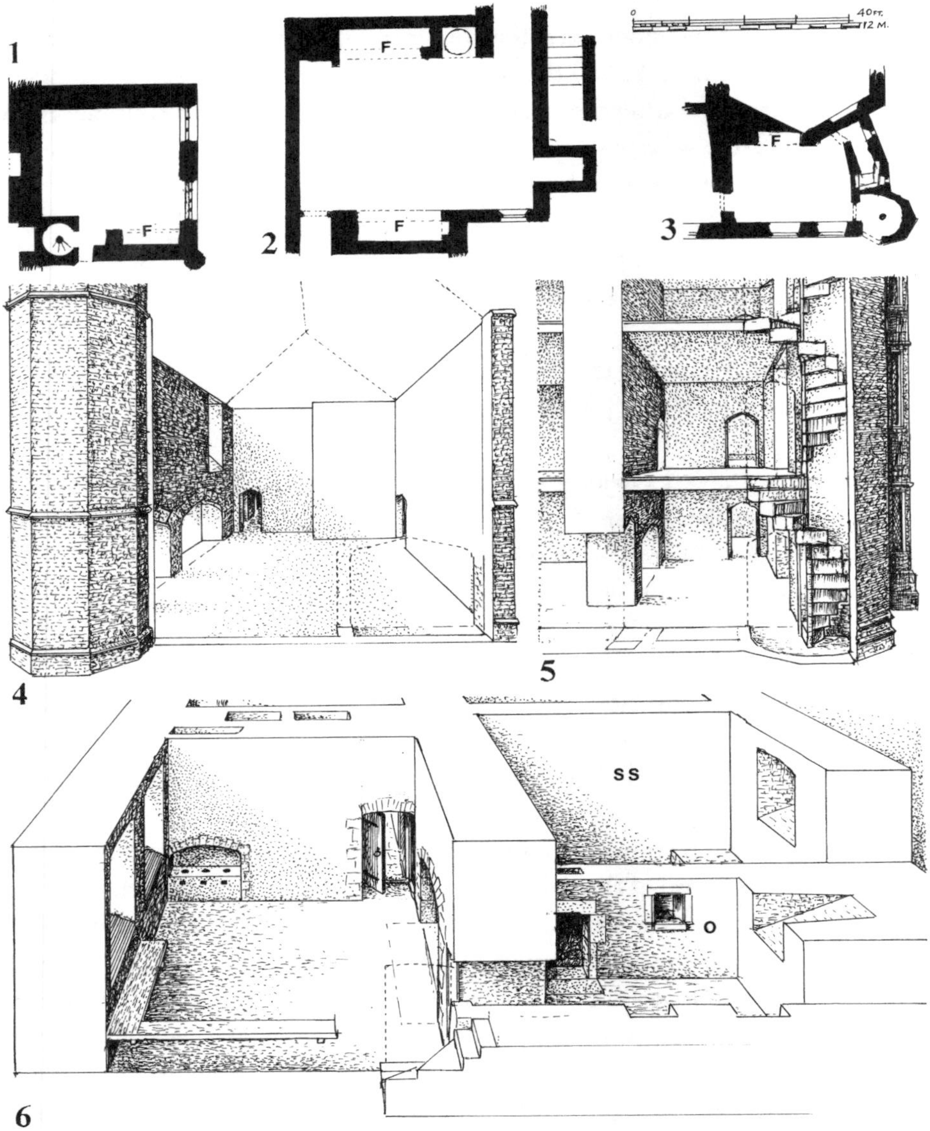

Figure 44. Privy kitchens. Privy kitchens provided an improved level of convenience and security to monarchs and great lords. (1) Hampton Court Palace, 1526; (2) York Place, Westminster, 1528; (3) Cowdray House, Sussex, 1530s; (4) Greenwich Palace, early 16th cent.; (5) Temple Newsam, Leeds, c. 1513; (6) Bolsover Castle, Derbys., c. 1627. (F: Fireplace; O: Office; SS: Silver Scullery.)

hall (the hall-place kitchen), the courtiers in their chamber (the lords'-side kitchen), and the monarchs in their privy chambers (the privy kitchens). The hall-place and lords'-side kitchens were essentially enormous versions of those used by the nobility, their many fireplaces providing a 90-foot length of cooking space at Hampton Court Palace, for example.[4] Built as huge barn-like structures open to the roof, they remained cool and well ventilated as the great fires sucked in vast volumes of fresh air from outside and expelled them as smoke from ranks of magnificently decorated brick chimneys. In winter time they could be so cold that steam rising from the pots into the roofspace froze and fell as snow, as I know from the times I used to cook there.

PRIVY KITCHENS

In order to work efficiently, major households had to maintain strictly regulated daily timetables, especially for mealtimes, where any sudden changes could easily lead to confusion and waste. The household kitchens were ideal for producing ordinary, routine meals at set times, but could not satisfy the particular needs of their lords and masters, who demanded both a superior diet and meals served as and when most convenient. If their activities meant that they missed their usual mealtimes, for example, they were not prepared to wait until the next one turned up, while they also required facilities to satisfy their particular dietary needs. The solution to these problems was to set up a privy kitchen with its own staff. Not only did this provide the maximum flexibility of mealtimes and choice of food, but it provided its master with additional status and a greater security against poisoning.

In planning his ideal house Francis Bacon, Lord Verulam, stated that the privy kitchen, with its buttery and pantry, should be 'sunk underground' beneath the parlours and other living-rooms.[5] If in a basement or on the ground floor beneath the master's privy apartments, it was not only ideally placed for the service of fresh, hot foods, but also provided him with a most comforting form of under-floor heating. The only problems could be the noise and smell, which 'reboundeth uppe into the closette [so that Queen Elizabeth I] cannot sytt quiet nor without ill saver' at Hampton Court. As a result of this, she had a new privy kitchen built some distance away, where it can still be seen today.[6]

Some of the largest privy kitchens for royal use were almost freestanding structures: that built for Henry VII at Greenwich forming a block measuring approximately 40 by 25 feet, extending from his chamber and study. Equipped with three large fireplaces, it was ideal to serve the needs of the royal family, but Henry VIII added a separate privy kitchen close by for Catherine of Aragon in 1516.[7] At Hampton Court, the greatest of the new Tudor palaces, Henry VIII

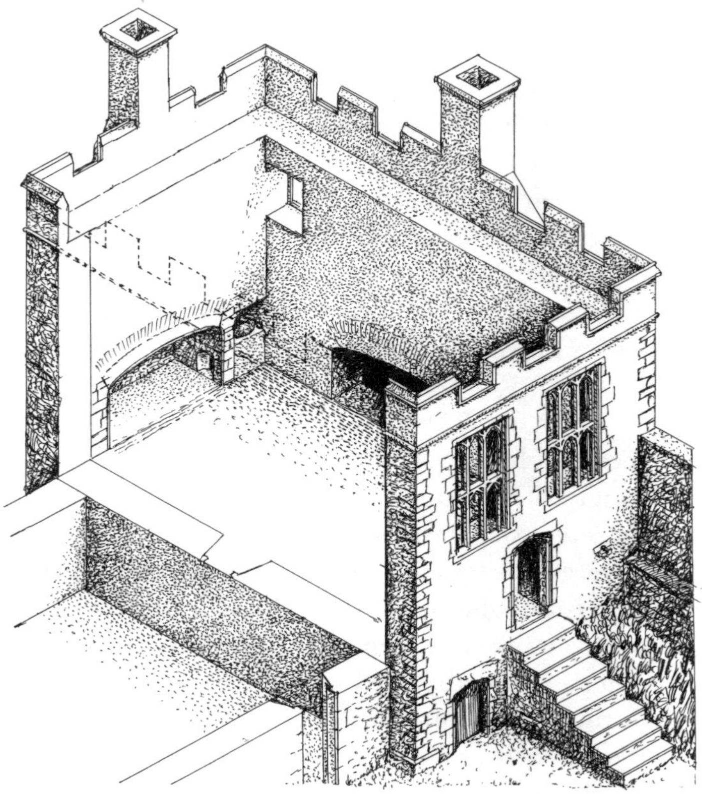

Figure 45. The kitchen, Wharton Hall, Westmorland. As Warden of the Western Marches in the 1540s, Thomas, Lord Wharton, had to extend and fortify his house as a base for his military operations. His new kitchen was therefore built as a tall and strong corner tower.

took over Cardinal Wolsey's privy kitchen of 1526, this being a ground-floor room some 25 feet square, provided with a huge fireplace for cooking, and a spiral stair up to the closet before the door of the king's dining-room. A new privy kitchen for the Queen was built in 1533, similarly on the ground floor with a spiral stair up to her dining chamber, the same arrangement being followed for Henry's new privy kitchen of 1537.[8]

When building their great houses, Henrician courtiers incorporated their own privy kitchens, which may be recognized from both archival and architectural sources. The 1520 inventory of Lord Darcy's Temple Newsam, Leeds, which he built around 1513, shows that his occupied the ground floor beneath the gentlewomen's chamber, a spiral stair enabling food to be carried up from the 'surveying burd' and along to Darcy's bedchamber and great chamber.[9] At Cowdray House, Sussex, the large fireplace in a room below the great chamber suite suggests that this too had been built as a mid-sixteenth-century privy kitchen, particularly since it was directly linked to the chambers by a spiral stair.

These single-room privy kitchens were ideal for the use of small noble families, but could not cope with the demands created by a royal visit. Those who courted advancement in this way had to invest in much larger facilities. In order to accommodate Queen Elizabeth, Robert Dudley had two privy kitchens at Kenilworth Castle, one measuring 45 by 18 feet, with two fireplaces, and another 42 by 19 feet described as 'very handsome' in a survey of 1563.[10] When William Cavendish decided to build at Bolsover Castle in 1627, ready to receive Charles I and Henrietta Maria, he included a semi-basement privy kitchen comprising three rooms. The kitchen itself had one fireplace for boiling and roasting, another for a stewing stove, and a long wall-bench or dresser on which to marshal the various foods. One door leads off into a secure room which probably served as a silver scullery, from where an internal hatch enabled the dishes to be passed into an adjacent clerks' office before being issued for use. The office door, meanwhile, would serve as an excellent dresser office, supervising the waiters as they carried the dishes up the adjacent staircase to the royal apartments.

CASTLE KITCHENS

Following the Wars of the Roses and the accession of Henry VII, there was little need to build any more castles, except those required for external defence. This became a matter of priority in the 1530s, when Henry VIII expected invasions from both France and Scotland, leading him to construct a series of state-of-the-art artillery forts along the Channel. Since they did not have to house large numbers of troops, their catering facilities were quite modest. At Portland Castle, Dorset, a typical example of 1539, there was a regular garrison of fifteen, for example. They were served by a 25-by-19-foot kitchen set within its massive stone walls, equipped with an 8-foot fireplace including a baking oven, ideal for providing basic food through a passage into a 31-foot octagonal dining hall.

Privately built castles, perhaps better described as defensible manor-houses, tended to have kitchens of a civilian scale, being intended to serve a domestic household rather than a large regular garrison. That at Compton Castle, largely rebuilt around 1520 a few miles inland from Torbay, is a tall stone-built ground-level structure measuring some 20 by 15 feet. Its fireplace occupies the whole width of one end, a double-height relieving arch taking the weight of its long timber lintel. Large beehive ovens set into each end of the hearth provided ample facilities for baking. When Thomas, Lord Wharton, decided to extend and defend Wharton Hall, Cumbria, as a base for his actions against the Scots, he included

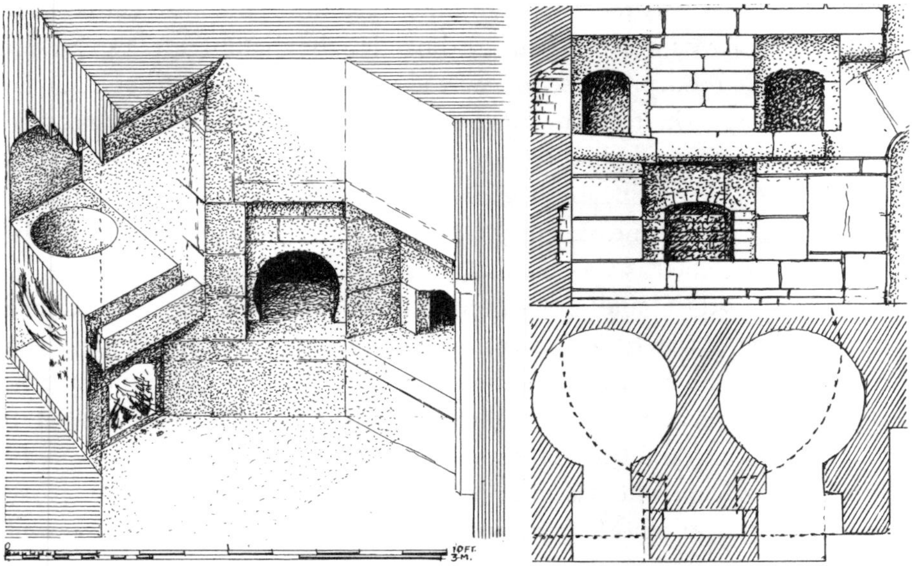

Figure 46. Lodge kitchens. The need to provide lots of good food in small lodge kitchens led architects to devise compact arrangements of ovens and other components. At Lyveden New Bield, Northamptonshire, c. 1594 (left), the boiler with its front drain and the two ovens all stand beneath a single smoke-hood, while the three ovens at Lodge Park, Gloucestershire, c. 1630 (right) each have their own smoke hood.

a hall measuring 68 by 27 feet to accommodate his large retinue of soldiery. Like the hall, the adjoining kitchen is raised over a basement, then continued upwards for a further 25 feet to the top of its battlements. Its 36-by-17-foot interior has two fireplaces, 13 feet and 11 feet in width, together with provision for a 3-foot boiling furnace, but without any ovens. The boiler would be ideal for cooking the messes of beef and pottage expected by the soldiers. The lack of an oven means that, as northerners, they probably received oatcakes rather than bread, unless there was a separate bakehouse elsewhere on the site.

LODGE KITCHENS

The lodges built to provide supplementary accommodation to a great house, or to serve fashionable hunting or fishing parties, were relatively small in area, but built to the highest standards of architectural style. This presented a real challenge to their builders, since they had to incorporate facilities capable of producing huge, high-quality meals within very small suites of kitchen offices. Since they were intensely used for only short periods, and were within a short ride of a family's major seat, they had no need for bakehouses, brewhouses or larders, for all the bread, beer, wine and other raw ingredients could be carted in as needed. They therefore only needed a pantry in which to store their pre-cooked foodstuffs along with those about to be cooked in their kitchens. Since boiling, grilling, roasting and baking had all to be carried out in the minimum of space, the finest lodges incorporated ingeniously contrived ovens and boilers. At Lyveden New Bield in Northamptonshire, for example, the 7-foot-wide octagonal basement of a turret housed a pair of ovens and a boiler, together with a duct to carry off all steam and smells. It would have been ideal to serve Sir Thomas Tresham's fine lodge, which has remained unfinished since 1605. John Dutton's Lodge Park, Gloucestershire, built in 1634, also had its kitchen in the basement, the short wall, at the side of the fireplaces having two 3-foot 6-inch pastry ovens set directly over a 6-foot oven in order to make maximum use of the available space.

Whatever the size and status of a kitchen, it had such features as fireplaces, floors and roofs particularly suited to its situation, as described in the following sections.

FIREPLACES

Throughout most parts of late medieval and Tudor England the great development in the comfort and convenience of most cottage homes was the disappearance of the cooking fireplace from the centre of the kitchen floor. Having occupied this location for millenniums, it was now placed along one of the walls and provided with a wide flue to carry off its swirling wood smoke and peat-reek. This immediately improved the cleanliness and atmosphere of the kitchen/living-room, made the fire easier to control, and rendered it possible to add a first floor above. The form of the new fireplaces differed from one region to another. In the south and south-east, for example, smoke-bays were preferred, these being half-timbered walls rising above mantle-beams parallel to a gable end and set a short distance away from it. A typical though late example may be seen at the Weald and Downland Museum's 'Poplar Cottage', which dates from around 1630–1650. Here the smoke bay is only about four feet wide, its central hearth being partitioned off at one end to form a lobby entrance, and at the other to provide space for a staircase. In the north, smoke-hoods were preferred. These too had a mantle-beam running from one side-wall to the other, but instead of a rectangular chimney shaft rising above, they had a wide pyramidal wattle-and-daubed hood which conducted the smoke up to a narrow chimney. At floor level, one end was partitioned off by a 'heck' or screen to form an entry from a cross-passage behind the hearth, while a 'fire-window' at the other end provided a useful source of daylight.

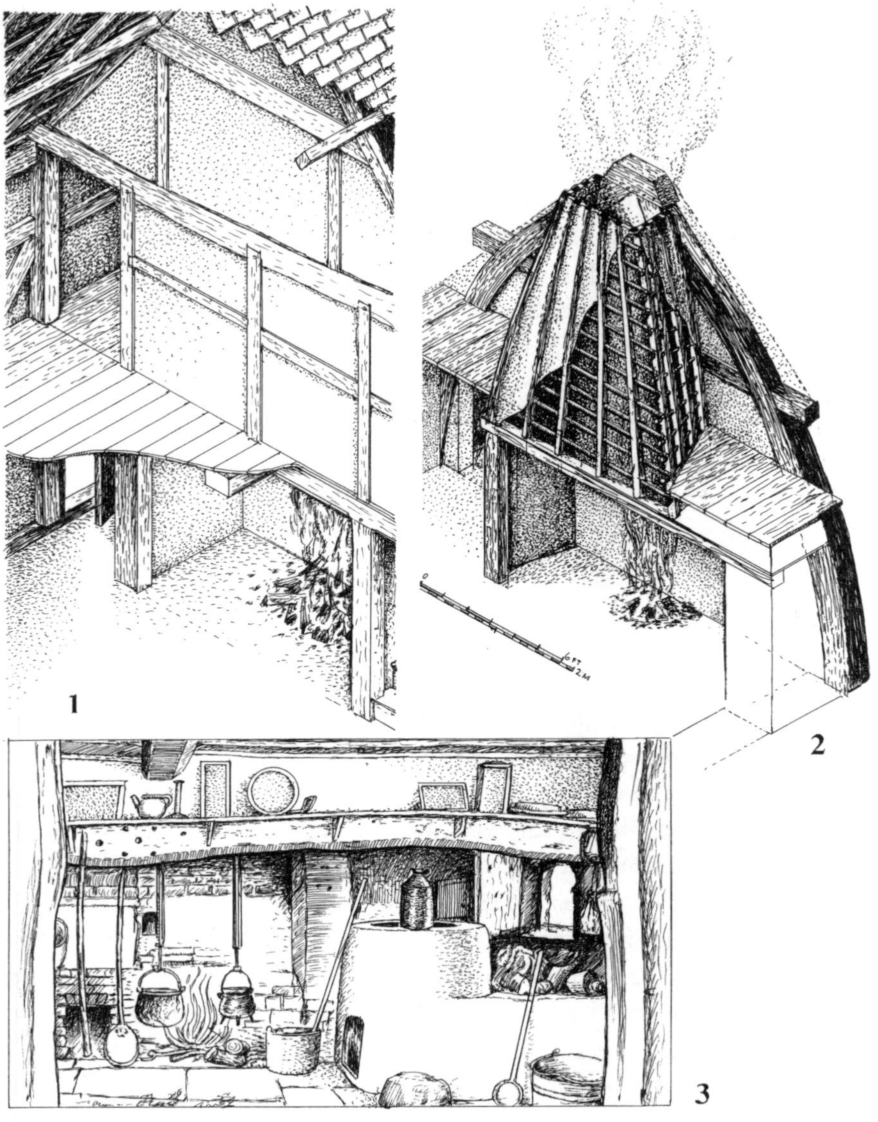

Figure 47. Basic fireplaces. The early 16th century saw the widespread introduction of chimneys into many cottages and small houses. In the southern counties they usually took the form of a smoke-bay, as at Poplar Cottage, Sussex, of c. 1630–50 (1), while in the northern and upland counties timber-framed smoke-hoods predominated. That in a cottage at Old Malton, Yorkshire (2), was recorded by Dr John Kirk around 1920. Where masonry chimney stacks were constructed, wide 'inglenook' hearths were bridged by either masonry arches or, as at Woolsthorpe Manor, Lincolnshire (3), by a timber lintel. Note the boiler, the fire-window above, the oven to the left, and the fixings for a clockwork jack bored into the lintel.

In most new houses occupied by families of yeoman and minor gentry status, kitchen chimneys were built of brick or stone, their wide hearths being bridged by either timber lintels or masonry arches, as already well established in later medieval great houses.[11] Some had single flues rising up their chimney stacks, while others had their flues divided into two or three ducts by cross-walls called midfeathers. These both strengthened their structure, and probably helped to prevent down-draughts. In Essex a number of brick fireplaces of the late sixteenth and early seventeenth centuries were built with two or three open ducts running up the upper half of their firebacks. It is difficult to explain their use, but again they were probably intended to prevent down-draughts.[12]

The simplest way to support the masonry chimney breast over the hearth was to use a massive timber beam as a lintel. Since it was well ventilated and some two yards above the flames, it presented no fire-risk but, unless topped by a strong relieving arch, it was liable to sag and cause structural problems. Large stone lintels were comparatively rare, a better solution being to use cantilevered half-lintels, the outer end of each block being firmly held in place by the weight of the masonry above. A pair of mid to late sixteenth-century kitchen fireplaces at Saltram House near Plymouth were built in this way, using the robust local granite. John Smythson's Slingsby Castle kitchen of the 1620s is an extremely impressive example of this type, each cantilever measuring some 8 foot 6 inches by 2 feet in order to create a fireplace a full 12 feet wide.

Arched fireplaces with typical 'Tudor' four-centred arches had been built in the late medieval period, as at Herstmonceux and Durham castles. Immensely strong, they were ideal for supporting massive chimney stacks. One in Cardinal Wolsey's kitchen at Hampton Court dates to around 1515–20, is over 15 feet wide, its stone voussoirs being notched into each other, and its keystone carried up to gain additional support from a higher relieving arch of brick. When fireplaces were built in the adjacent kitchen for Henry VIII in 1529–30, the masons were far more confident, creating an 18-foot arch of un-notched voussoirs with a relieving arch in the higher brickwork. By the late sixteenth century, fashionable kitchen fireplaces tended to adopt a three-centred or elliptical shape, ideal for creating relatively shallow, wide arches. Those built by Robert Smythson at Wollaton Hall, Nottingham, in the early 1580s are 12 feet wide, their voussoirs being finished with a simple internal chamfer. In contrast, those designed by his son John at Bolsover *c.* 1613–1630 were rather more elegant, having either arches with alternating long and short voussoirs, or else voussoirs cut level at the bottom to create a rectangular fireplace opening. These were among the best kitchen fireplaces of their period, but others of very good quality were now being made by masons in all parts of the country, each working in his particular vernacular tradition.

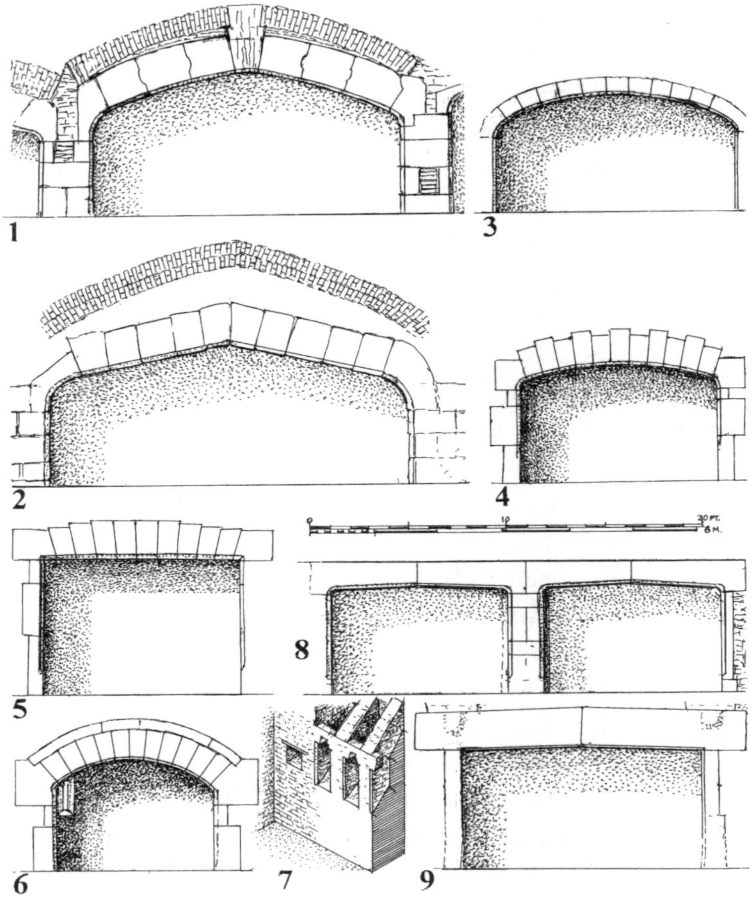

Figure 48. Fireplaces. Spanning a hearth in such a manner as to withstand constant changes of temperature and still carry the weight of a massive chimney stack presented considerable challenges. The 1515–20 arch at Cardinal Wolsey's Hampton Court (1) had its keystone supported by a strong relieving arch of brick, its voussoirs having joggled joints to prevent slippage. The arch in Henry VIII's adjacent kitchen of 1529–30 (2) demonstrates more confidence, relying largely on its brick relieving arch. Robert Smythson's arch at Wollaton Hall, Nottingham of the 1580s (3) adopted an efficient elliptical form, while those of his son John at Bolsover Castle, Derbyshire of 1630 and 1613 (4 & 5) show the adoption of flatter arches. At the vernacular level, segmented arches remained popular, as at Heaton Royds Farmhouse, Yorkshire, of 1634 (6), but some masons adopted more experimental approaches, as in Essex around 1600 (7). Flatter arches, more effective in containing the smoke, were sometimes made as pairs of cantilevered blocks as at Saltram, Devon, in the late 16th century (8) and John Smythson's Slingsby Castle, Yorkshire of c. 1630 (9).

Figure 49. The kitchen, Parham House, Sussex. Built in 1577, this kitchen was provided with two major stone-arched fireplaces, that on the left having an oven to one side and a boiling furnace to the right.

While kitchen fires still burned on the hearth, rather than in a grate, the masonry at the back of the fireplace was always liable to be spalled and cracked by the intense heat. The best solution to this problem was to protect it with a large slab of cast iron. Many of the firebacks made by the Sussex founders bore elaborate designs, and were clearly intended for use in parlours and chambers. Others, probably much plainer, were made for kitchen chimneys, as is shown by the following entry of 1655 from the account book of the Rev. Giles Moore: 'I paid to James Cripps for a plate cast for my kitchen, weighing 100lb and 3 qu. marked G.M.S besides two shillings given to the founders for casting. 13s.'[13]

FLOORS

According to popular history, Tudor kitchens were squalid places and all their food was rotten. Propaganda for this opinion is provided by Erasmus, who complained that the English were 'sluttish within doors. The floors are commonly of clay, strewed with rushes, under which lies unmolested an ancient collection of beer, grease, fragments, bones, spittle, excrement of dogs and cats, and everything which is nasty.' In contrast, there is plenty of evidence to show that English kitchens at all levels of society were remarkably clean. All excavations of peasant

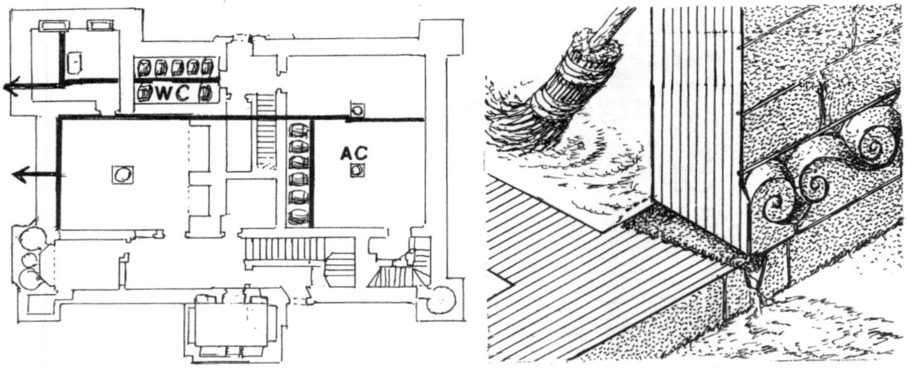

Figure 50. Floor-washing. The better kitchens had shallow gullies set into their paved floors, as at Bolsover Castle, Derbyshire, in 1613 (left), or spouts cut through external walls, as at East Riddlesden Hall, Yorkshire, in 1648 (right). These enabled their floors to be efficiently scrubbed and swilled clean.

houses, such as those at Wharram Percy in East Yorkshire, show their unpaved floors to have been well-brushed and clean, with not a trace of supposed layers of putrefying filth. In the kitchens of most gentry and noble houses, the floors were neatly paved in stone, brick or tile so that they could be constantly washed down and scrubbed clean. Ideally they were laid with a slight slope so that, having had bucketfuls of water thrown across them, it could be brushed down into a 'sink', this being the Tudor term for a drain set into the floor. At Hampton Court, an iron grille covered a stone sink in the centre of the kitchen floor, so that the waste could be discharged into the great conduit below. This magnificent feat of engineering was 14 feet high by 10 feet wide, and led beneath the moat to enter the Thames. All the palaces had similar arrangements, as did many great houses. On a smaller scale, manor houses such as the old Wollaton Hall, Nottingham, had pipes made of bored-out tree-trunks to carry water from their kitchen sinks.[14] Some kitchens, such as the Smythsons' Bolsover and Slingsby castles, had gullies laid throughout their various rooms, these eventually draining through an external wall, while others, as at East Riddlesden Hall, Yorkshire, had only a shallow-arched duct through its wall to drain its flat, flagged floor.

It is difficult to determine when 'sinks' changed from being drains to become bench-level receptacles for holding water for washing purposes. References such as '2 alter stones one Mr. Sheffield haithe made a sinck of in a kitchin' in 1566, 'a sinke, or washing stone in a kitchen' in 1611, or 'a grate for the sincke' of 1634 might still represent the medieval floor-level draining areas as seen in the Glastonbury Abbey and Warkworth Castle kitchens, for example.[15] To date no conclusive archaeological evidence for a pre-Civil War kitchen sink in the modern

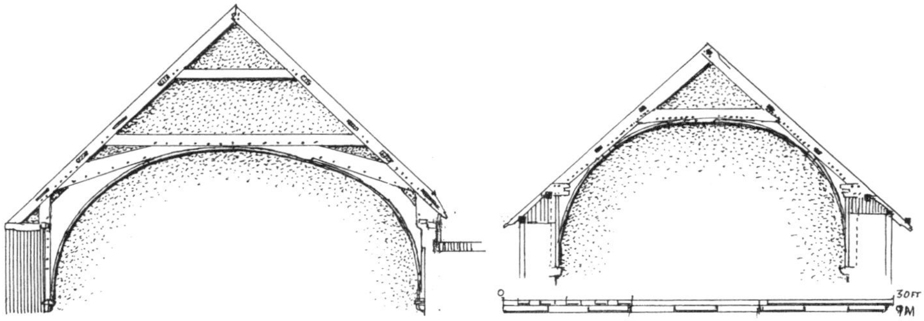

Figure 51. Kitchen roof trusses. Major Tudor kitchens might have high-quality timber roofs, these examples being at Hampton Court of 1529–30 (left), and Sizergh Castle, Cumbria, of the mid-16th century (right).

sense appears to have been found, although they had probably developed from the conduit-basins for clean water found beneath most pumps and taps.

However much effort went into cleaning the kitchen, the presence of food ensured the constant risk of invasion by rats and mice. Domestic cats and dogs appear to have proved largely ineffective, and so most sets of household accounts include payments made to professional rat-catchers. At Haddon Hall in Derbyshire, 'a Man yt Kylled Ratts & Myesse' in July 1549 was paid 16*d*. for his trouble, while at Valdey in 1561 Mistress Broadbank received 3*s*. 6*d*. 'in reward for kytchinge forty-four rattes' – clearing up a major infestation.[16] Rat-traps had been used in England from at least the fifteenth century, these probably being of the traditional forms of an iron gin-trap, or a wooden 'dead-fall' in which a nibbling rodent released a crushing weight from above. The preferred method appears to have been arsenic-poisoned food, as when a rat-catcher 'baited the house' at Althorp in 1623.[17] This could easily lead to the accidental and often fatal poisoning of humans.

ROOFS

The roofs of most peasant cottage living-room-kitchens were constructed of rough rafters mounted on a few purlins supported by cruck frames or simple trusses. From below, the underside of the roof covering was open to view, whether of turfs or thatch, both of which accumulated dirt and smoke ready to fall into the food. One advantage of this kind of roof was that sparrows roosted under the eaves, where they could be caught in nets or riddles; or they nested in the thatch, often in sparrow-pots specially placed here so that they could be taken when needed for food.

Figure 52. The kitchen, Burghley House, Lincolnshire. Here the magnificent fan-vaulting of the 1550s is of unparalleled height and quality for its date. It terminates in a ventilation shaft rising to the roof.

In most well-built houses, the ceiling was formed by the underside of the beams and joists of the floor above, often lathed and plastered for additional cleanliness. Only in the very largest kitchens were there fully framed roofs based on series of huge arched trusses. Those in Wolsey's and Henry VIII's kitchens at Hampton Court, erected around 1515 and 1530 respectively, are perhaps the finest surviving today, each spanning the nigh-on 47-foot width between the side walls. The trusses concealed above later ceilings at Sizergh Castle, Westmorland, built by Walter Strickland in the 1550s, are much plainer, since they were never intended to be seen. Rows of mortices along the sides of their tie-beams and the tops of the wall-plates show that it was built to receive a lath and plaster ceiling.

A number of the finest late medieval kitchens had demonstrated their architectural status and quality in the form of elaborately louvred and vaulted roofs, as may still be seen at Glastonbury Abbey, Durham Cathedral and Raby Castle. By the sixteenth century such kitchens were no longer being built, perhaps because they offered their owners little opportunity for public display and were extremely expensive to construct. However, just one magnificently successful attempt was made to not only rival, but to completely outdo the best of the medieval kitchens.

Figure 53. Vaulted basement kitchens. At Wollaton Hall, Nottingham (top) and Slingsby Castle (bottom), the use of basement kitchens provided a substantial fireproof plinth on which to raise up the state rooms above.

This was the kitchen built from around 1552 by Sir William Cecil, later Lord Burghley, at his new Burghley House, Lincolnshire. Occupying the cool north-eastern corner of this great courtyard house, it measures some 50 by 30 feet, its crowning glory being a soaring multi-ribbed fan vault springing from each corner to terminate in a ventilating louvre which carried off all smoke and steam. Executed in fine cream-coloured Barnack ragstone, it remains one of the most impressive sixteenth-century kitchens in the whole of Europe.

Kitchens covered by masonry vaults had always been quite rare, but as kitchens retreated into the basement storeys, these began to be constructed for purely practical purposes. Not only did they strengthen the superstructure, but they were fireproof and provided a firm foundation for stone-paved floors above. Their use was promoted by the Smythson dynasty of architects, Robert designing

Figure 54. Kitchen classicism. The columns at Hardwick New Hall of the early 1590s (1) and Wollaton Hall (2 & 3) were designed by Robert Smythson. Those of his son John at Bolsover Castle of the mid-1630s (4) and Slingsby Castle, c. 1630 (5) have octagonal shafts with an unusual form of consoled capitals.

them for Wollaton Hall in the mid-1580s, and for Welbeck, Blackwell-in-the-Peak, and his preliminary scheme for Slingsby Castle in 1599.[18] Each of his round Tuscan columns supported a semi-circular cross-vault, strong, functional, and devoid of all ribs or other decorative features. The same details are not to be found in the kitchen of the Little Castle at Bolsover, commenced in 1612 since it was almost certainly built by his son John, who preferred octagonal columns with characteristic consoles on each diagonal face of their capitals. John also used this unique design in his kitchens in the Terrace Range at Bolsover, of *c.* 1627–30, and at Slingsby Castle in *c.* 1630. William Arnold, the leading contemporary architect in Somerset and Dorset, also built vaulted basement kitchens, perhaps his finest being at Cranbourne Manor, Dorset, which he remodelled for the Earl of Salisbury *c.* 1608–11.[19] Here the columns are square with a narrow chamfer down each corner and a simple variety of dentil moulding serving as a capital. The cross-vaults they support have a shallow four-centred profile, the ribs along their groins joining central fluted bosses enriched with finely modelled leaves to complete a highly functional yet elegant design. Vaulted kitchens remained a rarity in England, however, most houses of any quality having their

Figure 55. Cranbourne Manor, Dorset. Built c. 1608–11 by William Arnold for the Earl of Salisbury, demonstrates the advantages of three-centred vaults to reduce their height. Note the dresser hatch by the door.

ceilings lathed, plastered and whitewashed, a simple yet effective means of preventing cooking smells from seeping upstairs, and grit and dirt falling down between the floorboards.

WINDOWS

In all prosperous kitchens, whether vaulted, ceiled, or open to the roof-timbers, the windows were usually set as high as possible, with deep, sloping sills, so as to throw the maximum amount of light across the floor and worktops. Instead of being shuttered or partly glazed, they were now usually fully glazed, with leaded lights set either into the masonry or into opening iron casements. Archival evidence for this change includes accounts from London houses for,

> 26 quayrelles of Englisshe glass sett in the said Kytchin wyndow, price every fote 1*d*: 2*s* 2*d*
> 8 sawdclette barres [glazing bars] for the kytchin wyndows: 8*d*[20]

One area where good light was essential for fine cookery was the stewing stove, and so some small stoves were set into the flat table-height sills of windows set

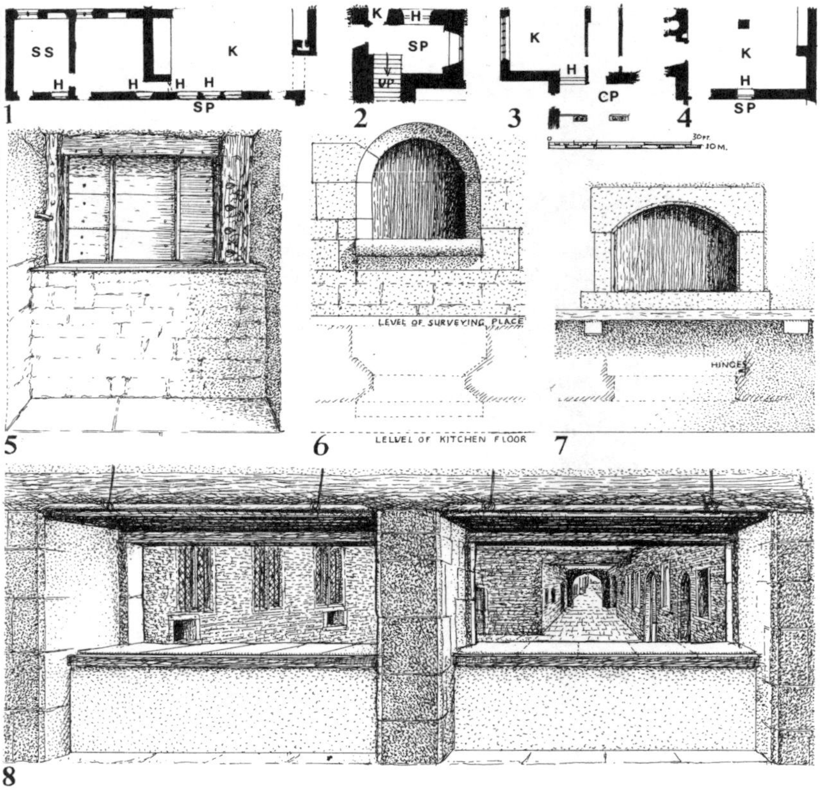

Figure 56. Dresser hatches. (1) lords'-side, Hampton Court, c. 1515–1520s; (2) Sizergh Castle, Cumbria, mid-16th cent.; (3 & 5) Oakwell Hall, Yorkshire, 1583; (4 & 7) Bolsover Castle, Derbyshire, mid-1630s; (6) Lodge Park, Gloucestershire, c. 1630; (8) hall-place, Hampton Court, 1529–30. (CP: Cross Passage; H: Hatch; K: Kitchen; SP: Surveying Place; SS: Silver Scullery.)

at a lower level. Larger stoves might be placed directly beneath high-level windows, as in the Terrace Range and the garden stillhouse at Bolsover. Some architects provided even better stove-top lighting by setting the stoves in deep fireplaces, the back wall of which was pierced by large glazed windows to the open air. These can be seen at Cowdray House in Sussex, and also in the back of the northern 'fireplace' in the ruins of Slingsby Castle, Yorkshire, showing that it was intended to house an impressive 12-foot stove.

DRESSERS

Following well-established medieval practice, dressers with serving hatches through which laden dishes could be passed out to waiters in an adjacent 'surveying place' were essential in all great houses. Since their shutters or doors were only opened at mealtimes, they prevented any wasteful and unauthorized distribution or theft of food, as well as excluding all hungry interlopers. In addition, they provided an important facility for checking the food when ready for service, so that both the cooks and the clerks could ensure that it was of the specified quality and quantity. As recorded in Henry VIII's household ordinances, the clerks of the kitchen were to 'daily sett out at the dresser to the King's Chamber and the Queen's, and to all other the Ordinarie of the Household, to see that none of them doe lack any of their Ordinances which is set for them.' They were further instructed to supervise the Master Cooks as they served food from the dresser 'without embesselling or takeing away any parte of the same, according to the old custome of the King's house.'[21] For the Privy Kitchen, these duties were directly supervised by Edward Weldon and Eustace Sulliard, Surveyors at Dresser for Henry VIII.[22]

The dresser hatches built at Hampton Court for Cardinal Wolsey in the years around 1520 still survive today as a 10-foot-wide opening in the eastern wall of the kitchen. Its table-height base is formed of broad planks of wood and its flat top from a stout wooden lintel surmounted by a pair of relieving arches in the brick wall above. On the kitchen side, a pair of heavy shutters hinge down from the lintel, each being raised at mealtimes and secured by '3 houcks of irne servyng to hold up the dresser window.'[23] Outside, in the 'Great Space' or surveying place, the two dresser windows, separated by a great oak pillar, are finished with elaborate mouldings. Since this kitchen served lavish foods dished on silver, two separate offices were set just to the south of this dresser, the first being a silver scullery, where the dishes were cleaned and stored ready for use. From here they were passed through an internal doorway into the dresser office where the clerk of the kitchen and his staff presumably recorded them before passing them out through a hatch next to the dresser, into the hands of the cooks, who filled them and set them out in order. When all was ready, the hatches would be opened, each waiter taking a dish in its correct order and having it inspected at the separate dresser-office hatch before carrying it up to the dining tables. Afterwards, the soiled silver would then be returned to the hatch into the silver scullery, so that the whole operation could commence once more.

Some major courtiers incorporated similar facilities into their newly built kitchens. At Sir David Owen's Cowdray House, Sussex, in the 1520s, the 7-foot-wide dresser hatch faced into a large triangular surveying place, still open to the sky in the medieval tradition. Having collected their dishes, the waiters then passed a clerk seated in a small doorway, the upper half of the door being fully open so that he could record the food before it was served into the hall and chambers. The soiled plates were then returned to a room to one side of the

Figure 57. Dinner service at Cowdray House, Sussex. Having been washed and polished in the spicery/pantry (1) the dishes were passed out of its hatch (2) and into the kitchen hatch (3). Here the cooks filled them with food (4) and passed them to the gentleman waiters through the dresser hatch (5). The waiters then carried each dish to be surveyed by the clerk in his hatch (6) before continuing through the open-air surveying place (7) and along the kitchen passage (8) into the hall (11). Ale and beer drawn from the cellar (9) was kept in the buttery (10) ready for issuing in tankards and other vessels into the hall.

kitchen passage, there to be cleaned and polished on work-benches set beneath a large window. When required again, the dishes were passed through a hatch at the end of the bench, across a narrow corner of the surveying place, and through a further hatch back into the kitchen, ready to be refilled and sent out once more. Other large houses had simpler arrangements, with their dresser-hatches leading directly into open-air or roofed surveying-places. Sometimes their outer faces were provided with a projecting wooden bench, as in the Terrace Range at Bolsover Castle, but otherwise they were simple arched or flat-topped openings flush with the wall. There was no general rule for the form of their wooden doors, some swinging up internally as at Hampton Court, some being hinged from the side, as at Bolsover, and some sliding to one side, as at Skipton Castle, North Yorkshire. Accounts for the works undertaken at Windsor Castle in 1534–5 include details of a more interesting arrangement there which had 'a new leved Dore and a Wykett in the same ffor the great Kechyn with a ffoldynd Dresser upon the said Wykett to sett mette upon at the serves time.'[24]

Where major households occupied quite small buildings, such as lodges, many still required a dresser/serving hatch to ensure the security of their food and tableware, as shown by examples at Lodge Park in Gloucestershire, or Dob Park, Otley, in Yorkshire. They were also provided in some privy kitchens, as at Hampton Court.[25] In contrast, the food in most gentry houses appears to have been issued directly from the kitchen door, across the cross-passage and on into the hall and parlours. Apparently these households had no need for a dresser and serving hatch for the controlled distribution of their meals, although a few did. At Oakwell Hall in West Yorkshire, for example, the Batt family included a serving hatch leading directly from the kitchen into the cross-passage in their stone-built H-plan house of 1583. Their contemporary, Thomas Smalman, Justice to the Council of the Marches of Wales, demanded even greater control of his kitchens and their contents when building Wilderhope, Shropshire, in the 1580s. Those entering the south porch could only turn into the hall, for the cross-passage was permanently blocked by a solid wall, its northern end forming a very secure lockable service entry-cum-surveying place for the kitchen. It is regrettable that the National Trust has destroyed this rare feature.

Today all the dressers and serving hatches are silent, for no longer do master cooks pound the woodwork with their ladles to announce that all the food was ready to be served. As a character queried in Leigh's *Armorie* of 1597, 'What meaneth this drumme said I. Quod he, this was to warn gentlemen [waiters] of the household to repair to the dresser.'[26] Another cries 'Hark, they knock to the dresser', while Massinger, in his *Unnatural Combat* of 1619, hospitably explained:

I'd undertake to stand at push of pike
With an enemy in the breach, that undermin'd too,
And cannon playing on it, than to stop
One harpy, your perpetual guest, from entrance,
When the dresser, the cook's drum, thunders, Come on,
The service will be lost else,[27]

Before leaving the kitchens, it is interesting to consider who was to control and manage them. In the largest houses it was the master cook, as will be described later, while in the smaller ones it was the mistress of the house, chiefly the wife of the master and mother of his children. When her husband died, the title of the property usually passed to his eldest son, whose wife became the new mistress. This placed her mother-in-law in a different position, potentially homeless and devoid of all support. This problem was usually solved through provisions made in the husband's will. To describe a typical arrangement, a yeoman living at Lythe Hill in Surrey in 1571 instructed that his widow should occupy the ground-floor parlour, first-floor chamber and second-floor garret to the west of his hall, the lofts over the hall and kitchen, and room and fire in the hall and *half* the kitchen. Here she was to have access 'to dresse meate and drincke, bake and brewe ... at all tymes.' Furthermore, she was to have brass pots, two kettles, a posnet and a skillet to cook with, and half the kitchen hen-coop in which to keep her poultry, as well as a good selection of tableware. In this way she would be able to continue a virtually independent household, notionally quite separate from that of her daughter-in-law, but still in the same rooms. In practice, however, much mutual respect and restraint would be required to maintain a peaceful family life.[28] The alternative adopted by some families in which husbands and wives of different generations occupied the same house was to set up separate kitchens, greatly reducing the risk of bitter and stressful disagreement.

CHAPTER ELEVEN

Kitchen Furniture

Of all the furniture which might be found in a Tudor or early Stuart kitchen, the most important was the dresser on which, as its name confirms, all manner of foods were prepared for use. Today the 'dresser' is usually perceived as a piece of living-room furniture, its run of cupboards and drawers being surmounted by a tall plate-rack, all beautifully polished. In contrast, the original kitchen dressers were no more than great, thick planks of planed wood raised to table height on either pillars or trestles.

Since they were essential in almost every kitchen, it should be expected that they would appear in every probate inventory, since they listed everything it contained, but often this is not the case. The reason for this is that probate inventories only included moveable goods, all fixtures being ignored, since they formed part of the freehold of the property. Where no dressers were listed, it usually meant that they were built into the walls and floors of the kitchen. This practice is clearly illustrated in the list of fixtures at Bedford House, Exeter, compiled in 1594:

> One great planck standing in the midest of the kitchen, standing on two tresells made fast in the grownd.
> A long planck standing by the glasse windowes side standing on fowre tressels made fast in the grownd.
> A planck by the dresser Window, made fast in the Wall in ech end belonging to the dresser.
> One other short planck under the dresser planck one end made fast in the Wall the other end standeth upon tressles made fast in the grownd.
> A long shelfe by the Windowes standing on five corbells.
> One little shelfe over the Sestren on two corbells.
> A shelfe made fast in the Wall by the beef pann.[1]

Being part of the structure, the construction of such fixed dressers sometimes appears in building accounts, as when Ashley House, Walton-on-Thames, was being completed in 1604:

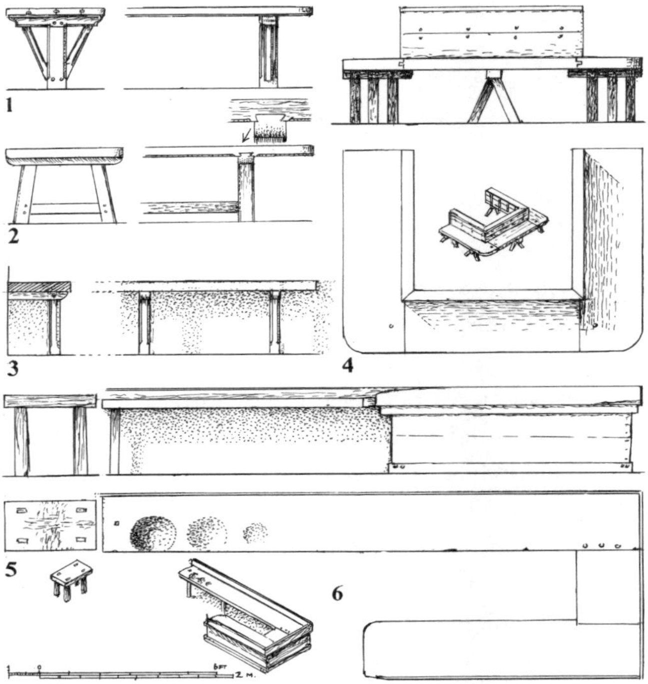

Figure 58. Kitchen furniture: dressers. (1) Rockingham Castle, Northamptonshire, mid-16th century?; (2 & 3) Hampton Court Palace, 1530?; (4) Cowdray House, Sussex, mid-16th century?; (5) the Mary Rose*, 1545; (6) Haddon Hall, Derbyshire, mid-16th century?*

R. from London out of olde Jurye 3 dresser plankes of beeche for the pastrye and Kitchin and 1 Kitchin boorde of elme.
P. for 2 dresser boordes for the Kitchin, 1 for the pastrye of beeche and one elme plancke for the Kitchin boorde with the cariage out of the olde Jurye to the water side 27*s*. 10*d*.
P. to Tho. Taylor of Chobham for 2 beechen planckes for dresser boordes for the Larder ... 6*s*. 8*d*.[2]

Evidence for the appearance of such dressers when free-standing and 'made fast in the grownd' is very scarce, since most have been destroyed. However, a very rare survival still stands in the kitchen of Rockingham Castle in Northamptonshire. Its three great square posts and braced crosspieces probably date from the construction of the kitchen around 1550, although the top may have been replaced by Anthony Salvin when he restored the Castle in the Victorian period.

The sockets by which dresser-boards were mounted on stout beams built into the walls, their ends supported by posts set into the ground, can be seen in a number of ruined kitchens, such as those in the Terrace Range at Bolsover Castle, Derbyshire. Fortunately a few dresser-boards of this type still survive *in situ*, as at Hampton Court Palace (*c.* 1530?) and Ham House, Surrey (*c.* 1610?, with later drawers). The finest example, however, is in the kitchen at Haddon Hall in Derbyshire, which has a single board measuring some 18 feet by 2 feet by over 3 inches in thickness running along one wall. At its left-hand end are three round hollows where food has been repeatedly chopped, while its right end is extended to produce an efficient U-shaped dresser. A deep plank mounted above its outer edge prevented any food or utensils from rolling off onto the floor, while boarding beneath created a useful storage space, also helping to shield the cooks from chilling draughts.

Where the dressers were freestanding and, despite their great weight, relatively portable, they were listed in inventories as 'boards' or 'dresser-boards', as in: 'fyve long bordes' (Chatsworth, 1601); 'dresser bordes 4, formes of tressels 2' (Wollaton, 1601); or the '2 greate planks with feet' (Broadclyst, 1579).[3] One at Hampton Court Palace has its massive top supported on a pair of strong trestles, their top rails being cut to a dovetail profile and slid into a slot cut into its underside, thus preventing it from warping. Another Tudor example in the kitchen of Cowdray House in Sussex, now only known from its description as 'three great dressers' in an inventory of 1682 and a watercolour by S.H. Grimm, was constructed to form three sides of a square surrounding a tall stone conduit. It was supported on five three-legged trestles and had a boarded back and shelf around its inner edges for the convenience of the cooks. References to 'folding boards' or 'falling boards' suggest that some dresser-boards were designed to fold down when out of use, but nothing is known of their construction.[4] Although dresser-boards continued in use throughout this period, some households were replacing them with tables mounted on joiner-made frames from the later sixteenth century, Alice Aldworth of Reading having one in her kitchen in 1586, for example.[5]

Some dresser-boards were intended to serve specific purposes. There was an 'oysterboard 5*s.* 6*d.*' at Petworth House in 1574; '2 chopping bordes' at John West's house in Exeter in 1569; and '3 chopping stools 12*d.*' in Alice Aldworth's kitchen in Reading in 1586.[6] Only one fully provenanced example of the latter appears to have survived; made of a thick oak board mounted on four stout through-tenoned legs, it was recovered from the hold next to the galley on the *Mary Rose*, which sank in 1545. Cut-marks running both across and along its upper surface show where the meat and fish was chopped before being plunged into the boiling furnace nearby.[7]

Another probably smaller and lighter kitchen-board was used to hold the dishes and impedimenta, this being known as a dish-bink in the north and a dish-board in the south, or else as a dish-cradle or a dish-cratch. Keeping this neat and tidy was seen as a measure of good housekeeping, Fitzherbert advising housewives to 'dresse up thy dysshborde.'[8] Individual kitchens might have a number of other pieces of furniture in which to store their utensils and ingredients, such as cupboards, arks (large plank-built chests), or shelves. There might be an aumbrey or food-cupboard, such as the 'ambry half laticed for pans' which stood in Thomas Cromwell's kitchen in 1527.[9] Salt was often stored in cooper-made salt-barrels, salt-kits, or salt-pies, or else in salt-boxes.[10] Only the major kitchens possessed purpose-made spice-boxes from which to season their food. There was a 'little trunck to kepe spyce in the Kytchen 3*s.*' at Petworth House in 1599.[11] Within a few years spice boxes had developed into small square cupboards, their lockable doors opening to reveal perhaps eight or more drawers to hold individual spices. Due to the costly nature of their contents, such spice-boxes were usually fine examples of joinery, made in oak, elm or fruitwood and decorated with carving, mouldings or turned split-balusters.[12]

Today we find it unacceptable to keep livestock in the kitchen, but this was not the case with previous generations. In many cottages poultry roamed free across the kitchen floor, as I remember still seeing in Hampshire in the 1960s. In Brompton, North Yorkshire, William Ryman had a 'caul 4*d.*' in his living room in 1498, for example, this being a dresser having a cage to hold his cock and hen incorporated into its base. Many others in this area had similar cauls well into the Stuart period.[13] Thus housed indoors, the poultry were warm and safe for, as Thomas Tusser warned:

> Where pullen use nightly to perch in the yard,
> There two-legged foxes keep watches and ward.[14]

The practice of keeping poultry in the kitchen was found in many of the most prosperous households. Some in Elizabethan Exeter had 'a cage for poultrye' in their kitchens, while more had 'a Coope for Capons 3*s.* 4*d.*' or 'a Capon Cage 10*s.*' there.[15] These were specifically used to hold capons or cocks as they were crammed with food to fatten them up for the table even though to,

> Leave capon unmeet, Dear fed is unsweet,
> Though fat fed is dainty, yet this I thee warn,
> Be cunning in fatting, for robbing thy barn[16]

The remaining furniture usually found in kitchens was largely devoted to seating. This often comprised just a few stools or chairs suitable for rough usage, rather than anything of good quality.

CHAPTER TWELVE

Of Cooks

Cooks in all major households worked under the direct control of the clerk of the kitchen. He was the senior officer who organized the supply of ingredients, the bills of fare, the quantities to be cooked, the payment of most bills, and the inter-related activities of each culinary department. To undertake these duties he had to understand every managerial and practical aspect of the cook's work, thus ensuring that, as stated in royal household ordinances of 1526:

> every of the master cookes give their dayly attendance ... that their meates be good and sweete, and to see the same well dressed; and to cause the cookes under them to see all such victualls as shall come to their hands be well and seasonably dressed, and the same to serve out at the dressours by the oversight of the said clerke of the kitchen, without embesselling or takeing away any parte of the same; according to the old custome of the King's house.[1]

The careers of most professional kitchen staff started with their appointment as young 'boys' or 'children' of the kitchen. Their wages were usually between £1 and £2 each year, plus their food.[2] The Eltham ordinances of 1526 recorded how the junior kitchen staff in the royal household worked either naked 'or in garments of such vileness as they now doe, and have been accustomed to doe [and] lie in the nights and dayes in the kitchens or ground by the fire-side'. To remedy this situation it was ordered that in future they should 'be found with honest and whole coarse garments, without such uncleannesse as may be the annoyance of those by whom they shall pass, and so be brought up in that business, as they may have been chosen for that purpose may learne hereafter to be cookes ... a certaine number alternately to be deputed shall daily, once in the forenoone and once in the afternoone, sweepe and make cleane the courts, outward galleryes, and other places of the court, as there remaine no filth or uncleannesse in the same ... overseene to be done by the serjeant of the hall or some officer of the same by him appointed.'[3] To pay for the new clothing, each of the three master cooks was given twenty marks, £13 6*s*. 8*d*., each year from 1526. By 1541 the master cook was spending £50 'for appareling of 33 galapines for one year fully to be run at Christmas next coming', suggesting that each set of clothing cost some £1 10*s*. 4*d*.[4]

This new policy of clothing the kitchen boys had already been common practice in many lesser households. In 1520 the Le Stranges' of Hunstanton were already paying 11*s*. for three yards of red cloth to dress their cook, as well as the following for their boy of the kitchen:[5]

2yds. Canvas for a shirt	8*d*.
4yds. Frieze for a coat	2*s*. 0*d*.
Robert Tailor making his coat & doublet	6*d*.
1 ell blanket for his hose	11*d*.
1 pair of hose	8*d*.
1 pair of shoes	6*d*.
clout leather [for patching them]	5*d*.
	5*s*. 8*d*.

The Earl of Leicester's three boys of the kitchen were being smartly dressed in well-made and fully lined clothes around 1560, their coats apparently being black, and their hose russet:[6]

5yds. Sheep russet at 2s. the yd.	10*s*.
3yds. Welsh plain lining for the same hose	2*s*. 6*d*.
8yds. Black frieze at 16*d*. the yd.	10*s*. 8*d*.
for making 3 pairs of hose	
for cloth lining & making coats & hose	£1 12*s*.0*d*.

Along with the other junior kitchen staff, the boys were allocated the most basic of sleeping accommodation. At Wollaton Hall in 1599 they were provided with an old mattress, an old quilt, and an old coverlet in a room away from the main house.[7] References to 'straw for the children of the kitchens beddes 2*s*.' suggest a minimum level of comfort.[8]

Kitchen boys were rarely selected on the basis of their intelligence and energy. When Edmund Verney tried to find a worthwhile occupation for one dull youth, he considered that since 'Nedd is so thick-sculled a fellow, without any apprehension, & so indoseable, a cook is the easiest trade I can think on for him', and put him under the direction of his head cook. Even so, 'Nedd' refused to do any work, or learn to read and write, until his articles of apprenticeship had been signed. The exasperated Edmund therefore recommended that he should either be beaten into action with a ladle, or else be turned out as a labourer to wear a fool's coat and collar.[9]

Whether employed in a royal or private household, or in the shop of a professional city cook, kitchen boys would be expected to enter into a formal apprenticeship with their master, this being recorded in the registers of a cooks' guild. That in London had been established in the early fourteenth century, gaining its grant of arms in 1461 and its incorporation as a City Company in 1482.[10] Similar cooks' guilds also operated as part of the civic administration of most other major cities, regulating the training and working practices of all their members, and protecting their interests. Only master cooks were able to practise their trade within the limits of their particular city, but this still left them free to work in private households. Even so, most people preferred to employ fully trained master cooks who had earned the membership of their guild through apprenticeship, otherwise called servitude. The only other methods of becoming a master cook were by patrimony, where one's father was a freeman of the city, or by purchase, paying a sizeable fee into the guild's coffers.

As their levels of skill, strength and usefulness gradually developed during their years of training, the kitchen boys would rise through the ranks of turnspit, groom, yeoman and sergeant cooks in their kitchens. They were still subject to the disdain of the clerks, however, as may be seen by some sets of accounts which record payments to characters such as 'Roger Platterface' of the scullery, 'gregorie one-eye' of the bakehouse, or just 'the fooles of the kechin'.[11]

Despite such insults, some households gave great encouragement to likely youths who showed real skill in cookery. Some time around the early years of the sixteenth century John Smythson was born as the illegitimate son of an officer of Henry VII's wardrobe and one of the royal laundrywomen, perhaps not the best start in life. Having been trained, however, he rose to become Master Cook to Elizabeth I by 1562, with an annual salary of £11 8*s.* 1½*d.*, five dishes at every meal, the income from the sale of beef fat and lambskins from the Privy and Queen's Side Kitchens, a house in Eltham and land in Westminster, and his own coat of arms, raising him to the rank of gentleman. His portrait, painted in 1568 (figure 59), presents him as a well-dressed courtier, gold rings on his fingers and gold chains round his neck, very prosperous and successful.[12]

Similarly, having been initially instructed by his master-cook father, the fourteen-year-old Robert May was sent off by Lady Dormer to train in France in 1601. Here he joined the household of Achille de Harlay, president of the Parliament of Paris, where he spent five years learning the language, reading their culinary manuscripts and printed recipe books, and gaining kitchen experience. On returning to England he was bound over to Arthur Hollinsworth, cook to the Grocers' Company and the Star Chamber, and almost certainly a master cook in the Cooks' Company of London.[13] After completing his

Figure 59. John Smythson (c. 1523–c. 1590), Master Cook to Elizabeth I. The son of two royal servants and probably trained as a kitchen boy in the royal household, his rise to Master Cook brought him great wealth and properties including Millbank and a vineyard in Westminster and a house and lands in Eltham, Kent. Note his fashionable dress, gold chains and elaborate ring.

apprenticeship, May would also have become a master cook, but unfortunately the Company's registers which would have recorded this were destroyed by enemy action in 1940. However, he went on to become one of the most celebrated cooks of his age and author of *The Accomplisht Cook*, the major work on early seventeenth-century English cookery.

William Rabisha's career had followed a similar route. His upbringing commenced in the household of an honourable lady, 'who spared no cost nor charge for my instruction in the said Art,' first in her own kitchens, and then in those associated with Charles II's court in exile in France. He went on to work as master cook for a number of families.[14] These probably included those of the Duchesses of Richmond and of Buckingham, and Ladies Lane, Tufton and Walker, all 'upholders and nourishers of ... the said Mystery of Cookery' to whom he dedicated his *Whole Body of Cookery Dissected* of 1661.

In return for their great responsibilities, master cooks could expect high wages, in addition to free bed, board and clothing. In the royal household in 1551 the master cook for the King's mouth received £30 a year, master cooks £20 and other cooks £6.[15] In the 1580s the Earl of Leicester's personal cook earned £8, and others £2, while in the early seventeenth century the Earl of Northumberland's master cooks earned £10, and others £5.[16] In addition, such men could expect to receive considerable extra income. Each New Year the monarch gave each master cook a gift of silver-gilt in return for presents in the form of marchpanes; in 1561 Elizabeth I gave George Webster an 8oz tankard and in 1578 John Smithson 8oz in gilt plate.[17] The leading courtiers did the same, Leicester giving the royal Privy, Queen's and Lords'-side cooks £2 each at New Year, along with further gifts to everyone else in the various offices of the kitchen.[18] The master cooks might also be permitted to hire themselves out to provide feasts for others. When entertaining Elizabeth in 1577, for example, Lord North had to pay £4 to the Earl of Leicester's cook, and a further £21 to the cooks of London, vast sums for that period.[19] Such income might be expected on a regular basis, but there might also be infrequent gifts of even greater value from time to time. In 1541 John Bricket, Henry VIII's Master Cook, was granted the stewardship of Caversham in Oxfordshire to supplement his wages, along with an annuity for life paid out of the tax income from the counties of Cheshire and Flint.[20] It was the policy of the court to promote its staff according to their merits rather than favouritism, 'so that the King's house [is] the myrrour and example of all others within this realme.'[21]

The master cooks in the royal household were so greatly favoured by Queen Elizabeth that she attended their great feast at Mile End in March, 1559. From her gallery, she observed the procession of gunners, great guns, halberdiers, musicians, a great dancing giant, a team of morris dancers, a cart bearing two bears and another with great mastiffs. These were followed by 'the master cooks rydying in cottes in brodere, and cheynes of gold, and mony of the quen['s] servandes in ther levery.' The repeated firing of the great guns, the music, dancing and bear-bating ensured that this was a memorable day, as did the accompanying dinner of 'all manner of mett and drynke.'[22] With such rewards openly displayed for all to see, the competition for any senior post that fell vacant must have been extremely fierce.

As befitted their status, master cooks in great households wore expensive, fashionable clothing. Cardinal Wolsey's master cook wore damask satin or velvet with a gold chain around his neck, for example, while Queen Elizabeth's master cook had his coat of marble cloth embellished with velvet, all fabrics forbidden to the lower classes.[23] These excesses disappeared with the early Stuarts, Robert

Figure 60. Robert May, master cook. His Accomplisht Cook *of 1660 remains one of the finest cookery books in the English language.*

May's portrait of 1660 showing him wearing a plain jacket from which emerges the broad collar and tasselled cords of his linen shirt. He sports a neat moustache and shoulder-length hair. This contrasts to the short hair and clean-shaven face recommended by some authors who quoted the advice of Heliogobalus: if he vomited, he wished to 'be well assuryd that it came not by no heer [hair] from his cokes heddes.'[24]

Dressed in the finest of clothes, well paid, well fed and well housed, armed with a formidable degree of practical skill and book knowledge, and in charge of considerable human and material resources, it is not surprising to find that Tudor and Stuart master cooks thought highly of themselves. A poem of around 1524 likens them to heathen priests:

To god of the belly, gluttons a temple make
Of the smoky kitchin, for temple it them take.
Within this temple minister bawdy cookes,
And yong scolions with fendes of their lookes;
The solemne aulter is the boorde or table,
With dishes charged twentie in a rable;
The beestes offred in sacrifice or hoste
In divers sortes of sodden and of roste;
The sawce is insence, or of the meate the smell,
And of this temple these be the vessell;
Platters and dishes, morter and potcrokes,
Pottes and pestels, broches and fleshe hokes,
And many mo els then I can count or tell
They know the best which in the kitchen mell,
For God of the wombe this service they prepare,
As for their true God full little is their care.[25]

The master cooks' own opinion of their intellectual and practical abilities is best described by Ben Jonson in his masque of *Neptune's Triumph* presented at court for Twelfth Night, 1623–4. In its opening scene Jonson meets the master cook in the banqueting house, where he is informed:

> Sir, this is my room, and region too ... And in matter of feast, the solemnity, nothing is to be presented here, but with my acquaintance and allowance ... a good Poet differs nothing at all from a Master-Cook. Either's art is wisdom of the mind ... I am by my place to know how to please the palates of the guests ... the study of several tastes, what every nation, the Spaniard, the Dutch, the French, the Walloon, the Neopolitan, the Britan, the Sicilian, can expect ...
>
> Expectation ... is a powerful great Lady, Sir, at all times, and must be satisfied; so must her sister, Madam Curiosity, who hath as dainty a palate as she ... For there is a palate of the understanding as well as of the senses. The taste is taken from the good relish, the sight with fair objects, the hearing with delicate sounds, the smelling with pure scents, the feeling with soft and plump bodies, but the understanding with all these ... you must begin in the kitchen. There the art of Poetry was learn'd and found out, or nowhere, and the same day with the art of Cookery ...
>
> A boiler, range and dresser were the foundations
> Of all the knowledge in the universe,
> And that's the kitchen. What! A Master-Cook! ...

A Master-Cook! why, he's the man of men
For a professor! he designs, he draws,
He paints, he carves, he fortifies,
Makes citadels of curious fowl and fish,
Some he dry-ditches, some motes around with broths,
Mounts marrow-bones, cuts fifty-angled custards;
Rears bulwark pies; and for his outer-works,
He raises ramparts of immortal crust;
And teaches all the tactics at one dinner,
What ranks, what files, to put the dishes in,
The whole art military! then he knows
The influence of stars upon his meats,
And all their seasons, tempers, qualities,
And so to fit his relish to his sauces!
He has Nature in a pot 'bove all the chemists,
Or bare-breech'd brethren of the Rosy-cross!
He is an architect, an engineer,
A soldier, a physician, a philosopher,
A general mathematician ...

I would you have your isle brought floating in now
In a brave broth, and of sprightly green,
Just to the colour of the sea; and then
Some twenty Syrens, singing in the kettle,
With an Arion mounted on the back
Of a grown conger, but in such a posture
As all the world would take him for a dolphin ... [26]

Those who observed such master cooks in action in the kitchen might temper such high-flown and boastful philosophizing with the brutality of their methods, which even included cutting up live animals.[27] John Earle's cook in his *Microcosmographie* of 1628 presents a more realistic portrait:

> The kitchen is his hell, and he the devil in it, where his meat and he fry together. His revenues are showered down from the fat of the land, and he interlards his own grease among to help the drippings. Choleric he is, not by nature so much as his art, and it is a shrewd temptation that the chopping knife is so near. His weapons of war offensive are a mess of hot broth and scalding water, and woe be to him that comes in his way. In the kitchen he will domineer and rule the roast, in spite of his master, and curses is the very

> dialect of his calling. His labour is mere blustering and fury, and his speech like that of sailors in a storm, a thousand businesses at once; yet in all this tumult he does not love combustion, but will be the first man that shall go and quench it. He is never good Christian till a hissing pot of ale has slaked him, like water cast on a firebrand, and for that time he is tame and dispossessed. His cunning is not small in architecture, for he builds strange fabrics in paste, towers and castles, which are offered to the assault of valiant teeth, and like Darius his palace, in one banquet demolished. He is a pitiless murderer of innocents, and he mangles poor fowls with unheard of tortures, and it is thought the martyr's persecutions were derived from hence; sure we are Saint Lawrence his gridiron came out of his kitchen. His best faculty is at the dresser, where he seems to have great skill in the tactics, ranging his dishes in order military and placing with great discretion in the fore-front meats more strong and hardy, and the more cold and cowardly in the rear, as quaking tarts, and quivering custards, and such milk-sop dishes which scape many times the fury of the encounter. But now the second course is gone up, and he down into the cellar; where he drinks and sleeps till four o'clock in the afternoon, and then returns again to his regiment.[28]

The fuming anger of master cooks was already a well-known characteristic of their profession. Then, as now, their choice of abusive words was legendary. As Beaumont and Fletcher's Diagoras exclaimed in *The Maid's Tragedy* when trying to repel a crowd; 'I pray you, can you help me to the speech of the master-cook?' In 1625 Massinger introduced Furnace the Cook into a country household near Nottingham. In response to the usher's observation that 'Cooks, by their places may be choleric', Furnace replied:

> Twit me with the authority of the kitchen!
> At all hours, and all places I'll be angry;
> And thus provoked, when I am at my prayers
> I will be angry … I am angry with my Lady …
> I was entertained by her to please her palate,
> And, till she foreswore eating, I performed it, now
> Though I crack my brains to find out tempting sauces …
> … when I am three parts roasted
> And the fourth part parboiled, to prepare her viands
> She keeps her chamber, dines with a panada
> Or water-gruel, my sweat is never enough [thought] on.[29]

The inflaming effects of heat, drink and temper appear to have worked havoc on the cook's complexion. This is clearly demonstrated in Sir Thomas Salusbury's *Twelfth Night Masque* at Knowsley, especially composed for the Great Stanley in 1640, and featuring raucous in-jokes directed against his household officers. As it marked the end of the Christmas revels, Father Christmas declared his bequests to Dr Almanac, leaving the fawning, swaggering steward and comptroller, 'One new booke of Tackticks to learn a new march up with my Lord's mace.' The curmudgeonly, censorious Andrew Broome, clerk of the kitchen, received 'one new booke of Arithmeticke and one other new booke of the Poetrie of theise times: hee may censure and damme all as he pleaseth.' In contrast, Peter the cook inherited a face-pack in the form of 'three whole pounds of Fuller's earth, together with a pattent of reformacon to mend ill faces: I would have him to try the receipt upon his own first, and so goe on with his commission as hee shall see cause.' As the crowded hall rocked with laughter, under-cooks and kitchen boys must have dreaded the ensuing retribution below stairs!

The skills of master cooks were great. Writing in 1584, Thomas Cogan noted how 'it is saide a good Cooke can make you good meate of a whetstone, even so it may be that suche fish and flesh as is of its own nature unwholesome and unpleasant, by the skill of dressing may be made both wholesome and pleasant.' He had experienced this when eating a pie in which tough, dry stockfish had been rendered extremely savoury.[30] Regrettably some cooks were unable to perform such miracles, hence the Elizabethan proverbs 'God sendeth us meate, and the Devil Cookes' and, from 1552, 'He is an evyle cooke that cannot lycke his own fyngers.'[31] The latter was taken up by Shakespeare in *Romeo and Juliet*:

> *Capulet* Sirrah, go hire me twenty cunning cooks.
> *Servant* You shall have none ill, sir, for I'll try if they lick their fingers.
> *Capulet* How can'st thou try them so?
> *Servant* Marry , sir, 'tis an ill cook that cannot lick his own fingers; therefore
> he that cannot lick his fingers goes not with me.[32]

Even with a bad cook, there was little real risk of being deliberately poisoned in England, since the punishment for doing so was particularly appropriate and horrific. The cook who poisoned broth intended for the Bishop of Rochester, but killed his servants instead, was found guilty and therefore 'boylyd in a cauderne [of brass] in Smythfeld' in 1531.[33] Even so, in 1599 John Danyell requested Robert Cecil to instruct the master cook and other officers dealing with Queen Elizabeth's food to prepare it personally, 'To prevent others their wicked practices,' also warning Cecil that he too may be poisoned.[34] Maids who were found guilty of poisoning were not boiled alive, but their punishments were still quite horrific, one being set in the pillory one day to be branded on the forehead and have an ear cut off, then brought back the next day to lose her other ear. Another who 'putt in to a pott serten powyssun' which caused her masters and fellow-servants 'to swell and vomett peteusle' had her ears nailed to the pillory before both her hands were cut off.[35]

FRENCH COOKS AND COOKERY

The practice of employing a French cook to prepare the meals served to the monarch appears to have started in the reign of Henry VII, for whom Perot le Doulce was 'cook pro oro'. He went on to serve Henry VIII as Yeoman Cook for the King's Mouth, being granted 'his dwelling in one of the new houses at Charing Cross' in 1533, and being paid £3 6*s.* 8*d.* a year in 1540. As French cook to Edward VI in the early 1550s, he appears to have completed around half a century of continuous service in the privy kitchen.[36] Edward's successor, Mary I, similarly employed the Frenchmen Estienne Havet and Astyan Hana as her master cooks.[37] Both Elizabeth I and James I appear to have preferred English master cooks, but Jehan Rivière was performing this role for Henrietta Maria (herself of course French) in the 1630s, with W. la Montague [W.M.] as her 'escuyer de cuisine.'[38]

The fashion for employing French cooks was already well established in noble families. Robert Dudley, Earl of Leicester, had Philippe as his French cook in the 1550s and '60s, followed by Piero Moerew in the 1580s. The Earl of Northumberland had Robert Jaggard 'the French cook' at £10 a year from 1623 to 1630, and Lady Portland her 'French cook' about the same time.[39]

A taste for French cookery had also been promoted through diplomatic contacts. Between around 1617 and 1657 Thomas Barker of Shrewsbury, though no great traveller, had 'been admitted into most Ambassador's Kitchins that have come into England ... and do wait upon them still at the Lord Protector's charge, and I am duly paid for it.'[40] By contrast, Lord Herbert of Cherbury had to ensure that his cooks could produce feasts 'to the manner of France' while serving as ambassador to Paris from 1619 to 1624. Here, to impress the Spanish Count de Gondomer's gentlemen, he gave them a tour of the kitchens where:

> after my usual manner, were three spitts full of meat, divers pots of boiled meat, and an oven with a store of pies in it, and a dresser board covered with all manner of good fowl, and some tarts, pans with tarts in them, after the French manner.[41]

Others who travelled to France found many of its dishes flimsy and insubstantial in comparison to their solid English fare. In 1644, having retreated to Rouen to escape the Civil War, Sir Ralph Verney bemoaned his new French diet:

> I know noe English maide will be content with our diet and way of living: for my part, since this time twelvemonth, I have not had one bit of Rost meate to dinner, and now of late, I rost but one night in a weeke for Suppers, which were strange in an English maide's oppinion.[42]

His particular dislikes included the numerous *légumes* and *potages*. However, by the time he had returned to England in 1653, his appreciation of French cuisine had developed considerably, his garden now being planted with 'Cordon d'Espaigne' (cardoons), both Roman and frisée lettuces, cabbages of Milan and also frisée, melons and dessert grapes.[43] These, along with other French foods, were now to be incorporated into his daily fare, with Michel Durand eventually being employed as his French cook.[44]

From the 1580s French dishes had already started to infiltrate cookery books printed in England, these including fricassees and others cooked 'in the French fashion.'[45] John Murrell's *A New Book of Cookery … all set forth according to the new English and French Fashion* appeared in 1617, but it was not until 1653 that the first complete French cookery book was translated into English. This was François Pierre (alias) La Varenne's *The French Cook*. Dedicated to the Earl of Thanet, it claimed that 'Of all Cooks in the World the French are estemm'd the best, and of all Cooks that ever *France* bred up, this may very well challenge the first place.' This statement, though an excellent copy-writer's boast, would certainly be seriously challenged in many English households, where, although open to new ideas, there was great pride in the high standards of the native tradition.

ROYAL, NOBLE AND GENTLE LADY COOKS

It would be difficult to imagine Queen Elizabeth stirring pots in the kitchen, but Henrietta Maria was a highly skilled cook, as were many ladies of the powerful upper classes. Contemporary opinion on such practical involvement in household affairs was strongly divided. When setting down important advice to his son in 1595, Henry Percy, Earl of Northumberland, dreaded the consequences of allowing noble ladies to do anything more than raising and educating the children, keeping the linen sweet, entertaining strangers, and carving at table. Some might be efficient at keeping household accounts, but savings on food would be squandered on new clothes and jewels. Most importantly, 'The kitching, buttry, or pantry, are not places proper for them,' he wrote, as we have already observed, although allowing them a place in the dairy.[46] Territorial master cooks and other professional servants would also find an inquisitive and troublesome lady intruding into their offices particularly unwelcome. In contrast, John Milton thought that,

... nothing lovelier can be found
In woman than to study household good,
And good works in her husband to promote,
Yet not so strictly hath our Lord imposed
Labour as to debar us when we need
Refreshment, whether food, or talk between ... [47]

Ladies of high status certainly did not intend to enter into the world of everyday catering and its massive bulk food production. Instead, they wished to concentrate on delicate small-scale cookery, using recipes and ingredients of greater refinement, intricacy and interest. The lives they lived within their richly furnished parlours and chambers could be oppressively claustrophobic; practical cookery with a few friends offered an attractive, stimulating escape.

The great ladies of earlier centuries had never cooked, since their kitchens were staffed entirely by men, who often worked in the nude. The reason why Elizabethan ladies moved into cookery most probably stemmed from the Dissolution of the Monasteries in the 1530s. Up to this time religious houses had provided the only medical care available to most of the community; when they were closed down, their workload tended to be transferred to the ladies of the nearest major house. In 1539, as the last of the monasteries were being suppressed, two of the first London-printed books of medical advice were published, these being *The Treasure of Poor Men* and Sir Thomas Elyot's *Castel of Helthe*. These were followed in 1558 by the *Secretes* of Alexis of Piedmont, which included general remedies, perfumes, household recipes, general science and sugar confectionery, here considered in terms of its medicinal benefits. The book which had first demonstrated that fine cookery and sugar confectionery were, 'Mete and necessary for the profitable use of all estates both men and women: and also pleasant to recreation,' was John Partridge's *Treasurie of Commodious Conceits and Hidden Secrets* of 1573. This was so popular that it was consistently republished over the next 64 years. Many books exploring the same themes, all written by men for the use of ladies, followed in the late sixteenth and seventeenth centuries. Most included a number of recipes from overseas, but volumes such as *Epulario or The Italian Banquet* of 1598 (from the Italian original of 1549), La Varenne's *The French Cook* of 1653 and *Archimagirus Anglo-Gallicus* of 1653 provided more specialized information.[48]

Using these published recipes, along with others obtained from family and friends and transcribed into manuscript recipe books, ladies now developed great skill in making their own medicines, toiletries, alcoholic drinks, sugar confectionery, preserves, bakery and fine cookery. Much of this activity took place either in purpose-built stillhouses or in the pastry, where they could easily work without interrupting the routine of the main household kitchens.

The range of dishes prepared by noble and royal ladies is demonstrated by *The Queen's Closet Opened*. From her arrival in England in 1625, Queen Henrietta Maria had collected dozens of recipes, which were transcribed into her recipe book by one 'W.M.', ready for her practical use.[49] In 1655, while still in exile in France, the Queen gave her consent for him to publish the manuscript, which was issued as a trilogy, *The Pearl of Practice* dealing with medical matters, *The Compleat Cook* of 164 general recipes, and another 164 in *A Queen's Delight*, largely devoted to confectionery. These cover every aspect of the fine cookery and stillroom products with which a great lady of the late sixteenth and seventeenth centuries would be expected to serve her family and entertain her guests, using her own compilation of recipes. To gain the necessary expertise, William Powell recommended that well-bred young girls should abandon all pretentious matters and instead:

> Let them learn plain works of all kind...Instead of song and music, let them learn cookery and laundry. And instead of reading Sir Philip Sydney's *Arcadia*, let them read the *Grounds of Good Housewifery*...If the mother of them be a good housewife...let her have the bringing up of them. Place the other[s] forth betimes [into other households] before they can judge of a good manly leg.[50]

WIVES AND MAIDS

In major kitchens the staff was entirely male, women only being hired in as and when required, as when the Le Stranges paid 'ye Nethered wife for 5 weeks helping ye Cooke in ye Kechyn' in 1519, or the cook to the Star Chamber employed 'a poor woman labouring in the kitchen during this term 21*d*.' in 1567.[51] The low wages paid to women were controlled by statute in the sixteenth century. An Act of 1515 set a maximum of ten shillings a year, plus four shillings for clothing, in addition to meat and drink. Their hours might be from 5 a.m. to 8 p.m., with half an hour for breakfast and an hour for dinner.[52]

In middle-class households the role of master cook was usually taken by a cook-maid. Ideally she should have all the qualities set out by Thomas Churchyard, some of which have already been mentioned in respect of the bakehouse (page 120, above):

> She was as good a maiden cook
> As ever dressed a piece of meat;
> And for a banquet, small or great...[53]

In other smaller houses it was the wife who performed every culinary task, as well as taking on the management of the entire domestic economy. Men freely set down their expectations of such women. In his *Book of Husbandry* of 1523 Sir Anthony Fitzherbert stated that she should rise early, say her prayers, and immediately start work. This included sweeping the floor, dressing the dishboard, tidying everything, milking the cows, straining the milk, dressing the children and cooking all the meals required in her household. She should then send the corn off to the mill, bake, brew, make butter and cheese, feed the pigs and poultry, gather the eggs, and drive away all kites, crows and polecates. In addition, Thomas Deloney demanded that:

> Her household folke from sloth to keepe
> She will indevour with good heede;
> At worke more wakeful than asleepe,
> With place and stuffe which housewifes need
> To be employde: her hands also
> The way to worke will others show.
>
> Her wit a common wealth maintaines
> Of needments for her household store,
> And, like a ship, herself contains
> The riches brought from forraine shore
> Arriving, with a bounteous hand
> Dispearsing treasure through the land.[54]

For her cooking, Gervase Markham further required that,

> First, shee must be cleanly both in body and garments, she must have a quicke eye, a curious nose, a perfect taste and a ready eare (she must not be butter fingered, sweet-toothed, nor faint hearted); for, the first will let everything fall, the second will consume what should increase, and the last will loose time with too much nicenesse ...[55]

Armed with all these qualities, Tudor and Stuart housewives ideally became extremely capable and confident, fully able to fulfil the multifarious roles demanded in keeping their households clean, well fed and healthy. To perform their tasks efficiently, they proved hard task-mistresses to their long-suffering maids. In Nicholas Breton's *The Court and Country* of 1618, Hylding the maid bitterly complained that:

> I must serve the Old Woman, I must learne to spinne, to reele, to carde, to boil ... bake, make Mault ... milke, serve Hogges, make clene theyr houses

> ... Then to the kitchen, turne the spitte, although it was but seldome, for we have not had roaste Meate often; then scoure Pottes, wash dishes, fetch the wood, make a fire, scald milke Pannes, wash the Cherne and butter dishes, ring up a Cheese clout, set everything in good order. And alas, to all this was but another Maid and I.[56]

Hopefully she still had the time and energy to maintain her personal hygiene, and that of her clothes, otherwise she might degenerate into the kind of maid described by Shakespeare as 'reechie necked Malkins', 'Kitchen Trulles', or, in *The Comedy of Errors*:

> Marry, sir, she's the kitchen maid and all grease; and I know not what use to put her to but to make a lamp of her and run fro her by her own light. I warrant her rags and the tallow in them will burn a Poland winter; if she lives till Domesday, she'll burn a week longer than the whole world.[57]

Maids were not the only ones to suffer from the beatings and tongue-lashings inflicted by formidable housewives. Despite having agreed to honour and obey their husbands, wives were quite able to see off any man who interfered with their culinary affairs. When the Cobbler of Colchester scoffed an apple pie without permission, his wife gave him a sound cudgelling as she screamed:

> Gip with a murraine knave! She cryes,
> Must your old chops be fed
> With custards and with apple pyes?
> A rope shall stretch your neck.
>
> I'll teach you take the browne rye loafe,
> And chaw the Essex cheese,
> As fitter for your rotten teeth
> Than any one of these!'[58]

To be fully efficient, domestic kitchens had to run to a strict timetable, to ensure that every meal could be served promptly. The exact routine would vary from one house to another, but the following proposal from Nicholas Breton's *Fantastickes* of 1626 was suggested for that of a prosperous gentleman or city merchant:

1 a.m. The bellman calls to the maids to look to their locks, their fire and their lights.

3 a.m. The milkmaids start work in the dairy, the housewife starts her housework, and the porridge pot is put over the fire for the servants' breakfast.

4 a.m. The servants have their breakfasts, and the milkmaids go into the fields to milk the cows.

5 a.m. The schoolboys are up and off to school, the maids are busy milking, the mistress makes her preparations, while the hogs, chickens and capons are fed.

6 a.m. School has started and the mistress has put her maids to their various tasks. In the City, the shops and markets are now open.

7 a.m. The milkmaids make butter and cheese in the dairy. Professional men now start work.

8 a.m. Breakfast [for the family?].

9 a.m. The markets are busy, and fresh fish is coming in.

10 a.m. The cook finishes the boiled and roast meats and cuts sops for the broth. The milkmaids clean their vessels.

11 a.m. Schoolboys, professional men, their guests and the labourers all come home for dinner, after which the cook clears up in the kitchen.

12 a.m. The first course of dinner has been served, the second now follows, to be followed by fruit, cheese, and the saying of grace.

Preparations for supper would then follow and, after it had been served, the kitchen cleaned again, and preparations made for re-starting the whole cycle early next morning.[59]

Throughout these long days the cook had been using his or her judgement in many different ways: gauging temperature of fires, ovens and pots purely by experience, and short times, since he or she had no watch, by those of everyday prayers. As John Hollybank advised in 1561, 'Let it so abyde the space of half a Pater-noster', for example, while a number of Pater-nosters could be used to judge longer times. Weights were little used, and were rare in most recipes, usually being given in terms of everyday objects, rather than pounds and ounces. Sir Hugh Plat used the weight of a groat, or that of a sixpence, for his smaller quantities.[60]

In terms of volume, the spoonful was about a modern 15ml tablespoonful, when measured with the average Tudor or Stuart spoon, but it is virtually impossible to convert either a ladleful or a handful into accurate modern alternatives. One is on much safer ground with direct comparisons with quantities described as being as big as (in ascending order) a hazelnut,[61] a nutmeg, a musket ball, a walnut, a hen's egg, a tennis ball, or 'your little finger'.[62] Similarly items may be cut as thin/thick as a shilling, half a crown, a trencher (but banqueting or table?), a quarter of an inch, half an inch,[63] or as big as a threepenny piece or a shilling.[64]

Whatever the status of the cook, from velvet-clad master to greasy maid, there was always a mass of work to be completed each day, yet with the exception of farmers, gardeners, and other food-producers, few other occupations contributed so much to the well-being of the entire population.

CHAPTER THIRTEEN

Boiling

The boiling house was essentially designed to serve the mass-catering needs of large households. Its output was therefore basic, rather than refined, as experienced by those who took their meals in Henry VIII's great halls around 1520:

> Thy fleshe is restie or leane, tough and olde,
> Or it come to borde unsavery and colde
> Sometimes twise sodden, and cleane without taste,
> Saused with coles and ashes all for haste ...
> Thy potage is made of wedes and with ashes,
> And between thy teeth oft times the coles crashes,
> Sometimes halfe sodden is bothe thy fleshe and broth;
> The water and hearbes together be so wroth
> That eche goeth aparte, they can not well agree,
> And ofte be they salte as water of the sea.[1]

In contrast to this rough fare, the foods boiled for those occupying the dining parlours in well-to-do homes throughout the country were of the best produce, all carefully cooked in small quantities and finely flavoured to provide a vast range of excellent dishes. To make them, a number of different boiling vessels were required, along with a few pieces of specialized equipment.

In medieval England, the primary boiling vessel in most homes had been the ceramic cooking pot. To those who do not understand the processes of potting, they look incredibly crude, just large cylindrical vessels of rough unglazed earthenware with simple rims and usually with sagging bottoms. In reality, however, they were consummate examples of the potter's skill, made with well-chosen blends of clays, grits and other bodies, and thrown with amazingly thin walls to enable them to hold their gallons of precious food directly over the flames of the fire without shattering. Their days were numbered, however, for they gradually died out during the sixteenth century. In their place, the potters developed more convenient shapes, with internal lead glazes to render them both waterproof and much easier to keep clean. Some were direct copies of

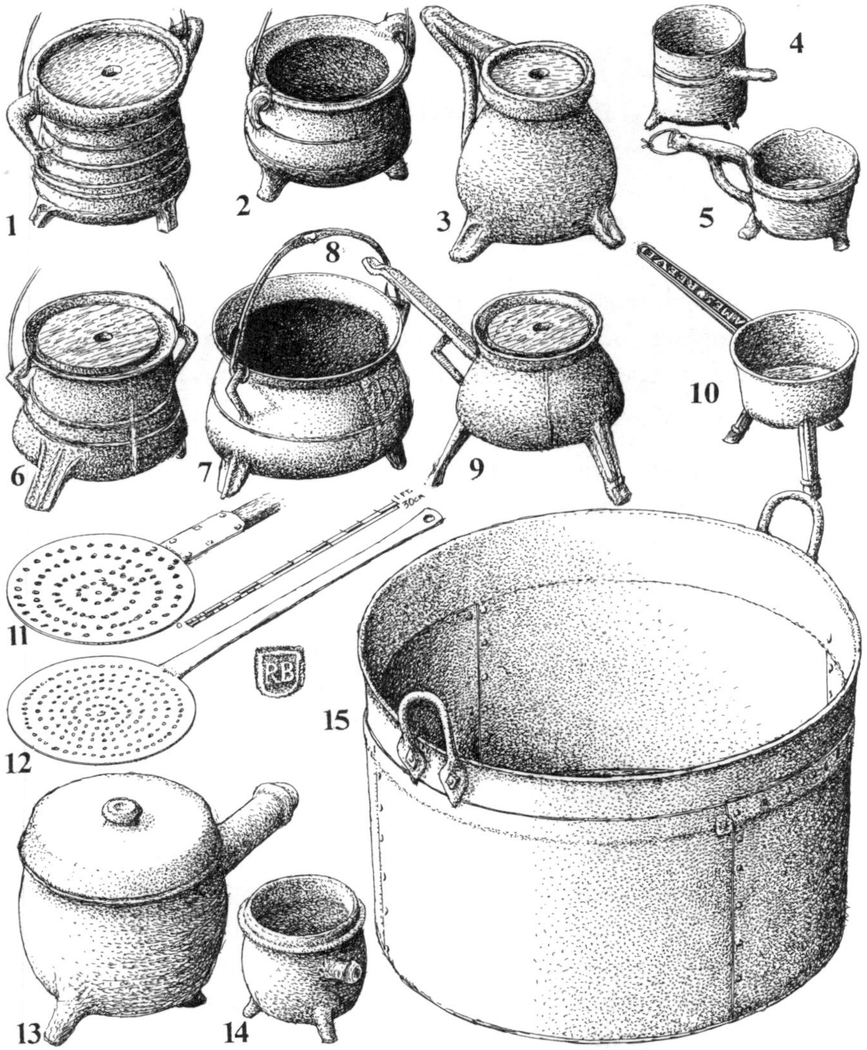

Figure 61. Boiling pots. Many earthenware pots were direct copies of their cast bronze contemporaries: (1 & 2) crock, Exeter, early 16th cent., and west-country bronze 15th–16th cent.; (3 & 4) Netherlands redware pot, Newcastle-upon-Tyne, mid-17th cent., and bronze, by Bernard Pennington of Bodmin, mid-17th cent.; with an iron potkilp (5) from Norwich, early 16th cent.; (6 & 7) coarse sandy posnet, late 16th cent., Exeter, and bronze, Birdsall Foundry, Exeter, 16th–early 17th cent.; (8, 9 & 10) skillet, Newcastle-upon-Tyne, mid-17th cent., London, mid-17th cent., and bronze, James Reeve (Kent?) c. *1642; (11 & 12) brass skimmers from Castle Rising, Norfolk, and made by 'R.B.' in the early–mid-17th cent.; (13 & 14) border ware lidded pipkins from London, mid-17th cent.; (15) Copper-alloy kettle from the* Mary Rose, *1545.*

contemporary bronze cooking pots, with a rim designed to take a lid, a pair of hanging loops at the sides, and three feet at the base.[2] Others, of similar form but with almost spherical bodies, were imported from the Netherlands into the eastern and southern sea-ports, where they have since been recovered from excavations.[3] Close copies of bronze posnets were also made, these having the same combination of a deep rounded body, a lid-seated rim and the three legs of cooking pots, but with a long handle projecting from one side, rather than loops for suspension.[4] For lesser quantities of food, smaller vessels called skillets were used, these having cylindrical bodies, or ones widening towards their plain rims, single projecting handles to one side, and three short legs.[5] The form of the bronze and earthenware cooking pots called pipkins is uncertain, but since they were later described in the East Midlands as red earthenware vessels holding up to two gallons (10l), they were probably identical to posnets. These new shapes were used in kitchens at all levels of society, some of their functions being described in the cook's accounts for the Star Chamber in 1568:

> Item. for earthen boiling pots for broths, salads etc.
> during the term. 2*s*. 10*d*. [6]

Since the Middle Ages, bell-founders had cast boiling pots in copper alloys variously called bronze, latten or brass. Their thin walls, sturdy shapes and very highly conductive metal made them ideal for general use, and well worth their relatively high prices. Those who required new pots usually sold their old ones to the founder at their scrap value, paying an enhanced rate for the extra new metal which would be required, since it included an allowance for the work required in the casting process. Details of such transactions often appear in household accounts, such as the following:

> '13th Oct. 1578 Paid Richard Hawtone of Ripon casting a great pot
> 3 dozen weight. master's metal 22½lb at 2*d*. a lb,
> rest at 6*d*. a lb. 13*s*. 4*d*.'[7]
> '14th Jan. 1612 Received of John Hyaley of Wigan 36*s*. 10*d*. and that
> was upon exchange of Pott brasse, vizt. old brasse
> which came from Barden with 4 new Pottes & a
> Mortar as he did bargain with Mr. Steward at 8*d*. per
> lb. new metal and 5*d*. per lb. old metal, we receiving
> of him new metall 11 stone at 14lb per stone and
> things of 5*d*. old metall 20 stone & 10lb upon the
> exchange at the sumes as aforsayed 36*s*. 10*d*.'[8]

Figure 62. Boiling utensils. This early 16th-century misericord in Bristol Cathedral (1) clearly illustrates a flat round wooden lid being taken off its pot – and the immediate consequences. Items lifted from pots and kettles were easily drained in the Netherlands red-ware strainers (2 & 3) found in many coastal English towns in the late 16th and early 17th centuries. Other utensils included iron bodkins, seen here stitching up a stuffed leg of mutton (4), flesh-forks for removing joints from the pots (5) and reckon-hooks, such as this 1507 example (6) from Norwich, for suspending the pots over the fire. Wooden ladles, similar to this of elm from the Mary Rose *(7), were essential for baling out the hot pottages and other liquid foods.*

As with other accounts of this period, the arithmetic of the last transaction is questionable. Two-hundred-and-ninety pounds of old metal at 5*d.* the pound is 120*s.* 10*d.*, while 154lb of new metal at 8*d.* is 102*s.* 8*d.*, so the sum returned should have been only 18*s.* 2*d.*

By the early seventeenth century, cast-iron pots were being made by a founder called John Browne, who had obtained a royal monopoly for their manufacture. His business practices proved very unpopular, however, complaints against him being brought before Parliament. Allegedly he had bought up the available iron, inhibited its import, raised prices from 16*s.* to 23*s.* a ton, and made his pots so thick-walled that they 'require more fire to heat them, [and] more labor to carry them off and on.' These protests proved ineffective, for in 1635 the Attorney General was ordered to grant him the sole rights to make iron ordnance, shot, pots and firebacks.[9]

In great contrast to these cast bronze and iron pots, the finest, intended for royal use, were cast in solid silver. Henry VIII's inventory of 1547 includes two boiling pots of silver, each with a bail or handle, one pot weighing 8lb 13oz, and the other 6lb 10oz. In addition to eliminating all risk of poisoning from verdigris, their high level of conductivity must have made them extremely efficient in the privy kitchens.[10]

Today collectors and others use the term 'cauldron' to describe cast bronze cooking pots, but in the Tudor and Stuart periods they were usually simply called 'pots' or 'crocks'. They were made in a variety of sizes to hold from around two pints up to around ten gallons (1.2–48l) to suit the needs of particular families. Each had a flared rim designed to receive a lid in the form of a disc of wood, a hole through its centre serving as a handle. One is illustrated in a misericord of *c.* 1520 at Bristol Cathedral, and examples have been found in excavations. Having used such lids practically, I found that they worked well, any warping due to the hot steam on the underside quickly being reversed by simply turning them over. They are also good insulators, retaining the heat within the pot.[11]

All pots required a number of associated pieces of equipment in order to work efficiently. Whether hung from a balk mounted across the inside of the chimney, or from a chimney-crane, they needed either a pot-hook of fixed length, or an adjustable reckon-hook for suspension. To link the hooked bottom ends of these wrought-iron devices with the hanging loops at each side of the rim of the pot required a pair of pot-kilps. This was a curved iron bar hooked at each end, a central hinge allowing it to be adjusted to fit pans of various diameters. Since the metal of their sides and rims became far too hot to be touched, the cooks lifted their pots on and off the fire with the use of hand-hooks. These were ovals of iron bar large enough to enclose the clenched palm, each with a projecting hook to grip the hanging loops on the pot rim. A pair at Speke Hall, Liverpool was valued at 4*d.* in 1624.[12]

As cooking proceeded, further items were needed. One of the most important of these was the pot-stick or slice, the wooden stick used to stir stews and other dishes of that nature to stop them sticking to the bottom of the pots and burning. Between 1531 and 1534 nine or ten heretics were burnt at the stake in England, a further twenty-five Anabaptists suffering the same fate on a single day in 1535. News of these unprecedented executions rapidly spread throughout the country, leading to the popular adoption of a new word into the English language. As William Tyndale explained in 1536:

> If the porage is burned to, or the meate over rosted, we say the bishop hath put his foot in the potte or the bishop hath played the cooke, because the bishops burn who they lust and whosoever displeaseth them.[13]

As a result, food burnt onto the pot continued to be described as 'bishoped' well into the twentieth century in the north.

As it was the English practice to have the liquids boiling in the pots as clear as possible, skimmers or scummers were required to remove all scum as the contents came to the boil. The different names both related to a single utensil with a perforated shallow disc mounted at the end of a long handle. Some were made of wood, others of metal. A typical example from Castle Rising, Norfolk, has its 8-inch (20cm) diameter sheet-brass head pierced by four concentric rings of small holes, a tubular ferule beneath enabling it to be mounted on a wooden handle.[14] By the early seventeenth century, others were having their heads riveted on to long brass handles, some examples being stamped with an 'R.B.' maker's mark. It should be stressed that skimmers were primarily designed to remove scum, rather than anything heavier. Flesh-hooks, with a number of sharp-pointed hooks mounted to one side of a long handle, were still used to remove hot joints from the pot in the early sixteenth century, but these were gradually replaced by flesh-forks. These had two-pronged heads, resembling miniature pitch-forks.[15]

Ladles were used to take liquids from the pot. Everyday examples were made of wood, probably with the same hemispherical turned bowls and carved handles as those used in various parts of the country up to the opening years of the twentieth century. Better ladles were made of brass, those supplied to the Earl of Northumberland by John Brodebanck the brazier in 1586 costing 2*s.* and 2*s.* 6*d.* each, while his skimmer cost 3*s.* 6*d.*[16] The price of Henry VIII's 22oz solid silver ladles is not recorded.[17]

Cauldrons and kettles are differentiated from pots and crocks in contemporary accounts, since they were usually made of sheet copper or brass fastened together with rivets, rather than being cast in moulds. As the sheets were produced by hammering, and were a speciality of producers in the Low Countries, cauldrons, kettles and other cookware were collectively known as either battery ware, or Flemish metal. They were light and efficient in use, and capable of being made in various sizes when strengthened with iron rims and encircling bands. Henry VIII's great kettle at Oatlands Manor, Surrey, had iron bands, feet and 'ears' for suspension, as did Thomas Hill's two-gallon (10l) kettle in his cottage at Knaresborough, North Yorkshire, demonstrating their widespread use.[18] Due to the amount of labour required in their production, they were relatively expensive in terms of their weight, costing some 2*s.* a pound in 1612, when cast pots were charged at 8*d.* the pound, a third of the price, but they were still good value since they provided a much greater capacity in relation to their weight.[19]

Very few cauldrons and kettles have survived through to the present day, the finest being those recovered from the wreck of the *Mary Rose*. One of 25 inches diameter by 17 inches (62.5 x 42.5cm) in height has a capacity of some 30 gallons (144l), while another, 23 inches by 14 inches (57.5 x 35cm), holds 20 gallons (96l), both with rolled rims, riveted joints, wrought iron 'ears' or loops for suspension, and flat bottoms intended to sit on wrought iron trivets or brandreths.[20]

Copper-alloy sheet metal was also used to make the bodies of posnets and pottingers, their supporting frames and handles being forged from wrought iron. As described in 1657, they were small boiling vessels with long iron handles, ideal for heating smaller amounts.[21] Some thought that this combination debased the use of the beautiful, highly polished sheet brass, asking how,

> Brass and old iron, who brought these two together?
> Brass thinketh scorn to see them brought so hither.
> Old iron is rusty and rotten to view,
> Brass with silver blanched and polished new.[22]

Whichever kind of cooking pot was being used, it was essential that its interior should be kept clean. This was particularly important for copper and brass vessels, since damp, food acids and salts readily caused them to produce pale green spots of verdigris. Ideally their interiors were tin-plated to prevent this happening, but tinning was always an expensive process, and could easily be damaged by rough use and over-cleaning. When handling metal cooking vessels of this period, especially those of cast brass or bronze, their interiors are usually exceptionally smooth and polished through years of constant use and cleaning. Their exteriors, however, are frequently as fresh and sharp as when they were first made, the texture of their loam or sand moulds and the fettling marks left by their makers retaining their every detail. Clearly many cooks followed the advice of Thomas Tusser:

> No scouring for pride; Spare kettle whole side.
> Though scouring be needful, yet scouring too much,
> Is pride without profit, and robbeth thine hutch.[23]

Having considered the utensils used for boiling and stewing, the following sections each describe how particular foods were cooked. It must be stressed that 'boiling' meat can never have meant immersing it in rapidly boiling water, for this hardens the meat, making it irredeemably tough. It is much better to appreciate that Tudor and Stuart 'boiling' should now be understood as 'poaching', with the water barely bubbling to keep everything moist and tender.

It was customary to serve most boiled and stewed foods on a layer of plain or toasted pieces of sliced bread called either sippets or sops, as may be done for all the following recipes. They soak up the juices, and make them much easier to spoon up from the dish either onto the plate or directly into the mouth. This was far in advance of modern table manners, which demand that many delicious sauces remain uneaten on the plate, inaccessible by both knife and fork.

BEEF

The plainer recipes for boiling joints of beef for the hall have already been given in Chapter Nine, above. The following examples, however, show how it was cooked for those in the higher-status dining parlours and chambers.

STEWED FILLET OF BEEF, ITALIAN FASHION[24]

3lb/1.4kg fillet of beef joint (or silverside or topside)
1 bottle dry white wine
1tsp ground black pepper, 2tbs salt
1tsp each coriander seed, aniseed, fennel seed and cinnamon, coarsely ground together with ½tsp cloves and ½tsp savory to make 'Tamara' powder
3 beef stock cubes (or stock)
1 blade of mace
6 cloves

Wipe the beef clean and dry, place in a close-fitting bowl or pan, pour in a little of the wine, and knead to soften the meat. Add the pepper, salt and 'Tamara' powder mixed with the remaining wine. Top with a small plate and put a weight on top to keep the joint submerged for 2 days.

Drain the joint, wipe dry, truss with string, put into a saucepan, cover with water, add the stock cubes, cloves and mace, cover, and simmer very gently for about 3 hours until tender. Transfer to a dish, pour some of the stock around it, and serve hot.

STEWED COLLOPS OF BEEF[25]

1lb/450g topside or silverside
4oz/100g butter
1 beef stock cube or stock
5tbs claret
pinch ground nutmeg
2tbs elderflower vinegar
2 cloves
1 orange, sliced
butter for garnishing

Slice the meat very thinly across the grain and gently fry it in the butter in batches, removing them to a saucepan as their juices begin to emerge and they start to brown. Add the pan juices, the stock cube dissolved in ½pt/300ml water, the claret, nutmeg, vinegar and cloves and stew gently for 30 minutes. Meanwhile simmer the orange slices separately in a little of the stock. When the meat is tender, pour into a dish, lay the orange on top, and dot with the softened butter.

A third recipe for a beef stew, this time in the French fashion, and finished with grapes or gooseberries, grated nutmeg and barberries, is given at page 298, below.[26] However, another recipe displaying foreign influences is the following:

A TURKISH DISH OF BEEF[27]

1lb/450g lean beef
2oz/50g short grain rice
2 onions, peeled
6 peppercorns, (1tsp salt)

Cut the beef into thin slices, add 1pt/600ml cold water, bring to the boil, skim, add the remaining ingredients, cover, and stew over a very gentle heat for about 2½ hours, until the meat is tender and the rice has thickened. Stir occasionally and add a little more water as needed.

A HASH OF RAW BEEF[28]

1lb/450g lean beef
2tbs suet
1 onion, peeled
1tsp mixed herbs
¼tsp each ground clove, mace, pepper & nutmeg
6 blanched chestnuts
1 beef stock cube
¼pt/150ml claret
gooseberries, grapes or barberries for garnish

Chop the meat very finely with the suet, place in a pan with the remaining ingredients, top up with sufficient water to cover everything, cover, stew for 3 hours, pour it into a dish, and add the garnish.

VENISON

ELIZABETH CROMWELL'S BOILED VENISON[29]

3lb/1.3kg joint of venison	*florets of 1 cauliflower*
3tbs fresh mixed herbs	*1 beef stock cube*
2oz/50g suet	*¼pt/150ml milk*
3 hard-boiled egg yolks	*3oz/75g butter*
1tsp ground ginger	*8oz/225g spinach*
½tsp ground nutmeg	*2tbs white wine vinegar*
½tsp ground black pepper	*¼tsp grated nutmeg*
1tsp salt	*sprigs of fresh parsley*

Rub the venison with coarse salt, leave overnight, and rinse just before cooking. Beat together the remaining ingredients in the first column above, stuff this into the centre of the joint, and truss it securely with string. Bring a pan of water to the boil, put in the venison, return to the boil, skim, cover, and reduce to a gentle simmer for some 1½ hours until tender.

Twenty minutes before serving, boil the cauliflower, with a little water, the stock cube and the milk for about 15 minutes, then drain, retaining the stock, and keeping the cauliflower hot, shaken with half the butter. Pour ¼pt of the stock into a separate pan, add the spinach, and boil for some 5 minutes until tender; drain and stir in the remaining butter with the vinegar and nutmeg.

Line the bottom of a dish with sippets, arrange the drained spinach around the edge as a border, place the venison in the centre, pour the cauliflower and its butter over the top, and finally garnish the brim with the parsley just before serving.

This was served at her table every day during the season since, 'her times destroyed the game yet cheapened and aviled venison and made it everyone's meat, which sordid example yet prevails among some proprietors of parks.'

MUTTON

Mutton was a favourite meat for stewing, best when a year or two old, rather than older, drier and tougher. Its fine texture and delicate flavour made it ideal for stewing with a variety of different flavourings, as demonstrated by the many recipes published in the sixteenth and early seventeenth centuries. The following selection shows the most usual methods used for boiling and stewing.

TO BOIL MUTTON FOR SUPPER[30]

3lb/1.3kg joint of mutton, trussed
1lb/450g onions, peeled & quartered
4tbs chopped parsley
2tsp salt
1tsp ground peppercorns
large pinch of saffron
6tbs vinegar

Barely cover the joint with water, bring to the boil, skim, add the remaining ingredients, cover, and simmer for about 3 hours until tender. Remove from the heat and stand for 10 minutes before dishing and serving.

TO BOIL MUTTON IN SEAU[31]

3 x 1lb/450kg joints of mutton, trussed
3 blades mace
12 peppercorns
6 cloves
2tsp salt
10 small or 5 large onions
½oz/12g each of fresh parsley, sorrel & spinach chopped
2tsp each savory & thyme, chopped
½oz/12g soft white breadcrumbs

Put the mutton, spices, salt and 5 small or 3 large whole peeled onions into a large pan. Cover with water, bring to the boil and simmer for 1 hour. Add the remaining ingredients chopped together finely, and continue simmering very gently for a further hour with the lid off, to reduce the stock, then dish and add a light sprinkling of salt.

TO FORCE A LEG OF MUTTON (1) [32]

3lb/1.8kg whole leg of lamb
2oz/50g suet
2oz/50g fresh white breadcrumbs
1oz/25g raisins
1oz/25g currants
½oz/12g orange peel, finely chopped
5 dates, finely chopped
½tsp each of sage, rosemary & thyme, chopped
1tsp ground ginger
½tsp grated nutmeg
½tsp salt
1 egg, beaten
2tbs single cream

for the garnish

¼tsp ground pepper, sliced lemon, grapes or gooseberries

Using a sharp knife, carefully peel back the skin from the large end to within 2in/5cm of the small end, keeping the skin as whole as possible. Cut the meat through to the bone just above the knuckle, and remove all the lower muscles, then cut through to the bone just above the kneecap, and remove the large thick muscles. Reserve one of these large muscles for any other dish, such as steaks or stews, but carefully cut the remainder of the meat into small cubes, removing all sinew and gristle, before mincing coarsely.

Mix the dry ingredients in a large bowl, add the egg, cream and minced lamb, and work thoroughly with the hands to form a uniform mixture. Pull the skin back up the bone, laying it flat with the longest part on the worktop. Pack in the mixture, and sew the skin around it using twine and a sharp bodkin.

Turn the joint over, and place on a trivet in a large pan. Cover with boiling water, bring to the boil, cover, and simmer very gently for 2 hours, then drain, garnish with sliced lemon, grapes or gooseberries, and serve hot on sippets with the following sauce:

¼pt/150ml strong lamb stock
¼pt/150ml white wine
¼tsp ground mace
1½tsp sugar
2 egg yolks
2tbs lemon juice (for verjuice)

Bring the stock, wine, mace and sugar to the boil, and set aside while beating the yolk into the lemon juice. Pour the hot stock over the yolks, replace over a gentle heat until thickened, but not curdled, and serve immediately.

TO FORCE A LEG OF MUTTON (2)[33]

Follow the recipe above, replacing the suet, dried fruits and spices with:

4oz/100g streaky bacon, very finely chopped	
3 cloves garlic, finely chopped	*¼tsp each of ground pepper,*
3 chestnuts, cooked & chopped	*cloves & mace*

and for the sauce,

½pt/300ml strong lamb stock	*6oz/150g apples or pears*
4 chestnuts, chopped	*peeled and chopped*
2tbs pistachio nuts or pine kernels	*pinch of salt*

Stew together for 30 minutes and pour hot (onto a layer of sippets?) into the dish, then place the forced leg on top.

Other legs of mutton were simmered long and slow, rendering their meat extremely delicate, as William Cartwright described in *The Ordinary* of 1634:

A gallant's like a leg of mutton boil'd
By a Spanish cook; take him by th' one end,
And shake him, all the flesh falls from the bones,
And leaves him bare immediately.

TO STEW LAMB STEAKS[34]

2lb/900g loin or leg joint	*4tbs lemon juice (for verjuice)*
2oz/50g pickled capers	*1tsp salt*
2oz/50g pickled samphire	*2oz/50g fresh parsley*
3 artichoke bottoms	*4oz/100g spinach*
½tsp crushed blade mace	*4oz/100g cooked gooseberries*
¼ of a nutmeg, grated	*1oz/25g butter*

Cut the trimmed joint into ¼in/6mm steaks across the grain. Put into a saucepan, cover with water, bring to the boil, skim, add the pickles, spices, artichoke bottoms, lemon juice and salt, cover, reduce to a gentle simmer, and cook for about an hour. Just before serving pick the coarse stalks from the parsley, then put into a pan with the spinach and a little water, cover and simmer for about 5 minutes, until tender. Pour off the liquid, add the gooseberries and butter, and stir until hot.

Drain the liquid from the lamb into the parsley, spinach and gooseberries, stir and bring up to the boil, before pouring over a bed of sippets of white bread in a deep dish. Carefully arrange the lamb steaks on top and serve immediately.

STEWED MUTTON STEAKS[35]

1lb/450g mutton or lamb steaks
½pt/300ml claret or white wine
1 onion, peeled
1 bundle of herbs
1 large blade of mace
1tsp salt

Place the steaks, wine and ½pt/300ml water into a pan, bring to the boil and skim. Add the remaining ingredients, cover, and simmer gently for 2 hours, turning the steaks from time to time. Serve on sippets of white bread.

TO BOIL A LEG OF MUTTON WITH LEMONS[36]

1lb/450g lean lamb or mutton
1 lemon
2oz/50g currants
¼tsp pepper
1 beef or lamb stock cube
2tsp wine vinegar
1tbs sugar
a few drops red food colour

Cube the mutton, thinly slice the lemon, cutting each slice into quarters, and place in a pan with the currants, pepper, stock cube and ¾pt/425ml cold water. Slowly bring to the boil, cover, and simmer very gently for 1½ hours. Stir in the remaining ingredients just before serving.

TO STEW STEAKS OF MUTTON IN BEER[37]

2lb/900g leg of lamb or mutton
1 large/2 small onions, thinly sliced
1pt/600ml brown ale
1oz/25g butter
1tsp salt
¼tsp ground pepper

Remove the bone, skin and fat from the leg, and cut the meat into thin slices across the grain. Place in a pan with the onions and beer, cover, and simmer for 1 hour. Add the butter, salt and pepper, and continue to simmer for a further 20–30 minutes until tender.

BALLS OF MUTTON[38]

Also known as Farts of Portingale, Spanish Balls or pears, these meatballs in broth had apparently been introduced from Iberia by the 1580s. Made 'as big as tennis balles', some were plain mixtures of mutton, bone-marrow and raw egg yolks, while others were spiced, or included dried fruit, fresh gooseberries or green grapes.

Balls

1lb/450g lean lamb, minced
3oz/75g suet
2tbs sugar
½tsp mixed ground ginger, clove & mace
½tsp salt
1 egg, beaten
flour for dusting

Broth

2 lamb stock cubes
1oz/25g currants
8 dates, sliced into 4
2 blades mace
1tsp salt
2 raw egg yolks, beaten
1tbs cider vinegar (for verjuice)

Mix the ingredients for the balls together and form into 1½in/4cm balls. Stir the stock cubes, dried fruit and salt into 1pt/600ml water, bring to the boil, drop in the balls, cover, and simmer for some 45 minutes until tender, ensuring that they do not stick to the bottom. Arrange the balls on the sops in a dish, pour the stock onto the yolks beaten with the vinegar, beat rapidly, then pour over the balls and serve.

PORK

As described in Chapter Nine, pigs provided cured bacon joints for labourers, along with brawns and boars' heads for the nobility and gentry. However, pork was hardly, if ever, used to make any other kind of boiled meat or stew.

POULTRY & GAMEBIRDS

Today the practice of simmering birds until moist and tender has fallen completely out of fashion, despite centuries of enthusiastic endorsement by generations of professional and domestic cooks. Being more practical, economic and foolproof than roasting, it also produced rich stocks to flavour nourishing soups and stews. The late Tudor and early Stuart period saw the development of many new recipes for boiling fowl of all kinds. The bird of choice for many households was the capon, frequently fattened by the cook within the actual kitchen, but many other birds were regularly eaten, including the cock, hen, chicken, duck, pheasant, partridge, quail, pigeon, woodcock, snipe, lark and sparrow.[39]

In most recipes the bird was simply simmered in a pot along with mutton on the bone and beef marrowbones to add flavour and a gelatinous smoothness to the stock (these being substituted by stock cubes and gelatin in the recipes below, to achieve similar effects in a more economical and convenient modern manner). Their additional flavours came from rich stocks which were cooked separately and usually thickened with sops of white bread, which were then laid on top of the bird just after it had been removed from the pot onto its dish. The range of flavours introduced into these stocks was extremely varied, enabling the cooks to provide diners with a constantly changing range of appetizing dishes using their seasonally available ingredients. It might appear strange that the sops were usually placed over the birds, rather than under them, but since boiled birds might appear rather bland, particularly when boiled white, they could improve their appearance at the table, and provide a good base for further garnishings.

The presentation of the birds was a matter of some importance, and so the final part of this section (see page 271) describes how the dishes should be garnished for service at formal meals. The recipes below have been selected to present a sample of the typical ingredients and methods used in this period, but it is worthwhile going back to the recipe books to try the many others which still lie there.

It is also always wise to use the best available poultry, so that it contributes its natural flavours to the dish, rather than being a tasteless recipient of added flavours. Of course, cooking times will vary according to the weight of the individual bird.

PLAIN-BOILING CHICKENS

1 chicken, oven-ready & trussed
2 beef or lamb stock cubes
3tsp or 3 small sheets gelatin
2tsp salt

Put the chicken, stock cubes, gelatin softened in water and salt into a close-fitting pan, cover with water, bring to the boil, skim, and simmer for about 50 minutes for a bird weighing 3lb/1.3kg; 1 hour for one weighing 3½lb/1.5kg; 1¼ hours for one weighing 4lb/1.8kg; and 1½–2 hours for something weighing 5lb/2kg. If in doubt, check with a thermometer probe to 90°C, and drain, place in a deep dish, and serve with one of the following sauces.

(1) CHICKEN WITH DRIED FRUITS[40]

1½oz/37g currants
1½oz/37g raisins
1½oz/37g dates
½ onion, finely chopped
1 beef or lamb stock cube
2oz fresh white breadcrumbs
10 prunes
¼tsp each ground pepper & mace
pinch ground clove
2tsp salt
2tbs wine vinegar (for verjuice)

Place the dried fruits and onion into a pan with the stock cube and ¾pt/450ml water, bring to the boil and simmer for 20 minutes until tender, then stir in the remaining ingredients, simmer for 5 minutes more, and pour over the boiled chicken.

(2) CHICKEN WITH LEMONS[41]

1 lemon, in ¼in/5mm slices
4tsp sugar
1tbs rosewater
a little white wine
1 beef or lamb stock cube
¼tsp black peppercorns
2oz/50g red currants

1oz/25g bone marrow or butter
½tsp blade mace
2tbs wine vinegar (for verjuice)
1tbs sugar

Place the lemon in a shallow pan with the contents of the left-hand column above and simmer for about 5 minutes until the peel is just tender. Stew the contents of the right-hand column with ½pt/300ml water for 5 minutes. When the chicken has been placed on its dish, use the stock to soak sops of white bread around its sides, then put the lemon slices and their syrup over the chicken breast.

(3) CHICKEN WITH ORANGES[42]

5 oranges
1 stock cube
1½oz/35g currants
1½oz/35g prunes
2oz/50g bone marrow (or butter)
2 blades mace
¾pt/450ml white wine or claret

1–2tbs wine vinegar (for verjuice)
½ loaf white bread, crustless & cubed into sops
1tbs sugar
⅛tsp each ground cinnamon & ginger

Plain-boil a chicken in stock, adding a whole orange 30 minutes before serving. Put the stock cube, currants, prunes, marrow, mace and juice of 3 oranges into the wine, cover, and simmer for 15 minutes. Thinly slice the remaining orange into a little water in another pan and stew gently for 5–10 minutes until tender, changing the water if bitter.

When the chicken is ready, place on its dish, cover with the bread sops soaked with the wine, prunes and other ingredients (sharpening this sauce with a little wine vinegar if preferred), sprinkle with the sugar mixed with the ginger and cinnamon and top with the orange slices.

(4) CHICKEN WITH GOOSEBERRIES OR GRAPES[43]

1pt/600ml white wine
½tsp blade mace
1 bundle sweet herbs
8oz/225g gooseberries or grapes
4tbs cider vinegar (for verjuice)
1oz/25g butter
1–2tbs sugar
2 hard-boiled egg yolks
2oz/50g fresh white breadcrumbs

Add the wine and mace to the stock when about to boil the chicken, and put the herbs inside it. Just before dishing the chicken, simmer the gooseberries or grapes with the vinegar, butter, sugar, and a little stock from the pot for 5 minutes, until tender. Mix about ¾pt/450ml more of the stock with the yolks and breadcrumbs, briefly re-heat while stirring, pour over the sops in a dish, place the chicken on top, and pour the gooseberries over all.

(5) CHICKEN WITH RICE[44]

4oz/100g short-grain rice
2pt/1.2l milk
½tsp ground mace
8oz/225g sugar
4tbs rosewater
4oz/100g ground almonds
¼pt/150ml cream

For this version, cook the chicken in just salted water.

Soak the rice in water overnight, then boil in plenty of water for 20 minutes, then drain, add the milk, mace, sugar and half the rosewater and continue cooking, stirring over a gentle heat, for a further 20 minutes until tender. Grind the almonds to a smooth paste with the cream and remaining rosewater.

Just before serving the chicken, gently warm the almond mixture. When the chicken has been placed on its dish, cover it with the rice, pour the almond mixture on top and serve immediately.

(6) CHICKEN WITH CARROTS OR LETTUCE[45]

Add prepared carrots or lettuce (such as 'Little Gem') to the chicken half-way through its cooking time, and serve with the chicken and some of its own broth, thickened with fresh white breadcrumbs and seasoned with mace, pepper, sugar and a little wine vinegar (for verjuice).

(7) MRS CROMWELL'S CHICKEN FRICASSEE[46]

¼pt/150ml white wine
1 whole onion, peeled
½tsp blade mace
½ a nutmeg, sliced
2 yolks of eggs
1oz/25g butter
2 anchovy fillets
1oz/50g capers, finely chopped
1 bundle of sweet herbs

Add the wine, onion, the mace and nutmeg tied in a piece of muslin, and the herbs when starting to cook the chicken. Dissolve the anchovy in ¼pt/150ml of the chicken stock, beat with the remaining ingredients, and the chopped spices from the stock and stir together over a gentle heat until thickened immediately before pouring over the chicken in its dish.

MRS CROMWELL'S BOILED CHICKEN OR PHEASANT[47]

4lb/1.8kg chicken, oven-ready
3oz/75g finely chopped bacon or suet
¼tsp each ground ginger & clove
½tsp each ground nutmeg & pepper
1tbs sugar
1tsp salt
2tsp mixed chopped herbs
3oz/75g gooseberries or grapes
2tbs pistachio nuts
1 yolk of egg

for the stock

1pt/600ml white wine
1oz/25g butter
1 bundle of herbs
3 stock cubes
5oz/150g gooseberries or grapes

to garnish

a lemon or currants

Place the chicken breast-down onto a board, make a cut from the vent up the spine towards the neck, and peel back the skin to each side. Continue turning the skin back, severing the wing joints, then the leg joints, until the carcass and breast may be lifted free from the skin, which still retains the wings and legs. Keep the skin as intact as possible. Remove all the breast and other meat from the carcass, mince it finely, then knead with the ingredients in the left-hand column above to form a forcemeat.

Lay the skin flat, breast-skin down, pack the forcemeat into the centre, gather the skin around it, and secure it in place, including the neck and vent, using either small skewers or stitches with twine. Turn it over and truss like a normal chicken.

Place breast upward in a large pan with the contents of the right-hand column above (and the carcass chopped in pieces), add sufficient water to cover, cover, bring to the boil, then simmer gently for about 1¾ hours. Lift out onto a bed of sops of white bread, garnish with slices of lemon or poached currants, pour over some of the stock, and serve hot.

BOILED PIGEONS[48]

2 pigeons, oven-ready & trussed
2oz/50g fresh parsley
4 rashers streaky bacon, chopped
6tbs wine vinegar
3 hard-boiled egg yolks
½tsp blade mace
8 black peppercorns
½tsp marjoram
1 chicken or lamb stock cube
1oz/25g butter

Put the parsley into the pigeons and simmer them in salted water for up to 1¾ hours until tender (depending on source and age). Fifteen minutes before serving add the remaining ingredients (except the butter) to ½pt/300ml water, and simmer together. Beat the butter into this sauce just before pouring it over the pigeons in their dish.

TO BOIL QUAIL (SPICED)[49]

4 quail, drawn, plucked & trussed, heads and legs removed
1 chicken stock cube
1 medium carrot, cut up
1tbs parsley, chopped
2tsp mixed herbs, chopped
1tsp salt
½tsp each ground ginger & cinnamon
¼ nutmeg, grated
pinch ground black pepper
4tbs cider vinegar (for verjuice)
cubed white bread for sops

Arrange the quail in the bottom of a pan, add the carrot, sufficient cold water to cover the birds, and the herbs, salt and spices. Cover the pan, bring to the boil, then simmer for some 35 minutes until they are tender. Set the quail on the sops in a dish, pour on sufficient stock to soak them, serve immediately.

TO BOIL QUAIL (SWEET)[50]

4 quail, as above
½pt/300ml white wine
2oz/50g currants
12 dates
1 blade mace
1oz/25g bone marrow (or butter)
½tsp salt
large pinch pepper
2oz/50g ground almonds
1tbs rosewater
1tbs sugar
cubed white bread sippets

Put the quail in a pan with the wine, dried fruit, salt and spices, add sufficient water to cover, cover the pan and simmer for some 35 minutes until tender. Strain the stock onto the almonds, grind (blend) until perfectly smooth, strain into a pan, rapidly re-heat with the rosewater and sugar, and pour over the quail and fruit arranged on sippets in a dish. Garnish with sliced lemon, barberries and sugar.

GARNISHING[51]

For any of the above dishes, garnish the rims of their dishes with any of the following:

fine sugar
pomegranate seeds
sliced lemon
par-boiled currants or prunes dusted with sugar
oysters fried in butter
boiled egg white minced with parsley
boiled blades of mace
quartered hard-boiled egg yolks
sugar-paste lozenges
ornamental shapes of puff paste
boiled sheep's tongue, sliced & fried in green butter
pickled barberries

OLLA PODRIDA

English cooks first became aware of this gargantuan dish in the opening decades of the seventeenth century, especially when Prince Charles was negotiating for the hand of the Spanish Infanta around 1620. The name itself comes from the Spanish *olla*, or cooking-pot, and *podrida* meaning rotten, referring to the delicate state of the meat after prolonged cooking. One of the best descriptions of the dish comes from Edward Herbert, Lord Herbert of Cherbury, in 1648. When entertained by the Spanish governor at Novara in northern Italy, the first course of 'the most sumptuous feast' he had ever seen was:

> three ollas podridas, consisting of all choice boiled meats, placed in three large silver chargers, which took up the length of a great table; the meat in it being heightened up artificially pyramid-wise, to a sparrow, which was on the top.[52]

A few years later, in 1654, James Howell described some of its properties to Lady Cornwallis:

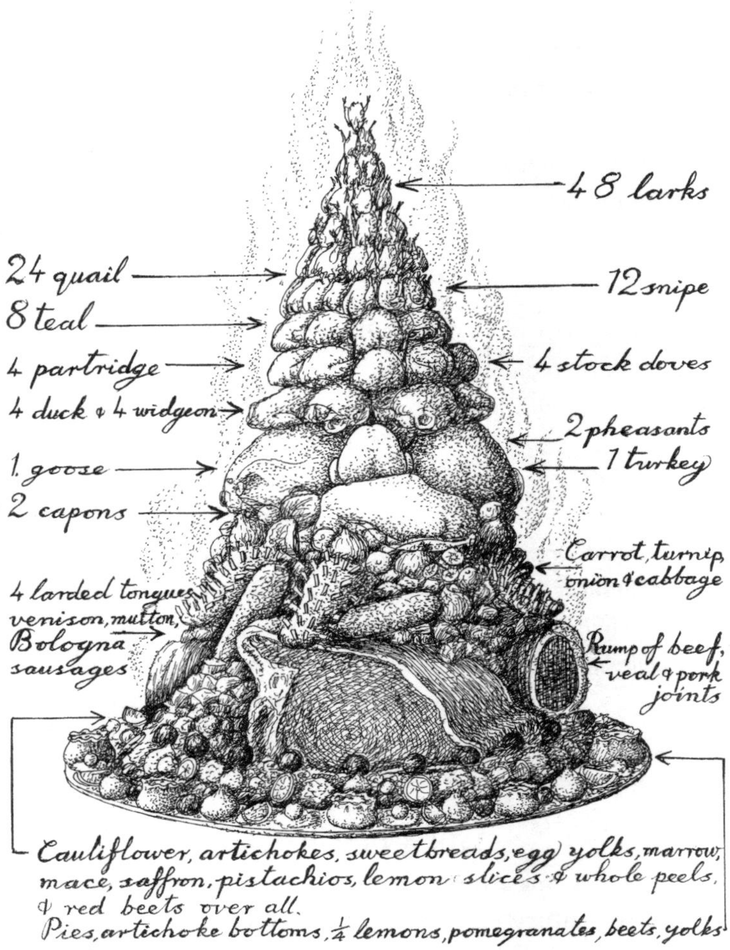

Figure 63. A Robert May Olla Podrida.

> You ask for a cook – here is one ... He is passing good for an Ollia, he will tell your Ladyship that the Reverend Matron Olla potrida hath intellectuals and senses. Mutton, Beef and Bacon are to her as ... understanding and memory are to the soul. Cabbage, turnip, Artichoke, Potatoes and water are her senses, and pepper the common sense. She must have her marrow to keep life in her, and some birds to make her light; by all means, she must go adorned with a chain of sausages.[53]

Robert May gives a number of recipes in the opening pages of his *Accomplisht Cook* of 1660, but a good impression of their appearance as presented on the table is provided in the accompanying drawing. The garnishing of some of May's olios was even more elaborate, comprising:

2 collars pig brawn	4 pies
2 marrow pies	2 salads
12 roast turtle doves in a pie	2 jellies of 2 colours
4 pies	2 forced meats
18 quails in a pie	2 tarts

SEA FISH

In his *Poly-Olbion* of 1612 Michael Drayton celebrated the wealth of sea-fish which provided England with one of its most important sources of food. These included :

... The Herring, King of the Sea
The faster-feeding Cod, the Mackrell brought by May,
The dainty Sole, and Plaice, the Dab, as of their blood;
The Conger finely sous'd, hot summer's coolest food;
The Whiting known to all, a general wholesome dish;
The Gurnet, Rocket, Maid, and Mullet, dainty fish:
The Haddock, Turbet, Bert, fish nourishing and strong;
The Thornback, and the Skate, provocative among;
The Weaver, although his prickles venom be,
By fishers cut away, which buyers seldom see
Yet for the fish he bears, 'tis not accounted bad;
The Sea-flounder is here as common as the Shad;
The Sturgeon cut to kegs, (too big to handle whole)
Gives many a dainty bit out of his lusty jole,
Yet of rich Neptune's store, whilst thus I idly chat,
Think that not all betwixt the Wherpoole [whale] and the Sprat
I go about to name, that were to take in hand...
I'll of our Shell-Fish speak, with those of scale and fin:
The sperm-increasing Crab, much cooking that doth ask,
The big-legg'd Lobster, fit for wanton Venus' task;
Voluptuaries oft take rather than for food.
And that the same effect which worketh in the blood
The rough long Oyster is, much alike the Lobster limb'd.
The Oyster hot as they, the Mussel oft trimm'd
With Orient pearl within, as thereby Nature show'd
That she some secret good had on that shell bestwo'd.
The Scallop cordial judg'd, the dainty Whelk and Limp,

> The Periwinkle, Prawn, the Cockle and the Shrimp
> For wanton Woman's tastes, or for weak stomach bought.[54]

This wealth of fish, freshly caught at coastal fishing ports, was available in all but the furthest inland parts. Following long-established trading and transport arrangements, it was rapidly carried to the markets of the major regional towns and cities within a day of landing, and then distributed further inland over the next day or two. Fish caught off the coast of North Yorkshire was packed into panniers and carried on horseback to be sold in York, some 50 miles away, by 11 a.m. next day. From here it was repacked and taken to West Riding towns such as Leeds, Bradford and Skipton, a further 25 to 40 miles inland. In this way those living about a hundred miles inland might receive fish only three days old, and still quite fresh, except during the hotter months of summer. The availability of fresh fish did not mean that it was readily accessible to all, however, for the cost of its long-distance rapid transportation could make it prohibitively expensive for many families. In addition to the problems of summer heat, many fish were subject to seasonal availability as their shoals came in reach of the coastal fishermen. Of these, the most important were the herring and the pilchard.

'The Herring, King of the Sea' arrived off Northumbria in mid-July, then migrated down the coast to East Anglia, from where it was fished until mid-November. As it was in great demand as both an important fish-day and Lenten food, it was mostly gutted, dry-salted, packed into barrels for a few days until it formed its own brine, and then sealed down. It might be re-packed at the ports, after sorting and re-packing in more salt, the great fair for barrels of salt or 'white' herring being on 29 September, St Michael's day, at Great Yarmouth. Since most were simply soaked in water and poached until tender, they were rarely, if ever, given specific recipes. The fresh, unsalted herrings might be stuffed with a mixture of their ground roes, almond milk, minced dates or figs, currants, cloves, mace, saffron, sugar, salt and breadcrumbs, and then poached in ale, chopped onions, raisins, mustard, saffron and breadcrumbs. Unfortunately the strong flavour of the hops added to modern beers makes it impossible to replicate this fine recipe today.[55]

At the other end of the country, in Cornwall, the pilchard shoals which arrived between mid-July and October were similarly preserved. After being salted and stacked in a cellar for ten days they were either packed in hogshead barrels in their own brine, for export to France, smoked for the Spanish and Italian markets, or pressed to extract their train-oil. Since the barrels required for the export trade made such great demands on this country's dwindling timber resources, an Act was passed in 1594 which ordered every foreign merchant to import two hundred clap-boards for cask-making for every six tons of fish he exported.[56] This may appear to be an over-reaction, until it is realized that, even in the 1640s, Mevagissey alone required 2,200 casks a year and over 14,000 bushels of salt to deal with the pilchards caught by its twenty-two seine nets.[57]

To meet an increasing demand for fish, west-country fishermen had begun to set up seasonal 'plantations' on the eastern coast of Newfoundland from around 1500. Here they could gut, de-spine, split and salt their rich catches of cod, wash them and lay out on racks to air-dry for long-term preservation and transport back to England. By around 1610 Barnstaple and Bideford men had settled in Fermeuse Bay, so that their equipment and gear could be maintained between visits of the fishery crews. Here Professor Peter Pope and his team from the University of St. Johns, Newfoundland, have recently excavated one of their pole-built cook-rooms, which still contained sherds of North Devon pottery cooking pots.[58] Accounts of the fish they brought back occur in Exeter inventories:

> 1564. 2 hundryd of Newland fyshe at 10*s*. the hundryd 20*s*.
> 1579. 116 cople Newland ffysh ... [59]

These were the basic air-dried cod, the other main product, salted and dried hake, being sold at higher prices under the name of Poor John. In contrast, the 'greenfish' which frequently appear in household accounts were usually Newfoundland cod which had been packed with salt into barrels, probably while still at sea, so that they became pickled in their own brine. As in the medieval period, ling, haberdine (large salted, dried cod) and buckhorn (whiting dried until as hard as an antler) were cooked as stockfish (see page 203, above), and eaten with strongly flavoured sauces such as mustard or greensauce.

The varieties of fresh marine fish caught off the coast of England were virtually the same as those still being harvested within living memory. Even in wealthy households most were simply simmered in salted water, perhaps with the peel of a lemon, and dished with slices of lemon and a hot sauce of melted butter, lemon-juice and nutmeg.[60] Alternatively they might be stewed in claret or white wine with butter, onion, nutmeg, sweet herbs, salt and pepper, or be cooked to specific recipes, such as the following.

TO BOIL TURBOT[61]

1 whole turbot, cleaned and gutted
1tbs salt
1 bottle white wine
a bundle of rosemary and bayleaves
1tsp ground ginger
1 lemon, sliced
6 oysters (taken from their shells), prawns or shrimps
1 raw egg yolk, beaten
4oz/100g butter, melted

Place the fish in the bottom of a large pan, add the salt, 1pt/600ml of the wine, the herbs, ginger and lemon, add just sufficient water to cover. Lift out the fish, bring the liquid up to the boil, replace the fish, cover, and simmer for some 10–15 minutes until tender. Meanwhile gently stew the shellfish in the remaining wine.

Dish the drained fish on a bed of sippets, pour the melted butter over the fish, then beat the egg yolk into the stewed shellfish and pour them over the fish just before serving. Garnish the fish with sliced lemon and fried bayleaves, with ground ginger sprinkled around the rim.

TO BOIL CONGER EEL TO BE EATEN HOT[62]

2lb/900g conger eel, after the head, vent and innards have been removed
white wine vinegar
1tbs salt
1 lemon, sliced
½tsp blade mace
1 slice root ginger
3 cloves
1 bottle white wine
juice of 1 bitter orange or a lemon
4oz/100g butter
root ginger and barberries for garnish

Scald the eel, wash it clean and marinade it for a few hours with the vinegar, half the salt, half the lemon and the spices. Drain the eel, put it into a clean pan, cover with half wine and water, then remove the fish while you bring the liquid to the boil, before adding it back, with the lemon and spices from the marinade, along with the rest of the salt, and simmer for 20–25 minutes until tender. Remove the eel on to a dish lined with sippets, pour on a sauce made by beating the orange or lemon juice with the warmed butter, garnish with the rest of the sliced lemon, barberries and sliced ginger and serve hot.

TO BOIL PLAICE[63]

1 3lb/1.35kg plaice
1tsp salt
juice & peel of 1 lemon, & 1 lemon sliced
2oz/50g butter
pinch grated nutmeg

Draw and wash the plaice, put into a large pan with the salt and lemon peel, and just cover with water. Then remove the plaice so as to bring the water to a boil, then replacing the fish and simmering gently for 15 minutes. Drain, dish, arrange sippets of bread around the sides, and lemon slices down the middle. Melt the butter, lemon juice and nutmeg together until just boiling, pour over the fish, and serve.

TO DRESS SOLES

1 sole
2–3tbs olive oil or clarified butter
½pt/300ml white wine
¼tsp grated/ground ginger
¼tsp garlic, chopped
6–8 anchovy fillets
juice of 1 bitter orange

Draw and wash the sole, pat dry with a cloth, and fry, brown side down, for 2 minutes. Bring the wine, ginger and garlic to the boil, add the sole (with added boiling water to cover it, if necessary) and simmer for a further 2 minutes. Using a knife and a fish-slice, separate the top fillets along the line from the head to the tail, turn each one back, arrange the anchovy fillets inside, replace the fillets, and stew for a further minute before dishing. Pour a little of the cooking liquor over the sole, along with the orange juice, and serve hot.

All forms of shellfish were also eaten, the most popular being the oyster. As Thomas Fuller stated in 1662:

> The best in England, fat, salt, green-finned, are bred near Colchester, where they have an excellent art to feed them in pits made for the purpose. King James was wont to say 'he was a very valiant man who first adventured on eating oysters ... Oysters are the only meat which man eat alive, and yet account it no cruelty.'[65]

They were also gathered from other parts of the coast, those of Wainsfleet in Kent, and from Cornwall being especially well known.

TO STEW OYSTERS[66]

12 oysters
¾pt/450ml white wine
¼tsp blade mace
6 peppercorns
1 small slice root ginger
pinch of salt
1tbs white wine vinegar
1 bundle sweet herbs
2oz/50g butter
½ lemon flesh, minced finely

Open the oysters, saving their liquor separately. Wash the oysters. Put the liquor, wine, spices, salt, vinegar, herbs, and half the butter into a pan, bring to the boil, add the oysters, and simmer gently for about 2 minutes until they are tender. Drain the oysters in a sieve, pour half the liquid into a clean pan with the remaining butter and the lemon, and bring to the boil. Dish the oysters, pour the lemon sauce over them, and serve hot, garnishing the dish with ground ginger.

TO STEW SCALLOPS[67]

8–10 scallops in their shells
½pt/300ml white wine
1tsp salt
2tbs elderflower (or wine) vinegar
3 whole cloves; 1 blade mace
2tsp mixed herbs
2oz/50g butter
juice of 1 orange

Scrub the shells under running water, discarding any that are open and do not close when tapped. Put them into a pan, cover them with the wine, topped up with water, and the salt, bring to the boil, simmer for about 5 minutes, until the shells open, then leave until cold. Using a knife, cut the scallops away from their rounded shells, prize the shells apart, breaking their hinges, then rinse them while still attached to their flat shells. Cut away the grey beard-like fringes, without detaching the orange roe or tearing the flesh, put a knife under the black thread to each side, and pull it gently off along with the black intestinal bag. Now cut the scallops from the bottom shells, rinse, and put into a clean pan.

Strain the liquid the scallops were cooked in, and pour in sufficient to just cover them, then add the vinegar, spices and herbs, slowly bring to the boil and simmer for about 5 minutes until tender (do not overcook or they will toughen). Remove the scallops, put 4 or 5 in two of the shells, and pour over the butter melted with the orange juice, and serve hot.

TO STEW COCKLES[68]

8oz/225g shelled cockles
¼pt/150ml claret
¼pt/150ml wine vinegar
2tbs capers
1oz fresh white breadcrumbs
¼tsp salt
pinch ground mace
pinch ground pepper
pinch thyme
1 hard-boiled egg yolk
1oz/25g butter
1 clove garlic

If you are using unprepared cockles, wash them, soak them for 2–3 hours in clean water, cook gently in water for about 5 minutes until the shells open, then remove the muscle from the shells.

Put all but the butter and garlic into a saucepan and stew for 4–5 minutes stirring gently from time to time, then shake in the butter. Rub a hot dish with the sliced garlic, line it with 2 or 3 toasts of white bread, and pour the cockles on top.

Alternatively they may be simmered in salted water for about 4 minutes after being removed from their shells.[69]

TO BOIL MUSSELS[70]

2lb/900g mussels
1 large onion, peeled & chopped
1oz/25g butter
1tsp dried yeast
¼tsp ground black pepper

Wash each mussel under running water, scraping off barnacles, seaweed and the beards. Discard any which are open but do not close when tapped. Place the mussels in a pan with the remaining ingredients, cover with water, bring to the boil and cook for 4–5 minutes until they open, frequently shaking the pan. Discard any which have not opened, and serve the rest in their shells.

TO STEW SHRIMPS OR PRAWNS[71]

8oz/225g shrimps or prawns, boiled and picked
¼pt/150ml white wine or cream
2oz/50g butter
pinch of ground nutmeg
¼tsp salt
juice of 1 bitter orange or lemon
scallop shells for display

Bring the wine or cream, half the butter, the nutmeg and salt to the boil, add the shrimps or prawns, return to the boil and simmer for 1–2 minutes until heated through. Pour into the scallop shells, pour over the remaining butter melted into the juice and serve hot.

TO STEW CRABS[72]

1 dressed crab, with its shell
1oz/25g butter
1tbs wine vinegar or fresh orange juice
pinch of ground cinnamon
pinch of ground ginger

Take all the meat out of the shell, put it into a saucepan with the other ingredients, and stir over a gentle heat until almost boiling, adding a little more butter and vinegar, and perhaps a little sugar if necessary to keep it moist. Wash the shell, put the meat back inside it, and dish with the legs to each side.

For great feasts, much larger and more expensive fish were acquired. In October 1567, for example, the Privy Council dined on a side of porpoise which cost 9*s.* 6*d.*, a whole one purchased in 1590 being 18*s.*[73] Some considered that it was 'nother praysed in the olde testament nor in physicke' and that its flesh was neither meat nor fish, having the characteristics of both.[74] It might be roasted, or else poached, drained, dished on three pleated napkins, and surrounded by a bed of parsley.[75]

The other great fish was the sturgeon, still to be caught in the estuaries and lower reaches of rivers of Stuart England. Even in the middle of a lively Civil War siege, there was time to go fishing for one. When, in 1644, Ferdinando, Lord Hastings, was defending Donington, ten miles upstream from Nottingham, he had on,

> Aug 10. A sturgeon taken today in the Trent above the boat at the Mills 7 foot and a half long. Cut into 10 pieces. Sent for the boiling of him 2 gallons of claret, 1 gallon and a half of wine vinegar (and 8 gallons of ale of my lady's own) and a pound and a half of bases [bass] to tie it up in pieces.[76]

The next day a nine-foot sturgeon was caught in the same place, and pickled in the identical manner. Usually households purchased their sturgeon already pickled and sold by the keg, cag or cask of some four or five gallons (22.5–24l) capacity:

> 1575 A barrel of Sturgeon £2 10 0*d.*[77]
> 1602 for 1 firkin and 1 keg of sturgeon spent this term 45*s.*[78]

Whether pickled or fresh, it was usually cut across the head end as joles, long fillets called rands, and the tail. Robert May published thirty-three recipes for its use, exploiting its texture, which was said to closely resemble that of veal.[79]

FRESHWATER FISH

Freshwater fish was caught both commercially and for sport, every variety finding its way onto the dining table. Before their habitats were rendered sterile by the industrial and sewage pollution of the nineteenth century, vast quantities of large fish could be found in every river and lake. Of these, the salmon was most prized, especially those taken in the Tweed and the Tyne on the Northumbrian coast. Here up to 300 might be caught on a single day or 2,000 per week, providing a good living for the local fishermen and their families.[80] They were also taken by the sporting angler using lines baited with lob-worms, gudgeon or flies, as described in *Barker's Delight or the Art of Angling*, published in 1651–7 by Thomas Barker, a Shrewsbury man living in Westminster, and *The Compleat Angler or the Contemplative Man's Recreation* published in 1653 by Izaak Walton. In Walton's view, there was 'no better Salmon than in *England*: and that though some of our northern counties have as fat and as large as the river *Thames*, yet none are so excellent a taste.'[81] They looked their best when cooked whole.

TO STEW A SALMON OR A TROUT[82]

1 salmon or trout
1pt/600ml white wine
4 cloves
½tsp blade mace
1 slice root ginger
6 peppercorns
½oz/12g butter
2 bay leaves
bundle of rosemary & thyme
2tbs (white) wine vinegar
½ an orange, unpeeled
1 lemon, sliced
ground ginger or sieved dry soft breadcrumbs for garnish

Slit the fish beneath the head and gills, cut out the entrails and discard, then rinse clean.

Make up sufficient stock (using the remaining ingredients except the lemon, ginger or breadcrumbs) to cover the fish, and bring to the boil. Put in the fish and poach gently for 7–8 minutes per lb/450g if to be eaten hot. If to be eaten cold allow 5 minutes for fish under 7lb/3.2kg, and 10–15 minutes if over that weight, allowing it to cool in its stock.

Place the hot or cold fish on a dish lined with sippets, lay on the sliced lemon, and pour over a little of its stock (or melted butter if hot) and garnish the rim with the ginger or breadcrumbs.

Fresh trout were held in similar esteem. Having caught a good dish-full for Edward, Lord Montagu, Thomas Barker, who took as much delight in the dressing of fish as he did in his angling, prepared them as follows:

TROUT IN BROTH[83]

1 trout, cleaned and gutted
1pt/600ml milk
½tsp blade mace
1½oz/35g butter
4 raw egg yolks
½ lemon, peeled, flesh finely chopped

Measure sufficient milk to cover the trout, bring it to the boil with the mace, put in the trout and simmer for about 10 minutes until tender. Put ½oz/12g of the butter into one yolk beaten with the lemon and set aside. Beat 3 yolks in a deep dish, stir in the milk from the trout, season with salt and pepper to taste, and serve as a broth, meanwhile keeping the trout warm. When the broth has been eaten, put the trout into a hot dish, top with the lemon mixture, stirring together as it melts, and serve immediately.

For the next course, further trout were 'calvered', a term which might apply to very freshly caught fish, but, as his recipe shows, it was also a method of sousing, by which they could be pickled for consumption over the next few days.

TO CALVER TROUT[84]

trout, cleaned and gutted
4tsp salt
bundle of rosemary, thyme and marjoram

Cut through the spine in 2 or 3 places, place in a deep dish, sprinkle with half the salt and leave in a cool place for at least an hour. Bring to the boil sufficient vinegar to half-cover the trout, pour it over the fish, and leave it for about 10 minutes. In a suitable pan, bring to the boil the same quantity of water as vinegar, with the remaining salt and herbs. Add the vinegar in which the fish has been soaking, bring back to the boil, then add the fish, which should be covered with liquid, and simmer for 15 minutes before setting aside to cool. Keep the fish submerged in the liquor and use over the next few days.

TROUT THE ITALIAN WAY[85]

1 trout
½pt/300ml white wine
4 cloves
¼tsp blade mace
½ nutmeg, sliced
a little root ginger
1oz/25g butter
juice of 1 lemon

Stew the trout in the wine and spices for about 10 minutes until tender. Pour the liquor into a hot dish, beat in the butter and lemon juice, add the trout and serve.

Other popular freshwater fish included perch, chub, bream and pike, as caught in most rivers and lakes. In contrast, carp and eels were also farmed in ponds or 'moats, whereon you may row with a Boat, and fish with nets.'[86] In the mid-seventeenth century, for example, Sir John Barrington of Hatfield Broad Oak in Essex paid,

For 14 stone eels put into the Moat Pond	1s.
For 500 store Carps	11s.
For mending the Great Dragge Net	6*d.*[87]

There were numerous recipes for stewing a carp, some splitting it or drawing its blood while still alive, some sealing it, some leaving the scales on, and all deploying a different range of flavourings. One of the simplest was used by Elizabeth Cromwell, wife of the Lord Protector.

TO STEW A CARP[88]

1 carp
coarse sea salt
¼pt/150ml wine vinegar
1 bottle white wine
1 slice root ginger, shredded
1 nutmeg, cut in four
1 clove garlic
1 onion, peeled and halved
1 bundle of herbs
8 anchovy fillets
butter
1 lemon, sliced or carved
grated white breadcrumbs

Cut the carp open along its underside, remove the entrails and gall bladder, but retain the spawn, milt and the 'rivet' or liver. Wash out with a little vinegar, retaining it with the blood, then rub the carp inside and out with coarse salt. Pour the wine into a large pan, adding sufficient water to cover the carp, the spices, garlic, onion, herbs and anchovies, and bring to the boil. Mop the carp with a clean cloth, put it into the wine and flavourings with the spawn, milt and liver, and simmer for 15–30 minutes, according to its size, until tender, then adding the blood and vinegar, and the butter. Remove the carp onto a dish, place the spawn, milt and liver on top. Pour some of the stock around it, to be eaten as a broth, and garnish the dish with the lemons and grated bread.

VEGETABLES

One of the great changes between the medieval and early post-medieval diet, particularly that of polite society, was the introduction of new vegetables, fostering a growing interest in gardening. The medieval staples of onions, beans, spinach, coleworts and peas retained their popularity, only leeks losing their former importance. The arrival of globe artichokes, lettuces, French, scarlet runner and haricot beans and improved carrots in the early sixteenth century, followed by asparagus, cauliflowers and sweet potatoes by the 1590s, brought an unprecedented range of new tastes and textures onto the table. Along with Jerusalem artichokes of the early seventeenth century and sugar peas in the 1650s, each new vegetable was initially treated as a rare, fashionable luxury. This led them to be cooked with a range of similarly expensive ingredients which frequently masked their true tastes, although still producing a number of flavoursome and delicious dishes.

ARTICHOKES (GLOBE)

Globe artichokes were introduced into England in the early sixteenth century, when they were a high-status vegetable found only in the gardens of the great. Henry VIII had a passion for them, his privy purse expenses recording their receipt as welcome gifts. As Henry Buttes wrote in 1599, they 'please the taste: provoke urine and Venus', beliefs which ensured their fashionable popularity into the early mid-sixteenth century.[89] The basic way of cooking them was to boil them for about half an hour, discard the leaves and other superfluities and eat the bottoms seasoned with salt and pepper, though Ben Jonson considered that a young artichoke 'always carries pepper and salt in itself.' However, as befitted such esteemed delicacies, they were also cooked with richly flavoured syrups.

TO STEW ARTICHOKES[90]

3 globe artichokes
3–4 slices white bread, crusts removed
2oz/50g beef marrow (or butter)
3 plums, halved and stoned
3oz/75g sugar
1tbs lemon juice (for verjuice)
½tsp blade mace

Cut the stalks off the artichokes, cover the heads with water and boil for 30 minutes until tender, when the leaves may be easily detached. Meanwhile poach the plums and sugar in a little water for 5–15 minutes, depending on their ripeness, until just tender. When the artichokes have cooked, remove the leaves and choke, slice the bottoms across horizontally, and each slice into quarters.

Place the bread over the bottom of the dish. Arrange the artichokes on top, and the plums in turn on top of them. Add the marrow, lemon juice and mace, and just cover with the syrup from the plums. Invert a second dish of the whole to act as a cover, then poach very gently over a low heat (or stand the dish over a pan of simmering water) for 2 hours, topping up with more syrup as necessary. Serve. It is a very rich and flavoursome dish, but one which masks much of the artichokes' original taste.

ARTICHOKES (JERUSALEM)

The name of this tuberous root is believed to come from the Italian *girasole articlocco*, or 'sunflower artichoke', as it was known in Rome, and has no connection with Jerusalem. Rather, it was introduced into Europe from tropical America in the early seventeenth century, when its rarity made it fashionable, while its ability to produce good crops soon caused it to become a much more common vegetable, simply boiled and eaten with butter, vinegar and pepper in the 1620s.[91]

JERUSALEM ARTICHOKES[92]

1½lb/675g Jerusalem artichokes
1tsp salt
2 hard-boiled egg yolks
6 dates
4oz/100g grapes or gooseberries
2oz/50g butter
1oz/25g sugar
½tsp salt
¾pt/450ml white wine
½ a lemon, sliced

Cover the artichokes with water, add the salt, bring to the boil, simmer for 10 minutes, then drain and leave to cool a little, then peel them. Place in a clean saucepan with the remaining ingredients, cover and stew for about 15 minutes, until the artichokes are tender. Pour into a dish, then top with knobs of softened butter and a sprinkle of caster sugar just before serving

ASPARAGUS

Previously known as sperage, and as sparrow-grass by 1650, asparagus was uncommon on English tables before the late sixteenth century. It then came into wider cultivation, Richard Brome publishing his play *Sparagus Garden* in 1653, when it had become popular.[93]

ASPARAGUS[94]

1lb/450g asparagus
2tbs olive oil
1tbs wine vinegar
salt & pepper to taste

Wash and trim the asparagus, tie in bundles of 6 to 8 stalks, stand vertically in a pan of boiling salted water, and simmer for 10–15 minutes until tender. (there is no need to change the water as in the original recipe). Shake the oil, vinegar, salt and pepper together and pour over the asparagus after it has been drained and dished.

BEANS

The broad bean was largely regarded as a subsistence dish for peasants, for although nutritious, 'it is good for plowmen to fyl the panche; it doth ingender grose humours, it doth replete a man with ventosyte.' One of its great advantages, however, was that it could be easily dried to provide a reliable source of food throughout the whole year, either in pottages, or as bean butter to replace real butter in Lent.[95] In the early sixteenth century kidney beans were being grown in English gardens, soon to be joined by new varieties from the Americas, including the French, scarlet runner and haricot beans, all suitable for more delicate cookery.

BROAD BEANS[96]

2lb/900g broad beans, shelled
1tsp dried marjoram
1tsp salt

Cover the ingredients with water, bring to the boil and simmer for 15–20 minutes until tender, then drain and serve. Alternatively omit the marjoram and dish dotted with butter and accompanied with salt and pepper.

DRIED BUTTER BEANS

8oz/225g dried butter beans
½tsp salt

Soak the beans in cold water for 18–24 hours, drain, cover with plenty of water and simmer gently for about an hour until tender, adding the salt about 10 minutes before serving, dotted with butter.

FRENCH OR RUNNER BEANS[97]

1½lb/700g French or runner beans, topped, tailed, and the strings removed
½tsp salt

Bring a pan of water to the boil, add the beans and salt, simmer for about 10 minutes until tender, then drain and serve dotted with butter, and a sprinkling of salt around the dish.

BROOM BUDS

Cook as French beans

CABBAGES

The colewort, with its coarse, open leaves, was a basic peasant vegetable, only the tender bud and long sprouts being considered fit for the table. To replicate them today, spring greens may be used.

COLEWORTS[98]

1 head spring greens
½pt/300ml meat stock
¼tsp salt
½tsp fennel seed
pinch ground black pepper

Trim the greens, cut across into broad strips, and boil in water for 10 minutes. Drain, press dry, add the remaining ingredients, and simmer for a further 10 minutes until tender.

'The great hard and compacted heads of cole, commonly called cabbage,' by the 1620s, had been in cultivation from the late medieval period. Simply boiled, it was a good everyday dish, but for polite use it was frequently cooked in stock or hollowed out and stuffed.

CABBAGE[99]

1 cabbage, trimmed
2 medium onions, peeled & chopped
1 leek, peeled & chopped
1 beef stock cube
pinch of saffron
pinch of cinnamon
1tsp sugar

Cut the cabbage vertically into four, remove most of the thick stalk, put in a pan with the vegetables, stock cube and saffron, and simmer for 10–15 minutes until tender. Drain, put into a dish and sprinkle with the cinnamon mixed into the sugar.

STUFFED CABBAGE[100]

1 large cabbage, trimmed
4oz/100g prunes, pre-soaked
2tbs raisins
1½tbs suet
3oz/75g fresh white breadcrumbs
¼tsp salt
pinch each of pepper, clove & mace
2 beef stock cubes
18in/50cm square of muslin

Make a deep cut all around the cabbage stalk and dig out the heart, leaving some 1½in/4cm all round. Trim the outer end of the stalk so that it may be replaced as a plug.

Dissolve one of the stock cubes in ¼pt/150ml hot water, and mix with the prunes, raisins, suet, crumbs, salt and spices, to form a stuffing. Pack this into the cabbage, replace the stalk end, place this on the muslin, gather tightly at the top, and tie securely with string. Bring a pan of water to the boil, add the remaining stock cube and the cabbage, cover, and simmer for some 45 minutes until tender, then drain and turn out onto a hot dish.

CARROTS

Red carrots were considered nutritious, but hardly appear in household accounts or other records before the mid-sixteenth century, when improved varieties began to be eaten.[101] A quantity were purchased for the Lords of the Star Chamber in 1567, for example.[102] Later they became a common garden vegetable. They might be boiled, peeled, pulped and heavily seasoned, or plain boiled whole for about 20 minutes until tender, the peel rubbed off, and dressed with oil, vinegar, mustard and coriander.[103]

CARROTS & ONIONS[104]

1lb/450g carrots	*1tsp parsley, chopped*
1 onion, sliced	*½tsp thyme*
1oz/25g butter	*½tsp savory*
1tsp salt	*pinch ground pepper*
4fl.oz/120ml white wine	*1 light stock cube*

Peel the carrots and cut into strips 1in x ¼in x ¼in/2.5cm x 6mm x 6mm. Add the remaining ingredients to ¾pt/450ml water, bring to the boil, simmer for 15 minutes, or until just tender, then dish on sops of white bread.

CAULIFLOWER

Cauliflowers were introduced into England in the late sixteenth century, the Star Chamber accounts of 1590 recording the purchase, perhaps for just one, at the high price of 2*s.*[105] By 1634, however, they cost 8*d.* each when purchased for use at Althorp, still a high price for a vegetable.[106]

BUTTERED CAULIFLOWERS[107]

1 medium cauliflower	*1 blade mace*
1pt/600ml milk	*1oz/25g butter*
½tsp ground mace	*2tsp sugar*
½pt/300ml single cream	*a little mixed salt & nutmeg*

Separate the florets and simmer in the milk and ground mace for 12–15 minutes, or until just tender. Meanwhile heat the cream, blade mace, butter and sugar until boiling. Drain the cauliflower, dish on sippets, pour the cream sauce on top, and finally sprinkle with the salt and nutmeg.

CAULIFLOWERS: AN ALTERNATIVE SAUCE[108]

⅛pt/15ml sherry	*1tbs white wine vinegar*
2oz/50g butter	*½ lemon, sliced very thinly*

Stir together until boiling, and pour over the dished cauliflower.

GARLIC

Garlic was popular in Tudor and Stuart cookery, even if some diners might have 'suche a garlicke breath as would have poisoned a dog.'[109] It was not only used to flavour other foodstuffs, Thomas Cromwell having 'a garlick mortar of wood, with a pestle' in his kitchen in 1527, but was plain-boiled until tender and eaten with oil and vinegar.[110]

LEEKS

As many new garden vegetables became popular, the leek lost its place as one of England's leading potherbs, its exceptional retention in Wales being a source of humour for Elizabethan playwrights. In *Henry V* Shakespeare's Fluellen takes great offence against Pistol who, along with other Englishmen of his generation, did not 'love it, nor your affections and your appetites and your digestions does not agree with it.'[111] It was this perceived indigestibility that Henry Buttes tried to counteract by boiling them twice, and eating them with almond oil. The French influence of the mid-seventeenth century introduced new leek pottages for use in Lent, as in the following example from La Varenne.

POTTAGE OF LEEKS WITH MILK[112]

1lb/450g leeks	*1tsp salt*
water in which peas have been cooked	*pepper*
½pt/300ml milk	*6 cloves*

Trim the leeks, chop them finely, put into cold water, bring to the boil and drain (this is unnecessary with young, tender leeks). Then put them in a pan with the pea stock (enough to cover), put on a lid, and simmer for about 20 minutes until tender. Add the remaining ingredients, cook for a further 5 minutes, then pour the liquid onto sops of bread in a deep dish, and top it with the leeks.

LETTUCE

Unlike most pot-herbs, lettuce was used as either an ingredient or a garnish, rather than a dish in its own right. In recipes for seething chickens with lettuce, or to boil mutton with lettuce, for example, it was simply washed and added to the boiling stock. Alternatively, lettuces were stewed in broth, cut in half and buttered to garnish pottages.[113]

MUSHROOMS

Rather surprisingly, mushrooms were rarely eaten in England before the second quarter of the seventeenth century.

MUSHROOMS[114]

1lb/450g field mushrooms
1tsp salt
1 onion, peeled & chopped
1 blade mace
2–3 cloves
¼tsp ground black pepper
1tbs fresh sweet herbs, chopped
2oz/50g butter
¼pt/150ml dry white wine
1oz/25g fresh white breadcrumbs
1 clove garlic
1 orange, thinly sliced

Peel the mushrooms, put into a shallow pan hollow side upwards, add the salt, onion, spices, sweet herbs and butter, cover, and stew for 5 minutes over a gentle heat. Stir in the wine and then the breadcrumbs and simmer for a further 10 minutes. Rub the dish with the garlic, pour in the mushrooms, and garnish with the slices of orange.

ONIONS

Onions are described in *The Countrie Farme* of 1626:

> The Onion, though it be a Countryman's meat, is better to use than to taste, that he that eateth everie day tender Onions, with Honey, to his Breakfast, shall live more healthfull, so that they be not too new; for the drie are more healthfull than the greene; the boyld than the raw; the preserved than the drie, wherefore the drie must be chosen to use in salads, fried Meats, Gallymawfries, baked Meats, Sawces, Beane Pottage, and other uses.[115]

As such a useful vegetable, onions were purchased in great quantities for the use of major households. As explained in the accounts of Robert Dudley, Earl of Leicester, both onions and garlic were sold in 'ropes' of fifteen heads, their stalks plaited together as in modern France. Every fifteen 'ropes' comprised a 'hundred' of onions or garlic, so that the 'hundred' actually totalled 225 heads.[116]

TO BOIL ONIONS[117]

1lb/450g onions
3oz/75g raisins
1tsp ground pepper
½tsp salt
1 egg yolk, beaten
1tbs white wine vinegar
1tbs sugar

Peel and quarter the onions, place in a pan with the raisins, pepper, salt, and ½pt/300ml water, and simmer for 15 minutes. Remove from the heat, stir in the mixed yolk, vinegar and sugar, and pour into a dish lined with sops of white bread.

A SOP OF ONIONS[118]

1lb/450g onions
2oz/50g butter
½tsp salt
pinch ground black pepper

Peel and slice the onions and fry in the butter until pale brown, stirring regularly. Add ½pt/300ml water to the pan and simmer for some 5 minutes until the onions are tender.

BUTTERED ONIONS[119]

4 small/medium onions
1 tbs/15g currants
pinch ground cinnamon
2tbs/30ml olive oil or butter
2tsp/10g sugar
1 thick slice white bread or toast

Peel the onions, place in a pan with the currants, cover with water, bring to the boil, and simmer for some 45 minutes until tender when tried with a skewer. Meanwhile cut the bread/toast into one-inch (2.5cm) squares, and place in a dish. Drain the water from the onions and currants, return them to the pan with the cinnamon and olive oil or butter, roll them around over a gentle heat until coated, then turn them out onto the bread, sprinkle with sugar and serve.

PARSNIPS

Along with Jerusalem artichokes, potatoes and skirrets, parsnips for fashionable tables might be plain-boiled, then stewed with dates, grapes, gooseberries, barberries, sliced lemons, salt, mace, cinnamon, butter, sugar and white wine, all of which would mask their original flavour.[120] Some of the French recipes introduced in the 1650s were much plainer, as in the following example from La Varenne.

PARSNIPS[121]

1lb/450g parsnips
2oz/50g butter
¼tsp salt
pinch of ground nutmeg
4–5tbs of strong meat stock, or wine vinegar or verjuice (lemon juice may replace the verjuice)

Boil the whole parsnips for about 20 minutes until just tender, drain, peel, cut into large pieces, put into a clean pan with the remaining ingredients and stir over a gentle heat for a few minutes until most of the liquid has been absorbed, then serve immediately.

PEAS

Fresh, young and tender peas were a great seasonal delicacy, dried peas then being used for pottages throughout the remainder of the year. Even though fresh peas had an excellent flavour and texture of their own, contemporary recipes cooked them in thick sauces.

TO BOIL FRESH YOUNG PEAS[122]

1lb/450g fresh peas
½pt/300ml milk
1 egg yolk
¼tsp salt
1oz/25g fresh white breadcrumbs
¼tsp ground ginger
1tbs fresh parsley, chopped
pinch of saffron

Cover the peas with water and simmer for some 15–20 minutes until tender, then drain. Mix the egg yolk, breadcrumbs and ginger, scald with boiling milk, and pass through a strainer onto the peas. Stir in the salt, parsley and saffron, re-heat (without boiling), and pour into a hot dish just before serving.

In June, 1654, a poor woman carried a basket of young peas to Whitehall as a present for the 'Protectoress' Elizabeth Cromwell, who sent out a mere 5s.

by way of reward. The woman was so disgusted with this beggarly insult, that she demanded the return of her peas, then selling them for double the price to a cook by the Savoy. Elizabeth Cromwell's own recipe for sugar peas, as mange tout were then know, shows that she was following the latest culinary fashions.

TO BOIL SUGAR PEAS[123]

1lb/450g mange tout
4oz/100g butter
2tbs olive oil
½tsp salt
large pinch each black pepper & mace
2 egg yolks
4 tbs sherry

Trim the stalks and strings from the pods. Bring the butter, oil, salt and spices to the boil in ¼pt/150ml water, put in the peas and simmer for about 3–4 minutes until tender. Remove from the heat, stir in the yolks and sherry beaten together, then pour over sops of bread in a dish. This formed a base for a boiled chicken or capon.

SWEET POTATOES

The first potatoes to arrive in England in the late sixteenth century were the sweet or Spanish kind, then being grown in Spain and Portugal as well as their native West Indies. As with most novel and expensive imports, they soon gained the reputation of being a strong aphrodisiac, Sir John Falstaff crying 'Let the sky rain potatoes' in his amorous exchange with Mistress Ford.[124] Fletcher's *Loyal Subject* of 1617 includes a pedlar who advertises his wares with a cry of,

I have fine potatoes, Ripe potatoes!
Will your Lordship please to taste a fine potato?
'Twill advance your wither'd state,
Fill your Honour full of noble itches.'[125]

'Potatoes of America or Virginia', but actually from Peru, were being grown as botanical specimens in England in the 1590s, but did not develop as a food-source until after the Civil War.[126]

TO STEW SPANISH POTATOES[127]

2lb/900g sweet potatoes
2 medium cooking apples
½tsp each ground cinnamon & ginger
4tbs lemon juice (for verjuice)
4oz/100g butter
strips of citron & candied orange peel
5tbs sugar

Cover the potatoes with water and boil for about 15 minutes. Drain, cool in cold water, peel and cut into ¼–½in/1cm slices. Put the slices into a clean pan, layering them with the apples, spices and half the lemon juice and butter before simmering very gently for 1 hour, until cooked through and tender. Transfer to a hot dish lined with sippets, pour on the remaining juice beaten into the remaining butter, stick with the candied peels, and finally add a sprinkling of caster sugar.

SPINACH

As Henry Buttes described in 1599, spinach was easily cooked 'with it owne juyce, without water: then condite with Oile, Sorrel-juyce, and Raysons of the sun.'[128] Most other contemporary recipes include similar delicious sour/fruity-sweet flavourings.

BOILED SPINACH[129]

8oz/225g spinach
2tbs raisins
pinch ground cinnamon & ginger
1tbs sugar
1tbs vinegar
juice of 1 orange
2tsp cornflour

Rinse the spinach, put into a pan, cover, and cook for 10 minutes, stirring occasionally, until tender, then drain, turn onto a board and chop it finely. Return it to the pan, stir in the remaining ingredients, and stir over a gentle heat until it simmers and thickens, before turning out onto a dish, which may be lined with buttered, toasted sippets.

BUTTERED SPINACH[130]

8oz/225g spinach
1oz/25g butter
3fl.oz./90ml white wine
¼tsp ground cinnamon
1tbs sugar
4 dates, sliced
1oz/25g currants
¼tsp salt
2 hard-boiled eggs, quartered

Plunge the spinach into 1pt/600ml boiling water, press down, leave for a minute to wilt, then drain and press dry in a sieve. Turn on to a board, chop finely, and place in a clean pan with all but the eggs. Stir, cover, simmer gently for 5 minutes, then turn on to a dish lined with sippets and arrange the egg segments around the edge.

TURNIPS

The simplest way of cooking turnips was to scrape them, boil them in water with a little salt and butter, perhaps with a little mustard, and served with grated nutmeg. To convert them into a far more luscious dish they could be stewed in butter over a gentle heat, a process quite different from frying.[131]

TURNIPS[132]

1lb/450g turnips	*¼tsp salt*
4oz/100g butter	*¼tsp ground ginger*
4tbs wine vinegar	*2tsp sugar*

½ light stock cube dissolved in 4tbs hot water

Peel the turnips, cut into strips 1in x ¼in x ¼in/2.5cm x 6mm x 6mm, place in a pan with the remaining ingredients on a very low heat. Stir gently about every 15 minutes for 2 hours, keeping the strips whole. This makes the turnip very tender and well flavoured without absorbing most of the butter. If preferred the butter may be poured off for frying or sauces before the turnip is dished on sops of white bread.

CHAPTER FOURTEEN

Pottages, Stews and Soups

In contrast to today, when the differences between a stew and a soup, for example, are clearly understood, there were few such certainties in the periods under discussion. English cookery was in a state of ever-evolving transition, partly from within its own traditions, and partly from those being introduced from Europe and beyond. This chapter deals with dishes made by cutting or forming various foods into small pieces and simmering them in liquids until tender, as well as those made by grinding them into smooth pastes. However, the meanings of their various titles can be extremely confusing–especially as virtually the same dish might be known by a number of quite different names. For this reason the following attempt to provide clearer definitions will precede the more practical arrangement of the recipes.

Pottage is a term greatly misunderstood by most academics and re-enactors, who consider it to be a meatless, unpalatable mass of boiled vegetables. The absence of protein in the diet of individuals, as proven by the analysis of their excavated skeletons, is frequently explained by their dependence on pottage. This clearly demonstrates crass ignorance, for pottage was anything cooked in a pot, frequently including meats, fish and dairy products all rich in proteins. Some were based on cereals and vegetables, but the pottages which survived from the medieval period were made by adding these to the stock obtained by boiling the same joints of meat which followed them to the table. From around the early seventeenth century, some pottages took the form of an enriched sauce used to soak a layer of sippets arranged in a dish. These provided a combined base and accompaniment to the joint which was placed on top. One version of this type, based on a leg of beef and marrow-bones, was known as 'skinke'.[1] Other pottages were rich stews of a main ingredient flavoured with various fruits, vegetables, herbs, spices, stocks or wines which would give the diners a surfeit of protein, rather than a lack of it.[2]

Today, 'stews' are made of food cut into small pieces before being simmered to tenderness, but formerly they also included large joints cooked whole, or 'boiled'. However, Tudor and Stuart stews were known by many other names. Some were partly defined by the way in which the meat had been cut up, perhaps as gobbins or 'gobbits as big as a pullet's egg', as 'square bits' (cubed), as 'thin slices cross of the grain' called 'collops', or as large thin slices to be stuffed and rolled as 'olives'.[3] 'Hashes' were usually made of raw rather than cooked meat cut up into small pieces.[4] If the meat was sliced, fried and served in a succulent sauce in the French manner it became a 'fricassee', while if it was minced and cooked with other ingredients to form a very thick semi-liquid it was a 'capilotado'.[5] Alternatively, if made with a variety of principal ingredients cut into small pieces all cooked together it became a hockpot or hochpotch.[6]

Some pottages were served as liquids, the rich, boiling-hot stocks poured over cubes of fresh or toasted bread known as 'sops' in medieval English cookery surviving into the Tudor period.[7] In France the identical '*soupes*' had already begun to discard their bread to become the purely liquid dishes which were introduced into this country as 'soups' in the early seventeenth century.[8] If made of a strong broth, boiled and strained, these might also be known as cullises.[9] In the following sections a typical range of pottage/stew recipes is given for each of the main types of raw ingredient. It can only present a limited number, but many others are to be found in the manuscript and printed cookery books of the period.

BEEF POTTAGES

Some of the earliest specially made 'soups' were simple stocks made from meat and/or bones stewed for about 5 or 6 hours in order to extract all their gelatin. Since the resulting stocks could be clarified to set as a clear jelly, they were considered particularly nutritious. The cook at the Star Chamber regularly purchased the 'pottegche flesche', 'marebonys' and 'necke of motton' for their preparation in 1518–19.[10]

TO STEW BONES OR GRISTLES OF BEEF[11]

beef bones & sinews, coarsely chopped
bundle of fresh rosemary sprigs
blades of mace
salt

Cover the bones and sinews with cold water, add rosemary and mace separately tied in pieces of muslin. Bring to the boil, skim carefully, cover and simmer gently for about 6 hours, topping up with boiling water as necessary. Remove the cover, boil until reduced by half, then strain into a clean pan, squeezing in the rosemary and mace juices. (This was originally intended to be poured over cooked meat.) Stir in salt to taste and serve hot.

Around 1600 writers such as Sir Hugh Plat began to explore the possibility of transforming this kind of broth into a concentrated, long-lasting tablet. In this form it would provide a useful 'Victual for Warr', 'dry gelly carried to sea' and a food for soldiers on the march, who could eat it raw. He had heard of men who had survived for some ten years solely on meat juices, and believed that such an invaluable resource should be produced for victualling by the Crown. The basic ingredients, the lower legs of beef and calves' feet, were relatively cheap, and only needed to be boiled, strained, and their stock boiled down to a stiff jelly, just as if making glue. When set on clean cloths and exposed to the wind in full shade, it dried to firmness, could be sliced into pieces with a wire, which were then dusted with flour to stop them sticking together. Various flavourings were also suggested, so that the pieces would produce a good broth merely by addition of hot water. Such 'Portable Soups' continued to be made up to the mid-eighteenth century, the belief in gelatin as an all-fulfilling source of nutrition continuing well into the twentieth century.[12]

Beef was not as popular as mutton for making stews, pottages and soups, a rather surprising fact considering the leading role that beef stews played in the Georgian and Victorian periods. Nothing, apparently, could be more English, but one of the earliest recipes for a beef and mixed vegetable stew, published in 1660, is actually entitled:

TO STEW BEEF IN GOBBETS IN THE FRENCH FASHION[13]

1½lb/700g braising or stewing steak, cubed
1 large carrot, cut in pieces
1 parsnip, cut in pieces
1 turnip, cut in pieces
1 whole onion, peeled
1tsp salt
6 peppercorns
3 cloves
1 blade mace
4oz/100g spinach
¼pt/150ml claret
2tsp mixed thyme, parsley, marjoram & savory

final garnish
grapes or gooseberries; boiled artichokes with beaten butter; grated nutmeg; barberries

Cover the beef, vegetables, salt and spices with cold water, bring to the boil, cover, simmer for 2 hours, then add the herbs, spinach and claret and continue simmering for a further 30 minutes until tender. Pour into a hot dish lined with sippets, and garnish with the grapes or other fruit before serving hot.

Other beef stews used either sliced or minced beef;

TO MAKE A HASH OF SLICED BEEF[14]

1lb/450g rump steak, in thin slices
4oz/100g streaky bacon
1 beef stock cube
½tsp salt
¼pt/150ml claret
3 cloves
1 blade mace
large pinch ground black pepper

Put all the ingredients into a pan, cover with water, bring to the boil, cover, and simmer for 1½–2 hours until tender, then serve on sippets.

TO HASH COOKED BEEF[15]

1lb/450g cooked beef cut in very thin slices
1 stock cube
1 onion, sliced thinly
½tsp salt
¼pt/150ml claret
1oz/25g softened butter
1 small lemon, sliced

Follow the recipe above, cooking for 45 minutes.

Tripe and other offal were greatly appreciated, particularly when simmered in rich sauces such as these.

TO DRESS TRIPE[16]

1lb/450g tripe
½ a stock cube
½tsp mustard powder
large pinch ground black pepper
2oz/50g butter
1 clove of crushed garlic
2 tsp (white) wine vinegar

Cut the tripe into finger-sized pieces, cover with water and stew for 30 minutes. Mix the stock cube, mustard, pepper, butter and most of the garlic with ¼pt/150ml water, and bring to the boil. Rub a hot dish with the remaining garlic, pour on the drained tripe, pour the sauce over the top, and sprinkle with the vinegar.

TO BOIL TRIPE[17]

1lb/450g tripe
1½pt/900ml mutton stock (or 2–3 stock cubes)
½tsp salt
2tbs malt vinegar (for verjuice)
1lb/450g mixed spinach & lettuce, finely shredded
¼tsp ground black pepper

Cut the tripe into finger-sized pieces, stew with all the ingredients except the pepper for about 25–30 minutes until tender, pour into a dish lined with sops of bread and sprinkle with the pepper.

TO BOIL SAUSAGES[18]

1lb/450g sausages, with or without their skins
1pt/600ml claret
2tsp mixed herbs
2 blades mace
¼tsp ground cinnamon
1–2tbs barberries
garnish with sugar, cinnamon & ginger

Bring the claret, herbs, spices and barberries to the boil, put in the separated sausages, cover and simmer for 15–20 minutes until tender, then serve with its stock on sops of bread.

MUTTON & LAMB POTTAGES

Cubed lamb or mutton formed the basis of many different stews and meaty broths, of which the following examples are typical.

WHITE MUTTON BROTH WITH ALMONDS[19]

2lb/900g leg of lamb, cubed
3 light stock cubes
½tsp salt
1oz/25g butter
blade of mace
1tbs cider vinegar
2oz/50g ground almonds
4tsp sugar
½tsp ground ginger
1tbs rosewater
1 orange, thinly sliced
bouquet of rosemary, thyme, hyssop & marjoram

Gently simmer the lamb, stock cubes, salt, butter, mace, vinegar and bouquet in 2pt/1.2l water in a covered pan for 2½–3 hours until tender. Beat the almonds in a mortar (or blend) with half the cooking liquid and strain it into a clean saucepan. Add the ginger, rosewater and half the sugar, bring rapidly to the boil and keep hot. Put the remaining sugar, the orange and sufficient stock to cover them in another pan, and simmer until tender.

Arrange the lamb on sops, pour the almond liquid on top, then the oranges, and serve hot.

Scotch collops had nothing to do with Scottish cookery, the name coming from the act of 'scotching' or scoring the thin mutton steaks using the back edge of a knife.

SCOTCH COLLOPS OF MUTTON[20]

1lb/450g leg of lamb or mutton	*4oz/100g butter*
1–2tsp salt	*¼pt/150ml lamb stock*

Cut the meat into large slices as thin as possible, across the grain, and sprinkle both sides with salt. Gently fry the slices in the butter on each side for about 5 minutes just until they give up their juices. Pour off all surplus butter, add the stock, shake over a gentle heat until just boiling, then serve.

If preferred, either the juice of an orange, a pinch of grated nutmeg and a little claret may be added with the stock, or a few capers, oysters, and thin slices of lemon.

Large slices of mutton were also stuffed, rolled and boiled to produce aloes or 'olives'.

ALOES OF MUTTON[21]

6 thin mutton leg steaks at least 4in/10cm across

1 lamb kidney, minced	*1tsp salt*
6oz/175g fresh white breadcrumbs	*¼tsp ground black pepper*
1 hard-boiled egg yolk	*2oz/50g prunes, chopped*
1tsp mixed parsley, thyme & hyssop	*1oz/25g raisins*
½tsp mixed ground ginger, mace & cinnamon	*2–3 beaten eggs*
	2oz/50g small gooseberries or grapes

Beat the steaks out with the back of a knife and set aside. Mix all the ingredients together except for the gooseberries or grapes, and the eggs. Mix in sufficient egg to form a soft paste, and carefully mix in the gooseberries or grapes. Spread the mixture on the steaks, roll up and secure with small skewers or small stitches of thread (and wrap in cling-film to take the place of pig's caul). Plunge into boiling water and simmer for about 40 minutes until tender, then drain (remove the cling-film) and serve hot.

Cooked slices of lamb or mutton were ideal for being re-heated in a spiced sauce to provide a quickly available extra dish for the table.

PEARS OF MUTTON[22]

the pears

1lb/450g minced lean lamb
2oz/50g suet
4oz/100g fresh white breadcrumbs
1tsp mixed thyme & parsley
½tsp salt
pinch of ground cloves
pinch of saffron
3 raw egg yolks
2oz/50g small grapes or gooseberries
sage stems

broth for cooking

3 beef stock cubes
1½tsp salt
6 cloves
2 blades mace
pinch saffron
3 raw egg yolks

Knead together all the ingredients (but not the sage stalks) for the 'pears', adding the grapes or gooseberries last of all. Bring the ingredients for the broth (except the yolks) to the boil in 1½pts water. Form the mixture into small pears, using the sage stems as stalks, and poach in the stock for 10–15 minutes until cooked through. Pour off half the stock onto the yolks, beat until thickened, and then pour onto the pears in a deep dish.

Cooked slices of lamb or mutton provided an easy and quickly prepared additional dish for the table when re-heated in a spicy sauce.

TO MAKE A RASHER OF MUTTON OR COLD LAMB[23]

8–12oz/225–325g sliced cooked mutton or lamb
½pt/300ml claret
1oz/25g butter
1 blade mace
1 nutmeg, sliced
1–2tsp sugar

Heat together in a shallow pan and serve hot.

In contrast, chopped lamb formed the base for delicious soups such as the following:

WHITE BROTH WITH ALMONDS[24]

1lb/450g lean lamb
2tsp salt
6in/15cm sprig of rosemary
4 sprigs marjoram & hyssop
3–4 blades mace
1oz/25g butter
2tbs lemon juice (for verjuice)
1½oz/36g ground almonds
½tsp ground ginger
1½tsp rosewater
1tbs sugar
½ an orange, sliced
sops of white bread

Cut the lamb into small pieces, put into 3pt/1.8l cold water with the salt, bring slowly to the boil, skim, and reduce to a gentle simmer. Add the herbs and mace, each tied in pieces of muslin, the butter and lemon juice, cover, and simmer for about 2½ hours until tender. Pour off half the cooking liquid, add the almonds, grind (or blend) together until smooth, and strain into a clean pan, adding the ginger, rosewater and half the sugar before bringing to the boil, and keeping hot. Add the remaining sugar to the orange in another pan, and simmer with a little of the cooking liquid until tender.

Line a dish with the sops, arrange the lamb on top, then the almond sauce, and finally the oranges.

CHICKEN POTTAGES

Most chickens were boiled whole, only being cut in pieces, sealed down with spices and dried fruits in a pastry-sealed flaggon and immersed in a boiling cauldron for hours when being prepared for the sick.[25] The delicacy of their flesh made them ideal for making capilotado, cullis, blancmange and mortis.

CAPILOTADO OF VEAL & FOWL[26]

1 small cooked chicken
6oz/175g cooked veal or lamb
3oz/75g short-grain rice
½oz/12g each pine kernels, blanched almonds & pistachio kernels
6 chestnuts, boiled tender & peeled
1½pt/900ml mutton stock (or with 3 stock cubes)
1½tsp salt
1½oz/35g butter
¼tsp ground cinnamon
2tbs sugar
¼tsp ground black pepper

Pull all the meat off the chicken, cut the veal or lamb into small pieces, mix and set aside. Simmer the rice and nuts in the stock for about 30 minutes, stirring from time to time, until thick and tender. Stir in the salt with half the butter, cinnamon and sugar and spread half the mixture across a hot dish. Arrange the chicken, veal or lamb on top, cover with the remaining rice, sprinkle on the remaining cinnamon and sugar. Dot with the remaining butter and serve hot.

Cullis, a rich, strained broth used to strengthen those who were weak or ill, was usually based on chicken stock, the chicken itself being served separately. The following example is typical of this period.

A CULLIS AS WHITE AS SNOW[27]

1 medium oven-ready chicken
1½pt/900ml white wine or white wine and water
1 egg white, lightly beaten
1pt/450ml double cream
½tsp ground ginger
2tbs sugar
1tbs rosewater

Simmer the chicken in the wine/wine and water for about 45–50 minutes until tender, then remove from the pan for use as required, and leave the remaining stock until tepid. Beat the egg white into the stock and heat gently whilst continuously whisking until it is ready to boil, then stop whisking immediately and allow the stock to rise to the top of the pan before instantly removing from the heat. Set aside for 5 minutes, then strain through a fine cloth into a clean pan. Return to the stove over a gentle heat, and stir continuously while pouring in the cream, then the ginger, sugar and rosewater. Bring to the boil and serve.

The Tudor and Stuart blancmange or mortis was a sweet rosewater-flavoured pâté, quite different from the modern cornflour blancmange of the same name. Having chopped the ingredients very finely, they were pounded to a smooth paste in a pestle and mortar, those of marble, stone or wood being much better for this purpose than brass, which tended to spoil the delicate taste. Today a food processor performs the same function with far less labour.

BLANCMANGE[28]

half a chicken
3oz/75g ground almonds
¼pt/150ml cream
whites of 2 eggs
2oz/50g fresh white breadcrumbs
1tbs sugar
2tbs rosewater

Cover the chicken with water, cover, and simmer for about 45 minutes until tender, then drain and cool. Meanwhile mix the almonds into the cream. Pick all the chicken from the bones, removing any gristle and skin, chop it small, grind with the almond mixture, egg whites, breadcrumbs and sugar, and stir over a gentle heat until thickened. When cold, rub through a sieve, mix in the rosewater and dish in three piles on a plate.

TO MAKE A MORTIS[29]

half a chicken
2oz/50g ground almonds
¼pt/150ml milk
1tbs sugar
1tbs rosewater

You can use a ready-cooked chicken or, if cooking from scratch, cover a raw half-chicken with water, cover and simmer for about 45 minutes. Leave to cool, then strip off all the meat. Finely chop the meat and mix in the almonds, milk and sugar. Either pound these in a mortar or blend or process them to a smooth paste, transfer to a pan and stir over a gentle heat for 10–15 minutes until thick. Cool the pan in a bowl of cold water, beat in the rosewater, then press the mortis into a deep bowl or form into a round cake on a dish, and serve when completely cold.

RABBIT POTTAGE

SMOTHERED RABBITS[30]

2 rabbits, cut into joints
½tsp salt
¼tsp ground black pepper
2lb/900g onions
2oz/50g butter
2oz/50g currants
⅛pt/75ml cider vinegar (for verjuice)

Rub the rabbit joints with the salt and pepper, peel and quarter the onions, place in a pan with the remaining ingredients, add sufficient cold water to cover, cover, simmer for about 1½ hours until tender, then serve hot.

FISH POTTAGES

Most fish were boiled whole, only some of the larger species such as salmon, pike and carp sometimes being cooked as fillets, steaks or minced.

SALMON IN SPICED FRUIT BROTH[31]

1½lb/625g salmon fillets or steaks
½pt/300ml claret
1oz/25g raisins
1oz/25g currants
12 prunes, pre-soaked
3 cloves
2in whole cinnamon stick
1 piece root ginger, sliced
¼tsp salt
3tbs flour
2tsp sugar
1 lemon, sliced

Simmer the wine, fruit, spices and salt together in ¾pt/450ml water for 5 minutes, then add the salmon and poach for 7–10 minutes until tender. Arrange the salmon on sippets, mix the flour and sugar with a little cold water, add to the stock and boil rapidly until it has thickened. Pour this over the salmon, garnish with the lemon, and serve immediately.

TO CALVER SALMON[32]

1½lb/625g skinned salmon fillets
½pt/300ml white wine
¼pt/150ml white wine vinegar
½tsp salt
1 sprig rosemary
3 cloves
1 piece root ginger, sliced
1 blade of mace
1 fresh lemon peel

Simmer all but the salmon with ½pt/300ml water in a covered pan for 5 minutes. Add the salmon fillets in batches, ensuring each is covered by the stock, and poach for 5–7 minutes, then remove and leave to cool. When the stock is cold, pour it over the fillets and leave to soak overnight, and eat within the next few days.

ALOES OF FRESH SALMON[33]

1lb/450g skinned salmon fillets
2 hard-boiled egg yolks
4tbs raisins
1oz/25g butter, softened
½tsp mixed ground mace, pepper & cloves
½pt/300ml claret
2 raw egg yolks
2tbs cider vinegar (for verjuice)

Cut six 6 x 3in/15 x 7.5cm slices, preferably from the side of the fillet closest to the skin. Chop the remainder very finely, and knead with the sieved hard-boiled egg yolks, butter and spices to form a smooth paste. Spread the paste over the slices, leaving 1in/2.5cm bare at one end, and roll up, with the bare end on the outside. Secure with a cocktail stick (this function was originally served by feathers).

Add the claret to ½pt/300ml water, bring to the boil, put in the rolled salmon and poach gently for about 7 minutes. Stir in the raw yolks beaten with the cider vinegar (do not boil thereafter), and pour into a dish lined with sops of bread.

TO DRESS A CARP[34]

1 4lb/2kg carp
4 hard-boiled egg yolks, sieved
8oz/225g butter
¾pt/450ml white wine
½tsp salt
2oz/50g prunes (quartered)
½tsp grated nutmeg
¼tsp ground ginger
¼tsp ground cinnamon

Cut the head and tail off the fish, plunge into boiling salted water, simmer for 3–4 minutes, then drain and set aside.

Remove the skin, bones and guts from the body of the fish, finely chop or mince the flesh, mix it with the remaining ingredients and stir over a gentle heat until the mixture has thickened. Transfer the mixture to a hot plate, re-form it into the shape of the carp's body, set the head and tail to each end, and serve.

PEASE POTTAGES

In addition to the vegetable pottages described in the previous chapter on boiling, there were also thick pease pottages, forerunners of modern pea soups.

PEASE POTTAGE[35]

8oz/225g fresh or frozen peas
½ beef stock cube
½tsp chopped parsley
½tsp chopped sage
1 thick slice white bread
salt & pepper to taste

Boil the peas and stock cube in ½pt/300ml water for 10 minutes if fresh, 5 minutes if frozen, and remove from the heat. Grind the herbs in a mortar. Cut the crusts off the bread, divide the crumb into cubes, place them in the mortar and add just enough water from the peas to soak them. Add two-thirds of the peas and grind together to make a smooth paste. Stir the paste into the remaining peas and water in the pan, re-heat while stirring continuously, adding salt and pepper to taste.

THICK PEA OR BEAN POTTAGE[36]

12oz/350g cooked peas or broad beans
½pt/300ml milk
2 egg yolks
1oz/25g fresh white breadcrumbs
1tsp salt
1tsp chopped parsley
½tsp ground ginger
pinch of saffron

Put the peas or beans into a large pan, cover with water, bring to the boil, and then drain. Beat the remaining ingredients together, and pour onto the peas or broad beans, stirring continuously as they thicken whilst being brought back to the boil, then serve.

CEREAL POTTAGES AND A NUT POTTAGE

All cereal grains are extremely difficult to eat in their natural state, but are transformed into nutritious, easily digested warm and comforting foods following a prolonged period of stewing. Some, such as wheat, barley and rice, were often cooked whole after their hard inner husks had been removed, but these and oats were also ground to produce smoother forms of pottage.

Oatmeal was the mainstay of many peasant communities up to the twentieth century, being made into:

MILK POTTAGE[37]

For two people, take:
2oz/50g coarse or medium oatmeal (NOT rolled oats)
¼pt/150ml milk or cream
1oz/25g butter (optional)
1tsp salt

Bring ½pt water to the boil in a pan, sprinkle in the oatmeal while stirring with a porridge-stick, thible or spurtle, and allow to simmer for 15–20 minutes stirring as it thickens, then stir in the other ingredients for a further 5 minutes before serving.

OATMEAL POTTAGE (WITH HERBS)[38]

8 spring onions
2oz/50g medium oatmeal
2 beef stock cubes
½tsp salt
4tbs finely chopped selection of parsley, spinach, strawberry leaves, marigold petals or other greenstuff

Chop all the ingredients together very finely, put into a pan with ¼pt/150ml cold water and mix to a smooth paste. Stir in a further 1pt/600ml water, bring to the boil and continue stirring for some 20 minutes before serving. Alternatively, you can add a (sliced) onion instead of the spring onion & herbs.

GRUEL POTTAGE (WITH RAISINS & SPICES)[39]

2oz/50g medium oatmeal
2tsp mixed herbs, tied in muslin
2oz/50g raisins
1 blade mace
pinch of salt
1oz/25g sugar
½oz/12g butter
pinch of saffron
2tsp rosewater

Bring 1pt/600ml water to the boil, sprinkle in the oatmeal while stirring, add the herbs and simmer gently while stirring for 20 minutes. Pass the mixture through a sieve into a clean pan, add everything except the rosewater, and simmer while stirring for a further 10 minutes, then stir in the rosewater and serve.

BARLEY BROTH[40]

4oz/100g pearl barley
1 large blade of mace
1 bundle of herbs
12 prunes (optional)
½tsp salt
2oz/50g raisins
2–3tbs marigold petals
1 knuckle of veal (or 8 sheets gelatin & 2 lamb stock cubes)

Stew the barley in 1pt/600ml water for 10 minutes, drain, stew for a further 10 minutes with a further 1pt/600ml water, and drain again. Add a further 1½pt/900ml water and the remaining ingredients (having pre-soaked the gelatin for 5 minutes in cold water) and simmer for another hour. Serve on sippets of white bread.

Furmety or frummety took its name from the Latin word for wheat, *frumentum*. It was made by removing the outer husk by soaking the grain overnight in water, putting it into a sack and beating it with a washing bat or beetle. In many yeoman, gentry and noble establishments this stage was completed by the use of a large stone mortar known as a knocking stone, accompanied by a wooden pestle. One in the kitchen at Speke Hall, near Liverpool, was described as 'one stone mortar to knock wheat in 8*d*.' showing that furmety was being made there in 1624. After rinsing off the inner husks it was covered with water and left to barely simmer over a low fire during a second night, and finally flavoured and cooked.

64. Pestle and mortar. This carving on an early 16th-century misericord at Beverley Minster shows food being ground in a mortar. The presence of the bag in the background and the form of the mortar as a north country stone 'knocking stone' might suggest that wheat was being de-husked for making frumenty.

FURMETY[41]

6oz/150g whole wheat grains
¼pt/150ml milk or cream
¼tsp ground mace
1 stick cinnamon
pinch of saffron
½tsp salt
sugar for garnishing
2 yolks of eggs, beaten (optional)

Place the wheat in a stone mortar and soak overnight, then work with a wooden pestle to grind off the husk, rather than pulp the grain. Alternatively, either place the grain in a food processor with ¾pt/450ml water and process for 15 minutes, or replace the wheat with soaked pearl barley. Pour the grain into a coarse sieve, rinse off the loosened husks, put into a clean pan with 1½pt/900ml water, and simmer gently while stirring for about an hour until it has formed a glutinous mass. (Alternatively, boil, remove from the heat, cover, and wrap in towels to cook in its own heat, re-heating as necessary).

When tender, mix in the milk or cream with the spices, salt (and yolks, if chosen), bring to the boil, simmer for about 5 minutes, then serve in a clean dish, sprinkling the sugar over the top.

BUTTERED RICE[42]

2oz/50g short-grain rice
1 slice white bread or toast
1tbs olive oil or butter
1–2tbs sugar
pinch of ground cinnamon

Bring 1½pt/900ml water to the boil, stir in the rice and simmer for about 15 minutes, stirring from time to time, until tender. Cut the bread or toast into sippets and use to line a dish. Stir the oil or butter into the rice, pour it onto the sippets, sprinkle with the sugar and cinnamon, and serve hot.

ALMOND POTTAGE[43]

4oz/100g almond paste	*¼tsp ground mace*
½pt/300ml milk	*pinch of salt*
1pt/600ml cream	*1tbs sugar*

Beat and knead the paste into the milk to form a smooth, thick liquid. Bring the cream to the boil, stir in the almond mixture, mace and salt, cook for 5 minutes while stirring, pour into a dish lined with sippets, sprinkle with the sugar, and serve.

PASTA

Pasta, which had been made in English kitchens from the fourteenth century, came back into fashion especially after the publication of *Epulario, or the Italian Banquet* in London in 1598. Translated from Venetian editions of 1549 or 1562, it described 'A devised meat after the Roman manner' made of flour and water, rolled around a staff, cut in pieces and either boiled in water or broth, or dried in the sun for long-term storage.[44] It was one of the dishes adopted by stylish young men, who, as Ben Jonson described in *Cynthia's Revels* of 1600, learned to eat 'anchovies, macaroni, buoli, fagioli and caviare.'[45] Sir Hugh Plat also promoted pasta for military use and consumption at sea. His own pasta press was shipped by Drake on one of his voyages.[46] The dried forms were usually imported, but English cooks also prepared their own, especially when making ravioli, square 'pasties' trimmed with a jagging-iron, and tortelleti, smaller, round 'pasties', both boiled in cream, milk or almond milk.

PASTA DOUGH

1lb/450g plain flour	*pinch of saffron, 1tsp salt*
4oz/100g butter	*3 egg yolks, beaten*

Mix the flour, saffron and salt in a bowl, and make a well in the centre. Warm the butter with ¼pt/150ml water, until just melted, pour into the flour, stir together, adding the yolks, to form a dough. Having worked in all the flour, turn out onto a floured board, knead for 5 minutes, then cover, leave for about an hour in a cool place, then use as directed.

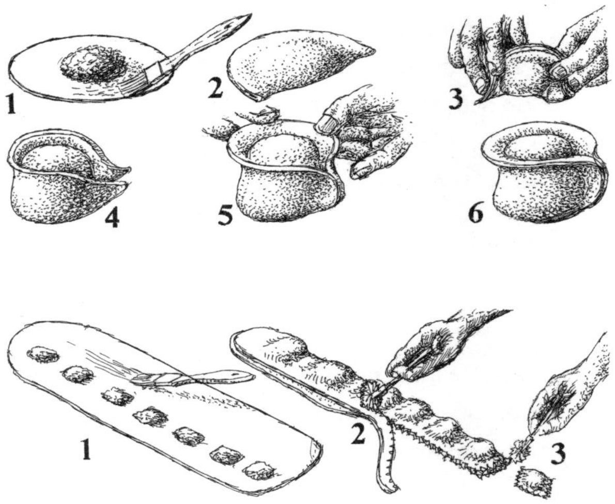

Figure 65. Pasta. Tortelleti (above) had a mound of the filling placed at the centre of a disc of dough, which was then moistened (1) and turned over to form a small pasty (2). The 'pasty' was then pressed down to give it a flattish base (3), the corners folded to one side (4) squeezed together and the top flap pinched out horizontally (5) to produce the finished result (6) ready for boiling. To make ravioli, portions of the filling were spaced out along one side of the strip of dough, and the other side moistened (1). The strip was then folded over, gently pressed around the filling, and the surplus cut off (2) before each one was separated (3).

This dough was then used to make ravioli or tortelleti, as in the following recipes.

TORTELLETI

Prepare the fillings by mixing together any of the following:

Bacon

4oz/100g streaky dry-salted bacon, finely chopped
2oz/50g roasted turnip or parsnip, rubbed through a sieve
½oz/12g currants
2oz/50g finely grated Parmesan cheese
pinch each of ground pepper, clove & nutmeg
2oz/50g sugar
1 egg, beaten

Chicken

8oz/225g cooked chicken or fish, ground to a smooth paste
1oz/25g bone marrow or butter
2oz/50g finely grated Parmesan
½oz/12g currants
pinch each of pepper, saffron, nutmeg & cinnamon
¼tsp each chopped mint & marjoram
1oz/25g sugar
1 egg, beaten

Spinach

8oz/225g spinach, chopped & fried in 1oz/25g butter
1tsp mixed chopped sage, marjoram & thyme
2oz/50g grated Parmesan cheese
¼tsp mixed ground cinnamon & clove
1oz/25g currants
pinch of pepper
pinch of saffron

Peas or beans

8oz/225g cooked peas, French or runner beans, ground & sieved
½ an onion, chopped & fried
3tbs sugar
2oz/50g grated Parmesan cheese
¼tsp mixed ground clove & cinnamon
pinch each ground pepper & nutmeg

Roll out the pasta dough as thinly as possible on a floured board, and cut into 3in/7.5cm discs. Place a teaspoonful of any of the mixtures in the centre, lightly brush the edge of the pasta with water, then fold over to form a small pasty. Stand the 'pasty' on its straight edge, and squeeze the pointed ends together, then fold back the top edge, as in the illustration opposite.

Plunge the tortelleti into boiling stock for 2 minutes, drain, dish, and sprinkle with grated Parmesan, sugar, and a pinch of ground cinnamon.

RAVIOLI

4oz/100g spinach (for beet leaves)
2tsp mixed herbs
4oz/100g butter (for butter & bone marrow)
2oz/50g raisins, finely chopped
2oz/50g dates, peeled & finely chopped
4oz/100g sponge finger biscuits, crushed
4oz/100g grated Parmesan
½tsp salt
1tsp sugar
pinch each ground nutmeg, cinnamon & ginger

Put the spinach and herbs into a pan with 2–3tbs water, cover, bring to the boil, simmer 5 minutes, drain and chop finely. Add the remaining ingredients and knead together to make a smooth paste.

Roll out a batch of the pasta dough, as detailed in the previous recipe, on a floured board to form a strip 3in/7.5cm wide. Arrange little gatherings of the mixture at 1½in/4cm centres along one half of the strip, brush the other half with cold water, fold over and seal down closely around each lump. Separate each square of ravioli using a pastry-wheel/jagging-iron, and, if possible, leave overnight. Plunge into boiling salted water and boil for about 10 minutes before serving.

CHAPTER FIFTEEN

Puddings

Today a pudding is usually any kind of sweet dish, but in Tudor England the same word was used to refer to the guts of man or beast, the stomach, or to any food which used these organs as a container. As Palsgrove explained in 1530, a sausage was a pudding, just like the black puddings and white puddings of modern times.[1] This explains Thomas Nash's amusing statement that 'every thing hath an end, and a pudding hath two!'[2] In towns and cities there were professional pudding-makers, but puddings were also made in most households, large or small. At Hampton Court in the 1530s there was a 'wif that makes the king's podonges', others being presented to him by Lady Weston.[3] The main types of this kind of pudding include those described in the following sections.

BOILING PUDDINGS TODAY

The recipes frequently refer to the use of sausage skins or casings, or of large guts, as appropriate. If these are not available when boiling, roll the mixtures either into lengths of plastic sheet cut from roasting bags, or into pieces of cling-film, tying up the ends. If of large diameter, these may also be further encased in a piece of fine cloth or muslin. For larger puddings, such as the haggis, the same materials may be used to line a square of fine cloth or muslin, or the cloth might be soaked in cold water, wrung out, spread flat, rubbed with butter, dusted with flour, and the surplus shaken off. Using the casing material or cloth to line a bowl, the pudding mixture can then be packed inside, the cloth gathered on top and tied with twine or string, and the complete pudding lifted free of the bowl for plunging directly into boiling water. A large, strong sieve provides a safe means of transferring a hot pudding from the pan and onto the dish, being doused with cold water as it passes between them.

BLACK PUDDINGS

Most everyday black puddings were probably made to basic local recipes from one generation to another purely through practical experience. Pig blood, carefully collected at the time of slaughter and stirred to keep it liquid before being flavoured, was packed into prepared guts and simmered until cooked through. Some had either raw oats, groats, oatmeal or oatmeal cooked in milk stirred in, with pieces of chopped pork fat or beef suet, clove, mace, pepper, salt and fennel seed, and perhaps milk, cream or beaten eggs too.[4]

The blood of other animals was also used to make black puddings, using the same basic methods, but with different seasonings. Ox-blood puddings included pennyroyal, rosemary, thyme, savory and fennel, for example, while those of sheep-blood might contain chopped leeks, and oatmeal soaked in hot mutton broth, along with similar blends of herbs and spices.[5] Swan or goose blood puddings were boiled in the birds' necks.[6]

The finished puddings were either sliced and fried as for a modern 'Full English' breakfast, or, as preferred by discerning Lancastrians today, simmered in hot water. 'Who comes yonder puffing as whot as a black pudding?' asked a character in Fulwell's *Like will to Like* of 1568, while those in Heywood's *Maidenhead* of 1634 sensibly demanded 'sixe Black-Puddings, to be served up in Sorrel-sops', presumably accompanied with a saucerful of mustard in the traditional manner.[7]

The theft of a black pudding was taken very seriously. In his *Catch that Catch can* of 1658 John Hilton recorded the fate that befell a cook who stole a black pudding from one of three cooks in Colebrook, Devon:

> And they fell on our Cook,
> And beat him sore that he did look
> As black as the pudding he took
> From one of the cooks of Colebrook.

LIVER PUDDINGS

The methods of making liver or liveridge puddings or sausages changed remarkably little from the sixteenth to the twentieth centuries, except for the original use of dried fruits and spices as may be seen in this recipe from 1591.

WHITE PUDDING OF HOG'S LIVER[8]

10oz/275g pig's liver
4oz/100g fresh white breadcrumbs
4oz/100g suet
1oz/25g chopped dates
1oz/25g raisins
1½tsp sugar
¼tsp mixed ground clove, mace & saffron
¼pt/150ml cream
3 yolks & 1 white of egg

Parboil the liver for 5–10 minutes, cool, chop and grind it to a smooth paste, mix with the dry ingredients, then with the cream and eggs beaten together. Pack into sausage skins and simmer for some 20 minutes. It may be served hot or cold, or cut into thick slices and fried until lightly browned.

SAUSAGES

Most sausages were made for frying (see page 356), but others were intended for boiling.

BEEF SAUSAGES[9]

1lb/450g lean beef	*½tsp ground mace*
6oz/175g suet	*¼tsp ground clove*
1tsp salt	*½tsp ground black pepper*

Finely mince the meat and grind, pound or mix with the remaining ingredients. Pack into a large gut, put into boiling water and simmer for about 2 hours. Serve hot or cold.

BOLOGNA/POLONY SAUSAGES

From at least the late sixteenth century, sausages from Bologna in northern Italy had been imported into England as an expensive luxury, but recipes for home-produced alternatives were appearing here from around 1600.[10] Sir Hugh Plat's version is entitled 'Sawsedges of Polonia', i.e. sausages of Poland, English cooks continuing to use both 'Bolognia' and 'Polony' quite indiscriminately over the next four centuries. The sausages were made of finely chopped pork fillet seasoned with sage and ginger, all packed into sheep-gut, brined, boiled, and hung up in a chimney to dry. Lasting up to six months, they were sliced as required for salads, to garnish boiled meats, or to provoke the appetite for drinking sessions.[11] By the mid-seventeenth century their recipes comprised lean pork, sometimes including lean beef, short strips of fat bacon, with pepper, clove, mace, nutmeg, salt, and either coriander or caraway. Packed into large guts and smoked, they were stored either in a cool larder or in a barrel of sifted wood-ash ready for use. Since they were not cooked before being stored, they are unsuitable for being home-made today.[12]

CERVELAT/SAVELOY SAUSAGES

'Carvels of pork', a dish of fried pigs' brains made in medieval England, took its name from the Latin *cerebellum*, the hinder part of the brain. On the Continent it had been made into sausages, but by 1653, when '*cervelats*' were introduced into England by La Varenne's *The French Cook*, it had been replaced by ground pork or mutton mixed with suet, onions, herbs, clove, salt and pepper, all packed into beef guts, and hung up to dry in a chimney for up to a month before being boiled for immediate use.[13]

CHITTERLINGS

Around the opening of the sixteenth century a distinctive form of gut pudding began to be made in England from 'big hogges gut stuffed with small guts ... cut into small pieces and seasoned with pepper and salt.' They were called either andoille, from the Latin *inductilia*, to insert, or chiveridge (cf. liveridge) puddings, made to recipes such as this one published by John Murrell in 1615.[14]

A CHIVERIDGE PUDDING[15]

> Lay the fattest Guts of your Hogge in fair water and Salt, to scoure them. Take the longest and the fattest gut, begin at the middle of the gut, and stuff it with Nutmeg, Sugar, Ginger, Pepper and sliced Dates, boyle it and serve it to Table.

Alternatively,

> When you use them, you may cut them in slices, and fry them, so serve them up with Mustard, but if you think they will serve you better, you may dip them in the yolks of eggs and so fry them.[16]

ISINGS

The first recipe for English isings was published in 1550, their title probably coming from contemporary Latin dictionaries which described *insicia* as a stuffing or forcemeat.[17] Alternative spellings were 'estings' or 'eisands', but most late Tudor recipes have almost the same blends of oatmeal groats, eggs, cream or milk, suet or fat, all boiled in guts. Later they became plain 'oatmeal puddings'.[18]

EISANDS WITH OATMEAL GROATS[19]

½pt/300ml single cream
8oz/225g pinhead oatmeal
4 egg yolks, beaten
1tsp mixed ground pepper, clove, mace & saffron
1tbs sugar
4oz/100g suet
2oz/50g raisins
4 dates, coarsely chopped

Bring the cream to the boil, remove from the heat, stir in the oatmeal, cover, and leave overnight. Mix the remaining ingredients, pack into large skins, plunge into boiling water and simmer for some 30 minutes, then remove and drain.

RICE PUDDINGS

Probably made here from the late sixteenth century as a more refined version of isings, rice puddings soon developed sweeter, richer and spicier flavours.[20]

RICE PUDDING[21]

3oz/75g short-grain rice
1pt/600ml milk
pinch ground mace
5oz/125g suet
5oz/125g currants
2 yolks & 1 white of egg, beaten
3oz/75g sugar
½tsp salt
¼tsp ground nutmeg
¼tsp ground cinnamon
3tbs rosewater

Plunge the rice into the boiling milk, stir once to loosen the grains at the bottom, then simmer uncovered for about 12 minutes, before draining in a sieve. When cool, mix with the remaining ingredients, pack into sausage skins, three-quarters filling each 12in/30cm link, tie the ends, plunge into boiling water, and simmer for 15 minutes before serving.

FRENCH BARLEY PUDDINGS

Puddings made with French or pearled barley cooked in skins were fashionable around the early mid-seventeenth century, probably representing a cheaper version of contemporary rice puddings.[22]

FRENCH BARLEY PUDDING[23]

3oz/75g pearl barley
2oz/50g ground almonds
¼pt/150ml cream
2 yolks & 1 white of egg
1tbs rosewater
2oz/50g fresh white breadcrumbs
¼tsp each ground nutmeg & mace
½tsp salt
2oz/50g suet

Boil the barley in 1pt/600ml water for about 20 minutes, meanwhile grinding the almonds into the cream, before beating in the eggs and rosewater. Mix in the drained barley, bread and remaining ingredients, pack into sausage skins, and simmer for 15 minutes before serving.

ALMOND PUDDINGS

Perhaps the most luxurious puddings were made with high percentages of almonds and sugar. This example comes from Elizabeth Cromwell, wife of the Lord Protector, being that 'which she usually had to her breakfast'.

ALMOND PUDDING[24]

4oz/100g ground almonds
1tbs rosewater
4oz/100g fresh white breadcrumbs
4oz/100g sugar
4oz/100g suet (for marrow)
¼tsp grated nutmeg
pinch of salt
(the original recipe included ambergris)

Grind the almonds with the rosewater 'in a stone or wooden mortar' (not in brass), mix with the remaining ingredients, pack into sausage skins and simmer for 15 minutes.

THE HAGGIS

The haggis, that truly English dish first mentioned in the treatise of Walter of Bibbesworth in the early 1230s, remained as popular as ever. It was not of the uniform kind made today, however, but embraced a much greater variety of ingredients and flavourings, all boiled in a stomach, or perhaps in a napkin.[25] Many were based on tender tripe obtained from calves' stomachs, otherwise known as haggis, which had been carefully cleaned, boiled and finely chopped. To these were added a fat in the form of suet, bone-marrow or butter, eggs, cream, salt, spices and either breadcrumbs or oatmeal as a binder. Some also added herbs, onions and dried fruits to provide more interesting flavours. The following examples represent the two main types, those made with bread and those made with oatmeal, the original sheep stomach or paunch here being replaced by a cling-film-lined cloth, which gives identical results in a domestic kitchen.

LORD RUTHVEN'S HAGGIS[26]

4oz/100g tripe, very finely minced
2oz/50g suet
6oz/175g fresh white breadcrumbs
2 yolks & 1 white of egg
1½oz/35g currants
2oz/50g sugar
½tsp grated nutmeg
½tsp each chopped marjoram, thyme & parsley
½pt/300ml double cream

Mix all the ingredients together. Place a square of fine cloth or muslin across a bowl, spread a piece of cling-film over it, then fill with the mixture. Gather the middle of each side of the cloth and film together over the top, then the corners, in order to form the mixture into a compact ball, and tie with string. Bring a large pan of water to the boil, put in the haggis, knot downwards, return to the boil and simmer for about 1½ hours until cooked through. Turn out onto a dish and serve. It makes a delicate light pudding.

A ROBERT MAY HAGGIS[27]

7oz/200g pinhead oatmeal
1 large onion, finely chopped
6oz/175g suet
2tsp parsley
1tsp thyme
1½tsp salt
¼tsp each ground clove & mace
2oz/50g butter
2 raw egg yolks
½tsp hyssop

Put all except the butter and yolks into a bowl and thoroughly mix together, then stirring in just sufficient cold water to make a moist dough. Follow the recipe above, boiling for 2½ hours. Turn out onto a dish, cut a well into the top, and pour in the butter and yolks beaten together over a gentle heat, taking care that it does not curdle due to over-heating.

These represent the two most common varieties of haggis, but some included shredded lemon peel and gammon and were baked in dishes, while others were made with parboiled mutton hearts, lights, kidneys and liver, or with blood, liver and oatmeal.[28]

HASLET

Taking its name from the Old French *hastelet* and Latin *hasta*, a spear or spit, the haslet was usually a composition based on minced pig's fry, which was also called a haslet when still in its raw state. It was minced, packed into a large gut or caul and originally spit-roasted before the fire. Superior versions made from pork or mutton were known in the Elizabethan period as searced puddings, haggis of Almain or mortatellys. Each was wrapped in a caul, and either boiled or oven-baked for serving hot or cold. The following example comes from the 1576 recipe book of Mrs Elizabeth Beale.

MORTATELLYS/HASLET[29]

1lb/450g lean pork, cubed
1lb/450g pig's liver, sliced
4oz/100g fresh breadcrumbs
4oz/100g grated cheese
1tsp ground black pepper
½tsp ground cinnamon
½tsp ground mace
¼tsp ground cloves
2 eggs, beaten
(1½tsp salt)

Cover the pork with water, bring to the boil and simmer for 2 hours until tender, similarly simmering the liver for 10 minutes in the same liquid. Drain the pork and liver, retaining the stock, leave to cool, grind smooth and mix and knead with the remaining ingredients and up to ½pt/300ml of the stock to produce a soft mixture. Pack into a roasting bag, excluding all the air, and bake at 180°C, 350° gas mark 4 for some 40 minutes until cooked through, then cool and serve in thin slices. Alternatively, it may be boiled in a cloth for about the same time.

BAGPUDDINGS

The preparation of animal stomachs and guts by repeatedly washing and soaking them to perfect cleanliness, ready to encase the pudding mixtures described above, was a time-consuming and laborious process. From the early fifteenth century, a number of recipes had instructed cooks to cook haggis or haslet-like mixtures either 'in a bleddur or in a bagge', or to 'fill the bage ther with and sow it'.[30] These and other similar sources show that the traditional stomachs were already being replaced with cloth pudding-bags. They were much easier to prepare, would never split, and could be used time after time perhaps for years on end. If their filling was particularly sloppy, they could be internally prepared by being rinsed, wrung out, sometimes buttered, floured, and the surplus shaken off. This provided an effective seal during the boiling process, and enabled the puddings to be cleanly turned out onto their dishes without sticking to the cloth. The use of pudding bags increased dramatically during the sixteenth century, laying the foundation for the great English tradition of boiled puddings which flourished here up to the middle of the twentieth century. Some were actually called bagpuddings, their swollen bodies, density and heaviness soon causing this word to become a byname for any paunchy dim-witted yokel.[31]

The following examples demonstrate the three major types of bagpudding; a delicate bread-based quaking or shaking pudding, one based on the whole grains of oats or barley, which could also be made with rice, and a substantial fruited and spiced bread and suet pudding .

A QUAKING PUDDING[32]

4oz/100g crustless white bread	*2oz/50g sugar*
1pt/600ml cream	*3tbs rosewater*
6 yolks & 3 whites of egg, beaten	*1tsp nutmeg*

Thinly slice the bread, put into the boiling cream, remove from the heat, cover, and leave for 3–4 hours. Beat it smooth with a fork or whisk, mix in the remaining ingredients. Wet and rinse a square of fine cloth, spread it flat, rub it with a little butter, sprinkle with flour, shake off the surplus, and arrange across a bowl. Pour in the mixture, gather the cloth together over the top, tie it with twine or string, lift from the bowl, plunge into boiling water and simmer for 1 hour. Turn out onto a dish and serve with a simple sauce made of 2oz/50g butter, 4tbs rosewater, and 1oz/25g sugar melted together.

The addition of ¼pt/150ml extra cream to this recipe produces a particularly delicate pudding.

OATMEAL PUDDING[33]

5oz/125g whole (or pinhead) oats (or pearl barley)

1pt/600ml milk	*½tsp ground mace*
1pt/600ml cream	*¼tsp ground cloves*
2 yolks & 1 white of egg	*pinch of saffron*
2oz/50g dates, sliced	*½tsp salt*
2oz/50g sugar	*(2oz/50g raisins, and/or 2tbs finely chopped sweet herbs, optional)*
(1tbs flour)	

Bring the oats and milk to the boil, remove from the heat, wrap in a few layers of towel and leave to soak overnight. Drain off the milk and mix the oats into the remaining ingredients. Prepare a pudding cloth and boil as for the quaking pudding above, but for 1½–2 hours, and allow to cool a little before turning out.

CAMBRIDGE PUDDING[34]

12oz/325g fresh white breadcrumbs
3oz/75g flour
4oz/100g sugar
5oz/150g currants
5oz/150g dates, chopped
1tsp ground cinnamon
1tsp ground nutmeg
3 yolks & 2 whites of egg
5oz/150g suet, melted
4oz/100g butter

Mix the dry ingredients, make a well in the centre, drop in the eggs, start to work into the mixture, then work in the suet, working or kneading together to form a uniform dough. Line a basin with a square of fine cloth or muslin, which has been rinsed, dusted with flour and the surplus shaken off. Pack half the mixture into the bottom of the cloth, place the lump of butter in the centre, cover with the remaining mixture, press together, smooth the exterior, gather the cloth around it, and tie with twine or string. Plunge into boiling water and simmer for 3½ hours. To serve, slice across and serve both halves side by side, the cut sides and their butter-filled hollows uppermost.

NORFOLK DUMPLINGS[35]

In John Day's *The Blind Beggar of Bednall-green* of 1600, one of the characters explained how, when 'mine Hostis came up to me I was as naked as your Norfolk Dumplin'. This is probably the earliest reference to this great regional speciality, and also one of the most informative. The dumpling was naked for, unlike the bagpudding, it never needed an enclosing cloth or bag. The reason for this was that it was no more than balls of risen bread-dough plunged into boiling water and boiled for some 20 minutes until cooked through.

A number of other sweet puddings were baked in dishes, as described on pages 180–181, above, in the chapter on the pastry. The final group of puddings are quite different from those we recognize as puddings today, for they were either sweet or savoury mixtures packed within small game, poultry and vegetables as a form of stuffing. Just four examples are given here to demonstrate the main types of pudding intended to be used in this way. The first was recommended for cucumbers, cauliflowers, cabbages, pumpkins, gourds, large onions, parsnips, turnips or carrots, as well as melons.

FORCING FOR A MELON[36]

1 canteloup melon
2oz/50g white breadcrumbs
1oz/25g ground almonds
2tbs rosewater
3tbs sugar
1oz/25g trifle sponge (biscuit bread)
1 egg yolk, beaten
½tsp ground mace
1tsp ground cinnamon
½tsp coriander seed
pinch of saffron
1oz/25g candied lemon peel, finely chopped
1oz/25g butter

Using a 2in/5cm biscuit/pastry cutter, remove one end of the melon, retaining it as a plug, and scoop out the seeds and sufficient pulp to leave a 1in/2.5cm layer next to the skin. Mix all the ingredients together, along with 2–3oz/50–75g of the pulp, to form a smooth mixture. Pack this into the melon, replace the plug, tie tightly in a cloth or muslin, plunge into a pan of boiling water and simmer for about 1½hours until tender, then turn out onto a dish, remove any of the mixture which has boiled out through the plug, and serve hot.

Alternatively, cut the melon across in slices about 1½in/4cm thick, stuff with the mixture, place on a well-buttered baking dish and bake at 190°C/375°F/gas mark 5 for 30 minutes and serve on sippets.

The melon was accompanied with a sauce made of:

¼pt/150ml white wine
1 light stock cube
3tbs ground almonds
2tbs sugar
½tsp ground cinnamon
1tbs caster sugar

Grind the wine, stock cube and almonds in ¼pt/150ml cold water until smooth, then strain hard through a cloth into a clean saucepan. Add the sugar and cinnamon, heat until dissolved, spoon over the baked melon, sprinkle with caster sugar, and return to the oven for 5 minutes before transferring to a dish and serving hot.

PUDDINGS IN CARROT ROOTS[37]

5 large carrots
8oz/225g pig liver
1oz/25g currants
6 dates, chopped
1tbs sugar
¼tsp ground black pepper
¼tsp ground mace
pinch ground cloves
1oz/25g butter
2oz/50g white breadcrumbs
1 light stock cube
1oz/25g currants
½tsp blade mace
1tsp salt
2tbs wine vinegar (for verjuice)
2tbs sugar

Using a narrow, pointed knife, preferably one with a straight cutting edge, cut the stem out of four of the carrots, then, gripping each carrot in turn (with a thick cloth for safety), rotate the knife whilst pushing it down the centres of the four carrots, to leave them hollow. Put the liver into simmering water for 1 minute, drain, chop or mince finely, mix with the remaining ingredients in the left-hand column above, knead together and pack into the carrots. Finally, carefully scrape the skin from the carrots.

Put the ingredients in the right-hand column into a pan with the remaining carrot sliced into rounds, and 1pt/600ml of water. Bring to the boil, put in the stuffed carrots, add more water to cover if necessary, and simmer for about 20 minutes until tender, then serve in a dish along with the broth.

PUDDINGS IN TURNIP ROOTS[38]

for the roots and the stuffing:
6 small white turnips
8oz/225g apples, peeled & minced
2oz/50g white breadcrumbs
2 hard-boiled egg yolks
3oz/75g currants
1tsp ground cinnamon
1tsp ground ginger

for the broth:
½pt/300ml claret
1tbs wine vinegar
1oz/25g currants
6 dates, chopped
2tsp sugar
½tsp blade mace
¼tsp dried rosemary, chopped
1oz/25g butter

Hollow the turnips, then follow the instructions in the recipe above.

TO BOIL A CONEY WITH A PUDDING IN HIS BELLY[39]

for the rabbit and stuffing:
1 oven-ready rabbit
2oz/50g suet
4oz/100g white breadcrumbs
2oz/50g dates, finely chopped
½tsp ground mace
¼tsp ground cloves
1½tbs sugar
½tsp salt
4fl.oz/120ml cream
1 raw egg yolk
1tbs mixed parsley, marjoram, savory, pennyroyal or mint, & spinach, finely chopped

for the broth:
2 light stock cubes
2oz/50g currants
4oz/100g gooseberries or grapes
1oz/25g white breadcrumbs
2tbs white wine vinegar
½tsp salt
1tbs sugar

Wash and dry the rabbit, mix together the ingredients in the left-hand column above, using this mixture to stuff the rabbit before sewing the belly together with strong thread.

Put the ingredients in the right-hand column into a pan with sufficient water to cover the rabbit. Bring to the boil, stir, put in the rabbit, cover, and simmer for about 1 hour until tender. Serve hot with its broth on a bed of sops.

As well as being boiled or baked, some puddings were roasted before the fire. Henry VIII's 'Instruments of silver and gilt supposed to be to roste puddinges' were quite exceptional, most cooks using ordinary small or bird spits.[40] Recipes such as 'to roast a pound of butter curiously and well' are found to be just as improbable as they sound, but others are more practical.[41]

TO ROAST A PUDDING ON A SPIT[42]

8oz/225g fine white breadcrumbs	*1 egg yolk*
2oz/50g currants	*½pt/300ml cream*
2oz/50g sugar	*spinach juice or saffron for colouring*
¼tsp salt	
1tsp mixed ground cinnamon, nutmeg & mace	

Mix the dry ingredients with the yolk and 1 tablespoonful of the cream. Knead together for 5 minutes, adding a little more cream if necessary, to produce a firm, cohesive dough. Clap three-quarters of this round a small spit (or a ¼in/6mm dowel) and roast, or bake at 180°C/350°F/gas mark 4 for about 40 minutes until it has set. Meanwhile knead the remaining mixture and just sufficient cream together to form a batter and use this to baste the set pudding, allowing each layer to set and brown before pouring on the next. The pudding resembles a modern hog's pudding, and is best served by being cut into slices and fried on both sides.

The puddings described in this chapter only represent a small sample of those being made in English homes in Tudor times. The boiled pudding currently appears to have been developed in this country to a far greater extent than in any other. By the time the Hanoverians were on the throne, it even became an accepted symbol of the nation, appearing alongside huge joints of roast beef in patriotic political cartoons during the Napoleonic wars.

CHAPTER SIXTEEN

Roasting

Roasting has always been one of the most prestigious methods of cookery. Not only did it demand a high level of expenditure in terms of equipment, fuel and labour, but it was only suitable for the most tender cuts of meat. Its chief characteristic was the sole use of the direct radiant heat of an open fire. Here the rush of fresh air feeding the fuel carried off all the coarser and heavier elements as they evaporated from the meat to reveal remarkably light and delicate flavours. This is in contrast to the usual modern practice of 'roasting' by baking the joints in an enclosed oven, which ensures that they absorb much of the flavour of their scorching fat. Producing the necessary degree of radiance was always problematic with wood fires, unless there was a truly prodigal wastage of logs, as in royal and noble households. Medieval depictions of roasting usually show just a single spit mounted only a few inches above the hearth, close to the glowing embers. This was still the general practice in early Tudor England, but environmental factors were soon to make it obsolete in all but the poorest houses.

Unlike most parts of continental Europe, this country had experienced a great shortage of firewood from the third quarter of the sixteenth century, thus making the use of coal essential. This new cooking fuel required a different kind of hearth, for whereas logs burned readily on a flat hearthstone, their ends perhaps elevated on andirons, coal required much more draught, and so had to be burnt in a vertical-sided iron firebasket, otherwise called a grate or a 'chimney'. English cooks therefore found that they had ready access to an efficient source of fierce, horizontal radiant heat, much more suitable for roasting than the earlier wood fires still used by their Continental counterparts. This facility was rapidly used to develop a whole series of new and interesting techniques, transforming the plain roasts of earlier generations into many uniquely English speciality dishes. The recipe books of the late Elizabethan period clearly demonstrate this change, but it is made even more apparent when reading the great French or French-inspired recipe books of the mid-seventeenth century.

François de la Varenne's *French Cook*, 'Englished by I.D.G.' in 1653, restricts roasting largely to poultry, game birds and sucking pigs, for example, most of

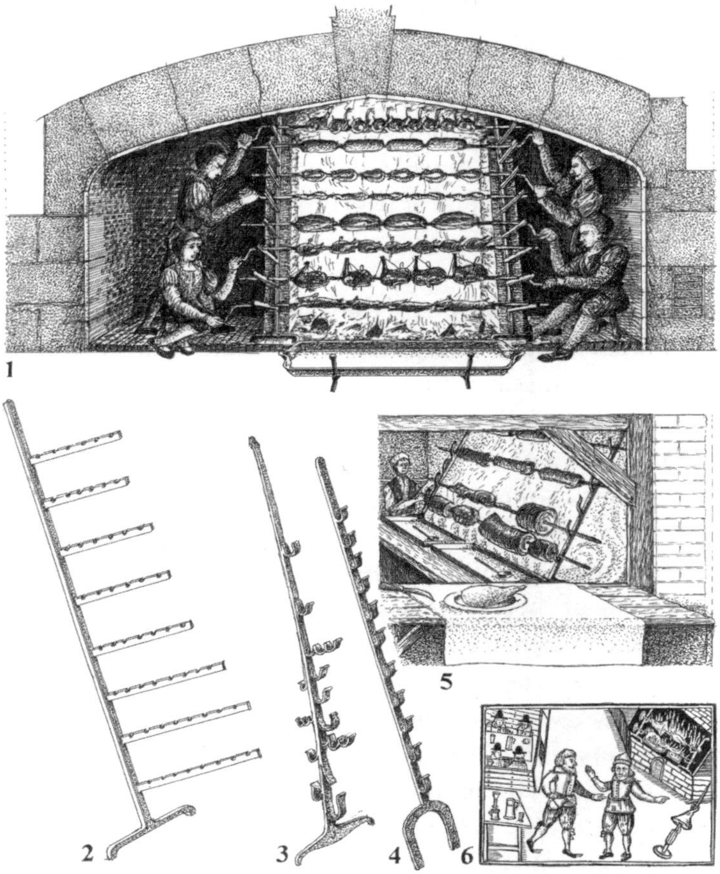

Figure 66. Roasting. Roasting at Hampton Court Palace (1); cob-irons at Hampton Court, early–mid-16th cent. (2); Plas Mawr, Conwy (3); and Cotehele, Cornwall (4); in use in Hoefnagel's Marriage Feast at Bermondsey *(c. 1570) (5); and the 1641 broadside of* Nick Froth the Tapster and Ruleroast the Cooke *(6).*

the recipes for red meats using roasting as a preparation for braising.[1] Basting is barely mentioned and only a couple use dredgings.[2] In contrast, Robert May's *Accomplisht Cook* of 1660 and William Rabisha's *Whole Body of Cookery Dissected* of 1661 both show a full mastery of every aspect of roasting.[3] Regrettably, their skills have now been largely forgotten. Well-baked 'roast' meats are still popular in many homes, public houses and similar establishments, but the restaurant industry has promoted an élitist fashion for serving many of their roast meats virtually raw. This practice certainly reduces fuel, time and labour to the ideal minimum, but has nothing to do with the excellent dishes produced by true roasting. Anyone who tries the period recipes given in this chapter will soon begin to appreciate the amazing range and quality of Elizabethan and Jacobean roasts.

In practical terms, roasting demanded that each joint should be in a state of constant rotation before the fire. This ensured that the fierce frontal heat was absorbed into its mass during the remainder of its turn away from the fire. If it stopped rotating for even a minute or two, this absorption ceased and the surface rapidly overcooked and charred. Not only did this spoil the appearance, texture and flavour of the joint, but it also converted the outer layer from being a conductor to an insulator of heat. This same characteristic demanded that meats were usually roasted a foot or more away from the fire in order to gently absorb the heat and cook through to tenderness, only being brought closer if a final golden brown finish was required. Any attempt to reverse this order could easily produce a over-roasted exterior, and an interior which remained stubbornly raw even if spit-roasting continued for several hours.

The simplest way to keep a joint rotating before the fire was to hang it up by a twisted skein of worsted yarn which constantly unwound and rewound itself if its momentum was regularly renewed by hand. All other methods required the use of a spit, a long iron rod, square or round in section, pointed like a spear at one end, and with a cranked handle at the other. Their size and number varied considerably according to the needs of individual establishments. In 1637–8 for example, William Carding of Roxwell, Essex, had just one spit and a dripping pan in his small cottage, while John George of Writtle had five spits and a dripping pan in his larger yeoman's house.[4] Lords such as Thomas Wharton of Healaugh, Yorkshire, might have twelve spits turning on two pairs of racks over two dripping pans, appropriate for his busy noble household.[5]

Such equipment was extremely expensive, Robert Dudley paying Leonard the Frenchman £4 10*s*. for a pair of racks and five spits weighing a total of 478lb/215kg in 1559. This is about the size illustrated by the pair of spit-racks which still remain in place in the Lords'-side kitchen at Hampton Court Palace. Here the central 6 feet (1.8m) of the roasting hearth is flanked by a pair of 9-inch (23cm) brick walls, their front faces sloping back at 20 degrees from the vertical. These enabled a great bonfire to rage between them, and also supported racks which were propped back against their fronts. Each rack had eight projecting arms forged with a total of 54 notches along their top edges, so that they were capable of supporting the spits in any of the 54 positions before the flames.[6] Exactly the same arrangement is shown in use in the Henrician painting of the kitchen erected at the Field of Cloth of Gold in 1520. Two men shelter behind the side walls, one standing, with the other sitting in front of him on a stool. By turning two spits each, and working from both sides, eight spits could operate simultaneously to provide some 50 feet (15.5m) of operational spit length to meet the needs of the courtiers' meals.[7]

For ordinary houses, where only one person turned the spit, hooks were forged on to the fronts or backs of the vertical posts of andirons, thus converting them into cob-irons or cobbards, the 'cobs' being the round knobs on their tops. These are frequently mentioned in inventories of this period, as well as being shown in woodcuts – Gervase Markham also stressing that the first stage of roasting was 'the cleanly keeping and scowring of the spits and cobirons'.[8] In the street-front kitchens of professional city cooks such cob-irons were used on table-height hearths, so that the roasts could be more easily managed without having to constantly stoop down to baste the joints and refuel the fire.

As in medieval times, men or boy servants called turnspits or turn-broaches still continued their boring, sweaty and thirst-creating labours. The simile 'as hot as a turnspit' was particularly appropriate.[9] Sometimes this task was offered to a passing beggar in return for the gift of a meal, 'Diccon the Bedlam', a rogue described in *Gammer Gurton's Needle* of 1575, described how he got into good men's houses in this way, where:[10]

> Many a gossip's cup in my time have I tasted
> And many a broche and spit I have both turned and basted.
> Many a piece of bacon have I cut out of the balks
> In runnyng over the countrey, with long and were walks.

Both men and boys were employed as spit-turners, Lord Middleton paying one Twyttchell and a boy 2*s*. each for turning the extra spits required over Christmas in 1573.[11] Similarly the great clothier, Jack of Newbury, maintained a number of poor children to turn his spits.[12] Such a charitable act was seen as a real responsibility of all those who kept a truly hospitable household. To install a mechanical replacement was therefore seen as a selfish dereliction of public duty. The true noble-hearted fellow who keeps house was recognized 'by want of whirligig-jacks in the kitchen'.[13] As a servant in Richard Brome's play *The Joviall Crew* of 1652 remembered, 'I myself was but a silly Lad when I come first a poor turn-spit Boy. Gentlemen kept no whirling Jacks then, to cozen poor People of Meat.[14]

In most kitchens the turn-spit boys had to try and keep cool by sitting by the walls which framed the fireplace opening. In larger houses they were provided with seats set into the walls at each end of the fireplace, being sheltered there by the wall which contained the fire and supported the cob-irons. A good example survives in the kitchen of Berry Pomeroy Castle, Devon, in the form of a two-foot wide seat set into a round-backed and round-headed niche.

The first effective substitute for the human turn-spit was a dog-wheel, an open-sided wooden drum about three feet in diameter by nine to almost twelve inches wide (*c.* 1m x 22–29cm). This was mounted on a horizontal axle to one side of the fireplace, usually about head-height to judge from later examples, so that it started to rotate once a small dog began to run inside it. This motion was then transferred by a continuous loop of cord or chain from a pulley fixed to the hub of the wheel to another pulley on the end of the spit. In order to ensure that there was no slippage, it was essential that the full weight of the pulley-end of the spit was carried by the jack-cord, otherwise the joint of meat would remain stationary and burn. Such dog-wheels were certainly in use in London before 1536, when Dr Caius' book on dogs stated that:

> There is comprehended under the curs of the coarsest kind a certaine dogge in kitchen service excellent. For when any meate is to bee roasted, they go into a wheele, which they turning rounde about with the weight of their bodies so diligently look to their business that no drudge or scullion can do the feat more cunningly, whom the popular sort hereupon call Turnspets.[15]

They continued to be used throughout this period, Samuel Harsnet describing how 'a Wheel is turned by a turnspit curre, that is put into it' in 1603, and Nathaniel Carpenter the 'Turn-spit-dogs labouring in their wheeles' in 1625.[16] Similarly, Peter Mindy, a Cornishman visiting Bristol in 1639, found that there was 'scarce a house that hath not a dogge to turn the spitte in a little wooden wheele.'[17]

To the economical householder, investment in a mechanical jack offered great benefits, ridding his kitchen of an apparently insatiable glutton, drunkard or causer of strife. Men of a scientific turn of mind explored a number of different sources of motive power. In his *Mathematicall Magick* of 1648, Bishop John Wilkins suggested setting a boiler in the fire, a small hole in its top forcing a jet of steam upwards to rotate 'sails in a chimney corner, the motion of which sails may be applied to the turning of a spit.'[18] This prototype of the steam turbine probably remained a theoretical proposal, rather than a practical solution to spit-turning. However the practice of using the strong updraught caused by the smoke and hot air from the fire rushing up the tall kitchen chimneys provided real potential. Woodcuts show that they were popular on the raised hearths of Continental kitchens. A vane or windmill blades were set on a vertical shaft above the hearth, gearing at the bottom of the shaft then turning the horizontal spits before the low fire of logs. These were already in use in south-eastern England by around 1500, a vertical smoke-jack shaft being excavated from the cellars of a house in Norwich which had been burnt down in 1507.[19]

In spite of these developments, the most efficient and relatively trouble-free form of jack was that powered by a weight-driven clockwork mechanism governed by a simple flywheel escapement. These were probably introduced in the mid-sixteenth century, many appearing in the probate inventories of those who died in the 1580s, such as:

> 'one Jacke to torne the spit 2*s* 6*d*' (Exeter);[20]
> 'The Jacke wiche turneth the broche' (Lancashire).

They were also described as fashionable kitchen accessories in the early seventeenth century:

> 1606 , 'an English Jack or Turne-spit, upon skrewes and vices' (Dekker);[21]
> 1606, 'Even as in a turne-spit called a Jacke ... the great Wheeles turning but softly, make the lesse to whirre' (Chapman);[22]
> 1615, 'The winding up of a Jacke is better than musicke to his eares in Lent' (Stephens);
> 1633, 'The Jacke plaies Musicke and the Spits Turne round too't – my stomach hath struck twelve' (Heywood).[23]

The acquisition of a jack was usually recorded in the household accounts. Entries such as 'one Jacke to torne the spitt 2*s*. 6*d*.' of the 1580s or the payment of £1 to William Hoppin for a new winding jack, the old one being taken in part-exchange in Exeter in 1640, are both typical.[24] In some instances the actual installation of a jack is detailed, as in Joyce Jeffreys' kitchen in Hereford in December 1638:

14th Dec. 1638	Robert Whittier buys the new brass jack in Oxford for 30*s*. and brings it to the house for 2*s*., where George Gillding, joiner nails it in place for 1*s*. 10*d*.
24th Dec. 1638	John Probin provides 38lb of lead for the weights for 6*s*. 8*d*., Harry the smith makes ironwork for hanging the weights for 2*d*. and also a cross-plate for the jack for 6*d*.
13th Nov. 1641	14 yards of small cord for the jack 1*s*.
10th Aug. 1642	mending and scouring the jack 1*s*.[25]

The mechanism of such a jack was relatively simple, as illustrated by a woodcut in Bishop Wilkins' book, and by early datable examples. The woodcut shows a primitive form of jack with three shafts mounted between two vertical bars. The lower shaft is fitted with a (wooden?) drum wound with a cord which descends to a heavy weight, and also has a large gear wheel. Meanwhile the upper two shafts have gear-trains which ensure that the lower shaft rotates far slower than the upper one. The escapement takes the form of a horizontal vane with a small disc at each end, its vertical shaft having a pinion engaging a gear on the top shaft. It therefore relied on the air-resistance on the vane and the friction of the speed-reducing gearing to ensure that the bottom shaft turned slowly and steadily. To illustrate its efficiency, Wilkins shows it acting in reverse, a human hair rotating the vane enabling it to lift the weight of a man.

Such jacks were soon replaced by others having simpler gearing, the shaft supporting the vane being forged as a worm-gear engaging with a gear-wheel on a single horizontal shaft over the winding drum. Fortunately the front bar and main gear-wheel of an example dated 1656 still survive.[26] This has enabled its mechanism to be readily reconstructed, complete with the jack-line or cord wound round its drum, and the loop of jack-chain descending from its back pulley to rotate the spit hanging below.

As proved by the nail-holes or lead-filled holes for bolts found in many historic kitchens, the jacks were mounted above and to one side of the fireplace opening. Here, although conveniently away from the working area of the fire, they were not high enough to allow the jack to run for a prolonged period before stopping as its weight touched the ground. The solution to this problem was to introduce a block and tackle onto the jack-line, so that by using a heavier weight and passing the line through two pulley-blocks, the jack could turn for much longer. This explains why Joyce Jeffreys' line was 42 feet long, about six times the distance between the jack and the floor. In contrast, the jack-chains which supported and rotated the spits were much shorter, one purchased in Exeter in 1640 being 13 feet 6 inches long, providing a loop which suspended the spit about 6 feet below the jack.[27]

As the spit-loads of meat rotated before the fire, their fats and juices, together with any additional bastings, fell down towards the hearth. Here they might still be collected by a masonry gutter which channelled them into a stone mortar or a pottery vessel embedded into the hearthstones. Good early sixteenth-century examples are still to be seen at Norham Castle and the Henrician tower to the west of Berwick town walls in Northumberland. However, most prosperous households used metal dripping pans instead.

The four large wrought iron dripping pans listed in the 1659 inventory of Hampton Court, but almost certainly dating from the 1530s, are probably identical to those shown in use in *The Field of the Cloth of Gold* painting. Some 5 feet long, their sides were forged into walls about 3 inches high, one end terminating in an ogee-shaped spout from which the dripping could be poured into a pot or tub. For noble households there might be five dripping pans of this

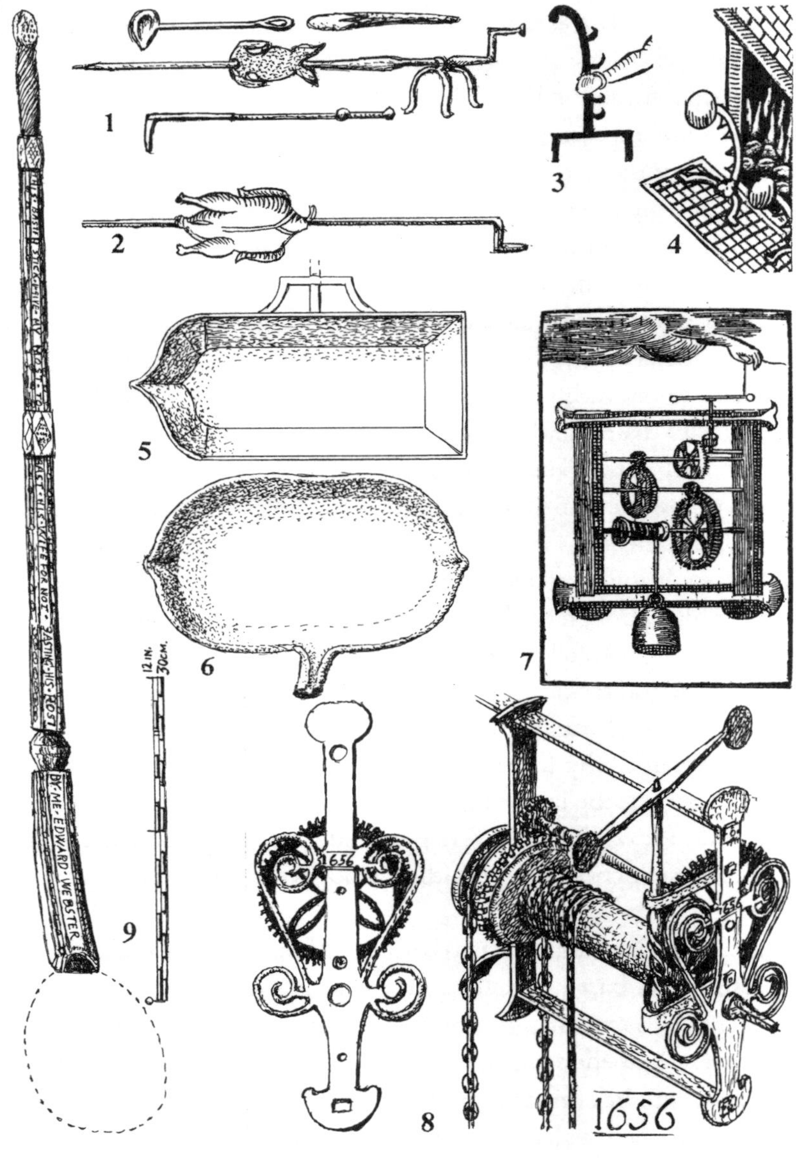

Figure 67. Roasting utensils. (1) a spit, basting ladle and brush, c. *1520–30, from a manuscript in the Bodleian Library, Oxford; (2 & 5) a spit and a dripping pan from* The English Irish Soldier *broadside of 1641; (3 & 4) cob-irons from the* Reply as True as Steele *and* Mistress Able, The Ship, Fish Street *broadsides both of 1641; (6) a glazed earthenware dripping pan from 16th-cent. Southampton; (7 & 8) a spit-jack illustrated in John Wilkins'* Mathematical Music *of 1648, and an example of 1656; (9) the carved yew handle for an iron-bowled basting ladle of 1646.*

type, as at Hardwick Old Hall, or two, as at Healaugh, near York, while most gentry found just one or two to be quite adequate.[28] By the early seventeenth century, lighter, brighter dripping pans were also being made of tinplate, probably with the traditional wire-edged rims to give them the required degree of rigidity.[29]

For those who could not afford dripping pans of this quality, potters, working particularly in the eastern counties from Yorkshire to Essex, still supplied earthenware alternatives. During the sixteenth and probably early seventeenth centuries, most were oval in plan, with a pouring lip at each end and a handle projecting from the middle of one side. Their internal lead glazes enabled them to retain the molten fats, and ensured that they could be easily cleaned after use.[30]

To keep the meat moist and to contribute to its flavour, it was repeatedly basted by having either its own fats and juices, or else additional ingredients, poured over it using a basting ladle which might be of brass, iron or wood.[31] A very fine example in the Pinto Collection had its heat- and fat-proof iron bowl secured into a long, curving yew handle, all magnificently chip-carved as a love-token and inscribed:

> THIS. BASTIN. STICK. I. GIVE. MY. HOST
> TO. BAST. HIS. WIFE. FOR. NOT. BASTIN. HIS. ROST
> BY. ME. EDWARD. WEBSTER. 1646.[32]

As the roast was about to be completed, it was often given a final period of basting, each coat being supplemented by a dusting of flour or breadcrumbs or other medium in order to build up a crisp outer shell called a froth. This required the use of a dredging-box, probably a cylindrical brass or sheet-iron container with a handle to one side and a slightly domed lid pierced all over in order to scatter its contents evenly.

When roasting animals such as suckling pigs before an open fire, the thin meat over the ribs would have become charred to blackness long before the thick shoulders and legs had even half cooked through. To prevent such wasteful disasters, it was customary to shield the tenderest parts of a joint from the fierce radiant heat by the use of strategically placed sheets of iron. None of these is known to survive, but they do appear in contemporary documents, being described as:

> 1 bar of iron to set before the meat 2*s*.
> 2 plates of iron to hang before the meat 6*d*. (Speke Hall, 1624)[33]

These should not be confused with the long, flat bars which could be hooked onto the front edge of large metal dripping pans to help prevent embers from falling in and stop their fats from dangerously overheating:

> an Ire to lie before the dripinge panns 10*d*. (Exeter 1575);[34]
> for an iron to stande before the dripping pans 4*s*. 3*d*. (London 1585).[35]

Having described the roasting equipment, practical uses can now be considered. The traditional methods used to prepare meat and game for roasting were robustly described by Thomas Heywood in 1633:[36]

> Certain creatures being brought in (to the kitchen) by some of the House; The Cooke being a Colleriche fellow, did Towse them and Tosse them, so Plucke them and Pull them, till he left them as naked as my Nailes, Pinioned some of them like Fellons; Cut the Spurres from others of their Heeles; Then downe went his spits, some of them he ranne in at the Throat, and out at the Back-side; About went his Basting-Ladle, where he did besawce them, that many a shrode turne they had amongst them.

This sounds efficiently rough and ready, but in practice the production of well-roasted meats involved much time, trouble and skill. For some meats it was customary to give them a preliminary salting or marinade. Beef might be rubbed with salt and left overnight before roasting, for example, so 'that the groose blode by salte may be exhausted … (to) make an Englysshe man stronge.'[37] In contrast joints of fresh pork could be tenderized and flavoured by half-submerging them in a mixture of wine vinegar, salt, bruised juniper-berries and garlic, and turning twice a day for eight to ten days.[38] Moisture could also be increased by parboiling or simmering, a particularly useful technique when dealing with meats such as venison or hare which could easily dry out or harden before the fire.[39] Larding was also practised, with narrow strips of fat pork, bacon or mutton inserted into the flesh by the use of a pointed wooden skewer called a larding pin, stick or prick.[40] The protruding ends of the lardons formed neat parallel rows across the surface of the meat, each shrivelling before the fire as their fat dissolved simultaneously to baste it both inside and out. The same method could use lardons of orange or lemon peel, anchovies, sprigs of herbs, oyster forcemeat, or whole cloves to impart their respective flavours.[41]

Further flavouring could be provided by stuffing the meat, especially the body cavities of poultry and game, which were then said to have 'a pudding in the belly.' Such stuffings were usually of fresh white breadcrumbs mixed with salt, spices, dried fruits, perhaps with sugar or suet too, all bound together with eggs and cream.[42] Other roasts, such as calves' heads, might also include their par-boiled and cubed brains and tongues in their stuffings. Rabbits, meanwhile, might have nothing more than a mixture of oysters, shredded onions, pepper, mace and thyme, and hens a piece of streaky bacon sprinkled with pepper and nutmeg, and stuck with cloves.[43] After their insertion, the skin was pulled back into place and secured with either a few stitches of linen thread or twine, or with skewers ready for the fire. Medieval cooks had developed the technique of stuffing beneath the skin, first cutting a small hole in a convenient place, then blowing air into it to raise it from the flesh to form a pocket. This was particularly useful for the drier meats, since the impervious skin held in not only their own fats and flavours, but also those incorporated into their stuffings. It also made them easier to serve, the cooked stuffing falling away from the meat, allowing both to be readily carved from the dish.[44] Taken one stage further, some recipes for legs of mutton remove all their meat, mince it, mix it with suet, herbs or spices, sugar, salt and dried fruits, and pack as much as possible back into the skin, skewering it in place before roasting. The surplus mixture was then baked in small pies to provide a further dish for the table.[45]

One of the most essential aspects of roasting was trussing, tying or skewering each item so that it cooked as evenly as possible, looked neat and tidy, and could be easily carved. Even more importantly, it ensured that they rotated with the spit. At this period large double-pronged 'holdfasts' were still unknown, and inexperienced cooks could come up against real problems as their meat remained stationary and scorching black before the fire, while the rotating spits passed uselessly through them. Solid joints usually required little more than to have their bones broken (excepting legs of mutton) and to be speared onto the spit, carefully avoiding the best parts.[46] Most game and poultry, however, had to be carefully trussed to hold them firmly together and in place. They then had the spit pushed through their hollow bodies, with a skewer under their wings and above their thighs, and another at their feet or rump, depending on their manner of trussing:[47]

Capon, chicken, turkey & pheasant

The pinions folded up, and legs extended backwards, the pheasant with a feather in its breast to avoid it being mistaken for a chicken.

Hen & dove

The pinions folded up, the legs cut off at the knees and tucked into their vents.

Quail & partridge

The pinions cut away and the legs extended, or the legs of the quail broken and 'knit together'.

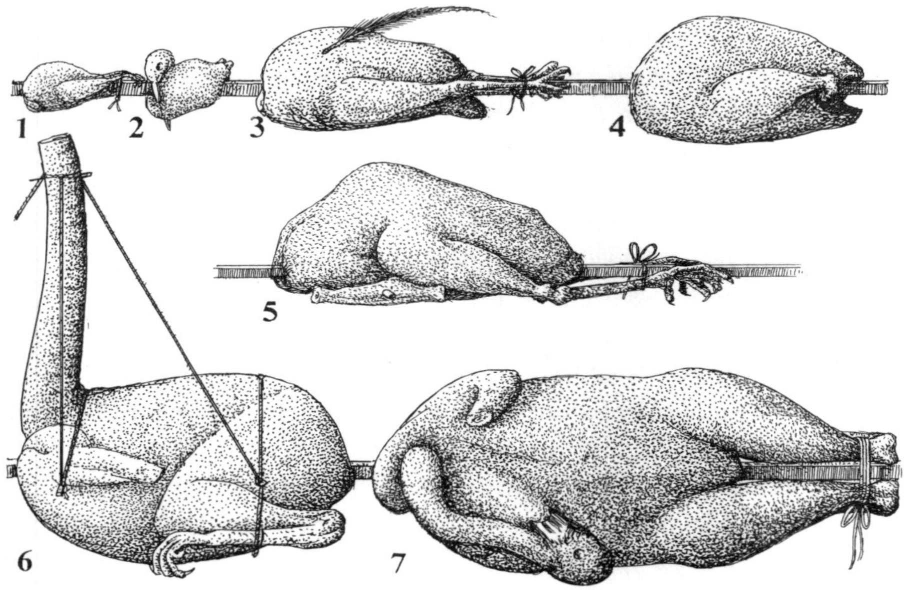

Figure 68. Trussing for poultry and game. (1) quail; (2) snipe; (3) pheasant; (4) hen; (5) turkey; (6) peacock; (7) heron.

Woodcock & snipe

The legs tucked into their vents, the heads left on and passed round the spit so that the bill could be stuck into the breast like a skewer. Alternatively the snipe's legs could be folded onto its breast.

Waterfowl

The pinions cut away, the legs turned backwards.

Plover

The head removed, the legs folded on their backs.

Crane & heron

The wings cut off at the joint closest to the body, the neck wound round about the spit and the bill stuck into the breast, and the legs turned up behind.

If these or any other joints failed to rotate with the spit, the solution was to place a narrow wooden lath down each side, tying the ends firmly to the spit to form an effective clamp.

Once placed before the fire, the meats were rotated until they were hot, at which point they began to be regularly basted with an appropriate liquid to keep them moist and impart extra flavour. The usual bastings were melted butter, a combination of cream and melted butter (especially for pigs), clarified suet or lard, olive oil, salted water, or claret applied with a bundle of sage, rosemary, thyme and parsley. Beaten egg yolks might also be used, sealing in the juices and giving an attractive golden yellow surface.[48]

Throughout the roasting time it was important to ensure that the fire was maintained at a suitable temperature. A good, steady slow fire was best for solid joints of meat and large birds which needed the application of long, gentle heat to cook them through. Smaller items needed a stronger, brighter fire, since they often had to be roasted relatively quickly, having to replace the first-course roasts before the fire, and yet be ready in time to be dished at the second course. Great care was taken to achieve the correct surface colouring, only venison, beef, pork, geese and the larger birds being roasted brown, everything else ideally remaining pale or 'white', even when cooked through. This stage was judged in a variety of ways. Large joints were ready when their steam was drawn upwards, they shrank from the spit, and they produced clear bloodless juices when a knife or skewer was stuck into them. Poultry was similarly judged by checking the tenderness of the thighs and the lack of any blood at the base of the pinions.[49]

Now it was time to apply a crisp outer coating to the roasts, this being called the dredging. It involved basting with fresh butter and immediately shaking over it grated breadcrumbs mixed with any of the following ingredients:[50]

1. flour, with either grated orange or lemon zest, or with ground cinnamon and sugar;
2. fennel seed, coriander seed, cinnamon and sugar;
3. the grated dried zest of oranges or lemons;
4. dried and powdered sweet herbs;
5. sugar and salt;
6. for pigs, flour, nutmeg, ginger, pepper and sugar, after a basting with orange or lemon juice beaten into the egg yolks.

A further basting and two or three turns before the fire set and crisped the dredging, after which the roast was slid off its spit onto a hot dish ready to be served immediately to the waiting diners. Even at this stage, however, many roasts remained incomplete, since they still had to receive their pre-prepared boiling-hot sauces, made, for example, by mixing the dripping-pan juices:

1. with capers, samphire and salt;
2. with sliced onions, claret, nutmeg and water;
3. with white wine with whole onions, pickled capers, pepper, mace and three or four slices of lemon;

4. with oyster-liquor and claret, with onions, capers nutmeg and salt;
5. with white wine, butter and mace, thickened with egg yolks;
6. with verjuice, butter, sugar and chopped parsley;
7. with wine vinegar and chopped parsley;
8. with orange juice with salt and pepper;
9. with wine and sugar with strained cooked prunes.

Having introduced the general practices of late Elizabethan and Jacobean roasting, the following recipes provide working examples taken from the cookery books of the period. Since very few kitchens now have facilities for spit-roasting, the cooking times and temperatures are those for basic ovens without fan assistance. Spit-roasting times are very similar, but it is advisable to check the internal temperatures using a probe. The guidelines are:

60°C/140°F	beef, rare
70°C/160°F	beef, medium
75°C/170°F	beef, well done, veal & ham
80°C/175°F	lamb & mutton
90°C/195°F	pork & poultry

Of all roast meats, venison was one of the most prestigious, only being available to those who could afford to maintain a deer-park and enjoy the sport of hunting. Since it tended to dry out on the spit, it was frequently par-boiled before being larded and roasted, as in the following recipe. Alternatively it might be larded and roasted directly, allowing 15–20 minutes per pound (450g) at 190°C/375°F/gas mark 5 if young and tender.

TO ROAST VENISON[51]

1 joint of venison
4oz/100g fat lamb or pork flesh or *streaky bacon*
c.20 cloves, or *sprigs of rosemary, thyme and savory*, or, *chopped mixed herbs and suet*

Weigh the joint and calculate the cooking time at 25 minutes per lb/450g plus 25 minutes. Wash and truss it, put it into a deep pan on a grid or a few pieces of steel cutlery to keep it from the bottom, cover with boiling water, cover, and simmer very gently for half its cooking time.

Remove from the pan and plunge it into cold water for a couple of minutes. Lard with the fat cut into strips, and stick with the cloves or herbs, having made holes with a skewer, or stab with a knife and pack in as much herb/

suet mixture as possible. Either spit-roast or bake on a grid in a roasting tin at 170°C/325°F/gas mark 3 for the remainder of the cooking time.

Sauces for roast venison

1. the pan juices with chopped sweet herbs, or with the juice of an orange or a lemon;
2. 3oz/75g fresh white breadcrumbs boiled and stirred continuously with 2oz/50g butter, 2tbs white wine vinegar, 2tbs sugar and ¼pt/150ml water until thick;
3. 3oz/75g fresh white breadcrumbs boiled with ½pt/300ml claret, 1tbs wine vinegar, ¼tsp ground ginger, ½tsp ground cinnamon and 2tbs sugar, stirred continuously, sieved, and re-heated with a few whole cloves and a sprig of rosemary.

Pour any of these sauces into a dish, place the roast venison on top, and serve hot.

Most roast beef was probably served only with the gravy or juices which collected in the dripping pan, accompanied by salt and perhaps mustard. For more impressive meals, however, a variety of different techniques were available. The chine, rib, loin and brisket cuts were all good for roasting, but the best by far was the whole fillet.

TO PLAIN-ROAST BEEF[52]

1 roasting joint
4oz/100g butter
½tbs fresh chopped parsley
1tsp fresh chopped mixed herbs
¼tsp black pepper
grated zest of an orange
1 small onion, finely chopped
1tbs wine vinegar
1 beef stock cube
2 raw egg yolks, beaten

Spit or bake the beef at 180°C/350°F/gas mark 4 on a grid in a roasting tin, basting regularly with the butter. Allow 20 minutes per lb/450g for a medium roast, or 5 minutes more or less per lb/450g for rare or well done respectively.

Fifteen minutes before it is to be served, remove the joint from the heat, and allow to rest. Meanwhile bring all the remaining ingredients (except the yolks) to the boil with ¾pt/450ml water and the juices from the roasting tin, simmering and stirring until the onion is tender. When ready to serve, return to the boil, remove from the heat, pour into the yolks beating rapidly, and pour over the beef.

TO ROAST BEEF WITH HERBS[53]

1 roasting joint, either plain, or rubbed with salt the previous day
sprigs of fresh rosemary, parsley, thyme, marjoram and sage
4oz/100g butter
¼pt/150ml wine vinegar, or the juice of 1 lemon and 1 orange

Stab the joint with a skewer, and push the sprigs of herbs deep into the meat, then cook as in the recipe above. For the sauce, simmer the juices from the roasting pan with either the vinegar and more of the herbs, or with the orange and lemon juices.

TO ROAST BEEF WITH SPICES[54]

1 roasting joint
¼pt/150ml claret
¼pt/150ml wine vinegar
2tbs rosewater
1tbs elderflower cordial
1tsp salt
4oz/100g butter
1tsp mixed ground clove, nutmeg pepper, cinnamon & ginger
½tsp ground coriander
½tsp ground fennel
juice of 1 orange or 1 lemon

Mix the salt and spices into the liquids in a deep dish, add the joint, and leave overnight, turning from time to time. Cook the joint as in the recipe above, basting it with the butter, and serve with the orange or lemon juice mixed into pan juices as its sauce.

Legs and shoulders of mutton provided some of the most popular and varied roasts, using methods totally unknown today. A shoulder in blood, for example, involved saving the blood from a freshly slaughtered sheep, mixing in minced thyme and using this mixture as both a stuffing and a coating, wrapping the joint in a caul and leaving it overnight to set before roasting.[55] Other techniques included plain roasting, larding, forcing, stuffing with oysters, and roasting in the French way, which involved stuffing beneath the skin with a mixture of minced mutton, sweet herbs, suet, shallots and nutmeg.[56]

LADY MARY LISTER'S ROASTED MUTTON[57]

1 leg of lamb
4oz/100g butter
3tbs chopped fresh parsley
2 medium onions, finely chopped
white wine vinegar

Spit the leg close to the bone, or place on a grid in a roasting tin and cook at 180°C/350°F/gas mark 4 for 25 minutes per lb/450g plus 25 minutes basting with the butter. Half-way through the cooking time, trim a piece from the joint, chop it finely, mix it with the parsley, onions and vinegar, together with the gravy (without the fat) from the roasting tin, and a little water, cover, and simmer gently until the roast is ready. Pour this sauce into a dish, put the roast on top, and serve hot.

Plain roast mutton or lamb was served with a number of other hot boiled sauces too, including;

1. gravy, capers, samphire and salt;
2. gravy, whole onions, capers, mace, pepper, lemon slices and white wine;
3. gravy, vinegar, salt, and onions chopped with sweet herbs;
4. gravy, lemon juice (for verjuice), chopped parsley, butter and sugar;
5. orange juice with salt and pepper;
6. sieved stewed prunes, (red) wine and sugar.

TO ROAST A LEG OF MUTTON TO BE EATEN COLD[58]

1 leg of lamb
4oz/100g fat pork or bacon
2tsp salt
2tsp mixed ground cloves, pepper, nutmeg & mace
1tsp thyme & marjoram
1 small onion, finely chopped
grated rind of 1 orange

Cut the fat into long narrow strips and roll in a mixture of the remaining ingredients before closely larding the leg. Coat the leg with the surplus mixture, place on a grid on a roasting tin, cover, and cook as in the recipe above, but without basting.

When cold, set on a dish garnished with two (carved) lemons, and accompanied by saucers of mustard and sugar.

TO FARCE A LEG OF MUTTON (PLUS MINCE PIES)[59]

For the leg of lamb:
1 5lb/2.2kg leg of lamb
14oz/400g suet
1lb/450g raisins
1lb/450g currants
6 dates, chopped
2tbs sugar
2tsp salt
2tbs rosewater
1tbs caraway seeds
½tsp each ground clove, mace & nutmeg
1 egg, beaten

For the pies:
2lb/900g flour
8oz/225g lard
2tsp salt
4tbs white wine
2tbs white wine vinegar
2tbs barberries or capers
1 egg yolk, hard-boiled

For garnishing:
sippets of white bread
1 sliced lemon
barberries or capers

Carefully slip a sharp knife between the skin and the flesh of the broad end of the leg of lamb (or mutton if you should be so lucky to find it), and cut around, separating the skin so that it can be pulled back, intact. Continue to within 2in/5cm of the pointed end, except where the lower leg-bone runs against the skin. Then, cut the flesh off the bone, except at the pointed end.

Finely chop, then mince the meat, thoroughly mix with all but the egg in the first column above, weigh off 2lb/900g of the mixture, and bind with the egg. Pack this into the skin, with the bone down one side, fold the excess flap of skin over the open end, and 'stitch' to the skin of the other side using a 6in/15cm narrow iron skewer. Place, skewer side down, on to a grid in a roasting tin holding 1pt/600ml water. Cook at 180°C/350°F/gas mark 4 for 1½ hours. Just before serving, place on a dish lined with the sippets, pour off most of the fat from the roasting tin, stir in the wine, vinegar and egg yolk, the barberries or capers, bring to the boil while stirring and pour through a strainer over the meat. Finally garnish with the lemon, the barberries or capers, and a sprinkle of sugar.

Meanwhile, using the list of ingredients for the pies in the right-hand column above, boil the lard and salt with ½pt/300ml water, pour into the flour, and mix to form a pastry. Use half to line six 4in/10cm greased pie or tart tins and fill these with the remaining meat mixture. Moisten the edges with a little water, cover with lids made of the remaining pastry, cut a ½in/1.5cm slit in the centres, surrounded with a narrow border, and bake at 190°C/375°F/gas mark 5 for 15 minutes, then reduce to 180°C/350°F/gas mark 4 for a further 45 minutes. Serve either hot or cold.

TO ROAST A SHOULDER OF MUTTON WITH OYSTERS[60]

1 shoulder of lamb
12 oysters
3–4tbs white wine vinegar
4 anchovy fillets, chopped
½tsp mixed ground black pepper & nutmeg
½tsp salt
1 sprig pickled samphire, chopped
10 capers, chopped
½pt/300ml white wine
3 raw egg yolks
sliced lemon for garnish
4oz/100g butter

Open the oysters, remove the beards, loosen from the shells, simmer in half their own liquor, for 3–4 minutes, retaining the remainder for the sauce. Drain the cooked oysters, retaining their liquor, rinse them in the vinegar, and wipe them dry.

Mix together the anchovies, spices, salt and pickles and bind with one of the yolks. Stab the shoulder-meat with a sharp knife, and stuff with this mixture and the cooked oysters, then place on a grid in a roasting tin and cook at 180°C/350°F/gas mark 4 for 25 minutes per lb/450g plus 25 minutes, regularly basting with the butter.

Just before serving, pour the juices (not the fat) from the roasting tin into a clean saucepan, add the remaining oyster liquor and white wine, simmer for 5 minutes, pour onto the remaining egg yolks, beaten, return to the pan, stir while re-heating (do not boil), and pour into the dish around the roast.

Suckling pigs a few weeks old were sometimes plain roasted, the skin being pulled off when half-cooked, or with its skin left on and just sage or pennyroyal and butter in its belly, or completely filled with a rich stuffing.[61] Since suckling pigs are not easily obtainable in Britain today, no recipe is given here. However, the following instructions are suitable for all pork roasting joints.

TO ROAST WILD-BOAR ... OR FRESH PORK[62]

1 roasting joint of pork
1pt/600ml wine vinegar
1tsp salt
1tbs juniper berries, bruised
3 cloves of garlic, bruised
2oz/50g lard

Place the joint in a deep stainless or ceramic pan or dish, and half submerge in the brine made by mixing together the vinegar, salt, juniper and garlic. Store in a cool place for a week, turning and rubbing it twice a day. Drain, and either spit or place on a grid in a roasting tin and cook at 180°C/350°F/gas mark 4 for 30 minutes per lb/450g plus 30 minutes, basting with the lard.

Alternatively the pork could be plain-roasted, stuck with sage leaves, and served with any of the following hot sauces:[63]

1. the pan juices with 2 large onions, chopped and stewed with 2–3tsp sage;
2. 1lb/450g peeled apples, quartered and stewed with 2oz/50g butter and 1tbs sugar for about 10 minutes until just tender;
3. the pan juices with onions, vinegar and pepper;
4. 2tbs mustard powder, 2tbs vinegar and ¼tsp pepper, mixed together to make a viciously pungent sauce.

Most poultry and game-birds were plain-roasted, sometimes with slices of streaky bacon over the breast, and a larger piece inside, or with salt, pepper and an onion stuck with cloves in the belly.[64]

TO ROAST HENS & CHICKENS[65]

1 oven-ready chicken, trussed as described on p. 337
2–3 slices streaky bacon *4oz/100g butter*

Either spit or set on a grid in a roasting tin and cook for 20 minutes per lb/450g plus 20 minutes, regularly basting with the butter.

There were many different sauces with which the cooks could make their roast chickens constantly interesting as they regularly appeared on the table. These included:[66]

1. the pan juices boiled with sliced onions, claret and salt sometimes supplemented by slices or the juice of oranges and lemons and a little grated nutmeg;
2. the pan juices boiled with butter and lemon juice (for verjuice);
3. butter creamed with orange or lemon juice, and claret or white wine;
4. the pan juices stewed with sieved hard-boiled egg yolks, grated lemon zest, salt and white wine.

In addition, roast poultry was still being served on 'sops' of sliced or cubed white bread in a continuation of the medieval tradition. In effect, they provided a very practical and flavoursome vehicle for the service of savoury sauces. These are three typical sops to go under chickens:

1. boil butter and vinegar together with a little sugar, poured over thin strips of white bread in a dish;

2. sliced orange, butter, white wine, rosewater, ground mace and ginger stewed to tenderness and poured over thin slices of white bread;
3. the pan juices mixed with the juice of washed, liquidized and strained sorrel leaves, vinegar, sugar, creamed butter and slices of orange or lemon, all poured over thin slices of white bread, and dusted with sugar and ground cinnamon.

TO ROAST A GOOSE[67]

1 oven-ready goose, trussed, with a handful of sea salt inside, and the internal fat pulled out

Prick the skin with a fork or skewer, spit or place on a grid in a roasting tin, and cook for 35 minutes per lb/450g plus 35 minutes, at 200°C/400°F/gas mark 4, regularly basting with its own fat.

Being a dense, fatty meat, goose required a contrasting sharp, lighter sauce, such as:

1. cooking apples or pippins boiled to a pulp in beer before having butter and sugar beaten in;
2. cooking apples or pippins roasted before the fire, at 200°C/400°F/gas mark 6 for 45–60minutes in the oven or scored around the middle and microwaved for 3–5 minutes The pulp is then scooped out and heated with the pan juices, sieved boiled onions, grated white breadcrumbs, barberries, ground cinnamon, mustard sugar and vinegar.

ROAST PHEASANT[68]

In the English tradition, the plucked and drawn pheasant had only its head removed, one of the tail feathers being stuck into its breast when it was about to be served. Those who followed the later French fashion plucked the back and breast, sticking it with lardons and protecting the feathered head, neck, tail and one wing with buttered paper before roasting.

1 pheasant, plucked, drawn & trussed (with a slice of bacon on the breast)

Spit roast (or bake at 180°C/350°F/gas mark 4) for about 45 minutes. For a sauce take:[69]

1 onion, peeled
½, chicken stock cube
2oz/50g white bread
¼of a nutmeg, grated
pinch of salt
1 raw egg yolk
3tbs fresh orange juice

Beat the yolk into the orange juice and set aside. Bring the onion, stock cube, nutmeg and salt to the boil in ½pt/300ml water, cover and leave for 10 minutes. Next remove the onion, add the bread, and pass the mixture through a sieve into a clean pan. Stir in the yolk and orange juice, finally re-heating with the juices of the dripping pan just before serving.

ROAST RABBIT[70]

2 oven-ready rabbits
4oz/100g white breadcrumbs
1oz/25g suet
2tbs currants
4 dates, finely chopped
¼tsp mixed ground clove & mace
2tsp mixed chopped parsley, savory, marjoram, spinach & pennyroyal (or mint)
¼tsp salt
2tsp sugar
1 raw egg yolk
up to ¼pt/150ml cream

Mix the dry ingredients with the yolk and sufficient cream to make a medium-soft mixture, pack this inside the rabbits, sew up with thread, and spit-roast or bake at 190°C/375°F/gas mark 5 for 35–45 minutes, depending on their size. Serve with the following sauce.

SAUCE FOR A ROASTED RABBIT USED BY KING HENRY VIII (BEFORE 1588) [71]

2oz/50g fresh parsley chopped very finely
2oz/50g butter
juice of 1 lemon (for verjuice)
1tsp sugar
pinch ground black pepper
1oz/25g white breadcrumbs

Gently stew the parsley in the butter and lemon juice for about 5 minutes while stirring, then add the remaining ingredients, continue stirring over a gentle heat for a further 2 minutes until thickened and beat together. Lay the sauce as a 2½in/6cm strip down the centre of a dish, with a roasted rabbit along each side.

For a number of roasts, the lean meat was separated from all skin, sinew and coarse fat and then finely minced and seasoned before being wrapped up and mounted on the spits. Haslets of pigs' fry were enclosed in cauls, the membranes which enclosed the intestines, for example, while legs of mutton could be minced and sewn into linen bags.

TO ROAST A GIGOT OF MUTTON (IN A BAG)[72]

1lb/450g lean minced lamb/mutton
2 raw egg yolks
4oz/100g suet
1oz/25g currants
½tsp ground clove & mace
¼tsp each of chopped dried rosemary, parsley & thyme

Thoroughly mix all the ingredients, form into a cylinder about 2in/5cm in diameter, and roll in a piece of fine buttered cotton cloth, tying both ends tightly. Place on a grid in a baking dish, and bake at 180°C/350°F/gas mark 4 for 1½ hours. Remove the cloth and serve either hot or cold.

Aloes, the Old French for the larks they originally imitated, were similarly made by spreading minced meat or other fillings on thin slices of raw beef or lamb, rolling them up, and roasting them on spits. 'Fricaselles of Italy' were similar, but were made of lark-sized pieces of calf's liver flavoured with aniseed, salt and pepper, wrapped in pieces of caul and roasted on small bird-spits.[73]

TO MAKE ALOES TO ROAST[74]

4 thin slices of raw beef steak or lamb, about 4in/10cm across

For the onion filling:
1 large onion, finely chopped
1tsp parsley, finely chopped
2tbs suet
1 hard-boiled egg, finely chopped
1 raw egg yolk, beaten

For the kidney filling:
1 lamb kidney, minced
4 prunes, chopped
1tbs raisins
pinch each parsley, thyme & hyssop
pinch each of clove, mace, cinnamon & ginger
½tsp salt
1oz/25g fresh white breadcrumbs
1 hard-boiled egg yolk
1 raw egg, beaten

Lightly beat the steaks out flat. Mix the ingredients for either or both the fillings, spread over the steaks, roll them up, and secure them with either small skewers, thread or thin twine. Either tie to a spit and roast before a fire, or prop on skewers across the rim of a roasting tin and oven-bake at 170°C/325°F/gas mark 3 for about 30 minutes, basting with a little fat, oil or butter from time to time.

When tender, remove the skewers or thread and serve immediately.

The following recipe is for a rather more luxurious version of aloes using steaks of venison. It was served to the Cromwells during the Protectorate.

TO ROAST VENISON (STEAKS)[75]

6 large steaks cut from the top of the leg of a haunch of venison, beaten out thin

6oz/175g fat bacon, cut in narrow strips	*½tsp each rosemary, savory, & marjoram*
2tbs fresh parsley	*pinch each of clove, cinnamon & nutmeg*
2tbs fresh spinach	*1 egg, beaten*
2tbs fresh thyme	*½ bottle claret*
2tsp salt	
2oz/50g suet	

Lard the steaks closely with the fat bacon, then lay each one out flat in a line, turn up the ends so that they are all of the same length, then double each one and slide it on to a small spit or large skewer, to form a long roast.

Mix together the remaining ingredients (except the claret) having finely chopped the herbs, pack into pockets formed by the steaks on the spit, and hold in place with thread stitched through their open ends. Prop the skewer across the rim of a roasting tin, pour in the claret, and bake at 170°C/325°F/ gas mark 3 for some 1–1½ hours until tender, basting with the claret.

Serve with the following sauce:

3oz/75g fresh white breadcrumbs	*1oz/25g sugar*
¾pt/450ml wine vinegar	*4oz/100g butter*
¼tsp ground cinnamon	

When the roast is ready, remove from the oven, place the roasting tin over a moderate heat, stir in the above ingredients, allow to boil, while stirring, for a minute, then put the roast on to a hot dish, remove the skewer, pour the sauce over the top, and serve immediately.

GRIDIRONS

Most steaks, fish, toasts and other foods that only needed to be grilled for a few minutes over a bed of embers or glowing charcoal were cooked on iron frames called gridirons. This process, called broiling or carbonadoing, was particularly useful in large households, where there was great demand for producing hot food as quickly and easily as possible. The largest gridirons appear to have been huge rectangular frames enclosing several parallel bars, all mounted on low

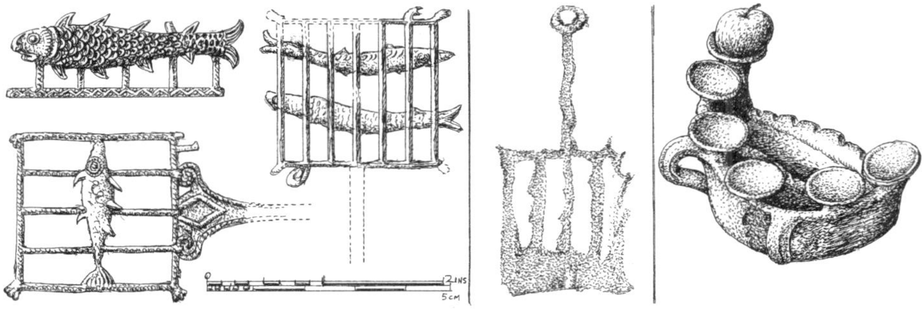

Figure 69. Gridirons and roasters. Toy gridirons, complete with their fish (left) have been excavated from 17th-cent. London, the outline of a full-size example (middle) being drawn with a sooty candle on a ceiling at Great Barton, Suffolk. The apple roaster (right) was found at Woolston, Somerset.

wheels. This enabled them to be laden with their raw meats or other fare, rolled over a bed of embers, and then rolled back again for their contents to be turned over or removed as necessary. A fine example of this type, regrettably undated, still survives in Cardinal Wolsey's kitchen at Christ Church, Oxford. For general use, gridirons were much smaller, perhaps a foot (30cm) square, with a long handle, and four low legs, those nearest the handle being shorter so that the fats ran back along the iron bars, rather than dripping into the fire. The modern preference for horizontal bars that ensure that meats and other candidates for the grill are given a coating of fine ash and give off the stench of burning fat was not acceptable in the past. The archaeological record presents little physical evidence for gridirons, but their appearance is confirmed by miniature versions made as toys in the seventeenth century, and by their depiction as protective symbols drawn with candle-smoke on East Anglian ceilings.[76]

CARBONADO OF BEEF (1)[77]

fillet or tender steaks cut ½in/12mm thick

claret	*nutmeg*
salt & pepper	*butter*

Season the claret with ¼tsp ground nutmeg, ¼tsp pepper & ½tsp salt per 1pt/600ml claret, and soak the steaks in this for about 1 hour. Drain and grill *very* gently on both sides until tender (about 10–15 minutes). Bring the claret mixture to the simmer and pour over the dish of steaks, and dot with softened butter.

CARBONADO OF BEEF (2)[78]

fillet or other tender steak cut ½in/12mm thick

½tsp salt	*1 beef stock cube*
2 onions	*¼tsp ground black pepper*
½pt/300ml white wine vinegar	

Sprinkle the steaks with salt on both sides, and set aside for 30 minutes before grilling it as in the recipe above. Meanwhile finely chop the onions, half-cover with wine vinegar and stew until tender. Dissolve the stock cube in ¼pt/150ml water to serve as a gravy. Dish the steaks with the onions and gravy, with a sprinkling of pepper.

Alternatively the steaks may be served with orange juice, nutmeg and gravy briefly simmered together.

CARBONADO OF PORK CHOPS[79]

Remove the skin from the chops, strew with fennel seeds, grill on both sides for some 10 minutes each side until tender, and serve with wine vinegar and pepper.

TO BROIL MACKEREL[80]

mackerel, gutted & washed	*vinegar*
sprigs of mint & hyssop	*butter*
salt	

Use thread to bind the herbs round the fish, plunge into boiling salted water, simmer for 2 minutes, then remove and grill on both sides until crisp and brown. Place on a dish, remove the thread, dot with butter, sprinkle first with vinegar and then with salt, and serve hot.

LORD D'AUBIGNY'S RED HERRING[81]

red herrings	*olive oil*
vinegar	

Beat equal parts of oil and vinegar together, soak the herrings in them for an hour, then grill lightly on both sides until hot but not dry. Return to the oil for a further hour, then grill again until 'short, crisp and savoury', then serve with some of the oil and vinegar mixture.

TOASTS

The usual way of toasting slices of bread in the Tudor and Stuart period was to support them either before the fire on the hooks of a toasting iron, or over the embers on the bars of a gridiron. If to be served as a dish in their own right, they were kept hot and soaked in butter or other rich liquids. According to Fynes Moryson, Cockneys born within the sound of Bow bells were also known as 'great eaters of buttered tostes.'[82] Having toasted rounds of fine manchet loaves, rolls or French bread, they had any of the following hot mixtures poured over them:

1. butter or olive oil, with sugar;
2. claret, or sack, flavoured with fresh orange juice and sugar.[83]

ROASTED APPLES

Roasted apples were used to make sauces, to add to bowls of hot spiced ale, and to make a hot dish in their own right. Since they had tender flesh, especially when starting to cook through, they were unsuitable for spit-roasting. Instead, special iron implements were used to hold them before the fire. Thomas Myddelton of West Applegarth in Swaledale had 'a playte for royestyng of appelles on 8*d*.' in 1564, for example, while Sir Thomas Kytson of Hengrave in Suffolk had 'one cradell of iron to roast appelles on' in 1603.[84] Similarly Thomas Prestwood of Exeter owned 'one apple roster 6*d*.' in 1577, demonstrating their widespread use throughout England.[85] Unfortunately not a single example appears to have survived, but they probably resembled earthenware examples such as those excavated in a 1660–1680 context in Goldsmith Street, Exeter, and from Woolston in Somerset. The first is a rectangular dish with a notched strip across its length on which to prop the apples. The second, meanwhile, is semicircular, with an identical strip across it, and six small saucer-like projections rising above the curved rim, each designed to hold an apple, and allow it to be turned so as to roast evenly.[86]

CHAPTER SEVENTEEN

Frying

The high temperature of boiling fat made it the ideal medium for cooking foods quickly and giving them a crisp, tasty surface, while retaining their inner moisture. The most common frying-fat was lard, the white parts of pig-flesh lying just beneath the skin. It was often preserved in this form ready for future use, as described by Mrs Elizabeth Beale in 1576. Having used a staff to stir salt into water to create a strong brine, the fresh lard was soaked for a night and a day to extract the blood. Having been drained, it was transferred to a tub of fresh brine where, held below the surface by wooden splints and covered by a lid, it would keep sweet and white for three or four years. She also noted Lady Weston's method. This required the removal of the skin, dry-salting with large-crystal sea salt, forming into a roll and leaving it beneath a heap of salt, where it would keep indefinitely.[1] Whichever method was used, pieces had only to be cut off as required, soaked in water, wiped dry, cut in pieces, and then baked in a dish. The hot, liquid lard could then be poured off, strained and either transferred to bladders for short-term storage, or used directly.

Dripping was also used for frying, but most recipes for good-quality dishes specify either clarified butter or olive oil. To clarify the butter, it was simply melted in a pan, perhaps with a little water, carefully skimmed, allowed to set, all its sediment removed, and then briefly boiled to evaporate any remaining moisture, after which it could be stored for use. Olive oil required no such preparation, being purchased either in 23-gallon barrels, or in the parsnip-shaped creamy-buff earthenware jars in which it had been imported from the Iberian peninsular.[2]

Deep-frying could be carried out in any cooking pot, or in deep, convex-bottomed wrought iron frying-pans, such as one recovered from the basement of a Norwich house which burnt down in 1507.[3] Many pans for shallow-frying were still being made of earthenware, their glazed interiors providing an impervious cooking surface. If used over the gentle warmth of glowing peats or wood-embers, they were relatively fire-proof, but the fierce heat of a coal fire would be far more likely to cause them to shatter. It is probably for this reason that their use declined as coal replaced wood in many areas from the late sixteenth

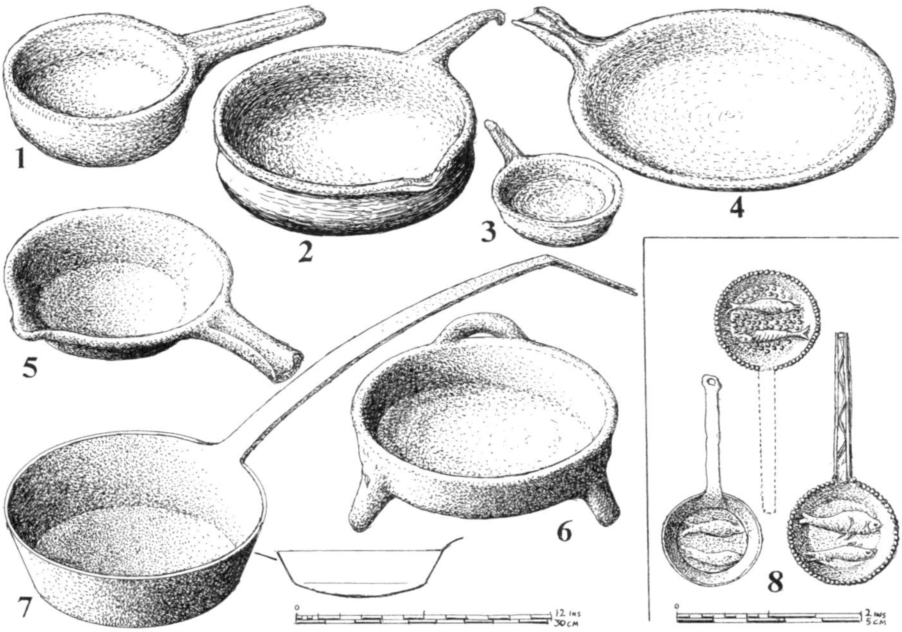

Figure 70. Frying-pans. (1) Sandal Castle, Yorkshire 16th cent.; (2 & 3) Norwich, 16th cent.; (4) Exeter, Devon, c. 1660; (5) Netherlands Redware, Newcastle-upon-Tyne, late 16th cent.; (6) Wrotham, Kent, 16–17th cent.; (7) Pottergate, Norwich, 1507; (8) toy frying-pans and their contents, London, early–mid-17th cent.

century. They survived for a while in rural areas such as Norfolk, Somerset and Cornwall, but even here had disappeared by the time of the Commonwealth.[4] They were largely replaced by metal frying-pans, each having a relatively flat base, a rim flaring out at about 45 degrees and a long, flat iron handle. Although few have been recovered from excavations, their shape is confirmed by miniature versions cast as toys and found in seventeenth-century contents in London and elsewhere.[5] Household accounts frequently record the purchase of frying-pans from their makers: for example, the Earl of Northumberland's steward paid John Brodebanck the London brazier 3*s.* 6*d.* for a pair in 1586.[6]

In many ordinary homes the frying-pan was in daily use, cooking that most characteristic English dish, bacon and eggs. As Andrew Boorde stated in 1542:

> Bacon is good for carters and plowmen, the whiche be ever labourynge in the earth or dunge ... wherfore I do say that collopes and egges is as holsome for them as talowe candell is good for a horse mouth.[7]

Bacon was so much a peasants' food that Shakespeare used the actual word to describe them in his *Henry IV*, Sir John Falstaff encouraging his bacon-fed knaves with the cry of 'On bacons, on!'[8] Thomas Dawson thought it best to thinly slice the bacon, cut away the lean, bruise it with the back of a knife, and fry it in butter.[9] For a more refined version, Gervase Markham soaked the rashers in hot water for an hour or two, drained them, and toasted them before the fire on a pewter dish before serving them with poached eggs.[10] To fry bread, slices of fine white rolls or manchets had their crusts chipped away before being quickly dipped in water, fried in clarified butter or oil, and sprinkled with sugar as they were piled one on top of another.[11]

Most sausages for frying were made of raw pork and pork fat flavoured with herbs and spices, some also incorporating beef suet, eggs or sack. Their mixtures might be packed into small guts by the use of a funnel, or else formed into rolls some four or five inches long by about an inch in diameter and fried without skins.[12] The following example is typical.

SAUSAGES[13]

1lb/450g lean raw pork
8oz/250g suet (or firm pork fat)
½tsp each ground clove & mace
2tsp finely chopped sage
½tsp ground black pepper
1tsp salt

Mince the pork (and pork fat) very finely, thoroughly mix in the remaining ingredients and either pack into prepared sausage skins, or form into rolls 4–5in/10–12cm long by about 1in/2.5cm diameter, and fry in lard for 5–10 minutes, turning from time to time, until cooked through. They may be served accompanied by either vinegar or the juice of bitter oranges.

Richer versions used finely ground pork fillet, and added nutmeg, savory, thyme and egg yolks to the above mixture.[14]

Offal such as kidneys, liver and tripe was also suitable for frying.

TO FRY TRIPE[15]

1lb/450g dressed tripe
2 small onions, sliced
4oz/100g clarified butter
1–2tbs vinegar (for verjuice)
a little ground ginger

Cut the tripe into strips about 1 x 2in/2.5 x 5cm. Fry the onions in the butter for a few minutes until softened, then add the tripe, stirring it from time to time until the mixture has thickened and turned golden brown. Turn onto a dish, sprinkle with the vinegar and ginger and serve hot.

The lamb-stones removed when castrating ram lambs each May and June were also fried. We have already described the elaborate service of these 'Anchitricoes' on Henry Best's East Riding farm (page 195, above),[16] but when fish was to be fried, the usual method was to simply dust it with flour and fry it in butter.[17] An accompanying sauce might be made at the same time, as in these examples.

TO FRY SALMON[18]

1lb/450g salmon steaks, ½in/1.25cm thick
2oz/50g clarified butter
3tbs claret
⅛tsp grated nutmeg
1tsp anchovy or fish sauce
2tbs wine vinegar
1 small orange, sliced thinly
sprigs fresh parsley & sage
orange & lemon quarters
2 pippins, sliced across
3–4 hard-boiled egg yolks

Put ½oz/12g butter, the claret, nutmeg, sauce, vinegar and sliced orange into a small pan, cover, and stew together for some 5 minutes, then set aside. Melt the remaining butter in a frying-pan and use to fry the salmon steaks for about 10 minutes, turning when half cooked, until the exterior is browned and crisped. Also fry the parsley and sage dipped in a little batter and the pippin slices. Arrange the salmon steaks on a hot dish, garnish the rim with the parsley, sage, pippin slices, orange and lemon quarters and yolks, pour the re-heated sauce over the salmon, and serve immediately.

TO FRY WHITING[19]

1½lb/675g whiting fillets
4oz/100g clarified butter or olive oil
8oz/225g apples or onions, peeled & finely chopped
½pt/300ml white wine
3–4tbs plain flour
1tbs white wine vinegar
¼tsp ground mace
¼tsp ground pepper
pinch ground cloves
1tsp salt

Fry the apples or onions in half the butter or oil until cooked but not brown, stir in the wine, wine vinegar, spices and salt, cook for a further 5 minutes, then keep hot for use. Skin the fillets, dust with flour, fry in a clean pan in the remaining butter or oil for 5–10 minutes, arrange on a dish and cover with the apple or onion mixture.

TO FRY TURBOT OR HALIBUT[20]

1lb/450g turbot or halibut fillets
2oz/50g butter
¼pt/150ml claret
4 anchovy fillets
1 slice root ginger
¼nutmeg, sliced
pinch of saffron
½tsp salt
flesh of 1 lemon, finely chopped

Cut the fillets into thin strips and toss in batches in half of the butter, removing them onto a hot plate as they become lightly browned. Clean the frying-pan, add the claret, anchovies, spices and salt, bring to the boil, add the fish and simmer for 5 minutes, add the butter and lemon, shake over the heat until just boiling, then dish and serve on a bed of sippets.

Since eggs cooked very quickly, they were ideal for frying by being simply dropped into hot fat in a frying-pan. Medieval cooks had also beaten them together with chopped meats or fried onions to make dishes such as froise or hanoney. As part of the increasing French influence of the early seventeenth century these were now replaced by a new and extremely versatile dish called the omelette. This might include all manner of savoury or sweet flavourings, Robert May offering twenty-one different recipes, such as the following.[21]

OMELETTES

1oz/25g clarified butter
6 eggs beaten with one of the following:

1. *4oz/100g finely diced and fried bacon with a pinch of salt (serve with wine vinegar for verjuice);*
2. *4oz/100g grated cheese and a pinch of salt;*
3. *4oz/100g mushrooms, chopped, stewed in a little salted water and drained (serve with some of the cooking liquid and a sprinkling of ground nutmeg);*
4. *4oz/100g leeks finely chopped, with a pinch of salt;*
5. *2oz/50g finely chopped fresh parsley with a pinch of salt;*
6. *the juice pressed out of 4oz/100g sweated spinach, plus 1oz/25g finely chopped fresh sorrel leaves and a pinch of salt (serve with a little greensauce, vinegar & sugar boiled together)*

Melt the butter in an omelette pan over a gentle heat, allowing time for the pan to heat through uniformly. Pour in the egg mixture and stir gently, drawing the liquid from the sides to the centre until it has just set, then stop stirring, cook for another minute until it is golden brown underneath and still creamy on top, then slide out onto a hot plate and serve.

Alternatively

Fry one of the following in the butter until tender before pouring in the eggs beaten with a pinch of salt:

7. *3 small pippins, sliced across (serve with sugar);*
8. *1 apple & 1 onion, peeled & sliced (serve with 1oz/25g butter, 2tbs wine vinegar, 2tsp sugar & ¼tsp mustard powder melted together);*
9. *4oz/100g asparagus, cut in small pieces, half-fried brown;*
10. *4oz/100g endive, cut in small pieces & fried with ¼tsp ground nutmeg (serve with sugar);*
11. *4oz/100g mix of pine kernels, currants and chopped candied lemon peel (roll this omelette into a cylinder when removing from the pan, then sprinkle with rosewater & sugar).*

Stuffed omelettes were called vaunts. They were made with dried fruits, spices and bone-marrow or meat, all bound with egg yolks and sandwiched between two layers of cooked eggs. The following is a simple version. More elaborate ones cut the top layer into narrow strips which were woven together to form a trellis pattern.

TO MAKE VAUNTS[22]

4oz/100g lean cooked veal (or lamb, or fish such as salmon)
2 eggs, separated
1 egg, beaten
1oz/25g dates, finely chopped
1oz/25g raisins
¼tsp each ground ginger & cinnamon
pinch of saffron
¼tsp salt
1tsp sugar
½oz/12g butter

Finely chop or mince the meat (or fish) and mix thoroughly with the two yolks, dates, raisins, spices, salt and sugar. Beat the egg and remaining whites together with a pinch of salt. Melt half the butter in a frying-pan over a gentle heat, pour in half the eggs to cover the base, leave until cooked through, then slide off onto a plate. Add the remaining butter to the pan, pour in the remaining egg, leave until just set, then spread the mixture on top in an even layer, covering it with the cooked disc of egg. Leave for about 5 minutes over a gentle heat until the filling has cooked through and set, then slide onto a hot dish and serve immediately. It may receive a final sprinkling of sugar and ginger.

TANSIES

Tansies were omelettes flavoured with the juices of the yellow-flowered herb *Tanacetum vulgare* or tansy. Its stems and foliage are extremely bitter, as anyone knows who has nibbled even a tiny piece, this strong flavour associating it with the bitter herbs customarily eaten at Passover and Easter. In the spring of 1559, six-pennyworth of wild tansy was purchased at Epsom for the Earl of Leicester, for example.[23] Recipes for tansies include a variety of different ingredients, some incorporating gooseberries, some violets and herbs, while others, such as one given by Izaak Walton, were made of minnows and the flowers of cowslips and primroses, all bound together with egg yolks.[24] The following recipe is much more typical of the tansies made in the early seventeenth century.

A TANSY[25]

a few stems of tansy
4 eggs plus one yolk, beaten
½pt/300ml thick cream
pinch of salt
½tsp each ground nutmeg, mace & cinnamon
a few drops green food colouring
2oz/50g fresh white breadcrumbs
3oz/75g clarified butter
2–3tbs caster sugar
juice of 2 oranges

Grind the tansy with 2–3tbs water, squeeze out the juice and mix it with the eggs, cream, salt, spices and green food colouring (replacing the juice of crushed green wheat stalks in the original recipe). Beat until completely smooth. Add the breadcrumbs and combine. Melt 1oz/25g of the butter in a 10in/25cm frying-pan over a gentle heat, pour in the mixture and stir it from the bottom continuously so that it does not stick. Cook until it has become quite firm. Remove from the heat, ease the sides free from the pan, place a buttered plate on top, invert both pan and plate, and work the tansy into a flat round shape. Clean the pan, melt another 1oz/25g butter, slide the tansy back in, and cook for a few minutes, gently shaking the pan to prevent it from sticking.

Cover the pan with a buttered plate once more, invert them both, remove the tansy, clean the pan once more, melt in the final 1oz/25g of butter, and slide in the tansy, cooking it again for a few minutes. Slide the tansy on to a hot plate, sprinkle with the sugar, then with the orange juice (or elder vinegar) and serve immediately. The tansy eats well, but great care must be taken each time it is inverted onto the plate, to prevent any accidental scalds of hot butter.

It was much simpler to merely stir beaten eggs and butter over a gentle heat until they scrambled. In the early sixteenth century, such buttered eggs were served as an aristocratic breakfast to the Earl of Northumberland and his chief officers.[26] In the 1650s they formed part of Elizabeth Cromwell's repertoire, her recipe being one of the first to dish them on toast.

TO BUTTER EGGS[27]

¼–½oz/10–15g butter per egg
toasted slices of white rolls or manchets

Gently melt half the butter in a small pan, pour in the beaten eggs and stir over a gentle heat until just cooked, but still soft. Stir in the remaining butter, turn out onto toasts and serve garnished with salt and ground pepper.

PANCAKES

In order to use up any eggs before the onset of Lent, it had become customary to make pancakes on Shrove Tuesday, the church bells which had formerly summoned congregations to confession now releasing them from work to kill and eat poultry and feast on pancakes and fritters. As Tusser advised:

> At Shrovetide to shroving, go thresh the fat hen,
> If blindfold can kill her, then give it thy men.
> Maids, fritters and pan-cakes inough see you make,
> Let slut have one pancake, for company sake.[28]

In his *Shoemaker's Holiday* of 1600 Thomas Dekker described how everyone cried 'The pan-cake bell rings, the Pancake bell! Trihill, my hearts!' while Firkin explained how,

> Every Shrove Tuesday is our year of Jubilee; and when the pancake bell rings, we are as free as my Lord mayor; we may shut up our shops, and make holiday.

And Eyre demanded the services of 'this swag-belly, this greasy kitchenstuff cook'.[29] Such a cook was,

> sole Monarch of the Mouth, high Steward of the Stomach, chief Ganimede to the Guts, prime peer of the Pallets, first favourite of the Frying-pans, great Bashaw to the Butter – bowles, Protector of the Pancakes, first Founder of the Fritters, Baron of Bacon-flitch, Earl of the Egge- baskets etc. This corpulent Commander of those choleric things called Cookes ... by his manner you may finde him better fed than taught wherever he comes.[30]

To make pancakes, he would take,

> a thing called wheaten floure, [mingled] with water, eggs, spice and other tragical, magicall inchantments, and they put it by little and little into a frying-pan of boiling suet, where it makes a confused dissmall hissing ... until at last, by the skill of the Cooke, it is transformed into the forme of a Flip-Jack, cal'd a Pancake, which with ominous incantation the ignorant people doe devoure very greedily.[31]

The cooks were not the only ones to make pancakes, however, since, as Pasquil's *Palanodia* of 1634 described:

> ... every man and maide doe take their turne,
> And tosse their pancakes up for feare they burne;
> And all the kitchen doth with laughter sound,
> To see the pancakes fall upon the ground.[32]

PANCAKES[33]

8oz/225g flour
½tsp salt
¼tsp each ground nutmeg, clove & mace
2 eggs
clarified butter (lard, or oil) for frying

Sift the dry ingredients into a bowl, make a well in the centre and drop in the eggs, beating them and drawing in the flour from the sides, while gradually adding 1pt/600ml cold water. Set aside for an hour or more. Heat a little of the butter (lard or oil) in a frying-pan, pour in a ladleful of the batter, rotating the pan to spread it to an even thickness. Cook for 1–2 minutes, toss over, cook the other side, and transfer to a hot plate. Serve sprinkled with caster sugar.

FRITTERS

The usual kinds of fritter-batter were made by mixing eggs, a cereal such as wheat flour or breadcrumbs and various flavourings with either shredded apples or spinach.

APPLE FRITTERS[34]

3fl.oz/90ml sherry
6fl.oz/180ml ale
3 eggs, beaten
5oz/150g peeled and finely chopped apple
¼tsp salt
½tsp dried yeast, first dissolved
2tsp ground ginger
6oz/175g flour
dripping or lard for frying

Dissolve the yeast in the ale, then mix with the sherry, eggs, salt and ginger. Pour into a well in the flour and beat to produce a smooth batter. Stir in the apple and set aside in a warm place for 2 hours to rise. Drop spoonfuls into the hot dripping or lard in a frying-pan, turn over, once the base has turned golden brown, and when cooked serve sprinkled with sugar.

SPINACH FRITTERS[35]

8oz/225g cooked & drained spinach
2oz/50g fresh white breadcrumbs
2 eggs, beaten
¼tsp ground cinnamon
¼tsp ground ginger
2oz/50g butter
2–3tbs sugar

Chop and mix the spinach, bread and spices to a smooth paste, then beat in the eggs. Heat the butter in a frying-pan, drop in tablespoons of the batter, spreading them with the back of the spoon and shaking the pan to stop them sticking. Fry on both sides, serve in a hot dish with a sprinkling of sugar.

Other fritters were made in ornamental shapes, either to be served as a separate dish, or to garnish others. The first continues the technique used for making 'cryspes' in the late fourteenth century.[36]

TO FRY PASTE OUT OF A SYRINGE OR BUTTER SQUIRT[37]

5oz/125g plain flour
1tsp dried yeast
¼tsp salt
pinch of saffron
1oz/25g butter
¼pt/150ml white wine
1tbs sugar
oil or clarified butter for frying

Mix the dry ingredients in a pan, make a well in the centre, pour in the wine and ¼pt/150ml water, and work to form a smooth mixture. Add the butter, and stir continuously until thick and boiling. Remove from the heat, allow to cool, then grind (or rub through a sieve) to banish all lumps. Beat in a little more flour or water to produce a thick, pipeable mixture. Use this to fill an icing bag or syringe with a ¾in/15mm nozzle, and pipe into a pan of hot oil or clarified butter.

It works best if the oil is about ½in/12mm deep, and the mixture is piped in a rosette or knot design, being turned over when firm, cooked on the other side, then removed to a wire rack using a pierced slice.

Figure 71. Robert May's stock-fritter moulds.

As a further development, special fritter-moulds had been introduced by the early seventeenth century. Most probably made of cast brass or bronze, each had its chosen design made up of a series of narrow strips, all mounted on a long metal handle. After being heated in a pan of hot fat or oil, their front and edges were dipped into a batter, and then plunged back into the pan. As a result, the batter was rapidly converted into a crisp fritter, quite stiff when removed from its mould.

STOCK FRITTERS[38]

8oz/225g plain flour
½pt/300ml cold water
1tsp dried yeast dissolved in the water

or

8oz/225g plain flour
¼pt/150ml almond milk
¼pt/150ml white wine
1tbs sugar
pinch of saffron
clarified butter or oil for frying

Put the flour into a bowl, make a well in the centre, pour in the remaining ingredients, work in to produce a smooth batter, cover, and set aside for at least an hour.

Heat at least 1in/2.5cm of clarified butter or oil in a pan. Take a fritter mould (such as the aluminium moulds used in modern times on the Continent), dip into the hot fat, lift out, shake dry, dip into the batter, leaving the top of the mould perfectly clean, and return to the fat until golden brown. Lift out, shake the fritter off onto a dish, and use to garnish any boiled or stewed food.

Alternatively, sprigs of sage or rosemary might be dipped in the batter and fried.

A further form of fritter was made by gently frying slices of bread in an egg and cream batter, this being a Tudor development of the medieval 'brown fries', and the ancestor of the Georgian 'pain-perdu'.[39] In the reign of Charles I it appears to have become associated with the twenty-six pensioner knights of the Order of the Garter, being popularly known as the Poor Knights of Windsor.

TO MAKE POOR KNIGHTS[40]

½pt/300ml single cream
3 eggs, beaten
pinch of ground nutmeg
a few slices of white bread with a firm, open crumb

for the sauce:
4tbs rosewater
1oz/25g butter
2tsp sugar
(butter for frying)

Pour the cream into a broad bowl or dish, dip the slices in on one side, and lay out, wet side up, on a board, until half the cream has been used. Beat the eggs and nutmeg into the cream, and set aside. Melt the butter in a frying-pan, without burning it, lay in the slices wet side down until lightly fried, pour the remaining egg and cream over them, turn them over to cook the other side, and transfer to a hot dish. Serve with the ingredients of the sauce melted, beaten together and brought up to almost boiling hot.

In contrast to such a basic recipe, others were more sophisticated. 'Peascods', for example, were small half-round pasties filled with sweetened and spiced bone-marrow, or herbed marrow and oysters and deep-fried.[41]

PEASCODS[42]

4oz/100g flour
2oz/50g butter
2tsp sugar
1 egg yolk
2oz/50g raisins
2oz/50g dates
½tsp ground cinnamon
fat (or oil) for frying

Rub three-quarters of the butter into the flour and half the sugar, mix in the yolk with 1tbs cold water to form a stiff dough. Chop the raisins, dates and cinnamon together, and work in the remaining butter and sugar to make a firm paste. Roll the pastry to about ⅛in/3mm thickness on a floured board and cut into 2½in/6.5cm rounds. Place a roll of the mixture down the centre of each one, moisten the edges, fold the pastry around it and seal the edges like a pea-pod. Heat the fat (at least ½in/12mm deep) in a small pan, put in batches of the peascods and gently shake until golden brown all over, then remove with a perforated spoon, drain, and serve hot sprinkled with cinnamon and sugar.

There were also 'kickshaws of paste', miniature puff-paste pasties filled with one of the following:

1. finely chopped (or pre-cooked) apples seasoned with cinnamon, ginger and sugar;
2. gooseberries seasoned with cinnamon, ginger, nutmeg and sugar;
3. curds made by mixing egg yolks and whites separately with cream, bringing them to the boil, draining, and mixing with sliced dates, parboiled currants or bits of bone-marrow (or butter);
4. almond paste beaten with rosewater and nutmeg and deep-fried for dinners and suppers.[43]

Further 'pasties' were enclosed in fruit, these including,

FRENCH PUFFS WITH GREEN HERBS[44]

1tbs each fresh, finely chopped spinach, parsley & endive
1tsp finely chopped savory | *1 egg, beaten*
1tsp sugar | *1 lemon*
pinch ground nutmeg & ginger | *lard for frying*

Mix the herbs, sugar and spices with just sufficient egg to make a soft paste. Cut the lemon across in thin round slices, remove the pips, and cover each one with a layer of the mixture. Shallow fry in the lard until the mixture has set, then turn over and briefly fry the other side before dishing and sprinkling with either sweet white wine or sherry-sack.

DROPPED RAISINS[45]

the same mixture as in the recipe above
large Lexia raisins

Slit each raisin down the side, open out and form into a disc, removing the seeds. Pack some of the mixture between a pair of raisins, seal the edges, and fry on each side in hot lard.

As with other recipes for fried dishes, these demonstrate how this method of cookery was ideal for producing hot, satisfying and sustaining dishes quickly and efficiently, a real boon in any busy kitchen.

CHAPTER EIGHTEEN

Salads, Pickles and Sauces

'Beware of sallettes & raw fruytes for they will make your soverayne seke,' advised Wynkyn de Worde in 1508.[1] After being popular or fashionable in the fourteenth and early fifteenth centuries, they were now considered as 'food more meet for hogs and savage beasts to feed upon than mankind.'[2] This appears to have surprised Catherine of Aragon, who demanded the services of a Dutch gardener to produce the salads she had been used to.[3] Perhaps because of her influence, attitudes began to change. By the 1540s Sir Thomas Elyot's *Castel of Helth* was recommending herbs such as rocket, savory, borage, purslane, onions and capers, along with imported olives, since they either 'stirred the appetite to meat' or promoted digestion.[4] In the 1550s salads had begun to be served as the first dish of the first course at both dinner and supper.[5] This now became their accepted place, John Gerard confirming in 1597 that 'Salad is served in these daies in the beginning of supper and eaten first before any other meat ... for being taken before meat it doth many time stir up appetite.' He also noted that 'if eaten after supper it keepeth away drunkennesse which cometh by the wine'.[6] By now the use of salads was 'not only resumed among the poor commons (ordinary folk), I mean of melons, pompions, gourds, cucumbers, radishes, skirrets, parsnips, carrots, cabbages, navews, turnips and all kinds of salad herbs – but also fed upon as dainty dishes at the table to delicate merchants, gentlemen and the nobility, who make their provision yearly for new seeds out of strange countries.'[7]

To ensure the best of supplies, most prosperous families employed gardeners to set up private vegetable and herb gardens, while professionals found it possible to set up commercial gardens to serve local markets. As a result, the 'Gardiners' Company of London received its royal charter in 1606. By this time the following herbs and vegetables were available to most cooks:

Alexander	*Onion*
Artichokes (globe)	*Parsley*
Asparagus	*Purslane*
Blessed thistle	*Radish*
Borage	*Rampion (wild garlic)*

Burnet
Carrot
Colewort
Cucumber
Cress
Endive
Garlic
Hops
Leeks
Lettuce
Mint
Mustard
Musk-melon
Rocket
Sage
Samphire
Scallion (spring onion)
Sea-holly
Skirret
Sorrel
Sperage
Spinach
Succory (chicory)
Tarragon
Violets

as well as imported capers, lemons, olives and oranges. This is not a comprehensive list, but clearly shows the great range of greenstuff now being grown for the table.[8]

As salads were among the first dishes seen by those assembled in the hall as the stately procession of waiters carried the lord's service through to his dining parlour, they had to develop an appropriately impressive appearance. Instead of being a random selection of herbs, salads had adopted fleur-de-lis or oakleaf designs by the 1590s, but these were superseded in the early seventeenth century by much more ornate 'Grand Salads'. These were huge chargers filled with salads enriched with nuts, dried fruits and other delicacies, all elaborately garnished with all manner of edible decorations chosen for their bright contrasting colours. Above rose some form of upstanding feature, perhaps a virtual bush of green rosemary sprigs studded with red cherries. A delight to both the appetite and the eye, they provided an ideal trophy to carry before the other dishes through the hall and then formed a significant feature on the dining table until its course was cleared away.

In contrast, the simplest salads were quite basic. Freshly gathered and washed chives, lettuces, purslane, radishes and other saladings were merely placed in dishes and dressed with wine vinegar, olive oil and sugar. Vegetables such as onions, asparagus, carrots and other delights were pre-cooked and served cold as 'boiled salads' dressed with wine vinegar, olive oil and pepper (see pages 369–375 for their recipes). Some of the mixed or compound salads were a springtime delicacy, being made of the finest young stalks and buds of herbs such as mint, lettuce, violets, marigold, spinach and other aromatics, all mixed together and dressed with vinegar, olive oil and sugar.[9] Others were more elaborate.

AN EXCELLENT COMPOUND SALAD[10]

1oz/25g each raisins, chopped dried figs, chopped blanched almonds & capers
2oz/50g currants
1pt/600ml mixed red sage & spinach leaves
2tbs olive oil
2tsp wine vinegar
1tbs sugar
2 oranges & 2 lemons
1 radiccio lettuce (for red cauliflower leaves)
1 small, crisp lettuce
6 pickled gherkins
20 olives

Mix the dried fruits, almonds, capers and sage and spinach leaves together, dress with the oil, vinegar and half the sugar, spread in a large dish and sprinkle with the remaining sugar. Pare the zest off the oranges and lemons, cut the flesh into thin slices and spread half of them over the fruit mixture. Add a layer of the radiccio leaves, then a layer of the thinly sliced heart of the lettuce, the olives and the gherkins cut into slices, arranged into a formal pattern. Finally garnish the top of the salad and the brim of the dish with the remaining orange and lemon slices.

ELIZABETH CROMWELL'S CHICKEN SALAD[11]

2 roasted chicken legs
1 lemon
1 dessert apple, peeled & chopped
1oz/25g onion, finely chopped
½tsp fresh parsley, finely chopped
pinch ground pepper
½tsp salt
1tsp wine vinegar
1tbs olive oil

Remove all the meat from the bones, chop it very finely, and trim the bones neatly. Pare the zest off the lemon, remove most of the pith, and slice the flesh thinly, removing all pips. Mix the chicken, lemon, apple, onion and parsley together, dress with the remaining ingredients and arrange on a dish. Use the bones and the lemon zest as garnishing.

PICKLED HERRING SALAD[12]

7 pickled herring fillets (rollmops)
1 large onion, finely chopped
1tbs fresh parsley, finely chopped
1tbs olive oil
1tsp wine vinegar

Chop two of the fillets and mix with the onion, parsley, oil and vinegar. Bend four of the fillets into cylinders (holding the ends together with a cocktail stick), arrange as an open square on a dish and fill with the mixture. Cut the remaining fillet into two strips and arrange like a snake between the rounds.

One of the main problems with salads was that they were largely seasonal, many of the best ingredients only being available during the summer. One solution was to use imported items such as olives and capers dressed together with oil and vinegar or as in the following.[13]

A SALAD OF PICKLED CAPERS[14]

4oz/100g capers
4oz/100g currants
2–3 small beetroots
1tbs olive oil
1tsp wine vinegar
1 lemon

Simmer the capers in their own liquor with the currants, until the latter are tender, then drain and cool, mix with the oil and vinegar and place in a dish. Slice the beetroots and lemon, cut their edges in V-shaped notches, and use to garnish the rim.

However, the growing popularity of salads led the cooks to develop ways of pickling and preserving their summer produce for winter use. The piquancy of the pickles soon led them to be used all the year round to add interesting flavours to fresh salads and other dishes, just as they are today. The following examples would have been made in all the kitchens required to serve the gentry and nobility.

BEETROOT[15]

Boil the beetroot for about 1½–2 hours until tender, cool, skin, and slice if large. Pack in jars and cover with white or malt vinegar with ½tsp salt and ½tsp peppercorns in each 1pt/600ml.

BROOM BUDS OR FLOWERS[16]

Pack the buds or flowers in layers of salt in a jar, let them stand for 24 hours, then top up with white wine vinegar (for verjuice) and seal down. Alternatively they may be pickled in a brine made of 2tsp sea salt to 1pt/600ml white wine vinegar (for verjuice).

CLOVE GILLIFLOWERS (PINKS OR CARNATIONS), ROSEBUDS ETC.[17]

Pick the flowers and put into a pickle made of 1tsp sugar dissolved in ½pt/300ml each of white wine and white wine vinegar along with 6 cloves, then seal down.

COWSLIP, VIOLET, MARIGOLD, BUGLOSS & BORAGE FLOWERS[18]

Shake 1oz/25g sugar with 1pt/600ml white wine vinegar in a jar until dissolved. Take the cowslip flowers, remove the green calyx and the green knob at their lower ends, and stir into the vinegar, seal, but stir twice daily until they settle at the bottom of the jar.

CUCUMBERS[19]

These were pickled in various ways, in brine flavoured with cucumber peelings or spare cucumbers, blanched, stuck with cloves and packed into seasoned vinegar, or flavoured with fennel or dill.

1lb/450g small cucumbers or gherkins
3oz/75g sea salt
¼pt/150ml malt vinegar or verjuice
a few sprigs or ½tsp seeds of fennel or dill

Boil the salt in ½pt/300ml water until dissolved, remove from the heat, add the vinegar, then the cucumbers, pack into jars with an inner weight on top of them to keep them submerged.

ELDER SPROUTS[20]

Gather the top 6in/15cm of the tender new shoots of elder bushes in March or April. Put into boiling water, bring to the boil, remove from the heat, and return again to the boil six times in all, then drain. Cover with a pickle made of 1tsp salt and ½tsp crushed peppercorns per 1pt/600ml malt or white wine vinegar, and seal down.

FLOWERS OF ALL KINDS[21]

Remove the stalks, calyx and any lower white parts of any flower, layer them in a jar with sugar, and top up with distilled vinegar before sealing down.

MUSHROOMS[22]

1½pt/675g button mushrooms
10 cloves
½ a nutmeg, crushed
¼tsp each ground mace & ginger
½tsp peppercorns
1tsp salt
1pt/600ml white wine vinegar

Peel the mushrooms and detach their stalks, plunge into boiling water, drain, pack into jars with the remaining ingredients and seal down.

PURSLANE STALKS[23]

The stalks and thick fleshy leaves of purslane were gathered from mid-July to August, to add a sharp and interesting flavour to salads. They were parboiled, dried on linen cloths and packed into jars with a cold pickle of 1tbs sugar boiled in 1pt/600ml white wine vinegar, and sealed down.

SAMPHIRE[24]

Pick off the coarser branches and dead leaves, put into a pan with equal parts of white wine vinegar and water, bring to the boil and simmer for 5–10 minutes until just tender. Drain, cool, pack into jars, cover with white wine vinegar and seal down.

Given the combination of these pickles with fresh salad vegetables and herbs, it was now possible to make much more decorative presentations, such as the following, dating from the 1590s.

CARROT SALAD[25]

1–2 large carrots
4oz/100g brown shrimps, cooked & peeled
1–2tbs olive oil
1–2tsp wine vinegar

Peel and chop the carrots very finely, mix with sufficient oil and vinegar to cause them to hold together, then model as a fleur-de-lis on a dish, garnishing its various parts with the shrimps.

This was only a start, however, for soon such dishes had been developed into truly impressive 'grand salads'. One of these, devised by William Rabisha, demanded both a structural base and an ornamental tower of pastry, and has already been described on page 166, above.[26] The following examples are typical.

A GRAND SALAD[27]

5 hard-boiled eggs
6 dates, in long slices
2oz/50g blanched almonds (in strips)
5 stems of rosemary
a few cocktail sticks
30 glacé or fresh cherries
5 lemons
large bowl of mixed salad herbs
2oz/50g raisins
2oz/50g currants
6 dried figs, sliced
3tbs sugar
2oz/50g capers
2oz/50g whole candied orange peel

Cut two of the eggs in half, place flat side down, stick their domed tops with a pattern of date and almond strips and set aside. Lay each rosemary stem on a chopping board, use a sharp knife to split it at three intervals along its length, insert a length of cocktail stick into each one, and stick a cherry onto each end of each stick. Slice three of the lemons in half, place five of them flat side down, and stick a rosemary stem upright into each one.

Mix the remaining salad herbs, dried fruit, almonds, sugar and half of the capers together, and lay in the bottom of a large dish. Set the lemons in the centre in a cross-shape, with a half egg between each of the outer four. Slice the remaining lemons, cut the remaining eggs into quarters, and arrange these alternately around the lemons as a circular border. Cut the orange peel into long slices (or, if unavailable, use fresh orange segments) and place alternately with small heaps of the remaining capers around the rim of the dish.

A GRAND SALAD[28]

6 figs, sliced
2oz/50g each, capers, currants & raisins
1oz/25g blanched almonds, cut in strips
4oz/100g each, cucumbers or gherkins, & small beetroots
1 small crisp lettuce, shredded
3 lemons
4oz/100g olives
2oz/50g candied orange peel
3tbs olive oil
3tsp vinegar
1tbs sugar (optional)

Arrange the figs in the centre of a dish. Mix the capers, currants and raisins with half the almonds, and arrange in a circle around the figs. Make cuts through the peel of the lemons from one end to the other, about ¼in/6mm apart at the centre, and peel off alternate strips, then cut across in thin slices. Arrange the cucumbers, gherkins, beetroots, lettuce, half the olives and half the lemon slices in segments around the capers and their neighbours. Stick

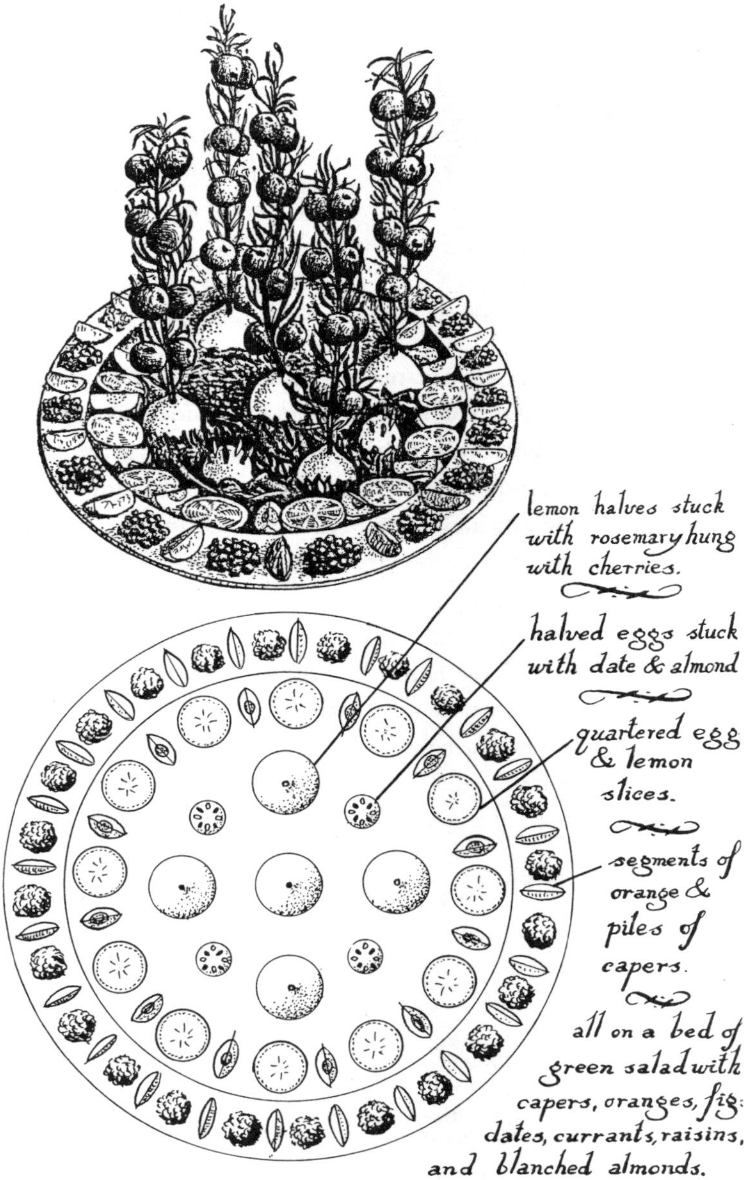

Figure 72. Robert May's Grand Salad.

the remaining almonds into the remaining olives, and alternate around the rim with the remaining lemon slices and orange peel. Beat the oil and vinegar together, pour over the food, and sprinkle with sugar if preferred.

GRAND SALAD OF DIVERS COMPOUNDS[29]

12oz/325g cold roast chicken, mutton, veal or tongue

1 onion, finely chopped	*3 oranges*
1 crisp lettuce, finely chopped	*3 lemons*
1tbs tarragon, finely chopped	*8oz/225g boiled potatoes*
2oz/50g olives	*1oz/25g raisins*
2oz/50g pickled samphire	*1oz/25g blanched almonds*
2oz/50g capers	*3tbs olive oil*
4 dried figs, quartered	*3tsp vinegar*

Cut the meat into small square slices, mix with the onion, lettuce, and tarragon, and heap in the centre of a large dish. Arrange the pickles, figs, segments of 2 oranges and 2 lemons, the diced or sliced potatoes, the raisins and the almonds in separate divisions around the sides, alternating their colours and flavours. Mix the oil and vinegar and pour over just before serving.

Perhaps the most delicate and attractive salads were those in which pickled flowers and buds were used to cover fruit dishes with floral designs which must have resembled those of contemporary stumpwork embroidery. Having set down purslane stalks to represent the stems and branches of the flowers, plain or jagged leaves cut from cucumber or gherkin were added, along with blooms made of red or pink gilliflowers (carnations), blue violets or bugloss, or yellow primroses or cowslips. These were depicted in bud, half-opened, fully blown, complete with calyxes made from purslane leaves. Such salads were not just for show, despite the hours taken in their preparation, 'for they are more excellent to taste than to look on.'[30] Other salads were used purely for decoration, being,

> made of Carret roots of sundrie colours well boiled and cut out into many shapes and proportions, as some into knots, some in the manner of Scutchions and Armes, some like Birds, and some like wilde beasts, according to the art and cunning of the workman and these for the most part are seasoned with Vinegar, Oyle, and a little pepper.[31]

ORANGES & LEMONS

Oranges and lemons had been imported from Spain from the late medieval period, but were now being grown in the most advanced gardens in Elizabethan England. Lord Burghley used Thomas Windebank to arrange for the purchase of the trees in Paris in 1561: 'I have already an orange tree, and if the price is not too much, I pray you procure me a Lemon, a Pomegranate and a myrtle tree.'

Such trees were very expensive, those housed in Henrietta Maria's orangery in early seventeenth-century Wimbledon being valued at £10 each.[32] Most people continued to buy the imported oranges sold by grocers and orange-wives through most of the year. In October and November the comfit-makers would also sell the pulp they removed from the Seville oranges when preparing the peels for candying. The pressed and strained juice was poured into bottles with a layer of olive oil on top to keep it airtight for long-term preservation.[33]

Andrew Boorde had advised that 'the Juce is a good sauce, and dothe provoke an appetyde', while the London merchant's wife described by Peter Erondell served it with her fat capon. She invited her guest to 'Take a wing of it, give here some Oranges ... Some beyond the sea did marvaile much how the Englishmen could eat their Capons without Oranges: but we should marvaile much more how they can eat their Oranges without Capons?'[34]

During the Commonwealth, when Cromwell broke off relations with Spain, both oranges and lemons became very scarce. As a result, his wife Elizabeth scolded him for wasting an orange just to sauce a loin of veal.[35]

For hot meats, oranges were also prepared as a hot sauce.

ORANGE SAUCE FOR A CAPON[36]

2 oranges, sliced	*½tsp mixed ground cinnamon & ginger*
½pt/300ml claret	*1–2tbs rosewater*

Stew the oranges in the claret and spices in a covered pan for about 20 minutes until tender, then stir in the rosewater just before serving in saucers.

In contrast, lemons made a delicious cool salad.

LEMON SALAD[37]

lemons	*icing sugar*

Make a series of cuts from one end of the lemon to the other, so that they are ¼in/6mm apart around the middle, then peel off alternate strips. Slice the lemons across very thinly, lay in a dish, decorating the rim with the strips, sprinkle with the sugar and leave for 10–15 minutes before serving.

VINEGARS

Vinegars were essential to provide sour flavours for sauces, dressings and many other dishes, as well as for making pickles. One of the most basic home-produced vinegars was called verjuice, its name coming from Old French meaning green or unripe juice. Unlike the French variety made from grapes, the English verjuice was made by crushing crab apples. As soon as their centres had turned black they were laid in a heap to sweat, had their stalks and any rotten parts removed, and were then beaten with heavy mallets in a long trough until reduced to a pulp. Having been packed into a square bag made of horsehair cloth they were then put under a press to extract their juices.[38] Many of the presses were quite simple affairs, just a large squarish slab of stone with a channel cut round its perimeter and a spout leaving from one side. Once the bag had been placed on top, a board was added, surmounted by a long lever or brake, one end fitting into a hole in an adjacent tree or wall, and the other being hung with a heavy weight to provide the necessary leverage.[39] As the juice was expressed, it was poured into barrels and kept for use. The fruit's sourness made it both an ideal accompaniment for the fatter meats, and an excellent adjective for describing anything or anyone with a sour disposition: 'Having a crabbed face of her own, she'll eat the less verjuice with her mutton,' wrote Thomas Middleton in 1626.[40]

Other vinegars were made by souring alcoholic liquors. Alegar was freshly brewed strong ale, sometimes mixed with a few handfuls of hot parched beans, salt and the yeast from ryebread dough, all barrelled up and set in the sun from May to August in order to turn sour.[41]

Some wine vinegars were economically made from wines which had turned sour by neglect or accident, these being reduced to two-thirds of their volume by boiling, then put into a barrel and left for a short time to mature. Alternatively the wine was deliberately soured, perhaps by being left in an unstopped firkin on the roof during the hot days of summer. It might also be poured into a vessel with salt, pepper and a piece of sourdough, heated by having a red-hot poker plunged into it, and again set in the sun to sour.[42] Wine vinegars were sometimes called 'winegars', as in the 1602 statement that 'The king calls for winegar to his sallet, because his sweet meate should have sower sauce.'[43]

The white wine vinegars, being the most delicate, were ideal for absorbing other tastes, the results adding delightfully subtle flavours when used to make or dress all manner of dishes. The main varieties comprised the following.

ELDER VINEGAR[44]

1pt/600ml white wine vinegar
1½oz/35g fresh or dried elderflowers, plucked off the stems of each head

Pack the vinegar and elderflowers into a jar, seal down, keep in a warm place for about a week, then strain into bottles, seal, store in a cool place for a week for the fine dregs to settle, then decant into clean bottles for use. A weaker batch of vinegar may be made from the remaining elderflowers.

ROSE VINEGAR[45]

As above, using the scented petals of damask roses, Markham demanding that those of four or five hundred damask roses should be left to soak for a month before the vinegar was poured off.

PEPPER VINEGAR[46]

As above, using 1tbs crushed black peppercorns, which may be loosely tied in a piece of muslin, and the jar regularly shaken.

There were also digestive vinegars, one soaking ¼oz/6g each of squills (sea-onions), pepper, onion, mint and juniper berries in 1pt/600ml white wine vinegar. For travellers who wished to take their vinegar with them without the weight or trouble of carrying a bottle, it could be made into dry balls to fit into the pocket. This was done by grinding either the blades of green wheat or rye, or else dried half-ripe blackberries, with strong vinegar to make a stiff paste, which was moulded and dried in direct sunlight. These could then be heated with wine to produce vinegar whenever it was needed.[47]

SAUCES

The liquids in which many foods were cooked provided flavoursome sauces appropriate to their respective dishes, but other sauces, the equivalent of today's bottled sauces and ketchups, were specially pre-prepared for more general use. In the royal and other large households these were made by a department called the saucery, that of Henry VIII using bread from the bakehouse, fifty poundsworth of mustard (seed), vinegar and verjuice, and four poundsworth of herbs.[48] These were ground, mixed, stored in jars and finally issued for use It was essential that each saucer-full of sauce was ready at mealtimes, the ordinances of Thomas, Lord Fairfax stating that; 'for the prevention of Errands, lett all Sauses be ready at the (Chamber) Door, for even one Message of Mustard will take a Man's Attendance from the Table.'[49]

MUSTARD

Of all the sauces, mustard was by far the most important in England. Mustard seeds were harvested both from the wild or 'treacle' mustard plants, and from field crops, especially those grown in Tewkesbury and Yorkshire.[50] 'His wit's as thick as Tewkesburie Mustard', cried Sir John Falstaff, describing Poins in *Henry IV*.[51] Those who were too fond of of it were warned, 'it will make you a red nose and a crimson face.'[52] To make it ready for the table the washed, drained and dried seeds were ground with a pestle and mortar, a small iron cannon-ball rolled around a wooden bowl, or a miniature mill called a mustard quern, along with a variety of liquids.

MUSTARD (CRUSHED GRAIN)[53]

4oz/100g black or white mustard seed
½–¾pt/300–450ml white wine vinegar, white wine, strong ale, verjuice, orange juice, cherry juice, milk or butter

Grind the seed, then grind with sufficient liquid to form a semi-liquid paste, then seal in jars.

FRENCH OR DIJON MUSTARD[54]

4oz/100g black or white mustard seed
1oz/25g honey
½oz/12g ground cinnamon
½–¾pt/300–450ml white wine vinegar

Follow the recipe above.

Finer mustards had the grain dried in a cool oven, ground to a fine meal, then shaken through a sieve to extract the fine flour, just the same as the commercially milled mustard powder still available today. This produced mustards of truly memorable power, which the unwary should treat with due respect.

SIR KENELM DIGBY'S STRONG MUSTARD[55]

1 large English onion
¼pt/150ml white wine vinegar
3tsp grated horseradish, or horseradish sauce
2–3tsp sugar
4oz/100g mustard powder
1tsp ground ginger
½tsp ground white pepper

Finely chop the peeled onion, soak it in the vinegar with the horseradish for at least 1 hour, but preferably much longer, then pour into a sieve over a bowl and use the back of a spoon or the fingers to press out all the juice. Mix the remaining ingredients into the juice (discarding the onion and horseradish pulps) and seal down in jars.

For smaller quantities of mustard for immediate use, the following recipe is very useful

LADY HOLMEBY'S MUSTARD[56]

4tbs mustard powder
2tbs honey
4–6tbs white wine vinegar

Mix together and use as needed. Larger quantities will keep if sealed in jars.

GREENSAUCE

Greensauce was a blend of finely ground fresh green herbs, vinegar and sufficient bread to produce a thick sauce. Its bright colour and piquancy rendered it ideal for fish, poultry, mutton or pork. Some recipes recommended mixes of betony, mint, basil, garlic and a few cloves ground with rose vinegar.[57] The principal ingredient, however, was usually common sorrel, *Rumex acetosa*, also known as greensauce, which has a refreshing, sharp taste. It was so popular that the besieged garrison of Pontefract during the Civil War sent a nine-year-old boy out of the castle to collect some for their dinner – with the result that he was 'dangerously shott in the belly'.

GREENSAUCE (1)[58]

3oz/75g sorrel
1 pippin, peeled & chopped
4oz/100g white breadcrumbs
1tsp sugar
6tbs white wine vinegar

Grind the sorrel, pippin, breadcrumbs and sugar together, adding just sufficient vinegar to form a thick ketchup-like mixture.

GREENSAUCE (2)[59]

2oz/50g sorrel
1oz/25g sage
1 hard-boiled egg yolk
4oz/100g white breadcrumbs
½tsp salt
¼tsp ground pepper
8tbs white wine vinegar

Grind all together, adding just sufficient vinegar to make a thick ketchup-like mixture.

SAUCE-ALONE

The tall hedge-weed *Sisymbrium Allaria*, otherwise garlic mustard or Jack-by-the hedge, had only to have its fresh leaves pounded to a smooth paste to make a piquant sauce, hence its name, sauce-alone. It was particularly suitable for accompanying salt fish.[60]

There was a well-established tradition of serving each different food with its particular standard sauce, the following list coming from *The Good Huswifes Handmaide to the Kitchin* of 1588.[61]

Meats
Beef: pepper & vinegar
Brawn: mustard
Capon: wine & salt
Duck: mustard & verjuice
Goose, green : sorrel sauce
Goose, stubble: mustard & vinegar
Peacock: wine & salt
Pheasant: water & salt
Rabbit: mustard & sugar
Swan: chaldron
Veal: oranges
Woodcock: mustard & sugar

Fish
Cod: greensauce
Crab: vinegar
Flounder: pike sauce
Halibut: vinegar
Herring, white: mustard
Ling: mustard
Mackerel: vinegar
Salmon, salt: mustard, verjuice & sugar
Shrimps: vinegar
Thornback: its liver, mustard, salt & pepper
Turbot: vinegar
Whiting: its liver, & mustard or verjuice

In addition to these usually cold sauces, a number of other hot sauces were made for use with particular kinds of meats, as in the following selection from the late sixteenth century.[62]

SAUCE FOR A CAPON

Claret, rosewater, sliced oranges, ground cinnamon & ginger heated and poured on the sops the capon is to stand on.

SAUCE FOR CAPON OR TURKEY

Thinly sliced onions boiled till dry added to gravy and coarsely ground black pepper.

SAUCE FOR ROAST DOVE/PIGEON

Minced onion boiled in claret until nearly dry, with vinegar, sugar, pepper, and juices from the dove/pigeon.

CHALDRON FOR A SWAN

Toasted white bread soaked in red wine, rubbed through a sieve, and boiled with sugar, ground cinnamon, ginger and pepper, and a little sugar.

SAUCE FOR MUTTON

Sliced onions stewed in verjuice with part of the almost-roasted joint minced and mixed in.

SAUCE FOR VENISON

White breadcrumbs mixed with vinegar and some of the joint's own juices, or with butter, sugar, ground cinnamon, ginger and pepper boiled together.

ONION SAUCE FOR ROAST CAPONS[63]

8oz/250g onions, thinly sliced
¼tsp ground black pepper
½tsp salt
1oz/25g white breadcrumbs
2tbs claret
juice of 1 orange
4 slices of lemon peel

Stew the onions, salt and pepper in a covered pan with ½pt/300ml water for about 45 minutes until tender. Add the remaining ingredients, stir until thick and hot, then pour over the capon after it has been broken up.

LA SAUCE POIGNANTE

When Edward Symmonds, a Royalist horsetrooper, was on campaign at Blandford in October, 1644, he devised this sauce in which to cook his mutton chops or beefsteaks in his frying-pan or pipkin over a quick fire: 'Compound the liquor of old sharpe beere; and some water, but more beere than water, a quantity of vinegar (wyne), a bunch tyed of parsley, tyme, rosemary, lemon, orange, 3 or 4 onions, cloves or other spices, store of salt.'[64]

BEATEN BUTTER

It will have been noticed that, unlike today, none of the above sauces had been thickened with flour, the English rejecting this stodgy French technique until later in the seventeenth century. If a thickened sauce was required, it was made by adding a little liquid to warm, softened butter and beating it together to form a smooth emulsion. Elizabeth Cromwell had made it by slowly melting thin slices of butter in a dish, adding two or three spoonfuls of water or vinegar, and then beating it until thick and white.[65] The best description, however, comes from Sir Kenelm Digby:

> Take two or three [table] spoons of [water or stock] into a pipkin; There must be no more, than even to cover the bottom of the pipkin. Make this boil by itself; as soon as it doth so, put to this half a pound of sweet butter, let it melt gently, or suddenly, it imports not, so as the liquor boiled, when you did put the butter in; when the butter is melted, then take it from the fire, and holding the handle in your hand, shake it round a good while and strongly, and it will come to be thick [as it cools], that you may almost cut it with a Knife. Then squeese juyce of Limon into it, or of sharp Orange, or Verjuyce or Vinegar; and heat it again as much as you please upon the fire. It will ever after continue thick, and never again, upon any heating, grow oily, though it be cold and heated again twenty times.[66]

This beaten butter, resembling a delicious mayonnaise, was used to both accompany and to garnish many different dishes. Given this and the many other sauces at their disposal, Tudor and Jacobean cooks were able to give all their dishes an even greater range of textures and flavours.

Figure 73. A first course just for show. This is Robert May's scheme for an inedible first course, which commenced with red-wine 'blood' flowing from the stag when the arrow was withdrawn, exchanges of cannon-fire between the ship and the castle, and finally the release of live birds and frogs from the pies.

CHAPTER NINETEEN

Planning Meals

What to eat, and when and where to serve each meal, were choices which individual families and sections of the community had to make in order to make the best use of their resources of income, foodstuffs and time. As in previous centuries, it was now virtually impossible to live entirely on wild plants and animals, although some of these might still supplement their everyday foods. Survival depended entirely on purposely grown herds, flocks and crops, whether raised for home consumption, or for sale to increasingly urbanized populations who earned their livings from craft or trade activities. By the middle of the sixteenth century a number of great social and economic changes were making it ever more difficult for most working families to maintain a good and varied diet. The dissolution of the monasteries had removed a source of charitable help to many of the poor, but more importantly had passed their vast estates into the hands of rapacious landlords who demanded vastly higher rents. As Bishop Latimer remembered, his father had paid an annual rental of only £3–£4 for his farm, which allowed him to educate his sons, provide dowries for his daughters, and keep 'hospitalitie for his pore neighbours and sum almes to the poore.' A few years later the next tenant had to pay £16 a year in rent 'and is not able to do anything for [his family] or geve a cup of drinke to the pore.'[1] The new landlords also found it profitable to enclose large areas of common land to increase their income, thus depriving the local cottagers of many essential resources, particularly grazing for their animals. Without their own cows, for example, they could no longer produce 'the white meats' of butter, cheese and other dairy goods which had made up a substantial part of their sustenance. Landlords also converted arable land into more profitable sheep-walks, reducing both the output of crops and the need for agricultural workers. Perhaps even more important was the debasement of the currency, leading to inflation and a rapid rise in the price of food.

For the first time, England experienced an appreciable level of unemployment, with sturdy beggars roaming the countryside and towns, openly begging and causing trouble. The poor laws of the mid-sixteenth century imposed physical punishment for vagrancy and authorized the establishment of houses of correction, but did not alleviate the basic problems. These continued through to the mid-seventeenth century, much of the population having lifestyles such as John Evelyn observed in Rutland in 1654, 'the people living as wretchedly as in the most impoverished parts of France, which they resemble, being idle and sluttish.'[2]

Many of the nobility and gentry still believed in performing one of the medieval Acts of Corporal Mercy, that of feeding the poor from their own houses. Supervised by the porter at the gate, perhaps alongside a domestic almoner, food left over from all meals was distributed to the waiting poor. In this they were following the practice of the royal household, in which 'all the said reliques and fragments be saved and gathered by the officers of the almonry, and from day to day be given to poore people at the utter court gate, by oversight of the under almoner.'[3] Others appear to have gone even further, as Richard Brome described in his play *The Joviall Crew or the Merry Beggars*, first published in 1652, but written in 1641. Master Oldrents was 'an ancient Gentleman and a great House-keeper [who kept] a Guest house for all Beggars far and neer, costs him a hundred a year, at least.' Randal, his groom, was responsible for obtaining the necessary supplies from the cook, pantler and butler, and delivering them to the old barns, where he had already:

> unloaden the Bread-basket, the Beef-kettle and the Beer-Bombards there amongst your Guests the Beggars. And they have all prayed for you ... our Master ... many from the teeth inwards 'tis enough to swallow your Alms; from whence I think their Prayers seldom come.

Meanwhile the beggars celebrated their lifestyle:

> From hunger and cold who lives more free,
> Or who more richly clad than wee!
> Our bellies are full; our flesh is warm,
> And, against pride, our rags are a charm,
> Enough is our feast, and for tomorrow
> Let rich men care, we feel no sorrow.

To Randal, as to many of his contemporaries, it was foolish to feed such beggars rather than the worthy poor. He had little appreciation for the fleas they left behind when he changed their straw for the fresh groups which arrived each night.[4]

FARM WORKERS

Most of the families of rural husbandmen and yeomen lived off the plainest of foods, as confirmed by a number of contemporary commentators:

> 'Husbandmen, and such as labour, can eat fat bacon, salt gross meat, hard cheese &c. coarse bread at all times, go to bed and labour upon a full stomach, which to some idle persons would be present death.' (1621)
> 'Browne bread … having moch branne [which] fylleth the belly with excrements, and shortly descendeth from the stomache.' (1584)
> 'White meats, milke, butter & cheese, which were woont to be accounted as one of the chief staites throughout the Iland, are now reported as food appertinent onelie to the inferiour sort.' (1577)[5]

These, with vegetables, and fruits that could be found in the locality, provided a relatively well-balanced diet, although its actual content could be subject to great regional variation. Oatmeal provided the main bread-corn and hot, sustaining porridge in the northern counties, for example, while wheat and vegetable pottages predominated further south. Their meal times however, would probably follow similar daily routines.

> The poorest sort they generally dine and sup when they may, so that to talk of their order of repast it were but a needless matter. The husbandmen dine also at high noon as they call it, and sup at seven or eight (Harrison, 1577)[6]

Such a timetable might look like this:

- 4 a.m. rise, prepare the horses and oxen;
- 6–6.30 a.m. breakfast;
- 7 a.m.–2 or 3 p.m. working in the fields, with a 30 minute break for dinner, the main meal of the day;
- 4 p.m. back to the stable, clean the horses and oxen, clean their stalls and feed all the livestock;
- 6 p.m. supper, followed by domestic chores such as dressing flax and hemp, stamping apples and crabs for cider or verjuice, grinding malt, making rushlights;
- 8 p.m. check the animals, refill their mangers, and go to bed.[7]

As stressed by Thomas Fuller in 1642, the yeoman's table bore no luxuries, just 'solid and substantial food; no servitors (more nimble with their hands than the guests with their feet) take away meat before stomachs [i.e. appetites] are taken away. Here you have that which in itself is good made better by store of it, and best by the welcome to it.' Here were 'no kickshaws [but] full dishes, whole bellyfulls.'[8]

As the agricultural year progressed, the completion of each major task was celebrated by a special meal. At the end of the corn harvest the workforce gathered at their master's house where at the hock-cart or harvest-home:

Ye shall see first the large and cheefe
Foundation of your Feast, Fat Beefe:
With Upper Stories, Mutton, Veale
And bacon (which makes full the meale)
With sev'rall dishes standing by,
As here a Custard, there a Pie,
And here all-tempting Frumetie,
And for to make the merry cheere
If smirking Wine be wanting here,
There's that which drowns all care, stout Beere.[9]

At Henry Best's East Riding farm the pea harvest ended with a meal of puddings, bacon or boiled beef, flesh or apple pies, and hot cakes which some cut up into platters of cream and scooped up with their spoons, all washed down with good ale. Those who washed his sheep were warmed with a posset of hot ale, milk, breadcrumbs, pepper and nutmeg, while his sheepshearers dined on roast mutton, with bread, ale, cheese and perhaps a cheesecake at noon. After gelding the lambs, there was a meal of testicles fried with parsley.[10] Shepherds also celebrated feasts at tables formed by cutting a trench around an area of land grass, 'With green-cheese, clouted cream, with flawns and custards stored [and] Whig, cider and thin whey' to drink, as Michael Drayton described in his *Poly-Olbion* of 1612.[11]

COUNTRY HOUSES

In the country houses of the gentry every locally grown fruit and vegetable, every farmed or wild animal, bird and fish, and most imported luxuries were readily available for the table. The meals served here were virtually identical to those of the upper and middle classes living in towns and cities. This is hardly surprising, since many prosperous families enjoyed the use of both town and country properties, regularly moving from one to another as they followed the seasonal round of hunting, assizes and assemblies. The daily timetable in a typical country house in 1626 was described in Nicholas Breton's *Fantasticks*:

- 3 a.m. milkmaids start work, the porridge pot is put on for the servants' breakfast;
- 4 a.m. milkmaids milking in the fields;
- 5 a.m. children getting up; the chickens and pigs are fed;
- 6 a.m. children at school; the housemaids set to work;
- 7 a.m. milkmaids start making butter and cheese;
- 8 a.m. breakfast;

10 a.m. upper servants set the family dining table, the cook completes her preparations and the waiters assemble; the house and yard dogs are kennelled;

11 a.m. the gates of the house are locked, the family sit down to the first course of dinner, the children having said grace; in a separate room [usually the Winter Parlour] the ploughmen, the senior farm workers, dine on porridge, a great loaf and a piece of cheese;

12 a.m. the second course is served to the family, wine poured into glasses half-filled with clean water; the final course of fruit and cheese is served, and grace said at the end of the meal; the ploughmen finish their dinner, while the farm labourers in the fields take their bread and cheese out of their bags, and start to eat.

Unfortunately he gave no details of the afternoon and evening activities, but it is probable that the family would have taken their supper around 4 or 5 p.m., and the servants, ploughmen and other staff about 6 p.m.

Within the towns, the merchant class found it most convenient to dine at noon and take their suppers at 6 p.m.[12] The course of a wealthy merchant's household day was full of a host of activities during the Elizabethan period:

6 a.m. the family rise, their servants already being at work;

7 a.m. the daughters' French tutor starts his 1 hour lesson; the merchant is in his shop, his son to school by 8 a.m.;

9 a.m. the daughters' dancing tutor starts his 1 hour lesson; the merchant and his wife may go to church;

10 a.m. the daughters' virginal tutor starts his 1 hour lesson;

10.30 a.m. or after: the wife receives guests invited to dinner, or goes shopping;

11 a.m. the butler starts preparing the dinner table in the great chamber;

12 noon–2 p.m. dinner for the family in the great chamber, and for the servants in the hall;.

Afternoon: walking, visits to gardens and the like; the daughters' lute and viol de gamba tutor comes at 4 p.m.;

6 p.m. supper;

Evening: dancing, cards, perhaps a masque;

10.30–11 p.m. all retire to bed.[13]

The dinners for this level of society comprised a selection of separate dishes served as first or second courses, their number being increased or decreased according to the number of diners. Suppers were similar, but were usually only of a single course. As William Harrison stated in 1577, the English, 'commonly begin with the most gross food, and end with the most delicate … We use also our wines by degrees, so that the hottest cometh last to the table.'[14] This is illustrated by the following menus:

A Proper New Booke of Cokerye (1545)

Dinner, first course	**Supper, first course**
Pottage	*Pottage or sewe*
Boiled or stewed meats	*Salad*
Chickens and bacon	*Pigs pettitoes*
Salt beef	*Sliced salt beef*
Pies	*Shoulder of mutton* or *breast of veal*
Goose	*Lamb*
Pig	*Custard*
Roast beef	
Roast veal	
Custard	

Dinner, second course	**Supper, second course**
Roast lamb	*Capon roasted*
Roast capons	*Coneys [rabbits] roasted*
Roast coneys [rabbits]	*Chickens roasted*
Peahens [roast]	*Pigeons roasted*
Baked venison	*Larks roasted*
Tart	*Pie of chicken or pigeons*
	Baked venison
	Tart

C. Hollyband, *The Citizen at Home* (1573)

Dinner, first course (for around 17 people)	**Wines**
[Pottage]	
Salt beef and mustard	*Malmsey*
Capon boiled with leeks	
Cabbages	
Turnips	
Leg of Mutton stuffed with garlic	

Dinner, second course	**Wines**
Larded Shoulder of Veal	
Turkey	
Ham	*Claret and water*
Venison pasty with mustard	
Minced meat pie	
Roast blackbird	
Roast larks	
Roast woodcock	
Larded partridge	
Hare with black sauce	
Boiled rabbits	
Fruit	
Roasted pears	*French wine*
Pippins	
Tarts	
Egg pies [custard]	
Cake	
Scraped cheese	

A.W., *A Book of Cookrye With the Serving in of the Table* (1591) [a repetition, for the most part, of *A Proper New Booke*, above]

Dinner, first course	**Supper, first course**
Pottage or stuffed broth	*Pottage or sew*
Boiled meat or stewed meat	*Salad*
Chickens and bacon	*Pigs pettitoes*
Salt beef	*Salt beef, sliced*
Pies	*Shoulder of mutton* or *breast of veal*
Geese	*Lamb*
Roast beef	*Custard*
Roast veal	
Custard	

Dinner, second course	**Supper, second course**
Roast Lamb	*Capons roasted*
Roast Capon	*Coneys [rabbits] roasted*
Chickens	*Chickens roasted*
Peaches	*Pie of pigeons or chickens*
Baked venison; Tart	*Baked venison; Tart*

Robert May,
The Accomplisht Cook (1660)

Dinner, first course
Oysters
Brawn and mustard
Neat's tongue and udder in stoffado
3 ducks in stoffado
Loin of mutton, roast
Venison pasty
Steak pie

Dinner, second course
A side of lamb
6 teals, 3 larded
Lambstone pie
200 asparagus
Warden pie
Flounders, marinated
Jellies, gingerbread, tarts royal

Ben Jonson,
Epigrams (1616)

Supper
Olives, capers or salad
Mutton
Hen, with lemon & wine
Coney
Partridge
Pheasant
Woodcock
Godwit, land or water rail or ruff
Pasties
Cheese
Fruit

THE ROYAL HOUSEHOLD

In the royal household of Henry VIII the servants and courtiers had breakfast just after rising, then dinner at 10 a.m. and supper at 2 p.m.[15] For the King, however, grooms arrived in his chambers at 6 a.m., to make the basic preparations of lighting fires and cleaning the rooms ready for the arrival of the chamber staff at 7 a.m. Breakfast would follow, but 'forasmuch as it is not convenient that any certain time should be prefixed for the King's goeing to dinner or supper' he had no regular mealtimes. These would have interfered with his 'walkeing, hunting, hauking or other disports.'[16] His privy kitchen was therefore required to provide dinners and suppers for Henry and his attendants as and when required. These comprised:

Dinner, first course
Pottage of flesh
Chines of beef
Rammuners (?) in stew
Venison in brewet
Red deer pestles [thighs]

Supper, first course
Pottage of flesh
Chickens, larks & sparrows, or stewed lamb with mutton chines
Legs of mutton or venison with cloves
Capons of grease

Mutton
Carp or young veal, farced
Swan, green goose, stork or capon
Coneys of grease
Fryanders, baked carp
Custard, garnished, or fritters

Coneys of grease
Pheasant, heron
Cocks, plovers or gulls
Sweet dowcets or oranges,
quinces or pippins

Dinner, second course
Jelly hippocras, cream of almonds
Pheasant, heron, bittern
Partridge, quail or
cocks, plovers or gulls
Kid, lamb or pigeons
Larks or rabbits
Snipes, pullets or chickens
Venison in fine paste
Tarts
Fritter
Fruit with powder or butter and eggs.[17]

Supper, second course
Blancmange or other dish
Kid, lamb, or pigeon
Partridge or quail
Godwits or teals, pullets
or chickens
Rabbits or larks
Tart
Fruit
Butter and eggs
Venison or other baked meats

In all there were 26 messes or dishes for dinner, and 20 for supper, far more than the king could ever eat; he would only be helped to those he wished to try, the remainder feeding those of his chamber staff who had served him at table. Other officers of the privy chamber, the masters of the household and the senior officers of the Greencloth had a more restricted range of dishes:

Dinner, first course
Beef
Mutton
Veal
Capon
Coneys
Fryandes

Supper, first course
Pottage of flesh
Mutton boiled
Mutton roast
Capons
Conies
Dowcets

Dinner, second course
Lamb, chicken, pigeon
Cocks, plovers
Tart
Fruit
Butter

Supper, second course
Lamb, chicken, rabbit
Cock, plover, teal
Tart
Fruit
Butter[18]

while the many minor officers, yeomen and grooms had:

Dinner	**Supper**
Beef	*Beef*
Veal or other roast	*Mutton roast*
Pig, goose, coney	*Lamb, coney*[19]

The dinners prepared for Elizabeth I in her privy kitchen were similar to those enjoyed by her father, but their ingredients were rather more delicate, as seen in this list for 19 November, 1571:

Dinner, first course	**Dinner, second course**
Mutton, boiled, 2f.	*Larks, 24*
Capon of grease, boiled, 1	*Snipes, 9*
Chickens, boiled, 4	*Partridges, 3*
Larks, boiled, 18	*Pheasants, 2*
Partridges, boiled, 2br.	*Coneys, 6*
Mutton, 1br.	*Pullets of grease, 2*
Beef, crop, boiled, 1	*Chicken pies, 1*
a surloin, ½	*Tart, 1*
Cignet, 1	*Fritter, 1f.*
Capon of grease, 2	*Butter, 14lb*
Veal, 8f.	*Eggs, 3q.*[20]
Mutton for aloes, 2f.	
Beef, chine, 1	
Cocks, 7	
Chickens, 9	
Plovers, 9	
Veal pies, 1	
Custard, 1	

These and other lists or menus of the period clearly demonstrate the lavish levels of food consumption and display to be found in all prosperous households. However, they appear quite modest when compared to those of the great feasts provided to entertain both monarchs and important embassies. The costs involved in entertaining Queen Elizabeth when on one of her progresses through the countryside were enormous and potentially crippling to her hosts. In many cases new suites of kitchen offices, both permanent and temporary, had to be built, armies of cooks and servants assembled, kitchen utensils and tableware borrowed or hired, and vast quantities of food brought together precisely in time for the arrival of the Queen and her huge, ravenous retinue. A four- or five-day stay in

1561 cost her hosts anything from £273–£389. In 1577, the cost might have been £577, while her three-day visit to Lord Keeper Egerton in 1602 rose to a staggering £2000.[21] James I continued to be entertained with similar magnificence. Here, for example, are the menus for his Sunday dinner and supper when he stayed at Houghton Tower in Lancashire in August 1617:

Dinner, first course
Salads
Capon, boiled
Mutton, cold
Chickens, boiled
Mutton, roast shoulder
Ducks, boiled
Veal, roast loin
Salads
Venison, roast haunch
Capon, soused
Venison pasty, hot
Turkey, roast
Veal, soused
Swan, roast & 1 for tomorrow
Chicken pie, hot
Goose, roast
Rabbits, cold
Mutton, boiled legs
Tripe pie
Veal, roast breast
Capons, roast
Salad
Beef, roast
Tongue pie, cold
Force, boiled
Herons, roast, cold
Curlew pie
Mince pie, hot
Custards
Pigs, roast

Supper, first course
Pullets
Capon, boiled
Mutton, cold
Mutton, roast shoulder
Chickens, boiled
Capon, cold
Veal, roast
Rabbits, boiled
Pullet
Turkey, roast
Venison pasty, hot
Venison, roast shoulder
Herons, cold
Beef, sliced
Umble pie
Ducks, boiled
Chickens, baked
Pullet
Neat's tongue pie, cold
Neat's tongue, roast
Salmon boiled
Curlew, baked, cold
Turkeys, baked, cold
Neat's feet
Rabbits, fried

Dinner, second course
Pheasant, hot + 1 for King
Quails, 6 for King
Partridge
Artichoke pie
Chickens
Curlews, roast
Peas, buttered
Rabbits
Duck
Plover
Red deer pie
Pig, soused
Herons, 3 roast hot
Lamb, roast
Gammons of bacon
Pigeons, roast
Made dish
Chickens, soused
Pear Tart
Pullets of grease
Tongues, dried
Turkey pie
Pheasant pie
Lyed tart
Hog's cheek, dryed
Turkey chicks, cold
Sturgeon

Supper, second course
Quails
Poults
Herons
Chickens
Pear tart
Rabbits
Peas, buttered
Made dish
Ducks
Gammon of bacon
Red deer pie
Pigeons
Wild-boar pie
Chicken
Neat's tongue, dry
Neat's tongue tart
Hog's cheek, dried
Red deer pie[22]

James's courtiers continued to entertain him with lavish feasts. In 1618 the Marquis of Buckingham arranged for Sir Thomas Edmonds, the former ambassador to France, to provide a supper 'much after the French' which cost £600.[23] The same year, in the less formal setting of Newmarket, the king and his companions each contributed a dish to a communal feast, the most memorably appropriate being Sir George Goring's representation of a carriage and horses – a huge bag pudding drawn by four huge hot brawny pigs, each bitted and harnessed with ropes of sausages![24]

Throughout the reigns of the Tudor and Stuart monarchs some of the most extravagant and impressive feasts were those designed to impress visiting

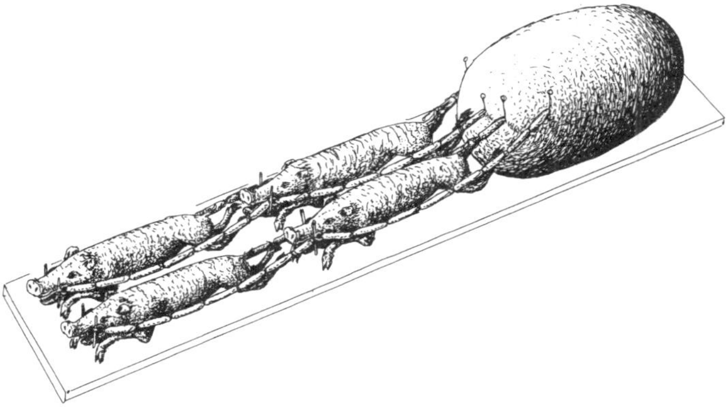

Figure 74. A dish for James I. This representation of a carriage and horses, with four cooked pigs drawing a huge bag pudding by means of links of sausages, was Sir George Goring's contribution to a feast for James I at Newmarket in 1618.

ambassadors. In January 1612, for example, it took a week to prepare the foods to be served to the French envoy, the Maréchal de Cadenet at Essex House. Forty master cooks and sixty under-cooks prepared the 1,600 separate dishes of beef, game, suckling pigs, swans, larks, salmon and other fishes. The first course, apparently of magnificent appearance and workmanship, was intended solely for show, being succeeded by a second to be enjoyed before the party proceeded upstairs for a masque followed by an elaborate banquet of sweetmeats. The ambigue, or course of cold meats, cost £300, and the banqueting stuff £500; the total cost including the wine and other extras amounting to a massive £3000.[25]

The best accounts of a Stuart first course designed to be seen rather than eaten comes from Robert May (figure 73). Its central dish was a pastry stag filled with claret and pierced by an arrow, this being flanked by piecrusts, one filled with live frogs and the other with live birds, like the 'four and twenty blackbirds' in *Sing a Song of Christmas*. At one end stood a ship in full sail, and at the other a castle, both sprouting cannon made from pasteboard tubes bound with packthread, all realistically finished in pastry and loaded with gunpowder. Both of these devices were set on great chargers full of salt, into which blown eggs full of rosewater were embedded. Once the company had taken their places a lady was requested to pull the arrow out of the stag, releasing its claret 'blood' to everyone's admiration. The guns on the castle were then fired towards the ship, which returned a broadside, both being turned round to deliver further discharges. As the candle-lit chamber was now filled with cannon-smoke, the ladies picked up the eggs and threw them at each other, to perfume the air. Believing all their dangers to be over, they began to wonder what was in the pies, which had previously had their top crusts cut around their edges to serve as lids. On the lids being lifted, the table and the floor were filled with leaping frogs, while the birds instinctively flocked around the candles, the only source of light, which they rapidly extinguished. All this made 'the Ladies to skip and shreek' and offered ample opportunity for the gentlemen to fumble where they wished. At length, the candles were re-lit, order restored, the dishes, frogs and birds turned out, and the second course of the banquet brought in with music. Having thus started the party, 'every one with much delight and content rehearses their actions in the former passages'[26]

WEEKDAY MEALS

The course of every week was punctuated by the serving of different foods. In most households the Christian prohibition of manual work on Sunday meant that there was more time available in which to prepare and enjoy a good dinner. It would also provide a welcome antidote to having been preached at in an uncomfortable cold church for an hour or more beforehand. As shown by the accounts of the Willoughby family more meat was consumed on Sunday than on any other day, even though no additional guests were being entertained.[27]

In the opening decades of the sixteenth century the full calendar of feast-days, fasts and fish-days of the Catholic church continued medieval practice. When totted up, almost half the days of the year were subject to dietary restrictions. Every Friday (the day of the crucifixion), Saturday (dedicated to the Virgin Mary), and Wednesday (when Judas accepted the thirty pieces of silver), was marked by abstinence from meat. On Fridays, as an additional penance, dinner was the only meal of the day. On Ember Days – the Wednesdays, Fridays and Saturdays following the first Sunday in Lent – on Whitsunday, Holy Cross Day (14 September) and St Lucia's Day (13 December), meat was forbidden, but dairy produce allowed. The great fasts of the year, however, were Lent, from Ash Wednesday to Easter, and Advent, which started on the fourth Sunday before Christmas. During all these days and weeks, fish was largely used as a substitute for meat, anyone discovered to have eaten extra meat being subject to punishment. At least, that was the usual practice. However, as John Skelton recorded in his criticism of the senior clergy:

> Howe some of you [bishops] dothe eate
> In Lenten season fleashe meate,
> Fesauntes, partryche and cranes;
> Men call you therefore prophanes.
> Ye pyke no shrympes nor pranes,
> Saltfysshe, stockfyssh nor herynge

It is not for your werynge –
Nor in holy Lenton season
Ye will neyther beanes nor peason,
But ye loke to be let lose
To a pygge or to a goose
Your gorge nat endued
Without a capon stued.
Or a stewed cocke
Under her surfled smocke
And her wanton wodicocke.[28]

It might have been expected that most of the fast- and fish-days would have been swept away, along with the monasteries, chantries and other institutions of Catholicism, at the Reformation, but this was not the case. The economic and political value of fish-days was far too important. In a statute of 1563 it was stressed that their continuance was 'not for any superstition to be maintained,' none the less, every Wednesday and Saturday was to be a fish-day unless they fell in the weeks of Christmas and Easter.[29] This would not only promote the fisheries, but also shipbuilding and the training of mariners for naval use. It also cut down on the consumption of cattle, a single fish-day a week sparing an estimated 135,000 head of beef each year.[30] Anyone found to have eaten meat on a fish-day was subject to a fine of £3 or three months' close imprisonment. The only exceptions were for the chronically sick, who might obtain a special licence from one of the clergy, or others who paid a set fee annually into support the poor of their parish: £1 6*s*. 8*d*. for peers, 13*s*. 4*d*. for knights and 6*s*. 8*d*. for those of lesser rank. The selling of meat on the prohibited days was also subject to punishment. When a wife of Hammersmith delivered a couple of pigs to a Smithfield carpenter in 1552, the authorities had them ridden through the City markets, each wearing a necklace of trotters, and a pig slung across their breast.[31]

Even with such penalties, it proved difficult to maintain two fish-days in every week and the Wednesday restrictions were lifted in 1585.[32] A further act in 1593 confirmed that anyone found eating fish on a fish-day should be fined £1, or a month in prison, while anyone who failed to inform on an offender was to be fined 13*s*. 4*d*.[33] The Lenten and Advent restrictions still remained in place, and it is easy to sympathize with all those who were subject to dine on nothing but second-rate cheap fish for weeks on end.

While [Advent] hast be within our house
We ete no puddinges ne no souse,
But stinking fish not worth a louse; ...

There was no fresh fish ferre ne nere;
Salt fish and samon was to dere;
And thus we have had hevy chere …
Thou has us fedde with plaices thinne,
Nothing on them but bone and skinne;
Therefore our love thou shalt not winne …
With muskelles gaping after the moone
Thou hast us fedde at night and noone
But ones a weke, and that too soone; …
Farewell fro us, both all and sam.[34]

For those with sufficient means, the fare could be much better. Henry VIII selected nineteen meat-free dishes for his first course at dinner with a further fifteen for his second. His fish included porpoise, salmon, sturgeon, halibut, lampreys, crabs, lobsters and shrimps, while his ordinary domestic servants had ling, cod, plaice and whiting.[35] The following menu of 1638 illustrates the range of dishes which might be served for a dinner on fish-days, fast-days, Ember Weeks and Lent:

First course	**Second course**
A dish of butter	*Carp, boiled*
Rice milk	*Eels, spitchocked*
Buttered eggs	*Stockfish, fried*
Oysters, stewed	*Eels, boiled*
Rocket or gurnard, boiled	*Baked puffs*
Salad of herbs, boiled	*Eels, roast*
Pike, boiled	*Parsnips, buttered*
Loaves, buttered	*Oysters, fried*
Ling or stockfish chuets [chewets]	*Blancmange in frying-pan*
Another salad	*Rocket, fried*
Trouts or smelts, stewed	*Oyster pie*
Stockfish, buttered	*Smelts, fried*
Salt eel or salt herring	*Pippin pie*
Jole of ling	*Flounders, fried*
Skirret pie	*Crabs, buttered*
Flounders or plaice, buttered	*Skirrets, fried*
Eel or carp pie	*Spinach or carrot tart*
Haddock, fresh cod or whiting	*Conger eel*
Salmon, salt	*Lobster or prawns*
Custard	*Oysters, pickled*[36]

The prohibition of suppers on Fridays, the eves of the major feasts, Wednesday and Saturdays in Ember Weeks and in Lent was still followed in the royal household and those of the peerage and gentry into the 1630s. Most others appear to have gradually abandoned this practice, unsurprisingly considering their hard manual labour, but an attempt to revive it was made during the food shortages of 1630. By royal proclamation neither families nor public houses were to have suppers on any of these days. In London, all City Company feasts were to be cancelled, half of the resulting savings to be given to the poor.[37]

CALENDAR CUSTOMS

The observance of the major feasts of the Christian church continued to be celebrated after the Reformation, only being temporarily suppressed during the Commonwealth. Most of them saw little change from the usual everyday diets, as restricted by the various fast- and fish-days. The major exception, however, was Christmas, which probably started on St Thomas's Day, 21 December, when the poor traditionally begged corn to make frumenty. Festivities commenced on Christmas Eve and continued for the twelve days up to Epiphany on 6 January, with every prosperous home providing hospitality for its friends and neighbours, both rich and poor, on most days. In 1507, for example, the Duke of Buckingham entertained 95 gentry, 107 yeomen or valets and 97 grooms for dinner on Christmas Day, with a further 84, 114 and 92 respectively for supper, a total of 589 meals.[38] Similar hospitality, on proportionally lesser scales, was provided in other houses, down to farmhouses where neighbours were feasted on:

> Good bread and good drink, a good fire in the hall,
> Brawn, pudding, and sowse, and good mustard withall.
> Beef, mutton and pork, shred pies of the best,
> Pig, veal, goose and capon, and turkey well drest,
> Cheese, apples and nuts, joly carols to hear
> As then in the country, is counted good cheer.[39]

This description of 1577 includes a number of dishes which had already become strongly associated with Christmas. Brawn (the soused shoulder of a boar), or a boar's head, from farmyard animals at this date, were regularly being served as a first course, accompanied by saucers of mustard. So too were roast geese and turkeys, suckling pigs and, if available, venison pasties.[40] The shred pies, otherwise called mince pies or Christmas pies, were made with minced meat flavoured with dried fruits and spices. Their crusts were so thick that it was 'as easy to win a Towne ... as to make a breach in the wall of a Christmas Pie.'[41]

The remaining contents of the Christmas meals, especially the larger ones served on Christmas Day, New Year's Day and Twelfth Night, were made up of dishes which might be seen on any ordinary dinner table. The menus given by Robert May, for example, have first and second courses of some twenty dishes of various meats, tarts, pies, jellies and custards. With the exception of Christmas Day itself, when meat would always be eaten, all the other weekly fish-days had to be observed throughout the whole of the twelve days.

Providing extra meals at this bleak midwinter period could stretch the resources of even wealthy households, but supplies of poultry and other useful foods were often brought in by the tenantry, either as boon-rents or gifts. In 1575, George Gascoigne had explained how, when '...tenants come to pay their quarter's rent, / They bring some fowls at Midsummer, a dish of fish in Lent; / At Christmas a capon, at Michaelmas a goose; / And somewhat else at New-Year's tide, for fear their lease fly loose.'[42] Abraham Cowley remembered how the tenants:

> ... used in the former days to fall
> Prostrate into your landlord in his hall,
> When with low legs and in an humble guise,
> Ye offered up a capon-sacrifice
> Unto his worship at New-Year's tide
> while Bishop Hall stressed how;
> Yet must he haunt his greedy landlord's hall
> With often presents at ech festivall;
> With crammed capons ev'ry New Yeares morne,
> Or with green-cheeses when his sheep are shorne.[43]

Similarly, the fathers of the young gentlemen who acted as serving men would 'gratifie their master's kindness at Christmas with a New Yeare's Gyft, at other festivall times with Pigg, Goose, Capon, or other such like household provision'. Courtiers and upper servants also exchanged New Year's gifts with their monarch, those from the master cooks to Queen Elizabeth usually being displays of culinary skill. In the 1570s–80s, for example, John Smythson presented her with marchpanes with a castle and with St George in the middle, and a 'fair pie of quinces orangeado'.[44]

Twelfth Night was celebrated with great ceremony in royal and noble households, this being one of the rare occasions when the sovereign or the lord and his lady dined in the hall. In the opening decade of the sixteenth century they sat on the dais at separate tables beneath the cloth of estate, here to take their suppers with all the usual formalities. The major difference, however, was that they were each served with their own wassail cake and a standing cup of wassail, and were provided with lively entertainment supervised by their master of the revels. This included dances by male and female disguisers, a morris dance and performance by men issuing from a large mock tower, and dances by the attending ladies and gentlemen, all accompanied by the household minstrels. The chapel choir also sang in the wassail, followed by carols.[45]

Similar ceremonies were being celebrated a century later, as recorded in Ben Jonson's *Christmas, His Masque* of 1616. Its introductory procession included 'Minced-pie', accompanied by a page 'bearing a browne bowle, drest with Ribbands, and Rosemarie'. As Robert Herrick explained:

> This I you tell, is our jolly Wassell,
> And for Twelfe-night more meat too ...
> Next crowne the bowle full
> With gentle lambs-wool;
> Adde sugar, nutmeg and ginger,
> With store of ale too;
> And thus ye must doe
> To make the wassaile a swinger.[46]

'Baby-Cake' was accompanied by an usher carrying,

> ... a great Cake with a beane, and a Pease';
> Now, now the mirth comes,
> With a cake full of plums,
> Where the beane's the king of the sport here.[47]

In Sir Robert Wroth's house, as in countless others across the country, his 'open hall' was filled with music, mirth and cheer as,

> The rout of rural folk come thronging in,
> (Their rudeness then is thought no sin)
> Thy noble spouse affords them welcome grace ...
> The jolly wassail walks the hall often round,
> And in their cups, their cares are drowned.[48]

RITES OF PASSAGE

Strongly held religious beliefs ensured that every birth, marriage and death was marked by a formal public service in church or chapel. This was deemed essential for the eternal life of the soul. However, to serve immediate temporal needs and aspirations, food was usually provided for the participants and their guests. At christenings, for example, early Tudor nobles set up pantries and cellars in the side-aisles of churches, so that kneeling gentlemen could bear laden spice-plates and wine cups to the officiating clergy and godparents, while a similar 'void' was being served to the other guests. A feast would follow back at the house.[49] The expenditure on the spices and other banqueting stuff could be considerable. In 1617 the steward of the Shuttleworth family purchased ten varieties of comfit, six varieties of fruit 'plates', plus suckets, biscuits, marchpane stuff, wines and caudel spices in London. Costing £5 2*s*. 4*d*., they were to be served 'at the tyme of my Mistress lying in child bedd'. In contrast, the ale and bread given for Widow Sonkie's childbirth celebrations cost a total of 3*s*. 8*d*.[50] Such fare was typical in lesser families. When trying to repulse a ravenous mob as it attempted to enter the palace after Princess Elizabeth's christening, a porter cried:

> ... You must see christenings?
> Do you look for Ale and Cakes heere, you rude Raskalls?'[51]

At early Tudor royal weddings the bride was fortified with wine and spices in the great chamber before her departure to the church. Here, after the service, cups of sops of white bread soaked in hippocras were handed round, before everyone returned to the palace for a dinner followed by dancing.[52] The household accounts of many noble and gentry families show that in their households too the wedding feast was one of the most lavish and expensive they would ever provide. When Elizabeth Nevile married Roger Rockley in 1526, her father lavished £16 11*s*. 4*d*. on their black velvet and satin wedding clothes, £10 on ale and wine, £2 16*s*. 8*d*. on wheat for bread and pastries, and £46 5*s*. 8*d*. for meat and fish, a total expenditure of £95 13*s*. 8*d*. The dinner served after the service was of thirty dishes. The first course opened with brawn and mustard served with malmsey, before moving on to venison, peacock, swan, pike, flampoints, fritters and the like, then a second course which included crane, heron, bittern, a great sturgeon, a whole baked roe deer, red deer, fallow deer, and finally apples and cheese strewn with sugar and sage. The dark January evening was enlivened with a play, then a masque, and a supper of a further 110 dishes all of meat, followed by dancing. The party did not break up until a week later, having consumed, among much else, 12 peacock, 252 rabbit, 366 mallard and teal, 15 deer, 2 oxen, a seal and a porpoise.[53] Such massive hospitality was typical of most prosperous Tudor and early Stuart households.

Since their ingredients were included in the general expenditure for foodstuffs, bridecakes rarely appear in the accounts, but they formed an important part of the celebrations. Robert Herrick described how milkmaids gossiped about,

> [the] talk of Brides; and who shall make
> That wedding-smock, this Bridal-cake ...
> That done we'l draw lots, who shall buy
> And guild the Baies and Rosemary ...
> And how the posset shall be made
> With Cream of Lillies (not of Kine).[54]

The bridecakes, huge ovals of fruited, sweetened and spiced bread, such as the Countess of Rutland made for the wedding of her daughter, Lady Chaworth (see p. 135) are shown in Joris Hoefnagel's painting *A Wedding Feast at Bermondsey* of *c.* 1570. Supported within napkins tied around the necks of two maids and two men, the four cakes lead the procession of musicians, a man brandishing the silver bride-cup of gilded rosemary and the bridal party. This is just as described in Thomas Deloney's *Pleasant History of John Winchcombe* of 1626, where the bride is led to the church with,

> a fair bride-cup of silver and gilt carried before her: wherein was a goodly branch of Rosemary gilded very faire, hung around with silken ribands of all colours: next was there a noyse of Musicians ... after her came all of the chiefest maydens ... some bearing great Bride Cakes, and some Garlands of wheate finely gilded.

Around the 1630s or '40s John Aubrey observed that in his native Wiltshire the bridecakes were stacked one upon another on the dinner table, the bride and groom kissing over them at the end of the meal.

The dinner might also include a specially made bride-pie, one of the most exotic products of the pastry. Robert May's version was a huge affair with concentric wells of lobed piecrusts all set on a single base, each containing a different filling. The centre one was baked hollow to receive live birds or snakes to startle the guests around the table, while others included ingredients such as the testicles of cocks and lambs, oysters and other tidbids, to enhance its aphrodisiac qualities.[55] Finally, at bed-time, came the wedding posset 'which is a kind of caudle, a potion made up of milk, wine, yolks of eggs, sugar, cinnamon, nutmeg and other spices'. This was presented to the young couple, who swallowed it as quickly as possible so that they might turn the guests out of their bedroom, and finally spend their first night together without further interruption.[56]

A similar level of entertainment was provided for those attending the funerals of wealthy individuals, mourners of any social standing being invited back to the house for one of the meals described by Henry Machin in the 1550s as 'a gret dener'.[57] For the poor, the will of the deceased often made provision for doles of bread, or perhaps of cakes and ale, to be distributed at the funeral.

Such provisions of food did not mark the end of the obsequies, for further communal meals were provided afterwards, often a week or a month after the funeral. In her will of 1544 Margaret Atkinson of London ordered that two dozen of bread, two gammons, three shoulders of mutton, two rabbits and 128 pints of ale should be set up on a table in the middle of her parish church on the following Sunday. This was to be partaken in her memory by both the rich and the poor. At the mass celebrated a month after the funeral, on the menning day or month's mind, similar meals were often provided. Robert Fabyan's will of 1511 instructed his executors to serve bread, roast ribs of beef, mutton, cheese and ale. Twenty-four poor people in his parish of Theydon Garnon in Essex were each to be given a piece of beef and mutton, a wooden platter and a wooden spoon.[58] Such hospitality in the churches was eventually to be swept away, however, due to the changes brought about by the Reformation and protestant legislation.

In the early seventeenth century, the magistrates of the West Riding of Yorkshire, along with others elsewhere, instructed that their order banning all wakes, feasts, help-ales and the like should be read out in all the churches and chapels where they had formerly been held.[59] In 1644 May games and maypoles were banned. In Canterbury, the banning of Christmas Day and all other superstitious festivals in 1647 had led to a riot, but by an order of parliament on 24 December 1652 it was proclaimed nationally,

> no Observation shall be had of the five and twentieth day of December, commonly called CHRISTMAS DAY; nor any solemnity used or exercised in Churches upon that day in respect thereof.[60]

This ban was abhorred by the bulk of the population, who ridiculed its sanctimonious, self-righteous display of repressive piety in verses such as these, published in 1656:[61]

> Christ-mass? give me my beads; the word implies
> A plot, by its ingredients, beef and pyes.
> The cloyster'd steaks with salt and pepper lye
> Like Nunnes with patches in a monastrie,
> Prophaneness in a conclave? Nay, much more,
> Idolatrie in a crust! Babylon's whore
> Rak'd from the grave, bak'd by hanches, then
> Serv'd up in coffins [crusts] to unholy men;
> Defil'd, with superstition, like the Gentiles
> Of old, that worship'd onions, roots and lentiles!

CHAPTER TWENTY

The Buttery and the Pantry

All the drinks and bread to be served at table had to be brought in from the cellars and bakehouse ready for service into the hall and chambers. Both required an office at the lower end of the hall, where they could be assembled, prepared, and issued at specific times and in specified quantities. Because of their physical attributes, drinks being wet and bread dry, it was often convenient to use the respective offices for other items which were best kept in wet or dry conditions, but this depended on the scale and practices of individual households. In royal palaces, for example, there was a separate office to serve each aspect of table-service, while in smaller houses the roles of the buttery and pantry were often combined within a single small room.

In the early sixteenth century the royal butteries were supervised by a sergeant of the cellar, who was responsible for overseeing three separate departments, commencing with the cellar itself. Here the casks of wine purchased by the purveyors, or received as gifts, were stored in the privy cellar, if for the King, or the great wine cellar if for general use. Having been set up horizontally on their stands or stillages, they were checked every day by a groom grobber, only being tapped by a yeoman tryer under the supervision of a clerk comptroller. Using a tarrier or augur, a hole would be bored in a slightly upwards direction some three inches above the bottom of the end of the cask and a cannel or bung-tap driven into it. A small spile-pin was then inserted into a gimlet hole in the top of the cask, to allow air to enter as the wine was drawn off by another servant, the tryer, who delivered it to the bar at the cellar door.

The ales and beer were controlled by a second department, the buttery. Having tasted these drinks and approved their quality at the brewhouses, the purveyors supervised the groom versours as they set up the barrels on their stillages in the privy buttery for the King, or the great buttery for general use. From here supplies were run off as required and delivered to the buttery bars.

The third department was called the pitcher house, responsible for carrying all the wines and ales and beers from their respective offices up to the hall and chambers. Each morning, its staff had to collect all the drinking vessels that had been used in the palace the previous day, count them, wash them, dry them on

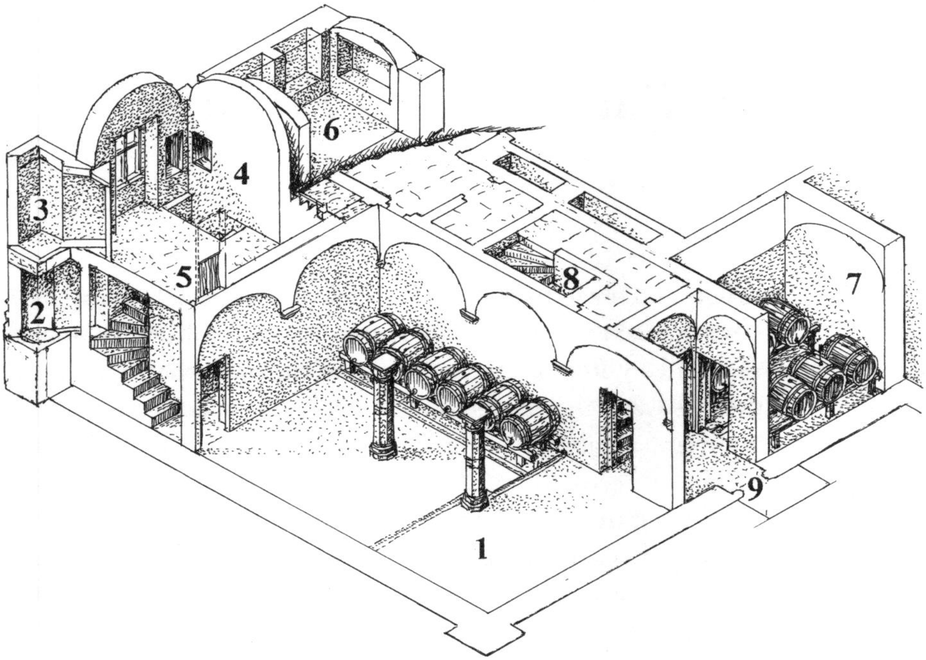

Figure 75. The cellars, buttery & pantry, Bolsover Castle, 1613. These were ingeniously planned to provide maximum efficiency and security for the Castle's staff, its drinks, and tablewares. (1) the great beer cellar; (2 & 3) close-stool closets; (4) the buttery; (5) the buttery bar in the hall; (6) the pantry; (7) the wine cellar; (8) stairs from the wine cellar to the hall dais & the chambers; (9) service entry to the cellars.

worn-out cloths provided by the Ewery, and re-distribute them into the hall and chambers.[1] The same departments continued to serve the courts of the later Tudor and early Stuart monarchs, with little change.[2]

In most noble houses, where scores rather than hundreds dined every day, the same duties were performed by a smaller staff. At Lord Montagu's Cowdray House, Sussex, the yeoman of the cellar had control of the wines, beers and drinking vessels, keeping records of their use and inventories of their content for submission to the clerk of the kitchen. He had to set the silver in place on the cupboard before meals, guard it while serving the wines during the meals, and return it to his service-room, here called 'the spicery', for washing and cleaning. The yeoman of the buttery assisted in these duties, being particularly concerned with 'the pewter pottes, tynne jugges, jackes, tubbes' and other vessels in the buttery, along with the issue of drinks into the hall. One of his other responsibilities was to provide refreshment at the buttery bar for any visitors arriving between mealtimes, always ensuring that none of the household servants tried to obtain unauthorized drinks.[3]

One unexpected role of the buttery was that of a reception-room for visitors who arrived between mealtimes. When a number of gentlemen came to a house in Richard Brome's *The Joviall Crew* of 1652, they were met by the usher, who took them to the buttery, where the butler asked,

> Please yee draw nearer my Office, and take a morning Drink in a Cup of Sack, if it please you ... Or perhaps you had rather drink White wine and Sugar. Please yourselves Gentlemen; here you may taste all Liquors ... Or had you rather take a Drink of Brown Ale with a Toast, or March Beer with Sugar and Nutmeg? or had you rather drink drink without Sugar.

Having decided on 'a Cup of your Household-Beer', the guests were next welcomed by the cook,

> Welcome Gentlemen! Brother Butler, lay a Napkin, I'll fetch a cut of the Surloyn to strengthen your patiences till my Master comes, Sirs, the Cook drinks to you.[4]

In *Twelfth Night* Maria, the waiting-gentlewoman, asks the recently arrived Sir Andrew Aguecheek, 'I pray you bring your hand to the Buttry bar, and let it drink', in allusion to this widely accepted custom.[5]

The yeoman of the pantry at Cowdray was entirely responsible for receiving bread from the bakehouse, recording, storing and preparing it, and issuing it into the hall and chambers. Just as important, however, was the care and setting out of the silver salts, plate trenchers, spoons and knives for his lordship's table, presumably as well as for those of lesser quality used in the hall. He too was to entertain strangers arriving at the buttery bar, providing bread, probably with cheese or cold meats, to accompany the yeoman of the buttery's wine, ale or beer.[6]

At Sir Francis Willoughby's Wollaton Hall, Nottingham, in 1572, the cellar, buttery and pantry were all placed under the supervision of a 'butler', rather than a number of yeomen. In addition to collecting, recording and distributing wines, ales, beer and bread, he was required to wash all the silver tableware and the cups with clean water twice a day, and keep the jacks used for serving drinks into the hall 'from furring and unsweet savour'. He was to provide and lay the table-linen in the chambers, while his under-butler did the same in the hall, also entertaining 'strangers of credit' at the buttery bar. Sir Francis's household regulations are of particular interest, since they specify the hours when the buttery bar was to open: from 8 to 9 a.m. it served breakfast, from 10 to 11 a.m.

Figure 76. The cellar and buttery. These woodcuts from the Roxburgh Ballads show a cellarer – and rats – in a typical cellar, and a range of the cups and tankards which would have been stored in the buttery.

for dinner, from 2 to 3.30 p.m. for drinkings and supper, and from 5 to 9 p.m., but was closed at all other times.[7]

As casks of wine, ale and beer were heavy, difficult to move, and had to be kept cool to reduce the risk of damaging secondary fermentations, it was essential that they should be stored in cellars. If the subsoil was dry and naturally well drained these might be set underground. However, many were either half-set into the earth, or placed at ground level, acting as a basement for butteries, pantries, or other rooms above. Their floors were frequently given a slight slope, with drainage channels below the positions intended for the barrel-taps, so that they could be readily washed down, and allow all accidental spillages to quickly run away. In some cellars short, low plinths projecting from the bases of the walls still survive, these being built to support a pair of long parallel beams, the stillages or stillings which supported rows of casks end-on, a foot or two above floor level. Elsewhere the stillages were entirely of wood, being mounted on short, stout posts or legs. If possible, the walls were pierced by small windows, just sufficient to give minimal natural daylight and ventilation, but still keeping out the hot rays of the sun. There might also be a number of small niches, handy for keeping taps, bungs, spiles, mallets, wedges and lanterns ready for immediate use. External doorways had to be wide enough for barrels to pass through, as at Cowdray House and Wollaton Hall. However, if not built that way, it was an easy task for a mason to cut back their jambs to produce an opening of sufficient width, as at Raglan Castle. Internal doors, meanwhile, needed to be only some 3–4 feet (90cm–1.2m) wide, just sufficient for the passage of the cellar staff bearing their tankards, black-jacks and flagons. Since wine was to be served in the chambers off the upper end of the hall, it was best to arrange for the wine cellar to lie beneath these rooms, its staircase emerging just where needed at chamber level.

WINES

The wines of this period were not 'vintage', but quite new, anything over eighteen months old being described as 'old', probably best used for making vinegar. The most popular, at the cheaper end of the market, were imported from Bordeaux, being described as either red wine, white wine, or claret, the latter, having a light amber to bright red colour, being considered the best. As Gervase Markham advised:

> See that in your choice of Gasconie wines, you observe that your Claret wines be fair coloured, and bright as a Ruby, not deep as an Amethyst: for though it may show strength, yet it wanteth neatness, also let it be as sweet as a Rose or a Violet, and in any case let it be short, for if it be long, then in no case meddle with it.

Dry white Rhenish wine, described by William Turner as 'small, white' in 1568, cost a little more, but was not as popular as the sack first imported in the early sixteenth century. This stronger Iberian dry, amber wine varied in quality according to its place of origin, that coming from the Canaries and the Xeres region of Andalusia being held in greatest repute. As Dr Venner described in 1622:

> Canary is of some termed sweet sack, yet improperly, for it differeth not only from sack in its sweetness and pleasantness of taste, but also in colour and consistence; for it is not so white nor so thin as sack, wherefore it is more nutritive than sack.[8]

The sack from Xeres was similarly superior, giving its name to the sherry-sack so beloved of Shakespeare's Sir John Falstaff. It was drunk cold, but when heated

Figure 77. The great wine cellar, Hampton Court Palace. Sir Hugh Askew shown as depicted on his monumental brass of 1562 at Bootle, Cumbria, was yeoman of the cellar to Catherine of Aragon, Henry VIII and Edward VI. Henry claimed 'I had the best wine when he was ith cellar: he is a gallant wine Taster.' He fought for the King at the battle of Pinkie Cleugh near Musselburgh, and at the siege of Boulogne in 1544.

it became 'burnt sack', or 'mulled sack'.[9] The stronger and heaviest wines, the sweet amber muscatels from Crete and Iberia, the sweet yellowish or amber malmseys from Greece, Crete, Smyrna and the Charneco from near Lisbon, among others, continued to be used both when banqueting, and as cooking ingredients when rich syrups were to be made.[10]

The cellar and buttery staff had not only to know how to keep their wines in good condition, but also how to doctor or improve them if they fell out of condition. This usually involved concoctions of egg white, brine, milk, rice, dregs, apples, or stewed damsons or bullaces.[11] Fruit wines and infused spirits such as usquebath (whisky) were largely the province of the lady of the house, who would

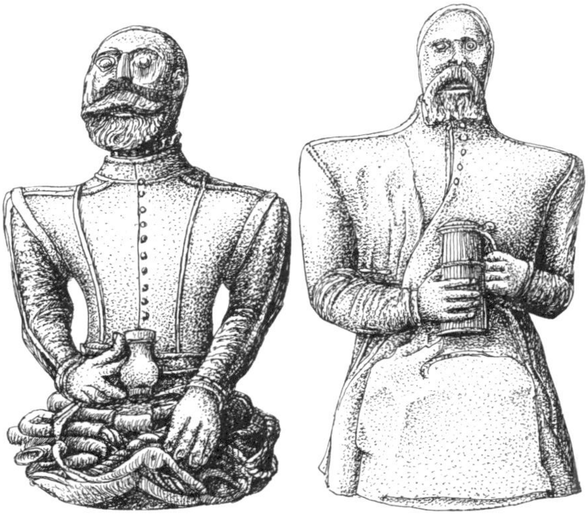

Figure 78. The buttery staff. These figures of officers of the royal buttery, now known as 'Gin' and 'Beer', date from c. 1550–1580. They are believed to have been carved for the buttery at Greenwich Palace.

prepare them in her stillhouse, but the cellar and buttery would have been expected to produce a number of sweetened and spiced wines for the household.

Hippocras, the sweet, spiced digestive liqueur of the medieval period, continued its popularity as an appetizer and as an accompaniment to the banquet course. It also became particularly associated with wedding feasts, for example when it was drunk by James I and Anne of Denmark.[12] Although it could be purchased, it was usually home-made just before being used, various combinations of spices being infused in either red or white wine for up to four days, then carefully filtered to clarity by being passed through one or more conical flannel filter-bags. These reputedly resembled the sleeves of Hippocrates, the ancient Greek physician. The recipes all contain cinnamon, ginger, cloves, peppercorns and sugar, along with more subtle flavourings, all in quantities which, given the strength of modern spices, would make the hippocras undrinkably strong. Even by halving the spicery, as in the following versions, it is still extremely well-flavoured and sweet.

HIPPOCRAS (METHOD)

Soak the various combinations of spices given below in 1pt/600ml white wine, Rhenish or claret in a lightly corked bottle for 1 to 4 days, then pour the settled and relatively clear liquid through a coffee filter-paper (as a substitute for the traditional flannel filter-bags).

Since modern sugar is highly refined, it may be stirred into the wine after filtering, rather than before, and the hippocras then either drunk immediately, or bottled for long-term storage in a cool place.

SWEET HIPPOCRAS[13]

1tsp cinnamon
2 cloves & 2 peppercorns, bruised
1tsp ginger
2oz/50g sugar

ROSE HIPPOCRAS[14]

2tsp cinnamon
¼tsp peppercorns & ½ a nutmeg, bruised
½tsp mace
½tsp ginger
1oz/25g sugar
a few rosemary flowers (or bruised leaves)
petals of 1 red rose

CREAM HIPPOCRAS[15]

3tsp cinnamon
¼tsp cloves
1tsp mace
2tsp ginger
1 peppercorn & ½ a nutmeg, bruised

Add 6oz/175g sugar and ½pt/300ml cream after filtering, and drink within the following day.

ROSEMARY HIPPOCRAS[16]

1tsp cinnamon
1tsp nutmeg
2 peppercorns, bruised
1tsp ginger
¼tsp cloves
a few sprigs of bruised rosemary
4oz/100g sugar

Gervase Markham used the same method to convert cider or perry into 'Rhenish wine'.

'RHENISH WINE'[17]

1pt/600ml cider or perry
dried peel of half a lemon
½tsp each cinnamon, mace & ginger
¼tsp cloves

Another sweetened wine was called raspis. Andrew Boorde stated, 'All maner of wynes be made of grapes, excepte respyse, whiche is made of a bery.'[18]

This was nothing more than an infusion of raspberries in white wine, easy to make, refreshing, and popular up to the middle of the seventeenth century.

RASPIS[19]

1lb/450g raspberries *4oz/100g sugar*
1pt/600ml Rhenish wine: hock

Using the back of a wooden spoon, crush the raspberries in a basin, mix with the wine, cover and leave in a cool place for two days. Pass the liquid through a filter-paper into a bottle, add the sugar, shake until dissolved, lightly cork, and leave in the cool for about a week to allow the sediment to settle. Decant the clear into a sterilized bottle, cork, and keep until required.

Since wines were delicious, relatively expensive, imported from exotic countries, stimulating, intoxicating, and appeared in rich, transparent colours in their drinking-glasses, they were the defining drink of the upper classes. However, their excessive consumption caused major problems. As Sir Walter Raleigh warned, it was essential to,

> Take especial care that thou delight not in wine, for there was not any man that came to honour or preferment that loved it; for it transformeth a man into a beast, decayeth health, poisoneth the breath, destroys natural heat, brings a man's stomach to an unnatural heat, deformeth the face, rotteth the teeth, and to conclude, maketh a man contemptible, soon old, and despised of all wise and worthy men.[20]

Fynes Morrison agreed, for 'in generall the greater and better part of the English hold all excess blameworthy, and drunkenness a reproachful vice.'[21] Many vulgar citizens, artisans, soldiers and gentry were inveterate drinkers. Even princes were diverted by the rich selection available for their delight:

> Ye shall have rumney and malmesine,
> Both ypocras and vernage wine,
> Mountrose and wine of Greke,
> Both algarde and respoce eke,
> Antioch and bastarde,
> Piment also and garnarde,
> Wine of Greke and muscadell,
> Both clare, piment and rockell,
> The reed your stomake to defye,
> And pots of osey set you by ... [22]

Wines could be considered beneficial, and were certainly warming and comforting when blended with other ingredients and served hot as possets and caudles. Frequently described today as cream or milk curdled with wine, they sound extremely unappetizing, but nothing could be further from the truth. The simplest were made by pouring about 1pt/600ml of hot, sweetened milk into about ¼pt/150ml of sack, claret, beer, ale or orange juice to produce a soft curd. These were definitely the poor relations of a true posset such as the following recipe, which dates from before 1636.

MY LORD OF CARLISLE'S SACK POSSET[23]

9 egg yolks & 4 whites
½pt/300ml dry sherry
¼tsp ground mace
¼tsp ground cinnamon
½tsp grated nutmeg
2pt/1.1l single cream
6oz/175g sugar

Beat the yolks, whites, sherry and spices together in a large saucepan, place over a gentle heat and stir constantly until warm, but not thickened. Meanwhile bring the cream and sugar to the boil in a separate pan, and as it rises to boil over, pour it from a height into the warm eggs and sherry. Tip immediately into a serving bowl, stand in a warm place for a few minutes, sprinkle with sugar, and serve.

The result is the most relaxing and soporific of all beverages, capable of rapidly turning a lively dinner-party into a group of dozing drones if served as a dessert, but the finest remedy for anyone arriving after a long, stressful winter journey, or approaching a cold bedroom. Robert May and other writers give a number of similarly excellent recipes.[24]

CIDER & PERRY

'In some place in England' wrote William Harrison in 1577, 'there is a kind of drink made of apples which they call cider or pomage, but that of pears is called perry, and both are ground and pressed on presses made for the nonce. Certes these two are very common in Sussex, Kent, Worcester, and other steeds where these sorts of fruits do abound.' Whether drunk neat or watered down, these beverages were held to be decidedly unhealthy, being cold, causing flatulence, wrinkled skin, pallour, stomach pains, rheums in the head, and violent toothache. To many they were only suitable for the poor who couldn't afford anything better. However, from the early seventeenth century, writers such as John Norden began to promote the development of orchards and the production of cider and perry as pleasant and health-promoting drinks. They became increasingly popular with polite society from around the 1620s, but the real expansion in their popularity took place after the Civil Wars, perhaps as a result of their being tried and enjoyed by the armies as they traversed the country.[25]

HYDROMEL, MEAD & METHEGLIN

Today many people believe that hydromel, mead and metheglin are sickly sweet blends of honey and wine, but these drinks were honey solutions fermented to produce much drier tastes. As Andrew Boorde defined them in 1542, 'Meade is made of honny and water boyled both together; yf it be fyned and pure, it preserveth helth,' while 'Metheglyn is made of honny and water, and herbes boyled and soden togyther; yf it be fyned and stale it is better ... than meade.'[26] Although the finished products would be stored in the wine cellar, they were often made by, or under the direct instruction of, the lady or gentleman of the house. Some twenty of the recipes collected by Sir Kenelm Digby came from the nobility and gentry.[27] Anyone wishing to make these or a number of other seventeenth-century versions should obtain a copy of Stuart Peachey's *The Tippler's Guide to the Mid-17th Century* of 1992. The following example comes from W.M.'s *Compleat Cook* of 1655.

METHEGLIN[28]

about 2oz/50g of mixed balm, mint, fennel, rosemary, angelica, thyme, hyssop, burnet and agrimony sprigs
3pt/1.8l honey
1tsp dried real-ale yeast
1oz/25g root ginger
4in/10cm stick cinnamon
6 cloves

Boil the herbs in 10pt/6l water for 15 minutes, remove from the heat, and pass through a strainer into a clean vessel. Next morning pour 8pt/4.8l into a large cooking pot, stir in the honey, cover, and boil for 1 hour, skimming off all scum as it rises. If preferred, the spices, tied in a piece of muslin, may be included in this boiling. Leave to cool to 16°C/60°F, remove the spices, stir in the yeast, cover with a cloth and leave in a warm place for 3 days to ferment. Skim off the yeast and transfer the clear to demijohns fitted with an airlock, adding the spices in muslin if not used previously. Leave in the cool until fermentation has ceased, then decant the clear into bottles, lightly cork if the bottles are made of glass, or screw down if plastic – which does not shatter should secondary fermentation take place.

As Mr Howell, Clerk of the Privy Council, wrote in 1640, such drinks were made of:

> The Juice of Bees, not Bacchus, here behold,
> Which British Bards were wont to quaff of old;
> The berries of the grape the Furies swell,
> But in the honeycombe the Graces dwell.[29]

ALE & BEER

The production of ale and beer has already been discussed in the chapter on the brewhouse. From there, the barrels were trundled into the ale and beer cellars close to the service rooms at the lower end of the hall, into which they would be served in quantity. Due to the rapid rate of consumption, the medium-strength and small beers would only need to be stored for anything from a few days to a few weeks, although the strong ales would keep almost indefinitely. With the exception of knowing how to keep these drinks in good condition, preventing secondary fermentation and fining them when cloudy, the cellar staff had little need to do any more before it was served onto the table. There, if good, it would draw appropriate praise for its beneficial effects. These were admirably described by John Taylor, the Water Poet:

> It is fragrant to the scent; it is most pleasant to the taste; the flowing and mantling of it ... with the verdant smile of it, is delightful to the sight; it is touching or feeling to the brain or heart; and to please the senses all, it provokes men to singing and mirth, which is contenting to the hearing ... it satiates and assuages hunger and cold; with a toast it is a poor man's comfort; it will set a bashful suitor a wooing; it heats the chill blood of the aged ... it is a friend to the muses ... it neither hurts nor kills any but those who abuse it unmeasurably and beyond bearing ... I could not, with mouth, pen, or inke, speake or write the true worthiness of ale.[30]

Drinking it to excess still caused unacceptable drunkenness, beer making 'a man fat, and doth inflate the bely.'[31]

Ale and beer were usually drunk when cool and freshly drawn from the barrels in the cellar, but during the last quarter of the sixteenth century it was also being served from bottles. These were not the large leather bottles for transporting and storing wines, as used by John Mawde, Henry VIII's groom of the bottles in 1545, but closely sealed glass bottles which had already come into use around 1580.[32] As Sir Hugh Plat described in 1600, when beer was ten or twelve days old it was put into glass bottles, corked, and left to ferment. Any attempt to bottle it on its first day led to excess gas and exploding bottles, but the slight delay enabled it to emerge as 'a most excellent and spritely drink'. Experience soon proved that sterilizing the bottles by baking in an oven or scalding the interior prevented them from turning musty and souring their contents.[33]

Various methods were used to flavour bottled ales. An orange stuck full with cloves might be hung in the cask before bottling, or one part of white hippocras would be added to eight parts of ale, or a few drops of the oils of mace, nutmeg or sage might flavour the brew.[34] These probably improved the weaker brews, sage ale selling at a penny a pint in mid-seventeenth-century London, while strong ale cost twice as much.[35] Ale was frequently served hot, as a warm and comforting drink, ideal for winter-time, as a nightcap or a stimulant after a cold journey. One of the most popular versions, as enjoyed by Robert Dudley, Earl of Leicester amongst others, was this:[36]

BUTTERED ALE[37]

1 egg yolk, beaten
1pt/600ml strong pale ale
1oz/25g butter
½oz/12g sugar
½tsp grated ginger or liquorice
(plus ½tsp long pepper or grains of paradise for a stronger flavour)

Beat the yolk into a little of the ale, bring the remainder of the ingredients to the boil, simmer for 2–3 minutes, then remove from the heat, beat in the yolk mixture, and serve immediately.

Another, dating from the early fifteenth century, was called:

ALEBERRY[38]

1pt/600ml strong brown ale
2tbs fine oatmeal
3tbs sugar
¼tsp ground cloves
¼tsp ground mace
8oz/225g crustless white bread cut in 1in/2.5cm cubes

Mix the oatmeal, spices and sugar in a pan with a little of the ale, then add the remaining ale, bring to the boil, and simmer while stirring for a further 10-15 minutes until thick and smooth, then pour over the bread in a deep bowl.

By the 1590s, if not much earlier, bowls of hot, spiced ale mixed with roasted

Figure 79. Wassail bowls & syllabub posset pots. Hot communal drinks were often served in specially made vessels. This early 17th-century wassail bowl (1) is a magnificent example of rose engine-turning in lignum vitae, one of the hardest and densest of woods. It has a nutmeg grater in the underside of its lid. Dipper-cups, such as this silver-mounted one (2) were used to scoop up the hot ale. Drinks such as syllabubs and some possets developed a creamy set curd over a fine liquid whey, therefore needing vessels with tubular mouthpieces which enabled the whey to be drunk before the curd was eaten with a spoon. Some were made in earthenware, as (3) of 1645, from Wrotham in Kent, or of 'delft', as in (4) of 1657 from Southwark.

crab apples were being served as 'lambswool', a name suggestive of its soft, warm and comforting nature. This frequently provided the contents of the wassail bowl at Christmas and was celebrated in verse, as in Robert Herrick's

> Then next I'le cause my hopeful Lad
> (If a wild Apple can be had)
> To crown the Hearth ...
> Then to infuse our browne Ale into the cruse;
> Which sweetly spice't, we'll first carouse
> Unto the *Genius* of the house
>
> Thy nut-brown mirth, thy russet wit,
> And no man pays too much for it ...
> Next crown the bowl full,
> With gentle Lamb's Wool,
> And sugar, nutmeg and ginger,

With store of ale too
And thus ye must doe,
To make the Wassaile a swinger[39]

Shakespeare's *Midsummer Night's Dream* confirms that crab apples in lambswool were left whole, rather than beaten in as a pulp:

Sometimes I lurk in gossip's bowl
In very likeness of a roasted crab,
And when she drinks, against her lips I bob,
And down her withered dewlap pours the ale

or when,

... Marion's nose looks red and raw,
When roasted crabs hiss in the bowl
Then nightly sings the staring owl,
To-whit!

Ulpian Fulwell's lines similarly request:

Good hostess, lay a crab in the fire, and broil a mess of a souse-a
That we may toss the bowl too and fro, and brinks them all carouse-a
And we'll pledge Tom Tosspot, till I be drunk as a mouse-a.[40]

Its alternative name appears to have been snapdragon:

'lambswool; the meekest meat in the world, 'twill let any man fleece it ... it was first invented by Pluto, to entertain Proserpina withal'

'I think not so ... for when Hercules had killed the flaming dragon of Hesperia with apples of that orchard, he made this fiery meat; in memory wherof he named it snapdragon.'[41]

No contemporary recipe appears to have survived, but lambswool can be easily made by bringing strong brown or pale ale to the boil with sugar, nutmeg and ginger to taste, and serving it in a large bowl with a number of crab apples which have either been roasted before the fire or oven-baked to tenderness. Traditionally everyone present scooped up an apple with their spoon, after which the bowl was passed around, each drinking from its brim.

According to Andrew Boorde, 'Poset ale is made with hote mylke & colde ale; it is good for a hote lyver and for hote fevers, specyally yf colde herbes be soden in it.'[42] Ale possets were generally viewed as being inferior to those made of sack. Today when ales and beers are more heavily hopped than in the Tudor and early Stuart period, it is difficult to obtain good, palatable results, but the following may be tried:

POSSET CURD[43]

1pt/600ml milk	*½pt/300ml beer or ale*
3 egg yolks	*1tbs sugar*
	¼tsp ground cinnamon

Beat the yolks into a little of the milk, bring the remaining milk almost to the boil, rapidly stir in the yolk mixture, and continue stirring over the heat until thickened. Meanwhile heat the beer or ale in a basin (originally over a chafing dish, more conveniently today in an oven at 140°C/275°F/gas mark 1), pour in the milk, cover and return to the heat for some 5–10 minutes until set. Sprinkle with the sugar and cinnamon, and serve hot.

CUPS

The cups in which all the drinks were served were stored and issued by the staff in the buttery. They were made in a variety of different materials.

WOODEN CUPS

The most common form of cup used by the bulk of the population in the first half of the sixteenth century was turned from woods such as ash, beech, elm, alder, birch and oak. Measuring about 8–9 inches (20–23cm) across and 3 inches (7.5cm) high, they were bowl-shaped, thinning around the rim for ease of drinking. Many examples have been excavated from wet or waterlogged sites, including 60 from the *Mary Rose*, but they remain largely unrecognized as cups, since archaeologists prefer to obscure their usual historic name and functions, and describe them as general-purpose 'bowls'. They are seen in use in contemporary illustrations, including the painting of *The Field of Cloth of Gold*, being raised to the lips within the open palm, the thumb just overlapping the rim. Archival sources usually refer to them as wooden cups, ashen cups, white cups, dishes, or, less commonly, bowls.[44] In many large households the state of these vessels, as issued from the buttery before every meal, left much to be desired, as outlined in this poem from *c.* 1524:

But if in court thou drinke both beare and ale,
Then is the colour troubled, black and pale.
Thinke not to drinke it in glasses, silver or golde,

The one may be stollen, and the other can not holde.
Of a trene vesell then must thou nedely drinke,
Olde, blacke and rustie, lately taken from some sinke:
And in suche vessell drinke shalt thou often time,
Which in the bottom is full of filth and slime,
And of that vessel thou drinkest ofte I wis,
In which some states or dames late did pis …
For moste parte thou muste drinke of a common boule,
And where gresy lippes and slimy bearde
Hath late bene dipped to make some mad afearde,
On that side muste thou thy lippes washe also,
Or els without drinke from diner muste thou go.

The quality of their washing and cleaning might also be unsatisfactory:

So cups and tankards in court as thou mayest thinke,
Wherein the commons are used for to drinke,
Are once in the yere empty and made clene
And scant that well, as oftentime is sene.[45]

The use of wooden cups was seen as a mark of low status, as in Richard Brome's depiction of an old beggar's wife in 1652. Entering 'with a wooden Bowle of Drink, She is drunk … She tosses off her bowl, falls back, and is carried out.'[46] Those who moved up the social ladder were keen to cast off their use. Even by 1547:

… they that of late did sup
Out of an ashen cup
Are wonderfully sprung up;
That nought was worth of late,
Hath now a cupboard of plate[47]

Similarly, in his *Richard II* of 1597 Shakespeare gave the deposed king the line 'My figured goblets [I'll exchange] for a dish of wood.'[48] Wooden cups continued to be used into the late seventeenth century, but had already begun to be replaced by ceramic cups from the late fifteenth century.

A second kind of wooden drinking vessel for individual use took the form of a coopered wooden tankard, one stave being carved as a handle on one side, its top providing the pivot for a hinged lid. Their capacity of some 60 cubic inches suggests that they were intended to hold about two old wine pints, or perhaps two pints each. The finest surviving examples have been recovered from

Figure 80. Cups. The 16th century saw the traditional wooden cups begin to be replaced by new ceramic alternatives, such as: (1) a wooden cup of the early 16th century, from Exeter; (2) a 'small beere bowl' of pewter, dated 1638; (3) a silver-mounted mazer of burr-maple from Epworth, Lincolnshire, 16th century; (4) wooden cups in use, from the painting The Field of the Cloth of Gold; *(5) a 'Cistercian ware' earthenware cup made at Potterton, Yorkshire, in the early 16th century; (6) a covered cup, of the same ware and date, from Potovens, Yorkshire; (7 & 8) 'Tudor Green' and green-glazed whiteware cups made in the potteries of the Hampshire/Surrey border, early 16th century; (9) a salt-glazed stoneware cup imported from Raeren into Exeter, early 16th century; (10) a 'Border-ware' cup of 'Tudor Green', of similar shape and date to no. 9; (11) a salt-glazed cup (from Cologne?) mounted with silver-gilt c. 1560; (12) a cup probably made by the first Venetian glass-blowers to settle in London, its mount being hall-marked for 1548–9.*

the wreck of the *Mary Rose*, some being carved with devices probably used to identify their original owners.[49] In addition to small wooden cups intended for individual use, larger ones were made for sharing. Measuring up to some 17–18 inches (43–47cm) across and 9 inches (23cm) high, they were often made of harder, better-quality woods.[50] 'Divers and sundry sorts we have, some of *Elme*, some of *Box*, some of *Maple*, some of *Holly* & *Mazers, Ale-bowles, Wassell-bowles*.'[51] In the early sixteenth century their role was becoming more formal and ceremonial, used for shared drinking as a symbol of good fellowship. For this purpose they were frequently enriched with finely engraved silver mounts, including a roundel or 'print' in the centre of their interiors, and bands at the rim and foot linked by a number of vertical strips. Such was the vessel described in Edmund Spenser's *Shepheardes Calender* of 1579 as,

> A mazer ywrought of the maple wood
> Whereon is enchased many a fair sight
> Of bears and tigers than man fierce war.[52]

or as Samuel Pepys used at Saffron Walden on 27 February 1660:

> They brought me a draught of their drink in a brown bowl, tipt with silver, which I drank off, and at the bottom was a picture of the Virgin with the child in her arms, done in silver.[53]

Some large houses kept such bowls for the Christmas wassail, Speke Hall near Liverpool having 'a great wassell bole 12*d*., a lyttle wassell bole 3*d*.' in 1624.[54] Poor families probably used one of their everyday wooden bowls for the same purpose when going a-wassailing for gifts to support their Christmas festivities, those who called on Sir John Franklin at Wilsden in 1625 receiving 1*s*. 6*d*. for their 'cupp'.[55]

CERAMIC CUPS

From the late fifteenth century wooden cups began to be replaced by those either imported from the salt-glazed stoneware potteries of Raeren, near Aachen, or made in English lead-glazed earthenware. Most would not be recognized as cups today. We would call them 'jugs' (a word first recorded in England in 1538) since they had bulbous bodies, narrower necks and a loop handle to one side. Such would be the '12 drynkyng Jugs, 3*s*. 10*d*.' purchased for Haddon Hall in November 1564.[56] They were among the most popular products of the 'Tudor Green' Border Ware potteries of the Hampshire-Surrey border, where they were made up to the early seventeenth century for the London market.[57] The problem with this form of cup was that it was difficult to clean the interior, or to see what it contained. They also had to be tipped up almost vertically, the brim pressing against the nose, to be fully drained. For these reasons cups with shallower bodies and wider rims were already being made in the last quarter of the fifteenth century.

In the north, two major communities of potters, one at Potovens near Wakefield, West Yorkshire, and the other at Ticknall in south Derbyshire, began to make ceramic cups on a truly industrial scale. Using local clays, lead glazes and new potting and firing techniques, they introduced an extremely fine, hard-wearing and practical range of drinking-cups. Since these were used in most of the great northern monasteries, they were christened 'Cistercian Ware' when first excavated in the late nineteenth century, but were used at all levels of society over an extremely wide area.[58] During the later sixteenth and seventeenth centuries more potteries adopted the same techniques, the form of the cups gradually changing up to the time of the Civil War. In other parts of the country, such as rural parts of the West Country, ceramic cups only appear to have been made from the seventeenth century.[59]

Most cups were undecorated, their brown or yellow colours being provided by applying transparent yellow lead glazes over their red or off-white firing clays, while green came from the addition of copper to the glaze. Blacks, meanwhile, were produced either by the addition of iron or manganese, or the absorption or iron from the underlying clay. Some of the finer Cistercian wares of the early sixteenth century had flattened pellets, narrow strips or other decorative devices added in a contrasting plastic clay. By the early or mid-seventeenth century, however, many potters were using liquid clay called slip to either pipe or 'trail' linear designs, or to give smooth dipped overall coatings which could be partly scratched away to reveal the darker clay beneath.

Some decorated cups were made for specific purposes, the two-handled, lidded forms of Cistercian wares being particularly suitable for hot liquids such as pottages, caudles or possets. Further decorated cups made from the early mid-seventeenth century, today frequently referred to as 'puzzle cups', since an internal tube ran from the base of the interior to a nozzle at the rim, were intended for caudles, possets and syllabubs. As these mixtures frequently separated into a watery whey at the bottom and a rich, smooth curd at the top, they enabled the drinker to first suck up the whey, before spooning out the curd. A description of certain posset cups in 1606 describes their 'libberd's faces and Lyon's heads with spouts in their mouths to let out the posset Ale.'[60]

Instead of using locally made earthenware cups, many preferred the stronger and more serviceable salt-glazed stoneware varieties made in the Low Countries and Germany. These are often described as 'cruses' in household accounts, using the Germanic word for a cup or drinking vessel. In 1512 the retinue of the Earl of Northumberland required 240 of the 'stoone Crozes', which were purchased at a halfpenny each.[61] Their shapes varied from one group of potters to another, but most followed the early 'jug' shape, rather than being open cups, into the early mid-seventeenth century. Basing House in the 1640s was still using such stoneware 'cups' imported from Raeren, Frechen (a centre of stoneware production close to Cologne) and Cologne.[62]

TANKARDS, BOMBARDS & PITCHERS

The serving of ale and beer in its carefully regulated quantities required a number of large, robust vessels that would bring it first from the cellar to the buttery, and then from the buttery onto the tables in the hall. Ideally each should hold sufficient for a single mess of (usually) four people sitting together, and from which they could help themselves, filling and refilling their cups until all was consumed. If made of wood, with vertical staves bound together with wooden or metal hoops, side handles and hinged lids, they were known as tankards, as listed in the naval accounts of 1485–95: 'Drynkyng botles of tree 20, Tankards … of a galon apece … 8.'[63] These were found on the *Mary Rose* (there mistakenly believed to be 'flagons'), but were also suitable for domestic use.[64] Similar vessels of pitch-lined leather were known by a variety of names, and were made in various sizes. In the Rutland's buttery in 1541 they were 'gispins': 'for 12 gyspyns of lether, whereof 4 of galons, 4 of potelles [½-gallons], and 4 of quartes.'[65] Their size and black cannon-like appearance gave them the alternative names of 'black-jack' and 'bombard': 'The great black jacks and bombards at the Court, which, when the Frenchmen first saw, they reported … that the Englishmen used to drink out of their bootes.'[66]

The ceramic vessels used for dispensing drinks were usually called pitchers. Most were tall and approximately baluster-shaped or cylindrical in profile, the smaller examples, such as the 1½pt/900ml Border ware pitchers, having a single handle placed directly opposite a pouring lip.[67] Larger ones, like the 1½gallon/6.6l pitchers from Sandal Castle, were too large for pouring, and so had a bung-hole just above the base to receive a wooden spigot-tap. This enabled quantities to be run off into the cups as required at the tables.[68]

VESSELS OF PRECIOUS MATERIALS

All the vessels described above were intended for use in the halls of great houses, or those of gentry and yeoman status. For use in the dining chambers reserved

Figure 81. Serving vessels. The top row shows a selection of vessels used to carry ale and beer from the cellar, through the buttery and into the hall: (1) a wooden tankard recovered from the Mary Rose*, 1545; (2) a leather black-jack or bombard from Bedford Street, London; (3) an earthenware pitcher from Sandal Castle, Yorkshire, 1645; (4) a 'Border-ware' pitcher or jug from 16th–17th century London.*

The flagons on the bottom row were used to carry wine into the chambers: (5–7) pewter flagons of c. *1500,* c. *1590–1610 and 1580–1620; (8) a silver flagon in the later cylindrical shape, 1616.*

for the lords and masters, and particularly for serving wines, it was fashionable to have both cups and flagons made of more expensive materials and displaying the highest standards of design and craftsmanship. The use of pewter, of silver, parcel gilt and gilt, or even gold vessels continued as in the medieval period, but the sixteenth century saw the arrival of new kinds of luxury ware, each imported from a different part of the world. In June 1518, for example, the pair of Venetian galleys paying their annual visit to Southampton invited Henry VIII and 300 of his courtiers on board for a sumptuous entertainment. A large platform along one deck was decorated with silks and tapestries, tables along the sides being laden with banqueting stuff and wine. At the end, the hosts presented their guests with the fine glass vessels they had used. As a result, Venetian glassware became instantly popular, future shipments being guaranteed excellent sales.[69] In 1577, William Harrison was horrified to find that here 'wherein gold and silver most aboundeth, how that our gentility, as loathing those metals, because of the plenty, do now generally choose rather the Venice glasses, both for our wine and beer.' The arrival of such wares stimulated the English glass industry, but it took many years before it could produce anything of really good quality. In the meantime the Venetian glassmaker Verzelini had set up his kiln at Crutched Friars in London in 1572, to serve the booming market for his native city's finely blown and beautifully engraved glassware. In the early seventeenth century, the English industry became dominated by Sir Robert Mansell. In 1623 he obtained a patent for making 'all manner of drinking glasses, broade glasses ... bottles, viols, or vessels whatsoever' in thin, almost colourless soda-lime glass. Examples of these, along with those made by his unauthorized imitators, have been excavated on a number of Civil War-period sites.[70]

In 1571 Jacob Jansen and Jasper Andries, Flemish makers of tin-glazed earthenware or 'delft', petitioned Elizabeth I for permission to set up a pottery on the banks of the Thames. As a result some thirteen Flemish potters came to work in the Aldgate area, probably in Duke's Place, the former Holy Trinity Priory, between 1571 and 1615. Here they made a range of wares decorated with attractive renaissance-style polychrome painting. Unfortunately, not many pieces have survived, but a plate inscribed 'THE ROSE IS RED, THE LEAVES ARE GREENE, GOD SAVE ELIZABETH OUR QUEENE, 1600' in the collections of the Museum of London clearly indicates their high quality. Later, the industry moved to Southwark and Lambeth, where most of its products – cups, mugs, wine-bottles and dishes – were covered in a glossy, opaque white tin-glaze painted with cobalt-blue inscriptions and designs.

Because of the immense distances involved, the porcelain of China and the Far East had always been of the greatest rarity in England. The hardness and glossiness of its glaze, the translucency of its fabric and the fine detail of its decoration were of an unbelievably high standard, especially when compared to the wares being made in this country. In 1587 Sir Francis Drake captured Philip of Spain's royal carrack the *San Felipe*, which had 1,800lb of oriental porcelain in its hold. This was one of the earliest major arrivals of porcelain into northern Europe. Most of the cargo went to the Crown or was sold in London and elsewhere at high prices, which it maintained.[71] Many owners further enriched their 'carracke' wares by adding mounts of precious metal, as shown by the

Figure 82. Wine cups & glasses. The cups made for ceremonial use at formal meals were amongst the finest examples of expensive materials and workmanship of their age. Covers were essential for the service of wine, acting as assay-cups when inverted. (1) a silver-gilt font cup of 1515; (2) the silver-gilt and ivory Howard Grace Cup of 1525–6; (3) a silver-gilt cup and cover of 1569.

Cups without covers were for use at more informal meals, those of glass becoming particularly fashionable. (4) a gold cup made in London 1599–1600; (5–6) a glass attributed to Jacopo Verzelini, London, 1581, and another of 1586; (7) a glass with a lion-mask baluster made in the Venetian tradition, probably in England, from Basing House, 1645; (8) an English glass from early 17th-century Exeter.

following list of those owned by Richard Bevys of Exeter in 1603:

> One Carricke Goblett wth. A foote of silver gilte 26*s.* 8*d.*
> One other Carricke Goblett with a silver foote £1
> Tenn flatt Carricke Dishes, Tenn deep little Carricke dishes, two Basons and Ewers and two other Carricke dishes.[72]

As trade links developed, porcelain came into wider use in the second quarter of the seventeenth century, but still retained its original prestige.

Although not of the same rarity and value, some of the finer salt-glazed stoneware cups imported from Raeren, Frechen and Cologne were similarly embellished with silver and gilt mounts.[73] As shown in the following accounts, the mounts cost far more than the cups:

> 3 stones coppes 18*d.* (1572);
> A whyte stone Cuppe as yt ys thought 13*s.* 4*d.* (1563);
> a stone cupp with a cover and foote of sylver conteynes 5 ounces at 4*s.* 6*d.* the ounce 22*s.* 6*d.* (1571).[74]

FLAGONS

Whether made of pewter or precious metals, the flagons used to carry wine from the buttery to the cupboards were usually of a more elegant design and superior workmanship to the tankards and other vessels used for ale and beer in the hall. Most Tudor examples have a bold baluster-shaped body mounted on a tall base, these being gradually replaced by those of tall, almost cylindrical form around 1600. They were apparently kept cool in the buttery and chambers by being immersed in purposely made cisterns. At the Howard family's Naworth Castle in Cumbria, two sets were purchased in 1629–30:

> For a litle copper sesterne to sett flaggons in in the great chamber, weighing 30 pounds and a halfe 43*s.* 4*d.*
> For 2 pewter flaggons weighinge 25 poundes and a halfe at 14*s.* a pounde 39*s.* 10*d.* For one pewter sesterne weighinge 35 pounds and three quarters at 15*d.* a pounde 44*s.* 7*d.*[75]

BREAD

> The smell of newe bread is comfortable to the heade and to the harte [but] Hote breade is unholsom for any man. [It should be] a daye and a nyght olde, nor is it not good when it is past 4 or 5 dayes olde.[76]

Following this advice from Andrew Boorde and other physicians, the fresh bread delivered from the bakehouse to the buttery had to be stored for a period before being issued. For this purpose the butteries were provided with containers such as the 'lytle Byn, Which keeps my little loaf of Bread , Unchipt, unflead' in Robert Herrick's buttery.[77] The alternatives included 'pipes' or barrels, chests called arks, or cupboards called hutches. When about to be served, the 'Pantler and Bread Chopper' took up a pair of chipping-knives, either provided by the household,

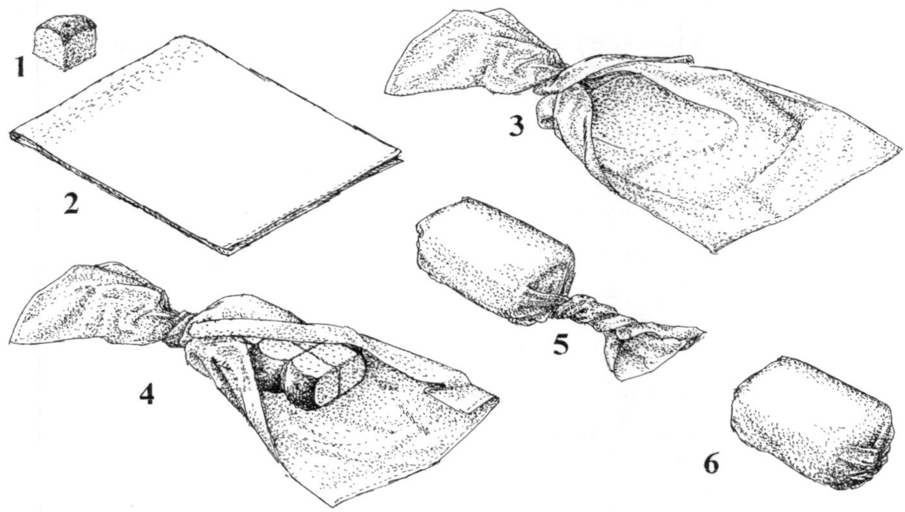

Figure 83. The portpain. For use in a portpain, the manchet loaves were first cut about 6ins/15cm square (1). The portpain was then folded end-to-end (2), the folded end twisted and placed under a weight, and the upper half folded back over it (3). The manchets were then inserted (4), the twisted end tucked underneath and the other end twisted (5), and also tucked underneath, to completely enclose the bread (6).

or, as in Elizabeth I's pantry, purchased by the pantlers in return for the trimmings of the loaves, and began to chip off parts of the outer crusts.[78] Continuing medieval practice, this was largely concerned with the cutting of the round manchets into square shapes, so that they could be arranged into a neat block of six, and then wrapped in 'A porte payne to beare bread fro the pantree to the table with.'[79] This was a piece of fine linen some 7 feet 6 inches by 3 feet (2.3m x 90cm) on which they were laid, before being covered and the ends twisted like a toffee-paper to form a neat parcel.[80] Portpains remained in use at formal meals up to the mid-seventeenth century.

The loaves of coarse wholewheat bread intended to serve as trenchers from which food would be eaten at table had to be cut into squares perhaps 4 inches (10cm) wide by half an inch (1.2cm) thick using a special trencher-knife. Bread trenchers were still being made in some houses in the early mid-sixteenth century, but were rapidly passing out of general use. Their replacements were practical, economic and permanent alternatives made of wood, pewter or precious metals, each still retaining the name of 'trencher'.

CHARGERS, PLATTERS & DISHES

These were the vessels in which food was presented at the table. If for a king, queen, lord or lady, he or she would be served with some of their contents, the remainder being eaten shortly afterwards by the upper servants. For all others, they would be placed on the table, so that everyone might help themselves. Their different names indicate different sizes and shapes. Largest of all were the chargers weighing about 70oz if of silver, and probably some 20–22 inches in diameter, with flat bases, and a medium-height 'bouge' rising up to a flat brim. These were ideal for serving large items of food, as well as decorating the shelves of a sideboard in the hall or chamber.[81] Next came platters at some 40–45oz and around 18 inches in diameter, again with flat bases, but only a shallow bouge: much better for the larger standing dishes such as roasts, leaving them more freestanding and easily accessible to the carving knife.[82] Last came dishes of various sizes, with relatively deep bouges so as to contain liquid and semi-liquid dishes such as pottages, stews or sops, the latter probably supporting various roasts or boiled joints.[83] The bases of most medieval dishes appear to have been fairly flat, but from the early sixteenth century they rose up as a shallow dome. Examples of this form were found on the *Mary Rose*, but the finest set, made for Sir Christopher Harris of Radford, Devon, between 1581 and 1602, was discovered in a cave being enlarged as a potato-store near Yealmpton on Dartmoor in 1827.[84] Each dish has a convex base about a quarter of its total diameter, a broad concave bouge, and a flat, slightly rising brim with a beaded edge. The set comprises:

	Dishes						*Saucers*
Weight (oz)	39.5	31	21	18	14½	11	4
diameter (in.)	15½	13½	12	10½	9½	8	4¾
inventory no.	1-2	3-6	7-10	11-15	16-21	22-27?	28-31
no. of	2	4	4	5	6	6?	4

These weights and dimensions make it possible to suggest the probable sizes of the dishes and chargers which, following the usual practice, were only accounted in terms of their numbers and total weights. When preparing for a visit from Queen Elizabeth in 1577, Lord North made the following purchases:[85]

Vessels	*No. of*	*Tot. weight*	*Weight each*	*Poss. diameter*
great chargers & platters	3	52 oz		20 inches
platters	6	145 oz	24.1 oz	13 inches?
greater dishes	13	219 oz	16.8 oz	10½ inches?
dishes	13	204 oz	15.7 oz	9½ inches?
saucers	8	43 oz	5.4 oz	6 inches?

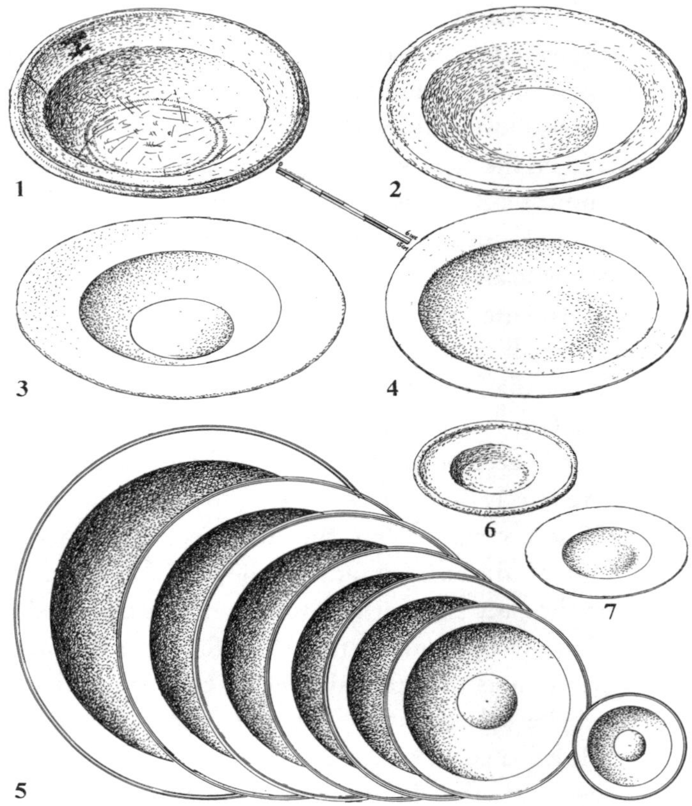

Figure 84. Chargers, dishes & saucers. The quality of wares used to serve foods on to the table varied according to the status of the diners. For the hall, wood, earthenware and sometimes pewter were in general use: (1) a wooden dish from the Mary Rose*, 1545; (2) one of the earthenware dishes introduced into late 16th-century London from the potteries of the Hampshire-Surrey borders; (3 & 4) broad- and narrow-rimmed pewter dishes from the* Mary Rose*, 1545; (5) part of a set of parcel-gilt dishes and a saucer made for Sir Richard Harris of Radford, Devon, between 1581 and 1602; (6) a Border-ware saucer of the late 16th–mid-17th centuries; (7) a pewter saucer of the 16th century.*

Clearly these can only be crude estimates, for differences in design and workmanship vary the relationship between the weight and the size of each set of dishes. The 1,023.5 oz of silver required to make Lord North's complete set was purchased at 4*s.* 10½*d.* the ounce, totalling £249 8*s.* 6*d.* To this had to be added 3*d.* the ounce for silversmithing, adding £12 16*s.* 9*d.*, giving a total cost of £262 13*s.* 9*d.*

A number of inventories and domestic accounts refer to dishes called 'doublers'. This does not appear to be an official term used by pewterers nationwide, but instead it was probably a dialect term restricted to the six northern counties of England. Here it was defined as a 'dish between the depth of a soup-plate and a punch-bowl, into which it was usual to dip for the liquid, whatever its nature whichever accompanied the solid victual.'[86] In other words, a large, deep, flat-bottomed dish, as was fashionable from the early seventeenth century. These, along with other dishes, chargers and platters, were frequently used in pairs, one being placed upside-down on top of the other to serve as a dish-cover when carrying food to the table.

Pewter chargers, platters and dishes were made in the same shapes and sizes as silver ones. As William Harrison stated in 1577:

> Such furniture of household of [pewter] as we commonly call by the name of vessel is sold usually by the garnish, which doth contain twelve platters, twelve dishes, twelve saucers, and those are either silver fashion, or else with broad or narrow rims and bought by the pound, which is now valued at six or seven pence, or peradventure at eight pence. In some places beyond the sea a garnish of good flat English pewter ... is esteemed almost so precious as [those] of fine silver. [Their] workmen are nothing so skilfull in that trade as ours, neither their metal so good, nor plenty so great, as we have here in England.[87]

The 1438 ordinances of the Pewterers' Company of London established their respective weights:[88]

chargers	3lb 4oz	platters (middle)	2lb
chargers (small)	2lb 12oz	dishes	1½lb
platters (large)	2lb 8oz	saucers	6oz

Their wooden equivalents, turned from ash, elm, alder, beech and similar timbers, were in regular use from before the Conquest through to the late nineteenth century, especially in poorer households, and on the tables of household servants. For example, there were four treen platters and a bread platter worth 4*d.* each at Speke Hall, Liverpool, in 1624.[89] One of the finest and earliest groups was recovered from the *Mary Rose* dating from 1545. Most are about 12 inches (30cm) in diameter, some being shaped rather like modern saucers, while others had flatter bottoms, with a bouge and a beaded rim resembling those of contemporary silver or pewter ware. Their interiors still bear the stab and cut marks inflicted as the sailors roughly cut their hunks from the joints of boiled meat or fish.[90]

Ceramic bowls were probably being used to serve foods in some peasant households of the fifteenth century, but vessels we can recognize as dishes only appeared in the late sixteenth century. They too appear to have taken their shapes from contemporary silver and pewter chargers and dishes, having flat bases and flattish beaded rims. Being cheap to produce, and having a glossy, usually yellow,

Figure 85. Dishes. Given their broad flat bases and rims, pottery dishes provided an ideal area for the display of decoration, both on the table and when displayed on the stages of a cupboard. (1, top left) a tin-glazed dish with polychrome decoration probably made at the Aldgate pottery of Jasper Andries and Jacob Jansen from Antwerp in 1602; (2, top right) a similarly made dish probably made at Christian Wilhelm's Pickleherring pottery in Southwark in 1635, the initials T/TM have been attributed to his daughter Maria and her husband Thomas Townsend; (3, bottom left) engraved pewter charger of 1656, decorated for David and Hannah Guy of Exeter, and (4, bottom right) c. 1640–60.

lead glaze which was easily washed, they soon became very popular, and have been found on most later Tudor and Stuart excavation sites. By the mid-seventeenth century, many were being decorated with liquid clays called slips, some applied as a surface layer, sometimes this being scratched away to show the contrasting colour beneath, or else slips were trailed or piped on using a goose-quill nozzle stuck in the end of a cow-horn reservoir. Though relatively crude, these techniques produced very attractive designs. The tin-glazed dishes made by the Flemish potters working in London from the 1570s were far more sophisticated, their patterned borders and pictorial centres being executed in elegant polychrome brushwork, ideal for both table and cupboard.

SAUCERS

As confirmed by their name, saucers were used to hold the cold 'bottle' sauces such as mustard or greensauce which accompanied all meats and fishes. Whether made of silver, pewter, glazed earthenware or perhaps of wood, they all have relatively small round bowls, disproportionately large rims, and diameters of around 4–6 inches (10–15cm).[91] They were ideal for their purpose, the bowl holding an economical quantity of sauce to be taken out on the point of an eating knife, and the rim providing a convenient handle for passing the saucer from one diner to another.

SALTS

In their simplest form, salts were simple, small squat cup-shaped vessels holding a few spoonfuls of salt, from which pinches might be taken and transferred onto a trencher or plate. Some wooden examples have been attributed to the early seventeenth century, but lead-glazed earthenware examples are well known from archaeological deposits from the late fifteenth and early sixteenth centuries.[92] Some of those made in the potteries of the north Midlands around 1500 were thrown in the shape of silver cup-salts, with faceted stems, round knops, and shallow conical lids, all made in yellow-glazed earthenware. Others produced at Potovens near Wakefield and Ticknall in Derbyshire in the 1530s–1560s were modelled as miniature ladies dressed in the height of fashion, each holding a bowl before her, full of salt.[93] Earthenware cup-salts continued to be made through to the mid-seventeenth century but probably fell out of use shortly afterwards.[94]

Superior salts of tin-glazed earthenware or delft were made in the London potteries, adopting a number of different shapes. Some mid-seventeenth-century examples were heart-shaped, while one for the Salters' Company, although only 4½ inches (11.5cm) high, has an elaborately scrolled triangular base supporting a trefoil-shaped recess for salt and the Company's coat of arms.

Silver salts, and their pewter imitators, were the most prestigious items on the dining table. As the manual *Ffor to Serve a Lord* of 1500 instructed:

> The boteler or panter shall bring forthe his principall salte ... he shall sette the [salt] saler in the myddys of the tabull accordyng to the place where the principall soverain shall sette ... then the seconde salte att the lower ende ... then salte selers shall be sette uppon the syde-tablys.

Figure 86. Salts. Salts were made for two distinct positions, either as the principal piece of tableware set before the head of the household, or as a utilitarian utensil for the other, lower-status tables. (1) pedestal salt of yellow-glazed earthenware, early 16th century, from Sandal Castle, Yorkshire; (2) a similar salt, always uncovered, from Coventry; (3) a 16th-century Border-ware salt from London; (4) a mid-16th-century salt found in Nottingham, and probably made at Ticknall, Derbyshire; (5) a turned sycamore salt of c. 1600; (6) a tin-glazed earthenware salt made at Southwark in the mid-17th century; (7) a similarly made Southwark salt, modelled on a contemporary silver example; (8) a silver trencher salt, imitating the form of earlier ones cut from the bread; (9) a silver trencher-salt of c. 1635; (10) a silver pulley-salt of c. 1625–60, with scrolls to support a dish; (11) the jewelled silver-gilt salt presented by Francis I of France to Henry VIII in 1535; (12) a silver-gilt salt made by William Cobbold of Norwich in 1568; (13) a silver-gilt bell-salt of 1613; (14) a silver-gilt pedestal salt of c. 1610.

Made in many individual designs, the salts tended to adopt a sequence of different forms as fashions changed from one generation to another. Up to around 1525 a waisted 'hour-glass' shape was popular, followed by cylindrical profiles c. 1550–1600, bell-shapes c. 1580–1620, and spool-shaped 'pulley' salts from c. 1625. The latter had three short scrolls rising above its broad, flat rim to hold a plate in lieu of a cover. These were only general trends, for the wealthy and great commissioned their goldsmiths to demonstrate the greatest displays of aesthetic design and technical ingenuity to grace the centres of their tables. A typical nobleman's collection of 1535 might include:[95]

4 square salts 2 bell salts with covers
1 salt of gold holden withby a shepherd
1 salt of gold borne by a foole
1 salt of gold like a shippe with perle and stone.

or at Hardwick Hall in 1601:[96]

a great guilt salt with a Cover & pictures	62oz
A great guilt salt with a Cover and tills	86oz
A Salt of golde and Christall enameled with a Cover with a talbott on top and stages beneath and with a Scutchion of my Lord and my Ladies Armes	5½oz

These were certainly impressive pieces of plate, but fade into insignificance when compared with those for royal use. Henry VIII had salts made of agate, beryl, rock crystal, ivory, jasper, chalcedony and serpentine, but his finest were of solid gold. His Morris Dance salt had sculptures of five morris dancers and a lady, the figures and their base being embellished with 10 sapphires, 52 diamonds, 95 rubies and 156 pearls, all set in some 147oz of solid gold.[97] Other salts incorporated a clock, one 'standing upon four Antiques' with pillars of rock crystal and silver gilt, and another with a man in armour brandishing a club and a shield.[98] Quite remarkably, the clock salt presented by Francis I to Henry in 1535 still survives in the collection of the Goldsmiths' Company. It appears to be his crystal salt described as having a base of six cameo heads near the top, garnishings of garnets, turquoises and ragged pearls, all mounted in silver-gilt, and weighing 115 ounces.[99]

CHAFING DISHES

Chafing dishes were useful for keeping dishes of food hot on the table, or reheating it as it cooled. Most would be of the same design and construction as those used in the kitchens, but superior versions were made for use in the dining

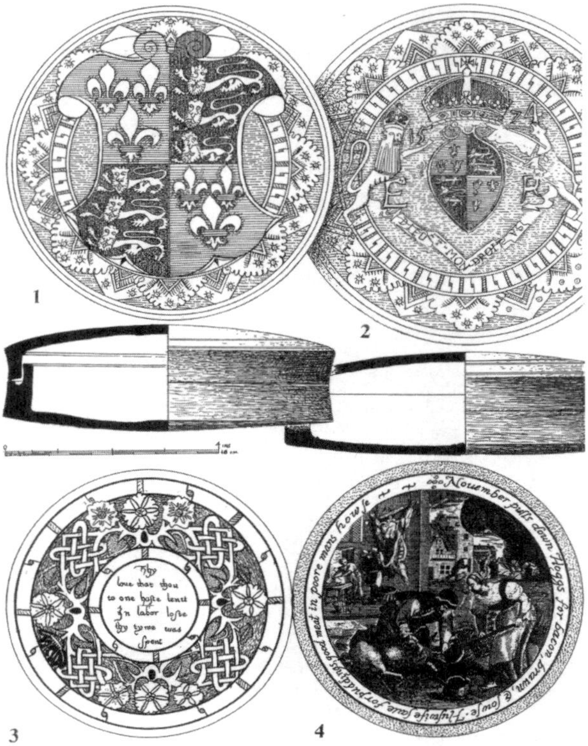

Figure 87. Banqueting trenchers. Used when eating cheese or fruit, some sets of banqueting trenchers came in purposely designed boxes (1 & 2) of 1574. Many of the trenchers bear painted designs and texts (3) suggesting that they were made by two major workshops in London. Some early 17th-century examples had engravings depicting the months pasted into the centre of a painted verse, this example being originally owned by the Harington family of Lincolnshire.

chambers of the wealthy. Those used at Hardwick Hall were made from 28–55 ounces of solid silver.[100] Henry VIII also had them in silver, parcel-gilt and silver-gilt and weighing about 50 ounces, some bearing his arms, some lions heads, antique heads or leaves, most standing on three feet with a couple of side-handles or ears.[101]

TRENCHERS

Unlike plates, which had a raised brim around their edges to contain liquids or, later, an individual's portion of a course, trenchers were essentially flat. They were used as personal cutting-boards for pieces of solid meat or food taken from a communal dish as these were cut into smaller 'gobbets' suitable for raising to the mouth. They also held small heaps of salt or sauce into which the food might be dipped just before being eaten. The everyday trenchers used in most homes were simply small, thin slabs of wood, many being imported from the Baltic ports. In 1499–1500 the 2,500 shipped into Newcastle were valued at between sixteen and twenty-five for a penny.[102] Other accounts confirm their cheapness.[103]

1564	3 dosen of trenchures	3*d.*	(12 for 1*d.*)
1566	5 dusson of trenchers	3*d.*	(20 for 1*d.*)
1577	Sixe dosens of trenchers	12*d.*	(6 for 1*d.*)

Most appear to have been purchased from specialist makers, but some were certainly home-made, the Middleton family of Stockeld in Yorkshire paying one Haggerpennie 'for 17 dayes worke at 8*d.* the day makinge trenchers 11*s.* 4*d.*' in November 1654.[104] Large households used them in great numbers, perhaps because they were considered semi-disposable. The Percys at Petworth in Sussex had over a thousand in stock in 1632.[105] Most were probably tossed into the fire when discarded, and so their survival, even in archaeological contexts, is extremely rare. Only six were recovered from the *Mary Rose* (suggesting that most sailors took their meats and foods directly from their dishes or platters), these being some 4 inches (92–105mm) wide by 6 or 7 inches (151–187mm) long and ⅛–½ inch (4–12mm) in thickness. Made of oak, beech or pine, half of these trenchers are quite plain, the remainder having borders of chip-carved zig-zags around their edges.[106] Before leaving this class of trencher, it is important to correct two common misconceptions. Firstly, they were used to hold meats and other foods as they were cut up for eating, and were never 'side-plates' for bread. Secondly, those square 'Tudor' trenchers with turned hollows to hold food and a corner hollow for salt as are frequently made for museum displays and re-enactments, are no older than the eighteenth century.

Better quality wooden trenchers were also made for middle- and upper-class use, their value being about a penny or twopence each. The '8 doz. Maple trenchers 8*s.*' purchased for the Earl of Cumberland's household in 1607 were of this kind.[107] Most were probably still being set directly on top of the tablecloth, but from the early sixteenth century they had been placed within silver trenchers, protecting the latter from damaging knife-cuts and sauce-stains. Sir Thomas Brudenell had ordered his 'round trenchers of silver ... of 6 ounces [175g] the piece ... to lay a wooden trencher in the midst, as ye know the manner is, and about the edge would be some pretty print or work.'[108] This is a particularly useful quotation, since it marks the first stage in the replacement of the trencher with the 'plate' for individual use at table. In the 1540s the Earl of Rutland had

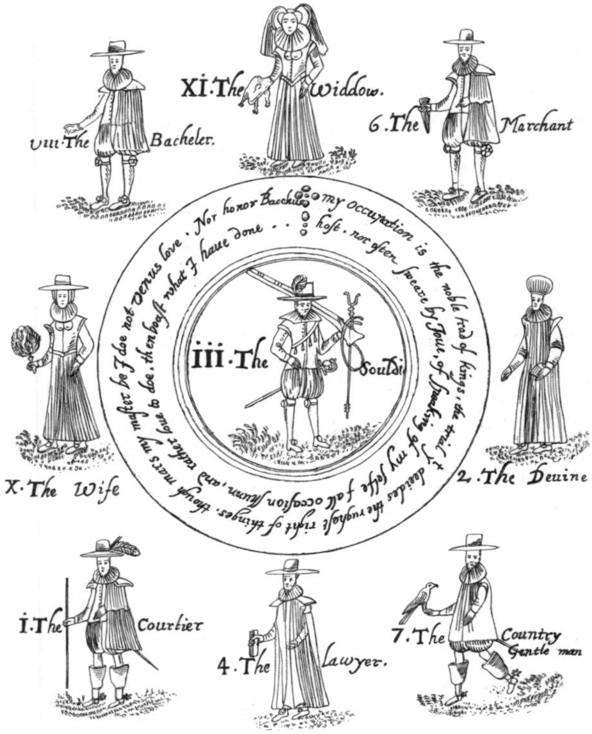

Figure 88. Banqueting trenchers. Characters from a set of twelve painted trenchers dating from the reign of James I and depicting various members of polite society.

owned two dozen of these parcel-gilt 'plates for trenchers', representing a practice which probably continued well into the seventeenth century.[109]

The use of metal trenchers, those made of pewter and silver, dated back to at least the fourteenth century, their flat, round or rectangular surfaces being surrounded by a slightly raised moulding.[110] They remained relatively uncommon until the early seventeenth century, not being included in any standard 'garnish' of pewter; no English pewter examples from earlier periods appear to be extant today.[111]

The most magnificent trenchers were made in precious metals for Henry VIII. His silver or silver-gilt plate-trenchers weighed some 8–10 ounces (225–275g), while his square standing trenchers with a salt in one corner and mounted on short legs weighed about 26 ounces (725g).[112] One silver-gilt example with a covered salt was 'holden upp by Greyhoundes and Dragons holding the kinges armes enameled.'[113] There were also six trenchers made of tin-glazed earthenware, fifteen of glass and twelve of marble garnished with silver-gilt, as well as fifteen 'cases of trenchers furnished all woode' for his use.[114]

The latter probably refers to a case of fruit or cheese trenchers, these being a superior kind made especially for use either at the end of formal meals or at sweetmeat banquets. They first appeared in the 1530s, Catherine of Aragon's 'one case of woode trenchiers, cont[aining] one dussen' being passed on to her successor Anne Boleyn after Catherine's death in 1536.[115] The earliest dated example, now in the Museum of London, is a turned wooden box with a slightly domed lid painted with the Tudor arms supported by a lion and a dragon beneath a large crown and the inscription 'E.R.' and '1574'. Its internal recess is only 1¼ inches (32mm) deep, but just sufficient to contain twelve 5½-inch (14cm) trenchers, each under one-tenth of an inch (2.5mm) in thickness. They appear in sixteenth and early mid-seventeenth century inventories throughout the country:[116]

(1569 Exeter)	A Doosen of fruite Trenchers in a Boxe 4*d*.
(1579 Exeter)	a dossen Box trenchers gilt 6*s*. 8*d*.
(1578 Yorkshire)	round trenchers in boxes 20.
(1603 Yorkshire)	a dossen of cheese trenchers & a cais 2*s*.
(1579 Exeter)	a dozen of ffyne trenchers paynted 10*s*.

The references to painting and gilding describe some of the methods used to decorate their upper faces. Borders of interlaced strapwork, fruit, nuts, leaves, texts, mottoes, or more formal motifs often enclose a central panel including more decorative painting and inscriptions. The majority appear to have been made by two 'factories' based in London, each using a distinctive selection of devices and verses, but others show a more individual approach. Some bear figurative paintings, some feature sprays of flowers, while later examples have specially printed engraved designs stuck onto them, or imitate the designs of imported oriental black lacquerwork. A number of the finest examples were not round, but rectangular, a fine set in the Bodleian Library, Oxford (on loan to the Ashmolean Museum) having its box made to look like an elaborately bound book, opening at one end.[117]

In use, these trenchers appear to have been handed round, probably painted side down, so that each individual could turn them over and read his or her verse or roundelay. In this way they were a Tudor/Stuart version of the 'jokes' found in Christmas crackers, but of higher quality and taste. The *Art of English Poesie* of 1589 described verses or epigrams 'to be printed or put upon banketting dishes of sugar plate, or of March paines, &c., and never contained above one verse, or two at most, but the shorter the better. We call them poesies, and do paint them now-a-dayes upon the back sides of our fruit-trenchers of wood.'[118] They covered subjects ranging from biblical texts, marital and single life, the months of the year, occupational characters, the sibylls, philosophy, to flowers, fruits and other ornament. A few examples demonstrate their character:

(With a painting of Dives and Lazarus)

Luke, XVI.

This lazar pore on hyearth had paine
but after deathe had Joy and reste:
The glotton riche had pleasares vaine
and after deathe hath hell posseste [119]

(With a painting of a bachelor)

The Bachelor

How many things as yet are deare alike to me,
The field, ye horse, ye dog, love, armes, or libertie,
I have no wife as yet, whome I may call my owne,
I have no children yet that by my name are knowne;
Yet if I married were, I would not wish to thrive,
If that I could not tame ye veriest shrew alive [120]

Now spend thy goods amongst thy frends
whilst life doth license lende
& let thy sonnes know how to gett
Before they know to spende [121]

Ask yu yr wyffe if she can tell
Whether yu in marriage haste spedd well;
And let her speake as she dothe knowe,
For XX pounde she will saye noo [122]

ROSE
Esteem of me as one in worth that standes,
Sweetes can I give you, and water for your hands [123]

Some of the designs show the influence of Continental artists, such as the Swiss Virgil Solis (1514–1562). His wood engravings published in the *Biblische Figuren dess Alten Testaments* (Frankfurt, 1565) were the source of a set of trenchers now in Strangers' Hall, Norwich.[124] Similarly, Jan van de Velde's 1621 engravings of *Aesop's Fables*, after 1569 originals by Marcus Gheeraerts, were pasted on trenchers and given English captions such as:

The Ape and Fox
The Ape would have halfe Leonord's tayle
To hide his bum nakt as his nayle.
The meaning is such as have store
Should be more liberall to the poore [125]

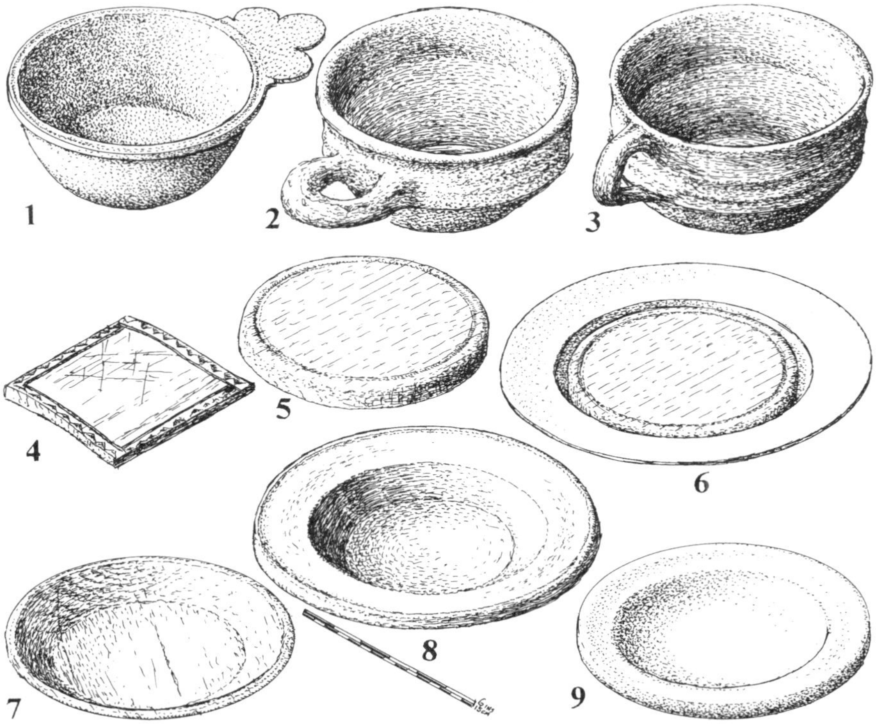

Figure 89. Porringers & plates. The 16th and early 17th centuries saw the development of new vessels reflecting the change from communal dishes to those for individual use. These porringers were used for liquid and semi-liquid foods, (1) being pewter of c. *1500–1550, (2) of late 16th century 'Border' earthenware, and (3) of earthenware from the Potovens pottery near Wakefield. Square wooden trenchers (4) from the* Mary Rose *of 1545 were now being made round to fit within pewter or silver trencher-plates (5 & 6 from the* Mary Rose*) to help contain the food, and to prevent the plates being damaged by knife cuts. Other plates were made of wood (7 from the* Mary Rose*) or glazed earthenware (8) late 16th century Border Ware, (9) from Sandal castle, Wakefield, 1645).*

PORRINGERS & PLATES

Throughout the medieval period liquid foods such as pottages were usually eaten from communal bowls or dishes, solid foods such as meats also being served on communal dishes before small portions were transferred to individual trenchers. These methods were ideal so long as it was the practice to serve food to 'messes' of four people. In some circumstances messing continued into the later seventeenth century, but from the early 1500s there was an increasing tendency for foods to be placed in or on smaller vessels intended for use by individuals. One of the first of the new vessels was the porringer or pottager, which came into increased use in pewter, silver and north-country 'Cistercian' earthenwares from the closing decades of the fifteenth century.[126] Pewter examples were found on the *Mary Rose*, while earthenware porringers, both of English manufacture and also imported from Dutch potteries, became popular in East Anglia, London and the south coast during the latter half of the sixteenth century. Most of those made on the Hampshire-Surrey border for the London market were yellow-glazed, with a loop handle set horizontally on one (rarely two) sides, and had a capacity of around a pint.

Plates, as replacements for trenchers, but with their flat bases surrounded by a raised rim in order to contain solid foods and some of the liquids from stews and runnier dishes, were introduced during the late sixteenth century. The first pewter and silver examples had broad, flat rims, which continued into the 1690s, and measured around 8–9 inches (20–23cm) across.[127] In order to accommodate the new kind of dining, in which a selection of foods were eaten off the same 'plate', wooden trenchers began to be made with raised rims and hollow, flat-bottomed centres. Such trenchers remained in use in cottages, farmhouses and servants halls through into the late nineteenth century. Most of the coarse lead-glazed earthenware potteries began to make ceramic plates for individual use from the mid-sixteenth century, demonstrating the decline in the practice of taking food from large communal dishes placed in the centre of the table in most middle- and lower-status homes. The broad, flat rim surrounding all plates, regardless of their quality or materials, was there to serve the very practical purpose of a handle. Specifically designed to allow the plates to be securely gripped between the thumb and crooked forefinger, it enabled them to be set in place or handed round without contaminating their contents. This was of great importance where foods were being distributed from the head of the table, or where one diner 'helped' another to a portion of something which was out of reach.

CUTLERY AND FLATWARE

Most individuals in medieval England, whatever their social status, had carried their personal eating knife at their belt, ready for use at table. This practice appears to have slowly died out in the early seventeenth century as households began to acquire sets of knives which were now placed beside each plate at the start of a meal. Perhaps leading this change, Henry VIII had owned at least a couple of dozen sets, each 'case' or 'stock' holding up to 24 matching knives.[128] Some cases also incorporated a number of carving knives, so that all the cutlery on the table appeared uniform, while others included a ginger-fork, and were most probably intended to be used at sweetmeat banquets.[129] Most were housed

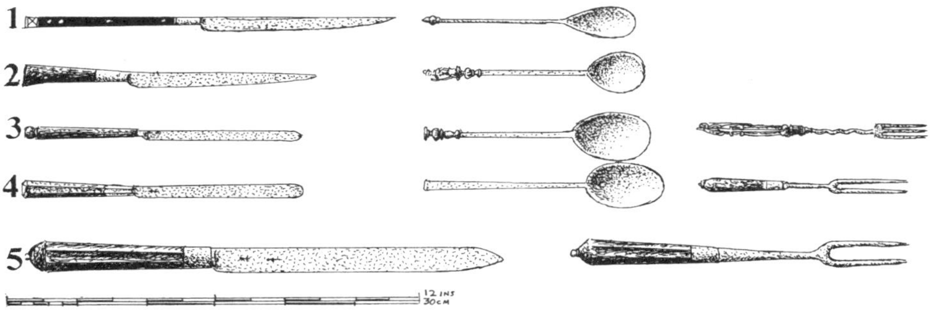

Figure 90. Cutlery. The general design of cutlery slowly evolved throughout the Tudor and early Stuart period. (1) c. 1500; *(2)* c. 1550; *(3)* c. 1600; *(4)* c. 1650; *(5) a carving knife and fork of* c. 1660.

in leather cases, but his finest cases took the form of a bejewelled silver-gilt woman or a dragon, weighing 86 and 176oz respectively.[130] These were of fabulous value, in contrast to the Lord Mayor of London's 'two cases with 16 knives 4*s*.' of 1577.[131]

Whether hafted with the rarest, most expensive and most beautiful of materials for the great, or of wood, bone or horn for the rest, the forged steel blades and overall dimensions of most knives followed some general trends. Up to around 1550 most eating knives were narrow and some 6–7½ inches (15–19cm) long with a sharply pointed straight or slightly convex back. Their tangs were usually forged flat to receive a pair of thin plates or 'scales' of wood, bone or horn, each held in place with brass rivets, although a few had their handles forged from the solid iron. In the latter half of the century the same techniques were followed, but with the shoulders and caps of the handles increasingly being forged integrally with the tang. The main change at this period was the elongation of the blade, which developed almost parallel edges and backs terminating in a sharp point, the total length being around 7-9½ inches (18–23cm). Some Elizabethan knives were made with a small decorative finial projecting from the bottom of their handles, this pulling out to reveal its sharp point, for use as a toothpick.

From the later sixteenth century, knives became a little shorter, some 7–8 inches (18–20cm) in length, with their parallel-sided blades finishing at an obtuse point. The handles, meanwhile, took on a slightly tapering profile, usually hexagonal or octagonal in section and mounted on a narrow tang. Many handles were elaborately decorated, perhaps being carved from solid ivory or boxwood, or inlaid with contrasting materials, with engraved silver mounts on the finest examples. Some of the most elaborate knives were made as wedding presents, made in pairs and fitted into a single sheath, as mentioned in contemporary literature. A lady in Thomas Dekker's *Match me in London* of 1620 states, 'see at my Girdle hang my wedding knives', while a character in Dekker, Rowley and Ford's *Witch of Edmonton* of 1621 sees 'the bridegroom and bride come, a new pair of Sheffield knives, fitted both in one sheath.'[132]

Just as knives were essential for cutting solid foods, spoons were necessary for all liquid and semi-liquid dishes. Some for use by those of lower status might be of wood, horn and bone, but those of pewter and silver were much more desirable, a silver spoon sometimes being the sole piece of precious metal in a yeoman's home. Most spoons measured about 6 inches (15cm) long, having a straight, narrow and parallel shaft to their handles, a shallow fig-shaped bowl at one end, and either a plain 'slip-top' or 'stump-top' at the other, or an ornamental finial. The earlier finials might include relatively plain baluster, acorn or melon shapes, or a maidenhead, bearded head, an alderman, apostle, saint, worthy, or heraldic device such as a lion. By the early seventeenth century some of these, particularly the apostles or elaborate renaissance balusters, were being topped with a small round disc to give a 'seal-top'. This provided an ideal place on which to engrave or stamp initials and dates as marks of ownership.

In order to lift pieces of preserved ginger and other wet suckets from their glutinous syrups, wealthy medieval diners had used long-handled two-pronged forks. The concept of using such a specialized implement to replace the fingers when dining was completely alien to most people in England. It removed most of the tactile enjoyment of dining, was far more likely to allow food and its juices to drop onto tablecloths and laps, and was just the kind of effeminate Continental affectation which every self-respecting Englishman should abhor. In his *Crudities* of 1611 Thomas Coryatt described how he had seen the Italians:

> at their meals use a little fork when they cut their meat. For while with their knife, which they hold in one [right] hand, they cut the meat out of the dish, they fasten their fork which they hold in their [left] hand upon the same dish, so that whatsoever he be that, sitting in the company of any other at meal, should unadvisably touch the dish of meat with his fingers from which all at the table do cut, he will give occasion of offence unto the company ... their forks [are] for the most part made of iron or steel, and some of silver, but those are used only by gentlemen ... I myself thought good to imitate the Italian fashion by this forked cutting of meat ... oftentimes since I came home ... [133]

This description shows that at this time the fork was solely used to replace the left hand (as used for toilet purposes) for gripping the food in the communal dish. Some years may have elapsed before it performed its modern role of replacing the right hand as a means of lifting food from the plate to the mouth. Some time after 1614, Ben Jonson recorded the adoption of the fork into fashionable circles. Having explained that he was trying to obtain a patent for forks, Meere is asked: 'Forks? What be they,' and replies,

> The laudable use of forks
> Brought into custom here, as they are in Italy,
> To th'sparing o' napkins.[134]

This was one of their main advantages, enabling diners to eat without soiling their fingers, and hence their napkins. Soon sets were being purchased for aristocratic use, the Howard family buying ten, each made from an ounce of silver, in April 1630 for £3 13*s*. 6*d*.[135] The earliest surviving English-made example, dating from 1632, was found beneath the floorboards of Haddon Hall, and remains in the collection of the Duke of Rutland. It should be stressed, however, that table-forks continued to be a rarity in this country throughout the seventeenth century. Most people preferred to continue using their fingers, this being a simple, practical, elegant and enjoyable experience for everyone trained in good manners.

TABLE LINEN

In many households of gentry and lower status the production of linen was the responsibility of the lady of the house. Having seen the flax and hemp sown in March and April, the plants were harvested in late summer. They were then rippled [combed], watered, washed, dried, braked [crushed], swingled [beaten], heckled [combed], dressed, spun, reeled, scoured, washed and bleached in the home.[136] The finished yarn was usually sent out to a weaver, who would convert it into cloth of the required weave. This constituted an appreciable outlay in time and money, linens representing a major household investment, being carefully laundered, ironed and stored to provide decades of regular use.

The finest linens were usually imported from Flanders, where there was greater expertise in weaving the best of yarns into pictorial designs called damask. These, although woven in uniform white yarn, had various twills which made the designs appear in relatively light and dark shades according to the fall of the light. The same effect was used to create diapers, all-over designs usually in diamond shapes. Plain-woven cloths were simply called 'linens', while 'canvases' were made of coarser-spun and mainly unbleached yarns of flax or hemp, also with a plain weave. As with all other aspects of material culture, the finest and most expensive linens were used by those of high status, and the coarsest by

Figure 91. Table linen. This damask napkin is woven with the arms as borne by both Henry VII and Henry VIII.

those below them. A few linen or diaper tablecloths and the like would be in regular use in most modest households, but the stocks maintained by the wealthy gentry and nobility were quite substantial. The following list, taken from the 1594 inventory of Sir William Fairfax of Gilling Castle, Yorkshire, is typical. Their lengths were:[137]

Tablecloths
5 damask woven with a spread eagle or a marigold and rose 14ft 9 in–21ft (4.5–6.4m)
and 1 square cloth
4 diaper 8ft 9in–25ft 6in (2.66–7.7m)
13 linen 7ft 6in–13ft 6in (2.28–4.1m)
7 square cloths, 5 hall cloths
12 canvas 7ft 6in–22ft 6in (2.28–6.86m)
2 drawing cloths 12ft–18ft (3.66–5.49m)
5 square cloths

Cupboard cloths	*Towels*	*Napkins*
2 damask	3 damask 12ft–15ft (3.66–4.57m)	60 damask
2 diaper	6 linen 12ft (3.66m)	12 diaper
10 linen 9ft (2.75m)	4 linen 6ft–9ft (1.83–2.75m)	144 linen

With damask valued at some 10*s.* a yard, diaper at 3*s.*, linen at 1*s.*–1*s.* 6*d.* and canvas at 3*s.*, the stock of linen amounted to £17 6*s.* 8*d.*.

All of these linens would be about a yard wide, hemmed at the ends and with a selvedge along both sides. Each would have been cut from a bolt of cloth such as the '25 yeardes of dammaske for table clothes at 10*s.* a yearde' purchased for the Howard family in 1634.[138] Its making up would then follow, the steward for the Earl of Leicester paying 'To Mistris Garner wch. she payd and others to goodwyf Smith for hemming and markyng of 53 dossen of napkyns and towels … £3 2 0*d.*'[139] It was comparatively rare to have a tablecloth made up to fit a round table, but they did exist, round tables for the chamber and round tablecloths being recorded in Elizabethan Exeter.[140]

Weaving wide tablecloths was a very expensive process before the invention of the flying shuttle, a worker being required on both sides of the loom to hurl the shuttle some 3 yards (2.75m) through the warps. Big, seamless tablecloths were therefore only found in the most important establishments. Those used by Henry VIII were usually some 24ft x 9ft (7.32 x 2.75m), with Stafford knots, lovers' knots, crowns and fleur de lis designs in damask.[141] His finest had their edges embroidered in black silk and gold thread, with a rich fringe; his napkins, each 3ft 9in x 2ft 3in (1.14 x 0.69m), having the royal arms or the Salutation of Our Lady in damask, or gold-thread embroidery and gold-fringed ends.[142] Most of the cupboard cloths were of diaper some 12ft x 6ft 4½in (3.66 x 1.95m) while the towels measured up to 60ft x 2ft 3in (18.3 x 0.69m), suitably long for use at great ceremonial feasts.[143] The towels worn by those serving at the royal table, called either sewers' or neck-towels, were of the usual size, being narrow strips 9ft 4½in x 4½in (2.86 x 0.11m) of plain-weave linen or nettlecloth.[144]

Further cupboard cloths, those set on first, before the linen cupboard cloths, were made of coloured turkey-work, woollen or worsted cloths in most wealthy households. Some were red or green 'Penistones' named after the Yorkshire Pennine town in which these baize-like woollens were made. They cost some 3*s.* 4*d.* a yard in 1630.[145] In the royal household they were of red, crimson or green figured velvet, 9ft 9in (2.97m) long by three breadths wide, provided with buttons and tassels of silk and gold to hold them in place.[146]

This was in great contrast to the simple length of coarse linen or canvas which served as tablecloths in the halls of most communal households.[147]

LINEN FOLDING

A number of contemporary paintings show a regular pattern of creases marking out the surface of tablecloths where they had been folded into a series of rectangles.

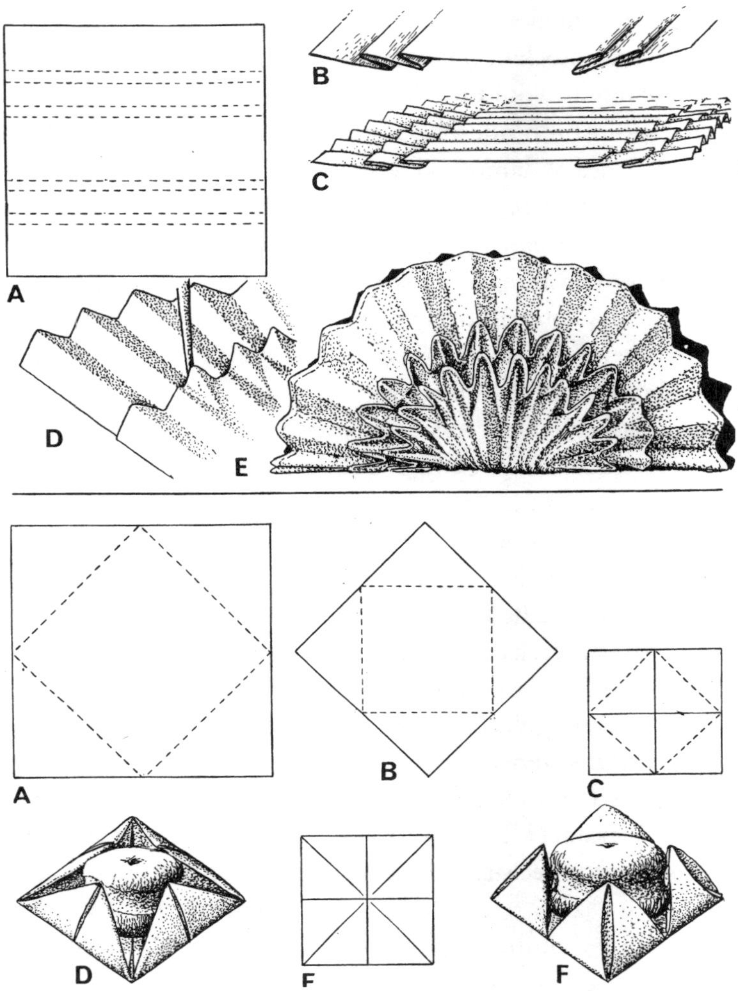

Figure 93. Napkin folding. These basic methods of napkin folding, though reflecting earlier practice, come from A perfect School for Officers of the Mouth *of 1682. To form a Cockleshell Double (top), take the open napkin (A) fold into 'bands' (B), and then into tight, narrow pleats at right-angles to the bands (C). Use a blunt point to lift up the folded edges of each band (D) and nip firmly in place. Finally turn the napkin upside down, squeeze the central part of the pleats tightly together, place a dinner- bun on them, then raise up each of the fan-like 'cockleshells' to the front and back (E).*

To make the Cross (bottom), fold each corner of the napkin to the centre (A), press down the folds, then turn it over and fold the corners to the centre once more (B). Turn over again and fold each corner upwards (C) to produce a Cross (D) to surround a bread-bun. This could be converted into a Cross of Lorraine by turning over once more and pulling up each corner around the bun.

Figure 92. Napkin folding. These designs, in Matthias Geigher's Li Tre Trattati *published in Padua in 1639, demonstrate the amazing achievements of professionally trained napkin folders.*

These were practical in a number of ways; they enabled large pieces of linen to be stored and carried efficiently, they provided a grid-pattern on which to set dishes and other tableware symmetrically in place, and they demonstrated a high standard of housekeeping.

In contrast, the folding of the crisply starched and smoothly ironed fine damask or diaper napkins developed into an extremely complex art-form, outclassing most modern Japanese origami. This was another of the butler's skilled tasks in a great house, for, as Robert Herrick noted,

> And the smirk Butler thinks it
> Sin, in's Naprie, not to express his wit;
> Each striving to devise
> Some gin [device] wherewith to catch your eyes.[148]

If a royal visit was anticipated, specialist linen-folders might be engaged, the Earl of Shrewsbury employing two Frenchmen to perform this service for a visit by Queen Anne of Denmark in June 1603.[149] Those who wished to learn this craft would have to find someone prepared to give them the necessary training. It was not until 1682 that the Continental manual of instruction entitled *A Perfect School for Officers of the Mouth* was first translated and published in London, but even then most of its directions for napkin 'nipping' or 'pinching' were completely unfathomable and beyond all practical understanding.

Figure 94. Ewers & basins. Used for ceremonial hand-washing before and at the close of formal meals, ewers and basins were of the finest design and workmanship. (1) Archbishop Parker's ewer of 1545; (2) the Henslowe ewer of 1562; (3 & 4) the ewer and basin probably made for Thomas, Earl of Arundel, by a Dutch goldsmith in 1617. They show the Triumph of Neptune. The silver gilt designs within the basin would have been given an additional combination of gleam and movement when seen beneath the crystal-clear rosewater.

TABLE CARPETS

Dining tables were usually covered with a table-carpet, the finest being knotted carpets imported from Turkey and the Middle East or Iberia, or of turkey-work, a form of embroidered woollen tapestry made in this country. Their rich colours and elaborate designs added to the impressive visual impact of every great dining chamber, such as those at Hardwick Hall.[150] Lesser tables were covered in green cloth carpets, the ancestors of the thick green baize cloths laid beneath every fine damask tablecloth up to the early mid-twentieth century.[151] These turkey and green cloth carpets made an enormous contribution to the dining experience. They muffled the sound of every dish as it was set in place, seemed to hold the tableware gently in place to prevent it wobbling and rattling, protected the linen cloth from the sharp corners and edges of the woodwork, prevented it from slipping off, and enabled it to lie smooth and even.

COVERPANES

As soon as the servants had laid the table for their sovereign or lord, they covered everything at his place-setting with a cloth called a coverpane. This was usually of the highest quality, such as a piece of coloured silk, but for royal use some were of the finest linens or silks embroidered in red, white, blue, gold and silver threads, with Venetian silver and gold braided sides and fringed ends. Their designs included the King's Beasts, crosses, knots, initials or inscriptions. Most measured about 3ft 9in x 3ft (1.14 x 0.91m), to cover a single setting, but another of 10ft 6in x 1ft 6in (3 x 0.46m) was probably intended to cover a number of settings of equal status.[152]

EWERS, BASINS & LAVERS

Since the hands would touch the food during the meal, it was essential that they should be washed immediately beforehand. For those in the hall, an ewer of water, a basin and coarse towels were placed at 'the towel' just within the screens passage or at the bottom end of the hall. Further washing facilities were set out on the cupboard for the use of the table-servants, while the finest ewer and basin would be carried from here directly up to the lord or lady in their inner chamber. For them, the staff of the ewery, or, lacking such a department, the butler, had to first prepare the hand-washing water. This might be distilled rosewater, such as the 'rosewater for the lords' table this term at 12*d*. The dinner for 15 dinners, 15*s*.' provided in 1590 for the Privy Council when dining in the Star Chamber.[153] As an alternative a handful of lavender flowers, a few cloves, a little orace powder and 4oz (100g) of gum benzoin (a Far Eastern or North American tree resin) might be distilled, and a little added to the hand-washing water.[154] If none of these was available, a few drops of the oils of clove, mace or nutmeg could be shaken in a bottle with a pint of water which 'you shall find very pleasing and delightful water to wash with ... before such time as your guests be ready to sit downe.'[155]

In cold weather, the water had to be heated for use. This was done by pouring it into a silver 'Chafer for water 81 ounces' at Hardwick Hall, or the three-legged chafers with single handles weighing some 35–50oz in the inventory of Henry VIII.[156] One reference to his 'skillet or Chafer' suggests that they resembled a three-legged saucepan which could hold the perfumed water over the heat of embers either on the hearth or in a chafing-dish.

The usual vessel used to dispense the water was an ewer, a form of spouted jug with a foot-rim that engaged on a central boss on its matching basin. Some were glass, tin, glazed earthenware or pewter, but the best were of silver, silver-gilt or gold, all designed and embellished to the highest standard. Queen Jane Seymour commissioned a set made from 109oz of solid gold: the ewer standing on three dragon-heads, its border chased with red and white Tudor roses and the royal motto in coloured enamels, its cover terminating in an angel bearing the king's arms.[157] Similar vessels, called lavers, could be even more magnificent. One owned by Henry VIII had a large mother-of-pearl shell mounted on an octagonal pedestal, a handle in the form of an antique man, and the spout and rim encased in gold. Complete with ten diamonds, twenty-eight rubies, seventeen emeralds, three sapphires and twenty-one pearls, it weighed 10lb, making a rich display of sparkling splendour when it appeared at the start and finish of a great feast.[158]

PERFUME PANS

In order to drive away any stale odours and perfume a chamber before use, it was customary to heat a number of scented substances over a small fire of glowing charcoal. In 1542 Andrew Boorde considered that contagion could be driven away by burning juniper, rosemary, rushes, bay-leaves, marjoram, frankincense (an aromatic gum resin), or gum benzoin every morning.[159] Alternatively one could,

> Lay two or three drops of liquid Amber upon a glowing coale or a piece of Lignum Aloes, Lignum Rhodium, or Storax.[160]

Or:

> Take of storax calamyte half an unce, of frankensence a unce, of the wodde of Aloes the weyghte of 6*d*; myxe al these togyther; Than cast half a sponefull of this in a chaffyng-dysshe of coles, And set it to fume abrode in the chambers & the hall ... [161]

The most basic fuming vessels were those made for the London market from the late sixteenth century to the mid-seventeenth. Of lead-glazed earthenware, these perfume pots resembled narrow chafing dishes, but with a high, narrower neck, and the sides and shoulders pierced with a number of holes. A hole in the base admitted fresh air which passed up through a small central hole (or group of holes) into the integral internal bowl which contained the glowing charcoal.[162] Sprigs of juniper or the other perfumes could be placed directly on the charcoal, but here the fierce heat could easily set them aflame, rather than to smoulder. This suggests that a number of other vessels made in the same potteries, deep, narrow cylindrical pots with broader rims and short handles which just fit into

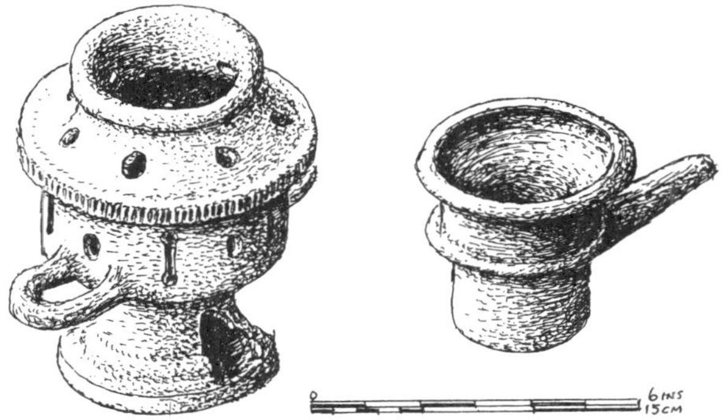

Figure 95. Perfuming. Having placed a few pieces of smouldering charcoal into the upper part of the perfume pot, sprigs of juniper or other scented substances might be placed on top, the gentle heat driving off their perfumes. It is probable that other perfumes such as resins, rosewater and perfumed vinegars were put inside the small pan and set into the top of the perfume pot, being left there to evaporate.

the necks of the perfume pots, were used to hold the odoriferous gums, juniper seeds and other agents.[163] Here measured quantities of the dry perfumes could be smouldered in a much more efficient and controlled manner, or rosewaters or vinegars evaporated to disperse their scents.[164]

In contrast, those in Henry VIII's inventory were of silver, or silver-gilt, some with columns, some with lids and some with three knobbed feet.[165] The finest of his perfume pans contained two separate pans for perfume, was decorated with the signs of the zodiac and a map, and weighed an impressive 92 ounces.[166]

CASTING BOTTLES

In Bess of Hardwick's inventory of 1601, there were three silver-gilt casting bottles, each weighing between four and twelve ounces.[167] Their purpose was to hold perfumed waters and to sprinkle them around the chambers to sweeten their atmosphere. Their contents were prepared as follows.

SWEET WATER FOR A CASTING BOTTLE[168]

3/16oz oil of spickenard	*1/16oz oil of cloves*
1/16oz oil of thyme	*1g civet*
1/16oz oil of lemons	*1pt. rosewater*

Having mixed the oils together, a tiny amount, 3 grains or some 1/500 of an ounce, was put into a silver spoon, the rosewater being poured in in small batches and rubbed in with the finger before dropping into a silver bowl, until all was completely dissolved. Further civet might then be added if not sufficiently strong.

STREWING HERBS

'The chamber shuld be replenyshed with herbes & flowers of odyferouse savour' advised Andrew Boorde.[169] He was talking of the sick-room, but the same principal was followed in halls and chambers. The practice of strewing the narrow, round stemmed *Juncus* rushes of heaths, moors and wetland across the floors of halls and chambers continued at least up to the middle of the seventeenth century. As anyone knows who has attended a rushbearing service in the Lake District, they provide a pleasant, refreshing perfume of their own. Bents, or coarse grasses were also strewn, as at Naworth Castle, Cumberland:

Nov. 1620	For rushes for the chamber 4*d*.
July 1618	For bents to strew the chamber[170]

When these, or the strip-plaited rush mats from Norfolk, had dried out, some additional perfuming was needed, this taking the form of fresh herbs. The accounts of Robert Dudley, Earl of Leicester, confirm this practice,

1588–9	for erbes to trym the house
1588–9	for strewing herbs for your chamber 1*s*. 6*d*.[171]

while elsewhere there were payments such as,

1582	Paid for Jyneper to swetten the Hall 1*d*.
1620	to Ellwood ... for cutting juniper 4*d*.[172]

All scented herbs, including lavender, rosemary, thyme and the like were used in this way to keep the dining areas sweet and fresh to the nose.

VOIDERS

At the end of a course, a servant would come to the table bearing a shallow tray of wood, pewter or silver called a voider, along with a voiding knife of wood, or a voiding skimmer of silver.[173] Using the knife or skimmer, he gathered the crumbs together on the tablecloth and scooped them into the voider, along with the soiled bread-trenchers, loaves and other detritus, thus leaving the cloth clean before the towels were spread along it for the final hand-washing ceremony.

WASHING-UP

After being carried back from the tables into the buttery, all the tableware had to be washed in hot water, the addition of bran acting as a mild soap and soft abrasive. In the Verney household, the following method was used:

> For your plaites if they be well washed every meal with water and bran so hott as their hands can indure it, then well rinsed in faire water, and soe sett one by one before the fire, as they may drie quick, I am confident they will drie without spots, for I never knew any sawce staine soe except it be pickled rabbits, which stand upon the plaite awhile so they will staine them filthyly.[174]

The alternative was to dry and polish the dishes using coarse cloths called rubbers.[175] If further polishing was required, 'a store of chawke for the buttry plate' mixed with oil proved effective, with fine sand for the rougher vessels.[176]

This description of the contents and the use of the buttery and pantry clearly demonstrates their essential roles in preparing, maintaining and housing every utensil and supply required by those dining both in hall and in chamber. It remains incomplete however, since other items of tableware and condiments, all forms of table lighting, and the pens, ink, ledgers and tally sticks used to control its activities have been omitted, along with the barrels of wine, ale, vinegar and verjuice frequently stored there.

96. A family at dinner. The late-Elizabethan introduction of porringers, a concept imported from the Netherlands, enabled diners to take their pottage individually, rather than from the medieval shared mess of pottage. The children stand at the table as was usual at this time.

Figure 97. School dinners. Where pupils had their dinners at school, they sat around their master's table.

CHAPTER TWENTY-ONE

Table Manners

During the twentieth and early twenty-first centuries, virtually every film, stage-play and television programme has represented the table manners of the Tudor and early Stuart periods as being crude, coarse and disgusting by modern standards. This is due to a combination of gross ignorance and the commercial need to put dramatic effect before historical truth and accuracy. All the available evidence confirms that the ability to dine politely and elegantly was an essential social skill, one which had to be carefully learned in childhood, and maintained throughout adulthood. The degree of expertise required to dine and serve at table varied according to status. In most ordinary families, and those of yeomen, minor gentry and merchants, it was probably acceptable to know little more than how to sit at table and eat politely without causing offence to others. Dining and serving at a noble or royal table was a completely different matter, however, requiring years of careful training in etiquette, manual skills and vocabulary. This was passed on from one generation to another through the practice of sending sons, and sometimes daughters, away from home before they were teenagers to live with a family of higher status. There, as a combination of servant and surrogate child of their new guardians, they learned how to handle themselves in society. Those children who stayed at home with their parents were treated in a similar way; they served their parents at table, and gave them great respect. The modern method of having parents act as servants and waiters to their children would have appeared inconceivably ridiculous to most Tudor and Stuart families.

BASIC TABLE MANNERS

Being largely illiterate and rarely, if ever, invited to participate at polite dining tables, the ordinary working population needed no manners-books, and left no descriptions of how they took their meals. The best available evidence probably comes from accounts of working-class habits of the early nineteenth century. At that time only adults sat at table in many households, while forks might only be used to transfer food from dish to plate, the only personal cutlery being a spoon and a knife.[1] There appear to be few arguments against similar practices being followed in the sixteenth and seventeenth centuries.

As far as general table manners are concerned, those of 'the meaner sort of husbandman and country inhabitants' still left much to be desired, since they were guilty of,

> very much babbling, with whom he is thought to be the merriest that talketh of most ribaldry, or the wisest man that speaketh fastest among them, and now and then surfeiting and drunkenness ... Divers of them living at home, with hard and pinching diet, small drink, and some of them having scarce enough of that, are soonest overtaken when they come into ... banquets; howbeit they take it generally as no small disgrace if they happen to be cupshotten ... the poorest sort they generally dine and sup when they may, so to talk of the order of their repast it were but a needless matter. Husbandmen dine high noon ... and sup at seven or eight.[2]

Given this background, it is hardly surprising that most of the working population were unable to successfully manoeuvre their way through a formal meal without causing great embarrassment to both themselves and their hosts. Theirs would be a quite different experience, however, if they had been trained from childhood to observe the following basic table manners:

Demeanour

1. stand straight at table, with feet close together, if a child;
2. if taking a seat, let your betters sit above you;
3. don't pick your ears, nose or ears, particularly not your teeth with your knife;
4. wipe your nose on a handkerchief, don't blow aloud, sneeze away from the company;
5. don't rest elbows or fists on the table;
6. don't spit, if you have to, do it modestly and rub it into the floor with your foot; never spit into the basins used for hand-washing;
7. if yawning, turn away from the company and cover your mouth with your napkin;
8. don't belch;
9. fart silently;
10. don't scratch yourself under the table.

Conversation

11. don't speak until addressed by one's better;
12. don't speak with your mouth full;

13. don't whisper to your neighbour;
14. don't talk too much, it is better to be silent;
15. don't swear.

Taking Food

16. take salt from the salt cellar on the tip of your knife and put a little on your trencher;
17. wait a short while before starting to eat;
18. don't break your bread, cut it not too thin from the loaf or manchet;
19. spoon your pottage to your lips, don't drink it from the pottage dish or porringer, and don't spill it;
20. don't leave your spoon in the pottage dish;
21. cut your meat with your knife, never bite it, and take the food with your fingers [in practice, this meant that any piece of solid food in a communal dish was taken by gripping the required piece with the thumb and two forefingers of the left hand. The knife held with the thumb and forefingers of the right hand was then being used to cut it off, so that it could be placed on one's trencher];
22. cut meats and other foods, in small morsels on the trencher, using the fingers and knife as in 21, then prop the knife on the trencher and use the thumb and two forefingers of the right (clean) hand to raise them to the mouth, so that the left hand (used for dirty, toilet purposes) never approaches the lips;
23. never put the fingers into any dish;
24. don't dip your meat into the salt-cellar, only into the salt on your trencher;
25. only eat small morsels of meat;
26. don't cram your mouth;
27. don't blow your food;
28. don't smack the lips;
29. don't gnaw bones;
30. don't return any bones or scraps from your trencher back into their dishes or onto the floor, but put them into the communal voider;
31. keep your trencher clean, and don't spill anything onto the tablecloth;
32. don't wipe your knife (or spoon) on the tablecloth (but on a morsel of bread, which you then eat);
33. keep your fingers clean, mopping them on your napkin (which is kept in long, folded form over the left forearm or left shoulder).

Drinking

34. wipe your mouth on your napkin before drinking;

35. hold your cup with both hands;
36. don't drink with your mouth full;
37. mop your mouth with your napkin after drinking.

The abandonment of most of these basics may now be observed in any modern fast-food outlet, on the current Shakespearian stage, and on television's so-called history programmes.[3]

BASIC TRAINING

In middle- and upper-class homes a sound training in table manners was considered absolutely essential, commencing in early childhood. Any child might still have quite a different experience at mealtimes, sometimes being treated as a guest, and at others as servants. In one city merchant's house in 1573, for example, his nine-and-a-half-year-old son Henry and younger daughter were summoned into the dining-room by a pageboy just before midday. Passing the fifteen or sixteen guests, they approached their father at the table, where Henry bowed and took off his cap, while his sister made a curtsy. After Henry had said grace, his father asked him to read the second chapter of St John's gospel, which described how Jesus turned water into wine at a marriage feast at Cana in Galilee. Meanwhile a small round table was set up at the end of the main dining table, so that the children might eat on their own. After dinner had been served and the tables cleared, the merchant called Henry once more, first to say grace, and then to 'repeat some fair saying or sentence, that we may see what you have learned'. Eager to show off, Henry then asked 'What shall I say Father? A sentence, a proverb, a fable, an epigramme, or an apopthegme?' Given a free choice, he quoted, 'For one pleasure, a thousand sorrows', gaining general approval. Compared to some children in similar households, he had had very little to do, for many parents treated their sons as table-servants, this being the best way of providing them with the social skills and good manners which would be essential for their future success.[4]

A number of training manuals were published to give all the required information, one of the most useful being Francis Seager's *The School of Vertue, and booke of good Nourture for chyldren, and youth to learne theyr dutie by*, published in London in 1557. In it he described how boys should set their family dining table, wash and dry their hands and, when the family and their guests had taken their places, stand in front of their parents. Holding up their hands together, they had to recite grace:

Give thanks to God with one accord
For what shall be set on this board,
And be not careful [fussy] what to eat,
To each thing living the Lord sends meat.
For food he will not see you perish
But will you feed, foster and cherish.
Take well in worth what he has sent
At this time be therewith content
    Praising God, Amen.[5]

If he was younger, he might have chosen:

Here a little child I stand,
Heaving up my either hand,
Cold as paddocks [frogs] though they be,
Still I raise them up to thee
For a benison [blessing] to fall
On our meat, and on us all, Amen.[6]

After bowing to his parents and wishing them 'Much good may it do you', he went down to the kitchen and brought up the dishes of food, carefully placing each one in the correct position on the table, without any spillage. Even when he sat down to eat his dinner, he had to watch what was happening, constantly getting up to fetch more food, clean trenchers, and napkins, and fresh bread, and to carry away the dirty dishes and the 'voider' when it had been filled with bones and table-scraps. Once everyone had finished their meal, he then had to carry the salt cellar back to the cupboard, bring up a large voider (dish), pile all the dirty trenchers and napkins into it, along with the crumbs and other detritus he had swept from the cloth with a clean napkin, and then set it down at the end of the table. Next he served the banquet course, putting a clean trencher in front of each person, the most important first, and placing dishes of fruit, biscuits, sugar-coated caraway seeds and cheese on the table before serving glasses of wine, ale or beer. After these had been consumed, he carried away the dishes and glasses, put the trenchers into the voider, and then took that away too to leave nothing but the tablecloth. In order to prevent any crumbs falling onto the floor, the front and back of the tablecloth were folded into the middle part, and then it was neatly folded from the left end, to expose the bare table-top. For hand-washing, he first laid a long white linen towel along the table, with a basin and an ewer of water at its centre. His parents then stood up and held their hands over the basin, rinsing them as he trickled the water from the ewer. When they had dried their hands on the towel, he then carried everything back to the cupboard, made a deep bow to his parents and waited until they had left the room. All these chores were carried out at every dinner and supper, not just on special occasions, to make sure that boys learned good manners, and did not show themselves to be ignorant when dining with other families.[7]

SCHOOL MEALS

In Tudor England, most schools only taught boys, girls being instructed at home. After a light breakfast, probably of wholemeal bread and butter or fruit, the boys had to be at school between 8 and 9 o'clock, although some schools started as early as 6 o'clock every morning. At 11 a.m., some boys went home for their dinner, while the remainder took theirs around the classroom table. On Mondays, Tuesdays and Thursdays they would have a pottage (broth) of turnips, cabbages or other vegetables, all thickened with ground oats, barley or wheat, and then a dish of fine wheat flour and eggs. On the 'fasting days' of Wednesdays, Fridays and Saturdays, and during Lent and Advent, they had porringers full of pieces of bread soaked in warm skimmed milk, followed by fresh or salt fish, and finally dishes of peas and beans. There were also pieces of wholemeal bread and glasses of beer and water to accompany every dinner.

The next break, between 3 and 3.15 p.m., was called 'drinkings', and comprised a small piece of bread, with apples, pears, cherries and prunes in summer, or dried figs, raisins and almonds in winter, all eaten along with glasses of weak beer.

Finally, at 5 p.m., lessons ended, and all those who lived nearby went home for their suppers, only those boarded with the schoolmaster taking this meal around the classroom table. A fresh salad dressed with oil and vinegar came first, then boiled mutton with dry prunes, and small root vegetables or chopped green vegetables, or else some roast veal or kid, or dishes of minced meat or gallimafrie (hash). Finally, there was cheese and two nuts for everyone. On fasting days the second course of meats was replaced by one of fish or of eggs, either roasted, fried, poached or made into pancakes (these being sprinkled with vinegar) just as each boy wished.[8]

Instead of going to school, the children of the wealthier families were home-educated by private tutors. The relationship was not an easy one for the tutor, since, being of lower status than his pupils, he had to take on an appropriately subservient role to them. As Joseph Hall described in the early seventeenth century:

First, that he lie upon the truckle-bed
Whiles his yeoman master lieth o'er his head.
Second, that he do on no default
Ever presume to sit above the salt.
Third, he never change his trencher twice.
Fourth, that he use all common courtesies,
Sit bare at meals, and one half rise and wait ...
All these observed, he could contented be
To [receive] five marks and winter livery.

This verse is of particular interest, showing that trenchers were changed as each dish or course was finished, indicating that they were communal, rather than personal items of tableware.[9]

FAMILY MEALS

After a light breakfast, both gentry families and students usually took their dinners at 11 a.m., and suppers at 5 or between 5 and 6 p.m. In contrast, city merchants dined around midday and had their suppers at 6 p.m., giving them more time for trading and other business each morning. In 1605 Peter Erondell, a Huguenot refugee who ran a school in London, published *The French Garden*. This aid to the teaching of French to the twelve-year-old sons of the merchant class took a conversational approach, based on the everyday home-life of his pupils. In this way, unintentionally, he provided future generations with a unique insight into how meals were served and taken in typical middle-class homes of the early Jacobean period.

Having usually risen at 6 a.m., the lady of the house had set her maids to work in the kitchen and nursery, seen the French, dancing, singing and music tutors attend her daughters, and gone on a shopping expedition to the Royal Exchange, all before she and her guests returned home shortly before noon. Although the butler had laid a plain-woven cloth on the table in the great chamber, she still had to instruct him to complete his preparations with the following:

1. lay the cloth and napkins of damask linen;
2. bring out more plate trenchers;
3. set a knife, spoon and silver fork by each plate trencher;
4. take the cover off the salt-cellar, on the table;
5. put the pepper-box on the table;

6. place three basins, three ewers and three towels on the cupboard, together with:
7. the gold cup at its centre;
8. the silver-gilt cups;
9. the silver pots (flagons) filled with wine;
10. the silver chafing dish;
11. the drinking glasses;
12. the little silver casting-bottle full of rose vinegar;
13. a copper tub or cistern of water in which to cool the wine;
14. a wooden tub of water for rinsing the glasses and cups;
15. the knife-case, which must be removed once the knives had been laid on the table.

It was then proposed that the oysters should be eaten first, for otherwise the diners would have to wash their hands a second time before the first course. The meal, therefore, proceeded in this sequence:

1. Oysters, in their shells, set on a dish on a round table in the middle of the room, accompanied by brown bread, and saucers of vinegar seasoned with [sliced?] onions and pepper; however, since no one wishes to try the oysters, they remain unopened.
2. Handwashing. Although there were three basins, ewers and towels on the cupboard, the lady, her two lady and one gentleman guests decide to wash four to a basin, her daughter and an unmarried gentleman guest washing in another.
3. The lady and her guests take their places around the table, with the chief diners on chairs and the others on stools with cushions.
4. One of the gentlemen has to say grace, since no chaplain was present:

   O Lord, which giv'st thy creatures our food,
   Hearbs, beastes, birdes, fish, & other giftes of thine,
   Bless these thy giftes, that they might doe us good,
   And we may live, to praise thy name divine.
   And when the time is come this life to end:
   Vouchsafe our soules to heaven may ascend.

5. The lady helps her guests to the dishes laid on the table in the usual order. The first mess was made up of:
6. a first course of boiled dishes; broth, with white meat of a capon, a hen boiled with leeks or rice, turnips grown from seed brought from Caen, Normandy, salt beef with Tewkesbury or Dijon mustard. These were then cleared away and replaced by:

7. a second course of roasted dishes; beef, veal, leg of mutton with galentine, pies and artichokes, sauce. To drink, white wine, Graves, claret, Orleans, delicate Blois and strong Spanish or Greek wines offered, with water mainly for the younger daughter. One daughter calls for small beer, since the double-beer is too strong.
8. The second mess is served, a lady guest acting as carver. It comprises:
9. the third course of baked turkey and baked peacock cooked with pepper, ginger, clove, mace, nutmeg, cinnamon, saffron and sugar, roasted wild boar pig, imported from France, and other roasts of lamb, pheasant, quail, lark, chicken, woodcock, snipe, wood pigeon, rail, teal, heron, young capon, baby rabbits and leverets. A leg of capon was sent down to the cook to be carbonadoed (grilled) with a little wine, salt and pepper.

   These were accompanied by sliced oranges, olives, capers, cucumbers, green peas and salads of crimped lettuce, spinach, endive, borage flowers, bugloss, sage, rosemary and violet buds.

   On a fish day these would be replaced by salmon, sturgeon, lobster, shrimps, sole, gurnard, turbot, smelts, whiting, pike, carp, bream, tench, eel, along with vinegar served in saucers, all then being cleared away.
10. The fourth course follows, of quince pie, almond tart, cherry tart, gooseberry tart and prune tart.
11. Cheese is served, Angelot and Auvergne from France, Italian Parmesan, Holland cheese, and mild Banbury cheese. Some of the harder cheeses are grated and mixed with sage and sugar.
12. The fruit or banquet course is served, including strawberries and raspberries with cream, large peaches, home-grown apricots, plums, pears, apples, green walnuts, chestnuts if available.
13. All wash their hands at the table, using rosewater or another sweet water in the ewers.
14. Grace is said:

    O Lord our God, we yield thee prayse,
    For this thy gracious store:
    Praying that we may have the grace
    To keep thy lawes and lore,
    And when this life shall flitte away:
    Graunt us to live with thee for aye.

15. Instead of leaving the table at this point, everyone remains seated, for according to an English proverb,

    After Dinner sit a while;
    After Supper walke a mile.

The party rose about 2 p.m. then spent the afternoon walking in the garden, admiring its orchard, watercresses and fishpond, presumably having their suppers before an evening of dancing and games, finally going to bed just before 11 p.m.

With the exception of the unrealistically large number of individual dishes, which Erondell must have introduced to extend his pupils' vocabularies, his description covers many of the table manners followed by most middle-class Elizabethan families. One which he omitted was holding up the hands and spoons as an acknowledgement and salute to absent friends. In January 1615, Robert Heyricke, a Leicester alderman, wrote to his brother Sir William in London, to inform him how, on Boxing Day, his family had been,

> busy with holding up hands and spoons to yow,
> out of porredge and pyes, to the remembraunce
> of yowre gt. Lyberality of frute and spice,
> which God send yow long lyffe to contynew

As this and the following chapters clearly show, the table manners of the gentry, nobility and royalty of Tudor England were elegant, refined and tasteful. The Venetian Francesco Chiergato certainly found them to be so in 1517, when he noted that,

> In short, the wealth and civilization of all the world are here, and those who call the English barbarians appear to render themselves such. I perceive very elegant manners and politeness,

Most stage, film and television directors, presenters, celebrity chefs and all others depicting this period still fall into Chiergato's definition of a barbarian.

MEALS & MANNERS OUT OF DOORS

> Now doth the broad oak comfort the weary labourer, while under his shady boughs he sits singing to his bread and cheese.

Farm workers took impromptu snacks in the fields most months of the year, perhaps a little bread and cheese with small beer or ale. These would have been taken in the identical manner to that still used up to the mid-twentieth century, and as I was taught in Hampshire. The piece of cheese was gripped between the thumb and first two fingers of the left hand, the third and fourth fingers holding the hunk of bread against the heel of the palm. Alternate pieces were then cut off with a knife held in the right hand, being eaten directly from its back edge, where it had been held in place with the thumb. The meals served at

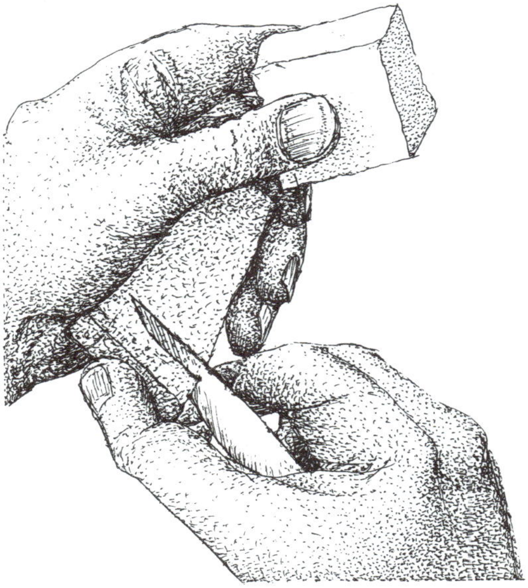

Figure 98. Eating out of doors. The traditional way of eating bread and cheese out in the fields saw the cheese grasped between the thumb and forefingers, and the bread between the palm and two small fingers, of the left hand. Alternate pieces were cut off between the knife and thumb of the right hand.

particularly busy times of the year would be eaten in the same way, including the bread and cheese, cheesecake and ale given to sheep-clippers in June, or the additional tempsed (hair-sieved wheat) loaf, cheese and meat pie provided in the corn harvest.

Other outdoor meals required holes to be dug into the ground. The New Year's Day meal taken by the shepherds at Hutton Conyers, Yorkshire, appears to have continued a late-medieval practice into a nineteenth-century custom. Having eaten their bread and cheese (as described above) a pot of mustard-flavoured frumenty was placed into a close-fitting hole, which supported it up to the rim. Each shepherd in order of precedence then used his wooden spoon to scoop up a mouthful, anyone who had forgotten their spoon having to lie down and eat theirs directly out of the pot. A much larger hole was required for taking meals at Dover's Games, the grand outdoor sporting event of the Cotswolds. High on the hill over Chipping Campden, Gloucestershire, amid the dancing, tumbling, wrestling, sword-play, quarter-staff, cudgel-play and various races, a long rectangular pit about 18 inches (45cm) deep was excavated to form a ground-level bench around a long central strip, which served as a table-top. As illustrated in a woodcut of 1636, it was used for drinking sessions,

Figure 99. A dining table at Dover's Games. Here a rectangular cut into the ground enabled the diners to sit around their earthen table.

Figure 100. An Elizabethan hunt dinner. Here the Queen is being served with the usual ceremonies, by a kneeling gentleman and a cup-bearer with his napkin over his right wrist. To the bottom right a youth approaches with a pair of black-jacks or bombards for ale or beer, while an officer of the cellar fills a glass from a wine flask taken from its cooling stream.

bearing two enormous tankards which were probably used to fill individual glasses.

Rustic arbours and tents had been used for outdoor meals for centuries, but these were inadequate for the great pre-planned entertainments prepared for royal receptions. Probably the most lavish were those erected for the meeting of Henry VIII and Francis I at the Field of the Cloth of Gold in June 1520. Smaller, but still extensive temporary pavilions were also set up by the aristocracy for state visits by their monarchs. Those prepared by the Earl of Hertford for the reception of Elizabeth I at Elvetham in Hampshire in 1591 were suitably grand:

> First there was made a room of estate for the nobles, and at the end thereof a withdrawing place for Her Majesty. The outsides of the walls were all covered with boughs and clusters of ripe hazelnuts, the insides with arras, the roof of the place with work of ivy leaves, the floor with sweet herbs and green rushes. Near unto this were many offices newly builded, as namely, spicery, lardery, chaundery, wine-cellar, ewery, and pantry; all of which were tiled. Not far off was erected a large hall for entertainment of knights, ladies and gentlemen of chief account.

These, with further rooms, for all others to dine in, contained nearly seventy feet of tables, all served with a complete suite of kitchen and service offices. Although very expensive, such pavilions were far cheaper than extending a house to palatial scale and being impoverished by its future upkeep.

The hunting lodges erected in major parks and chases provided excellent small-scale cooking and dining facilities. Men such as Sir Thomas Wortley of Wharncliffe Chase near Sheffield, really enjoyed such locations; in 1510 he 'cawsyd a loge to be made hon thys crag ne mydys of Wancliff, for his plesor to he[a]r the hartes bel', as he inscribed on the adjacent rocks. It might be pleasurable to take a meal out-of-doors, but this did not bring any diminution in the standards of either food or service. As George Turbeville described in his *Noble Art of Venerie of Hunting* of 1575:

> That done he spreads his cloth upon the grassy bank
> And sets to show his dainty drinks, to win his Prince's thanke,
> Then comes the captain cook, with many a warlike wight,
> Which armour bring and weapons both, with hunger for to fight,
> For while cold loins of Veal, cold Capon, Beef and Goose,
> With Pidgeon pies and mutton cold, are set on hunger loose.
> First neats tongues powdered well, and jambons of the hog,
> Then sausages and savoury knacks, to set men's minds a gog.

> Then King or comely queen, then Lords and Ladies look
> To see which side will bear the bell, the Butler or the Cook.
> At last the Cook takes flight, the butlers still abide
> And sound their drums, and make retreat, with bottles by their side.

John Milton chose to set Satan's temptation of Christ in the same kind of setting in *Paradise Regained:*

> In ample space under broadest shade
> A table richly spread in regal mode.
> With dishes piled of meats of noblest sort
> And savour – beasts of chase, or fowl of game,
> In pastry built, or from the spit, or boiled,
> Gris-amber-steamed; all fish, from sea or shore,
> Freshet or purling brook of shell or fin,
> And exquisitest name, for which was drained
> Pontus, and Lucrine bay, and Afric coast ...
> And at a stately sideboard, by the wine,
> That fragrant smell diffused, in order stood
> Tall stripling youths rich-clad, of fairer hue
> Than Ganymed or Hylas ...

These would have brought great delight to James I when out hunting. As the parson of Fordham in Cambridgeshire recorded in his parish register on 27 February 1604, 'ye High and mighty Prince James ... did hunt ye hare with his own hounds in our Fields of Fordham and did kill six near a place called Blackland and did take his repast in ye same Fields at a Bush near unto King's Path'.

At the end of a deer-hunt, the preparation of the carcass for culinary use took place in the field, each action being formalized into a precise ceremony, as Erasmus described in his *Praise of Folly* of 1500:

> And then what pleasure they take to see a Buck or the like unlac'd. Let ordinary fellows cut up an Ox or a wether, 'twere a crime to have this done by anything less than a gentleman, Who, with his hat off, on his bare knee, and a cuttoe [a short, hollow-ground hunting sword] for that purpose (for every sword or knife is not allowable), with a curious superstition and certain posture, layes open the several parts in their respective order, while they that hem him in admire it with silence, as some new religeous Ceremony, though perhaps they have seen it a hundred times before.
>
> And if any of 'em chance to get the least piece of it, he presently thinks himself no small Gentleman.

CHAPTER TWENTY-TWO

Dining in the Hall

The largest, highest and most dominant room in any sizeable house was the hall, its large windows, high roof and, in the best, tall louvre topped by glittering weather-vanes, being instantly recognizable from a distance. Usually entering by a porch at its ceremonial lower end, every visitor would pass through its door into a cross-passage, from which doors on one side led back to the buttery, kitchen and pantry, while openings in the screen on the other gave access to the hall itself. The first view into it was intended to be as impressive as possible, ensuring instant recognition of the quality of both its family and its household. A gallery above the screens-passage provided a platform for minstrels, as well as for dining tables for those of lowest rank at times of great feasting. Most of the earlier halls were open to their great timber-framed roofs, and had the window sills of their side walls set high above head height, but these were replaced by flat ceilings and lower windows in many houses built from the 1580s, when upper floors were increasingly constructed over the halls. A central open hearth in the medieval tradition might be placed towards the upper end of the hall, but these were gradually being replaced by fireplaces with chimneys in the side or lower-end walls.

The upper end of the hall, although part of the same space, was treated as a separate, higher-status room. It might be demarcated by having a raised dais, or a large full-height bay window to one side, illuminating it almost as if it were a stage. Here there were doors leading through into the chambers, and perhaps also to stairs leading either down to the wine cellars, or up to the higher chambers.

Despite its grandeur, the hall had already been used almost exclusively as a servants' hall for centuries, for here all the household servants took their meals, only the family and their most important guests dining beyond in the parlours or chambers, and the scullions and kitchen boys back in the kitchens. The furniture used in the hall was usually quite sparse and utilitarian, as illustrated by inventories, for example:

> 1 little table, 1 chair, 2 buffet stools, 2 long tables and the forms belonging to them, 2 cupboards & a little counter (Ripon Park, 1559);[1]
>
> 1 table across the end of the hall, 1 chair, 2 side tables, 8 forms & 1 cupboard in the bay (Sizergh Castle, 1569);[2]

Figure 101. The hall, Cowdray House, Sussex. Bare walls, the steward and senior officers on the top table, clerks, cooks and minor officials at one table, and a vacant table awaiting the arrival of the lord's waiters and the left-overs from his dinner. With virtual silence, no music, most likely no heat, and no external views, this was the usual appearance of every hall, a great contrast to the scenes of unbridled debauchery and drunkenness usually depicted in modern period dramas.

> 3 long tables & 6 forms (Hardwick Hall, 1601);[3]
>
> 2 long tables, 7 forms & 1 cupboard (Chatsworth, 1601);[4]
>
> 1 round table, 5 chairs & 1 buffet stool, 1 long table & 1 long form, 1 counter & 2 trestles, 1 cupboard (Eccleshill, 1612);[5]
>
> 1 round table, 30 high buffet stools, some newly made, 2 tables, 1 long table with a long form and a bench fastened into the ground. 1 wainscot bench (Walton, 1624).[6]

As these few entries show, halls could be used in a variety of ways. In some (Ripon Park and Sizergh Castle), there was a top table across the end of the hall, with a chair and stools and forms for those sitting behind it, with two long tables in the body of the hall, where lower servants sat on benches. In some great houses of the late sixteenth century (Hardwick and Chatsworth) there was no top table, since the upper servants were dining in a separate chamber or parlour. In smaller houses of the same period (Eccleshill, W. Yorkshire) the long top table and single chair might be replaced by a round table surrounded by a number of chairs, while the lower servants sat on a form at one side of a single long table. The same kind of round table, this time surrounded with stools, is seen in Sir William Fairfax's house (Walton), with the lower servants sitting on forms or benches at both sides of a single long table.

The mention of 'a bench fastened into the ground' (Walton) shows that earth-set furniture was still in use in halls of the early seventeenth century. Easton Lodge in Essex, for example, had 'two longe Tables in the hall fastened to Tressells set in the ground' in 1637. The tables in the hall at Henry VIII's The More, Hertfordshire, were similarly set into the ground.[7] The advantages of this practice were that the furniture remained firmly in place and, since it required no supporting frames, it left more room for the legs and feet, and also made it easier to sweep the floor beneath. In some halls the tops of both the tables and their forms were set on a common frame to give particularly stable results. In others, framed forms or benches were fixed to the walls, one across the upper end of the hall at Oakwell Hall, Gomersal in Yorkshire, being for those sitting at the top table. The late medieval timber-framed canopies of estate which curved forward high above the top table continued to be built into the early sixteenth century, but then passed completely out of fashion.

In contrast to the usual kinds of hall described above, some of the highest status were furnished and used as great chambers. In 1527 that of Thomas Cromwell was particularly lavish, being hung in paned red and green saye (a cloth, usually containing silk, of high quality), those dining on its large oak trestle table being seated on a great gilded chair, three small gilded chairs for women, six gilded stools and footstools, along with two Flemish chairs and three long settles. Even the cupboard had been gilded, its cover being Levant carpet.[8] Such halls were truly exceptional.

SEATING IN THE HALL

As the head of the household and his close family dined within their chambers, the top table in the hall was usually occupied by his chief officers, the two parallel tables being occupied by two groups of lesser officers and servants. The second or waiters' table, vacant at the start of each meal, was for those who had served in the chamber before retiring here to dine on the food left over from the chamber table, sometimes supplemented by more hot dishes. The third or clerk's table was where most of the remaining household staff dined, their food being the basic messes of pottage, boiled meat or fish, and bread and cheese. The arrangements for Viscount Montagu's hall in 1595 were typical:

Top Table

Left to right: gentlemen strangers, the steward in his gown, the comptroller, the high steward, the auditor, the receiver general, the secretary (if a chief officer), the solicitor, the secretary (if not a chief officer).

Second or Waiters' Table	***Third or Clerk of the Kitchen's Table***
(to the steward's right, top to bottom)	(to the steward's left, top to bottom)
gentleman usher	clerk of the kitchen
carver	usher of the hall
sewer	chief cook
2 gentlemen of the chamber	yeoman of the cellar
gentleman of the horse	yeoman of the ewery
6 gentlemen waiters (by seniority)	yeoman of the pantry
yeoman usher of the chamber	yeoman of the buttery
2 chief yeomen of the chamber	second cook
clerk of the officers' chamber	baker
yeoman of the horse	brewer
yeoman of the wardrobe	gentlemen's servants[9]
yeoman of the chamber	
yeomen waiters (by seniority)	
porter	
granator	
bailiff of husbandry	
2 grooms of the chamber	

Figure 102. The hall, Parham House, Sussex. Built in 1577, this hall has a fashionable flat plaster ceiling to support an upper floor, marking the gradual decline of the traditional great hall, which had been open to an elaborate timber-framed roof.

Each household instituted seating arrangements to meet its particular requirements, as this second example shows. In the Earl of Worcester's chamber in 1641 there was one table for the family and nobility with another for knights and honourable gentlemen, one in Mrs Watson's apartment, one in the housekeeper's room for ladies' women, and three in the hall:

> ***Top Table***: the steward, the comptroller, the master of horse, the master of fish-ponds, Lord Herbert's preceptor and gentlemen who were not knights, all served by footmen

2nd Table (24 in total)	***3rd Table***
sewer	clerk of the kitchen
daily waiters	yeomen officers of the house
my Lady's gentleman usher	2 grooms of the chambers
my Lord's gentlemen of the chamber	and others[10]
pages	

In contrast, the steward and chief officers of the Earl of Dorset at Knole, Kent, in 1613–24 all dined in the chamber, and not in the hall. It appears that the two clerks of the kitchen presided there, probably occupying the top tables along

Figure 103. Hall furniture. Some of the earlier top tables for the dais had been extremely elaborate. The example of c. 1500 *from Durham Cathedral (1) having a top which hinged out at both ends to double its length. Many great Jacobean houses had matching sets of trestle tables and benches for their halls, this one (2) being made for Hatfield House, Hertfordshire, around 1611. The plainer example from Yorkshire (3) had a completely loose top, which would have made it easy to slide forwards or back as people took their seats. Elsewhere combined tables and benches were framed together, as at (4) Gawthorpe Hall, Lancashire,* c. *1605?, and (5) Landkey Parish Room, Devon, of 1655.*

with their four cooks, the baker and under-baker, brewer and under-brewer, the pastryman and other members of their department, totalling 21 servants. A further 47 servants, mainly yeomen and grooms, both indoor and outdoor, dined at the long table in the hall, obviously occupying both sides of it to accommodate their number, and seated in order of precedence. The location of the laundry-maids' table, where twelve dined, was either at the lower end of the hall or, more probably, in a separate room. Here, a lady's maid, the dairy maid, 'Grace Gibson, a Blackamoor', and a lone man, William Lewis the porter, are named as partaking. Presumably the six kitchen and scullery staff, with 'John Morochoe, a Blackamoor', took their meals in the kitchen, their constant attendance there being essential for the efficient service of each dinner and supper.[11]

The overall management of the serving of meals, along with all other domestic service, was the responsibility of the steward. One named Order in Massinger's *A New Way to Pay Old Debts* stated that his duty was to,

> Set all things right, or, as my name is Order,
> And by this staff of office that commands you,
> This chain and double ruff, symbols of power.
> Whoever misses in this function
> For one whole week makes forfeit his breakfast
> And priviledge of the wine cellar.[12]

In practice, the hall was managed by a marshal of the hall in the greatest houses, or a yeoman usher of the hall elsewhere. According to John Skelton, he should be,

> A red angry man, but easy to intrete
> An usher of the hall fayn wold I get
> To poynt this proude page a place and a rome
> For Jak wold be a Jentylman, that late was a grome,[13]

for, as Thomas, Lord Fairfax instructed 'If any unworthy Fellow do sitt himself down before his betters he must take him up and place him lower.'[14] A sure knowledge of precedence, and the boldness to enforce it, was a prime requirement for a good usher of the hall, so that he 'places strangers, and see them served att meales, and breakfast accordinge to their degrees: that he remove unfit and disordered persons.'[15] Those visitors who were of good standing were usually sure of a hospitable reception, having been set in their appropriate place by the usher either at the end of the top table, or at the waiters' or clerk's table further down. Here, as Ben Jonson found at an upper table at Jacobean Penshurst,

> ... comes no guest, but is allowed to eat,
> Without his fear, and of thy lord's own meat,
> Where the same beer, and bread, and self-same wine,
> That is his lordshipe's, shall be also mine ...
> Here no man tells my cups; nor, standing by
> A waiter, doth my gluttony envy,
> But gives me what I call, and lets me eat
> He knows, below, he shall find plenty of meat,

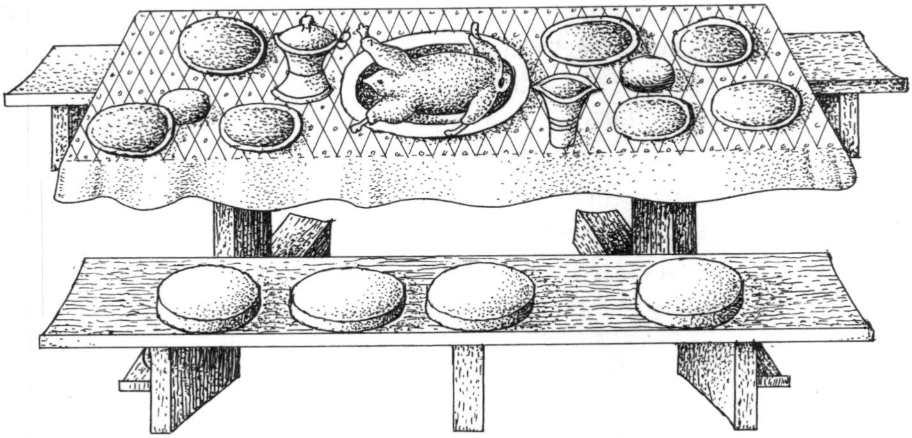

Figure 104. A hall table? early 16th cent. This illumination from a herbal in the Bodleian Library, Oxford, shows seven places set down the sides of a trestle table. Note the pewter salt to the left, and the squab cushions on the bench.

> Thy tables hoard not up for the next day,
> Nor, when I take my lodging, need I pray
> For fire, or lights, or livery, all is there.[16]

The practical duties of the yeoman usher of the hall also included many other areas; he had to ensure that it was kept clean and that the fires were maintained over the coldest winter period by his yeomen and grooms of the hall. He also had to command order and silence at all times, a difficult task where the yeomen waiters were liable to use 'uncomely gestures or actions (as laughing, harkeninge to tales and the like) whereby they may neglecte or hinder their dutyes.'[17] In addition to announcing the passage of his lord's service through the hall, he had to supervise all service to the steward, chief officers and gentlemen strangers who were to dine at the top table. After the lord's table had been prepared, he ordered the yeomen of the ewery and pantry to lay the cloth on the top table and set out the salt and trenchers, making sure that no one took their seats here until their food had been set down. Having called for an ewer and basin from the ewery, he then held the towel as the almoner poured the water over the hands of the steward and officers before they sat down.[18] The messes of food served to the top table, along with the drinks issued from the hall cupboard, were all carried up by the personal servants of the steward, chief officers and gentlemen, under the supervision of the usher. Even when he had taken his place just below the clerk of the kitchen at the clerk's table, he had to regularly get up from his meal to ensure that all at the top table were being served properly.[19]

When those who were to take their meals in the body of the hall had entered, washed their hands at the ewer or laver, basin and towels at the lower end, and taken their places beside the long, coarse linen or canvas-covered tables, grace was said, and they sat down on their stools or benches. The usher then called the pantler to set out the bread, with manchets for individual upper servants, and a communal cheat loaf for each mess of four lower servants. He then called the butler to set out his pitchers, one for every mess at the lower tables, after which the food was served. As it was eaten, the usher kept his place in the middle of the hall.[20]

All those dining in the hall had to be familiar with the practice of taking their meals in messes, each usually comprising four people sharing communal dishes of food and pitchers of drink. Since most carried their own eating knives and sometimes their spoons, cutlery was rarely set on the table, just a wooden trencher, a cup and, probably only for the officers and upper servants, a napkin at each place, along with the bread, drink, a saucer of sauce and a small salt. The initial dish of pottage, along with subsequent spoonable foods, was placed at the centre of each mess, so that each person might spoon it directly up to their lips. All the accompanying slices of bread were sliced from the manchet or cheat loaf while it was placed on a trencher, never on the tablecloth. Pieces of bread might then be dropped into the pottage in the dish before being spooned up, but none might be crumbled in, since this would contaminate it with grease or other undesirables from the fingers. Having finished the contents of the dish, a morsel of bread was used to wipe the bowl of the spoon perfectly clean for re-use in other dishes, and this then being eaten, keeping the table and its contents perfectly clean and tidy. Each required portion of solid food, such as a piece of a communal joint of boiled meat, was gripped with the thumb and two forefingers of the left hand, and then transferred to the individual's trencher. There it was cut into small gobbets, dipped into a little salt or mustard which had been transferred from the cellar or saucer to the trencher on the tip of the knife, and lifted to the lips with the thumb and two forefingers of the right hand. While taking their food in this way, and while filling their cups from the pitcher, a strict order of precedence was followed, the worthiest of each mess taking first place. Those upstarts such as Jack who,

> counteth in his coutenaunce to check with the best ...
> In a dysh dare he rush at the rypest ...

were considered extremely ill-mannered.[21]

Once the gentleman usher and all the others had finished serving their lord and his family in the chamber, they retired to the waiters' table in the hall as an

Figure 105. Dining in hall, early–mid-16th century. The mess of pottage has just been served, the cheat loaf is being cut into gobbets, and the cups have been filled with ale or beer.

orderly procession; 'march in order, and retire in battle array' as Jenkin instructed his fellow servants in Thomas Heywood's *A Woman Killed with Kindness*, 'now spread for the serving men in the hall! Butler, it belongs to your office … the rest be ready to prepare their stomachs! More lights in the hall, there!'[22]

After everyone had finished their meals, the steward's top table and the clerk's table served from the kitchen and the waiters' table from their lord's table in the chamber, the usher of the hall and his grooms helped 'to take awaye, and all broken meate in that place to bee putt into the amnorie, and from thence to bee bestowed on the poore by the amnor and porter.'[23]

DINING IN ROYAL HALLS

In the earlier years of the reign of Henry VIII the lower servants and members of the court dined in the hall in most of the royal palaces. In the Eltham ordinances of 1526, however, he specified that the hall was only to be kept in his six greatest houses, Greenwich, Eltham, Richmond, Beaulieu, Woodstock and Hampton Court.[24] In each of these everything was supervised by a marshal of the hall, or one of his ushers.

Before each meal two yeomen and two groom ewerers of the hall, assisted by their page, laid the long linen tablecloths on the tops of the trestle tables, these being changed at least twice a week, or more often if soiled.[25] This was the regulation, but those dining at court might find that they were,

> … unto the plank cleveing,
> So black, so baudic, so foule and ill seming,
> Of sight and of scent so vile and abominable,
> Till scant a man discerne them from the table …
> Touch them, then shall they unto thy fingers cleve,
> And then muste thou wipe thy handes on thy sleve …
> That as many men as on his skirtes looke
> Count him a scoleon or els a greesy cooke.

in contrast to those of the chamber, where

> … table cloths be kept white and clene,
> Finer then silke, and chaunged every day.[26]

The groom ewerers of the hall next laid a napkin at each place, as well as ewers, basins and towels on an ewery table called 'The Towel' close to the screen at the lower end of the hall, not too distant from the tables at which they dined. Cheat loaves and pewter salt cellars for every mess were then put in place by yeomen or grooms of the pantry, and a wooden trencher and wooden cup by a yeoman of the pitcher house.[27] These too were appropriately coarse, for,

> Thy breade is blacke, of ill sapour and taste,
> And harde as a flint because thou none should waste,
> That scant be thy teeth able it to break;
> Dip it in pottage if thou no shift can make;[28]

while as far as the cups are concerned, one need look no further than the poem already quoted in the earlier discussion of their qualities.[29]

Having taken their places at the tables, said grace and sat down, the food was served, commencing with the pottage and mess-pieces of boiled meats or fish. The waiters had a reputation for being careless, inattentive and clumsy:

> At borde be men set as thicke as they may be,
> The platters shall passe oft times to and fro,
> And over the shoulders and head shall they go;
> And oft all the broth and the licour fat
> Is spilt on thy gowne, thy bonet, and thy hat … [30]
> Sometime thou wantest eyther bread or wine,

> But nought dare thou aske if thou should never dine.
> Demaunde salt, trencher, spone, or other thing,
> Then art thou importune, and evermore craving;[31]

Since the waiters expected to eat and drink all that was left after a meal, they considered everyone at table to be robbing them of their just perquisites. They therefore carried away all the best dishes before anyone could help themselves:

> The hungry servers which at the table stande
> At every morsel hath eye unto thy hande,
> So much on thy morsell distract their minde …
> Because that thy leaving is onely their part
> If thou feede thee well, sore grieved is their heart;
> Namely of a dish costly and deynteous,
> Eche pece that thou cuttest is to them tedious
> … if it fortune, as seldome doth befall,
> that at beginning come best of all …
> Slowe be the servers in serving in always
> But swifte be they after taking thy meate away.[32]

There were similar delays in serving the drinks, the cups not being filled until the meal was half-eaten, while fresh water was not available, anyone calling for it to mix with their wine in the usual way being served with that in which the cups had been rinsed.[33]

In such circumstances, it is hardly surprising that each person seated at the tables put hunger before manners and grabbed whatever they could from every dish within reach:

> If the dish is pleasaunt, eyther fleshe or fishe,
> Ten handes at once swarme in the dishe,
> And if it be fleshe, ten knives shalt thou see,
> Mangling the flesh and in the platters flee:
> To put there thy handes is perill without fayle,
> Without a gauntlet or els a glove of mayle.
> Among all these knives thou one of both must have,
> Or els it is harde thy fingers whole to save:
> Oft in such dishes in court it is seene
> Some leve their fingers, eche knife is so kene,
> On a finger gnaweth some hasty glutton,
> Supposing it is a piece of biefe or mutton.[34]

Even the cheese eaten with bread at the end of the meal was a challenge, being:

All full of magots, and like to the raynebowe,
Of divers colours, as red, grene and yelowe,
On eche side gnawen with mise or with rattes,
Or with vile wormes, with dogges or with cattes;
Unclean and scorvy, and hard as the stone,
It loketh so well thou wouldest it were gone
If thou have butter, then shall it be as ill
Or worse than thy chese, but hunger hath no skill.[35]

Clearly written as a humorous satire, these lines from *The Cytezen and Uplondyshman* of c. 1524 are not to be taken as an entirely factual record of what it was like to dine in a royal hall. Even so, there must have been much truth in its content, certainly sufficient to warrant its composition. It provides a quite different view of the efficiency of the culinary divisions of the royal household to that presented in its ordinances or regulations. Providing two major meals every day for the 600 men entitled to eat in the hall would provide huge challenges even to the most efficient and experienced of organizations.[36]

CHAPTER TWENTY-THREE

Dining in the Chamber

Today it is still popularly believed that kings and queens, and lords and ladies, always dined on the raised dais in their 'banqueting hall', quaffing their ale and wine as minstrels led the dancing of raucous peasants in scenes of bucolic abandon. Factual history presents a quite different picture. The heads of major households had already abandoned regular use of the dais in the fourteenth century, leaving their steward or other senior officers to take their place there. From that time they had taken their meals more privately in a large apartment off the upper end of the hall, this combined living-dining-bed-room being called the solar or chamber. Over the course of the following centuries the function of this single room remained unchanged in many small and medium-sized houses, as indicated by the furniture listed in contemporary inventories. In larger houses, however, the 'chamber' expanded to occupy a number of rooms, each offering a greater degree of separation from the lower servants and others occupying the hall. The first or 'great' chamber might still house a fine bed in the 1540s, but was increasingly used as a dining room.[1] In 1588, for example, Sir Cotton Gargrave's great chamber at Nostel was furnished with two long table-tops on frames, three forms, twelve high and six shorter stools, a small square table, three chairs and a cupboard.[2] This shows that he, his family and upper servants were all dining here at separate tables, a relatively common arrangement. At Knole in Kent in 1613, the Earl of Dorset and seven of his family dined at 'My Lord's Table', while six gentlewomen, six chief officers, nine gentlemen, the Earl's attendant, and the three gentlemen and three pages who served the Countess dined at 'The Parlour Table'.[3]

At Raglan Castle the Earl of Worcester's table, and his Lady's table with the rest of his family were set up at the upper end of the parlour, while at the lower end a third table was set up for the Countess's gentlewomen, other resident gentlewomen, and any gentlewoman strangers who happened to be present. A further description of Raglan stated that the first table in the dining room was for the Earl and his family, with all other nobles, while the second table there was occupied by knights and honourable gentlemen, demonstrating the flexibility of this arrangement.[4]

In the great houses of the Elizabethan aristocracy the chamber suites were of the most magnificent construction and furnishing. The best preserved of these occupies the second storey of Bess of Hardwick's Hardwick Hall, Derbyshire of 1590–97. Designed for the most important of occasions, it commenced with a halfpace at the head of the main staircase, where a square table and forms were ready for the servants who were to serve in the meals and other foods, and provide space for them to marshal themselves and their burdens before entering the high great chamber. This huge room, decorated with brightly coloured tapestries hung beneath a deep, richly modelled plaster frieze, was furnished with a long wooden table with six forms, a square table, sixteen stools, a gilded cupboard, and a wicker screen, showing that it was to be used as an outer dining chamber. Beyond this lay the withdrawing chamber, hung in velvet cloth of gold and in arras, all embroidered with classical and biblical characters. Here stood the magnificent drawing-table supported on four sea-dogs, a richly upholstered chair with footstool and foot carpet, eleven stools, a little inlaid board, and another gilded cupboard. This was clearly intended for a very important person to dine 'in public' with the full panoply of table-servants. Next came the best bed-chamber, hung in embroidered cloth of gold and silver, and housing one of the finest gilded state beds also hung in cloth of gold and silver. Here too were a square table, a great and a smaller chair, five stools, a cupboard and a screen, suitable for when dining as in a privy chamber.[5] Clearly these chambers were built and furnished to impress even those who were familiar with the greatest of royal and aristocratic interiors. The formal dining ceremonies expected to take place here, as in all other great chambers, had to be conducted to an equal level of precise observance, one which demanded long years of training and practical experience gained in an aristocratic household.

GENTLEMEN OF THE CHAMBER

In Tudor England the medieval practice of maintaining resident staff of gentlemen servants to perform a mix of administrative, menial, and recreational services for the head of a socially superior household was commonplace. Such servants usually had their own houses, lands and local responsibilities, only acting as servants for part of the year. They had most probably inherited their prestigious yet servile duties from their fathers, who, like them, had been sent out to a superior house in late childhood, to gain a training in social skills and manners through acting as a privileged servant and to gain patronage for future advancement. In the household of the Earl of Worcester in 1641, his duty waiters were 'many gentlemen's sons of £200–£700 per annum bred up in the castle'.[6] Similarly, Sir William Wentworth advised in 1604 that,

> For servants be very careful to keep only those that be born of good and honest friends and be willing, humble, diligent and honest. [With] some ancient honest servants of your father's whose wealth and credit depend most upon your house and are seated on your ground [and] are like to be fast and true to you.[7]

The role of such servants as captains of a lord's private army had disappeared under Henry VII's administration, although they might still serve in this capacity if their lord was given a military role by the king. This aspect of their potential use was still apparent to men like Francis Bacon, who believed that,

> the state of free servants and attendants upon noblemen and gentlemen, which are in no ways inferior unto the yeomanry for arms, and therefore out of all question the splendour and magnificence of great retinues, the hospitality of noblemen and gentlemen received into custom, do much to conduce unto martial greatness, whereas, contrariwise, the close and reserved living of noblemen [without such chamber servants] causes penury to military forces.[8]

For a lord or prosperous gentleman, the acquisition of a group of serving men had many advantages. It enabled them to exert their control over their own lands and regions of influence by having locally important men perform some of their domestic tasks. Having the head of one's distant estate or castle regularly serve at table, for example, made sure that he knew his place, and maintained an appropriate level of respect, even when he had returned to his base. As such men were educated and enjoyed the same sports, pastimes and interests as their lord, they also offered him a welcome degree of social companionship. From the servant's point of view, there were advantages in having the protection, prestige and patronage of a powerful superior, who might have useful offices in his gift, or perhaps a profitable marriage.

In addition to being provided with good food and accommodation while on duty, these upper servants, known as either gentlemen or ladies of the chamber, usually received a cash wage. Those serving in Sir Thomas Lovell's household were paid the following rates in 1536–7:

10 gentlemen waiters	£2 13*s*. 4*d*. per annum
1 gentleman usher	£2 13*s*. 4*d*. per annum
12 yeomen ushers of the chamber	£2 0*s*. 0*d*. per annum
1 groom of the chamber	£1 6*s*. 8*d*. to £2 0*s*. 0*d*. per annum

and to serve his wife: '3 gentlewomen waiters, £2 0*s*. 0*d*. per annum.'[9]

Before describing the duties of the chamber staff, it is apposite to gain an overall impression of how they were expected to behave to maintain the dignity of each meal. At Denton, Yorkshire, Thomas, Lord Fairfax instructed that,

> the best fashioned and apparelled Servants [should serve] above the Salt, the rest below. If one servant have occasion to speak to another about Service of the Table, let him wisper, for noyse is uncivil. If any Servant have occasion to goe forth of the Chamber for anything, let him make haste, and see that no more than twoe be absent. And for the prevention of Errands, lett all Sauces be ready at the Door, for even one Message of Mustard will take a Man's Attendance from the Table ... have a good eye for the bord for empty dishes, and placing of others, and let not the Bord be unfurnished.
>
> Once again let me admonish Silence, for it is the greatest part of Civility.[10]

The latter instructions had been emphasized by William Harrison in 1577:

> I might here talk somewhat of the great silence that is used at the tables of the honourable and wiser sort generally over all the realm, likewise of moderate eating and drinking that is daily seen, and finally the regard that each one hath to keep himself from the note of surfeiting and drunkenness.[11]

Dignity, elegance, meticulous manners and calm order ruled in the chamber when meals were served, certainly not the loud, ignorant vulgarity displayed in most modern representations of the Tudor and Stuart period. Those who demonstrated their lack of the expected social skills were a source of mocking amusement. Thomas Dekker's *The Guls Horne Booke* of 1609, in the chapter on 'How a Yong Gallant should behave himself at an Ordinary', sarcastically advises them to enter the dining room and 'walke up and downe by the rest as scornfully and carelessly as a Gentleman Usher' and boast to all present. Then,

> When you are set downe to dinner you must eate as impudently as can be (for that's most gentleman-like) when your knight is upon his stewed mutton, be you presently (though you be but a Captain) in the bosome of your goose; and when your Justice of Peace is knuckle deep in goose, you may ... fall very manfully to your woodcock.

Such behaviour was abominably annoying, but other ignorant diners at least provided a rich source of amusement for both family and servants. Philip Massinger's Marrall, an attorney and creature of the grasping lawyer Sir Giles Overeach in *A New Way to Pay Old Debts* of 1625, fulfilled this role admirably when at Lady Allworth's table. As Amble, the gentleman usher, reported to the

Figure 106. The Bretton Hall cupboard. Now at Temple Newsam House, Leeds, this was originally built into Sir Thomas Wentworth's little chamber in the 1530s. He appears between two of his relatives, above the Wentworth, Dronsfield and Fitzwilliam coats of arms. Since he was Knight Marshal to Henry VIII it is probable that it was made by joiners serving members of the royal court.

servants, while bursting with laughter: 'He thinks he's at the cook's shop in Ram Alley ... and feeds so slovenly!' As his hostess had raised her glass to drink to him, he had pledged her by supping from a dish containing the broth left over from a capon. When Amble had served him with a cup of wine, instead of taking it, he had left his stool, knelt before him once or twice, and thanked 'His Worship'! Clearly he did not realize that 'Manners Maketh Man', and that he had destroyed any social reputation he might have aspired to.

CHAMBER FURNITURE

On entering a chamber, a gentleman would expect to find a number of essential pieces of furniture ready for use. Of these, the most impressive was the cupboard, already spread with a soft and coloured cover, topped by a neatly creased white linen cloth. At its most basic, the cupboard might still be a flat-topped side-table, but to this might be added tiers or stages, rather like a long, narrow-stepped staircase, rising along its back, against the wall. The purpose was to display tableware both for use and purely for show: the higher the status of the owner, the greater the number of stages. From this simple origin, the cupboard began to adopt a number of different forms. Those of the early sixteenth century often had a semi-octagonal table-top set over a number of 'aumbries', 'tills', or small cupboards, a flat carved back rising above, terminating in a miniature wooden canopy of estate. Probably the finest example from this period is now at Temple Newsam, Leeds. It was made for Sir Thomas Wentworth of Bretton, Henry VIII's Knight Marshal around 1531. It has a lower shelf for display, a long semi-octagonal top with both cupboards and tills [drawers] and a canopied carved back including the owner's arms, his portrait, and those of his family all in the finest of 'Romayne' design and construction.[12]

Most of the later cupboards are rectangular in plan, some having three great shelves or platforms supported by stout corner posts. Although still being made up to the the mid-seventeenth century, these soon began to incorporate smaller cupboards between their middle and top stages, and eventually turned into totally enclosed cupboards. Many have simple plank tops, intended to be hidden beneath their cupboard-cloths, but now provided with cornices added during Victorian restorations. There are very few representations of cupboards in actual use, but among the more useful are a number of cast white-metal toys probably made in London in the late sixteenth and early seventeenth centuries. They show single-staged tops, some diapered like their linen cupboard-cloths, and symmetrical arrangements of ewers, dishes and candlesticks, showing how their full-sized equivalents were set out. The same founders also made miniature ewers.[13]

Figure 107. Cupboards. These are typical English examples of the early 16th century (left) and around 1600 (right).

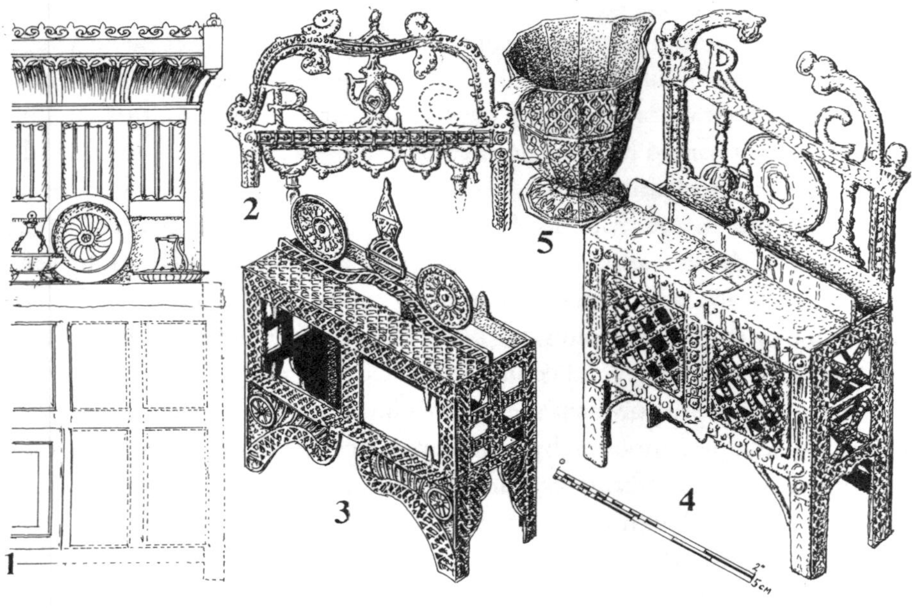

Figure 108. Furnishing the dresser. Having been covered with a rich and soft cupboard cover and a linen cupboard cloth, the top and its shelves or stages were used to display ewers, basins and other tablewares. Hans Holbein the younger drew Sir Thomas More's cupboard in the 1530s (1), the others (2–4) being made as pewter toys, the R.C. initials probably referring to Sir Richard Champion, Lord Mayor of London in 1565–6. The pewter toy ewer (5) probably dates from the 1640s.

The quantity of silver or gold, itself known as 'a cupboard of plate' displayed on the cupboard could be quite considerable, as shown by many inventories. It would certainly include a basin and ewer, flagons for wine and ale, cups and standing cups, salts, spoons and candlesticks.[14]

When Massinger's Overeach was about to entertain, he instructed his servants to,

> Spare no cost; let my dressers crack with the weight of curious viands,
> And let no plate be seen but what's pure gold,
> Or such whose workmanship exceeds the matter
> That it is made of. Let my choicest linen
> Perfume the room and, when we wash, the water
> With precious powders mixed, so please my lord,
> That he may with envy wish to bathe for ever.

The dining table in the chamber, typically placed across and in front of the fireplace, was usually a board some 24–30 inches (60–76cm) wide – anything broader making it very difficult for a kneeling carver to reach his master's trencher.

Continuing established medieval practice, many dining tables had long, rectangular planked tops supported on two or more trestles or 'dormers', made with a horizontal wooden bar supported on three or four legs, as demonstrated by the unique examples recovered from the *Mary Rose*, wrecked in 1545.[15] That with three legs had fox-wedged joints which made it impossible to dismantle, but the other one had its four legs topped with tenons which were only held in place by the weight of the cross-bar and table-top. This enabled it to be instantly reduced to five short lengths of wood which would stack away neatly behind the wall hangings when not in use. Since they were to be covered with cloths, such simple trestle-tables could be found even in the most prestigious of rooms, even Henry VIII's privy and withdrawing chambers.[16] Whenever any important individual had finished his meal, the servants first removed the table, so he could stand up, then 'lay some of the tables [tops] on the floor, and remove[d] the trestles'.

There is an early seventeenth-century description of James I standing on such a dismantled table while washing his hands after a meal.[17] Its trestles may have been of the usual kind, or of a lighter and more elegant design introduced by the 1540s, since also found on the *Mary Rose*. It comprised two open rectangular frames; one hinging within the other to fold flat, or open up to an X-shape to support a table top. One is shown in use in the campaign tent of Sir Anthony Mildmay in his portrait of *c.* 1596.[18] The next development was to reduce each trestle to a simple rectangular frame hinged to the underside of the table-top,

Figure 109. Chamber furniture. (1–3) a table and bench from Ilminster, Somerset, and a stool and arm chair all of the early–mid-16th century; (4–6) a table, bench, stool and Yorkshire arm chair, of the early–mid-17th century; (7) a 'Spanish' table, numbers of these being suitable for forming long runs of table for varying numbers of diners.

holding it in place with a folding iron stay. Known as Spanish tables, they were first mentioned in England by John Lyly (?1554–1608) when describing the preparations for a visit by James I:

> All hands to work! Let no man stand!
> Set me fine Spanish tables in the hall,
> See they be fitted all;
> Let there be room to eat ... [19]

Each one was short enough to be carried by one person, but they readily combined to produce dining tables of any length or conformation. Such tables remained in use in country houses over the succeeding centuries. A number remain at Cotehele in Cornwall, and another in the National Trust's tearoom at Hardwick Hall. It is very difficult to date existing examples, however, for any Georgian or early Victorian estate carpenter could easily make extra ones to match, which now have a genuine patination of age.

Dormant tables, which had their tops permanently fixed to a mortised frame, became more common from the mid-sixteenth century. They appear high in comparison with modern dining tables, around 33 inches (84cm) or more, and have bottom rails perhaps 6 inches (15cm) from floor level. For this reason they are frequently mis-identified as 'side-tables', items virtually unknown at this date. The reason why they appear impossible to use with stools and chairs, is that most of these have had their legs shortened for use at Victorian tables. At their original height they were ideal for use at the taller tables, the bottom rails acting as foot rests, keeping the feet well above the layers of rushes which covered the floors. One example of this type, now in St Anthony's Hall, York, has an excellent provenance. Made for the city's Joiners' and Carpenters' Company in 1608, it was used by James I in 1617, and still remains in its original condition. Drawing tables with rigid frames holding tops which could be lengthened or shortened had already been introduced by the 1540s.

The large fabric-covered bankers or benches on which medieval magnates had sat at table were passing rapidly out of use by 1500, being replaced by simple arm chairs, their oak frames being filled in with linen-fold panels. These in turn were superseded by open-framed armchairs from around the 1530s or '40s, their quality and design then improving to create great armchairs on which the lord or master sat, on his deeply upholstered and richly embroidered cushion. Set centrally on one side of the table, it gave its occupant the expected degree of status. From the early mid-seventeenth century upholstered seats covered in velvets, turkey-work or similar rich fabrics became more common, the best having deep fringes to increase their opulence. Those sitting to each side of the chair usually sat on tall stools, benches or forms, their plank tops being covered with fine cushions for essential comfort.

Since the seated diners had their backs to the fireplace it became necessary to provide fire-screens to protect them from the fierce heat of the flaming logs. As seen in a number of late medieval illustrations, these took the form of a large vertical disc of lip-work (straw rope, as in traditional bee-skeps) or wicker mounted on a vertical post. These continued in use through into the mid-seventeenth century, a rare example surviving at Haddon Hall, Derbyshire.

Figure 110. Preparing the dining chamber in 1655. This woodcut in Jan Amos Comenius' The Visible World *contains a wealth of interesting detail. A staged cupboard covered with its cloth and holding a flagon and rows of cups stands to the left behind a servant who fills a glass held by its base. A laver and basin stands to the right, behind a servant with an ewer and basin. A waiter carrying a pair of doubled dishes approaches the table, its square-creased cloth having a place-setting at the nearest end, its square-folded napkin put half-way across the plate.*

This completed the essential furnishing of the chamber, but other pieces were added according to the needs of the household. Beds might still be found here up to the early mid-seventeenth century, along with further chests, chairs, desks and other items. Additional tables might also be present either to accommodate secondary groups of diners, or to serve as ewery or other service tables.

CHAMBER STAFF

There are several 'breviates' or 'ordinances' which describe the duties of the individual officers and servants of the chamber. These were intended to be read by each one, in order that he might perform his particular duties efficiently, but it can be very difficult to assemble the pieces of this complex jig-saw into a coherent whole. One of the most useful general descriptions of table-service in a chamber was published in Hugh Rhodes' *Booke of Nurture* of 1568:

[Laying the Table.]

When your master will go to his meat, take a towel about your neck, then take a cupboard cloth, a basin and an ewer, and a towel to array your cupboard, then cover your table, and set on salt, bread, and trenchers, the salt before the bread, and the trenchers before the salt, and set your napkins and spoons on the cupboard ready, and lay every man a trencher, and napkin, and a spoon. And if ye have more messes than one at your master's table, consider what degree the persons are of, and thereafter you may serve them: and then set down everything at that mess as before, except your carving knives. If there be many gentlemen or yeomen, then set on bread, salt, trenchers, spoons, after they be set, or else after the custom of the house. And some do use to set before every man a loaf of bread and his cup, and some use the contrary. Thus you must have respect to the custom of your house. And in some places it is used to set drink and a loaf or two.

[Carving & Serving.]

Also you shall understand that in some place the carver doth use to shew and set down, and goeth before the course, and beareth no dish, and in some places he beareth the first dish, and maketh obeisance to his master, and setteth it down covered before the degree of a knight, or else not used, and take off the covers and set them by. Also the carver hath authority to carve to all at his master's mess in special, and also unto other that sit joining by them if he list. Also see ye have voiders in a readiness for to avoid the morsels they do leave on their trenchers. Then with your trencher knife take off such fragments, and put them in your voider, and set them clean again. And whether your sovereign move trenchers or bread, void them once or twice, specially when they are wet, or give him clean, and as ye see men leave eating of the first and second dish, so avoid them from the table. And then if so be ye have any more courses than one or two, ye may make the more haste in voiding, and ever let one dish or two stand till the next course, and then take up all, and set down fresh and clean voiders withal, and let them not be too full before ye empty them, and then set clean again. And look what sauce is ordained for any meat, void the sauce thereof when ye take away the meat; and at the degree of a knight ye may set down your cup covered, and lift off the cover and set it on again, and when he listeth to drink and taketh off the cover, take the cover in thy hand and set it on again. And when he hath drunken, look the cup of wine or ale be not empty, but oft renewed. Also the carver shall break his dish before his master, or at a side cupboard, with clean knives, and see there be no lack of bread or ale;

[Voiding.]

And when men have well eaten, and do begin to wax weary of eating, or if ye perceive by the countenance of your master when ye shall take up the meat and void the table, begin at the lowest mess, take away your spoons, if there be any, howbeit ye may avoid them, after broths and bake meats are past. Then take away your voiders and then your dishes of meat, as they were set down, so take them up in order.

[Cheese or Fruit.]

And then set down cheese or fruits, and that ended, avoid your cheese or fruits, and cover your cup, ale or wine; first avoid the ale, and then the wine: then set on a broad voider and put therein the small pieces of bread, and small crumbs, with trenchers and napkins, and with your trencher knife or napkin make clean the table, then set away your bread whole, and also your voider, then take up the salt, and make obeisance.

[Washing.]

Mark if your master use to wash at the table or standing; if he be at the table, cast a clean towel upon your tablecloth, and set down your basin and ewer before your sovereign, and take the ewer in your hand, and give them water. Then avoid your basin and ewer, and fold the board cloth together with your towel therein, and so take them off the board. And when your sovereign shall wash, set your towel on the left hand of him, and the water before you at dinner or supper; if it be to bedward, set up your basin and towel on the board again.

[After Dinner.]

And if your master will have any conceits after dinner, as apples, nuts or cream, then lay forth a towel on the board, and set thereon a loaf or two, see that ye have your trenchers and spoons in a readiness if need require, then serve forth your master well, and so take it up again with a voider.[20]

Although this provides a good introduction to dining in the chamber, it omits many of the procedures and practical details which were essential for the service of a dinner or supper in a noble household. Since these are very difficult to understand when delivered in written form, they are here presented in the form of a strip-cartoon, using two complementary sources. The main one is the *Booke of Orders and Rules* established for Anthony, Viscount Montagu, of Cowdray House, Sussex, and drawn up in 1595, supplemented by the anonymous *Breviate touching the Order and Governmente of a Nobleman's House* of 1605.[21]

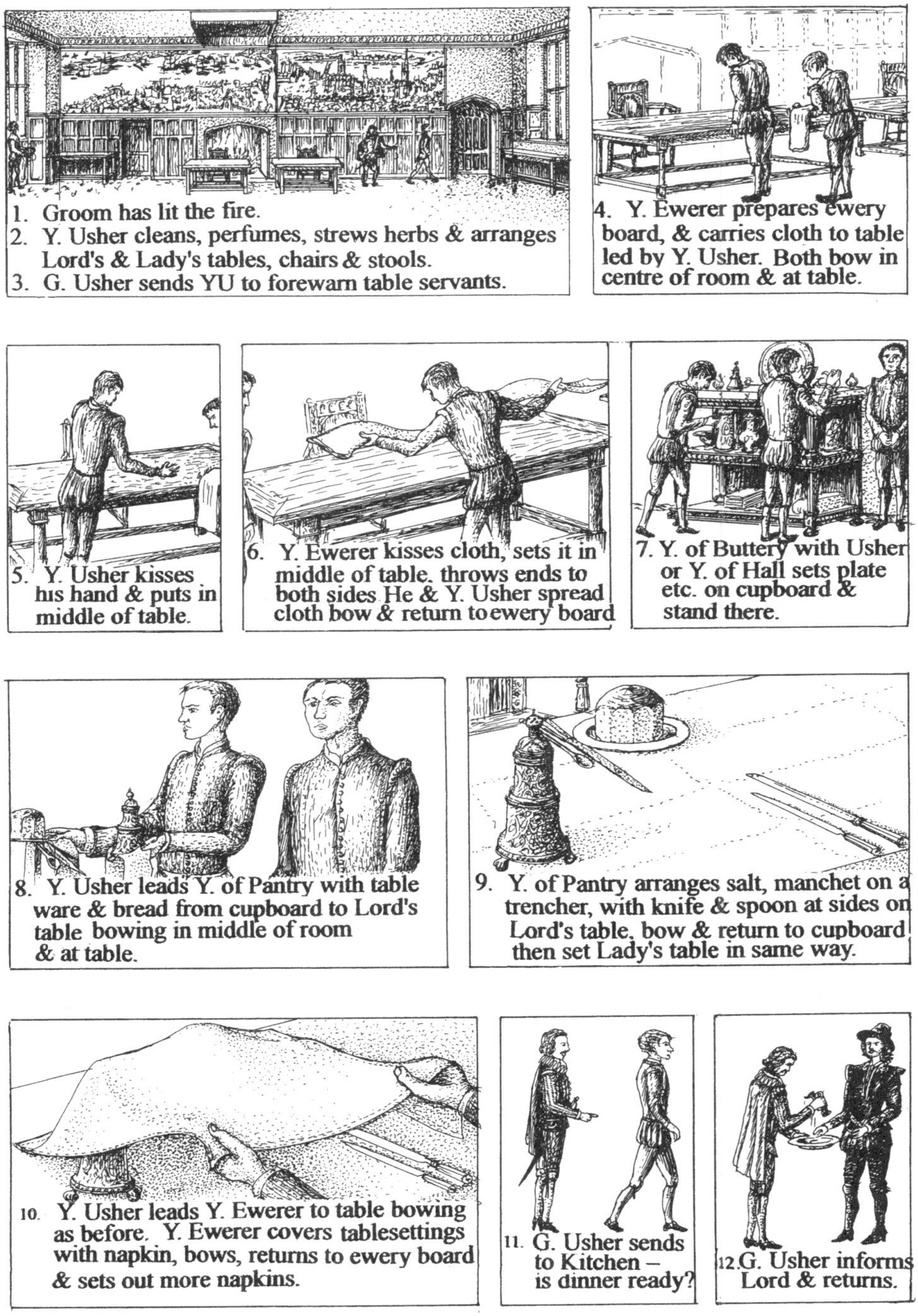

Figure 111–1. Dinner in the chamber at Cowdray House, Sussex, in the 1590s.

Figure 111–2. Dinner in the chamber at Cowdray House, Sussex, in the 1590s.

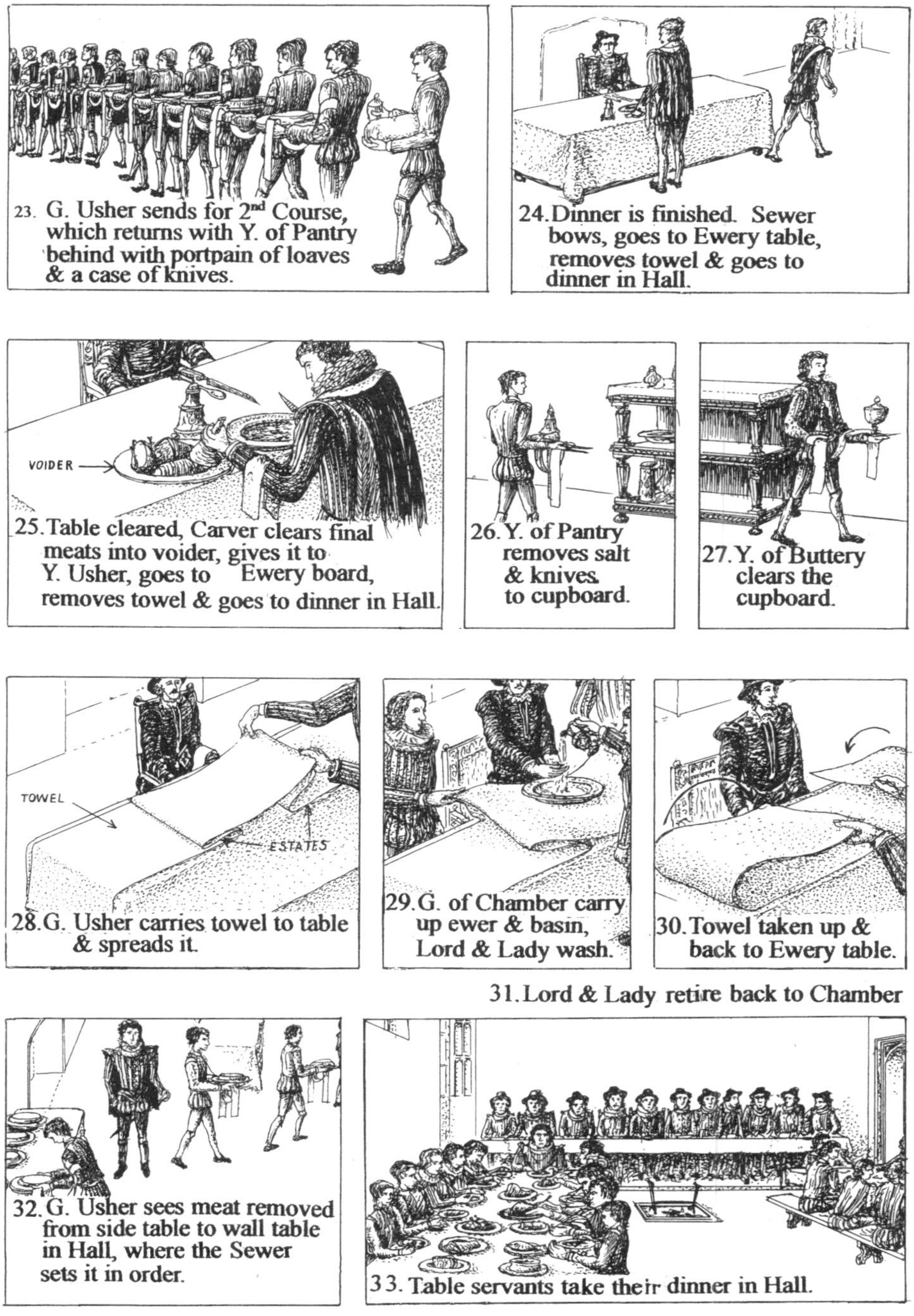

Figure 111–3. Dinner in the chamber at Cowdray House, Sussex, in the 1590s.

Figure 112. A wealthy man dining in his chamber. From Thomas Trevelion's Miscellany *of 1616.*

While performing his duties at the table, the carver had to be familiar with the vocabulary of his craft, as already established in the fifteenth century. Some lists provided up to forty-one verbs, each referring to the act of carving a different creature, but most included a fairly uniform group of thirty-seven. They appear in Wynkyn de Worde's *The manere of hawkynge & hunting* of 1496, his *Boke of Kervynge* of 1508, Abraham Vele's *Boke of St Albans c.* 1560, Edward Allde's *Hawking, Hunting and Fishing* of 1586, and, as below, John Helme's *Jewell for Gentrie* of 1614.

1. *a deer broken*
2. *a goose reared*
3. *an egg tyred*
4. *a fritter timbered*
5. *a salmon chined*
6. *a pike splatted*
7. *a haddock sided*
8. *a chevin (chub) finned*
9. *a sole loined*
10. *a gurnard chined*
11. *a tench sauced*
20. *a crane displayed*
21. *a curlew imjointed*
22. *a pheasant alayed*
23. *a quail winged*
24. *a plover monced*
25. *a pigeon thighed*
26. *a brawn leached*
27. *a swan lifted*
28. *a lamb shouldered*
29. *a kid shouldered*
30. *a hen spoiled*

12. *an eel traunch*
13. *a bream splayed*
14. *a barbel tusked*
15. *a trout gobbetted*
16. *a pig headed and sided*
17. *a capon sauced*
18. *a chevin (chub) frushed*
19. *a cony unlaced*
31. *a mallard unbraced*
32. *a heron dismembered*
33. *a peacock disfigured*
34. *a bittern untached*
35. *a partridge allayed*
36. *a rail breasted*
37. *a woodcock thighed*

other terms included:

a crab tamed
a chicken frust
a turkey cut up
a trout culponed
a sturgeon tranched
a pasty bordered[22]
a lobster barbed
a lamprey stringed
a bustard cut up
a teal broken
a deer broken

DINING IN ROYAL CHAMBERS

The service of meals to Henry VIII required a substantial number of privy chamber staff, who received only their daily 'Bouche of Court' allowance of bread, ale, wine, lighting and fuel, their meals and accommodation.[23] His three cup-bearers and three carvers and three sewers were usually lords or knights, his eighteen gentlemen and two gentlemen ushers of the privy chamber were knights, while his four gentlemen ushers daily waiters and four grooms of the privy chamber were untitled.[24] Of these, however, one cup-bearer, carver and sewer, six gentlemen, two ushers and four grooms were in attendance on a normal day, as they worked rotating terms with their fellow officers.[25]

In the palaces used by Henry VIII, the chamber was made up of three linked rooms, each of successively higher status. The first, called the great watching or guard chamber, was a large reception room. Next came the second or presence chamber, or chamber of estate, which housed a cloth of estate beneath which the King could dine when, hardly ever, he chose to dine in public. The third chamber, the King's or privy chamber, having both a cloth of estate and a bed in the 1520s, was where he usually took his meals with the minimum number of lords and servants. The dining furniture in the privy chamber at the end of his reign are recorded in his inventory of 1547. At Hampton Court, for example, that on the King's Side included:

Figure 113. Henry VIII dining in a chamber. Probably drawn several decades after the King's death, this drawing may present a relatively accurate depiction of Henry at table. Note the three-staged cupboard, the sewer with a towel over his right shoulder, and a canopy of estate with its pendant sparver.

2 wainscot cupboards	4 joined stools
1 table with a green cloth	1 triangular wainscot stool covered in green cloth
2 joined forms	

and the Queen's Side:

2 cupboards	2 forms
1 table on 2 trestles	1 wicker screen[26]

As the chamber suite was used as a dormitory for the chamber staff, the first task every morning was to pack away the 'pallet' beds and bedding between 7 and 8 a.m. Pages then lit the fires, shook the carpets, strewed the floors with rushes, and made everything clean and ready for the grooms to erect the dining tables. These had been stacked behind the arras or wall-hangings, two grooms holding these up as the table-tops, trestles and other furnishings were brought out.

Between 8 and 9 a.m. the yeomen ushers of the chamber arrived, supervising the door into the great chamber, along with the gentleman usher, who manned the door into the King's chamber. Approaching the Lord Chamberlain, the gentleman usher was informed of the time at which the King had ordered his dinner to be served, which lords were to sit at his board's end, who were to be his carver, sewer and cup-bearer, and if he required the heralds or minstrels to be in attendance. The ewerer then set out the ewery table (in the presence chamber?) with all the tablecloths, towels, ewers, basins and water required for dinner.

In the King's chamber the yeomen ushers of the chamber helped the ewerer to lay the cloth on the King's table, which stood on a carpet beneath the cloth of estate. The sewer and carver washed their hands at the ewery table, donned their towels of office, and the carver took his place at the King's board-end. The gentleman usher and a knight also went to the ewery table, the former collecting the King's towel, and kissing it for assay, while the latter collected the King's basin [and ewer], and its water for assay. Going through to the King and his lords, the gentleman usher passed the towel to the senior lord, who held it before the King's hands as he washed his hands at the knights' basin [and ewer], which were then carried back to the ewery table. The sewer for the board's end now took his place in front of the King's table.

On the command of the gentleman usher the sewer led a procession of yeomen daily waiters, grooms and pages to the kitchen dresser, where the dishes were collected and carried back under the supervision of an additional steward, who ensured that there was no pilfering or tampering with the food. If it was dark, the steward leading this procession was preceded by a groom carrying a flaming torch.

As the King approached his table, two gentlemen ushers, one at each end, lifted it forwards until he had seated himself in his chair, and then set it back in place before him. Now everyone left the King's chamber, leaving only the lords who were to dine at his board's end, his henchmen, carver, sewer, cup-bearer, butler, pantler, and a gentleman usher, who stood just within the door, to restrict all access. The hands of the lords were then washed, and their forms and stools put in place by yeomen ushers (who also departed) so that they could take their places at the board's end.

Now the King was served in the usual manner, his pottage being presented to him by an esquire of the body. All the following dishes then being presented by a kneeling waiter to the kneeling sewer, and on to the kneeling carver, who cut assay pieces from each one and saw them eaten by the waiter and sewer before cutting gobbets from any which the King wished to enjoy. The ceremonial of serving Henry VIII's meals appears to have followed the same format as those

Figure 114. Dining at the Field of the Cloth of Gold. Here, in a tent, a group of senior courtiers dine as if in a chamber, complete with a cupboard and a waiter with his towel hanging from his left shoulder. The bearded figure at the end of the table strongly resembles Charles Brandon, Duke of Suffolk and Lord Great Master, and therefore responsible for all the culinary activities shown behind him in the original painting of c. 1545.

of late medieval monarchs and prelates, as described in my *Food and Cooking in Medieval England* of 2008. At the end of dinner, the gentlemen ushers removed the tablecloths, bringing water from the King's chamber door for the King to wash his hands, yeomen ushers then taking the hand-washing water to the lords at the board's end. Two yeomen then entered, dismantled the table-top and its trestles, and carried them away (into the presence chamber?), bringing dinner to an end. The same procedure was followed later in the afternoon, when supper was served.

Having retreated into the presence chamber, the Lord Chamberlain and the remaining lords stood at its lower end as two yeomen held the basins, ewers and towels for them to wash their hands. A yeoman usher meanwhile removed everyone who had not obtained permission to dine there, leaving only the Lord Chamberlain and his three servants, the Vice Chamberlain with his two servants, the Captain of the Guard with his servant, and their sewers, butler, pantler, ewerer, grooms of the chamber, and other lords, knights, squires, chaplains and gentlemen as permitted by the Lord Chamberlain. Further tables were set up in the great watching chamber, probably one for the lords not dining with the Lord Chancellor, one for the chaplain and those of his rank, and one for the gentlemen ushers and people of like standing. The yeomen ushers and yeomen of the chamber, meanwhile, dined at a table just outside the King's or privy chamber door, the tables for the chamber staff being used after they had completed their duties at the King's table. Once those dining at the Lord Chamberlain's, chaplain's and gentlemen ushers' tables had finished their dinners, their tables were voided, towels laid, and water set before them so that they might wash their hands and go about their duties. The grooms then dismantled all the tables and trestles and packed them away behind the arras, ready to be brought out again for supper, taken in the late afternoon in exactly the same manner. Finally the grooms and pages retired to the groom porter's room, to take their dinners there.[27]

Over the succeeding years the staffing and operation of the privy chamber department was modified to suit the King's changing needs. In 1526 there was a staff of fifteen, rising to twenty by 1530 and twenty-eight by 1539, further rooms being added to the later privy chamber suites as their operation became increasingly complex. Their basic purpose remained the same, however; to provide Henry with a means of dining privately, while using the outer chambers as a means of giving or withdrawing favour to his senior courtiers.[28]

Under Elizabeth I, the manner of serving meals to the monarch was completely changed, since she was served there by her ladies in waiting. The ceremonial in the outer presence or audience chamber commenced after the Queen had retired within her privy chamber, as Thomas Platter observed in 1599. First the guard entered, wearing their red gold-embroidered liveries and bearing tables which they set up in the recently vacated place beneath the canopy of estate. Two more guards followed, each bearing a mace, bowing at the entrance, the middle of the chamber and in front of the table, before laying the table and retiring. The next two guards bowed in a similar manner, bearing plates to the table, two more carrying in and setting down the bread and salt. A gentleman with a mace, with a gentlewoman or lady in waiting joined the last two before the table, there to act as sewer and carver for the Queen's service.

At this stage the most impressive part of the ceremony took place, as about forty of the guard, each one carrying a covered dish, and with their tabbards folded back, marched up from the dresser of the privy kitchen, up through the great chamber into the presence chamber. Probably kneeling beside the lady in waiting, each held up his dish while the gentleman removed its cover and the lady in waiting cut off assays and put them into the guard's mouth. They were

Figure 115. James I and the Spanish ambassadors. To reflect their relative status, the King occupies a chair, the ambassadors sit on stools, and the Prince of Wales stands at table, probably serving as carver, a waiter presenting a dish to his right. The laden table confirms that the English were dining in this manner long before the term 'à la Francaise' was imported from the Continent.

supposed to eat them, but generally took the assay-piece out or merely tasted a morsel. Two more guards then brought in the wine and beer which was poured out and tasted for assay. Each of the dishes was carried in so that the Queen could make her selection, the remainder being sent back and carried out for service at the Lord Chamberlain's table. The second course, including huge joints of beef, all kinds of game, pasties and tarts, a third course, and a third 'void' or 'banquet' course were all served in the identical manner. Finally the Queen's musicians appeared and performed on their trumpets and shawms, after which everyone left and the tables were carried away.[29]

Baron Waldstein observed the same ceremony in July 1600, as did Paul Hentzner in 1598, when he added the following details:

> the Yeoman of the Guard entered, bareheaded, cloathed in Scarlet, with a Golden Rose upon their Backs, bringing in at each Turn a Coarse of twenty-four Dishes, served in Plate, most of it gild. These dishes were received by a Gentleman in the same Order they were brought, and placed upon the Table,

> while the Lady-taster gave to each of the Guards a mouthful to eat, of the particular dish he had brought, for Fear any Poison.

On 27 December 1584, Lupold von Wedel was present when the Queen was actually at table, where after the preliminaries described so far:

> A young gentleman habited in black carved the meats for the Queen and a gentleman of about the same age arranged in green served her beverages. This gentleman had to remain kneeling as long as she was drinking: when she had finished, he rose and removed the goblet.
>
> At her table, to her right, stood gentlemen of rank ... white staffs in their hands. [When summoned, one of them knelt until commanded to rise, bowed, bowed again in the centre of the chamber, then ordered the next course to be carried in.] Four gentlemen with sceptres also walked before the dish bearers.
>
> [After dining sparingly from a few of the dishes, the Queen rose, five countesses who had been seated near the door then] made a deep courtesy to the Queen, and passed over to the other side. The Queen arose and turned her back upon the table, whereupon two bishops stepped forward and said grace. After them came three earls ... These three then took a large basin, which was covered like a meat dish and of gilt silver, and two of the old gentlemen held the towel. The five of them then advanced to the Queen and knelt down before her. They then raised the lid from the basin ... A third poured water over the Queen's hands, who before washing her hands drew off a ring and handed it to the Lord Chamberlain. After washing her hands she again drew on the ring.[30]

On the accession of James I, royal table service largely reverted to Henrician practices, his table being served with the usual group of gentlemen, gentlemen ushers, daily and quarterly waiters, carvers, cup-bearers, sewers, yeomen ushers, grooms and pages of the Privy Chamber.[31] He dined in a much more informal and public manner, however, and even enjoyed constant conversation throughout his dinners and suppers, in rejection of English good manners:

> The King's table was a trial of wits. The reading of some books before him was very frequent, while he was at his repast. Otherwise he collected knowledge by variety of questions, which he carved out to the capacity of his understanding writers. Methought his hunting humour was not off so long as his courtiers, I mean the learned, stood about him at his board. He was ever in chase after some disputable doubts, which he would wind and turn about with the most stabbing objections that ever I heard. And was as pleasant and fellow-like in

Figure 116. Waiters for Charles I. Here, in Gerrit Houckgeest's painting of 1635, the sewer leads the procession of guard/waiters up to the royal table. Each bears one or two pairs of dishes, the upper dishes acting as dish-covers to keep their contents clean and hot.

Figure 117. Charles I, Henrietta Maria & Charles, Prince of Wales, at table. Note the White Stick to the left, the carver to the right, the square-creased linen cloth, and the piles of covered dishes on the table.

all those discourses as with his huntsmen in the field. They that in many such genial and convivial conferences were ripe and weighty in their answers were indubiously designed to some place of credit and profit.[32]

Under Charles I there was a rather more formal approach to dining, which still took place in (restricted) public, and yet might be full of incident. Gerritt Houckgeest's 1635 painting of the King, Queen and Prince of Wales at table shows a royal greyhound, spaniel and other dogs close by, while the Queen's pet monkey sits on the carver's shoulder, distracting him from his work (W.H. Pyne could clearly see this monkey on the painting in 1819, but it is barely visible there today). Other features are highly informative. The chamber has a symmetrical plan, its service door being in the centre of the wall at its lower end, directly opposite the fireplace set between doors which presumably led into the privy chambers beyond its upper end. Entering the service door, a pair of cupboards stand to each side, their richly embroidered and deeply fringed covers protected by white linen cupboard-cloths freshly pressed into neat rectangles. Each cupboard has a single raised stage or shelf across its back, bearing large dishes, while below, on their flat tops, are covered standing cups, dishes and probably cutlery ready for use. Before the cupboard in the foreground a huge gadrooned gilt cistern contains square glass flagons of wine in their cold water, from which an approaching cup-bearer is about to refill what appears to be a tall glass-covered cup.

A short-cloaked sewer is leading in a single file of waiters, probably of the guard, since they are wearing red liveries embroidered with royal emblems and are armed with swords. Each carries a single dish with a second dish inverted over it to serve as a cover. Interestingly, only the sewer is now wearing a narrow linen towel of office, the rest of the procession carrying their dishes in their bare hands.

Following medieval practice, the royal table is set parallel to the fireplace, and about a couple of yards in front of it. It stands on a foot-carpet, here defining the area of honour which was previously indicated by a canopy or cloth of estate. Here too there is a neatly creased linen cloth placed over a deeply fringed table cover. Charles I sits with his back to the fire, with Henrietta Maria to his reward or second-mess (left), and Charles, Prince of Wales beyond, seated at the end of the table. A group of gentlemen and ladies of the chamber stand behind the King and Queen, along with one of the 'white sticks' bearing his rod of office, all being here to serve the royal couple, and act as human fireguards, since no screen is present. Standing at the opposite side of the table, a short-cloaked carver wearing a short linen towel of office is busy carving from a dish, another uncovered dish standing to his left. Most of the other dishes, and a shaped pie, remain covered, some being stacked two deep, these suggesting that the dishes of each course were carved as required for the monarchs, then re-covered until cleared away.

The Civil Wars and the institution of the Commonwealth disrupted such everyday ceremonials, their trained noble officers and salaried servants being scattered. In December 1653, Cromwell was declared Lord Protector and given the use of all the major palaces, which were cleared of their existing occupants. Whitehall became his principal residence, he and his family dining there from April 1654, using two services of plate worth over £3,000.[33] His meals were taken in a relatively informal manner, unless he dined in public, when most of the former royal ceremonies were revived, requiring gentlemen of the chamber, gentlemen ushers, gentlemen waiters, and up to forty of the guard to bring up his dishes.[34] From before his investiture as Lord Protector, a replica royal household was in place, headed by a Lord Chamberlain, operating a new Board of the Greencloth.[35]

The practical details of Cromwell's culinary arrangements were published in a news-sheet of March 1654. After stating that the Protector's privy lodgings and those for his wife had been established at Whitehall, it described 'the privy kitchen and other kitchens, butteries, and offices' and that the 'tables for diet prepared are these':

A table for his Highness
A table for the Protectress
A table for the Chaplains and Strangers
A table for the Steward and Gentlemen
A table for the Gentlemen
A table for the coachmen, grooms and other domestic servants
A table for Inferiors, or sub-servants[36]

Here he entertained the officers of his army once a week, his diet being 'spare not curious', for 'at his private table very rarely, or never, were our French *quelque choses* suffered by him, or any such modern gustos.'[37] The recipes published in *The Court and Kitchen of Elizabeth commonly called Joan Cromwell* in 1664 have usually been discredited as being part of a satirical retribution against the libels of the late usurper. Anyone who has tried them, and read their texts, soon realizes that they are no hack's compilation, but those of a practical and skilled lady. The author of the published version considered them 'ordinary and vulgar', since, as we should expect, they include no 'French *quelque choses*'.[38] In fact, they are all good, workable recipes, as may be seen by some of those given elsewhere in this book, and, if they are those of Elizabeth Cromwell, they should bring her praise, not condemnation. After Cromwell's death in September 1658, the days of the Commonwealth were numbered, the Restoration of Charles II in 1660 finally dispersing the Protector's court, as a royal court was re-established.

THE DECLINE OF SERVING MEN

Society saw gentlemen servants in an increasingly critical light from the later sixteenth century. Richard Brome's *Northerne Lasse* of 1632 describes a 'Gentleman Usher, his duties be in eight parts':

> Boldness, Neatness, Flatterie and Secresie, [all] rewarded, Diligence, Obedience, Truth, and Honestie, unrewarded. His dexteritie in carving and his discretion in marshalling of meats; to give every mess the due service, and everie dish his lawfull preheminence [which is rewarded double] at board and at bed, by good bits, and the love of a Chambermaid.[39]

John Lyly's *Serving-Man's Song* pursues a similar vein:

> Granichus: O! for a bowl of fat Canary,
> Rich Palermo, sparkling Sherry,
> Some nectar else, from Juno's dairy,
> O! these draughts would make us merry.
>
> Psyllus: O! for a wench (I deal in faces,
> And in other daintier things).
> Tickled am I by her embraces,
> Fine dancing in such fairy rings.
>
> Manes: O! for a plump fat leg of mutton,
> Veal, lamb, capon, pig and coney;
> None is happy but a glutton
> None as ass but who wants money.
>
> Chorus: Wines (indeed) and girls are good,
> But brave victuals feast the blood;
> For wenches, wine and lusty cheer
> Jove would leap down to surfeit here.[40]

In the first half of the sixteenth century the position of gentlemen servants was well-defined and secure, their role cementing personal and family relationships and preserving a closely defined social hierarchy. Henry VII's policies had diminished their military role, but the great upheavals following the Dissolution of the monasteries were to considerably weaken it. In brief, former monastic land rapidly passed into the hands of gentlemen who developed its economic potential to great profit. This could not be fully enjoyed out on remote country estates, but offered much scope for a luxurious city life. Here were the law courts, the shops, the entertainments, the lively company, and everything else a *nouveau riche* family demanded. As a result, those who could afford it spent an increasing part of their year in London or, if not the capital, in their major regional city. Unlike the old aristocracy and gentry, they did not wish to pay for tiers of gentlemen servants; they had no need to build up the old-fashioned family and geographical links, and saw such people less as supporters, more as expensive parasites. Any money paid to them meant less for living the high-life in town. In this increasingly competitive age, in which the display of material wealth and conspicuous consumption was being valued at least as much as status and lineage, there was little need for a full chamber of gentlemen servants. The royal family and the grandest of grandees continued to use them up to the Restoration, but their decline was already obvious sixty years earlier. I.M.'s *A Health to the Gentlemanly Profession of Serving-Men* of 1598 discusses this situation in detail, its conclusions condensed into these verses:

> When Countreys causes did require,
> Each Nobleman to keep his house.
> Then Blewcoats [serving men] had what they desyre,
> Good cheare, with many a full carouse;
> But now not as it wont to be,
> For dead is Liberalitie.
>
> The Hall boardes-ende is taken up,
> No Dogges do differ for the bones,
> Black-Jacke is lefte, now Glasse or Cup,
> It makes mee sigh with many groones,
> To think what was, now thus to be,
> By death of Liberalitie.
>
> Thus you have heard, the death of Liberalitie to be one of the especiall occasions that hath wrought the utter overthrow, ruine, & subversion of Servingmens estate.[41]

Similarly, in 'A new guyse now a Dayes', we read that:

> Temporal lords be well nigh gone:
> Householdes keepe they fewe or none,
> Which causeth many a poore man
>   For to begge his bread.
> If he steale for his necessity
> There is none other remedy,
> But the law will very shortly
>   Hang him all save the head.[42]

Without the greater household, there was no need to build suites of chambers and great halls. The new cheap, ill-trained employees, both men-servants and even cheaper serving-maids, were of a different calibre, and were best kept as far away from their employers as possible. Architects such as Sir Roger Pratt clearly recognized this, removing them from the hall down into a meaner, smaller servants' hall in the basement, and providing back-stairs to keep them out of the public rooms. They were unable to perform the former rites of service at the table in the chamber, leading to completely new methods of polite dining after the Restoration.

Figure 118. Sir Henry Unton's banquet, c. 1596. Sir Henry, his family and guests, sit around the table, the men with their napkins over their left shoulders, and the ladies with theirs on their laps. Each person has a square or round trencher before them, but there is no evidence of cutlery. A cupboard stands in the background, with a covered table just outside the chamber to hold additional or used tableware. As the musicians play, the masques march in, lit by pairs of children bearing long flaming torches, in this unique depiction of a formal banquet.

CHAPTER TWENTY-FOUR

The Banquet

In the late medieval period a 'voidee' or 'void' was a digestive course of spices, sweetmeats and spiced wines taken when standing at the table at the end of a feast, just before hands were washed and the tablecloth removed. It was still being served in this way at great feasts in the 1540s, as at Anne Boleyn's coronation feast, or at the reception of an embassy, for which it might comprise sixty dishes. By this time it had also begun to develop into a separate event in its own right, Henry VIII's entertainments of masques and dances concluding with 'a voidy of spices'.[1] These usually took place in the great chambers, after the feast, as Shakespeare described in *All is True*, where, in 1527, the masked king and his fellows entered Wolsey's feast, leading the cardinal to ask, 'Sir Thomas Lovell, is the banquet ready, i'th privy chamber?'[2] Here Wolsey was using the word 'banquet' in its new and specific meaning of a luxurious, select course of sweetmeats and delicacies: the successor of the voidee.

There were a number of reasons for the introduction of such banquets. Since feasts were highly formalized displays of ceremony and power, every detail faultlessly performed by trained gentlemen to impress all observers, they stifled all informal interaction between those at the top table. Any conversations, or even glances between participants, would have been immediately noted by the servants, and most probably their content rapidly reported around the household and beyond. In contrast, a banquet solely of the select few, totally unobserved, held in the most sumptuous and closely controlled of locations, and consuming the most costly and rarest of foods and drinks, offered much scope for real enjoyment. It also provided a uniquely powerful means of demonstrating who was in favour and who was not in this most status-aware of societies. For his own use, Henry VIII built special rooms in the grounds of his major palaces in which to hold banquets. One of 1533–4 at Hampton Court took the form of an onion-domed polygonal garden tower, while that at Greenwich was a long rectangular block set between the tiltyard and great garden.[3] Perhaps his finest was set on a hill next to Nonsuch Palace. High on its brick-walled platform with circular corner-bastions, it was made of lead-clad timber framing. The lowest storey was a large hall with cellars below and eight rooms in two storeys

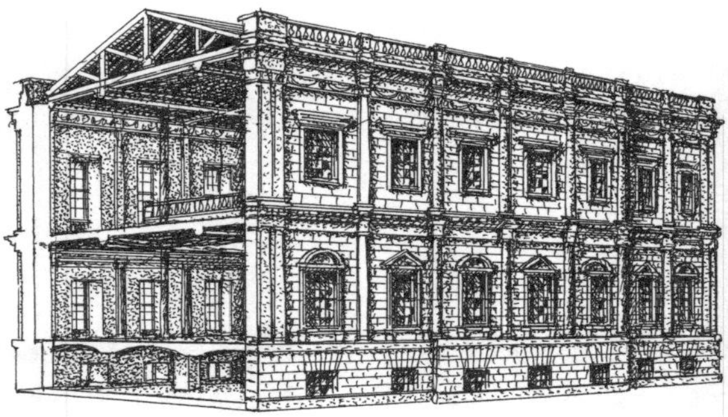

Figure 119. The Banqueting House, Whitehall. Built by Inigo Jones for James I in 1622, this was the prime location for state ceremonies and entertainments, including the incomparable masques written by Ben Jonson and set against Jones's spectacular scenery. The banquets which followed were often set out in the basement, which was decorated as a shell grotto, similar to the contemporary example, probably also by Isaac de Caus, which survives at Skipton Castle (right). Here, with candle-light reflecting from the pearly shells and figures, the jollity and drinking continued into the early hours of the following day.

above, all oak-panelled and with large glazed windows. A lead-covered lantern and prospect balcony at each corner formed the roof. Close by was a bakehouse, a well and a wash-house to service this impressive banqueting house.[4]

The fashion for banqueting houses spread rapidly down the social scale, John Stow complaining in 1598 that around London,

> wee see a thing in worse case than ever, by means of inclosure for Gardens wherein are builded many fayre summer houses, and as in other places of the Suburbs, some of them like Midsummer Pageants, with Towers, Turrets, and Chimney tops, not so much for use or profite, as for shew and pleasure, bewraying the variety of men's mindes [in] allies, Gardens, banquetting houses and bowling places.[5]

Philip Stubbes had no doubt as to their real purpose, describing in his *Anatomy of Abuses* of 1583 how the women,

> have their banqueting houses with galleries, turrets, and what not, therein sumptuously erected, wherein they may many of them play the filthy persons. And for that their gardens are locked, some of them have three or four keyes a piece, whereof one they keep for themselves, the other their paramours have to goe in before them, least happily they might be perceived, for then were all the sport dasht ...

Raucous behaviour was not the sole preserve of the middle classes, however, particularly after James I injected a completely new standard of debauchery into the dignified court of his predecessor. When being entertained along with Christian IV of Denmark at Hatfield House in 1606, the wine flowed aplenty, and they embraced lovingly at table. At the subsequent representation of Solomon receiving the Queen of Sheba,

> The lady who did play the Queen's part did carry most precious gifts to both their Majesties: but, forgetting the steps arising to the canopy, overset her caskets into his Danish Majesty's lap, and fell at his feet, though I rather think it was in his face. Much was the hurry and confusion; cloths and napkins were at hand, to make all clean. His Majesty then got up and would dance with the Queen of Sheba; but he fell down and humbled himself before her, and was carried to an inner chamber and laid on a bed of state, which was not a little defiled with the presents of the Queen which had been bestowed on his garments, such as wine, cream, jelly, beverage, cakes, spices and other good matters. The entertainment and show went forward, and most of the presenters went backward, or fell down, wine did so occupy their upper chambers.
>
> Now did appear, in rich dress, Hope, Faith and Charity. Hope did essay to speak, but wine rendered her endeavours so feeble that she withdrew, and hoped the King would excuse her brevity. Faith was then all alone, for I am certain she was not joined with good works; and left the Court in a staggering condition. Charity came to the King's feet, and seemed to cover a multitude of sins her sisters had committed; in some sort she made obeisance and brought gifts, but said she would return home again, as there was no gift which Heaven had not already given his Majesty; she then returned to Hope and Faith, who were both sick and spewing in the lower hall.[6]

'Victory' had to be led off to sleep, while 'Peace' used her olive-branch to swipe the heads of those who tried to hold her back.

The first banqueting house in Whitehall Palace was a timber-framed building, covered with canvas painted to represent masonry, erected in 1581. Its successor of 1606, a classical galleried hall 120 feet long which burnt down in 1619, had been replaced by the present Banqueting House designed by Inigo Jones by 1622. Here the great court masques were performed, James enjoying the unique combination of Jones as deviser of scenic effects and Ben Jonson as playwright for the many performances which were followed by sweetmeat banquets. Some must have taken place in the shellwork grotto which Isaac de Caus built in the undercroft in 1623–6.[7]

Figure 120. Rooftop banqueting houses. These locations offered great privacy and great views. At Longleat in 1569 (top) the banqueting houses were small domed pavilions at the stair-heads, but later examples took the advantage of large areas of flat-lead roofs, as at Hardwick Hall of 1590–97 (left). At Wollaton Hall (right) there were two levels for banqueting, the lower one being some 40ft above the ground, and the higher, a further 45ft above, with an intimate banqueting house in each of the spectacular corner bartizans.

One of the first English grottoes, presumably also intended for banqueting, was at Robert Cecil's Theobalds where, in 1600, Baron Waldstein had admired

> different kinds of semi-transparent stones, and roofed over with pieces of coral, crystal, and all kinds of metallic ore ... A number of columns by the windows support the mighty [rock-work] structure of the room: these columns are covered with the bark of trees, so they do in fact look exactly like oaks and pines.[8]

Today only two of these early grottoes can still be seen, one by de Caus from the 1630s at Woburn Abbey, and the other, probably also by him, in the gatehouse at Skipton Castle, Yorkshire. Both are clad in pearly shells to give a rich, dramatic and mysterious atmosphere, particularly when candle-lit for an evening banquet.

Instead of banqueting in gloom, many preferred a much lighter, higher location, one which offered the advantages of privacy and fine views from roof level. When set on top of a tower or in a rooftop turret, the participants could neither be overlooked nor overheard, but might enjoy a birds-eye view over the formal gardens, orchards, and surrounding landscape. Sir William Sharington's tower at Lacock Abbey, Wiltshire, has two banqueting houses in its upper storeys, each capable of holding half a dozen people, access to the lower one being from the house, and to the upper one only by a walk across the leads. When Longleat, Wiltshire, was being remodelled in *c.* 1569, it was specified that all the stairs were 'to Royse above the house and to be typed [domed] and 4 to have lytle staires wonne from the roof so as they may serve as banketting howses' [where they still remain].[9] Similar small banqueting houses were built on the roofs of houses such as Heath Old Hall, Yorkshire, and Barlborough Hall, Derbyshire, both of the 1580s, and Doddington Hall, Lincolnshire, *c.* 1593–1600. Much larger ones were built at Hardwick Hall, Derbyshire, in 1590–97, where they were up to some 25 feet by 15 feet (6.1 by 5.7m), with high ceilings and four great windows being capable of accommodating large numbers as they promenaded the broad lead roof. Others, as at Wollaton Hall, Nottingham, *c.* 1580, and Bolsover Little Castle, *c.* 1612, are tiny, with just sufficient space for an intimate couple.

In a number of houses, long lofts under pitched roofs were apparently used as banqueting houses. One at the former Grove House, Woodford, Essex, had a flat ceiling, sloping eaves, and walls which sloped inwards as they approached the floor. When built by a merchant adventurer and grocer in 1580, its eaves were painted with a series of appropriate rural scenes, one showing an outdoor music party with a servant replenishing wine glasses from lidded containers standing in a long basket.[10] A much more impressive example still survives at Apethorpe Hall, Northamptonshire. Built in the 1620s above the long gallery, it too has sloping eaves and walls, but extends for some 160 feet (48m) along the entire east front. Inside, it had three marble tables for drinks and sweetmeats, while three gabled porches gave access to a long parapet walk providing excellent views over the formal gardens to an avenue, river, and rolling landscape extending to the horizon.[11]

A detached banqueting house offered a similar retreat from the formality of life in the chambers, and away from the prying eyes and ears of the servants. Many were designed to punctuate the layout of the garden, or to provide amenities for bowling greens and other garden features. If large, they also served as lodges, capable of housing a separate, compact household. That for Holdenby, Northamptonshire, pre-1587, was a compact three-storey H-plan topped by two small banqueting houses, and might easily have been taken for a separate residence, were it not for the great house close by.[12] Most, however, had only a few rooms,

Figure 121. A garden banquet. This scene was painted on the walls of the banqueting house in the roof of Grove House, Woodford, Essex, in 1580.

and were of one or two storeys, always of interesting design and good quality construction.

Some were built on islands to give an even greater sense of isolation, to enjoy the movement and reflection of the water, and to facilitate angling. Francis Bacon's island banqueting house was in Roman style, paved with black and white marble, roofed in Cornish slate, and oak panelled, while one proposed by Richard Carew for Antony, Cornwall, was to be of wood. Its round room set within a square building, surmounted by a square room set within a round turret, was a typically intriguing device.[13] The brick foundations of a fishing banqueting house still survive as an island in a former pond at Norton Conyers, Yorkshire.

Another rather unexpected location for a banqueting house was up a tree. At Cobham Hall, Kent, the branches of a lime tree were entwined to form an arbour at ground level, then two storeys of rooms up above with boarded floors, all linked by stairs to accommodate a total of 25 people. Another lime tree set on top of a mound at Pitchford Hall, Shropshire, had branches formed to cradle a 10-foot square timber-framed banqueting house, crowned with a pyramid-shaped tiled roof. Banquets here would be delightful, shaded and largely hidden by the leaves, yet high enough to enjoy the views.

The banqueting houses of England were admired by many visitors from the Continent. While Paul Hentzner was at Theobalds in the late sixteenth century he was led by the gardener

> into the summer house, in the lower part of which, built semicircularly, are the twelve Roman emperors in white marble and a table of touchstone, the upper part of it set round with cisterns of lead, into which water is conveyed through the pipes, so that fish may be kept in them, and in summer time they are very convenient for bathing, and another room for entertaining very near this, and joined to it by a little bridge, was an oval table of red marble.[14]

Whatever their form, any of these banqueting houses would be suitable for fulfilling their principal purposes as locations in which to enjoy a course of sweetmeats and for lust. As Corsica offered in Massinger's *The Bondman* of 1623:

> I have a couch and a banqueting-house in my orchard,
> Where many a man of honour has not scorn'd
> To spend the afternoon.

Or, as Robert Davenport's Antonio explained to Phillipe in his *City Nightcap* of 1661: 'Garden-houses are not truer bawds to cuckold-making, than I will be to thee and thy stratagem.'[15]

Some of the earlier banqueting houses, put up before they gained their later reputation, were temporary structures for short-term use. In July 1502, for example, 'certain labourers' were paid 4*s*. 6*d*. 'to make an herbour in the litle parke of Windsore for a banket for the Quene' Elizabeth of York.[16] When entertaining a French embassy at Greenwich in 1560, Elizabeth I had another banqueting house 'made with fir poles and decked with birch branches and all manner of flowers both of the field and of the garden; as roses, july flowers, lavender, marygolds and all manner of strewing herbs and rushes.'[17] Ordinary people made their own communal 'summer halls, their bowers, arbours and banqueting houses set up, wherein they feast, banquet and dance all [May] day, and, peradventure all night too,' in their churchyards, according to the puritanical Philip Stubbes.

The furniture used at banquets as depicted in contemporary paintings comprised a cloth-covered rectangular table surrounded by a number of stools, which may have been brought from the chambers as required. One of the few

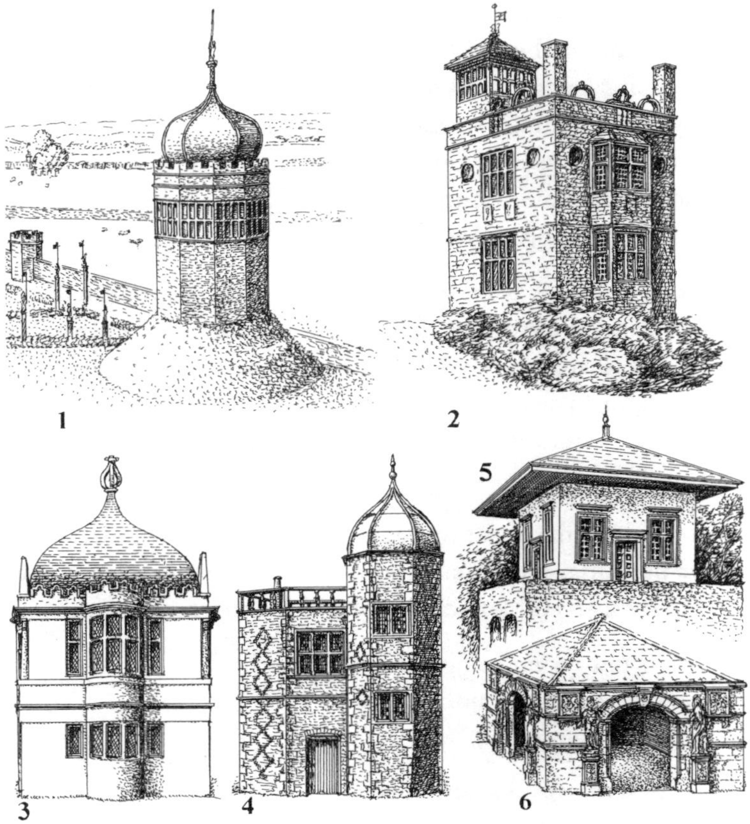

Figure 122. Garden banqueting houses. (1) Henry VIII's banqueting house of 1536–7 at Hampton Court; (2) Weston Park, Otley, Yorkshire, late 16th century; (3) Montacute House, Somerset, 1590s; (4) Eyton-on-Severn, Shropshire, 1607; (5) Becket House, Shrivenham, Oxfordshire, c. 1632, by Inigo Jones?; (6) Knostrop Hall, Leeds, mid-17th cent.

banquet-house tables to remain in place is in Sir William Sharington's tower at Lacock Abbey, Wiltshire, its octagonal stone top being supported on an octagonal base, four figures in elaborate arches being separated by alternate, appropriately naked, male and female terms. A magnificent carved wooden banqueting table still survives at Norton Conyers, Yorkshire, where it has been for over 200 years, probably being used in the island banqueting house which once stood there. Dating from the late sixteenth century, and likely of London manufacture, it is square, with a panel of marble set into its centre for flagons and glasses, and a cupboard in its square pedestal for banqueting stuff.

It is probable that a number of suites of English-made back-stools or armchairs of elaborately carved Italianate design were for use at banquets, their shell- or cherub-topped backs, complex scrolled and swagged supports, being ideal for such entertainments. One set is provenanced to Holland House, London, a further two sets of nine at Petworth House, Sussex, being purchased by Algernon Percy, tenth Earl of Northumberland as 'backstools of Italian fashion' in 1635–6. According to Horace Walpole, these were 'undoubtedly' designed by Francis Cleyn.

By the early seventeenth century, Dudley, Lord North was able to report that a new custom had sprung up:

> Now all are Banquets ... ordained for merry humours, some being used even at Funeralls ... How like Epicurists do some persons drink at a Funeral, as if they were met there to be merry, and make it a matter of rejoicing that they have got rid of their Friends and Relations.[18]

For most people, the cost involved in purchasing expensive sweetmeats for a funeral banquet was prohibitive, the anonymous *Whimsies or a New Cost of Characters* of 1631 describing a Londoner who had 'so much she hath reserved out of the labours of her life, as will buy some small portion of Diet Bread, Comfits and Burnt Claret, to welcome in her Neighbours now at her departing, of whose cost they never so freely tasted while she was living.'

It might have been thought that all frivolous entertainments such as banquets would have been suppressed by the Commonwealth government, but this was not the case. When at the final course of a feast for the French ambassador in 1656, the Lord Protector's wife requested a few dried candied apricots from an adjacent table. Hearing this Colonel Pride

> threw into her apron a conserve of wet, with both his hands, and stained it all over; when, as if that had been a sign, Oliver catches up his napkin and throws it at Pride, he at him again, while all of that table were engaged in the scuffle. [The party then went] to this pastime of gambols and be spectators of his Highness's frolics.[19]

Figure 123. Banqueting furniture. Italian-style chairs, such as those from Holland House, London (left), and purchased by Algernon, 10th Earl of Northumberland in 1635–6 now at Petworth House, Sussex (right), were ideal for use in banqueting houses. Their shell motifs followed the theme of shell-lined grottoes while their bright colouring and gilding echoed that of the elaborate sweetmeats. The carved stone table stands in the centre of Sir William Sharington's 1549–53 banqueting house at Lacock Abbey, Wiltshire.

Figure 124. A banquet. Painted on the walls of Knightlands Farm, Potters Bar, Hertfordshire, this scene shows a banquet taking place outside a tavern – the maid to the right is marking up her slate. Meanwhile, beneath their vine-hung bower, a merry group of banqueters 'play the filthy persons' with lots of tongue-action.

CHAPTER TWENTY-FIVE

Banqueting Stuff

The foods set out in the banqueting houses before the arrival of the participants had to meet a number of criteria. It had to be luxurious and attractive to the eye, bright, delicate and elegant; it had to be suitable for everyone to help themselves whether sitting, standing or moving around, since servants would usually be absent; and it had to promote the hot and moist humours of lust. In addition, it had to demonstrate the wealth, conspicuous consumption, and frequently the confectionery skills of its provider. To do this it used large quantities of expensive sugar, spices, fruits and alcohol, along with various perfumed ingredients, colourings and gold leaf, all worked up into delectable sweetmeats.

At the opening of the sixteenth century most of the sugar used in England was imported from the Middle East and Mediterranean by the Venetians in a refined or semi-refined form. The canes had been crushed to extract the juice, which was then boiled with lime to throw off its thick scum, and poured into conical earthenware moulds before standing for a few days to set. Holes in their bases were then unblocked so that the surplus syrup and molasses could drain down into collecting jars. A liquid mixture of fine white clay might be poured on top, so that its water could seep through the sugar to purify it. This process was repeated several times before the mould was put into hot and dry conditions until a complete, dense, marble-like sugar-loaf could be unmoulded and tied in paper ready for sale.

Having been carried to the New World by Columbus, sugar began to be cultivated by the Spanish in the Caribbean, Mexico, Paraguay and the Pacific coast of South America, while the Portuguese grew it in Brazil. These new supplies of sugar arrived in Europe from 1515 onwards, but it was not until 1551 that Captain Thomas Wyndham brought the first cargo of sugar into England in an English ship, and this was from Morocco. Before this time, however, considerable quantities of New World sugars had become available here through piracy. In 1591 a Spanish spy was reporting that 'English booty in West India produce is so great that sugar is cheaper in London than it is in Lisbon or the Indies themselves.' The acquisition of Barbados in 1625 enabled England to import its own sugar for the first time, 6,667 tons of muscovado and 283 tons of clayed sugars arriving from there in 1655. In the same year Jamaica was invaded, bringing even more plantations under English control.

The first sugar refinery in London had been established in 1544, this expanding after the sack of Antwerp in 1576 to become the largest centre of sugar refining in the whole of Europe.[1] Further refineries were later set up in cities such as Bristol, and York. The increasing availability of sugar should have brought a reduction in prices, but this was not the case here, William Cholmley complaining in 1553 that 'The sugar that I have known at 4*d*. the lb., is now at 14*d*.', rising to 18*d*. around 1600.[2] The reason for this was the ever-increasing demand, as people at all levels of society developed a taste for this exotic product. Evidence for this is provided by excavated teeth which show a pronounced development in dental caries from the sixteenth century.

Since the wealthiest people could afford to eat the most sugar, they also developed the greatest tooth decay, and hence the need for tooth-picks. Some were small splits of wood, specially made and sold in boxes, Robert Dudley, Earl of Leicester, regularly buying 'boxis of tothe pickes' costing between 6*d*. and 7*d*. each.[3] Others were made of precious metals, such as the 'tothe pyke of silver' bequested to Robert Toutte in 1579.[4] These became fashion icons, flourished with pride, demonstrating that their owners had joined the ranks of the banqueters, eaten quantities of costly sugar, and had the bad teeth to prove it. Contemporary writers adopted the toothpick as a metaphor for a swaggering gentleman:[5]

> 'My case of toothpicks, and my silver fork' (Massinger);
> 'You shall find him in St Paul's, with a toothpick in his hat' (Sir Thomas Overbury);
> 'His toothpick bears a great part in his discourse' (Bishop Earle);
> 'Just like the brooch and toothpick, which we wear not now'
> (Shakespeare, *All's Well that Ends Well*).

The sugar consumed at banquets was usually purchased either from a grocer or from one of the professional confectioners who had set up in business from the mid-sixteenth century. It came in a number of different forms, such as:[6]

Cassonade: muscovado clarified with egg whites and limewater 'not so white and partly pulverized into crass lumps'.
Common sugar : an off-white sugar.
Madeira and Canary sugar : extraordinarily white.
Sugar candy: common sugar dissolved in water, (clarified) boiled, and allowed

to stand in a warm place for a few days until it formed large crystals around fine sticks.

Sugar-loaves: conical loaves of hard sugar, of variable stages of refinement.

For service at banquets, these had then to be combined with all manner of other ingredients, as both a flavouring and as a uniquely effective preservative. Those listed by Thomas Dawson in 1596 included,

> ... cinnomon, liquorice, pepper, nutmegs, all kinds of saffron, sanders, comfits, aniseeds, coriander, oranges, pomegranate seeds, damask [rose] water, turnsole, lemons, prunes, [ordinary] rosewater, dates, currants, raisins, cherries conserved, barberries, rye flour, ginger, sweet oranges, pepper white and brown, mace, wafers.[7]

In this way sugar added its moist humour to the hot and dry spices, and its hot humour to the cold and moist fruits, rendering both more suitable for banqueting in the dietetic theories of the day.

In smaller households sugar confectionery, fruits and distilled waters were usually purchased ready-made from professional confectioners, as shown in the following account for the Yorkshire wedding of Gervase Clifton and Mary Nevile in 1530:

2lb Marmalet *2s.*	3lb Green Ginger *4s.*
1lb Biskets *1s.*	3lb Suckets *4s.*
1lb Carraway Seeds *2s.*	4lb Oranges in Syrup *5s. 11d.*[8]

If collected from York, the syrupy ginger suckets and oranges would have been packed into glazed earthenware galley-pots, with covers tied down with string over their rounded rims like those of jam-jars. A quantity of these in two sizes, made in the early seventeenth century, were found when a cellar in Pavement in the city was broken into in 1885. For larger establishments, however, it was preferable to buy in the raw ingredients and process them in a private stillhouse.

THE STILLHOUSE

At the opening of the sixteenth century the production of distilled herbal waters for medicinal use was an area of male expertise, particularly in monasteries and great households. In 1512 the Earl of Northumberland had a still which used 30 sacks of charcoal to produce 28 different 'waters' each year, while the Willoughby family's chaplain, Sir William Webster, was distilling their strawberry water and similar substances in the 1520s. After the Dissolution the art of distilling passed to professionals working in the major cities, and to the wives

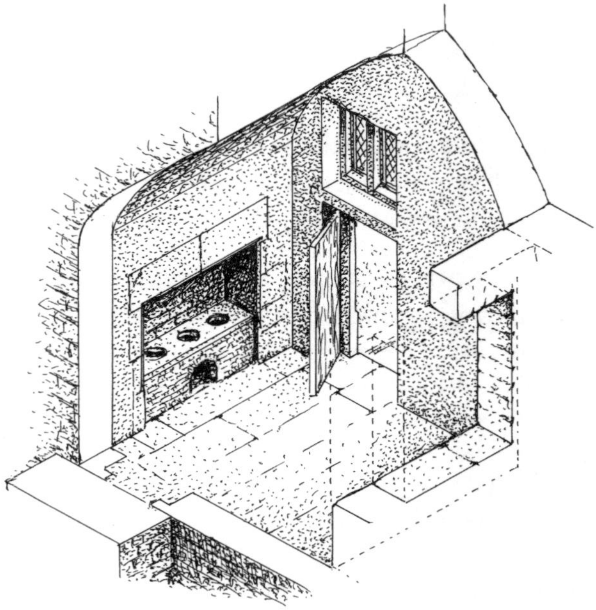

Figure 125. The stillhouse, Bolsover Castle. Built in a programme of works commenced in 1612, this stillhouse was set in a garden wall, its stove (restored in this drawing) enjoyed plenty of daylight from the adjacent door and high-level window. A wall-cupboard was let into the nearest wall, while the door to the left led out into the Wilderness, probably a good source of herbs and flowers.

of the aristocracy and gentry who had taken over the monastic role as provider of health-care both for their own families and the community at large. Aided by earlier distillers and books such as *The vertuose book of the Dystillacion of the Waters of all maner of Herbes* of 1527, ladies now set up their own stills. Lady Hewett, probably the wife of Sir William, Lord Mayor of London in 1559, produced a 'Great Cordial Water' the recipe of which circulated for at least 120 years. She was of the generation of older ladies of Queen Elizabeth's court who William Harrison stated were 'skilful in surgery and distillation of waters'. During the later sixteenth century, lady distillers started to make their own alcoholic aqua vitaes, each flavoured with spices or herbs both for medicinal use and to supplement the spiced hippocras served at banquets. *Rosa solis*, for example, the herb *Drosera rotundifolia* or sundew, added a stimulating aphrodisiac quality to the spirits, although its excessive use was dangerous.[9]

The arrival of James I and his spirit-drinking wife Anne of Denmark in 1603 saw aqua vitaes being increasingly used for social drinking, especially at banquets. They could be purchased ready-made from town-based distillers, but not without risk. In London many were established in the parish of St Giles, Cripplegate, where,

> dyversse of greedye and covetous myndes, for their owne lucre and gaine – without the dew regarde of the health and wellfayre of our subjects, or the p'fit and benefit wch may grow to us and our Commonwealth, by the trew right making of the same trew and wholsome lyquor – have, do use the foresayde drynkes and sauces of most corrupt, noysom, and lothsom stuff, viz, the washing [of] tonnes, colebacks, laggedragge, tylts, and droppings of tuppes, and such other noysom stuff used in tymes past to feed the swyne.[10]

Instead of buying such products of hog-wash and other excrescences, it was far safer to make one's own spirits from wine dregs, malt liquors, fermented fruits and other garden produce. A further advantage of this practice was that by setting up a stillhouse a lady gained a rare private space into which she could retreat with a companion or two, well away from the constraints of her chambers and the constant attendance of servants and family. Here, in her own private world, she could enjoy the practical activity of distilling and experimentation just as she wished.

The ninth Earl of Northumberland had advised his son that noble ladies should avoid the household kitchen, where their intervention caused mayhem, but there was no harm in letting them escape into the more peaceful dairy. Presumably the ladies who had used the various recipe books published for them in the late sixteenth century had used their household kitchens, probably being welcomed and accommodated there by master cooks who, in reality, would have been glad to see the back of them, and set everything back into working order. Given the use of a stillhouse, however, it rapidly became obvious that this was the best place in which a lady could conduct all the other activities necessary for making every item of banqueting stuff. This expansion of use had already taken place at Hengrave Hall, Essex, by 1603, where the stillhouse was the venue for 'preparing and keeping biskett cakes, marchpanes, herbs, spicebreads, conserves and other sweetmeats.[11] In the same year James I paid a visit to Apethorpe, Northamptonshire, where,

> The tables were newly covered with costly banquets wherein everything that was most delicious for taste prooved more delicate to the Arte that made it seeme beauteous to the eye; the lady of the house being one of the most excellent Confectioners in England, though I confesse many honourable women very expert.[12]

To undertake confectionery of this quality sufficient to serve the royal entourage in her huge roof-level banqueting house, Lady Grace Mildmay must have had the use of a very substantial stillhouse.

Many of the stillhouses were separate buildings set in the formal gardens which surrounded their mansion. William Lawson's *New Orchard and Garden* of 1618 shows a pair set on mounts at each end of a moat in front of the house, a typical position. Most have been modernized over succeeding centuries, but an almost complete example remains in the wall of the fountain garden at Bolsover Castle, Derbyshire. Built *c.* 1612, it has a fireplace with a chimney to carry off the fumes from the stove, this being illuminated by a high-level window. On the opposite wall is a recess for a wall-cupboard for the storage of equipment and bottles of waters and the like, while a door in the back wall leads directly into the wilderness garden, ideal for the collection of herbs and other plants.

At Chatsworth in 1601 the garden stillhouse occupied a two-storey turret, with four stills, two pewter pots, a cupboard to set glasses on, a pair of tongs and a bed on the ground floor, and a bed, a chest and two boards in the room above.[13] This stillhouse was obviously being used by a household servant for the distillation of waters, its contents being particularly sparse when compared to those in the stillhouse at Hengrave, Suffolk, in 1603:

Stilling & Cooking	*Storage*
1 great brass pot for distilling	1 tin cover for earthen pans
5 stills with 5 lead weights	6 white earthen pans to preserve in
1 alembic [still-head] of tin	1 basket to keep marchpanes in
1 great pan of latten with an iron furnace pan to hold fire	1 round maund for herbs 1 sheet to keep roses in
5 skillets of brass	1 locked coffer for spicebread
1 cradle to roast apples on	1 boarded chest for fruit
3 pairs of wafer irons	Galleypots & other pots for conserves

Preparation
2 great mortars & pestles
3 moulds of tin to make biscuit cakes
2 mustard mills

Service
Six Venice [glass] banqueting dishes[14]

This was clearly a fully equipped stillhouse capable of making all kinds of banqueting stuff. Details of the required utensils were given in Richard Tomlinson's *Medical Dispensatory* of 1657, and included:

A Dish can be brazen in which … fruits [are] condited. It has two handles that it may be set on the fire, upon a three-footed iron instrument.
A Pottenger is a small vessel with a long ferrous handle that it may be set on the fire, used for small amounts.
Sieves. Rustic sieves are made with leather skin with many holes to purge corn in. Other sieves are made of horse-hair (interwoven) … These are also made of wood fibre laced in lattices.
Tamis … is made of horse-hair, or fine linen, or silk which is woven and above and below is a piece of rams skin upon a bending of wood, so that the powder may pass from one section to the other without loss [i.e. a drum-sieve].
Another kind of Sieve is in the form of a great box, in which the whole middle is a great web through which the powder falls.
Strainers … of silk, linen, canvas and wood gives various densities, which also depends on the age of the strainer … Wool strainers are long and pyramidal, and are used to concoct hippocras wine … .
Mortars … of brass: one very ample for such things as are large or hard, and one very small. [Pestles are] brasen for brasen, but iron fits all metals, and a wooden pestle for a stone mortar for new herbs. The mortar must be covered with paper or leather for pulverising dry things, lest the powder fly out and perish or trouble the nose and eyes.
Spatulas and Spoons. … Table spoons are made of silver or wood for the rustick poorer people. They make little ones of ivory and horn, that serve for measuring all powders and putting them on the scales.
Containers. Bottles of glass or clay for distilled water. Ligneus [wooden] vessels: baskets, chests and boxes. Baskets of rushes or boughs to keep fruits therein. [Five-plank] chests in which flowers, horns [etc.] are reposed. Boxes are round and profound; either thrown [turned] or composed of a thin broad chip brought to a round form, wherein sugars, gummes [etc.] are kept. Dry things are sometimes kept in chests and sometimes in bags.[15]

Armed with this extensive range of equipment, a stewing stove, an oven and a worktable, together with a collection of recipes garnered from friends, relations and published cookery books, any competent lady could furnish all manner of confectionery or 'banqueting stuff' for her fashionable entertainments.

FRUIT

The medieval belief that raw fruits were positively dangerous continued as strongly as ever, despite the great developments in gardening and orchards from the Elizabethan period. In 1583, readers of *The Schoolmaster or Teacher of Table*

Philosophie were told how Galen, the great second-century philosopher, only 'fell into sundry, and long continuing diseases' after eating raw fruits, but after giving them up 'had never any sickness.' For this reason most fruits were eaten after being either cooked for immediate consumption, or preserved so that they could be enjoyed throughout the whole year, rather than just within their own limited seasons. During the third quarter of the sixteenth century many new recipes were developed for preparing fruits for banquets, these then being published in a series of innovative cookery books specially written for the benefit of fashionable and wealthy ladies. A selection taken from these now follows, considering each fruit in turn.

APPLES

Tudor and early Stuart households had access to a good selection of apples for eating (despite being considered unhealthy by some) and cooking, including the large five-sided costard, the john-apple, best when two years old, the June-ripening sweet jenneting, the summer and winter pearmains, pippins, and the hard or under-ripe codlings and crabs which could only be eaten when cooked.

Whether grown in private orchards, or bought at the market or from hawkers, apples had to be carefully stored to ensure their long-term preservation. The actual method depended largely on personal preference and experience:

> Lay them dark as wind may not come near,
> And do fair straw upon them, fleyk them under,
> Or in heaps save, a little space asunder
> These heaps must ye now and now divide,
> Yet there be divers folk say diverse wise,
> And all in pitched potts will they hide,
> Another of clay, another grease,
> Yet hath a third for them a fresh devise,
> Only the little feet [base or stalk] to cleme in clay
> And on a floor with chaff bestrewn to lay.
> And other dip her little feet in pitch all warme,
> And so in order lay them on a form.

The alternative to stacking in straw on slatted racks, in heaps, or sealed in jars perhaps for burying in the ground was to,

> pare them, take out the coars, and slice them in thin slices, laying them to dry in the Sun in some stone or metalline dishes, or upon a high frame covered with coarse canvas, now & then turning them, and so they will keep all the yeer.[16]

Fresh, raw apples were considered to be a real risk to health, corrupting the blood and aggravating weak stomachs, only becoming edible after a year in store, and eaten with fennel or caraway seeds to counteract their 'windy nature'; 'Nay, you shall see my orchard, where in an arbor we will eat a last year's pippin of mine own grafting with a dish of caraways.'[17] Alternatively they were roasted before the fire, baked or stewed, and scattered with sugar and aniseed comfits. These are the forms in which they popularly appeared at the close of dinner, just as they had at earlier, medieval meals. Apples could be roasted by simply threading them on a long string and dangling them in front of the fire, cooking them evenly by occasionally twisting the string to keep them rotating, and placing a dish beneath to catch their juices. Better-equipped kitchens used specially designed apple roasters. We have already mentioned Thomas Myddelton's in Swaledale in 1564 (page 353, above) and another example is Sir Thomas Fairfax, in his Walton kitchen (in Yorkshire too), who had 'An apple cradle' in 1624. However, there are no indications of the design and construction of these devices.[18]

The best-known recipes for roasted or boiled apples were:

APPLEMOYSE[19]

1½lb/675g apples	*2tbs sugar*
2 egg yolks	*1oz/25g butter*
2tbs rosewater	*ground ginger & cinnamon*

Either place the apples in a dish with a little water and bake at 180°C/350°F/gas mark 4 for some 40 minutes, or peel, core, slice and simmer with 3tbs water until tender, then rub the pulp through a sieve.

Beat the yolks with the rosewater in a pan, stir in the apple pulp, then the sugar and butter, and heat slowly to boiling point, sprinkle with a little ginger and cinnamon, and serve either hot or cold.

POMAGES[20]

1½lb/675g 'waterish apples' (Bramleys)	*2oz/50g sugar*
1pt/600ml red wine	*½tsp ground cinnamon*
6oz/175g crustless white bread	*½tsp ground ginger*

1tbs sugar, ¼tsp ground cinnamon & ¼tsp ginger for dredging

Peel, core and chop the apples, simmer with the red wine for 10–15 minutes until they are very soft, then stir in the thinly sliced bread to form a smooth, soft paste.

Rub the apple mixture through a sieve, return to the pan with the sugar and spices, and boil, stirring continuously until thickened.

Pour into a dish, sprinkle with the sugar and spice mixture, and serve either hot or cold.

APRICOTS

The apricot was introduced into England by Henry VIII's gardener in 1542, its perfume, colour and succulence ensuring its rapid spread into many private orchards.[21] Shakespeare assumed that they were native fruits, having them grow in the fourteenth-century Duke of York's garden where he instructed the gardener,

> Go, bind up young dangling apricocks,
> Which like unruly children make their sire
> Stoop with oppression of their prodigal weight
> Give some supportance to the bending twigs ... [22]

When the fruit ripened at the end of May or beginning of June, it was either eaten fresh, or preserved with sugar as,

PRESERVED APRICOTS[23]

1lb/450g apricots *1lb/450g sugar*

(Plunge the apricots into boiling water for a minute, drain, and pull off their skins), then split them and remove their stones.

Layer the apricots with the sugar and leave overnight in a pan.

Very gently heat the pan for an hour until all the sugar has dissolved, cover, and leave in a cool place for two days.

Return to the boil, pour into jars, and seal down.

TO DRY APRICOTS[24]

1lb/450g apricots *8oz/225g sugar*

(Plunge the apricots into boiling water for a minute, drain, and pull off their skins), then split them and remove their stones.

Layer the apricots with the sugar and leave overnight in a pan. Simmer gently until tender, and leave in a cool place for 2 days.

Drain the apricots from their syrup, arrange on a wire grid, place in an oven at 110°C/225°F/gas mark ¼ for 30 minutes, remove, allow to cool, and then turn over. Repeat this, or set the grid in an airing cupboard or over a radiator, turning them from time to time, until the apricots are dry, then store in a warm, dry, ventilated place, or in a sealed jar.

LADY WINDEBANK'S PASTE OF APRICOTS[25]

12oz/325g apricots *3oz/75g sugar*

(Plunge the apricots into boiling water for a minute, drain, pull off their skins), then remove their stones and slice them.

Put the apricots into a deep jar, seal the top (with a piece of cooking foil), and stand in a pan of simmering water for up to an hour, until they are reduced to a pulp.

Put the pulp into a small pan, and stir continuously over a moderate heat until it becomes very thick, then add the sugar, and work the paste with a wooden spatula until it has to be spread across the bottom of the pan, and is very thick once more.

Turn the paste on to a greased plate, form into a slab, and leave to cool.

CHERRIES

Cherries had the reputation of being easily digested, acting as an effective appetizer if eaten in moderation, and as a purgative if taken in excess. When 'Athenians' (i.e. Cambridge academics) over-indulged at Cherry-Hinton, they were 'so overcome by cherryes, that they can hardly convey them cleanly home to Athens'[26] to take corrective medicines. When preserved, cherries provided an excellent, richly coloured addition to the banquet course.

PRESERVED CHERRIES[27]

3lb/1.3kg cherries *2½lb/1.2kg sugar*

Stone all the cherries, put one-third of them in a pan with 1pt/600ml water, boil them for 20 minutes until very soft, then strain the juice through a muslin into a clean jug.

Layer the sugar and remaining cherries in a pan, pour in the strained juice, and boil rapidly until the liquid sets as jelly.

TO DRY CHERRIES[28]

1lb/450g cherries *12oz/325g sugar*

Stone all the cherries, layer them with the sugar and 45ml/3tbs water in a small pan, place over a very gentle heat, shaking them from time to time, until they are clear and tender.

When lukewarm, spoon each cherry separately onto a wire grid, not touching one other, and leave to drain, then place the grid over a radiator, or in an airing cupboard, for a few days, turning them from time to time, until dry, then store in a warm, dry place.

QUIDONY OF CHERRIES[29]

1lb/450g cherries | *1lb/450g sugar*

Stone the cherries, put in a pan, just cover with water, and boil until broken.

Pass the pulp through a sieve, add the sugar, and continue boiling until it will set as a firm paste, then pot and seal. To deepen the flavour, a little rosewater, ground clove and cinnamon, may be added after sieving.

CURRANTS – (RED)

These were first cultivated in England shortly before 1578, but although they probably were preserved from about this time, the first recipes for their culinary use only appear in the 1660s, in the works of William Rabisha and Sir Kenelm Digby.[30]

JELLY OF REDCURRANTS[31]

redcurrants | *sugar*

Gently heat the currants in a pan, stirring them from time to time, and squeezing out the juice by pressing them against the side with a spoon, then squeeze out the juice through a piece of muslin.

Weigh the juice, add three-quarters of its weight of sugar, then boil and skim to setting point. Pour into jars and seal down.

MARMALADE OF REDCURRANTS[32]

Make as above, but keep about a quarter of the currants whole, and add to the juices before weighing and boiling. Bruise them against the side of the pan as they cook.

DAMSONS

Damsons and their wild relatives bullaces, both with black and white varieties, were widely available. Damsons could be eaten before meals as an appetizer, dried to resemble figs, or preserved in syrup.[33]

PRESERVED DAMSONS OR PLUMS[34]

1lb/450g damsons or plums *1lb 4oz/550g sugar*

Put the fruit and sugar in a pan, just cover them with water and/or rosewater, then remove the fruit, and simmer the liquid to form a syrup.

Return the fruit to the pan, simmer until tender, then transfer to jars and seal down.

DATES

Raw dates were considered hard to digest, but this could be corrected by simmering them in syrup (say 8oz/225g sugar to 1pt/600ml water) for a few minutes, until they became tender. They were also served with a sprinkling of finely chopped preserved ginger.[35]

DATE LEACH[36]

4oz/100g stoned dates *2oz/50g caster sugar*

Pick the fibrous white lining out of the dates, finely chop the pulp, and grind it in a mortar to form a smooth paste with the sugar.

Form into a rectangular block and wrap in waxed paper (or foil) ready for slicing as required.

FIGS

Andrew Boorde described how Moorish slaves in Barbary, the north African coast, were in the habit of wiping their bottoms with the figs they gathered, before putting them into their baskets, but this did not prevent this dried fruit being a popular digestive and aphrodisiac. Some of the best came from Malaga.[37] If taken as an appetizer, they were eaten with ginger or pepper, or powdered thyme or pennyroyal, but if for the banquet course they could be either roasted or stewed.[38]

GOOSEBERRIES

The culinary use of gooseberries in England starts in the late sixteenth century. Perhaps because it was one of the most astringent of cultivated berries, it was one of the first to be made into creams and fools.

TO PRESERVE GOOSEBERRIES [WHOLE][39]

gooseberries, topped and tailed	*sugar*

Note the weight of the gooseberries.

Chop one-third of the gooseberries and stew for 10–15 minutes in a little water, to form a soft pulp, then strain the juice into a clean pan.

Add the original weight of gooseberries in sugar, and the whole gooseberries, simmer until they are just tender, then pour into jars and seal down.

TO PRESERVE GOOSEBERRIES[40]

1½lb/675g gooseberries	*1½lb/675g sugar*

Top and tail the gooseberries , scald with boiling water, leave for 15 minutes, then drain.

Layer the gooseberries with the sugar in a pan with 3tbs water, leave on a very low heat until the sugar has dissolved, then boil until thick, pour into jars and seal down.

ELIZABETH CROMWELL'S GOOSEBERRY CREAM[41]

8oz/225g preserved gooseberries	*3tbs sugar*
1pt/600ml single cream	*2tbs rosewater*
5 egg yolks, lightly beaten	
pinch of ground cinnamon, nutmeg and mace	

Heat the eggs, sugar, rosewater and spices while stirring until it has thickened, but not reached boiling point, then pour through a sieve into a broad dish, and leave to cool and set.

Use a pin to arrange the gooseberries in concentric circles on top of the cream, and sprinkle with sugar just before serving.

GOOSEBERRY FOOL[42]

1lb/450g gooseberries
4tbs sugar
3 egg yolks, beaten

Top, tail and coarsely chop the gooseberries, simmer with a little water, stirring to form a smooth pulp, then remove from the heat, and stir in the sugar.

Beat in the egg yolks, return to the heat and stir until just boiling, then pour into a broad dish, and stand in a cool place until required.

LEMONS

Lemons had become increasingly available throughout the late medieval period, but it was the sixteenth century that saw their large-scale importation from Portugal. Both their pulp and their peels were used as confections.

MARMALADE OF LEMONS OR ORANGES[43]

5 large lemons or oranges
3 apples (e.g. Cox's pippins)
c. *1lb/450g sugar*

Cover the fruit with water, cover and simmer for about an hour until the peels are very tender when tried with a skewer, then remove from the heat, drain, and rub the fruit and peels through a sieve.

Weigh the pulp, add its weight of sugar and stir over a gentle heat until very stiff before pouring into an airtight box or jar, and sealing down.

Alternatively, mould the thick marmalade as half-inch slabs on greased glazed plates or tiles (originally glass plates), place in an oven at 110°C/225°F/gas mark ¼ for 30 minutes, remove, allow to cool, then turn over, repeating this until it forms a firm, dry-surfaced slab.

SUCADE OF LEMON [OR ORANGE] PEELS[44]

3 lemons
2tbs rosewater
8oz/225g sugar

Quarter the lemons from top to bottom, remove the segments, and scrape the inner side of the peels clear of any membranes. Simmer the peels for 30 minutes until tender (originally the water was changed three times to remove their bitterness). Simmer the peels with sugar, rosewater and 300ml/½pt water, until they become transparent and the syrup is as thin as honey, then pot and seal down.

MEDLARS

Today's medlars are smaller than those available to Stuart cooks, since early gardeners had discovered that they could grow as large as an apple when grafted onto a white-thorn stock, hence Henry Buttes' description of them as 'Great, full and plumpe; with little kernels.' Unlike other fruits, the medlars are inedibly hard when ripe for harvesting, and have to be left for some months until their flesh has rotted to a richly flavoured brown pulp.[45] Shakespeare was well aware of this quality, using lines such as 'You'l be rotten ere you be half ripe, and that's the right virtue for the Medler' (i.e. meddler), or 'The usurer be like the medlar, he be no good till he be rotten.'[46] They were usually eaten uncooked, their pulp being spooned directly from their skins after cutting away their five-lobed tips, the source of some colourful anatomically allusive dialect names.

ORANGES

Henry Buttes described this fruit as being 'like Golde. Whence they are called *Aurantia* of *Aurum*, gold in Latine, and in Greek *Chrysomela*, golden apples. In English properly and truly *Aurange*, but … we both speake and write it Orange.'[47] They were chiefly in demand for their juice, which was taken either with a little toast, sugar, ground cinnamon and dried mint stirred into it as an appetizer, or as the essential sauce to accompany a capon, but both of these left a good supply of peels which retained much of the fruit's characteristic flavour. In 1508 Lord Huntingdon paid 3*s.* 4*d.* 'for 20 great oranges to send down into the country to preserve', and 3*s.* 'for half a hundred of ordinary oranges'.[48] The methods used would have been either marmalading, as for lemons, or as wet suckets, those 'Orange pils condite, which are good for the stomacke'. These kept the peels complete, converting them into richly coloured glossy spheres. These were expensive when bought from the confectioner, 4lb costing 5*s.* 11*d.* in 1530, for example, but could also be made at home.[49] Since contemporary oranges, particularly the Seville, had quite bitter peels, they might be simmered in a succession of ten or twelve waters to render them fit for use, but this is usually unnecessary when using modern sweet oranges.

ORANGES PRESERVED PORTUGAL FASHION[50]

6 oranges with thick skins

1lb 6oz/625g sugar

Use a pastry cutter to remove a small disc of peel from around the stalk of each orange, push a finger deep into the pulp, catching the juice in a soup dish. Place a muslin-lined sieve over a bowl to one side, in which to collect the juice and pulp. Next push a finger between the pulp and the pith, and remove all the pulp into the sieve.

Place all the empty peels in a large pan, with their 'plugs' of peel, pour in sufficient boiling water to fill them and cover them, then simmer gently for about 45 minutes until they are tender.

Drain the peels, chop three of them finely, and either grind them in a mortar, or in a food processor, to make a smooth paste with 6oz/175g of the sugar.

Pack the whole peels with the orange-peel paste, place in a small pan just large enough to hold them vertically, with the hole uppermost, and just cover with a syrup made by dissolving the remaining sugar in 1pt/600ml hot water. Add the 'plugs' of peel, and simmer gently for a further 30 minutes, before allowing to cool in the pan.

When quite cold, use a slotted spoon to remove each orange from the syrup, seal its hole with a 'plug' of peel, place in a broad-mouthed pot or jar, then bring the remaining syrup to the boil, pour over each orange, seal down, and keep for use.

TO PRESERVE ORANGES[51]

Follow the first two stages above, drain the peels, return to the pan, cover with a syrup, allowing 1lb/450g sugar to 1pt/600ml water, simmer gently for 30 minutes, and leave in the syrup overnight. Next morning remove and drain the peels, pack into broad-mouthed pots or jars, re-boil the syrup and pour it over the peels before sealing down.

PEACHES

Peaches were being grown in London in the late thirteenth century, but then appear to have fallen out of cultivation until the early sixteenth century, when Wolf, Henry VIII's gardener, is reputed to have reintroduced them from France. Believed to be cold and moist, they could be preserved for banquets.

PRESERVED PEACHES THE VENETIAN WAY[52]

6 peaches and their weight of sugar
2tbs rosewater

Split the peaches, remove their stones, layer with the sugar in a deep bowl, and leave overnight to extract the juices.

Slowly bring the fruit, syrup and rosewater to the boil and simmer for 10 minutes, then cover, and leave in a cool place for two or three days.

Drain the peaches, pack into jars, re-boil the syrup, pour onto the peaches to cover them, and seal down.

MARMALADE OF PEACHES OR APRICOTS[53]

1lb/450g peach or apricot flesh the stones and peel removed
8oz/225g sugar
3tbs rosewater

Chop and blend the fruit, then rub through a sieve to form a smooth purée.

Boil the purée with the sugar and rosewater, stirring continuously until it is very stiff and has to be worked across the bottom of the pan.

Turn the dark orange-coloured paste onto greased plates or tiles, form into rectangular slabs, allow to cool, then store in a dry place wrapped in waxed paper (or foil).

PEARS

Together with their hard cooking variety, the warden, pears were roasted, stewed or baked and eaten with comfits to settle the stomach after meals.[54]

CONSERVED WARDENS [PEARS][55]

1½lb/675g hard pears
8oz/225g sugar
5tbs rosewater
½tsp cloves
1 stick cinnamon

Place the pears in a casserole and bake at 180°C/350°F/gas mark 4 for 1–1½ hours until just tender.

When cool, pull off the peel, and pour any juices from them into a pan.

Simmer the juices, rosewater and spices with ¾pt/425ml water for 10–15 minutes until well flavoured, add the pears, simmer for 5 minutes more, then pack into jars, cover with the syrup, and seal down.

PRUNES

In the sixteenth and seventeenth centuries, 'prunes' might be plums, damsons (Damask plums), or dried plums (dry or French plums), many of their recipes suggesting that the raw fruit was mainly used in cookery.

CONSERVE OF PRUNES OR DAMSONS[56]

damsons *sugar* *red wine*

Cover the damsons with water, stew until they break, pour into a colander, allow to cool, then remove the skins and stones.

Weigh the fruit, and set aside the same weight of sugar.

Stir the pulp over a high heat with a little red wine until it is quite stiff, then stir in the sugar and continue boiling until it is smooth and thick. Pour into jars and seal.

Alternatively the dried prunes could be prepared as follows.

PRUNES IN SYRUP[57]

8oz/225g prunes
¾pt/425ml claret
4oz/100g sugar

Soak the prunes overnight in the claret.

Add the sugar, and stew gently until the prunes are swollen and tender, then either pour into a dish, or seal down into sterilized jars while still hot.

The placement of a dish of prunes could be quite significant, for if set on a window sill it advertised that the house was a brothel![58]

QUINCES

Rarely used today, this five-sided yellow pear-shaped fruit was one of the most popular preserving fruits of the period, for it had a fine taste, perfume and pink colour when cooked. Henry Buttes claimed that it recreated the heart, comforted, strengthened and closed the mouth of the stomach, especially when boiled with honey or made into marmalade and eaten at the end of the meal.[59]

TO PRESERVE QUINCES[60]

12 quinces, peeled and cored
3lb/1.35kg sugar
6tbs rosewater
2 sticks cinnamon

Bring the quinces, sugar and ¾pt/425ml water to the boil, skim, and continue simmering until they are just tender.

Lift out the quinces carefully with a slotted spoon and strain the syrup. Then return all to the pan with the rosewater and continue simmering until the syrup forms a soft jelly when tried on a cold plate. Seal down in sterilized jars with some cinnamon.

QUIDONY OF QUINCES[61]

2lb/900g quinces, peeled & cored *1lb/450g sugar*

Chop the quinces, boil until tender in 2pt/1.2l water, stir in the sugar and half a pint of water, and continue boiling until the fruit falls to the bottom of the pan.

Strain the syrup through a muslin into a clean pan, and boil until it will set as a jelly, then pour into jars or boxes, and seal down.

MARMALADE OF QUINCES[62]

3lb/1.35kg quinces *3lb/1.35kg sugar*
6tbs rosewater

Pare, quarter and core the quinces, boil them with the sugar in 1¾pt water until they are soft and the colour deepens.

Add the rosewater, and continue boiling and stirring until it is stiff, and leaves the bottom of the pan, then pour into jars or boxes, and seal down.

QUINCE CREAM[63]

1lb/450g quinces *¾pt/450ml double cream*
4tbs sugar *1 stick cinnamon*

Bring the cream to the boil with the cinnamon, cover, and leave to cool.

Cover the quinces with water, simmer until tender, then peel them and rub their pulp through a sieve into a clean pan.

Beat in the sugar and cream, having removed the cinnamon, and pour into a deep dish.

RAISINS

Great raisins, in contrast to the small raisins of Corinth (currants), made the stomach firm and strong, promoting the appetite, and so were eaten before meals.[64]

RASPBERRIES

The raspberry or framboysberry, usually in its red form, but also as a white variety, appears to have been the source of raspis wine, a sweet wine recorded from the mid-fifteenth century (see page 415, above), only entering culinary use in the early seventeenth century as a preserve or jelly.[65]

PRESERVED RASPBERRIES[66]

1½lb/625g raspberries *1lb/450g sugar*

Crush one-third of the raspberries and squeeze out their juice through a muslin, or heat them with a little water to extract their juice before straining.

Bring the juice, sugar and ¼pt/150ml water to the boil, skim, add the remaining raspberries, and simmer gently for 5 minutes before pouring into jars and sealing.

QUIDONY OF RASPBERRIES[67]

1½lb/625g raspberries *8oz/225g sugar*

Either crush the raspberries with 3tbs water, or gently simmer them in the water to extract their juices, then hang up in a muslin to strain into a clean pan.

Add the sugar to the juice, and boil until the jelly sets when tried on a cold plate. Pour into jars and seal down.

STRAWBERRIES

Strawberries were enjoyed at all levels of society, 'Rawe crayme undecocted, eaten with strawberries ... is a rurall mannes banket' wrote Andrew Boorde. Dr Butler considered that, 'Doubtless God could have made a better berry, but doubtless God never did', while James I was so ravenous for them, that whenever Mr French of his spicery tried to introduce the first of the new season's crop with a small speech, 'the King never had the patience to hear him one word, but his hand was in the basket.'[68] Up to the early seventeenth century all the strawberries grown in England were the small, brilliantly scarlet wild variety, whether gathered from the countryside or grown in the garden, but then the larger, juicier; but not so finely flavoured American variety was introduced, the ancestor of our modern strawberries.

CONSERVE OF STRAWBERRIES[69]

1lb/450g strawberries *12oz/325g sugar*
5tbs (sweet red) wine

Rub the strawberries through a sieve, mix the pulp with the sugar and wine, boil gently until it sets when tried on a cold plate, then pour into jars and seal down.

These were the main fruits to be preserved, but there were others, such as the grapes described by Robert Herrick:

> Put Purple Grapes, or Cherries in –
> To Glasse, and they will send
> More beauty to commend
> Them, from that cleane and subtile skin
> Than if they naked stood.[70]

ALMONDS

ALMOND CREAM JELLY FOR SUBTLETIES[71]

12tsp/16 leaves gelatin
6tbs rosewater
2pt/1.2l cream
4oz/100g shop-bought white marzipan
3oz/75g ground almonds
2oz/50g icing sugar

Soak the gelatin in the rosewater for 10 minutes, then warm and stir until completely melted. Rapidly beat in a quarter of the cream and the remaining ingredients, then beat thoroughly to form a smooth mixture, finally beating in the remaining cream. Leave in a cool place until just beginning to set, then pour into moulds and leave overnight to set completely, before turning out.

Some of the moulds for this jelly were plaster-casts taken of young rabbits, woodcock and other small animals, dried out and given an internal coating of lard before use. Other moulds of carved wood (and pewter) were brushed beforehand with almond oil to act as a separator. Moulds taken in wax apparently needed no such preparation. When the rabbit or other figure had been turned out onto their dishes, they were sometimes dredged with a mixture of bread-crumbs, ground cinnamon and sugar boiled together with a little water (or rosewater), so that they looked as if they had been roasted.

FLOWERS

Just as flowers were pickled for salads, they were candied or preserved for banquets. Many different methods were used, only three of the most practical for modern use being given here.

TO CANDY FLOWERS (1)[72]

flowers of violets, primroses *1tbs rosewater*
½ sheet gelatin *4tbs icing sugar*

Lay the gelatin on a small plate, cover with the rosewater and leave to soak for some minutes until soft. Place over a pan of hot water and stir a little until dissolved, then leave to cool. When tepid beat into the sugar in a small bowl to make a smooth cream. Lay the flowers on a sheet of white paper on a baking sheet and coat their upper surfaces with the mixture, using a soft brush. At this point the flowers on their paper were placed to dry before the fire for an hour, the best modern alternatives being in the hot sun or on top of a radiator, until dry, then turn over and coat the other side, and dry again; 'and when they be thorough dry they will have there owne couler and smell and be finelie canded.' Store in an airtight container.

They may also be dried as in the recipe below.

TO CANDY FLOWERS (2)[73]

small flowers, still on their stalks
2oz/50g sugar *2tsp rosewater*

Boil the sugar in the rosewater until dissolved, then leave until warm, dip in each flower individually, and allow the surplus to drain off. Have a wire sieve propped over an electric ring set on its lowest setting to provide a gentle, warm up-draught. Place the dipped flowers separately on the sieve, and leave to dry for about an hour before cooling and storing in an airtight container.

For a crystalline effect, the flowers may be dusted in granulated sugar just after draining.

TO PRESERVE ROSE PETALS OR ANY OTHER FLOWERS[74]

1oz/25g red rose petals, with the white parts removed
3oz/75g sugar *5tbs rosewater*

Dissolve the sugar in the rosewater over a gentle heat, allow to cool, then add the petals, shaking the pan until all are covered with the syrup. Cover the pan, cook on the lowest heat for 2 hours, then pour into a jar and seal down.

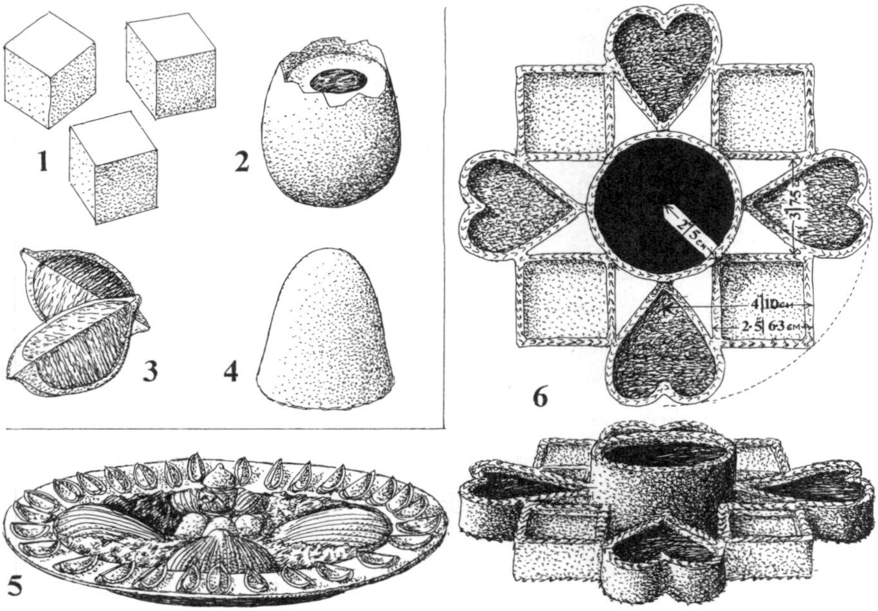

Figure 126. Jellies. Jellies might be cut into cubes and gilded with gold leaf as a leach (1), made into replica boiled eggs (2), cast in lemons (3) or in wineglasses (4). Robert May's great dish of jelly (5) could be served from its dish, while William Rabisha's laid tart of jellies could be readily cut into nine self-contained portions (6).

JELLIES

By boiling and straining bones, calves' feet, knuckles of veal, fish such as barbell, eel or plaice, fish skins and other discards, late-medieval cooks had been able to produce both opaque and crystal-clear jellies. These ingredients produced a reasonably firm set, but were difficult to use with milk or cream, since when they were mixed with hot gelatinous stocks they tended to form a curd. By the 1590s, however, when Thomas Dawson published his recipe for white leach, isinglass, the swim-bladder of the sturgeon, had come into use, enabling milk jelly stocks to be boiled without curdling.[75] Most Tudor jellies were served in dishes, probably because they were relatively soft, those stiff enough to be turned out or cut into cubes being introduced around the end of the sixteenth century. In the following recipes, the jellied mediums once produced in home kitchens have been replaced by readily available modern forms (i.e. gelatin, etc.), essentially the same product, but already clarified and of known strength.

In the Eltham Ordinances of 1526 the menus for both Henry VIII and Catherine of Aragon commence with jelly hippocras, which cost 8*d*.[76]

JELLY HIPPOCRAS[77]

½pt/300ml claret
4oz/100g sugar
2–3 pieces root ginger
2in/5cm stick of cinnamon
¼ nutmeg, crushed
6 cloves
¼tsp coriander seeds
pinch of salt
4tsp/5 leaves gelatin

Lightly bruise the spices and gently simmer with the salt in ½pt/300ml water for 10 minutes. Pour the claret into a pan, stir in the gelatin, and leave to soak for 10 minutes. Strain the spiced water through a fine cloth (or coffee filter paper) into the pan, stir in the sugar and gelatin mixture and gently heat while stirring until fully dissolved, then pour into a dish and leave to set.

Similar jellies were made with red or white wines through to the mid-seventeenth century, the following being used by Mrs Elizabeth Cromwell.

EXCELLENT JELLY[78]

5tsp/7 leaves gelatin
2in/5cm stick cinnamon
¼pt/150ml dry sherry
3tbs sugar

Soak the gelatin in ¼pt/150ml cold water for 10 minutes, meanwhile simmering the cinnamon in ¾pt/450ml water for the same time. Strain the cinnamon water on to the gelatin, stir until dissolved, stir in the sherry and sugar, then turn into a dish or wine glasses and leave to set.

STRAWBERRY, MULBERRY OR RASPBERRY JELLY[79]

1lb/450g soft fruit
¼pt/150ml rosewater
4oz/100g sugar
5tsp/7 leaves gelatin

Grind or liquidize the fruit, rosewater and sugar, bring to the boil and strain through a piece of fine cloth or muslin into a clean pan. Soak the gelatin in ¼pt/150ml water for 10 minutes, gently heat and stir until dissolved, stir in the fruit mixture and pour into a dish to set.

WHITE LEACH[80]

1pt/600ml whole milk
6–7tsp/8–10 leaves gelatin
1½tsp rosewater
4oz/100g sugar
real gold leaf (optional)

Soak the gelatin in a quarter of the milk in a pan, add the remaining milk, rosewater and sugar and heat gently while stirring until dissolved. Use a sugar-boiling thermometer to ensure that the temperature does not exceed 60°C. Leave until cool, then pour it 1in/2.5cm deep into a very lightly greased container and leave to set overnight. Turn out onto a freshly rinsed smooth cloth and cut into cubes with a knife dipped in warm water. Arrange as an open chequerboard pattern on a dish and apply the gold leaf.

QUEEN HENRIETTA MARIA'S PIRAMIDIS CREAM[81]

2oz/50g ground almonds
5tsp/7 leaves gelatin
a few pine kernels and a little cream for garnishing
2tbs rosewater
½pt/300ml cream
2oz/50g sugar

Grind the almonds in ½pt/300ml water until creamy, then strain the liquid through muslin into a pan. Stir in the gelatin, rosewater, cream and sugar, and leave to soak for 10 minutes. Stir over a gentle heat until completely dissolved using a sugar-boiling thermometer to ensure that the temperature remains below 60°C, then leave to cool. Pour into wine glasses, leave overnight to set, then warm the glasses and turn the creams out onto a dish. Stick them with pine kernels and serve with cream.

In the early seventeenth century wine jellies similar to the Jelly Hippocras and Excellent Jelly above, sometimes flavoured with rosemary, were coloured red with alkanet, purple with turnsole or yellow with saffron. These, along with clear, orange, lemon and white leach jellies, providing an attractive range of colours which could be used in a variety of ways. William Rabisha put contrasting jellies into pastry cases which could be cut into nine separate, individual servings (see the illustration).[82] Robert May, meanwhile, moulded them in the shells of scallops, cockles, whelks, winkles, mussels and eggs, in scooped-out whole or halved oranges or lemons, or in wooden or tin moulds. He also recommended serving them in little round glasses four or five in a dish on silver or glass trencher-plates, or in galley pots.[83] Rebecca Price's mother, Ann Ingham, used to 'lay some Lemon Peele at ye bottome of your dish; and ye jelly upon it in careless lumps.' For a more impressive effect, a plate was inverted over the centre of a large dish, and quarters of red, yellow, white and another colour piled upon it in lumps. A carved lemon filled with jelly was then set up in the centre, and quarters (i.e. halved halfs) of orange and lemon jellies set in their peels arranged around the sides. Further recipes for the jellies of this period may be found in my *Jellies & their Moulds* (Totnes 2010).

Figure 127. Subtleties. There are no depictions of the wax or sugarwork subtleties served in the Tudor court, but this woodcut from Hans Springlee's The Battle before Rouanne *of 1526 shows their scale and detail.*

SUBTLETIES

In late medieval England many subtleties, the sculptured dishes served at the start and sometimes the close of a course, were made of edible substances which were intended to be consumed. Some of these were still being produced in the early sixteenth century, the following being proposed for a wedding feast:

First Course

Brawn, with a boar's head, on a field surrounded with a scroll with the text: 'Welcome your bretheren godely in this hall, / Joy be unto you all that en this day it is now fall! / That worthy lorde that lay in an Oxe stalle / mayntayne your husbande and you, with your gystys [guests] alle!'

And to finish, a great custard with a lamb, within a scroll: 'I mekely unto you, sovrayne, am sente, / to dwell with you, and ever be present.

Second Course

A leach damask with an antelope sitting on a seal inscribed: 'beith all gladd & mery that sitteth at this messe / and prayeth for the king and all his.'

Figure 128. Subtleties for the French embassy of 1527. By combining George Cavendish's description of the subtleties prepared for the great feast at Hampton Court with contemporary illustrations, the author was able to recreate just a few of its 'personages most lively made.'

Figure 129. The subtlety of St Paul's Cathedral. The 1527 feast featured 'powlles Chirche & steple in proporcion for the quantitie as well counterfeited as the paynter should have paynted it upon a cloth.' The author made this subtlety of the subject in 2002.

Third Course

A pie bearing an angel with: 'thanke all, god, of this feste.'

Void

A cake with a wife lying in child-bed, with: 'yf ye dirste onys loke to me warde, / I wene ye nedys muste.'[84]

Such edible subtleties were rapidly passing out of fashion, however, being replaced with ones which were either made of totally inedible materials, or else of sugar or almond paste which were intended merely to be seen as displays of wealth and skill, and not to be eaten at the table. Anne Boleyn's coronation feast in June 1533 had included 'subtleties and shippes made of waxe, marvylous, gorgeous to behold', for example, while Henrician Garter feasts featured 'A George on Horseback.'[85] When King Philip and Queen Mary were entertained by the officers of the law in Inner Temple Hall, their subtleties included:

A Standing Dish of Wax, representing the Court of Common Pleas, artificially made, the chardge thereof £4.
A Standing Dish of Wax, to each mess one £4.[86]

The number and variety of subtleties prepared for great feasts was truly astounding. When planning for the reception of the French embassy of 1527 at Hampton Court Palace, Cardinal Wolsey

> sent for all the expertest Cookes ... that they could gett in all England ... to serve to garnysshe this feast. The purveyours brought and sent in suche plenty of costly provysion as ye wold wonder at the same. The Cookes wrought bothe nyght & day dyvers subtiltes and many crafty devisis where lakked nother gold, sylver ne any other costly thing maete [suitable] for ther purpose.

When all were seated in the Presence Chamber,

> ther servyce was brought uppe in suche order & Aboundaunce both Costly & full of subtilties wt. suche a pleasaunt noyce of dyvers Instrumentes of musyke that the Frenche men (as it semyd) ware rapte in an hevynly paradice.

This was only a preliminary for the second course, with its

> so many disshes, subtilties, & curious devysis wch. ware above [a hundred] in nomber so goodly proporcion and costly that I suppose the Frenchmen never saw the lyke; there ware Castelles wt. Images in the same/powlles [St Paul's] Chirche & steple in proporcion for the quantitie as well counterfeited as the paynter shold have paynted it uppon a clothe or wall. There ware

> beastes, byrdes, fowles of dyvers kyndes And personages most lyvely made & counterfet in Dysshes, some fighting (as it ware) wt. swordes, some wt. Gonnes and Crosebow. Some vaughtyng & leapyng. Some dauncyng wt. ladyes. Some in complett harnes justing wt. speres, And wt. many more devysis than I am able wt. my wytt to describbe.

One particularly fine piece was a chessboard of spiced sugar-plate, which Wolsey ordered to be fitted into a case so that it could be safely carried back to France as a gift.[87]

Similar selections of sugarwork continued to be made for great entertainments, as shown by the following list of the subtleties made for Queen Elizabeth's reception at Elvetham:

> The arms of Her Majesty and all the nobility;
> Many men and women, hand-modelled;
> Castles, forts, guns, drummers, soldiers of all sorts;
> Lions, unicorns, bears, horses, camels, bulls, rams, dogs, tigers, elephants, antelopes, dromedaries, apes and all other beasts;
> Eagles, falcons, cranes, bustards, herons, bitterns, pheasants, partridges, quails, sparrows, pigeons, cocks, owls, and all other birds;
> Snakes, adders, vipers, frogs, toads and all sorts of worms;
> Mermaids, whales, dolphins, conger-eels, sturgeons, pikes, carps, breams and all sorts of fishes.[88]

Under James I, classical themes were adopted, those made for the dinner for the Duke of Württemberg in 1603 including 'the figures and shapes of several kinds of beasts and birds, and also the statues of Hercules, Minerva, Mercury, and other famous personages.'[89]

Over and above these purely ornamental and symbolic subtleties, others appear to have been made as the inedible decorations for the edible marchpanes. Some of these were made by the royal master-cooks as New Year's gifts to the sovereign. John Smythson's presentations of marchpanes to Queen Elizabeth I have already been referred to (page 402, above), while George Webster presented her with 'a marchpane being a chessboard'.[90] Her surveyor of the works similarly gave her 'a very faire marshpaine made like a tower with men and artillery in it.'[91] In return, the Queen presented her servants with an item made of silver-gilt, each usually weighing some four to eight ounces.[92] When served onto the banquet table, it would be easy to break or cut off pieces of the marchpane base, while still leaving the decorative parts intact, and probably suitable for re-cycling at subsequent events.

SUGAR-PLATE

As larger quantities of sugar became available from the early sixteenth century, an impressive range of new methods of using it was introduced into England. Perhaps first appearing in the shops of professional confectioners in London, they rapidly spread to the stillrooms of many fashionable ladies, for whom the later sixteenth and early seventeenth century publishers produced a number of specialized recipe books. One of these, Wyllyam Warde's *The Secrets of the Reverende Master Alexis of Piedmont*, published in London in 1562, included the following instructions:

> Take Gomme dragante steeped and tempered in Rose water until it be soft and whyte, make therof as it were past; and take of it the bignes of a hasel nut, bray it in a brazen mortar, putting to it a lyttle moulder of good sugre, and half a graine of fine musk steeped and tempered with Rose water, mixe all welle together. And if you wyll have it better, put to it more muske and sugre, and tan as much mace beaten in poulder as will lye upon a pennye, and mixe it again well together, then put to it a little Amylum [fine wheat starch] beaten in powder, but it were better to putte in redde Sandal[wood], wel broken in sonde indifferentlye, and put it in by little and lytle, so much that a manne may make of it a conveniente paste, the whyche you shal cut after your fantasye and drye it in the shaddowe.[93]

In England, this versatile 'sugar-plate' was usually made to this recipe:

SUGAR- PLATE[94]

½tsp gum tragacanth	*½ egg white, lightly beaten*
1tsp lemon juice	*12–16oz/250–450g icing sugar*
2tsp rosewater	

Stir the gum into the lemon juice and rosewater in a small basin, soak for 30 minutes, then place over a pan of hot water and stir until completely dissolved. Stir in the egg white, then beat in the sugar little by little until it forms a pliable dough, then knead until completely smooth.

These points should be noted:

1. Keep closely covered at all times, as the surface rapidly dries out to rock hardness.
2. Use sterilized egg white if raw whites are unacceptable.
3. Dust all equipment and sugar-plate with either fine icing sugar, cornflour or finely ground spices while shaping.
4. Commercially made packs of pastillage or Mexican paste produced by companies such as Squire's Kitchen of Farnham already contain gum

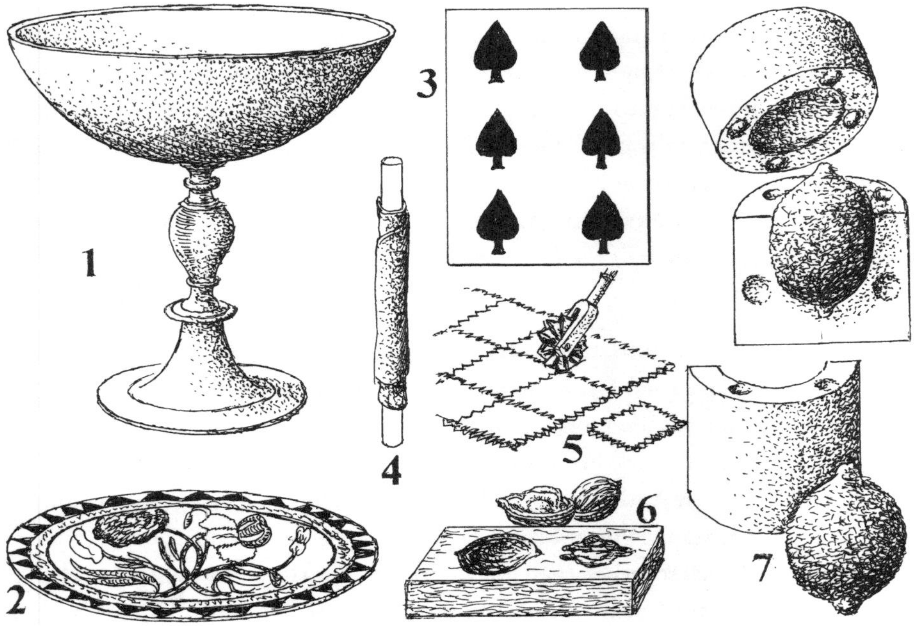

Figure 130. Sugarwork. Sugarplate made of finely ground sugar and gum tragacanth was ideal for making: (1) drinking cups; (2) banquet trenchers; (3) playing cards; (4) cinnamon sticks; (5) kissing comfits; (6) walnuts. Boiled sugars could be cast in plaster moulds to make artificial lemons and similar objects (7).

tragacanth, and produce excellent results if made up with lemon juice and rosewater.

5. Dry, powdered spices may be mixed into the sugar-plate at the same time as the sugar.
6. Since some of the original, period colours, such as sap green, are poisonous, and others, such as crushed bluebottles (cornflowers) are not generally available, they are easily replaced by safe, modern colourings, always in their paste (not liquid) form, kneaded in. Liquid food colours may be used to paint decoration onto dry sugar-plate, if the brush is kept relatively dry.

This sugar-plate was used in the following ways:

CARDS[95]

Roll the plate out thinly on smooth paper, cut to the shape of playing cards, leave until perfectly dry, then paint with hearts, clubs and the other suits as playing cards.

TRENCHERS, SAUCERS, DISHES & BOWLS[96]

Roll the plate out thinly on paper, then cut out 3–5in/7.5–12.5cm discs, dry completely and paint as banqueting trenchers. Alternatively, press gently into saucers, dishes or bowls, trim the edges, and leave to dry, then invert onto a board to dry out completely, before using to hold fruits or sweetmeats at the banquet.

CUPS & GLASSES[97]

Press the rolled-out plate into the bowls of cups or glasses, model their feet and stems and, when both are dry, stick them together with a little moist plate. When completely dry these will hold all cold liquids – I have left wine in a cup for a day or more without it collapsing. The advantage of sugar tableware was that it could be broken up and eaten at the end of the banquet.

MUSCADINES OR KISSING COMFITS[98]

Work different food colours (or the petals of violets, marigolds, cowslips, primroses, bugloss and other edible flowers ground with icing sugar) into the plate, roll each one out on a sheet of paper, cut into small diamonds with a jagging-iron, and leave to dry.

CINNAMON STICKS[99]

Mix sufficient ground ginger and cinnamon into the icing sugar when making the plate to produce a medium brown colour. Roll out thinly, dusting it with the same spices, then roll pieces around a pencil (originally the shaft of an arrow) to produce realistic, edible sticks of cinnamon.

ARTIFICIAL WALNUTS[100]

Carve wood or plaster blocks into the negative shapes of a walnut shell and a kernel. Use these to mould hollow shells of cinnamon-flavoured and coloured plate, to enclose kernels moulded in white plate. These were also used to contain comfits or other small sweets, stiff fruit pastes or marmalades, or verses written on small scrolls, before each pair of shells was stuck together.

MOULDED SUGAR-PLATE[101]

Plain, coloured or spice-flavoured sugar-plate was pressed into wooden moulds previously dusted with a little icing sugar shaken through a piece of fine muslin or linen. Having trimmed off the surplus, invert the mould over a board, tapping it on the board to release the moulded sugar-plate. If the mould is deep it might need to have the plate loosened with the point of a knife, lifting it from the surface of the mould before inverting it.

COMFITS

Comfits were small seeds of caraway, coriander, fennel or aniseed, or splinters of cinnamon stick, small cubes of root ginger, or blanched almonds, given a dense, smooth coating of sugar. They were used both as sweetmeats in their own right, and as garnishing for dishes of a contrasting colour. The basic equipment comprised a brass or latten basin or skillet to hold sugar syrup, a brass ladle to measure the syrup into a broad, shallow brass or latten basin suspended over the gentle heat of a chafing dish. A brass slice or scraper was also useful for removing surplus sugar from the broad basin.[102] For modern use, the broad basin may be replaced by a large wok over an electric stove on its lowest setting. A further requirement is plenty of uninterrupted time and patience; the process cannot be rushed, and is mind-numbingly boring, yet demanding considerable skill.

COMFITS[103]

3tsp seeds (see above) *⅓pt/200ml water*
1lb/450g cane sugar or icing sugar

Dry and heat the seeds by stirring them in a broad, shallow metal bowl or wok over an electric ring on its lowest setting. Meanwhile heat the sugar and water together, stirring until just dissolved, then remove from the heat and keep warm.

Pour a teaspoonful of the syrup into the seeds, rapidly stirring them with the left hand while shaking the bowl with the right, continuing until all the seeds are lightly coated, separated and dry before adding a further spoonful, and stirring and shaking them as before. Continue until all the syrup has been used up to produce small comfits. If required to be larger, a further batch of sugar might be added in the same way.

Because of the high sugar content of the syrup, this recipe produces rough white comfits. The use of ½pt/300ml water to each 1lb/450g sugar takes longer to apply, but gives smoother results. It may be stained with food colouring for the outer coats, in order to produce coloured comfits.

BOILED SUGAR

The use of sugar syrups boiled until they set clear and rock-hard on cooling was well-established in medieval England. From the sixteenth century they were being made into a confection called manus Christi, and cast in moulds to replicate natural fruits and other edible items.

MANUS CHRISTI[104]

Literally the 'hand of Christ', this 'wholesome and comfortable' sweetmeat was considered to be a tonic, taking the form of a sugar-drop including gold leaf, sometimes flavoured with oils of spices and perfumed with musk or ambergris.

8oz/225g cane sugar
¼pt/150ml rosewater
red gold leaf, cut into small pieces

Dissolve the sugar in the rosewater over a gentle heat, then bring to the boil without stirring, and continue until it reaches 143°C/290°F on a sugar thermometer. Add the gold leaf, remove from the heat and stir rapidly with a wooden spatula until it lightens in tone as small crystals form. Return to the heat for a few moments while still stirring, then drop as small round cakes (perhaps up to 1in/2.5cm diameter) on a surface which has been lightly oiled and dusted with either icing sugar or fine rice flour. Store in an airtight container.

CAST SUGAR[105]

Sugar boiled as just described, but without the gold leaf, was poured into moulds made either of carved wood, stone or plaster of Paris which had been soaked in water for three or four hours, and mopped dry with a linen cloth. Other moulds were made of pewter. By tying two sections of a piece-mould together with tape, pouring in a quantity of hot sugar, clamping on the final section, and then swinging it 'up and downe in your hand, turning it round, and bringing the neather part sometimes to bee the upper part in the turning' it was possible to cast three-dimensional pieces, such as pears, oranges and lemons (see the illustration). Removed when cold and completely set, these artificial fruits could be realistically painted using saffron and other colourings steeped in rosewater.

ALMOND PASTE

To make almond paste, the almonds were removed from their shells, soaked in boiling water (preferably for at least 15 minutes), and their brown skins pinched off. While still moist, they were then ground to a smooth paste using a pestle and stone mortar, a little rosewater being added to keep the almond oil as an emulsion. This was a skilled operation, for if the almond oil separated out it left an irretrievably useless mess. At this stage the almonds were weighed and half their weight of icing sugar beaten in to produce a smooth paste, suitable for modelling.

Figure 131. A mould for marchpanes. Carved in England in the early 16th century, this mould bears the sacred IHS monogram and the inscription 'An harte that is wyse wyll obstine from sinnes and increas in the workes of God.'

ALMOND PASTE[106]

To use modern marzipan or almond paste for historic recipes, its sugar content should be checked. Instead of the original 30%, today it is usually 60% or 75%, requiring 80% or 125% of its weight of additional ground almonds to be kneaded in with a few drops of rosewater to produce a stiff, workable paste. This could be modelled into pies, birds, fruits or flowers, before being dried off in a stove, or used to make any of the following.

MARCHPANES

Marchpanes were important items of banqueting stuff, being large discs of almond paste with a hand-raised vertical rim like that of a tart, glazed with icing sugar and richly decorated. They were made in various sizes, the smaller costing some 2*s*. 6*d*., and the larger 10*s*. or more in 1577.[107] Since they had to be dried off in an oven, they were underlain by a layer of wafers, each cut square and its edges moistened and overlapped with others to build up the required area.[108]

A MARCHPANE[109]

1lb/450g almond paste of 30% sugar content (see above)
8 wafers (or a 10in/25cm round of rice paper)
4tsp rosewater *5oz/125g icing sugar*

Moisten the edges of the wafers and overlap to form a large, flat round base, or lay out the rice paper, on a baking sheet. Place the almond paste in the centre as a ball, then press down and shape with the fingers to make a flat, round base about ¼in/7mm thick, with a 1in/2.5cm vertical wall around it. Smooth the top of the wall, then pinch like a pie crust. Bake at 110°C/225°F/gas mark ¼ for about 15–20 minutes, without browning the rim, then remove and leave to cool and dry off. Beat the rosewater and sugar to produce a very thick creamy mixture, and apply this evenly to the base and walls of the marchpane with a bristle brush, then return to the oven for a further 15–20 minutes until the sugar has turned opaque. Remove from the oven and leave to cool completely before transferring to a wire cooling grid. The marchpane improves if left for a time under a piece of paper in a dry atmosphere: 'The cleerer it is like a Lanterne horne, so much the more commended. If it be through dried, and kept in a dry and warme ayr, a Marchpane will last many years'. (One made thirty years ago is still in good condition.)

Marchpanes were decorated in various ways, including being studded with comfits when finally removed from the oven or, when cold, ornamented with kissing-comfits/lozenges, knot or jumble biscuits, or 'standards', three-dimensional models in cast sugar or marchpane paste.[110] They were also decorated with devices such as animals or the sacred IHS monogram in gold leaf applied to their moistened surfaces through cut-paper stencils. Some marchpanes appear to have been cast in carved wooden moulds, one early sixteenth-century example being illustrated at figure 131, opposite.

ALMOND PASTE BACON[111]

almond paste, prepared as above *red food colour (for sanders)*

Work the food colour into half of the paste, and roll out both the red and the white pastes to some ⅛–¼in/4–8mm thick, and cut into four red and three white rectangles of identical size. Dampen their surfaces and assemble in layers of 'lean' and 'fat'. Roll the remaining white to a thick layer of the same size, and place on top as a thick outer layer of fat, then slice vertically to produce 'rashers of bacon'. A thin layer of the paste coloured with cinnamon or ginger may be added as a 'rind', and matching eggs made by inserting saffron-coloured 'yolks' into white paste 'whites', and then cut into quarters.

CALISHONES[112]

8oz/225g almond paste | *1tsp ground coriander*

Knead together, print in moulds, and leave to dry until firm.

Leach Lombard is made in the same way, replacing coriander with 2–3 tsp cinnamon.

MOULDED ALMOND PASTE

'Print off this Marchpane paste in your moulds for banquetting dishes; and of this paste our comfitmakers at this day make their letters, knots, Arms, Escocheons, beasts, birds, and other fancies,' wrote Sir Hugh Plat in 1600.[113]

WHITE GINGERBREAD[114]

8oz/225g almond paste
2tsp ground ginger
1lb/450g sugar-plate (p. 559)
2tsp ground cinnamon

Knead the spices into the almond paste and roll out ⅛in/3mm thick. Cut the sugar-plate in half, and roll each one to the same size as the almond paste. Very slightly moisten the sides of the almond paste, applying a layer of sugar-plate to each side to form a sandwich. Roll out to about ⅛in/3mm thick, press into moulds, cut off the surplus and leave to dry. When eaten, the crisp, sweet rosewater taste of the exterior gradually gives way to reveal the hot, gingery interior. (The trimmings may be kneaded together and moulded separately).

Almonds were also made into almond butter, a luxuriously cool, smooth and sweet addition to the banquet table. A recipe for this has been given earlier, on page 96, above.

GINGERBREADS

Tudor and Stuart gingerbreads were nothing like the modern cakes of the same name, but were stiff doughs of sweetened and spiced breadcrumbs. They were defined in the 1570s as 'a kind of cake or paste made to comfort the stomacke'. Their principle ingredient was stale manchets, a character in Beaumont and Fletcher's *Coxcomb* of 1613 requiring 'two or three grating loaves out of the kitching to make gingerbread of.'[116]

RED GINGERBREAD AS USED AT COURT[117]

8oz/225g fresh white breadcrumbs *¼pt/150ml claret*
1tsp each ground ginger, cinnamon, aniseed & liquorice
1oz/25g sugar

Spread the crumbs on a baking tray and dry off under a cool grill or oven, stirring from time to time, until perfectly dry, but not browned, then pound smooth and pass through a sieve. Mix with the remaining ingredients in a saucepan, and simmer while stirring continuously until it forms a paste, then reducing the heat and continue to work in the pan until very stiff. This takes time and energy, since it readily burns and sticks to the bottom of the pan. When cold, dust with ground ginger and cinnamon, roll out, ¼in/5mm thick, and either print in carved moulds or cut in small pieces and leave in a dry place to harden.

Variations on this basic recipe include replacing half the breadcrumbs with ground almonds, or the sugar with clarified honey, or adding egg yolks, lemon juice, rosewater, or saunders to the initial mixture. The dried gingerbreads might also be gilded with real gold leaf, which greatly enhanced the definition of the moulded details.[118]

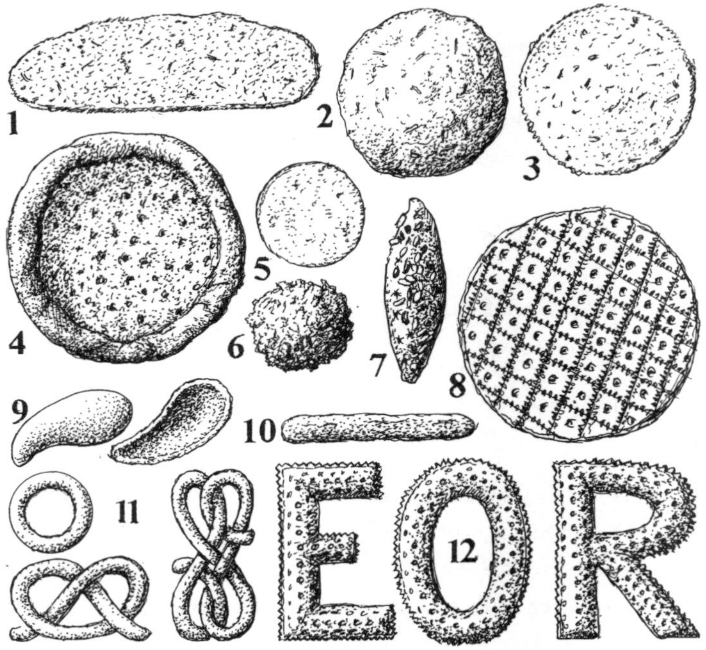

132. Biscuits. Among the rich, crisp biscuits of the period were: (1) biscuit bread; (2) English biscuit; (3) French biscuit; (4) cracknel; (5) shortcake; (6) bean bread; (7) Italian crust biscuit; (8) Shrewsbury cake; (9) shell bread; (10) macaroon; (11) knots or jumbles; (12) letters filled with almond paste.

BISCUITS

In 1569, Crawley described a bread 'as was provided to serve at neede, or in warres, for it was Bisket, that is twice-baked, and without leaven or salt.'[119] If made of fine flour, such bread was considered to be 'slowe of dygsetyon, but it doth nourysshe moche yf it be truly ordered and well baken.'[120] Since it was usually required in vast quantities to feed both soldiers and sailors about a pound a day over long periods, this form of biscuit was produced by large-scale contractors rather than domestic bakers.[121] One Robert Donne baked almost 23 tons of it to supply Henry VIII's forces at Boulogne in 1545, for example.[122] Unfortunately the quality was rarely of the best, and it provoked many complaints from those who had to rely on it as a major part of their diet.[123]

From the early sixteenth century finer varieties of biscuit were developed for high-quality entertainments, their textures and flavours being improved by the addition of sugar, eggs, almonds, spices and rosewater. Partly because of the substantial cost of their ingredients, the skill and time required for their preparation, and their delicious flavours, it eventually proved necessary to store them in particularly secure locations. Robert May advised the cook to 'dry them in a stove, and put them in a square latten box, and lay white papers between every range or rank, have a padlock to it, and set it over a warm oven, so keep them ... set them in a temparate place where they may not give [i.e. soften] with every change of weather, and thus you may keep them very long.'[124] This explains why the confectionery at Hampton Court was set over the pastry bakehouse, or that a dry storage chamber was built over the pastry ovens at Slingsby Castle.

Basic biscuit bread was made by baking a white loaf flavoured with seeds, slicing it, and oven-drying it with sprinklings of sugar.

BISCUIT BREAD OR FRENCH BISCUITS[125]

1½lb/675g flour
2tbs caraway seeds
1tbs aniseed
1½tsp dried yeast
1 egg white
6oz/150g caster sugar

Mix the flour and seeds, prepare the yeast according to the manufacturer's instructions, and work into the flour with 14fl.oz/420ml warm water. Knead for 5 minutes, then form into a roll 4in/10cm diameter on a baking sheet, cover with a light cloth, and leave to rise in a warm place for some 30 minutes until doubled in size. (This is for one-eighth of the original quantity, which was made up 'as big as your thigh'.) Bake at 220°C/425°F/gas mark 7 for 40 minutes, then remove, cool, and leave overnight.

The next day, pare off the crust and cut the remainder into thin rounds. Rub the sugar into both sides, and place on a wire grid in an oven at 150°C/300°F/gas mark 2 for 10 minutes. Remove, allow to cool, then repeat this process until the biscuits are perfectly crisp and dry.

FINE BISCUIT BREAD[126]

4oz/100g flour
4oz/100g caster sugar
1½tbs aniseed
2 eggs, separated
2tsp rosewater

Instead of beating the mixture for 2 hours, as instructed in the original recipe, beat the egg white to stiffness, then add the yolks, rosewater and sugar little by little, and fold in the flour and aniseed. Pour into a buttered and floured loaf tin and bake at 180°C/350°F/gas mark 4 for 25 minutes. When cold, cut into thin slices and dry in the oven at its lowest setting for 10 minutes.

It is particularly interesting to find that by the late Elizabethan period English biscuits had developed into something much more delicate, light and crisp. Instead of being baked as huge rolls, they were now baked in saucers or plates to produce individual cakes. Today we would recognize them as crisp, spongy buns or cup-cakes, of which they were the direct ancestor.

ENGLISH BISCUITS[127]

8oz/200g flour | *4 yolks & 2 whites of egg*
4oz/100g caster sugar | *a little butter*
1tsp caraway, fennel, and bruised coriander seeds

Place the flour in a baking dish, bake at 150°C/300°F/gas mark 2 for 10 minutes, remove, leave to cool, then pass through a sieve. Beat the eggs (with the sugar) for about 15 minutes until light and creamy, then fold in the flour and seeds (the original beats the eggs separately, adds the sugar and flour, before beating for 1 hour more), and pour into a buttered plate or 10 bun-tins which have been brushed with melted butter. Bake at 180°C/350°F/gas mark 4 for 20 minutes.

Similar versions such as Prince Biscuits or Biscuite du Roy were baked in tinplate 'coffins' or baking tins brushed with butter. This enabled them to be turned out as rectangular blocks, easier to store and serve.[128] Some forms of biscuits had their pastes boiled rather than baked before being finished in the oven. One of the simplest and most popular of these was the cracknell, so called since it produced a sharp cracking sound when either bitten or broken. Another was French biscuit.

CRACKNELS[129]

1lb/450g plain flour | *2tsp rosewater*
2oz/50g caster sugar | *1 egg, beaten*
1tsp mixed ground clove, mace, nutmeg, cinnamon & ginger
up to ¼pt/150ml single cream

Mix the sugar and spices into the flour, make a well in the centre, pour in the rosewater, egg and half the cream, and work in: adding just sufficient additional cream to produce a stiff dough. Knead the dough, form into six balls, roll each one flat and trim to 6in/15cm diameter, then pinch up the rim to resemble a tart. Prick the base all over with a sharp skewer. Bring a large pan of water to the boil, drop a cracknel in, rim side down, and boil for 1½ minutes, then remove with a slice, and invert, rim up, onto a wire tray to cool. When all have been boiled and cooled, place on floured paper on a baking sheet, and bake at 200°C/400°F/gas mark 6 for 15–20 minutes, until the interior is pale golden brown. Serve when cold.

FRENCH BISCUITS[130]

8oz/225g flour | *1 egg, beaten*
1oz/25g caster sugar | *about 6tbs rosewater*
1tsp each fennel, caraway and bruised coriander seeds
4oz/100g sugar boiled with 1fl.oz./30ml rosewater for glaze

Mix the flour, sugar and spices, work in the egg and just enough rosewater to give a medium soft dough. Form into a cylinder 4in/10cm long, roll in a piece of buttered and floured cloth, tie up the ends, plunge into boiling water, and boil for 45 minutes (the original recipe was for eight times this amount, 'as big as your Legge', and required 2 hours boiling). Remove from the pot, unroll, leave to cool, then cut across into ⅛in/3–4mm slices with a freshly rinsed knife. Place on a wire grid, and bake at 150°C/300°F/gas mark 2 for 10 minutes, leave to cool, and repeat this process until the biscuits are perfectly dry and crisp.

Stir the sugar and rosewater together over a medium heat until melted together, leave until it rises in the pan, then remove from the heat. Gripping each biscuit in turn between a pair of forks, coat both sides in the syrup, and place on a wire rack to drain. Replace in the oven for 10 minutes, remove and cool, turn over, and repeat the process until all are perfectly dry, then store in an airtight tin.

By the late sixteenth century crisp, light and delicate shortcakes had been developed, some using a combination of pre-baked flour, sugar, cream and egg yolks, while others had simpler doughs of flour, sugar and butter.[131]

SUGAR [SHORT] CAKES[132]

12oz/300g flour | *8oz/200g butter*
4oz/100g caster sugar | *1tbs rosewater*
½tsp each ground clove & mace

Mix the flour, sugar and spices, make a well in the centre and pour in the butter after it has been melted and allowed to cool, but not set. Work together with the rosewater to form a dough. Turn this out onto a floured board, and press out with the hands until ¼in/6mm thick, and cut into 2½in/6.5cm rounds. Slide a spatula underneath, transfer to a baking sheet covered with paper, and bake at 150°C/300°F/gas mark 2 for 20 minutes, so that they are cooked through but not browned.

In 1602 Lord Herbert of Cherbury sent a present of similar biscuits to these sugar cakes to his guardian Sir George More, his covering letter explaining: 'I have sent you some bread, which I am sure will be dainty … it is a kind of cake which our countrey people use and made in no place in England but in Shrewsbury. [It] is brittle, but the form of it … is circular'.[133] In the town itself they were known as fine cakes, the food shortages of 1596 causing the bakers to stop making them unless their customers provided the necessary quantity of butter. In the first published recipe for Shrewsbury cakes, which appeared in 1617, they are described as being 3 or 4 inches in diameter by around an eighth of an inch in thickness, white in colour and unpricked, so that the cook had to 'clap down' any blisters as they rose up in the oven. By the 1650s they had grown to about 5 inches in diameter, under a quarter of an inch in thickness and 2oz in weight. They had also acquired a pricked surface which enabled them to be broken up into neat squares for nibbling, just like a modern chocolate bar.

SHROPSHIRE CAKES[134]

1lb/450g plain flour
8oz/225g butter
8oz/225g caster sugar
1 egg, beaten
1tsp rosewater
½tsp ground cinnamon or nutmeg

Rub the butter into the dry ingredients, work in the egg and rosewater and knead lightly to form a stiff dough. Divide into 16 pieces, roll each into a ball, place on buttered paper or a piece of non-stick baking parchment, and cut out to about 5in/13cm diameter. Use a clean comb to mark the surface into a pattern of small squares, going half-way through, then use a wooden skewer to make a hole in the centre of each square. Bake at 180°C/350°F/gas mark 4 for some 10–15 minutes until cooked but not browned.

Various combinations of flour, sugar, butter and eggs were used to make biscuits which displayed great individuality in their taste, texture and appearance, as illustrated in the following examples.

ITALIAN CRUST [BISCUITS][135]

8oz/200g flour
4oz/100g caster sugar
½tsp each ground ginger & nutmeg
4tbs caraway comfits
¼tsp grated orange zest
2oz/50g butter
2 egg whites
a little egg white for glazing

Mix the flour, sugar, spices and zest, rub in the butter, work in most of the egg whites, with a little water if necessary to form a soft dough. Divide into eight, roll each piece into a ball, then roll out to about 4in/10cm long, thick in the middle and pointed at the ends. Prick all over with a sharp skewer, brush with a little egg white, sprinkle the comfits on top, place on a baking sheet, and bake at 180°C/350°F/gas mark 4 for about 25 minutes, until cooked through, but not browned.

KNOTS OR JUMBLES (1)[136]

1½oz/40g butter
1tbs rosewater
4oz/100g caster sugar
1tsp each aniseed, caraway seed & ground mace
2 eggs, beaten
8oz/200g flour

Beat the butter and rosewater until smooth, then cream with the sugar, and work in the eggs, little by little, before mixing in the flour to form a stiff dough. Roll out into long ropes about ¼in/6mm in diameter and form into letters, knots or rings before baking at 180°C/350°F/gas mark 4 for 15–20 minutes.

KNOTS OR JUMBLES (2)[137]

2 eggs, beaten
4oz/100g caster sugar
1tbs aniseed or caraway seed
6oz/175g plain flour

Beat the sugar into the eggs until dissolved and creamy, then work in the seeds and flour to form a stiff dough. Divide into 10 pieces, roll each one out to form a narrow rope, tie into a knot, and plunge half of them into a pan of boiling water. As they sink to the bottom, move them with a wooden spoon to prevent them from sticking to the bottom. When all have returned to the surface, remove them with a slotted spoon on to a cloth to dry, then boil the rest in the same way. Transfer onto a greased baking sheet, and bake at 180°C/350°F/gas mark 4 for 15 minutes, then turn over and return to the oven for a further 10–15 minutes until golden.

SHELL BREAD [BISCUITS][138]

4oz/100g flour
4oz/100g rice flour
2 egg yolks, beaten
4tbs rosewater
8oz/200g sugar

Mix the flours, make a well in the centre, pour in the yolks and work them into the flour with just sufficient rosewater to form a stiff dough. Roll this out very thinly on a floured board, then use to line cleaned mussel shells which have been very thinly smeared with butter. Prick the inside all over with a sharp skewer. Place on a baking sheet and bake at 150°C/300°F/gas mark 2 for 10 minutes. Bring the sugar to the boil with ¼pt/150ml water, until it rises as a froth, remove the biscuits from the shells, and boil them in batches for 3–4 minutes before removing them with a pierced spoon and arranging them separately on a wire grid. This will give them a shiny glaze, as if they were pottery. Store in a warm, dry and ventilated place for a few days until perfectly crisp and dry, then store in an airtight tin until required.

LETTERS & KNOTS IN ALMOND PASTE[139]

4oz/100g flour
4oz/100g icing sugar
1oz/25g butter
1 egg white
4oz/100g ground almonds
2oz/50g caster sugar
2tbs rosewater

Place the flour on a baking dish, bake at 150°C/300°F/gas mark 2 for 10 minutes, remove, leave to cool, and sift into a bowl. Work the almonds, caster sugar and rosewater together to form a stiff dough, and roll out into ropes ½in/12mm in diameter. Mix the icing sugar into the flour, rub in the butter, and work in the egg white to form a dough, kneading it until smooth. Roll out very thinly, and cut into strips 1¾in/4.5cm wide. Dampen the edges of the pastry, place the almond paste down the centre, fold the pastry over it, seal the edges and trim off the surplus with a jagging iron. Form the roll into letters about 4in/10cm high, dampening the cut parts when joining them together and making sure that no almond paste is left exposed. Prick all over neatly with a sharp skewer and bake on buttered paper at 180°C/350°F/gas mark 4 for 15–20 minutes until hard, but not coloured. Leave to cool before removing from the baking sheet.

Almond paste based on blanched almonds ground to a smooth paste with a little rosewater, sugar beaten to dust and egg whites, was used to make macaroons in England from the opening of the seventeenth century. Most recipes used uncoloured pastes, but green macaroons used sap green, a ferment of buck-thorn berries.

MACAROONS[140]

5oz/125g ground almonds	*1 egg white*
3oz/75g icing sugar	*1tsp rosewater*

Beat the eggs to stiffness, beat in half the sugar, then the remaining sugar and rosewater until smooth, and finally the ground almonds, to form a dough. Form into rolls 3in/7.5cm long by ½in/12mm in diameter. Originally these were baked on wafers, but now rice paper or non-stick baking parchment may be used. Bake at 150°C/300°F/gas mark 2 for 10–15 minutes until pale brown.

By replacing the ground almonds with those which had been sliced, and changing the proportions of sugar and egg, these rather solid macaroons were converted into much lighter and more delicate 'bean-bread' which tastes much better than its name suggests.

BEAN BREAD[141]

6½oz/190g flaked almonds	*1 egg white*
6½oz/190g icing sugar	*1 tsp rosewater*
1tsp aniseed	

Beat the eggs to stiffness, beat in half the sugar, then the remainder with the rosewater, and finally the almonds and aniseed, mixing or kneading to produce a very stiff paste. Form into domed cakes about the size of a walnut and set 2in/5cm apart on a greased baking sheet. Bake at 150°C/300°F/gas mark 2 for 20 minutes, until puffed out and very pale brown.

WAFERS

Thin, crisp and delicately flavoured, wafers were made by cooking a batter between the heated faces of a pair of wafer-irons. Since they required great experience and skill to make successfully, many were made by professional waferers and hawked by their wafer-women.[142] In the largest households a separate kitchen called a wafery was set up, that in the royal household being operated by a yeoman and a groom, 'making wafyrs, and saufely and clenely to

Figure 133. Wafers. Cooked in engraved iron wafer-tongs, crisp delicately flavoured wafers were the high-status accompaniment to wines such as hippocras.

kepe them covered, and under locke, and by assay'.[143] They were reserved for the use of the royal family, dukes, earls, White Sticks, the cofferer and a few others, largely for service with hippocras at the end of dinners and suppers. The rest of the household received wafers only on the four great feasts of the year, since they were always considered to be a luxury. They were made either round or rectangular, flat or rolled, flat ones being essential for providing a base for marchpanes.

TO MAKE WAFERS[144]

8oz/225g plain flour
¼tsp ground cinnamon
2tbs sugar
2 egg yolks
¼pt/150ml cream
2tbs rosewater
1oz/25g cold butter

Mix the flour, cinnamon & sugar, make a well in the centre, pour in the yolks, cream and rosewater, and beat in to form a stiff batter. Heat the closed wafer-irons on both sides. Wrap the butter in a small piece of cloth, and use to very lightly grease the inside faces of the irons. Ladle a small pool of batter onto the middle of the inside of one iron, quickly close the irons together and keep pressed firmly together as the wafer cooks, sending out spurts of squeaking steam and batter. As the steam subsides, and before there is any smell of scorching, open the irons and remove the wafer. Either remove flat, or rapidly roll off around the handle of a wooden spoon, then leave to cool and dry. The wafers should be crisp and light-coloured, but this requires much experience in mixing the batter to the best consistency, and in judging the temperature of the irons.

DISHING AND SETTING OUT

Having prepared all manner of banqueting stuff, it had to be assembled and dished ready for serving in vessels of the greatest magnificence. If to be served as a void on the dinner or supper table, a selection of spiced sweetmeats was arranged on spice-plates. Most of the silver and silver-gilt examples weighed around 16–20oz, some 'standing' examples being raised on a central foot, and some having elaborate cupboards.[145] One silver-gilt example of 1532–3 has a broad bowl of 8½ inches (20.7cm) diameter, its surface being worked as a number of shallow hollows which would enable both dry and syrupy sweetmeats to remain in place while being handed to the diners.[146] The finest spice dishes were even more impressive, one of Henry VIII's being of grey stone, probably agate, standing on four silver-gilt heads, a further three jewelled heads along with roses and fleur-de-lis and a man bearing a staff and shield decorating the cover.[147] Unfortunately very few banqueting dishes of this quality have survived, an exceptional example being a 1611 group of elegantly engraved rock crystal flagon, tazza, cup, spoons and forks, all richly garnished in silver-gilt, now at Hatfield House.

In households without access to such expensive and prestigious tableware, banqueting dishes were often of glassware and polychrome tin-glazed (i.e. 'painted') earthenware. At Speke Hall, Liverpool, in 1624, these were stored ready for use:

2 blue glass dishes gilt 5*s.*
18 bigg glass plates 4s. 6*d.*
4 dozen litle glasse plates 8*s.*
2 broad bankett dishes 10*s.*
1 gilt lether dish 4*d.*
2 dozen payneted dishes
& 3 odd ones 12*s.*
40 Venise glasses for wyne & beere,
some lesse than the other 30*s.*[148]
a sillibub glasse 2*d.*
9 little glass bottells 12*d.*
46 pottes & glasses for
preserved stuffe 4*s.*
3 barrells for fruit 9*d.*

Having assembled the dishes, each was filled in a set order:

> March-panes have the first place, the middle place, and last place; your preserved fruites shall be disht up first, your Pastes next, your wet Suckets

Figure 134. Tableware for banquets. These were made of the most expensive materials and finest craftsmanship, as seen in: (1) a spice-dish made in silver-gilt in London in 1528–9: the knob is purposely designed to hold the towel which was wrapped around it when presented at the table; (2) a tazza of engraved rock crystal with silver-gilt mounts – it was made in 1611 and is now at Hatfield House; (3) a Venetian glass tazza of c. 1600; (4–5) banquet dishes of silver/gilt taken from sets of twelve made in London by Roger Flynt in 1573–4 and 1568–9: (4) shows the sacrifice of Isaac amid a border of sea monsters, which would have been both magnified and enhanced when filled with a clear jelly; (5) shows a banquet in progress, with flagons cooling in their cistern in the foreground.

> after them, then your dried Suckets, then your Marmalades and Goodiniakes, then your Cumfets of all kindes, next your Pears, Apples, Wardens bak'd, raw or roasted, and your Oranges and Lemmons sliced; and lastly your Wafer cakes.

They were then carried into the banqueting house:

> when they goe to the table you shall first send forth a dish made for shew only, as a beast, bird, fish, or Fowl according to invention, then your Marchpane,

> then Preserved fruit, then a Paste, then a wet Sucket, then a drie Sucket, Marmelade, Cumfets, Apples, Peares, Wardens, Oranges and Lemmons sliced; and then Wafers, and another dish of preserved fruits, and so consequently all the rest before: no two dishes of one kinde going or standing together, and this will not only appeare delicate to the eye, but invite the appetite with the mich varietie therof.[149]

The tables used at major royal banquets were huge, one at St James's Palace in 1610 measuring 120 feet long, to provide sufficient food for the company through to three o'clock the next morning. A similar banquet in the Banqueting House in 1605 came to a sudden and disastrous end, being 'so furiously assaulted that doon went table and trestles before one bit was touched', an enormous waste of effort and valuable resources.[150]

To those who only heard second-hand reports of the gilded triumphs of confectionery, the magnificent dishes and boisterous, witty activities of the great, their banquets must have represented luxurious lifestyles almost beyond imagination. To those who were actually there, however, the internal politics and social aspirations of the banqueters frequently soured what should have been unbridled freedom and joy. Sir Thomas Wyatt, who in 1554 rebelled against the advent of the Spanish King Philip of Spain as co-ruler of England, described how he had,

> In court to serve decked with fresh array
> Of sugar'd meats feeling the sweet repast;
> The life in banquets, and sundry kinds of play
> Amid the press of lordly looks to waste:
> Hath with it join'd oft times such bitter taste,
> That who so joys such kind of life to hold,
> In prison joys fetter'd with chains of gold.[151]

Figure 135. Twelfth Night at Wressle Castle. Here the hall is seen as prepared for the feast. (1) kitchen; (2) pastry; (3) surveying place; (4) buttery; (5) pantry; (6) ewery?; (7) screens passage; (8) hall; (9) dais; (10) knights' chamber. Furniture etc.: A: carpet; B: hearth; C: Earl's table; D: Countess' table; E: chamberlain; F: gentlemen; G: ladies; H: gentleman strangers; I: comptroller's board with head officers; J: dean & chapel's board; K: household officers?; L: stair accessing the gallery; M: gallery over screens passage with tables for lower-status guests.

CHAPTER TWENTY-SIX

Feasts

Hospitality, especially in the plentiful provision of food and drink, was seen as an important Christian and social responsibility in early modern England. It brought praise and esteem to its providers, giving them a unique opportunity for displaying their wealth and power, while encouraging feelings of gratitude and loyalty in its recipients. Robert Herrick described the hospitable host as being,

> ... like a *Roman Tribune*, thou thy gate
> Early sets ope to feast, and late;
> Keeping no *currish Waiter* to affright,
> With blasting eye, the appetite ...
> No, no, thy bread, thy wine, thy jocund Beere
> Is not reserv'd for Trebius here,
> But all, who at thy table seated are,
> Find equall freedome, equall fare;
> And thou, like to that *Hospitable God*,
> Jove, joy'st when guests make their abode
> To eat thy bullocks thighs, thy Veales, thy fat
> Weathers and never grudged at
> The *Pheasant, Partridge, Godwit, Reeve, Ruffe, Raile*,
> The *Cock*, the *Curlew* and the *quaile*
> These and thy choicest viands do extend
> Their tastes unto the lower end
> Of thy glad table; not a dish more known
> To thee, than unto any one.[1]

No event gave a greater demonstration of hospitality than a feast. It might also be called a banquet, using that word in its continuing usage as a major ceremonial meal, but here it will be described as a feast, thus avoiding confusion with the sweetmeat banquets described in previous chapters. They varied considerably in their scale and quality, some being arranged to celebrate christenings, and weddings, some for special times of the year, and others for matters of state and international diplomacy.

This chapter will consider a few prime examples of major feasts to illustrate something of their ceremonial character. It is important to appreciate that the modern perception of a feast as a display of drunken debauchery, repulsive manners and lechery is the creation of ignorant directors who use the media to propagate their own fantasies and not historical accuracy. The feast was certainly an enjoyable experience, but it also incorporated a high degree of formality and ceremonial which could only be successfully accomplished by nobles, gentry and upper servants meticulously trained in all its complex refinements. It was also a feast for all the senses, each carefully orchestrated to achieve the richest displays of opulence and magnificence equalling, perhaps even surpassing, those of the great services of the Church. Today, four or five hundred years after they took place, their written descriptions still continue to amaze us. To those who witnessed them in person, however, they must have provided a wonderfully rich experience, a unique blend of superb food, glittering tableware, the finest and most colourful of clothing and tapestries, superb choral and instrumental music, and the constant flow of processions and ceremonies. This was the golden age of the feast, one which was to largely disappear in the mid-seventeenth century.

THE FEAST OF CHRISTMAS

The twelve days of Christmas, celebrated from Christmas Eve through to Twelfth Night on 6 January, remained one of the few times of the year in which the hall of every major house became crowded with the common folk who worked in the surrounding estates and villages. Many of them arrived with foodstuffs which, as customary tenants, they were bound to pay as boon-rents, this input of fresh comestibles being essential for providing open, seasonal hospitality. The usual order of precedence was largely set aside, as at Sir Robert Wroth's hall at Durants, Enfield, Middlesex,

> where Comus, god of revelry;
> … fills thy open hall with mirth, and cheer,
> As if in Saturn's reign it were;
> Apollo's harp, and Hermes' lyre resound,
> Nor are the muses strangers found;
> The rout of rural folk come thronging in,
> (Their rudeness then is thought no sin)
> Thy noblest spouse affords them welcome grace;
> And the great heroes of her race [the Sydneys]
> Sit mixed with loss of state, or reverence.

Freedom doth with degrees dispense
The jolly wassail walks the often round,
And in their cups, their cares are drowned ... [2]

and, as Thomas Tusser advised:

At Christmas we banquet, the rich with the poor
Who then, but the miser, but openeth his door? ...
At Christmas be merry, and thankful withall,
And feast thy poor neighbour, the great with the small ...
Good bread and good drink, a good fire in the hall,
Brawn, pudding, and souse, and good mustard withall ... [3]

The effects of the presence of a crowd of country folk were obvious on their departure, for they left,

The hall-floor pecked and dinted like a mill-stone,
Made with their high shoes. Though their skill be small,
Yet they tread heavy where their hobnails fall.[4]

Such were the rustic feasts given in manor houses and farmhouses throughout the country. The same open-handed hospitality also prevailed in great houses and palaces, but with the addition of appropriately aristocratic entertainments. In 1512, for example, when Henry VIII celebrated his Christmas at Greenwich, 'was such abundance of viands served to all comers of any honest behaviour as hath been few times seen.' One of the major features of the New Year's Eve feast held in the hall was,

a castle, gates, towers and dungeon, garnished with artillery and weapons after the most warlike fashion: and on the front of the castle written *Le fortresse dangereaux*, and within the castle were six ladies clothed in russet satin, laid all over with leaves of gold, and every one knit with laces of blue silk and gold. On their heads, coifs and caps all of gold. After this castle had been carried about the hall, and the Queen had beheld it, in came the King with five others apparelled in coats, the one half of russet satin, the other half of rich cloth of gold; on their heads caps of russet satin embroidered with works of fine gold bullion.

These six assaulted the castle. The ladies seeing them so lusty and courageous, were content to solace with them, and upon further communication to yield the castle, and so they came down and danced a long space. And after the ladies led the knights into the castle, and then the castle suddenly vanished out of their sights.[5]

Such artificial castles might appear at other feasts, Sir Thomas Pope providing one made of cloth of gold for a Shrovetide masque for Elizabeth I at Hatfield in 1566.[6] Another appeared at the Twelfth Night feast described in the following account taken from the household book of Henry 'The Magnificent' Earl of Northumberland. Devised for use at his castles of Wressle and Leconfield in Yorkshire in the opening years of the sixteenth century, it was copied from a contemporary source, perhaps that of a Marquis.[7] When combined with the known dimensions and architectural details of the hall at Wressle, it provides a remarkably complete description of a Christmas feast (see figure 135). For this, the usually bare walls of the hall were hung in arras, with a canopy of state or 'selour' of arras, counterfeit arras or fine arras against its southern wall behind the dais and over the tables of the Earl and Countess. Its lower end would be rolled up above the fireplace here, so that the nobles might benefit from the radiant heat so necessary on this cold night in early January.

The boarded floor of the hall, which measured 67 by 33 feet (20 x 10m), would have already have had its surface covered with a layer of *Juncus* rushes, but over its central area, extending from the screens passage up to the fireplace before the dais, a great carpet was rolled out. Its dimensions, some 35 by 12 feet (10.5 x 3.6m), show it to have been one of the largest foot-carpets in the country, equal to those of the royal household, and obviously one of the finest products of Middle Eastern or Iberian industry. Its elaborate designs and blazing colours would have introduced a rare element of opulence and luxury into this normally spartan interior.

Six trestle tables were then set up, three to each side of the carpet, their dimensions being some 13 by 2 feet (4 x 0.6m), as indicated by the known size of their linen tablecloths. Each one was initially covered with a table carpet, then a white diaper linen cloth, and were prepared following a strict order of precedence:

1. The Steward's Board (south-east corner) had the chamberlain at its board's end, with knights and gentlemen along its eastern side, and the ladies opposite. Their two covered salts and twelve spoons were of silver-gilt, a gentleman waiter and a yeoman usher of the chamber serving as waiters.
2. The Comptroller's Board (south-west corner) was for the Earl's steward, treasurer, head officers and council. Their two uncovered salts and twelve spoons were also of silver-gilt, and a gentleman waiter and yeoman usher of the chamber served as waiters.
3. The Gentleman Stranger's Table (middle of the east side) seated those gentlemen whose lower status barred them from the Steward's Board.

Their uncovered salts and twelve spoons were of parcel-gilt, a yeoman waiter acting as their waiter.

4. The Dean & Chapel's Board (middle of the west side) was occupied by the dean, gentlemen and children of the chapel, also with three uncovered salts and twelve spoons of parcel-gilt, and a yeoman of the chamber was their waiter.

5 & 6. Boards at the north-east and north-west corners of the hall were presumably occupied by those household officers of lower status who dined in hall throughout the year.

Other strangers who could not be seated in the hall were sent up to the gallery over the screens passage. Here two yeomen ushers and a groom of the hall had set up a number of tables which were to be served 'out of the little door of the backside the kitching towards the court' and up its narrow spiral staircase. This ensured that the main surveying place and kitchen passage were kept clear for those serving the hall.

The cupboard, probably a six-foot long narrow table set to one side of the dais, had its top, sides and ends covered with a great carpet overlaid with a diaper cupboard cloth. On top of this was placed a 'great stage' of five receding stages or shelves, all covered in a six-foot square of white linen cloth. The first stage was set with pots for ale and beer, the second with flagons for wine, the third with bowls, the fourth with goblets, and the fifth with standing cups, all of silver gilt or parcel gilt. The top of the cupboard in front of the stages was used to hold further standing cups, bowls and the like which were required for serving ale, beer and wine to the tables. Once this mass of magnificent gold and silver had been arranged, one of the cellar staff stood guard beside it.

On the dais, two short carpet-covered tables were set up side by side under the cloth of estate, one for the Earl, perhaps with his eldest son or a baron, and one for the Countess, no one else dining with them at this feast. The cloth for the Earl's table was brought up by one of the ewery staff. It was then spread by a gentleman usher and a yeoman usher or, if no gentleman usher was available, by two yeomen ushers and the man from the ewery. Only when the Earl's cloth had been laid could they cover the Countess' table in the same way, with the same order of precedence.

Two cushions were placed at each side of the Earl's, and of the Countess' place-settings, at their side of their tables, 'for theame to lean uppon' (these may have been put in place before the cloths were laid, but this appears to be impractical). Their carpet-covered benches were provided with pairs of cushions, one to sit on, and the other to support their backs.

Having made all the necessary preparations, four yeomen of the chamber or yeomen waiters entered the hall from the chamber, each bearing a long wax and resin torch or link called a standard, mounted on a long shaft, two standing along each side to provide illumination. Those entitled to sit at the lower, northern end of the hall were then admitted, two yeomen of the chamber checking that only those authorized by the marshals of the hall and the gentlemen ushers were able to enter and take their places.

The Earl's procession now entered the hall from the chamber suite in the following order:

1. The Dean and Chapel.
2. The Gentlemen.
3. The Head officers, Treasurer, Comptroller, etc., and Council.
4. The Steward.
5. The Herald.
6. Three yeomen of the chamber or yeomen waiters bearing torches.
7. The Earl, followed by the Chamberlain, then any of the Earl's brothers or sons that might be present.
8. Two torches (as 6).
9. The Countess followed by any of her daughters, if of age, or gentlemen of the Earl's family.
10. Other gentlewomen in order of their precedence.

Having taken their places, the second procession, that of 'making the cupboard' now entered the hall from the cellar and screens passage. First came a yeoman bearing a torch, then a yeoman of the cellar carrying the Earl's covered cup and cup of assay in both hands, and next a groom of the mouth of the cellar with the Countess' cups borne in the same way. At the hall door, the marshal of the hall followed by two yeomen ushers of the hall and two groom ushers preceded the torchbearer and his colleagues up to the cupboard. Once there the cups were set on the stages, the pairs of yeomen ushers of the hall and groom ushers departed, and the cellar staff remained there to serve the ale, beer and wines to the various tables.

Next came the play, interlude, comedy or tragedy. Some were composed by one of his household chaplains, 'a maker of interludes ... to have a Servaunte to th' entente for writing of the parties' [i.e. parts]. Others were performed by visiting groups of players.

This was followed by the disguising, a masque or masquerade of elaborately clothed and masked performers. The wardrobe of his contemporary, Thomas, Lord Wharton contained all the necessary properties: fool's coats, paper hats, bishops' mitres, peers' caps, wooden swords, false beards, visors, and red and yellow scarves for masking. The Earl's four minstrels, already standing in the hall, stood aside and began to play as the disguisers were led in by three yeomen waiters carrying torches. If the party included women, they entered and danced first, before bowing and standing aside, half the minstrels then playing in the male dancers, similarly preceded by three torches. On the completion of the dances, the disguisers split into two groups, one standing on each side of the hall.

When the disguising had finished, the minstrels struck up once more as a sequence of morris dancers issued one by one from a large mock castle, to which they returned after their performances had finished. The gentlemen seated at the tables now got up, approached the ladies, bowed, took their hands, and led them through a number of rounds, in which couples danced in a ring, as devised by the master of revels. The gentlemen then escorted their partners back to their places, returned to their own, and resumed their seats ready for the meal.

Now a pair of gentlemen ushers or yeomen ushers preceded the Earl's and Countess' yeomen up to their respective tables and folded estates into their tablecloths. Two yeomen waiters with torches, two gentlemen ushers and two yeomen ushers then led two almoners, each bearing lighted candles in their sticks, from the ewery table to the nobles' tables. Having set their lights in place, the servants returned to their duties.

The procession bearing tableware for the Earl and Countess now assembled in this order:

1. A yeoman usher of the chamber.
2. Two marshals of the hall.
3. Two gentlemen ushers.
4. Two yeomen of the chamber.
5. A yeoman of the pantry carrying the Earl's standing salt of gold, silver gilt or silver, a small golden salt for assay, a gold spoon, a pair of parcel gilt carving knives, manchet loaves and trenchers.
6. A groom with a towel on his (left) shoulder and carrying a wassail cake.
7. As 5, but for the Countess.
8. As 6, but for the Countess.

At each of the two top tables the yeomen of the pantry set down the salts, spoon, carving knives, bread and trenchers, along with a wassail cake taken from the groom. Having bowed, the yeoman usher, marshals, gentlemen ushers and yeomen of the chamber bowed and departed, only the yeoman of the pantry remaining by the table. Two identical processions now formed at the screens passage, each consisting of:

1. A yeoman usher.
2. A yeoman bearing a torch.
3. A marshal or Gentleman usher.
4. An almoner.
5. A carver.

That for the Earl marched up the east side of the hall, that for the Countess up the west side, and a short distance behind, until they reached their respective tables, where the carver bowed. The almoners then led the carvers to the ewery table with the yeomen bearing the torches, there washing their hands and donning their towels of office. The yeomen ushers and two gentlemen ushers led the carvers to the tables. Here a gentleman usher folded estates in each tablecloth, and a carver bowed before their respective tables [then kneeling] cut the bread and gave assays of bread and salt to the waiting yeoman of the pantry, who then departed with the ushers.

Now that the top tables had been prepared, the wassail, presumably the traditional vessel of spiced ale, could be brought in, along with the dishes of meats and foods. This was the main element in the whole evening, since it formally ended the twelve-day feast of Christmas, and so required the most impressive procession of all, consisting of:

1. Two yeomen ushers of the hall to make room.
2. Two yeomen ushers of the chamber, each carrying their rods with the pointed ends down.
3. Two gentlemen ushers [with their rods?].
4. The marshal of the hall with his rod.
5. The Earl's herald.
6. The treasurer and comptroller.
7. The steward.
8. Two sewars their towels over their right shoulders and knotted at their left hips, each carrying a wassail [bowl?], one for the Earl, and one for the Countess.
9. As many gentlemen as were available, to carry the dishes up to the top tables.

Once assembled at the dresser, and marshalled into the correct order, the procession marched into the hall. As soon as the steward emerged from the screens he 'must crie three tymes, Wassell, wassell, wassell, and then the chappel to answere with a good songe … And that doone than all the mynstrallis and trumpettes to play till the wassail be voided from the bourde of the lorde and laidy'. At the top tables, the officers in the procession bowed [and stood aside] so that the sewers [and gentlemen?] might bow, come up to their respective tables, bow again, set their dishes down and uncover them so that the carver could take assays for them to eat, then re-cover each dish so that the almoner could set it down on the table, or remove it if instructed to do so.

At this point the Earl and Countess appear to have dined with their usual level of formal service, ending with the voiding of the dishes from their tables. Two gentlemen ushers then led the lord's and lady's cupbearers to the cupboard to take up their covered cups and cups of assay which they then carried to their respective tables, raised and replaced their covers, and returned them to the cupboard. All this time the chapel sang carols, or the minstrels played suitably festive pieces. Meanwhile the Earl's and Countess' tables were each carried away by a gentleman usher and two yeomen ushers.

While this was happening, the spice plates were being prepared in the pantry, one for the Earl and one for the Countess, both ready for being served in an identical manner, but with separate processions, that of the Earl taking precedence. Each spice plate had a cover topped with a knob, around which a folded towel was carefully wrapped. The gentleman who bore it tied one end of his narrow towel around the upper part of his right arm, the other end crossing his right palm and fingers, so that he could grasp the base of the spice plate without actually touching it. He then took his place in the Earl's and Countess' processions, consisting of:

1. Two yeomen ushers of the chamber.
2. Two gentlemen ushers.
3. A marshal.
4. The treasurer and comptroller.
5. The steward.
6. The herald.
7. The gentleman with the spice plate.
8. (Two?) gentlemen to serve the spice plate.
9. Four gentlemen with uncovered spice plates for the top four tables in the body of the hall.

Having marched up to the cupboard, lit with a couple of torches, the processions were joined by cupbearers bearing cups [probably of hippocras], after which they continued up to the Earl's and Countess' tables and bowed. The gentleman with the spice plate approached the lord or lady, where one of the accompanying gentlemen unwrapped the towel from its knob, placed it on his shoulder and unfolded it. Another gentleman then took off the cover, handed it to a third gentleman, and fed samples of the spices to the gentleman who carried it, by way of assay. The spice plate was then held before the Earl until he had taken whatever he wished, after which its cover was replaced. Having stepped back and stood still, the place of the gentleman with the spice plate was taken by the cupbearer. The cupbearer first removed the cover from the cup, poured a little of its contents into his cup of assay, drank it off as assay, and replaced the cover. Having uncovered the cup once more, the cup bearer offered it to the Earl to drink, holding the cup of assay beneath his lips to catch any drops. Once he had retreated to stand beside the gentleman with the spice plate, the gentleman with the towel offered the towels from his shoulder to the Earl to mop his lips, then re-folding it and wrapping it once more about the knob of the spice plate. The identical ceremony was next performed for the Countess, her procession then retreated a little further back than his, all standing there while the four spice plates of comfits and cups of hippocras were served to the ladies and gentlemen on the upper tables. After this, the processions returned to the cupboard to deposit the spice plates and cups.

When the Earl and Countess were ready to leave the hall, the men and boys of the chapel left their table and formed a procession, probably at the west (Countess') side of the dais. From here, singing a carol, they preceded the couple back into the knights' chamber, where they divided, half standing against the side walls, still singing as the Earl and Countess walked between them, back into their great chamber. The chapel then returned back into their lodgings, while back in the hall two grooms or gentlemen's servants held two standard torches 'for the disguisars to daunce their for their pastyme as long as it shall list theame' and so make an end of Christmas.[8]

A LORD MAYOR'S FEAST

On 13 October 1599, Thomas Platter, a German visitor, was invited to dine with the Lord Mayor of London. On arriving, the swordbearer led him to a handsome apartment where he was welcomed by a gentleman, while the women received him with a kiss. Musk-scented water was handed to him for handwashing, after which, along with others, he took his place at the table while still wearing his cloak. Once the Lord Mayor's son had said grace,

> Straightway all manner of lavish dishes were served most decorously. And there were two servers or carvers who removed one plate after another from the table to another covered table nearby, and this did nothing else but carve and serve. They laid the food on small pewter bowls, placing these before each person upon plates, one course after another, all most perfectly and richly

prepared and served with delightful sauces, while diverse other dishes to stimulate the appetite surround one.

The drinks consisted of the best beer and all manner of heavy and light wines to follow, as for instance Greek, Spanish, Malmsey, Lanquedoc, French and German, for in England all kinds of wine can be had for comparatively little, many because of low freightage at sea.

After two helpings of roasts, stews and other things [a sweetmeat banquet] was served [with] tarts and pastries, not to be compared for delicacy with the first courses ... And the banquet continued until towards evening, when once again we were accompanied home.[9]

A CORONATION FEAST

Although the ceremonial feasts of noble families were lavish to a fault, they appear quite modest when compared to those of the royal household. In order to demonstrate its power and prestige, it had to outshine all others at a national or international level in terms of size, provisions, splendour and magnificence. Centuries before the development of effective communicative journalism, it was vital that as many significant people as possible actually witnessed great affairs of state, were impressed by them, and carried their impressions back into the regions. One of the most significant public ceremonies of the reign of Henry VIII was the coronation of his new queen, Anne Boleyn, in 1533. This marked the success of the King's personal and diplomatic policies which had effectively ended his first marriage, broken all links with the Church of Rome, seen him become supreme head of the Church of England, and offered the potential of fathering a son and heir. The couple had married secretly on 25 January 1533, and Anne was already five months pregnant when crowned in a blaze of publicity on 1 June of that year.

After the coronation service in Westminster Abbey, the table servants and guests took their places in Westminster Hall, while the Queen retired to her chamber. One table had been set up on the dais at the south end, with a throne beneath a cloth of estate at its centre for Anne, and a chair to its east side for the Archbishop of Canterbury. Her cupboard, supervised by the Earl of Arundel, as chief butler, with the assistance of twelve citizens of London, would be in the south-eastern corner of the dais [perhaps with a separate cupboard for the Archbishop in the north-eastern corner?]. From here the Earl of Derby, as cupbearer, would serve the Queen's wines, the drinks for those in the body of the hall being controlled by the Mayor of Oxford at the buttery bar in its north-western corner. At the lower, north end of the hall the Duke of Suffolk, High

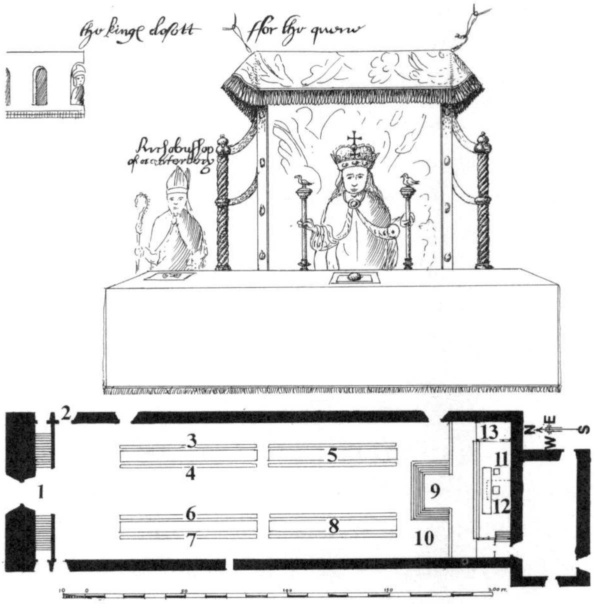

Figure 136. Anne Boleyn's coronation feast, Westminster Hall, 1533. (1) north door, with trumpeters over; (2) buttery bar; (3) Lord Chancellor and temporal lords in surcoats on the wall side; (4) bishops and abbots in parliament robes, then judges, sergeants, the King's council and, after carrying in the dishes of food, the knights of the Bath; (5) barons of the Cinque Ports, masters and clerks of the Chancery, doctors and gentlemen; (6) vacant; (7) duchesses, marchionesses, countesses, baronesses in robes, ladies in surcoats, gentlewomen in gowns; (8) Lord Mayor, aldermen, chamberlain & councillors of the City of London, then substantial merchants and worshipful persons; (9) the halfpace; (10) the cupboard; (11) Archbishop of Canterbury at the board's end; (12) Anne Boleyn, beneath the cloth of estate; (13) The King's closet (above).

Steward of England, sat on his great horse, he being gowned in crimson velvet and holding his long white stick of office in his hand. His horse, meanwhile, was covered in a trapper of matching velvet, 'full of letters of Goldsmithes work'. To his left Lord William Howard, deputizing for his father, the Duke of Norfolk, wore a gown of purple velvet and held his father's rod as Earl Marshal. His horse having its trapper of 'purple velvet cut on white satten embrodered with white Lyons'.

When all were in place, the Queen entered, walking beneath a canopy of estate, and took her throne. The Countess of Worcester stood to the east and the Dowager Countess of Oxford stood to the west, 'which divers tymes in the dynar tyme did hold a fyne cloth before the quenes face when she list to spet or do otherwise at her pleasure'. Further to the west, between the Queen and the Archbishop, stood the Earl of Oxford, holding his long white stick as High Chamberlain. Beneath the table at the Queen's feet sat two gentlewomen, while before her [knelt] the Earl of Essex, her carver.

Now, as fanfares rang out from the trumpeters standing in the bottom of the window at the bottom, north end of the hall, the first service was carried in in the following procession:

1. Sergeants of Arms.
2. The mounted Duke of Suffolk and Lord William Howard.
3. The Earl of Sussex, as Sewer.
4. The Knights of the Bath carrying 28 dishes for the Queen, with subtleties and 'ships made of wax marveilous gorgious to beholde'.
5. To their west side, level with the Queen's third dish, came the Archbishop's service, led by his sewer.

As the Queen and Archbishop were served, waiters brought in the dishes to those sitting in the body of the hall, the Lord Mayor of London and the Council each being served with thirty-three dishes at two courses, for example, 'The servitors gave such good attendance, that meate or drynke ne any thyng els, nede not be called for, whiche in so greate a multitude was marvaille: As touching the fare ther could be devised no more costlier dishes nor subtilties'.

After the Queen had completed her second course of twenty-four dishes, the Kings of Arms cried 'Largess!' in three parts of the hall, as at the Garter feasts, before retiring to stand by the King's Bench. The Queen then received her third course of thirty dishes, while Suffolk and Lord William continued to ride around the hall cheering on the lords, ladies and civic dignitaries. When all had finished, and taken their wafers and hippocras, they were commanded to rise and stand in their places, before their tables, or upon their forms, so that they might see the end of the Queen's service. Having taken her wafers and hippocras, her table was cleared, the Earl of Rutland laid the surnap at its west end, while Master Rode, marshal of the hall, drew it along with his rod [and folded the estates?]. Thomas Wyatt, as chief ewerer, brought the ewer and basin for her to wash her hands, after which the Archbishop washed his, and the surnap was removed. The Queen then stood as the Earl of Sussex, as sewer, brought her a spice plate of spices and comfits, and the Lord Mayor a standing gold cup of wine set in a golden cup of assay. After drinking, she presented the cup and cup of assay to the Lord Mayor along with her thanks for all the help provided by him and his fellow-councillors. This completed the feast, the Queen now returning to her chamber beneath her canopy of estate.

Figure 137. Garter Feasts. These early 16th-century illustrations of the investiture of Maximilian I (left) and Ferdinand I, Archduke of Austria (right) show the tables set with rectangular trenchers, single or pairs of eating knives, chipped manchet loaves and standing salts, both covered and open. Note the small trencher-salt of bread in front of Maximilian's trencher. Curiously, the carver is wearing his towel as if he were a butler, suggesting that the artist was unfamiliar with his subject. The wooden barrier enclosing Ferdinand's table is of particular interest, rare evidence for the use of such a fitting in England.

Throughout the entire feast a little closet or gallery erected over the south-west corner of the dais had been occupied by Henry and various ambassadors, so that they could observe everything in detail without being visibly present.[10]

GARTER FEASTS

In the early sixteenth century the dinners served on the feast day of the Order of the Garter took place in St George's Hall at Windsor Castle. As the sovereign's procession entered, first the alms-knights, then the prebends and the officers of arms fell off to the right-hand side of the lower end of the hall. Led by two junior knights and then the other knights companion in order of seniority, the knights continued to process into the hall until they were alongside the alms-knights and their party, then stopped and turned right to form a passage through which the officers of the order conducted the sovereign up to his table beneath the canopy of estate. Once there he turned about, received the bows of the knights, and bowed to them in acknowledgement. Three great nobles then brought up the ewer, basin and towel with three reverences, so that the sovereign could wash his hands, after which grace was said and he took his place in his ceremonial chair, its back carved with a depiction of St George and the dragon. Instead of dining alone, he was usually accompanied by up to three of four favoured companions who shared the services of his carver, sewer and cupbearer. Their first course of eighteen dishes commenced with a subtlety of St George on horseback, a variety of poultry, game and fish, and specially made dishes including a custard planted with Garters, a tart closed with arms, and a fritter in the shape of a lion.

After the first course had been cleared, the officers of arms, first Garter, then Clarenceaux and Norroy, pairs of heralds and pairs of pursuivants assembled at the lower end of the hall. Having bowed to the sovereign where they stood, in the middle of the hall, and just below the dais, Garter shouted 'Largess!' three times and proclaimed the sovereign's titles in Latin. After he and his procession had bowed again, Garter proclaimed the titles in French, followed by more bows, and then the same in English. After all had shouted 'Largess!' three times more, and bowed again, the treasurer of the household put £10 in gold into Garter's hat. Still facing the sovereign, the procession retreated for three yards, bowed, and then went back to their places. The second course of a subtlety and seventeen further dishes was then served to the top table.

After the sovereign had taken his place at the start of the dinner, the knight companions had replaced their caps and stood back against their table on the left side of the hall as each pair was served with an ewer, basin and towel borne by gentlemen and washed their hands. Having taken their places along the wall sides of the table, they were served with a first course of eleven varieties of poultry, game, fish custard and fritters, then a second course of thirteen varieties of similar foods, including venison pasties, baked oranges and leach.

Meanwhile tables down the right side of the hall had been occupied by the following, in order of seniority from the end nearest to the dais:

The Lord Steward	The Registrar
French hostages	Garter
Earls	Black Rod
Lords	Strangers
Dean of Windsor	Divers Knights
Two Abbots	Officers of Arms
The Choir	Gentlemen

Here they were served with a first course of eight varieties of pottage, poultry, meat, lamprey, leach and so forth, and a second course of lamb, poultry, venison, crayfish and leach or fritters.

When the second course had been finished, the tables were dismantled and removed, the knights companions remaining seated on their forms until the sovereign's table was taken up, when they rose, went together, and bowed to him. The prelate then said grace, and the sovereign washed his hands with the usual ceremony. Having received further bows from the knights-companions, he then doffed his cap and bowed to them, before retreating to the presence chamber, preceded by all those on the lower tables in the same order as they had entered.

These feasts continued to be held annually up to the outbreak of the Civil War, their ceremonies and locations being gradually modified over the intervening years. Under James I and Charles I, for example, they frequently took place in the Banqueting House in Whitehall. They were always considered to be one of the greatest of royal ceremonies, the opportunity of viewing their spectacle being extended to a select few. Catherine of Aragon and her ladies had observed them from the gallery at the end of the hall, while James I had invited the ambassadors of either France, Poland or Spain to stand by his table for about an hour.

Catering for a Garter feast was always a major undertaking, the food purchased for that of 1520 including 24 beefs, 92 muttons, 36 cygnets, 36 cranes, 16 peacocks with their tails, 200 apples, 300 oranges, and countless other items costing a total of £431 3*s*. 9*d*. Not all of this was consumed by the participants, however, for large quantities were cooked especially for distribution as 'waste'. Of this, 120 messes of beef, veal, geese and capons were to be given away by the great officers, while a massive 400 messes of beef, veal, venison and baked meats were to be dispensed to the poor at the castle gates.[11]

DIPLOMATIC FEASTS

Of all the feasts held during the Tudor and early Stuart periods, the greatest by far were those made to impress visiting monarchs and their embassies. Vast sums were expended in creating huge and astonishingly lavish settings, the most astounding quality of service, and in the production of gargantuan quantities of fine and elaborately dressed foods. The following examples have been selected to illustrate something of their magnificence.

The French Embassy of 1517

In July 1517 Francesco Chiergato, the Venetian Ambassador, was present at the feast provided for the reception of an embassy from France. He was clearly impressed, even though well aware of the feasts provided in his native city-state, reporting how,

> There was a buffet [cupboard] set out, 30 feet in length and 20 feet high, with silver gilt vases and vases of gold, worth vast treasure, none of which were touched. All the small platters used for the table service, namely dishes, basins, plates, saltcellars and goblets were all of pure gold. The large vases were all of silver gilt, very costly and precious.
>
> The guests remained at table for seven hours by the clock. All the viands placed before the King were borne by an elephant, or by lions, or panthers or other animals, marvellously designed. The removal and replacement of dishes the whole time was incessant, the hall in every direction being full of fresh viands on their way to the table. Every imaginable sort of meat known in the kingdom was served, and fish in like manner, even down to prawn pasties; but the jellies, of some 20 sorts perhaps, surpassed everything; they were made in the shape of castles and of animals of various descriptions, as beautiful and admirable as can be imagined.[12]

The Banqueting House of 1520

In 1519 Charles, Duke of Burgundy, King of Castile and Aragon, inherited the title of Holy Roman Emperor, thus becoming one of the greatest European magnates. A year later on 26 May, 1520 he and his retinue landed at Dover to be greeted by Wolsey, Henry arriving to embrace him at the castle early next morning. Over the next three weeks the King provided the Emperor with lavish entertainment, the climax to be a magnificent feast held on the evening of 12 July, just before their departure from London to Dover and embarkation to Calais. The banqueting house for this feast was of unparalleled construction and quality, greatly impressing the Venetian ambassador, who sent a detailed description back to his masters.

Its outer shell was a huge sixteen-sided timber-framed cylinder, 80 feet (24m) in diameter, 250 feet (75m) in circumference, and some 50 feet (15m) high, entered through a 30 by 15 foot (9 x 4.5m) vestibule. Its entrance featured three major statues, a central King Arthur flanked by Hercules and an English soldier, all with scrolls bearing inscriptions celebrating friendship. Between them Henry's red dragon bore the arms of England and the Emperor's black eagle, his coat of arms. Three gilded statues of kings lined each of the side walls, while above the entrance into the interior the god of love stood between the figures of a Continental Landsknecht soldier and an English bowman.

The first things seen on entering the central area were an open square of tables prepared for the monarchs, with further tables for other guests spaced

Figure 138. The Banqueting House of 1520. Over 80ft in diameter and some 50ft or more high, much larger than the Shakespearian Globe theatre, this magnificent building was constructed for a single diplomatic supper.

all around. Behind this square, rose a great stepped cupboard, probably of twelve stages, all laden with gold or silver-gilt tableware, a glittering display of wealth, taste and craftsmanship. Surrounding the tables rose a vast amphitheatre to house the trumpeters, musicians and all those invited to observe the feast. Each of the three tiers stood 10 feet (3m) high, having a 6-foot (2m) border of white cloth bearing white roses and gilded rosettes, all bordered in green ivy. The outer walls above the top tier formed a 250 foot-long (75m) frieze, all worked in scintillating silk taffeta, padded out in relief to represent a continuous landscape of mountains, woods, forests and meadows. Rising behind them a painted canvas depicted the sea and waves and the sky with clouds and blowing winds, then a deep cornice of flames, gilded ornaments and roses. Four circular globes depicted the four elements: 'Earth' with windmills, towers, houses, trees and animals; 'Water' with sea, ships, fishes and sea monsters; 'Air' with clouds, winds and birds; and 'Fire' as a blank. This was because 'in England they are still of the opinion that fire does not generate or nourish any animal soever'.

Above all of these decorations, closing the top of the amphitheatre, an azure-coloured sky hung from a great central mast and a ring of lesser masts, its surface garnished with gold stars and mirror planets. Since it was to be used in the evening, there were no windows, the illumination being provided by sixteen huge chandeliers, one hung at each angle of the outer wall. Between each pair alternate wicker-work male or female figures clad in silk and cloth were suspended, their torches providing further light. Lower down, cornucopias with foliage were fixed to the masts to serve as chandeliers.

The whole effect must have been enchanting, magical and wonderful, but regrettably it was never used. A westerly gale stripped off the roof, cornice, frieze and globes, so that the feast had to be rapidly transferred to the Exchequer.[13]

The Feast for the French Embassy of 1527

In February 1527 a French embassy arrived in England to negotiate a peace treaty combined with the proposed marriage of Princess Mary into the French royal family. In January, preparing for its anticipated completion, Henry VIII commissioned a 'Long House' for masking and disguising at the northern end of his tiltyard gallery at the palace at Greenwich. Timber-framed and boarded, with a canvas roof, and clerestory windows, it measured 100 feet by 30 (30 x 9m). It was entered via a long, narrow gallery leading from the palace, its doorway lined in white sarcenet, its door and lintel decorated with green foil.

Inside, the ceiling of stretched linen cloth was painted by Hans Holbein the younger with a mixture of pink, sinoper, vermilion, sanders and roset to produce a red background for roses and pomegranates painted in gold. Next, beneath the tall windows, framed with elaborately carved and gilded mouldings, came a corbelled frieze. This supported candlesticks carved in antique style, polished like amber, and each bearing small torches of white wax. Below this line the walls were hung with the most costly tapestry in England, representing the history of David. To one side stood a great nine-stage cupboard holding high pots, flagons and bowls of silver and gilt. Opposite, a seven-stage cupboard 13 feet (4m) long, was set with standing cups, bowls, flagons and great pots of gold, some garnished with precious stones and pearls. Here, too, were three ewery boards. The first of these held nine great ewers and basins and three pairs of covered basins and cups of assay, all silver-gilt, while the third had nine basins, two pairs of covered basins and cups of assay all of pure gold. Some of these vessels were so massive 'that every Lord grudged to beare them ... thei troubled sore the bearers'. Between the cupboards, the trestle tables and forms had been set out by four grooms, probably in the form of an open square. The practice of seating alternate male and female guests was already established in Henry's court. The Venetian ambassador described how, at a supper given by Wolsey in January 1527, everyone had 'a very beautiful damsel, each of the guests having one to his share'.

Beneath the tables, and across the whole floor, fresh green *Juncus* rushes had been spread, filling the room with their cool moisture and delicate scent. In preparation for the supper two men were stationed at each of the two doors and at the barriers at the stair head, to maintain security. Sixteen men with torches stood at the barriers [round the tables?] in order to provide the required illumination.

Back in the kitchens, the cooks had been working for days, the quantities of food being enormous, considering that only 31 people were to be fed. Little would be wasted, however, after the table-servants had presumably dined on the remains in the usual manner. There is no surviving menu, but the following list of ingredients gives a clear reckoning of what was served to the supper and its following sweetmeat banquet:

Meat	*Poultry*	*Game*
8 muttons	36 fat capons	18 cranes
3 veals	360 chickens	24 herons
2 fat hogs	18 chicken peepers	15 peacocks
34 ox tongues	108 green geese	22 pheasants
120 calves tongues	108 'renners'	222 pigeons
288 flail bones	(i.e. free-range hens)	
8 lambs		
16 kids		

Fish	*Dairy*	*Fruit & Vegetables*
24 great carp	466 dishes of butter	103 quarters of apples
2 calver salmon	3 dishes 'grease' butter	400 pippins
9 turbot	32 gallons cream	lettuce, spinach &
14 conger eel	15 gallons milk	carrots from Flanders
13 pike	3,857 eggs	1800 oranges
24 bream	1 great Parmesan cheese	10 pomegranates
10 tench		

Flour & Breads
20 bushels flour
297 cheat loaves
9½lb rice flour

Ale & Beer
377 gallons ale
52½ gallons beer

Wine
13 gallons French & Gascoigne wine
4 gallons Malmsey
3 gallons Rumney

Spices
2lb aniseed powder
6lb caraway seed
1lb cinnamon powder
1lb cinnamon 'elect'
8oz galingale
9lb ginger
3lb grains of Paradise
2lb liquorice powder
1lb 2oz mace
2lb 8oz nutmeg
4lb 8oz pepper
1lb saffron

Dried Fruits & Nuts
64lb almonds
27lb currants
2lb dates
24lb prunes

Sweetmeats
4lb comfits, long
4lb green ginger
7½lb marmalade
8lb orange-flower conserve
4lb sucket

Sugars & Colourings
14lb sugar
6 galleypot sugar
9½lb turnsole
1lb saunders

For Jellies
60lb isinglass
80 gang calves' feet
6 gang ox feet
4 yards cotton cloth for jelly

Rosewater (some for handwashing?)
2 gallons rosewater
2 gallons damask water

Vinegars
20 gallons vinegar
verjuice

On its completion, each item was dished in a vessel of pure gold and passed on to the processions of sewers and waiters who were to carry them in to the supper table. Now all the guests took their places and the supper was served in the usual manner.

Having talked for a while, the party then rose and walked to the bottom end of the room. Here three pillars carved full of gargoyles and serpents supported a pair of arches decorated with armoury, all gilded, and supporting 'many sondri Antikes & devises'. On passing through into the gallery, Henry asked his guests to turn around and look above the arches, for here Holbein had painted a depiction of the Siege of Thérouanne, one of his victories in France in 1513 – an unexpected choice for entertaining a French embassy.

At the end of the gallery a masonry doorway embattled with jasper led into a domed porch with gilt crockets. Beyond, a magnificent disguising house had been constructed for further entertainment. Its roof, designed by Nicolaus Kratzer, the royal astronomer, and painted by Holbein, had,

> on the grounde of the rose ... the hole earth environed with the Sea, like a very Mappe or Carte, and by a conning makyng of another cloth, the zodiacke with 12 Signes, and the five circles or girdelles and the two poles apered on the earth and water compassing the same, and in the zodiac were the twelve signes, curiously made, and, above this were made the seven planettes, as Mars, Jupiter, Sol, Mercurius, Venus, Saternus, and Luna ...

The walls below were lined with five tiers of galleries for spectators, each painted as marble with rails like white marble. These were supported by sky-blue pillars decorated with gilded stars of cast lead and topped by silvered latten basins holding great branches of white wax candles. In the middle of the chamber stood an ornamental arch, all gilded and topped by depictions of heroes such as Hercules, Scipio, Julius Caesar and Pompey. There was a cloth of estate too, over thrones prepared for Henry and Catherine. Having taken their places, the party was entertained with an oration on the benefits of peace between England and France, songs from the Chapel, a dialogue between riches and love, a mock battle performed by six knights, and the conclusion of the dialogue: princes need both love and riches.

After the fight, a curtain at the lower end of the room was let down to reveal a great rock. Based on a wooden frame and hoops, this had been modelled in grey paper and flour paste painted with Spanish White, verdegris and other pigments to resemble a 'mount set ful of Christal coralles, & rich rockes of rubie cureously counterfaited & full of roses & pomegranates as though they grew.'

It also featured real blooms and boughs, along with daffodils, primroses, other flowers and leaves all cut out of paper and realistically coloured. Orsidue, an alloy of copper and zinc beaten to a thin foil, added additional sparkle. The rock was finally defended by a fortress with towers all covered in gold and green foils. Eight lords, each dressed in cloth of tissue with quartrefoils gold on silver, and silver on gold set on white satin, wearing black satin cloaks and black velvet caps decorated with pearls and precious stones, appeared sitting on top of the rock. Princess Mary and seven of her ladies all 'appareled after the romayne fashion in riche cloth of gold of tissue & Crimosin tinsel bendy & their heres in calles of golde with bonetes of Crimosin velvet full of pearle and stone' now emerged from a cave at the bottom of the rock. As they danced with the lords, six persons dressed in cloth of silver and black tinsel satin cut long in the Icelandic fashion, their heads covered in cloth of gold tippets and masked with silver beards suddenly came in and danced lustily with further ladies.

Meanwhile Henry and the 'Viscount of Torayne' and six companions had retired to change into masking clothes of gold and purple tinsel satin in the

Venetian fashion, great robes and masks with beards of gold. Re-entering the room, they now danced with the ladies. When the Queen plucked off the King's mask, the other ladies removed those of their partners, so that all were recognized.

'Then the kyng, quene and the ambassadours returned to the banket chamber, where thei found a banket ready set on the borde, of so many & marveilous dishes, that it was wonder to se, then the kyng sat doune and there was joy, myrth and melody'. The banquet included the comfits, green ginger, marmalades, orange-flower conserve and other sweetmeats prepared by the cooks, but the main features (if not already served at the earlier supper) were a number of huge marchpanes. The largest pair were based on a thousand wafers, which, allowing each wafer as a four-inch square plus overlapping edges, gives a diameter of over eight feet. They required the work of seven cooks over four days, one being garnished with a dungeon [i.e. a tower] and the other with a manor surrounded by a moat with swimming swans and cygnets. Others, made by Princess Mary's master cook Hugh, included two four-foot square chessboards with chessmen garnished with gold leaf, and a tower to set on a marchpane. The marchpanes were brightly coloured using white, green, red, gold and silver papers, vermillion, sinoper (red), bisse (blue or green) and green pigments along with further silver and gold.

At the end of the banquet, as dawn was breaking, everyone retired to bed. Over the following three or four days this magnificent suite of rooms was left intact for all to see, but then the interior decorations were largely stripped out. The structures remained in place, however, being occasionally re-used for other entertainments over the next decades.[14]

As this and the other descriptions of feasts clearly show, they were among the greatest artistic achievements of their age, combinations of the most advanced and sophisticated tastes in art, design, performance, music, manners and amazing culinary skills. They demanded the resources of the wealthiest monarchs and magnates who clearly appreciated that such impressive displays of expenditure and prodigal hospitality were essential for maintaining their influence, reputation and political power. It is perhaps for this reason that they flourished in periods when monarchy was all-powerful, declining in magnificence as the wider polity gained increasing constitutional control. Even at a much lower level, that of the gentry and wealthier yeomanry, the generous, open-handed hospitality of the Tudor and early Stuart periods was also to shrink to a great extent over the following century as these groups acquired more metropolitan tastes and manners.

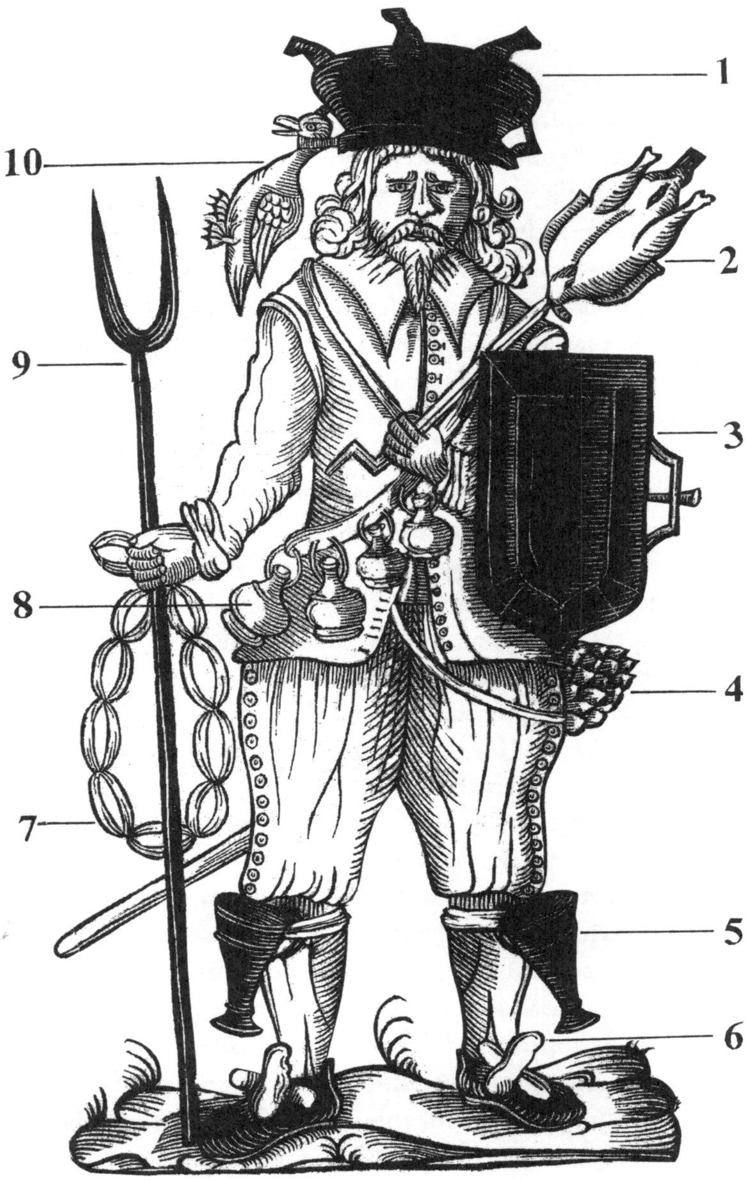

Figure 139. The English-Irish soldier of 1642. Designed to demonstrate the pitiless looting of the Royalist soldiery, it shows one of them wearing: (1) a cooking pot of hens and bacon as helmet; (2) a spit-roast goose as musket; (3) a dripping-pan as target or shield; (4) an artichoke as basket-hilted sword; (5) black pots as garters; (6) toasts as shoe-strings; (7) sausages or puddings as match; (8) bottles of Canary wine as bandoliers; (9) a fire-fork as musket-rest; (10) a goose as a feather in his cap.

CHAPTER TWENTY-SEVEN

The End of an Era

The Dissolution of the Monasteries in the late 1530s had seen their vast estates pass into the hands of the aristocracy and gentry. As a result, the relatively stable and passive management practices of the Church were replaced by more aggressive methods of increasing revenue including the raising of rents and agricultural and industrial development. The squirearchy and merchant class were among the greatest beneficiaries of this new economic environment, their growing wealth enabling them to enjoy higher standards of living. In addition to building new houses, they spent lavishly on furnishings, dress, food, drink, entertainment, recreation and the education of their sons. It was now possible for them to leave their isolated country estates to enjoy the high life in London and the major regional capitals, and also to increase their role in local and national administration.

The growing power of the new middle class posed a real threat to the aristocracy. Their traditional roles as military leaders and suppressors of revolt, enforced by their own armed retinues, had now been largely taken over by the state. They still had to attend court, fulfil royal appointments, maintain their expensive town and country houses, and employ large households of gentry, yeoman and groom servants, while trying to outspend the middle classes, who had far fewer financial and social or familial responsibilities. In former years the gentry and yeomanry had been proud to provide residential domestic service to their superiors, and to wear their liveries, since this had given them prestige, protection and an income, none of which they now needed.

In the early seventeenth century the tensions caused by these social and economic changes began to be resolved by drastically reducing the numbers of polite serving men in most of the great households. It was far more efficient and economical to replace them with a few professional stewards and clerks assisted by smaller numbers of cheap working-class male and female servants to perform all the menial tasks. The elaborate table-service which had graced the chambers for centuries had to be greatly simplified, while the top and side tables for servants in the great halls were gradually vacated. Now, for the first time, servants began to be hidden away from sight in subterranean or back-room servants' halls,

Figure 140. Cooking under bombardment. (1–2) Sandal Castle, near Wakefield in Yorkshire, the keep, July 1645, with its fireplace in use; (3) the keep, mid-September 1645, bombarded to ground level, with the defenders manning a trench cut deep into its floor; (4) The bombardment had already half-filled the trench with masonry, cannon-balls and a sword, but the defenders are still there, cooking their food on a small fire. A final cannon-ball brings down the last section of wall just before the surrender on 1 October. This sealed everything until the excavations of 1967.

concealed back-stairs and back-passages. As their masters' food was no longer paraded before them every mealtime, elaborate dishes such as grand salads now fell out of use. The abandonment of the hall had further significance, indicating that the free, open-handed hospitality so valued by previous generations had been largely withdrawn, only being extended to those who had been specifically invited. With fewer numbers to feed, kitchens might now be made much smaller, some being relegated to the basements in order to save space.

In many households these developments did not take place by gradual transition, but by sudden hostile intrusion. The social changes of the early seventeenth century had built up increasing tensions between those who still supported an all-powerful traditional monarchy, and those who demanded a far more democratic form of government. These flared up into the full-blown Civil War which disrupted all aspects of life intermittently from 1642 to 1651. Households on both sides still tried to provide hospitality for those of their own faction who were on campaign, but they were constantly under the threat of devastating enemy action. This took many forms, ranging from bitter sieges which often terminated in the total destruction of properties by bombardment or fire, in the looting of every creature, crop and possession and in having to provide free food, drink and accommodation for the thieving, rapacious soldiery. With many husbands away on military service, their wives and mothers were often left to defend their homes against all forms of aggression, displaying amazing levels of indomitable courage, loyalty and practicality. The end of military action in 1652 brought no end to their problems, at least on the Royalist side, as a vengeful Parliament imposed crippling fines on and confiscated the properties of their defeated opponents.

In 1653 there were attempts to return to something approaching normality. Having accepted the title of Lord Protector, Cromwell set up his version of the former royal household, with pairs of clerks of the kitchen managing the hall-place kitchens and privy kitchens at Whitehall and Hampton Court.[1] Families tried to carry on their lives as best they could, re-establishing their households if possible, but this was beyond the resources of many of those who had seen the destruction of their houses, the death of close relatives, the loss of trusted servants, and the disappearance of their accumulated capital and revenues. There was also a great feeling of uncertainty as the Commonwealth government became increasingly unpopular, promoting the likelihood of a return to monarchy.

In 1659 the Protectorate collapsed, Charles II and his court in exile returning to take power in May 1660. Once again there had to be a major re-distribution of property, as Royalist families tried to dislodge those who had taken over their houses and lands. It was not a simple matter of moving back in, for they had to prove their titles at law, a difficult matter when many original deeds had been destroyed. Legal costs and the need to sell lands to recoup Interregnum expenses could prove crippling.

As a result of these upheavals, the final vestiges of the late medieval, Tudor and early Stuart household traditions were largely extinguished. As previously described, large, expensive households of upper servants/retainers had disappeared, along with everyday ceremonial table service, many of the huge and elaborate dishes of food, and generous hospitality. Society now demanded more economical, smaller-scale and more intimate ways of dining, one largely based on the practices of the Tudor merchant class. Instead of sitting in splendour at one side of the formal table, set on a dais beneath a cloth of estate backing onto the fireplace wall of the chamber, even great lords now joined their families and select guests around tables placed in the centre of their dining rooms. Their retinues of stewards, ushers, carvers, sewers and cup-bearers were no longer required, except for great ceremonial feasts, their place being taken by a butler and a few low-status footmen. Now many relatively small dishes of food were placed on the table in two or three courses, each being helped either by a diner or a footman in a much less rigid manner. These permanent changes relegated most of the strict formalities of the past into obscurity, replacing them with the relaxed, boisterous, joyous meals so characteristic of Restoration England.

The methods used in cookery were also changing as many of the dishes which had survived from the late medieval period were replaced by others either of English invention, or imported from the Continent.

When in 1515 Sir Nicholas Carew, Francis Brian and their companions had returned from France, they were 'all Frenche, in eatying, drynkyng and apparrell, yea, and in French vices and bragges.' Instead of receiving the respect and influence they expected, however, they merely provided the Henrician court with a welcome source of hearty ridicule.[2] Diplomatic and military expeditions into France in the early mid-sixteenth century brought relatively few culinary influences into England, but this situation began to change after the accession of James I. Around 1602, for example, the fourteen-year-old Robert May was sent into the kitchens of Achille de Harlay, first President of the Paris Parliament, to start his training. On returning around 1607 he was apprenticed to Arthur Hollingsworth, cook to the Grocers' Company and the Star Chamber at Westminster. Then, as a fully qualified cook, he joined the household of Elizabeth, Baroness Dormer, daughter-in-law of his original patroness.[3] Presumably he was not alone in being partially trained in France, and in bringing French dishes and practices back into this country.

Further popularization of French cuisine appears to be largely attributable to James Hay, a Scot brought up in France, who joined James I in London in 1603. Over the following years he became increasingly involved in diplomacy, including periods in France in 1616, and also in the provision of lavish entertainments for the King, the Prince of Wales and leading courtiers. His greatest feast took place at Essex House in early January 1621, when the Maréchal de Cadenet, French Ambassador Extraordinary, and the royal party were served 'with that sumptuous superfluity that the like hath not been seen nor heard in these parts.' Six thousand ounces of gilt plate was set out as a present to the Ambassador, but the food was equally impressive. A hundred cooks had worked for eight days on 1,600 dishes, some comprising 12 pheasants, others 24 partridges, 144 larks, 2 swans, or 2 pigs respectively. Six six-feet salmon had been imported from Russia. The total bill amounted to a massive £3,300, which included £300 for 6lb of ambergris and £500 for banqueting stuff. This was one of the first significant feasts at which an ante-supper was served in England, a huge and succulent course of cold foods set before the guests merely to delight the eye and promote the appetite. Before it could be touched, this was rapidly whisked away, only to be replaced by another course of hot foods of even greater magnificence.[4]

Such influential feasts would have been well known to Princess Henrietta Maria, who married Charles I in 1625, but since her French companions were expelled the following year, her culinary influence was probably quite restricted. Interested in cookery, she was presented with several recipes that her 'Escuyer de Cuisine' W. la Montague [W.M.] transcribed into her book, retaining the originals as his 'Reliques' of the Queen after her departure to France in 1644. In 1655, anticipating his departure from 'this troublesome world', he had them published as *The Queen's Closet Opened.* Of the 163 recipes for general cookery, only 9 were French, the rest being typically English.

As the Royalist faction began to anticipate defeat in the Civil War, some of its leading members began to plan their escape across to the Continent. In 1643, for example, Sir Ralph Verney of Claydon had his household effects shipped to Amsterdam and Rotterdam, made the required financial arrangements, and obtained passes in the name of 'Smith' to allow him and his wife to enter France, whither they departed by the end of the year.[5] Similarly Sir Kenelm Digby departed to Paris, becoming Chancellor to Henrietta Maria in 1644. Prince Charles, the Duke of Buckingham, Lord Percy and other leading Royalists followed in 1646. Over the next fourteen years the future Charles II and his court in exile grew accustomed to their predominantly French cuisine, which they brought back into England at the Restoration of 1660. The most significant new collection of French recipes, François Pierre de la Varenne's *Le Cuisinier françois* of 1651 had already proved extremely popular, its fourth edition appearing in 1653, the same year that its translation *The French Cook* was published in London. Its 'Alphabetical table for the explaining of the hard and strange words contained in this book' included the haricots, bards, fricasees, hashes, lardons, ragouts, ramekins, and other French terms, often found in later English recipe books.

In the year of the Restoration, Robert May's *Accomplisht Cook* included many French dishes, ranging from the elaborate *Entre de table* to simpler bisks, puffs and the like. It remained more retrospective than innovative, however, recording the predominantly English tradition of the early Stuart great house. His French experience was already over fifty years old, but that of others was far more up-to-date. William Rabisha, for example, had followed his training in England with work 'abroad in the late King's Court ... and at the entertainment of Embassadors ... and with Embassadors and other Nobles in certain forreign Parts'. Following his return to this country and 'that happy and blessed restauration of our long-exiled Royal luminaries' he published his *Whole Body of Cookery Dissected ... of English, French, Italian, Dutch, &c.* recipes in 1661.

A superficial examination of later cookery books, such as Patrick Lamb's *Royal Cookery*, published in 1710, but recording recipes from his entry into Charles II's kitchens in the 1660s, is littered with *à la* dishes, bisques, amlets, fricasees, cullises, and so forth. These clearly demonstrate the adoption of many French dishes into the English repertoire as the less fashionable native dishes, especially those of sweetened and spiced meats, passed out of use. It would be a great mistake, however, to see this as the abandonment of innovative English cookery. As early as 1673 the later editions of La Varenne were incorporating decidedly English recipes, now fashionably re-named in French, such as *Pike boyl'd a la mode de Londres*, or *Steak Pies* à *mode de Paris*. This continued over the next two hundred years or more, as French became the accepted international language for all culinary matters, thus disguising the English origins of many fine dishes. The Boeuf Wellington, Boeuf Nelson and various dishes à la Chesterfield of the classical repertoire clearly illustrate this practice.

In the centuries following the Restoration, knowledge of the food and cookery of the Tudor and Stuart periods was almost completely forgotten. There was no academic study of the subject, and a similar lack of popular interest. In 1933, this vacuum was filled by the release of Alexander Korda's *The Private Life of Henry VIII*, with Charles Laughton in the title role. Extremely popular, this film provided all future directors with a ready-made set of concepts of Tudor life, food and manners, which they continue to follow. Gross food is heaped on dishes from which it is torn by the fistful, bitten off in mouth-cramming lumps, chewed open-lipped and then the bones thrown either over the shoulder or onto the floor. At best, actors gnaw like grinning rats on chicken legs. Most people now honestly believe that these fictions are true representations of historical realities, ones in which they may even participate at commercial 'recreations' of 'medieval' or 'Tudor' feasts. They are, however, mere figments of over-heated and ignorant imaginations aimed more at commercial success than truth and accuracy. This practice is still continued by some of today's 'celebrity chefs', their personal 'twists' are self-proclaimed as the 'THE ULTIMATE!' or 'BEST EVER!' of their kind. Such are truly nauseating to anyone who has a deep understanding of historical food, cookery and manners.

Interest in the true history of Tudor and early Stuart food began to develop in the 1950s and '60s with the appearance of books such as André Simon's *The Star Chamber Dinner Accounts* and F.G. Emmison's *Tudor Food and Pastimes*. 1973 saw the publication of perhaps the most important pioneering study of English food history, C. Anne Wilson's *Food and Drink in Britain*, based on the study of hundreds of recipe books housed in Leeds University's Brotherton Library. It remains an invaluable work of reference. Over the following years a number of reproductions and reprints of recipe books of the period began to appear, the series edited by Stuart Peachey in Bristol being particularly useful in making authentic information immediately accessible for practical use by historical re-enactors and others. The fine hardback reproductions of *A Book of Fruits and Flowers*, W.M.'s *The Compleat Cook and A Queens Delight*, Robert May's *The Accomplisht Cook*, William Rabisha's *The Whole Body of Cookery Dissected* and *The Closet of Sir Kenelme Digby Kt. Opened* by Prospect Books similarly made a wealth of period recipes readily available to all. In 2007 the finest and most complete study of any period of English foodstuffs and their uses finally appeared in print. This was Joan Thirsk's *Food in Early Modern England, Phases, Fads, Fashions, 1500–1760*. Breathtaking in its breadth, depth and closely referenced detail, it benefits from her knowledge as Britain's leading agricultural historian, but goes far beyond food production to emerge as one of the best of all culinary history books.

As a distinct discipline, history is based largely on the written word, and must therefore remain only one of the available sources from which we might reconstruct the life of past ages. Vast amounts of additional information can only be provided by archaeology, the study of structures and artefacts in their particular contexts. Architectural studies are equally necessary, particularly those concerned with the efficient planning of the domestic offices and the rooms in which meals were served. Knowledge of the decorative arts, far too often considered in terms of 'connoisseurship' and style, but often blinkered in terms of practical usage, is also invaluable. A true, rounded understanding of food history can only be achieved by combining all of these sources of information with the greatly under-appreciated (often academically despised) and infrequently followed technique of practical experience. Only by using buildings, artefacts (usually reproduction, for conservation reasons), and fuels as they were originally intended can the ways in which they were designed to work together be fully experienced. Purely historical research is excellent for stimulating the intellect and supplying contemporary context, but it cannot inform the vital senses of taste, texture, temperature, aroma, light and colour.

When the dishes of the Tudor and early Stuart period are accurately cooked, served and eaten in the authentic manner, their exceptional standard becomes self-evident. This is the food of Shakespeare, Jonson, Herrick and Tusser, of Drake and Raleigh, Wolsey, More and Cranmer, as well as of some of our most significant monarchs, and Cromwell too. It should be treated with the respect it deserves, presented neither as the crude fare of mannerless, loutish actors, nor as the pantomime whimsies of ill-informed chefs. It needs none of their perverse attentions, for it represents a golden age of English cookery, one which needs only to be accurately recreated to reveal its own high standards, richly flavoured, colourful, satisfying and often spectacular.

Figure 141. The feast has ended; the guests are replete, and the cooks relax. Back in the scullery, the boys of the kitchen now face a mountainous heap of washing-up, each kneeling before his kettle of hot water, dishcloth in hand, as seen on this misericord of 1520 in Beverley Minster, Yorkshire.

Notes

The sources most generally used have been abbreviated as follows:

EDD Wright, J. (ed.), *The English Dialect Dictionary* (Oxford 1923).
HMC Historical Manuscripts Commission.
HO *The Society of Antiquaries of London A Collection of Ordinances ... for the Government of the Royal Household* (1790).
NHB Percy, T. (ed.), *The Regulations and Establishment of the Household of Henry Algernon Percy, the fifth Earl of Northumberland at his Castles of Wressle and Leconfield in Yorkshire Begun anno domini MDXII (The Northumberland Household Book)* (1905 edition).
L & P *Letters & Papers Foreign & Domestic of the Reign of Henry VIII*, catalogued J.S. Brewer, 2nd edition, revised and enlarged R.H. Brodie (1861–3).
OED *The Oxford English Dictionary.*

INTRODUCTION

1. *L & P* 1540, 163b; Collier (1857) 147; *OED* 'Gigot'.
2. *OED* 'Fart'; A.W. 33; Anon, (1588) 15.
3. E.g. AW33; May 1, 98; Herbert 63.
4. Murrell (1615) 49; May 77, 84, 109, 114, 119, 124, 128, 171, 186, 73; A.W. 30; Clinton 44; May 116.
5. May 117, 119, 38.
6. Ibid. 443.
7. Heywood 14.
8. Haywood 119.
9. Wright 240–42.
10. I.M.H.
11. Markland 339–341.
12. Fussell 47.
13. Meads, general refs.
14. Anon. (1588) in Alnwick Castle Library, Press Mark 560.
15. M.R. Title page.
16. Percy, 371; Wilson 170–71; Dawson (2009) 143, 148, 170.
17. Meads 30/1/1600 etc.
18. See entries in *OED*.
19. Salaman (1949) 434, 436.
20. Ibid. 430.
21. Ibid. 439.
22. Warner xviii; Simon (1959) 9.
23. May 458; Simon (1959) 13.
24. Ibid. 416.
25. *HO* 137–240.

CHAPTER I

THE COUNTING HOUSE

1. Boorde 237.
2. Whateley 320.
3. Gray (1996) XV; Somerset County Record Office DD. H1, 303.
4. Hope (1919) 124.
5. E.g. Gray (1996) 217, 220, 314.
6. E.g. Raine (1836) 183 & Hope 129.
7. Batho 104.
8. Thurley (1993) 147.
9. Thurley (1990) 17.
10. Kingsford 24.
11. HMC Rutland IV 335.
12. Juddery 53.
13. *HO* 163.
14. *HO* 137–161.
15. *HO* 162–240.
16. *HO* 299–312.
17. Garfitt 210.
18. Yorkshire Archaeological Society DD 121/36 A.
19. Charles 1.
20. E.g. Gray (1995) 1–105 and (1996) for the Countess of Bath.
21. Chinnery 287–9.

22. Tinniswood 26.

CHAPTER 2

PLANNING FOR COOKING

1. Boorde 233–8.
2. Wotton 8.
3. Whateley 463–7.
4. Thurley (1993) 45, 64–5; Howard 69.
5. Thurley (1990) 12–17; (1993) 150.
6. Hope 81–2.
7. Howard 90, 215.
8. Anon, (19) I 326; Howard 212.
9. Goodall 204.
10. Howard 155, 202.
11. Duke of Northumberland MS.
12. (Anon) (19) II 386.
13. Drury 44–7.
14. Heal 45; Brears, unpublished survey of Temple Newsam.
15. Compton 308–11; Essex Record Office Publication 22; Howard 87, 203.
16. Girouard (1962) 104 & plate 109.
17. Girouard (1983) 137; Dodd 6; Anon (19) II 374; Girouard (1962).
18. Brears, unpublished survey, MS plans at Parham House; Ambler 74.
19. Plan of Shaw House by John Howard Building Surveys Ltd.; copy of Thomas Dolman's 1622 inventory at Shaw House; Girouard (1983) 66–8.
20. Girouard (1983) 122, 188; Rowell 8.
21. Girouard (1983) 111.
22. Ibid. 145.
23. Ibid. 155.
24. Brears, unpublished survey; Girouard (1983) 257–60.
25. Faulkner 18.
26. Harris (1973) 190.
27. Ibid. 204–5.
28. Gunther 64; also plan in *Vitruvius Britannicus* WGI.PL.65.
29. Girouard (1983) 108.
30. Ryder 58.
31. Girouard (1983) 239.
32. Ibid. 10; J. Haworth and the National Trust's plans of Lodge Park.
33. The National Trust, Newark Park; Brears, unpublished survey of Dob Park.
34. Ryan 15.
35. Martin 85.
36. Giles 142–3; Ryan 16.

CHAPTER 3

WOOD, COALS, TURVES AND FIRES

1. Lillywhite 662.
2. 34–5 Henry VIII c.3, 43; Elizabeth I c.14.
3. Adams 27.
4. Banks 374.
5. Ornsby 102, 272.
6. Juddery, 3.
7. Yorkshire Archaeological Society MS DD 121/36A. 19/9/1607, 27/9/1607, 14/10/1607; Tusser 164.
8. Brears (1972) 91; *OED* 'Peat'; Raine 93, 226, 260.
9. Ornsby 65.
10. Kaner 165, 257.
11. Brears (2009) 60.
12. Yorkshire Archaeological Society MS DD 121/36A. 3/4/1607.
13. Banks 373.
14. *HO* 227; Adams 28.
15. Simon (1959) 47; Emison 64–5.
16. *HO* 227.
17. Thurley (1993) 149.
18. Banks 374–5; Tusser 89.
19. Tusser 164.
20. Ibid. 157.
21. Ibid. 184, 189.
22. Banks 375.
23. Harrison (1587) 280, in Barnwell & Airs 23.
24. Walford 123.
25. Brears (2008) 58–9.
26. *NHB* 20–21, 100.
27. Gurney 471.
28. Nef 159.
29. Ibid. 19.
30. Ibid. 21.
31. Ibid. 247; BL MS 669 f.10.
32. Nef 157.
33. Barnwell & Airs 23.
34. Nef 247.
35. Kingsford 37; *OED* 'Grate'.
36. Brears (2009) 17, 86.

37. RIBA Smythson Drawing III/1 no. 12.
38. Carew's *Cornwall*; D. King & J. Hall quoted in Tinniswood 56, 42.
39. p. 201.
40. Wrathmell 24.
41. Gurney 433.
42. Tusser 21–3.
43. *Maison Rustique, or the Country Farme* quoted in Wilson (2006) 197.
44. Tomlinson 486.
45. Sandys 22; Walton ii 58; Arnold (2007) 105.
46. British Museum 1900 · 10 · 1–3 & Ludlow Museum.
47. Pearce nos. 186–192; Coleman–Smith 149 nos. 9/1–9.
48. For traditional kindling see Brears (2008) 61.
49. Seymour-Lindsay 54–5.
50. Juddery 137.
51. Simon (1959) 57.
52. Brears (1999) 53–5; Juddery 8, 79.
53. HMC Rutland MS IV (1928) 312.

CHAPTER 4
WATER SUPPLIES

1. Boorde 233, 252.
2. Borthwick Institute of Historical Research, York, Dean & Chapter Wills & Inventories Folder 1580.
3. Thurley (1993) 164 & Blackman 21.
4. Thurley (1993) 163–4.
5. Ibid. 168.
6. Anon (1779) 432.
7. Batho 103 & Taylor, Jerome & Allnut 1.
8. Stallybrass 369.
9. Thurley (1990) 16.
10. Emmison 23.
11. Hope 86.
12. Robins 134–8.
13. Ibid. 155–60.
14. White 116.
15. Donno 72.
16. Platter.
17. Robins 151.
18. Dodsley, VI 403.
19. Evans 44.
20. *OED* 'Soe'.
21. HMC Rutland MS IV 310 & II 245.
22. Chambers 293.
23. Gurney 562.
24. Rowntree 147.
25. *OED* 'Winch'.
26. Anon (1779) 435.
27. Richard II, IV 185.
28. Curtis Museum, Alton, Hants.
29. *OED* 'Treadwheel'.
30. Chandler 106.
31. Brunner & Major 142.
32. *OED* 'Plump' & 'Well' (12).
33. Thurley (1990) 16.
34. Thurley (1993) 163.
35. Green 24, 91.
36. Robins 155.
37. Ibid. 155 &157.

CHAPTER 5
THE DAIRY

1. Fussell (1953) 96. See also Shakespeare *A Winters' Tale* IV 4.
2. Ibid. 62.
3. Markland 340.
4. *OED* 'Milkmaid'.
5. Chappell 295–6.
6. Markham 108; Breton *Fantasticks* (1626).
7. Woodward 140.
8. Drummond & Wilbraham 72, Boorde 267.
9. Elyot II 35b.
10. Markham 109.
11. Leeds, Brotherton Library MS 621 p. 20.
12. Ornsby 217.
13. Santon 133.
14. Leeds, Brotherton Library MS 621 p. 20.
15. Markham 110.
16. Boorde 267.
17. Herrick (Hayward) 127, 139, 64.
18. *OED* 'Wassail Bowl'.
19. Hazlitt 3.
20. May 296.
21. Chambers I 571.
22. Wright (1976) 207, 213.
23. *OED* 'Churn' 5.
24. Woodward 98.

25. Herrick (Hayward) 170.
26. Ahmed 49.
27. May 279.
28. Ibid. 284.
29. Digby 98.
30. May 283.
31. Digby 268.
32. Ibid. 99.
33. Ibid. 95.
34. Saxton, 133; Day (1996) 33.
35. Day (1996) 33; Digby 99.
36. W.M. 53.
37. Digby 95.
38. Peachey (1994) 17.
39. May 296.
40. Clinton 76.
41. Ibid. 17; Ruthven 216.
42. May 278–9.
43. Cogan 179.
44. May 282–3; Digby 96–7; W.M. 30–31.
45. Juddery 79.
46. Grant plate 2; Ruthven 187; W.M. 30–37.
47. May 283; see also Spurling 115; Digby 99; Buttes 'Milke'.
48. Sarsby 19–23.
49. Googe 146b.
50. Markham 111.
51. Hone (1832) 150–153.
52. Platt 77.
53. Leeds, Brotherton Library MS 621 p. 20.
54. Boorde 147, 265.
55. Thirsk 40.
56. Williams 193.
57. III vi.
58. 14 Charles II c.26 (1662); *OED* 'Disk'; Charles 163.
59. Leeds University Brotherton Library MS 621; Saxton 133; Markham 114.
60. Markham 113.
61. Juddery 40, 52, 69, 78, 79.
62. Platt (1948) 77.
63. Markham 114.
64. Boorde 266.
65. Wilson (1976) 145.
66. Googe 147b.
67. Simon (1959) 88.
68. *Merry Wives of Windsor* I i 19.
69. Byrne 70; Wilson 159.
70. Peachey (1992) 38.
71. Markham 115–118.
72. HMC Hastings MS I (1928) 290.
73. Weddell 119.
74. Saxton 133; *OED* 'Cheese', 'Safe'.
75. Giles 64.
76. W.M. 42, 122; *OED* 'Eddish'; Markham 119.
77. Markham 119.
78. Markham 118.
79. Digby 186–9; Spurling 114; Ruthven 198.
80. Byrne 33; Ruthven 198; Peachey (1993) 16; W.M. 70.
81. Boorde 266.
82. Markham 120; Digby 191.
83. Dawson (1596) I 15b, 32; Peachey (1992) 52.
84. Ibid.
85. Boorde 267–8.
86. May 285.

CHAPTER 6

THE BREWHOUSE

1. Boorde 326.
2. Chandler 80, 296; *OED* 'Dagger' 11.
3. Greene 42.
4. Bosworth 34.
5. Bickerdyke 47.
6. Raine 218–9.
7. Bickerdyke 121.
8. Raine 110; *OED* 'Steep' 5.
9. Carrington 72.
10. Bickerdyke 122.
11. Brears (1972) 1, 6, 37, 52.
12. Walker, J.W., 142.
13. Bennet & Elton, 221.
14. Kaner, 69, 90, 96, 10.2, 146
15. Bennet & Elton, 221.
16. HMC Rutland IV (1905) 303; Raine 183–4.
17. Rowntree 146.
18. Harrison, J.K., 57.
19. Brears (1972) 98.
20. Bickerdyke 56.
21. Ornsby 227.
22. Allan (2006) 241 – 264.
23. Patents 1635 nos. 78 & 83; 1660 no. 129.
24. Batho 123.

25. Saxton 134.
26. Palmer 49.
27. *OED* 'Scurvy-grass' 4; Galpin 291.
28. Ornsby 359.
29. Bickerdyke 413.
30. Wright (1983) 218.
31. Brears (1984) 102.
32. Digby 88 (see also 9 & 11).
33. Boorde 122; Bickerdyke 163.
34. Bickerdyke 70.
35. Stevenson 292, 297 & Ornsby 34. See Bickerdyke 76–78 for Thomas Tusser's advice for growing hops in 1580.
36. Berry 104–112.
37. Bickerdyke 155.
38. Ibid. 106.
39. Ibid. 54–6.
40. Markham 123–4.
41. Markham 123–4.
42. Markham 123–4.
43. Bickerdyke 106; Allan 263.
44. Boorde 251.
45. Palmer 98.
46. Digby 43, 51, 53.
47. Digby 43, 51, 53.
48. Digby 43, 51, 53.
49. Smith (1964) 126.
50. Boorde 256.
51. Davies (1993) 84.
52. *OED* 'Ciderkin'.
53. Davies (1993) 83.
54. Digby 81, 84.
55. Markham 124–5.
56. Digby 82.

CHAPTER 7

THE BAKEHOUSE

1. Leviticus XXVI.26; Psalms CV.16; Ezekiel IV.16; *OED* 'Staff' 4c.
2. Boorde 260–61.
3. Markham 125.
4. Fairholt XL.
5. *HO* 160, 195, 232, 282–84.
6. Batho 157, 160.
7. HMC Rutland IV 314.
8. Girouard (1987) 130.
9. Wright 187–8.
10. Spence (2005) 52; Peachey 61.
11. Thurley (1993) Plan 1, 31, 19; National Trust *Lacock Abbey* (1997) 7, 21.
12. Thurley (1990) 21–22.
13. Tusser 43, 47.
14. Woodward 108–10; Kaner 53.
15. Saxton 134.
16. Raine (1853).
17. Halifax Antiquarian Society HAS/B: 13/42.
18. *OED* 'Bolting'; Kaner 217, 53, 113.
19. Kirkland 21.
20. Levey 29.
21. Woodward 110.
22. Batho 121; Kaner 96.
23. YAS, DD 121/36A 8/11/1607; Collier 347.
24. Grant 55; David 179.
25. Tusser 40, 175.
26. *OED* 'Malkin' 3.
27. Boorde 258.
28. David xxi, quoting Muffet of 1595.
29. David 335, quoting Markham, 1615.
30. David 334, quoting *Good Huswifes Handmaide to the Kitchen* 1594; Amyot 287; *HO* 294; Lorwin 37; Spence (2005) 52.
31. David 335, quoting Countess of Kent, 1653; Walford 150.
32. May 239.
33. Walford 150.
34. David xx–xxi quoting Muffet of 1595.
35. Spence (2005) 52.
36. Walford 150.
37. *OED* 'Brown Bread'.
38. Walford 150.
39. Vaughan xx.
40. Wilson 221 (quoting Harrison).
41. Woodward 109.
42. *OED* 'Spice-cake'.
43. White (2000) 105.
44. Walford 83.
45. Ruthven 194.
46. W.M. (1655) (1671 ed.) 13.
47. *A Queen's Delight* (1671) 62.
48. Adair 221–2.
49. Lewer 1.
50. *OED* 'Bridecake'.
51. Charsley 45.

52. W.M. (1655) (1671 ed.) 109–110.
53. W.M. (1655) (1671 ed.) 9, 16, 18, 19, Ruthven 195; Murrell (1638) 139; A.W. (1591) 33; Fettiplace 61; *Good Huswifes Handmaide* 47.
54. *Good Huswifes Handmaide* 62.
55. Woodward 217.
56. David 528.
57. Roeder 51–52.
58. *EDD* 'Bannock'.
59. Kaner 136, 151, 234; *OED* 'Bakeboard', 'Bakestone'.
60. Brears (1974) 57.
61. *OED* 'Havercake'.
62. Brears (1972) 102, 114.
63. Brears (1974) 58.
64. Brears (2008) 112–13.
65. *OED* 'Bake' 6.
66. Grant 56.
67. David 179; Brears (1998) 31.
68. Harland 339.

CHAPTER 8
THE PASTRY

1. Brears (2008) 125–6.
2. *HO* 143, 252; Brears (1999) 86.
3. Thurley (1990) 16.
4. Copy of inventory at Temple Newsam House.
5. Boorde 238.
6. *Romeo & Juliet* IV iv 2.
7. Thorpe, J., Architectural drawing no. T239.
8. Alcock (2003) frontispiece.
9. *OED* 'Bake-pan'; Dawson (1596) II 18b.
10. Grant 56; Brears (1971) 71, 247.
11. Thomson 20.
12. Levey 29.
13. Hastings Library HA/inventories Box 1 no. 1.
14. May 238, 262, 211, 343, 32, 239, 274.
15. Batho 110.
16. Girouard (1987) 130.
17. Moorhouse (1971) 55.
18. Brears (2008) 128, 138.
19. May 123, 321.
20. La Varenne 248, 149–50.
21. Pearce 54 no. 74; May 334.
22. May 234.
23. May 229; Rabisha 88.
24. Markham 65.
25. La Varenne 65.
26. Weddell 173.
27. Markham 65.
28. Peachey (1992) 22.
29. May 237; Peachey (1992) 31.
30. May 211, 214.
31. Dawson (1596) II 17; Rabisha 227; Peachey (1992) 22.
32. Rabisha 240.
33. Peachey (1992) 20.
34. Ibid.
35. Clinton 73; Rabisha 227; May 212.
36. May 211.
37. May 211.
38. A.W. 33; Markham 65; La Varenne 200.
39. Peachey (1993) 11, (1994) 4; Clinton 77; May 262 (3).
40. Yorkshire Archaeological Society DD 121/36A, 17/8/1628.
41. Boorde 274–5.
42. Emmison 52, 47; Dawson (2009) 225.
43. May 229.
44. Peachey (1992) 27; Clinton 73; A.W. 20–21; Rabisha 222.
45. For pastry paper see Simon 47, 48, 57, 62; Clinton 73.
46. Dawson (2009) 184.
47. May 288.
48. *A New way to Pay Old Debts* (1625) I iii.
49. May 231; Digby 173.
50. May 231; La Varenne 176.
51. Emmison 48; Platt 99; May 99; Rabisha 231.
52. Rabisha 244.
53. Ibid. 93.
54. May 228.
55. Ibid. 338.
56. Dawson (1596) II 31.
57. May, plates at pp. 224 & 240.
58. Turner 166; May 347.
59. May 227.
60. Ibid. 226.
61. Rabisha 225.
62. Markham 68.
63. A.W. 17b.

64. Dawson (1596) II 30.
65. Murrell (1638) 24.
66. May 338.
67. Pritchard 71.
68. Emmison 47–8.
69. A.W. 24b; Clinton 80; Rabisha 254.
70. May 246.
71. Tusser 73.
72. Garrett 384.
73. Hone (1828) I 419.
74. Hazlitt 294.
75. Carrington 69.
76. A.W. 17.
77. E.g. *OED* 'Potatoes 1', 'Eringoes'.
78. Chambers I 374–5.
79. Dawson (1596) I 20b.
80. May 234–6.
81. Salaman (1949) 432.
82. Rabisha 236.
83. Girouard (1983) 218–9.
84. Brears (2008) 137.
85. Dodsley V 143.
86. Act I scene ii.
87. May 8.
88. Ibid. introduction.
89. Rabisha 228.
90. Ibid. 240.
91. Ibid. 179–80.
92. Brears (2008) 143.
93. May 378.
94. Ibid. 232, 339; Murrell (1638) 24, 28; Peachey (1992) 23–4.
95. *OED* 'Florentine'.
96. *EDD* 'Florentine'; Clinton 50.
97. Rabisha 112, 111.
98. Digby 141.
99. May, plate before p. 225.
100. Ibid. 265.
101. Rabisha 110.
102. Ibid. 254.
103. A.W. 27.
104. Rabisha 246.
105. A.W. 27b; Dawson (1596) II 18.
106. May 246.
107. Clinton 81–2; Rabisha 253.
108. May, plate after p. 240.
109. Ibid., & 247.
110. Rabisha 255.
111. Ibid. 250; Peachey (1993) 18.
112. Rabisha 251.
113. May 249.
114. Peachey (1993) 19; May 250.
115. Ibid. 18.
116. May 247, 249, 251.
117. Dawson (1596) I 17, II 73; Peachey (1992) 35.
118. May, plate after 251.
119. Ibid. 237.
120. Dawson (1596) I 112; Markham 67.
121. Ahmed 47.
122. Dawson (1596) II 63; Peachey (1992) 31.
123. Brears (2008) 132.
124. May 291.
125. Clinton 78.
126. May 290.
127. May 211.
128. Rabisha 89–90.
129. Ibid., & Digby 171.
130. Rabisha 77–81.
131. Digby 174.
132. Kaner 342.
133. May 21, 82, 182, 183, 265, 266, etc.
134. Staffordshire CRO MS 1346.
135. May 189.
136. *OED* 'Whitepot'.
137. Spurling 213.
138. Clinton 46; May 295.
139. Pearce 75,98.
140. Allan (1984) 226 no. 2912.
141. Spurling 213; Clinton 46; Digby 123, 163; May 295.

CHAPTER 9

THE BOILING HOUSE

1. Hodgson (1914) 17–18.
2. *HO* 196.
3. Ornsby 26.
4. Thurley (1993) 156.
5. I am grateful to Mr J. Allan for showing me the kitchens here.
6. Brears (1972) 31; Peacock 132; Marshall (1996) 98.
7. *Devon & Cornwall Notes & Queries* XVII April 23 1932. 19; Levey 56.

8. Levey 56.
9. Gordon Slade 33.
10. Thurley (1990) 16.
11. HO 252, 288, 287, 296.
12. Gray (1996) 99.
13. Boorde 271.
14. Buttes 'beefe'; see also Elyot (1547) 12–14, 16.
15. Drummond & Wilbraham 97.
16. Holmes, J.M., in Woodfield (1981) 135.
17. Tusser 46, 49.
18. Clinton 54.
19. Markham 47–48.
20. Clinton 55.
21. Drummond & Wilbraham 97.
22. Peachey 16.
23. Boorde 271.
24. Brears (1972) 12, 16, 85, 81, 103.
25. Digby (1997) 178.
26. Williams (1990) 237; (1998) 55; Hall 45; Waterhouse 26.
27. Woodward 26; May 168.
28. Elyot II 29; Holmes, in Woodfield 130, found 65% of mutton was 3–4 years old at Coventry Free Grammar School c. 1550.
29. 25 Henry VIII cap. 13 (1533).
30. May 134–35.
31. Holmes, in Woodfield 130–34.
32. May 49, 50.
33. *OED* 'Mutton' 2b.
34. Tusser 37.
35. Peachey 16.
36. May 94.
37. Dawson (1596) II 19; Peachey 16, 21; Alnwick Castle Library press mark 560, 49.
38. Muffet 147.
39. Harrison 158.
40. May 194–5.
41. Clinton 45.
42. Ibid.
43. May 194.
44. Brears (2008) 167–71.
45. HMC Rutland MS IV (1905) 324 & Brears (1999) 134.
46. Hone I 168.
47. Garrett I 384.
48. Brears (1999) 134.
49. May 169.
50. Clinton 72–3.
51. 2 Eliz.cap. 5 (1562); 27 Eliz.cap. 8 (1585); 35 Eliz.cap.7 (1593).
52. Stephenson 293; Yorks. Arch. Soc. DD 121/36A.
53. Hone II 569–70.
54. See note 50 above.
55. Boorde 142.
56. *OED* 'Organ Ling'; see also *All's Well That Ends Well* III 2.
57. Owen 42; for prices see Sandys 23–24.
58. *HO* 175–6.
59. *HO* 289.
60. Tusser 178, 190, 61.
61. Dawson (1596) I 10, 11; Peachey 43; Digby (1997) 155–7.
62. Jonson *Every man Out of Humour* VI iii.
63. Digby (1997) 155.

CHAPTER 10

THE KITCHENS

1. Pearson 87, 86, 93.
2. Maguire & Gomme 58–68.
3. Batho (1959) 120.
4. Brears (1999) 111–132.
5. Whately 465.
6. Thurley (1993) 161.
7. Ibid. 160 & plan 3.
8. Thurley (1990) plan 7.
9. National Archives TNA. E 154/2/18.
10. National Library of Wales, Chirk Castle MS. F 13310.
11. Antrobus 21–31.
12. Hurst (2012) 26–7.
13. Blencowe (1848) 77.
14. Dawson (2009) 196.
15. *OED* 'Sink' (1c).
16. Carrington 68; HMC Ancaster (1907) 463.
17. *OED* 'Ratcatcher'.
18. Girouard (1983) 82, 183, 148, 179.
19. Ibid. 221.
20. Kingsford (1921) 45–9.
21. *HO* 236, 142.
22. *HO* 168.
23. Thurley (1990) 19.
24. Hope 94.

25. *HO* 1678.
26. *OED* 'Dresser'.
27. Dodsley X. 344.
28. Harrison (1972) 44.

CHAPTER 11
KITCHEN FURNITURE

1. *Devon & Cornwall Notes & Queries* XVII (1932) 18.
2. Blackman 26, 37.
3. Levey 29; Marshall 98; Juddery 78.
4. Juddery 51, 62.
5. Arnold 63.
6. Batho 75; Juddery 37; Arnold 63.
7. Mary Rose Trust 81 A 450.
8. *OED* 'Dish' 9.
9. *L & P* Henry VIII IV 1457.
10. Juddery 52; Berry 263; Peacock 132; Gray (1996) 218.
11. Batho 124.
12. Chinnery 331–5.
13. Stell & Hampson 338; Woodward 240.
14. Tusser 265.
15. Juddery 95, 76, 119.
16. Tusser 261–3.

CHAPTER 12
OF COOKS

1. *HO* 142.
2. *Archaeologia* XV (1806) 81; Dawson (2009) 203; Gurney 425.
3. *HO* 148.
4. *L & P* 1541, 140.
5. Gurney 419, 433, 445.
6. Adams 418.
7. Dawson (2009) 203.
8. Marshall (1949) 13.
9. Verney 172.
10. Borg 27, 39, 40.
11. Anon. *English Homes* II 366; Gurney 547.
12. Borg 64, 51; see Adams 442–4 for his embarkation with Robert Dudley in 1587.
13. May [14].
14. Rabisha [29], [31].
15. Collier (1863) 3.
16. Adams 342, 406; Batho 149–164.
17. Nichols (1788) III, 11, 19; II 88.
18. Adams 149, 162.
19. Stevenson 296, 197.
20. *L & P* 1541, 878 (58), 141, 1226 (24).
21. *HO* 146.
22. Nichols 191.
23. Furnivall (1868) LXX; BL Egerton MS 2806 f.25.
24. Boorde 309.
25. Fairholt XXXIII
26. Nichols (1828) 948–951.
27. Ahmed 50.
28. Wilson (1949) 288.
29. Massinger *A New Way to Pay Old Debts* I ii; and for the masque at Knowsley see Broadbent (1883).
30. Cogan 150.
31. Byrne 25; Gascoigne 33; Tavener.
32. *Romeo and Juliet* IV ii 2–8.
33. Camden (1556) 35.
34. *Calendar State Papers Domestic,* Elizabeth, CCLXXIII (1869) 355–367.
35. Nichols 196–7, 235–6.
36. *L & P* Henry VIII 1533 VI (1882) 306–13; *L & P* Henry VIII XV (1898) 178–210; Collier (1863) 3, 146; Digby 125.
37. Borg 63.
38. Richardson & Isabell 41.
39. Adams 138, 234, 241, 406, 442–4, 480; Richardson & Isabell 41; Batho 156; Digby 291.
40. Barker 20.
41. Herbert, E., 76, 89.
42. Verney 47.
43. Verney 88.
44. Verney 158.
45. Wilson (1979 & 1980) for further details.
46. Markland 337–342.
47. *Paradise Lost Book* IX lines 232–237.
48. Oxford 41–73.
49. Digby 130, 208.
50. Powell (1631).
51. Gurney 422; Simon (1959) 48.
52. Stuart 35.
53. Wright (1976) 187.
54. Fairholt 91.
55. Markham 39.
56. Fussell (1953) 66.

57. *Coriolanus* II ii 42; *Cymbeline* V v 177; *Comedy of Errors* III ii 96.
58. Fairholt 34.
59. Pritchard 13–18.
60. Platt C3, F4.
61. Platt 3.
62. May 171, 393, 143, 32, 127.
63. May 89, 120.
64. May 62, 239.

CHAPTER 13
BOILING

1. Fairholt xxxix.
2. Allan (1984) 156, fig. 71 no. 1663.
3. Harbottle & Emmison 133, fig. 22 no. 177.
4. Allan (1984) 171, fig. 85 no. 1970; McCarthy & Brooks nos. 398, 457–8; Pearce 56–58, nos. 134–168.
5. McCarthy & Brooks 448, fig. 280 no. 2185; Pearce 59, fig. 30 nos. 172–185.
6. Simon (1959) 50.
7. Bosworth *et.al.* 2.
8. Yorks. Arch. Soc. DD 121/36A/4.
9. Jansson 22–3.
10. Starkey (1998) nos. 1801–2.
11. See Butler & Green (2003).
12. Saxton 136.
13. *OED* 'Bishop' 5.
14. Morley & Gurney 90; Mary Rose Trust 82A 5102.
15. *OED* 'Flesh-fork' & 'Flesh-hook'.
16. Batho, 53.
17. Starkey (1998) nos. 1841, 1917.
18. Starkey (1998) no. 12862; Collins 223.
19. Ornsby 248.
20. Mary Rose Trust 82A 2340 & 81A 3277.
21. Tomlinson 483.
22. Heywood (1562) 39.
23. Tusser 256.
24. Clinton 54.
25. May 117, & Clinton 56.
26. Clinton 56.
27. Clinton 53.
28. May 118.
29. Clinton 72.
30. Dawson (1596) II 3.
31. Murrell (1623) no. 22.
32. May 30.
33. May 30.
34. Cooper 10.
35. May 15.
36. A.W. 10.
37. Ahmed 79.
38. Anon. (1588), 7, 15, 53; A.W. 11; Dawson (1596–7) II 6.
39. Clinton 52; Dawson (1596–7) I 121.
40. A.W. 4.
41. A.W. 4.
42. Anon. (1588) 7.
43. Murrell (1638) I 20.
44. Murrell (1615) 56.
45. A.W. 7–8.
46. Clinton 67.
47. Clinton 52.
48. Cooper 17.
49. A.W. 8; Dawson (1596–7) I 7.
50. May 73.
51. Murrell (1615) 54; Cooper 15, 3–4.
52. Herbert 63.
53. Campbell 433.
54. Wright (1983) 210.
55. Peachey (1992) 44.
56. Peachey (2009) 32.
57. Chambers 235.
58. Information from Prof. Peter Pope.
59. Juddery 14, 80.
60. E.g. May 347; Clinton 76.
61. Rabisha [191]; May 344.
62. May 359; Murrell (1615) 82.
63. May 346.
64. W.M. 68.
65. Peachey (2009) 60.
66. Cooper 32.
67. May 400.
68. Cooper 33; May 399.
69. Dawson (1596) II 62.
70. Dawson (1596) I 10.
71. May 401.
72. May 410.
73. Simon (1959) 45, 53.
74. Boorde 268; *OED* 'Porpoise'.
75. La Varenne 171–2.
76. HMC Hastings MS. I (1892) 392.
77. Stevenson 297.

78. Simon (1959) 63.
79. May 367–80.
80. Chandler 48; Hodgson 29.
81. Walton 100.
82. May 332; see also Walton 234.
83. Barker 14.
84. Barker 16.
85. Barker 19.
86. Lawson 63.
87. Galpin 292.
88. Clinton 80.
89. Buttes 'Artichoke'; *OED* 'Artichoke'.
90. Cooper 35.
91. *OED* 'Artichoke' (2).
92. May 448.
93. *OED* 'Asparagus'.
94. Buttes 'Sparaye'.
95. Boorde 268; Buttes 'Beanes'.
96. May 429.
97. May 429.
98. Buttes 'Colewort'.
99. Simon (1959 82.
100. Dawson (1596) II 7.
101. Elyot II 26.
102. Simon (1959) 25.
103. May 426; Buttes 'Carot'.
104. Murrell (1623) 39.
105. Simon (1959) 25.
106. *OED* 'Cabbage' (1).
107. Murrell (1623) 38.
108. Murrell (1623) 38.
109. Buttes 'Garlic'; *OED* 'Garlic' (2); *Coriolanus* 4–6–102.
110. *L & P.* Hen. VIII VI pt 2. 1457.
111. *Henry V* V. ii 24–6.
112. La Varenne 217–8, also 133, 137, 213.
113. Peachey (1992) 11, 6; La Varenne 186.
114. May 398.
115. Simon (1959) 26.
116. Adams 28.
117. Dawson (1596) II 57.
118. Dawson (1596) II 57.
119. May 426.
120. May 426.
121. La Varenne 187.
122. A.W. 30.
123. Clinton 38–9, 61.
124. *Merry Wives of Windsor* V. v. 19.
125. Act 3 scene 5.
126. Richardson & Isabell 51.
127. Cooper 36.
128. Buttes 'Spinache'.
129. A.W. 14; Dawson (1596) II 58.
130. May 426.
131. La Varenne 188.
132. Murrell (1623) 39.

CHAPTER 14
POTTAGES, STEWS AND SOUPS

1. May 115.
2. May 77–8, 93–4, etc.
3. May 117, 93, 118; Clinton 54.
4. *OED*. 'Hachy', 'Hash'.
5. May 81–3.
6. *OED* 'Hockpot', Hochpotch'.
7. Brears (2008) 282–6; Ahmed 65.
8. Murrell (1615) 59.
9. *OED* 'Cullis'.
10. Heath 9–10.
11. Ahmed 77.
12. Potter 83–95; Thick (2004) 145–7.
13. Clinton 54; May 117.
14. May 119.
15. May 119.
16. May 127.
17. Peachey (1992) 12
18. Murrell (1615) 66.
19. Dawson (1596) I 27.
20. May 59.
21. Dawson (1596) II 13.
22. Dawson (1596) I 6.
23. Murrell (1613) I 113.
24. Dawson (1596) I 27.
25. May 450–51.
26. May 81.
27. Platt A55.
28. Peachey (1992) 17 (see Dawson (1596) I 7).
29. Dawson (1596) I 7.
30. *The Good Hous-wives Treasurie.*
31. May 335.
32. May 331.
33. Dawson (1596) II 31.
34. Dawson (1596) II 27.
35. Simon (1959) 76.

36. A.W. 30.
37. May 420.
38. Markham 47.
39. May 41.
40. May 13.
41. May 420.
42. May 428.
43. May 422.
44. Brears (2008) 280; Thirsk 33.
45. Act 2. scene 1.
46. Thick 147.
47. May 66.
48. May 65–6.
49. May 83–4.

CHAPTER 15
PUDDINGS

1. *OED* 'Pudding'.
2. *Four Letters Confuted* (1593).
3. Nicolas 83,89.
4. May 190; A.W. 12; Cooper 148.
5. May 126; Dawson (1596) 10; Driver 109.
6. May 184.
7. *OED* 'Black Pudding'.
8. A.W. 12; see also May 26, 184; Clinton 69.
9. May 37.
10. *OED* 'Bolognian'; Thirsk 139.
11. Platt c.12.
12. May 36; Clinton 36; Thirsk 144.
13. La Varenne 14, 44.
14. *OED* 'Chitterlings', 'Andoille'; May 22, 183.
15. Murrell (1615) 39.
16. Rabisha 152.
17. *OED* 'Ising'.
18. May 22; Anon (1588) 59; Dawson (1596) I 16; Cooper 146.
19. A.W. (1591) 12b.
20. Murrell (1615) 39.
21. May 182–3.
22. May 186.
23. Cooper 139, 144.
24. Clinton 47.
25. May 25.
26. Peachey (1994) 13.
27. May 25.
28. MS Recipe book of Elizabeth Seton (1669) Private collection; Markham 178; Dawson (1596) II 54; Spurling 207.
29. Alnwick Castle Library, Press Mark 560.
30. *HO.* 438; Napier 120.
31. *OED* 'Bagpudding'.
32. Cooper 162; May 179.
33. May 187.
34. Murrell (1615) 37.
35. II. ii (1881) 35.
36. May 27.
37. A.W. 13b.
38. May 27.
39. A.W. 7.
40. Starkey nos. 1978 & 16586.
41. Markham 58.
42. Markham 58.

CHAPTER 16
ROASTING

1. La Varenne 45, 48–9, 75.
2. Ibid. 49, 77.
3. May 136–154; Rabisha 183–190.
4. Steer (1950) 71, 83.
5. Brears (1972) 52.
6. Adams 102.
7. Brears (1999) 127.
8. Markham 53.
9. *OED* 'Turnspit' 2.
10. Anon. (1825) II 7.
11. HMC Middleton 441.
12. Wright (1976) 197.
13. Wilson (1949) 286.
14. Brome 414.
15. Chambers I 490.
16. *OED* 'Turnspit'.
17. Mundy 11.
18. Wilkins 149.
19. Atkin, Carter & Evans fig. 60–62.
20. Juddery 38.
21. *OED* 'Jack'.
22. Chapman III 1.
23. Heywood 13.
24. Juddery 110; Ponsonby 51.
25. Spicksley 159, 213, 227.
26. Weston (2009) 14–26.
27. Ponsonby 51.
28. Levey 56; Brears (1972) 32, 114.
29. Vasey 53.

30. McCarthy & Brooks 393, 396, 411, 416, 418, 424, 425, 430.
31. Saxton 217.
32. Pinto 133 fig. 133.
33. Saxton 136.
34. Juddery 50.
35. Batho 53.
36. Heywood (1874) 26.
37. May 114; Boorde 271.
38. Digby (1910) 168.
39. A.W. 25; May 144.
40. *OED* 'Larding'
41. Clinton 70; May 113, 137, 139.
42. May 130.
43. Clinton 66; May 130, 147.
44. Markham 140; May 140.
45. Murrell (1638) II 94–5.
46. Markham 60.
47. A.W. 26; Markham 60; Peachey (1992) 41.
48. May 136; Markham 54.
49. Markham 54.
50. May 136.
51. Markham 59; May 144; A.W. 25; Rabisha 45; Ahmed 45.
52. May 113; W.M. I 96.
53. Clinton 70; May 138–9.
54. May 114.
55. W.M. I 77.
56. Clinton 44; Murrell (1615) 7.
57. Leeds University, Brotherton Library MS 621.
58. Murrell (1615) 78.
59. Murrell (1638) 94.
60. May 138; Clinton 70.
61. May 145–7.
62. Digby (1910) 168.
63. May 145.
64. La Varenne 67; May 149.
65. May 149–50.
66. May 150.
67. May 92.
68. A.W. 25; La Varenne 67.
69. May 151.
70. A.W. 7.
71. *Arch. Ael.* 2nd Series VI (1865) 17; Peachey (1992) 64.
72. Peachey (1992) 40.
73. Alnwick Castle Library, Press Mark 560.
74. Peachey (1992) 40; Dawson (1596) II 13.
75. Clinton 72.
76. Easton 27.
77. May 119.
78. May 119.
79. May 167.
80. Peachey (1993) 42.
81. Digby (1997) 144.
82. *OED* 'Toast'.
83. May 175–6.
84. Berry 127; Gage 36–7.
85. Juddery 51.
86. Allan no. 190; Somerset County Museum TTN CM 43/1997.

CHAPTER 17

FRYING

1. Alnwick Castle Library Press Mark 560 p. 49; Peachey (1992) 21.
2. Percy 12.
3. Atkin, Carter & Evans 38 fig. 41.
4. Mc Carthy & Brooks 406, 421, 462, 468.
5. Egan fig.20.
6. Batho 53.
7. Boorde 27.
8. *Henry VI pt. I.* II ii 82 & 87.
9. Dawson (1596) I 159.
10. Markham 43.
11. May 175.
12. Clinton 47; May 37.
13. Clinton 47; May 37, Peachey (1994) 13.
14. Weddell 112.
15. Ahmed 69.
16. Weddell 26, 102–3; May 168.
17. May 329, 336, 343, 346, etc.
18. May 335.
19. A.W. 36.
20. May 346.
21. May 430–34.
22. Peachey (1992) 47; A.W. 23.
23. Adams 62.
24. *OED* 'Tansy' 3; Walton; May 175.
25. May 174.
26. Percy 78.
27. Clinton 64.

28. Tusser 271.
29. Act II scene v.
30. Brand (1813) I 57.
31. Taylor (1636) 115.
32. Hone (1826) 246.
33. May 174.
34. W.M. I 55; see also Murrell (1615) 39.
35. Partridge (1885); May 171.
36. Brears (2008) 327.
37. May 173.
38. May 177.
39. Brears (2008) 329.
40. W.M. I 119. For a version covered with veal forcemeat see Murrell (1615) 40.
41. Ahmed 57; Murrell (1615) 41.
42. A.W. 23b.
43. Murrell (1615) 48.
44. Murrell (1615) 43.
45. Murrell (1615) 44.

CHAPTER 18

SALADS, PICKLES & SAUCES

1. Furnivall (1868) 152.
2. Harrison, in Lorwin 76.
3. O'Hara May 253.
4. Elyot 23–7.
5. Ahmed 63; A.W. 1, 2.
6. Lorwin 165.
7. Harrison, in Lorwin 76.
8. Buttes; Tusser; Thirsk 246, 253.
9. Markham 39.
10. Markham 40.
11. Clinton 64; also Digby (1997) 173.
12. Dawson (1596) II 29.
13. Dawson (1596) II 28.
14. May 162.
15. La Varenne 204.
16. Peachey (1994) 16; Platt (1600) A57; Murrell (1638) 38.
17. Rabisha [68]; Murrell (1638) 38.
18. Peachey (1994) 15.
19. La Varenne 203; Murrell (1638) 30; W.M. 26; Platt (1600) A36; Peachey (1994) 15.
20. Rabisha [68].
21. Markham 41.
22. Rabisha 2.
23. W.M. 123; Murrell (1638) 39.
24. May 162.
25. Dawson (1596) II 28.
26. Rabisha 179.
27. Murrell (1638) 116.
28. May 159.
29. May 158.
30. Markham 42.
31. Markham 42.
32. Bunyard 235.
33. Platt C 35.
34. Boorde 286; St Claire-Byrne (1949) 77.
35. Clinton 39.
36. A.W. 3.
37. Dawson (1596) I 26.
38. May 156.
39. Brears (1998) 74 no. 320.
40. *OED* 'Vinegar'.
41. May 155; Markham 81.
42. May 155.
43. *OED* 'Vinegar'.
44. Markham 81; May 158.
45. Markham 81, May 155.
46. May 155.
47. May 155.
48. Brears (1999) 62.
49. Smith, W., 254.
50. O'Hara-May 279.
51. 2 *Henry IV* II iv 242.
52. St Claire-Byrne 24.
53. May 156.
54. May 156.
55. Digby (1997) 162.
56. Digby (1997) 162.
57. Buttes 'Green Sauce'.
58. Drake 37.
59. May 154.
60. *OED* 'Sauce-alone'.
61. Peachey (1992) 63–4.
62. Peachey (1992) 63–4.
63. Markham 60.
64. Long 128.
65. Clinton 77.
66. Digby (1997 ed.) 160.

CHAPTER 19

PLANNING MEALS

1. Drummond & Wilbraham 27.

2. Ibid. 99.
3. *HO* 154.
4. Brome 362–6.
5. Drummond & Wilbraham 100, 74, 49.
6. Wilson (1949) 282.
7. Markham (1653), in Chambers I 96.
8. Fuller 106; Dekker, act 1 sc. 2.
9. Heywood (1961) 86.
10. Woodward 20, 26.
11. Wright (1976) 207.
12. Wilson (1949) 282.
13. Bryne 1–78.
14. Wilson (1949) 282.
15. *HO* 171.
16. *HO* 158.
17. *HO* 174.
18. *HO* 177.
19. *HO* 191.
20. Nichols (1788) 6.
21. Emmison (1964) 89–96.
22. Nichols (1828) 401.
23. Nichols (1828) 454.
24. Nichols (1828) 495.
25. Chamberlain II 69 note 13.
26. May, Introduction.
27. Dawson (2009) 224.
28. Skelton 101.
29. 5 Elizabeth Cap. 5.
30. Drummond & Wilbraham 64.
31. Ibid. 63–4.
32. 27 Elizabeth Cap. 18.
33. 35 Elizabeth Cap. 7.
34. Wright (1976) 133–4.
35. *HO* 175, 191.
36. Murrell (1638) 9.
37. Walford 159.
38. *Archaeologia* XXV (1834) 319.
39. Tusser 73.
40. May (intro.).
41. *OED* 'Christmas Pie'.
42. Chambers II 390.
43. *Archaeologia* XV (159).
44. Borg (2013) 193.
45. Bodleian Library, MS Eng. Hist. b. 208.
46. Jonson, *Works*, vol. VII 439, 445.
47. Henisch, 128.
48. Jonson, *Works*, vol. VII, 100.
49. See note 45 above.
50. Harland 1001.
51. *Henry VIII* V ii 10.
52. *HO* 128–9.
53. Smith (1883) 255–7.
54. Herrick (Hayward) 154.
55. May 234.
56. Pritchard 38.
57. Litten 152.
58. Brand (1849) 315–7.
59. Walker (1939) 424.
60. Hazlitt 261.
61. Robert Fletcher, *Christmas Day*, 1656.

CHAPTER 20
THE BUTTERY AND THE PANTRY

1. *HO* 76; Brears (1999) 157–60.
2. E.g. *HO* 215, 283; *Archaeologia* XVI (1806) 80–81.
3. Hope 129–30.
4. Brome 416–7.
5. *Twelfth Night* I i 66.
6. Hope 130.
7. Dawson (2009) 265–6.
8. Simon (1959) 38–41.
9. *OED* 'Sack' 1.
10. *OED* 'Muscatel', 'Bastard', 'Charneco'.
11. Harland 1110; Peachey (1992) 42–3, 47, 46.
12. *OED* 'Hippocras'.
13. A.W. 34.
14. Markham 70.
15. May 275.
16. May 275.
17. Peachey (1992) 38.
18. Boorde 254.
19. W.M. II 21; Digby (1997) 123.
20. Bunyard (1937) 260.
21. Ibid. 146.
22. Wright (1983) 129.
23. Digby (1997) 94.
24. May 423–5.
25. Davies 79–102.
26. Boorde 257.
27. Digby (1997) 288–90.
28. W.M. 94.
29. Gayre 91.
30. Bunyard (1937) 372.

31. Boorde 256.
32. *L & P* 1545 I 465 (10); *HO* 75; *OED* 'Bottle'.
33. Plat (1628 ed.) G 27–8.
34. Ibid. G. 32.
35. Bunyard (1937) 295.
36. Adams 138.
37. Cogan 1584, in Palmer 51; May 423–4.
38. Anon (1597) 26; see also May 423.
39. Herrick (Hayward) 115.
40. Palmer 137.
41. Dodsley V. 160.
42. Boorde 257.
43. Peachey (1992) 56.
44. Kaner 296, 2; Simon (1959) 51.
45. Fairholt XXXV–XXXVII.
46. Brome 390.
47. Tinniswood 65.
48. *Richard II* III iii 149.
49. Gardiner & Allen 451.
50. Gayre 146–9.
51. *Diary of Samuel Pepys* 27 Feb. 1660.
52. Gardiner & Allen 483.
53. Palmer 48.
54. Saxton 127.
55. *Archaeologia* XV, 159.
56. Carrington 76.
57. Pearce 90, 92, 96.
58. Brears (1971) 18–23; Spavold & Brown 181.
59. Draper & Griffith 37.
60. *OED* 'Posset'.
61. Percy 18.
62. Moorhouse (1970) 77, Gaimster 339–47.
63. *OED* 'Tankard'.
64. Gardiner & Allen 275, Fig 11 11.16.
65. HMC Rutland MS V (1905) 31.
66. *OED* 'Bombard'
67. Pearce 61, Figs. 32–34, nos. 207–237.
68. Mayes & Butler 222 Fig. 97 nos. 118–20.
69. Giustianino 193.
70. Moorhouse (1971) 63–7.
71. Allan (1984) 107.
72. Allan (1984) 107.
73. Gaimster 339–47.
74. Juddery 46, 8, 47.
75. Ormsby 265.
76. Boorde 261.
77. Herrick (Hayward) 195–6.
78. 2 *Henry IV*; Collier 127, *HO* 294.
79. *OED* 'Portpain'.
80. Brears (2003) 34.
81. Starkey (1998) 1807–9, 1814–5.
82. Ibid. 1805, 1807–8.
83. Ibid. 1794, 1804, 1806–7, 1831.
84. Thornton & Cowell 153.
85. Stevenson 294.
86. *EDD* 'Doubler'.
87. Hornsby 61.
88. Gardiner & Allen 424–5.
89. Saxton 134.
90. Gardiner & Allen 445.
91. Pearce 48 fig. 19 nos. 2–3, 5–6.
92. Levi 91 plate 7/1.1, 94 plate 7/7.
93. Mayes & Butler 218 no. 40; Spavold & Brown 99–105.
94. Pearce 38, 73 fig. 44 nos. 394–7; Moorhouse (1970) 49 fig. 11 32–3.
95. HMC Ancaster (1907) 452–3.
96. Levey 57.
97. Starkey (1998) 69.
98. Starkey (1998) 1376, 1384.
99. Starkey (1998) 1368.
100. Levey 60.
101. Starkey 1662, 1667, 1669, 1671.
102. Wade 263, 271.
103. Berry 142; Juddery 13, 52.
104. Bosworth 100.
105. Batho (1962) 121.
106. Gardiner & Allen 443–4.
107. Yorks. Arch. Soc. DD 12/36A. 23 Sept. 1609.
108. Winchester 146.
109. HMC Rutland IV (1905) 348.
110. *OED* 'Trencher' II; Hornsby 31.
111. Hornsby 38.
112. Starkey (1998) 1688, 1714, 1742–3.
113. Starkey (1998) 1694, 1700, 1710, 1718.
114. Starkey (1998) 10 943, 942, 1706, 15856.
115. *Camden Misc.* LXI (1854) 40; Nicholas (1827) 191.
116. Juddery 26, 74, 80; Bosworth 60, 101.
117. Pinto fig. 76.
118. *Gents. Mag.* (1797) 281.
119. Norwich, Strangers' Hall 435.76.94.

120. *Notes & Queries* XII (1855) 290.
121. British Museum 96. 8–7. 8.
122. V. & A. 6895.60.
123. *Gents. Mag.* (1794) 408–9.
124. Norwich, Strangers' Hall, 435.76.94.
125. Evan-Thomas 66.
126. Hornsby 36; Pearce 92–4.
127. Hornsby 38.
128. Starkey (1998) 1683–4, 1686, 1743–65.
129. Starkey (1998) 1754–6, 1762–3, 1751.
130. Starkey (1998) 1748–9.
131. Fairholt 329.
132. Dekker V (1631) 70; Dekker, Rowley, Ford II ii.
133. Wilson (1949) 285.
134. Jonson, *The Devil's an Ass* V v.
135. Ornsby 265.
136. Markham (1615) 91–104.
137. Peacock 133–4.
138. Ornsby 266.
139. Adams 328.
140. Juddery 62 & 24.
141. Starkey (1998) 1436–7.
142. Ibid. 17616–8, 1776, 17618–9.
143. Ibid. 11468, 11483.
144. Ibid. 11502–4; Ellis 24.
145. *OED* 'Cupboard'; Levey 52, 36; Ornesby 266.
146. Starkey (1998) 9874–5.
147. Ornsby 93; Gurney 474.
148. Herrick (Hayward) 97.
149. Worsley 108.
150. E.g. Levey 36, 47, 52.
151. Levey 24, 36.
152. Starkey 17218–33.
153. Simon (1959) 59.
154. Plat (1628) G2.
155. Plat (1628) G28.
156. Levey 60; Starkey (1998) 1803, 1810, 1912.
157. Starkey (1998) 156.
158. Ibid. 167.
159. Boorde 290.
160. Plat G31.
161. Boorde 290.
162. Pearce 40, 74 fig. 45 nos. 430–35, plate 5.
163. Ibid. 75 fig. 46 nos. 475–60.
164. *OED* 'Perfume' 1564–78.
165. Starkey (1998) 1929–30, 1935, 1952, 1972, 1979.
166. Ibid. 1983.
167. Levey 60; HMC Rutland IV (1905) 348.
168. Platt G29.
169. Boorde 302.
170. Ornsby 135, 94.
171. Adams 29, 64.
172. *OED* 'Juniper'; Ornsby 102.
173. Saxton 137; HMC IX Beaufort MS (1891) 18/7/1636; *OED* 'Voider'.
174. Fussell 69.
175. E.g. Ornsby 266.
176. Ornsby 42; Dawson (2009) 197.

CHAPTER 21

TABLE MANNERS

1. Brears *Traditional Food in Yorkshire* (2014).
2. Wilson (1949) 221, quoting William Harrison.
3. Furnivall (1868) 208, 221, 266.
4. Bryne (1949) 21–35.
5. Furnivall (1868) 229; Gray (1995) 251–2.
6. Haywood 203.
7. Furnivall (1868) 229–36.
8. Byrne (1949) 8–11.
9. Wright (1983) 222.

CHAPTER 22

DINING IN THE HALL

1. Brears (1972) 6.
2. Raine 222.
3. Levey 56.
4. Levey 27.
5. Brears (1972) 67.
6. Peacock 139.
7. Thornton 377 n. 6 & Thurley (1993) 243.
8. *L & P* 1527 no. 3197.
9. Hope
10. Percy 404.
11. Girouard (1987) 126–7.
12. Dunn 553.
13. Skelton 4.
14. Smith (1883) 254.
15. Hope 128.
16. Jonson, *Complete Poems* 97.
17. Hope 131.

18. Hope 128.
19. Hope 128.
20. Banks 333.
21. Skelton 6.
22. Dunn 165–6.
23. Banks 333; Hope 132.
24. Thurley (1993) 114.
25. *HO* 83–4.
26. Fairholt 38.
27. Brears (1999) 177.
28. Fairholt 40.
29. Ibid. xx.
30. Ibid. 47.
31. Ibid. 45.
32. Ibid. 46.
33. Ibid. 36–37.
34. Ibid. 56.
35. Ibid. 39.
36. Thurley (1993) 150.

CHAPTER 23
DINING IN THE CHAMBER

1. E.g. Brears (1972) 2.
2. *Yorks. Arch. Jnl.* XI (1890) 281.
3. Girouard (1987) 125–6.
4. Percy 404. (See also 139–40).
5. Levey 45–7, 55.
6. Percy 403.
7. Girouard (1987) 128–9.
8. Whateley 330.
9. HMC Rutland IV (1905) 284.
10. Smith (1883) 254.
11. Wilson (1949) 220.
12. Now at Temple Newsam House, Leeds; Brears (1972) 1–3.
13. Egan, figs. 22–23.
14. Leeds University, Brotherton Library MS 621 p. 160.
15. Knell 74, 77.
16. Starkey (1998) 9447, 9508.
17. Thornton 377 note 7.
18. Thornton 227.
19. Gardner 277.
20. Wilson (1949) 222–224.
21. Hope 125–134; Banks 315–389.
22. Hodkin 63.
23. *HO* 162–3.
24. *HO* 165–6.
25. *HO* 165–6.
26. Starkey (1998) 12248–59, 12387–91.
27. Grose & Astle II 184–206.
28. Thurley (1993) 136–9.
29. Williams (1937) 194.
30. Lorwin 189–190.
31. *Archaeologica* XV (1806) 79–80.
32. Pritchard 149.
33. Sherwood 15, 17, 21, 30.
34. Sherwood 70, 77, 85.
35. Sherwood 36, 41, 44.
36. Sherwood 146–7.
37. Sherwood 146–7.
38. Clinton 43.
39. Brome 69–79.
40. Gardner 90.
41. E2–3.
42. Fairholt 12.

CHAPTER 24
THE BANQUET

1. *OED* 'Voidee'.
2. *All is True* II i 101–2.
3. Thurley (1993) plan 2.
4. *Archaeologia* V. (1779) 434–35.
5. Stowe II 78 & 80.
6. Pritchard 150.
7. Harris, Orgel & Strong 118–20.
8. Groos 83.
9. *Archaeological Journal* CXVI 219.
10. *Gents. Mag.* CIII pt. 2 (1833) 393–4.
11. *English Heritage Research News* V (2006) 31, 27.
12. Girouard (1983) 153.
13. Girouard (1987) 154.
14. Hentzner 54–5.
15. Dodsley XI 366.
16. Nicholas 31.
17. Aiken 274.
18. North, Dudley, Lord North 105, 83.
19. Clinton 42.

CHAPTER 25
BANQUETING STUFF

1. Mintz 38, 45.
2. Drummond & Wilbraham 112.

3. Adams 49, 51, 57, 72, 78, 160.
4. *OED* 'Toothpick'.
5. Harland 1048.
6. Tomlinson 223.
7. Dawson (1596) c 7–8.
8. Smith (1883) 259.
9. Wilson (2006) 169–198.
10. Dyer 179.
11. Gage 236–7.
12. Tipping II 4.
13. Levey 30.
14. Gage 36–37.
15. Tomlinson 481–89.
16. Plat A47; Ruthven 20.
17. Elyot 23; Buttes 'Apples'; Boorde 284; 2 *Henry IV* V iii 1.
18. Berry 127; Peacock 147.
19. Frere 43; A.W. 31.
20. A.W. 32.
21. Byrne 70; Buttes C2.
22. *Richard II*, I v 29.
23. Anon. 1653.
24. Ruthven 17; A.W. 38; La Varenne 230–32.
25. Digby 212.
26. Buttes B6; Elyot 23; Boorde 283.
27. May 253; W.M. I 21; Dawson (1596) I 38.
28. Ruthven 19.
29. Ruthven 20; A.W. 35.
30. *OED* 'Currant' (2).
31. Digby 214.
32. Digby 215.
33. Boorde 285; Tusser 85; *OED* 'Damson'.
34. W.M. 35; Ruthven 6; May 235.
35. Elyot 20; Furnivall (1868) 166/18; Buttes, E.
36. Markham 75.
37. Boorde 212.
38. Elyot 21; Boorde 282.
39. Dawson (1596) I 39.
40. Ruthven 6.
41. Clinton 49.
42. Ruthven 193.
43. Plat 141; Ruthven 34; Brotherton MS 621.
44. Partridge.
45. Buttes, D1.
46. *As You Like It* III ii 125.
47. Buttes C3.
48. HMC Hastings MS I (1928) 364.
49. Smith (18) 256.
50. Plat A34.
51. Dawson (1596) I 37.
52. May 252.
53. Dawson (1596) II 76.
54. Boorde 284; Buttes C1.
55. Dawson (1596) II 597, 38.
56. Plat A50.
57. Partridge 57.
58. *Merry Wives of Windsor* I i 261; 2 *Henry IV* II iv 143.
59. Buttes C6.
60. Dawson (1596) II 71.
61. Ruthven 20; Plat A28.
62. Dawson (1596) 33; Plat A32.
63. May 278.
64. Boorde 282; Elyot 21.
65. Furnivall (1868) 9, 153.
66. May 254; W.M. II 3; Ruthven 10.
67. Ruthven 21; W.M. 74.
68. *OED* 'Strawberry'; Boorde 267; Lorwin 408.
69. Plat A51.
70. Haywood 65.
71. Plat B3–4.
72. Brotherton Library MS 621.
73. Ruthven 14.
74. Ruthven 7.
75. Dawson (1596) II 19.
76. *HO* 174.
77. A.W. 31.
78. Clinton 77.
79. Plat A29.
80. Dawson (1596) II 19.
81. W.M. I 32.
82. Rabisha 110.
83. May
84. Furnivall (1868) 358–60.
85. Grose & Astle III 244–6; Ashmole 606.
86. Dugdale 132.
87. Cavendish 68–71.
88. Nichols 20.
89. Nicholas 288–9.
90. Nicholas 105, 106, Borg 64.
91. Lorwin 388.

92. Nicholas 88.
93. Ibid. 53.
94. Dawson (1596) II 39.
95. Plat A13.
96. Plat A13.
97. Dawson (1596) II 39.
98. Plat A14.
99. Anon. (1611) 26.
100. Anon (1611) 33.
101. Plat A13.
102. Plat A24.
103. Plat A24.
104. Anon (1611); Dawson (1596) I 23.
105. Ruthven 22–3; Plat A34–5.
106. Ruthven 26.
107. Stevenson 285, 289.
108. HMC Ancaster (1907) 472.
109. Anon. (1600).
110. Plat A18.
111. W.M. II 69.
112. Murrell (1617) 85; Markham 73.
113. Plat A18.
114. A.W. 37.
115. Ruthven 195.
116. *OED* 'Gingerbread'.
117. Plat A22.
118. Plat A22; May 275; Markham 73.
119. *OED* 'Biscuit'.
120. Boorde 258.
121. Cruickshank 52.
122. Brears (2009) 314; *L & P* Henry VIII XX i. 1140, ii. 177, 430, 441.
123. Cruickshank 51.
124. May 274.
125. Plat 19.
126. Dawson (1596) 13.
127. Peachey (1993) 9.
128. Plat 20; May 274.
129. Peachey (1993) 11; Dawson (1596) I 12; May 276.
130. Peachey (1993) 10.
131. Peachey (1992) 61.
132. W.M. II 56.
133. Brears (2009) 95.
134. Brears (2009) 97.
135. Peachey (1993) 11.
136. Peachey (1993) 10; Weddell 65.
137. Dawson (1596) II
138. May 274.
139. Peachey (1993) 8.
140. Peachey (1993) 8; May 276, 273.
141. May 274.
142. *OED* 'Wafer'.
143. *HO* 118, 142, 167.
144. Plat A56.
145. Starkey (1998) 1097–1116.
146. Starkey (1991) 134.
147. Starkey (1998) 1118.
148. Saxton 127–8.
149. Markham 78.
150. Nicholas 282, 473.
151. Ellis II 48.

CHAPTER 26
FEASTS

1. Herrick (Hayward) 120.
2. Jonson, *Complete Poems* 99.
3. Tusser 70, 73, 76.
4. Dunn 142.
5. Hall, quoted in Strode 6–7.
6. Nicholas 19.
7. E.g. the MS describes a cupboard of 5 stages.
8. Bodleian library, Oxford, MS Eng. hist. b. 208.
9. Williams 158.
10. Hall 804–5.
11. Ashmole 589–603.
12. *Calendar of State Papers Venetian* III 400.
13. Ibid. 32–4.
14. Hall 722–724; *L & P* 18 Henry VIII 967–9, 1097–8; 19 Henry VIII 1390–92; *Calendar of State Papers Venetian* IV 2; Starkey (1991) 64–7.

CHAPTER 27
THE END OF AN ERA

1. Sherwood 35–6.
2. Hall 597.
3. May (14).
4. Stone 256.
5. Verney 38.

Bibliography

Adair, J., *By the Sword Divided* (2000).
Adams, S., *Household Accounts and Disbursement Books of Robert Dudley, Earl of Leicester, 1558–1561, 1584–1586*, Camden Soc. 5th Series VI (Cambridge 1995).
Ahmed, A. (ed.), *A Proper Newe Booke of Cokerye* (1545) (1557–8 ed.) (Cambridge 2002).
Aiken, L., *Memoirs of the Court of Queen Elizabeth* (1819).
Allan, J.P., *Medieval and Post Medieval Finds from Exeter* (Exeter 1984).
———, 'The Excavation of a Brewhouse at Buckland Abbey in 2005', *Proc. Devon Arch. Soc.* LXIV (2006) 241–265.
Ambler, L., *Old Halls & Manor Houses of Yorkshire* (1913).
Anon., *The Good Huswifes Handmaide to the Kitchen* (1588) (1594 ed. reprinted Bristol 1992).
———, *The Second Part of the Good Hus-wifes Jewell* (1597).
———, *The Treasurie of Hidden Secrets* (1600).
———, *A Closet for Ladies and Gentlewomen* (1611).
———, 'A Survey of Nonsuch House and Park … 1650', *Archaeologia* V (1779) 429–39.
———, *A Collection of Ordinances and Regulations for the Government of the Royal Household* (1790)
———, *English Homes* (1927).
Antrobus, A., 'Luminescence Dating of Brick Chimneys', *Vernacular Architecture* XXXV (2004) 21–31.
Arnold, H.G., '17–19 London Street, Reading', *Trans. Ancient Monuments Society* NS XXVI (1982) 63–7.
Arnold, J., 'A Cook's Inventory of 1576', *Petits Propos Culinaires* 82 (Totnes 2007) 104–8.
Ashdown, J., '17th century Pottery from Wrotham, Kent', *Kent Archaeological Review* XIV (1968) 13–116.
Ashmole, E., *The Institutions, Laws & Ceremonies of the Most Noble Order of the Garter* (1672).
Aubrey, J., *Remains of Gentilism and Judaism* (1687).
A.W., *A Book of Cookrye* (1591).
Banks, Sir J., 'A Breviate touching Order and Governments of a Nobleman's House &c.', *Archaeologia* XIII (1800) 315–389.
Barker, T., *Barker's Delight, or The Art of Angling* (1859).
Barnwell, P, S., & Airs, M., *Houses & the Hearth Tax* (York 2006).
Barrington, D., 'On the Progress of Gardening', *Archaeologia VII (1785) 113–130.*
Batho, G., 'Notes & Documents on Petworth House 1574–1632', *Sussex Arch. Coll.* XCVI (1959) 108–134.
———, *Household Papers of Henry Percy, 9th Earl of Northumberland*, Camden Soc. 3rd series CXIII (1962).
Bennett, R., & Elton, J., *History of Corn Milling* (1898).
Berry, E.K., *Swaledale Wills & Inventories 1522–1600*, Yorks. Record Series CLII (Leeds 1998).
Bickerdyke, J., *Curiosities of Ale and Beer* (n.d.).

Binns, J. (ed.), *The Memoirs and Memorials of Sir Hugh Cholmley of Whitby 1699–1657*, Yorks. Record Series CLIII (Leeds & Woodbridge 1997–8).
Blackman, M.E. (ed.), *Ashley House Building Accounts 1602–1607*, Surrey Record Society XXIX (Guildford 1977).
Blencowe, R.W., 'Extracts from the Journal & Accounts Book of the Rev. Giles Moor 1655–1679', *Sussex Arch. Coll.* I (1848) 65–127.
Boorde, A., *The fyrst boke of the Introduction of Knowledge made by Andrew Borde of physycke doctor: a compendyous regyment or a dyetary of helth made in Mountpyllier...* (1542) Furnivall, F.J. (ed.), EETS extra series 10 (1870).
Borg, A., *A History of the Worshipful Company of Cooks* (2011)
———, 'John Smythson, Master Cook to Queen Elizabeth I', *Jnl. Brit. Arch. Assoc.* CLXVI (2013) 189–198.
Bosworth, J., Hudson, P., Johnson, M., & Shillitoe, D., *The Middleton Papers*, Yorks. Record Series CLXI (Leeds & Woodbridge 2010).
Brand, J., *Observations on the Popular Antiquities of Great Britain* (1849).
Brears, P., 'Excavations at Potovens', *Post-Medieval Archaeology* I (1967) 3–43.
———, 'An early sixteenth-century building in the Market Place, Pontefract', *Pontefract. Arch. J.* (1968) 6–9.
———, *English Country Pottery* (Newton Abbot 1971).
———, 'Oatcake in the West Riding', *Folk Life* XII (Leeds 1974) 55–59.
———, 'Shibden Hall, Halifax', *Old West Riding* II (Huddersfield 1982) 15–21.
———, *The Gentlewoman's Kitchen* (Wakefield 1984).
———, *Traditional Food in Yorkshire* (Edinburgh 1987).
———, *The Old Devon Farmhouse* (Tiverton 1998).
———, *Ryedale Recipes* (Hutton-le-Hole 1998).
———, *All the King's Cooks* (1999).
———, *The Compleat Housekeeper* (Wakefield 2000).
———, *Cooking & Dining in Medieval England* (Totnes 2008).
———, *Traditional Food in Shropshire* (Ludlow 2009).
———, 'Food & Dining in Henry's Court' & 'To feed the King's Men', in Rimer, G., Richard, T. & Cooper, J.P.D. (eds.) *Henry VIII the Arms & the Man* (2009).
———, *Jellies & Their Moulds* (Totnes 2010).
Breton, Nicholas, *Fantasticks: seruing for a perpetuale Prognostication, etc.* (1626)
Brewer, S.J. (ed.), *Letters & Papers Foreign & Domestic of the Reign of Henry VIII* (1861–3).
Broadbent, R.J., 'A Masque at Knowsley', *Transactions of the Historic Society of Lancashire & Cheshire*, LXXVII (1883), 5.
Brome, R., *The Dramatic Works of Richard Brome* (1873).
Brooks, C., 'Aspects of Sugar Refining from the 16th to the 19th century', *Post-Med. Archaeology* XVII (1983) 1–14.
Brown, P. (ed.), *British Cutlery, An Illustrated History of Design, Evolution & Use.* (York 2001).
Brunner, H., & Major, J.K., 'Water Raising by Animal Power', *Industrial History* IX no.2 (1972) 117–151.
Bunyard, E. & L., *The Epicure's Companion* (1937).
Butler, R., & Green, C., *English Bronze Cooking Vessels & their Founders 1350–1830* (Honiton 2003).
Buttes, Henry, *Dyets Dry Dinner* (1599).
Byrne, M. St.C. (ed.), *The Elizabethan Home* (1949).

Camden, W., *Chronicles of the Friars* (1556).
Campbell, J., *The English Yeoman under Elizabeth and the Early Stuarts* (New Haven 1942).
Carrington, W.A., 'Selections from the Steward's Accounts Preserved at Haddon Hall … 1549–1564', *Jnl. Derbys. Arch. & Nat. Hist. Soc.* XVI (Derby 1894) 64–85.
Cartwright, J.J., 'Inventory … of Sir Cotton Gargrave of Nostell 1588', *Yorks. Arch. Jnl.* XI (1890) 279–286.
Cavendish, G., *The Life of Cardinal Wolsey* (1893) (1962 ed.).
Chamberlain. J., *The Letters of John Chamberlain* (McClure, N.E., ed, Philadelphia 1939).
Chambers, R., *The Book of Days* (1866).
Chandler, J., *Travels through Stuart Britain* (Stroud 1999).
Chapman, George, *The Gentleman Usher* (1606).
Chappell, William, *Popular Music of the Olden Time: a Collection of ancient Songs, Ballads, and Dance Tunes…*, vol. I (1855).
Charles, A.M., 'Mrs. Herbert's Kitchen Book', *English Literary Renaissance* 4 No. 1 (1974).
Charsley, S.R., *Wedding Cakes & Cultural History* (1992).
Chattle, G.H., & Leach, P., *Kirkby Hall* (1986).
Chinnery, V., *Oak Furniture, The British Tradition* (Woodbridge 1979).
Chope, R.P., *Devon & Cornwall Notes & Queries* XI (Exeter 1920–21).
Clinton, D. (ed.), *The Court and Kitchen of Elizabeth … Cromwell, 1664* (Peterborough 1983).
Cogan, T., *The Haven of Health* (1584) (1636 ed.).
Coleman-Smith, R., 'Excavations in the Donyatt Potteries Site', *Post-Med. Arch.* XXXVI (2002) 118–172.
Collier, J.P. (ed.), *The Egerton Papers*, Camden Soc. XII (1840) 340–357.
———, *Trevelyan Papers Prior to A.D. 1588*, Camden Soc. LXVII (1857), LXXXIV (1863).
Collins, F., *Wills & Administrations from Knaresborough Court Rolls I & II*, Surtees Soc. CIV (1902) & CX (1904).
Compton, W.B., *History of the Comptons of Compton Wynyates* (1930).
Cruickshank, C., *Henry VIII and the Invasion of France* (Stroud 1990).
Davies, S., 'Cider & Perry in the 17th Century', in Wilson, C.A., *Liquid Nourishment* (Edinburgh 1993).
Dawson, M., *Plenti and Grase* (Totnes 2009).
Dawson, T., *The Good Huswifes Jewell* (1596–7).
Day, I., 'Further Musings on Syllabub', *Petits Propos Culinaires* 53 (1996) 33–44.
Dekker, Thomas, Rowley, William and Ford, John, *The Witch of Edmonton* (1621).
Digby, Sir K., *The Closet of Sir Kenelm Digby Opened* (1669) (Reprinted 1997).
Dodd, D., *Montacute House* (1988).
Dodsley, R. (ed.), *A Select Collection of Old Plays* (1825–27).
Donno, E.S., *An Elizabethan in 1582* (1976).
Draper, J., & Copeland-Griffiths, P., *Dorset County Polling* (Marlborough 2002).
Drummond, J.C., & Wilbraham, A., *The Englishman's Food* (1957).
Drury, P.J. et. al., *Audley End* (1991).
Dugdale, William, *Origines Juridiciales, or Historical Memorials of English Laws…* (1666)
Dunn, E.C. (ed.) *Eight Famous Elizabethan Plays* (New York 1932).
Easton, T., 'Twelfth Night and the Lord of Misrule', *Weald & Downland Open Air Museum* (Autumn 2005) 27.
Egan, G., *Playthings from the Past* (Kensington 1996).
Ellis, G., *Specimens of the Early English Poets* (1811).

Elyot, T., *The Castel of Helth* (1547).
Emmison, F.G., *Tudor Food & Pastimes* (1964).
Evan-Thomas, O., *Domestic Utensils of Wood* (1937).
Evans, J., 'Account of the Expenses incurred at the Wedding of Mr. More of Losely, in 1517', *Archaeologia* 36 (1855) 33–52.
Fairholt, E.W. (ed.), 'The Cytizen and Uplondyshmen', *Percy Society* XXXI (London 1848).
Faulkener, P.A., *Bolsover Castle* (1988).
Fuller, T., *The Holy State* (1642).
Furnivall, F.J. (ed.), *Ballads from Manuscripts*, Ballad Society (1868–73).
———, *Early English Meals & Manners*, Early English Text Society XXXII (1868).
Fussell, G.E. & K.R., *The English Countrywoman* (1953).
Gage, J., *The History & Antiquities of Hengrave in Suffolk* (1822).
Gaimster, D., 'The Supply of Rhenish Stoneware to London, 1350–1600', *The London Archaeologist* V no. 13 (1987) 339.
Galpin, F.W., 'Household Papers of Sir John Barrington', *Trans. Essex. Arch. Soc.* New Series XIII (Colchester 1945) 280–297.
Gardiner, J., & Allen, M.J., *Before the Mast: Life Aboard the Mary Rose* (Portsmouth 2005).
Gardner, H., *The Oxford Book of English Verse 1250–1950* (Oxford 1972).
Garfitt, G. (ed.), *Ben Jonson. The Complete Poems* (Harmondsworth 1975).
Gascoigne, G., *Poems* (1575).
Gayre, G.R., *Wassail! In Mazers of Mead* (1948).
Giles, C., *Rural Houses of West Yorkshire 1400–1830* (1986).
Girouard, M., 'The Smythson Collection of the Royal Institute of British Architects', *Architectural History* V (1962).
———, *Life in the English Country House* (New Haven & London 1978).
———, *Robert Smythson & the Elizabethan Country House* (New Haven & London 1983).
———, *A Country House Companion* (New Haven & London 1987).
———, *Hardwick Hall* (1989).
Giustianino, S., *Four Years in the Court of Henry VIII* (1854).
Goodall, I., 'Privacy, Display and Over Extension; Walter Strickland's Rebuilding of Sizergh', *Antiquaries Journal* LXXXII (2002) 197–245.
Googe, B., *Heresbach's Husbandry* (1586) III.
Gordon Slade, Harry, *Berry Pomeroy Castle* (1990).
Grant, A., *North Devon Pottery: The Seventeenth Century* (Exeter 1983).
Gray, T., *Devon Household Accounts*, vol. I (Exeter 1995), vol. II (Exeter 1996).
Green, Lady E., *The Old Hall at Heath* (Wakefield 1903).
Greene, R., *A Quip for an Upstart Courtier* (1592).
Groos, G.W., *The Diary of Baron Waldstein* (1981).
Grose, F., & Astle, T., *The Antiquarian Repertory* (1808).
Gunter, R.T., *The Architecture of Sir Roger Pratt* (Oxford 1928).
Gurney, D., 'Extracts from the Household & Privy Purse Accounts of the Lestranges of Hunstanton from AD 1519 to AD 1578', *Archaeologia* XXV (1834) 411–569.
Hall, E., *Hall's Chronicle Containing the History of England* (1809).
Hall, R. de Z., 'A Preliminary Catalogue of Curing Chambers in Somerset', *Somerset Arch. & Nat. Hist.*, CXV (1971) 45–7.
Harbottle, B., & Emmison, B.A., 'An Excavation in the Castle Ditch, Newcastle-upon-Tyne 1974–6', *Archaeologia Aeliana* 5th Series IX 1 (1981) 75–250.

Harris, J., Orgel, S., & Strong, R., *The King's Arcadias Inigo Jones and the Stuart Courts* (1973).
Harris, R., *Weald & Downland Open Air Museum Guidebook* (Chichester 1999).
Harrison, B., & Hutton, B., *Vernacular Houses in North Yorkshire & Cleveland* (Edinburgh 1984).
Harrison, J.K., *Eight Centuries of Milling in North East Yorkshire* (2001).
Harrison, M., *The Kitchen in History* (1972).
Harrison, William, *An historicall description of the Islande of Britayne, etc.* In Holinshed (R.) *The Firste volume of the Chronicles of England, etc.* (1587, first published 1577)
Haworth, J., *Lodge Park* (2002).
Hazlitt, C., *Popular Antiquities of Great Britain* (1870).
Heal, F., *Hospitality in Early Modern England* (Oxford 1990).
Henisch, B.A., *Cakes & Characters* (1984).
Hentzner, P., *A Journey into England* (Walpole, H., ed.) (1757).
Herbert, E., *Autobiography of Lord Herbert of Cherburg* (1870).
Herrick, Robert, *Poems from Hesperides and Noble Numbers*, John Hayward ed. (Harmondsworth 1961).
Heywood, John, *Five Hundred Epigrams* (1562).
Heywood, T., *The Dramatic Works of Thomas Heywood* (1874).
Hodgkin, J., 'Tearmes of a Kerver'. *Trans. Philological Soc.* (1915) 52–94.
Hodgson, J.C. (ed.), *The Journal of Sir William Brereton 1635*, Surtees Soc. CXXIV (Durham 1914).
Hone, W., *The Everyday Book* (1826).
———, *The Year Book* (1832).
Hope, Sir W. St.J., *Cowdray & Easebourne Priory* (1919).
Hornsby, P.R.G., Weinstein, R., Homer, R.F., *Pewter; A Celebration of the Craft* (1990).
Howard, M., *The Early Tudor Country House* (1987).
Hurst, J.G., Rahtz, P.A., Wrathmell, S. (eds.), *Wharram: a Study of Settlement on the Yorkshire Wolds* VI (York 1989).
Hurst, M., 'Nostril Chimney Stacks in Essex', *V.A.G. Newsletter* LXII (2012) 26–7.
I.M., *A Health to the Gentlemanly Profession of Servingmen* (1598).
Jansson, M., *Two Diaries of the Long Parliament* (Gloucester 1984).
Jonson, Ben., *The Complete Poems*, G. Parfitt, ed. (Harmondsworth 1975).
———, *Works*, Herford, C.H., Simpson, P. & E., eds., 11 vols. (Oxford 1925–52, 1971 ed.).
Juddery, T.Z., *Exeter Orphan's Court Inventories 1560–1571* (Exeter 1990).
Kaner, J. (ed.), *Goods and Chattels 1552–1640* (Hull 1994).
Kingsford, C.L., 'Exeter House, formerly Leicester House', *Archaeologia* LXXIII (1923).
———, 'On some London Houses of the early Tudor Period', *Archaeologia* LXXI (1921) 17–54.
Kirkland, J., *The Modern Baker, Confectioner & Caterer* (1907).
Knell, D., 'Tudor Furniture from the Mary Rose', *Regional Furniture* XI (1997) 62–79.
La Varenne, François Pierre de, *The French Cook* (translated by I.D.G., 1653) (Lewes 2001).
Lawson, W., *The Country Housewife's Garden* (1617) (1983 ed.).
Levi, J., *Treen for the Table* (Woodbridge 1989).
Lewer, H.W. (ed.), *The Book of Simples* (1910).
Litton, J., *The English Way of Death* (1991).
Lloyd, C., & Thurley, S., *Henry VIII, Images of a Tudor King* (1990).
Loades, D., *The Tudor Court* (1986).
Long, C.E. (ed.), *Diary of the Marches of the Royal Army by Edward Symmonds*, Camden Soc. XXIV (1859).

Lorwin, M., *Dining with William Shakespeare* (New York 1976).
Lydgate, J., *Stans puer ad mensam* (1476) (1990 ed.).
McCarthy, M.R., & Brooks, C.M., *Medieval Pottery in Britain AD 900–1600* (Leicester 1988).
Maguire, A., & Gomme, A., 'Who needs Two Kitchens?', *Architectural History* XXXVIII (1995) 58–68.
Markham, G., *The English Hus-wife* (1615).
———, *Farewell to Husbandry* (1653).
Markland, J.H., 'Instructions by Henry Percy, ninth Earl of Northumberland', *Archaeologia* XXVII (1837) 306–344.
Marshall, D., *The English Domestic Servant in History* (1949).
Martin, D. & B., 'Detached Kitchens in Eastern Sussex', *Vernacular Architecture* XXVIII (1997) 85–91.
———, 'Detached Kitchens or Adjoining Houses? a Response', *ibid.* XXXII (2001) 20–33.
Massinger, P., *A New Way to Pay Old Debts* (1625).
May, R., *The Accomplisht Cook* (1660) (1685 ed., reprinted Totnes 1994).
Mayes, P., & Butler, L., *Sandal Castle Excavations 1964–1973* (Wakefield 1983).
Meades, D.M. (ed.), *The Diary of Lady Margaret Hoby* (1930).
Minet, W., 'A Steward's Accounts at Hadham Hall 1628–1629', *Trans. Essex Arch. Soc.* XV (Colchester 1921) 145.
Mintz, S.W., *Sweetness and Power* (New York 1985).
Moorhouse, S., 'Finds from Basing House', *Post-Med. Arch.* IV (1970–71) 31–91; V (1971) 35–76
———, & Roberts, I., *Wrenthorpe Pottery* (Wakefield 1992).
Morgan, B., & Brears, P., *Rockingham Castle* (Derby 2005).
Morley, B., & Gurney, D., 'Castle Rising, Norfolk', *East Anglian Archaeology* LXXXI (Norwich 1997).
Mountford, A.J., & Celoria, F., 'Some Examples of Sources', *Journal of Ceramic History* I (1968).
Muffet, Thomas, *Health's Improvement* (1655).
Murrell, J., *A New Booke of Cookrie* (1615).
———, *Murrells's Two Books of Cookrie and Carving* (1638 ed.).
Musgrave, Sir J.C., 'Extract from a MS Book of Accounts … [of] Chevalier Jeane Franklin au Wilsden (1624)', *Archaeologia* XV (1806) 157–163.
Napier, A., *A Noble Boke of Cookry* (1882).
National Trust, *Lacock Abbey* (1997).
Nef, J.U., *The Rise of the British Coal Industry* (1932).
Nicholas, N.H., *Privy Purse Expenses of Elizabeth of York* (1830).
Nichols, J., *The Progresses and Public Processions of Queen Elizabeth* (1778).
———, *The Progresses, Processions and Magnificent Festivities of King James the First* (1828).
Nichols, J.G. (ed.), *The Diary of Henry Machin*, Camden Soc. XLII (1848).
North, Dudley, Lord North, *Forest of Varieties* (1645).
Nott, J., *The Cook's Dictionary* (1726).
O'Hara-May, J., *Elizabethan Dyetary of Health* (Lawrence, Kansas, 1977).
Ornsby, G. (ed.), *The Howard Household Book*, Surtees Soc. LXVIII (Durham 1878).
Owen, G., *The Description of Pembrokeshire* (1693) (1891 ed.).
Oxford, A.W., *Notes from a Collector's Catalogue* (1909).
Palmer, K., *A Taste of Ale* (Lecklade 2000).
Peachey, S. (ed.), *The Good Huswifes Handmaide for the Kitchen* (1588) (Bristol 1992).

———, *The Tippler's Guide to the mid 17th Century* (Bristol 1992).
———, *Maritime Fish and Fishing 1580–1660* (Bristol 1992).
Peacock, E., 'Inventories made for Sir William and Sir Thomas Fairfax, Knights', *Archaeologia* XLVIII (1884) 121–156.
Pearce, J., *Border Wares* (1992).
Pearson, S., *Rural Houses of the Lancashire Pennines 1560–1760* (1985).
Percy, T. (ed.), *The Regulations and Establishment of the Household of Henry Algernon Percy, the fifth Earl of Northumberland at his Castles of Wressle and Leconfield in Yorkshire Begun anno domini MDXII (The Northumberland Household Book)* (1905 ed.).
Pinto, E.H., *Treen & other Wooden Bygones* (1969).
Plat, Sir H., *Delights for Ladies* (1600) (1628 ed. reprinted Brighton 2002).
Platter, T., *Thomas Platters des Jungeren Englandfaht in Jahr* (1598).
Ponsford, C.N., *Time in Exeter* (Exeter 1978).
Potter, D., 'English Portable Soup Receipts *c.* 1600–1750', *Petits Propos Culinaires* 76 (Totnes 2004). 82–95.
Pounds, N.J.G., 'Long Melford Hall', *Archaeological Journal* CIL (1992) 43–5.
Powell, W., *Tom of all Trades, or the Plain Pathway to Preferment* (1631).
Pritchard, R.E., *Shakespeare's England* (Stroud 1999).
Rabisha, W., *The Whole Body of Cookery Dissected* (1661) (reprinted Totnes 2003).
Raine, J., *Wills and Inventories from the Archdeaconry of Richmond* Surtees Soc. XXVI (Durham 1853).
Richardson, L.A., & Isabell, J.R., 'Joseph Cooper, Chief Cook to Charles I', *Petits Propos Culinaires* 18 (1984).
Robins, F.W., *The Story of Water Supply* (Oxford 1946).
Rowell, C., Moore, C., & Strachey, N., *Ham House* (1995).
Rowntree, A., *The History of Scarborough* (1931).
Ruthven, Lord Patrick (attrib.), *The Ladies Cabinet Opened* (1639) republished as *The Ladies Cabinet Enlarged and Opened* (1654).
Ryan, P., 'The Buildings of Rural Ingatestone, Essex, 1556–1601', *Vernacular Architecture* 31 (2000) 11–25.
Ryder, P.F., 'Oxspring Lodge', *Post-Medieval Archaeology* IXX (1985) 49–62.
Salaman, R.N., *The History & Influence of the Potato* (Cambridge 1949).
Sandys, W. (ed.), 'Inventory of Bishop Parker's Goods (1577)', *Archaeologia* XXX (1842) 19–28.
Sarsby, J., 'Butter-making the Devonshire Way', *Country Origins* (Nairn, Winter 1995) 19–23.
Saxton, E.B., 'A Speke Inventory of 1624', *Trans. Hist. Soc. Lancs. & Chesh.* XCVII (1946) 107–143.
Sherwood, Roy, *The Court of Oliver Cromwell* (Cambridge 1989).
Simon, A.L., *A Concise Encyclopaedia of Gastronomy* (1944).
———, *The Star Chamber Dinner Accounts* (1964)
———, *Wine in Shakespeare's Days & Shakespeare's Ways* (1964).
Skelton, John, *Poems*, R.S. Kinsman, ed. (Oxford 1969).
Smith, B.S., *A History of Malvern* (Leicester 1964).
Smith, W., *Old Yorkshire* (1883).
Spurling, H., *Elinor Fettiplace's Receipt Book* (1998).
Spavold, J., & Brown, S., *Ticknall Pots & Potters* (Ashbourne 2005).
Spence, R., *Londesborough House and its Community* [Hull? 2005].

Spicksley, J.M. (ed.), *The Business and Household Accounts of Joyce Jeffreys* (Oxford 2012).

Stallybrass, B., 'Bess of Hardwick's Building Accounts', *Archaeologia* LXIV (1913).

Starkey, D. (ed.), *The Inventory of King Henry VIII* (1998).

———, *Henry VIII. A European Court in Europe* (1991).

Stell, C., & Hampson, L. (eds.), *Probate Inventories of the Diocese of York 1350–1500* (York n.d.).

Stevenson, W. (ed.), 'Extracts from ... The Booke of the houshold Charges and other Paiments laid out by Lord North (1575)', *Archaeologia* IXX (1819) 283–307.

Stone, L., *The Crisis of the Aristocracy 1558–1641* (Oxford 1967).

Stow, J., *A Survey of London* (1598) (1908 ed.)

Strode, W., *Old Christmas* (n.d.).

Stuart, D.M., *The English Abigail* (1946).

Tavener, R., *Proverbs or Adagies ...* (1552).

Taylor, J., *Works* (1636).

Taylor, J.E., Jerome, D.A., & Allnut, A.G., 'Petworth Water Supply', *Sussex Industrial History* IX (1979).

Thick, M., 'Portable Soup', *Petits Propos Culinaires* 77 (2004) 145–7.

Thirsk, J., *Food in Early Modern England* (2007).

Thornton, D., & Cowell, M., 'The Armada Service; a set of Late Tudor Dining Silver', *Antiquaries Journal* LXXVI (1996) 153–180.

Thornton, P., *Seventeenth Century Interior Decoration in England, France & Holland* (New Haven & London 1983).

Thurley, S., 'The Sixteenth Century Kitchens at Hampton Court', *Jnl. Brit. Arch. Assoc.* CXLIII (1990) 1–28.

———, *The Royal Palaces of Tudor England* (New Haven & London 1993).

Tibbles, A.J., *Speke Hall* (1982).

Tinniswood, A., *A Life in the English Country Cottage* (1997).

Tipping, A., *English Homes* (1927).

Tomlinson, R. (trans. and revised), *Medical Dispensatory* (1657).

Tomlinson, W.W., *Life in Northumberland during the sixteenth century* (n.d.).

Turner, R., 'A Surfeit of Lampreys', *Archaeology of the Severn Estuary* XVII (Reading 2006) 161–168.

Tusser, T., *Five Hundred Points of Good Husbandry* (1557) (1812 ed.).

Vasey, D.G., *Probate Inventories of Lichfield & District 1568–1680* (Stafford 1969).

Verney, Sir H., *The Verneys of Claydon* (1968).

Wade, J.F. (ed.), *Customs Accounts of Newcastle upon Tyne 1454–1500*, Surtees Soc. CCII (Durham 1995).

Walford, C., 'Early Laws and Customs in Great Britain Regarding Food', *Trans. Royal Hist. Soc.* VIII (1880) 70–163.

Walker, J., 'Detached Kitchens', *Vernacular Architecture* XXXI (2000) 75–7.

Walker, J.W., *Wakefield, its History and its People* (Wakefield 1939).

Walton, I., *The Compleat Angler* (1653) (1948 ed.).

Warner, R., *Antiquitates Culinariae* (1791).

Waterhouse, R., 'Smoking Chambers in Devon', *Devon Buildings Group* XIV (1996) 25–31.

Weddell, G. (ed.), *Arcana Fairfaxiana* (Newcastle upon Tyne 1890).

Weston, A., 'English Roasting Jacks Part I', *Jnl. Ant. Metalwork Soc.* XVII (2009) 14–26.

Whateley, R. (ed.), *Bacon's Essays* (1899 ed.).

White, I., *Feeding the City, York* (Totnes 2000).

Wilkins, D., *Magnae Britannae et Hibernae Concilia* (1737).
Williams, C. (ed.), *Thomas Platter's Travels in England* (1937).
Williams, C.H., *English Historical Documents V 1485–1558* (1967).
Williams, E.H.D., 'Corn Drying Kilns', *Somerset Arch. & Nat. Hist.* CXVI (1972) 101–3 also CXX (1976) 57–61, & CXXI (1978) 53–5.
Wilson, C.A., *Food and Drink in Britain* (1976 ed.).
———, *Water of Life, A History of Wine-distilling and Spirits* (Totnes 2006).
———, 'The French Connection', I & II, *Petits Propos Culinaires* 2 (1979) 10–17, IV (1980) 8–20.
Wilson, J.D., *Life in Shakespeare's England* (Harmondsworth 1949 ed.).
Winchester, B., *Tudor Family Portrait* (1955).
W.M., *The Compleat Cook and Queen's Delight* (1655) (1661 ed.).
Woodfield, C., 'Finds from the Free Grammar School at the Whitefriars, Coventry, c. 1545–c. 1557/8. *Post-Med. Arch.* XV (1981) 81–159.
Woodfield, P., 'Yellow Glazed Wares of the Seventeenth Century', *Trans. Birmingham Arch. Soc.* LXXXI (Oxford 1966) 78–87.
Woodward, D. (ed.), *The Farming and Memorandum Book of Henry Best of Elmswell* (Oxford 1984).
Worsley, L., *Cavalier* (2007).
Wotton, Sir H., *The Ground Rules of Architecture* (1624).
Wrathmell, S., *Wharram, A Study of Settlement on the Yorkshire Wolds VI, Domestic Settlement 2: Medieval Peasant Farmsteads* (York 1989).
Wright, D., *The Penguin Book of Everyday Verse* (Harmondsworth 1976).
Wright, J., *The English Dialect Dictionary* (Oxford 1923).

General Index

This index includes names, places, subjects and foodstuffs that are discussed in the text, but not in the recipes. References to illustrations are to their page-numbers, and in bold type.

Index of Recipes